the INFLATION FIGHTER'S GUIDE to the Washington Metro Area

ANDREA LUBERSHANE
ERIK KANIN
CO-PUBLISHERS

Mary Ann Harden
Graphics

DISCLAIMER

The staff of this publication has personally checked information about each and every one of the shops listed. However, should there be any substantial errors of fact, we apologize for these inadvertent mistakes and promise, upon notification, to correct them in the next edition of this book.

Although paid advertising appears in this publication, this by no means influenced either the description of the merchandise or the store(s) listed in this publication. Claims made in the advertising material are neither accepted nor rejected by the publishers. Any omission of businesses was due entirely to editorial oversight. The publishers will make every effort to correct such oversights in future editions of this book.

For mail order copies and bulk orders call Erik Kanin (703) 548-1311 or write Andrik Associates, P.O. Box 5029, Alexandria, Va., 22305. For mail orders, enclose $5.95 plus $.75 postage and handling for each copy. In Virginia, add $.24 state sales tax, per copy.

Composition by van der Sluys graphics inc

Research Assistance
by Matt Roberts & Jody Silvio

Second (Revised) Printing

Copyright © June, 1980
Andrik Associates, Alexandria, Virginia
Library of Congress Catalogue Card Number 79-55706

TABLE OF CONTENTS

Preface 1

Introduction 3

Consumer Help 12

SHOPPING

Food, Drugs & Cosmetics 28

Clothing & Shoes 61

Linens & More for the Home 110

Fabrics & Yarn 118

Appliances & Electronics 127

Furniture, Bedding & Lighting 152

For the Office 194

Carpeting, Flooring & Wallpaper 202

Tires & Auto Parts 231

Surplus & Catalog Stores 250

Entertainment & Leisure 259

Auctions 301

Energy 317

Legal & Medical Services 335

Additions to the Second Printing 376

Maps 386

Glossary of Terms 425

Index to Stores 427

Preface

"You get what you pay for." That phrase has been around a long time. It implies that you can shop for quality or you can shop for price — but never the twain shall meet. But that old saw just doesn't always hold true, for the increase in the cost of retail goods and the consequent decline in purchases of those goods has sent many retail merchants scurrying. They are reducing their prices, holding frequent sales, or switching to a clearance or outlet store operation. And one major cause of this downturn in spending and increase in prices is inflation.

What does inflation mean to the consumer? Inflation means that the prices of consumer goods are being inflated — while the value of the dollar is deflated. The loaf of bread that used to cost 39c now costs 60c; the visit to the doctor that was once $10 is now $25; and the movie theater that only a few years ago charged a $1.50 general admission is now charging $3.50.

How does the consumer fight back? If he or she is wise, the fight begins by being selective — by cutting back on unnecessary and poorly-made or shoddy merchandise and frills, and by making sure that what is bought is of good quality.

But the selective consumer looks at more than the quality of what he or she buys — the price is important too. And one boon to the consumer which has resulted as a retail response to inflation has been the entry of a number of older retail stores and brand-new "discount" stores into the area marketplace. Now the consumer can get the best brands — not just the house brand of an inexpensive department store — at a discount.

The selective consumer is benefitting too by prepaying for packages of services — for legal and health service, for example. While these packages are available because they have been spurred on by federal legislation in recent years, the main reason for the growth of such plans can clearly be attributed to an economic need — people want to avoid expensive or catastrophic legal or medical expenses.

And the selective consumer can learn to get more for his or her entertainment dollar by learning when, where, and sometimes how to patronize theaters, shows, and other facilities while paying reduced or even no admission fee.

Many free services have often been neglected, but are coming to the fore as consumers seek ways to save their money. Advice from city, state, county, and federal sources are free. Associations and corporations offer all kinds of information on buying and maintaining their goods and services; and government at all levels makes available free facilities and programs in abundance.

This book directs you to all of the stores where you can find the best quality and selection of merchandise at great low prices — and tells you how to look for good quality in almost all of these items. This book tells you about free services, low cost entertainment, and how to lower the costs of health care and legal services. In short, we tell you how to fight inflation in many facets of your life — now. We offer no pie-in-the-sky ideas, no outlandish methods that require you to make drastic changes in your living style. The information is clear and concise on judging quality and helpful hints resonate throughout the book.

At the end of each of the shopping chapters is included additional mail order sources for the same goods and often for more interesting and unusual items as well.

And there are bibliographies sprinkled throughout the book so that you can learn more about selecting and purchasing quality goods and services.

Read any or every section of this book — and you will learn something about saving money in the Washington, DC area.

— Andrea Lubershane

Introduction

INTRODUCTION

How the Stores in This Book Were Chosen

The stores listed in this book were selected through a variety of means, including, but not limited to, advertising in the telephone book, newspapers, magazines, radio, and television; the listing of the store in a publication similar to this; word-of-mouth from interested consumers; recommendations from some of the other merchants who are included; personal experience; and serendipity.

Preliminary lists were compiled, then a researcher was sent to check out every store in person. Some of the stores had moved, others had converted to regular retail operations; some had closed their outlet stores; and some offered such low quality merchandise — or offered no bargains at all — that we deleted them from the list. We aimed to include stores with medium to high quality merchandise.

Although we used an extensive system for tracking down all of the stores which offered merchandise at low or discount prices, there was simply no way that we could include every one in the metropolitan area. We will appreciate it if readers or store owners contact us with such information for inclusion in the next edition of this book.

As an extra, we also included a number of establishments in the Baltimore area. Although some of these duplicate merchandise quality and price of stores in the DC area, and although it is plainly in the consumer's best interest to save gas by staying close to home, most of the Baltimore stores listed offer either a superior selection or quality of merchandise or a greater discount than most of the comparable DC metro area stores Hence the inclusion of these stores in this book.

How the Information about the Store Was Obtained

Each store in this book was contacted and visited at least once in the course of our research. Many were visited and the management interviewed twice; many were visited blind (that is, the management did not know of our research efforts at that time). The same questionnaire was used for each store, with the researcher making relevant notes and additions in spaces provided.

Obtaining the information presented some problems. Only a few of the hundreds of stores which we approached were unwilling to discuss their store's operations or merchandise with us. This was not the problem. Rather, the problem was getting consistent answers about exact items like average percent of discount offered, layaway, and return policies.

Another problem arose with stores that had more than two or three branches. In the larger stores, policy is generally made by a centralized management and theoretically carried out by on-line management. However, in many cases, this was only theoretical — as we often found line managers to give answers differing from those of central management. In cases where there was a difference between these two sources, the stores or consumer may find a discrepancy between actual practice and what we have printed. We apologize to both the consumer and to the store for any such inadvertent errors, and promise, upon notification, to correct them in the next edition of this book. This also goes for any store about which published information is incorrect.

How to Read the Store Descriptions in This Book

Each store is described in detail in the body of this book. A large number of questions were asked. In order to clarify the store listings, the following explanations are offered:

- **Address:** The address of each store which appears at the heading of the store description is the address of the store location that was visited. If two stores were visited, the second one will merely appear in the listing of additional stores in the text of the store description. For some stores with many branches, some of the branches further from the Washington area have been deleted.

- **Type of Merchandise:** The management was asked to describe the primary type of merchandise carried. This was verified by the researcher. Stores are arranged in this book by the primary type of merchandise which they carry. Because some have such differing merchandise, these have been grouped under "General Merchandise/ Catalogue Sales/Surplus" where feasible.

- **Quality of Merchandise:** The quality of the merchandise refers to how the lines found at this store compared to the vast range of merchandise available on the open market. Usually low quality means just that — inexpensively made. High or fine quality refers to the best or among the best that is made or is available. "First quality", on the other hand, means that the store is selling the merchandise (whether high, medium, or low quality) as unflawed, as opposed to "seconds", "as is" merchandise, etc.

- **Brand Names/Popular Brands:** Management was asked to relate what popular or well-known brands they carried. A number of these brands were listed in the description. But the store's inventory is not limited to those brands unless that is specified in the store description.

- **Discount:** A discussion of discount was difficult, since most stores work on a "mark-up" over their cost. But we urged management to try to classify the discount in terms of comparable retail, manufacturers' suggested retail, and manufacturer's list, which are used interchangeably in the descriptions of the discount in the store descriptions.

  We attempted to verify these discounts wherever possible, by comparing the price of the goods to those selling at full price stores, or to manufacturers' preprinted prices on labels. However, on some goods where almost no dealer sells at list — like stereos, auto parts, and carpeting — your best bet is to compare prices between stores on specific items.

  Also, in some cases, there is a wide range of "average" discounts noted — this occurs because a given store will carry a wide variety of items and manufacturers. Some manufacturers expect retailers to sell at a price twice the wholesale, while others allow for much smaller mark-ups. So, while the magnitude of the discount is of concern in most cases, don't forget to look at price in relation to the quality of the merchandise, and also in relation to the customary asking price.

- **In-stock/Special Order:** We asked stores to estimate what part of their trade was in-stock merchandise, and how much had to be special ordered. This is to give the consumer an indication of what type of store they would be shopping at — e.g., whether it was primarily special order or custom or whether they could expect to pick up or have their merchandise delivered instantly. In order to give more information, we also asked what the usual deposit was on special order merchandise.

- **Dressing Rooms:** Because many discount clothing stores have nonexistent or limited dressing room facilities — and because that just does not suit some of the more discriminating or hard-to-fit shoppers — we specified what type of fitting rooms were available.

- **Delivery:** Because free delivery is definitely an important factor in lowering the cost of an item, as well as eliminating the necessity for you to save a few dollars by schlepping a heavy package into and out of your car, we specified, where possible, which stores offered free delivery. Although nothing in this world is really free, you may find two stores that offer a given item at the same price, and with the same package of service and warranties — but that one will provide free delivery and the other will charge for it.

- **Catalogues:** We asked stores in the appropriate categories whether they provided store or manufacturers' catalogues, since such catalogues can be a great help to the consumer. Some are educational — they help you to learn about types of equipment available and price ranges, so that when you do go out to shop, you have an idea of what questions to ask and what sort of prices you will encounter. Catalogues from several dealers can enable you to do sit-at-home comparison shopping. And they're nice to have handy on rainy evenings when you've run out of books and nothing on television appeals to you!

- **Warranties/Guaranties:** We asked whether stores offered their own warranties, whether they extended the manufacturers', or whether they backed up the manufacturers. This question did help to point out those better stores which are willing to extend or offer their own warranties.

- **Repairs and Service:** It's good to know if the place you are buying some equipment from has the capability of repairing that equipment if something goes wrong with it — and also to know if they are an authorized warranty dealer — thus the inclusion of this information in each store listing where available or relevant.

- **Special sales:** Who doesn't want to know how to save more money? That's why we asked stores how often and when they have special sales or promotions — when prices are even lower than their normal discount prices. This information, where available, was included in the store description.

- **Mailing lists:** Of course, if you're interested in their merchandise, you will also want to know when they have special sales. Most stores with mailing lists give the people on these lists advance notice of special purchases and other sales — or just send them interesting catalogues. That's why we included mailing lists in the descriptions of the stores.

- **Hours:** We put down the hours of the location which was reviewed. We also noted whether or not the other locations kept the same hours.

- **Form of Payment:** We specify whether the store takes cash only, whether checks are accepted, and what credit cards are honored.

- **Layaway/Hold Policy:** Holds and layaway policy, unless clearly spelled out on a sign at the store, may vary slightly from those which are printed in the book. Many managers and owners pointed out that there was no firm policy on these — it just depended on the items and whether the purchaser was known to them or not.

- **Returns:** The subject of returns — whether for refunds, exchanges, or store credit — was another grey area. Some stores have clearly spelled-out policies — others go by situation. In cases where it is highly situational, we noted that you should check about this before you buy.

- **Parking:** We noted the magnitude and cost of parking facilities.

Despite the fact that the book was well-researched, details about the stores will change with time. One item which changes frequently — and often seasonally — is the hours which the store keeps. Always call in advance to make sure that they still maintain the same hours as in the book. Also, some discount stores have closed recently, and this trend may continue in the future — so check to make sure a store is still open, especially if it is some distance from you and/or you are unfamiliar with it.

General Shopping Tips

Throughout the course of researching and writing this book, we heard many hints and suggestions about shopping for the best buys and saving money; some of these were repeated many times over. The following section lists suggestions which we think are worthwhile.

- You should look for good quality to maximize the buying power of your dollar. Better merchandise lasts longer; looks, wears, or functions better; and usually turns out ot be the better buy.
- If you think that an item in a store is somehow not first quality merchandise, has a flaw, or (in the case of food) is beyond the pull date (but still edible), don't hesitate to ask the manager or buyer for a discount. Sometimes they can return the goods for credit from the supplier, but in many cases you will be doing them a favor by taking such merchandise off of their hands.
- Expect limited service in some of these stores — that is why you are getting a discount in many cases. Such stores hire less help and provide you with fewer extras. You pay for the extra personnel and services in customary retail stores through higher prices.
- Ask for a discount for paying with cash or check. If a store uses a credit card system, they are paying the credit card company a percentage of each charge sale. If you pay cash, you are saving them that payment. So at a store which accepts credit cards — especially American Express, which many stores claim charges the highest percentage of any credit card — you should ask for and expect a reduction in price — or a premium, such as a free item — especially if you are making a large purchase. (Bear in mind, however, that when you pay by check, unless you are already known at the store, they often must have the check verified by a system for which they also pay. They may therefore be more reluctant to give a discount for payment by check.)
- On many items, independent food stores — those not part of a chain — can offer better prices than large chain stores. While it may not be feasible (or economical) to shop independents for everything, you should consider them an alternative to check out.
- Consider the price of an item in relation to the service you are getting with it. For example, when buying a large appliance, if you find that two stores offer you the same model and make for a $10 difference, but the more expensive store is also offering you a warranty or delivery, weigh whether these services are not worth the extra $10.

- When doing things yourself, buy good materials and take your time. While the difference between buying the less expensive materials and the better ones may seem substantial now, when you figure out how long the product will last, it makes more sense to use higher quality materials. Also, if you don't do a skillful job, you aren't getting a bargain — you are just getting a cheap product.
- Use High Tech ideas — high tech means using items of a technology and adapting them to home (or office) use. If you see an item, for example, in a restaurant or office building — or even in a factory — that you think would suit a function in your home, call a commercial supplier and find out if you could purchase one yourself. Often you need to buy in quantity, and sometimes the price would be higher than that of an item designed for home use, but in the long run the industrial products are much sturdier and last longer.
- Shop rummage and church sales — you can often find buried antiques and curios, as well as more mundane things like books and records — at very low prices. Some sales tend to have outrageously high prices, but some are priced extraordinarily fairly. Our experience indicates that the price has little to do with the location of the sale. You have to shop these sales a bit in order to get an idea of the range of prices, but it can be well worth it.
- Consider trade-offs between your time and your money. Sometimes, it is just cheaper to buy something ready-made, rather than spend your time making it.
- Look for "storewide clearance" or "seasonal clearance" rather than "special purchase". "Special purchase" merchandise has usually been brought in by the retailer at a good price and is frequently merchandise of somewhat lower quality than the store's usual merchandise. Clearance merchandise comes from the store's first run lines and is just being cleared out.
- If a store advertises a special but does not put a limit on it like "subject to stock on hand", you should be sure to ask the manager for a raincheck if they have run out of it by the time you get to the store. If they do not give rainckecks, but there are other branches of the store, request that they check with the other addresses to see if they have the item in stock; it can then be sent to your branch or held for you at the other branch. Also ask that stores check with their warehouse if they can.
- If you feel that a store deliberately misrepresented merchandise — offering a great buy at a fantastic price, then trying to talk you into buying something else when you came in — this is called "bait and switch". Though illegal in most states, it occurs with some frequency. The best way to insist on the special (assuming of course that you want it) or just to shop elsewhere. If you feel that the "bait and switch" operation is deliberate, however, you might want to report it to your jurisdiction's consumer protection agency.

- Learn to compare — everything. You should learn which stores offer the best buys on a consistent basis, and you should also learn to compare individual item prices. Use the telephone frequently — most stores will be helpful. Check newspaper ads and rely on the experience of friends and relatives who have sought out and bought the same items.
- No matter what you are buying, stick to a shopping budget. Determine in advance about how much you want to spend on an item or on a group of items, then try to stick to your price range. If you go out with no specified dollar amount in mind, you might just say "Yeah, why not" to the most expensive — then kick yourself later.
- Learn to buy in anticipation of your needs — buy presents in advance; buy winter nightgowns (for example) in the late winter or early fall, when they are being cleared or when stores offer them at a special pre-season price. Buy Christmas presents any time during the year that you can get a good buy. Purchasing things like electric blankets in summer can make a lot of cents.
- By the same token, try to avoid buying when you are desperate. Don't wait until you run out of an item of food, for example, which you usually buy in a warehouse store, or nylon stockings, which you know you can buy in bulk at a teriffic price, and be forced to pay premium prices because you can't wait or shop around.
- Have a friend or relative "in the business" get an item for you wholesale. It may sound corny, but it still works.
- Buy bulk. Buy large quantities to take advantage of discounts. After all, if it is something like canned mushroom soup, which you use frequently and seem to have always used frequently, and if it has a long shelf life, go ahead and buy in quantity, because you will probably use it up before it could go bad. If you can't use all the entire quantity that must be purchased to get the discount, organize some friends, neighbors, and/or relatives to buy with you.
- Make a list of the desired features for each item for which you shop. When you go shopping, check to make sure that the item has the features, and check to make sure that you are not paying extra for an undesired or unnecessary feature. On large appliances, this can be an effective way to save money.
- When shopping at a discount store, buy only what that store specializes in. Some offer complementary accessories or goods at the full retail price. Unless you are in a hurry, buy your shoes at the discount shoe store, and your stockings at a store that discounts stockings.
- Familiarize yourself with brand names and learn to recognize quality. Then when you go shopping you don't need a label or a "comparable price" tag to tell you when you are getting a good buy.
- Make sure you get the details of what is included in your purchase — the warranty, delivery, and any accessories.

Hubbard-Dale Inc.

317 S. Washington Street
Alexandria, Virginia 22314
836-1111

1511 Quaker Lane
Alexandria, Virginia 22302
379-7977

Licensed in Virginia, Maryland, District of Columbia and Delaware

Hubbard-Dale REALTORS

SPECIALISTS IN FINE RESIDENTIAL PROPERTIES IN OLD TOWN AND NORTHERN VIRGINIA

- Inquire about mailing lists and frequency and dates of special sales — sometimes you will happen into a store only a week or even a couple of days before a sale event — and you would certainly wait that long for most items if you knew you could save 25% on the average.
- Don't underrate the value of a mailing list. You will get catalogues and mailers free — not only are they interesting to read, they help you to price items and/or tell you about special sales, sometimes giving you first crack at sale merchandise.
- Don't be pressured by salespeople, especially if they give you the line "Buy today, it's the last one" — it really may be the last one in cases like clothing or antique furniture, but rarely in the case of appliances or other mass market items. Take time to think over your large purchases.
- Don't hesitate to ask for discounts if merchandise appears to be worn out, out of season, etc.
- Beware door-to-door salespeople, except for those who sell well-known door-to-door products only (such as Avon, Electrolux, Fuller Brush, Tupperware, Encyclopedia Britannica, Grolier, etc.).
- Learn to complain if the product you buy is defective or doesn't hold up as long as it should — more on this subject is included in succeeding chapters.
- Barter when you can — bartering can save you money and help you get rid of something you no longer want or need. Or, you can get something you do need by trading some of your free time for someone else's free time and unique skills.
- On large purchases, avoid paying state sales tax by buying at an area store that is not incorporated (or not considered to be "doing business") in your state. Take advantage of this tri-state area and have something delivered for the cost of the tax. Even if you have to pay a delivery charge, it is often less than the tax; and if you don't have to pay for delivery, you've saved a bit.

RELATED PUBLICATIONS

Chilton Book Company, Radnor, Pennsylvania 19089, publishes a whole line of do-it-yourself, crafts, cooking, gardening, and car care books, among other things.

Dowd, Merle E. *How to Live Better and Spend 20% Less.* Parker Publishing Co., West Nyack, New York, 1979.

Inflation for Survival Letter, 901 North Washington Street, Alexandria, Virginia 22314, 836-3313. Published semi-weekly for $36 a year, this tells about finance, investments, gold and silver, food storing budget management, and the monetary crisis.

Money, 250 West 55th Street, New York, New York 10020.

Myerson, Bess. *The Complete Consumer Book: How to Buy Wisely and Well.* New York: Simon and Schuster, 1979.

Porter, Sylvia. *Sylvia Porter's New Money Book for the 80's.* New York: Doubleday, 1979.

Quinn, Jane Bryant. *Everyone's Money Book.* Delacorte Press, New York, 1979. Excellent, complete, and easy-to-read book on how to save money on almost everything and how to handle your money in savings, in investments, and in the marketplace.

Rowse, Arthur E. (ed.). *Help: The Useful Almanac.* Washington, DC: Consumer News, Inc., 1976. Truly excellent — covers a vast range of consumer concerns, including legislation and government action, with many informational charts and graphs.

Sunset Books, Lane Publishing Co., Willow and Middlefield Roads, Menlo Park, California 94025. Publishes a whole series of do-it-yourself building, remodeling, and home design books; cookbooks; garden and landscaping books; regional garden books; hobby and craft books; and travel and recreation books.

Tab Books, Blue Ridge Summit, Pennsylvania 17124. Publishes a whole range of do-it-yourself and learn-how books.

Toll-Free Digest. New York: Warner Books, 1979. Organized alphabetically by subject. Hotels-motels-inns take up fully 60% of the book. It's interesting if you like looking for strange new ideas of places to call — or if you really travel a lot.

Consumer Help

Is the US marketplace a jungle for consumers? It could be. If you don't watch out for yourself, you could find slinky snakelike salespeople promising you fantastic goods for a low price, beady-eyed sloths of merchandisers offering after-sale service — and never coming through with it; and tigerish businesspeople just looking for a weakened consumer to tear limb from limb.

But there is help for you out in that jungle — not only from consumer groups, but from the federal government, which has tried to make the marketplace safer for you by enacting some protective laws. Become familiar with these laws and you will have an edge in the jungle of the merchants and large corporations. These laws are meant to assure your protection: If you can prove that they have been broken or neglected, you can confront the merchant or manufacturer and get redress. You can get the federal government to enter the fray for you. Or you can just save yourself time and money by steering clear of the bad products — and advising others to do the same.

Not only does the federal government work in your behalf, but so do state and local governments and organizations. Local consumer protection groups, as well as the states' attorney generals' offices, all have established procedures whereby the consumer can either be helped, or be forewarned about problem merchandise.

Federal Involvement

The Federal Trade Commission (FTC) was created by the FTC Act of 1914. The FTC is an independent law-enforcement agency charged by Congress with protecting the public against anti-competitive behavior of companies, and against unfair and deceptive business practices.

Periodically, the FTC will issue "Trade Regulation Rules" and "Industry Guides" — lists of do's and don'ts for business. The Guides include explanations of legal and illegal practices. The FTC will also give advice on business to individuals or businesses, and these bits of advice are called Advisory Opinions. These Opinions are developed as preventive measures against unfair or deceptive practices; but, when sufficient cause is indicated, the FTC can use these as a basis upon which to take action. The FTC will recognize violations of these Opinions, and will investigate complaints about them with a view to correcting the problem, or stopping the company from continuing in an unacceptable practice. To do this, the FTC will issue complaints and enter orders to stop false advertising, fraudulent selling, or unfair tactics against competitors, for example. Since the Commission itself has no enforcement capacity, if these orders are ignored or violated, the Federal Court system will issue civil penalties to the offenders. The FTC can seek damages on behalf of the consumer who has been harmed by these unfair or deceptive acts or practices.

The FTC maintains regional offices at which to register complaints and from which to disseminate information on its regulations, provisions, updates, and consumer information.

Certain FTC Acts have had substantial impact on the consumer. Whether you know it or not, you have probably benefitted from their protection many times in your shopping.

The Fair Packaging and Labeling Act prohibits deceptive packaging and labeling of consumer products. It also requires the origin of manufacture, weight of contents, number of servings and their size, area of contents in their largest form (for example, 200 square feet of aluminum foil), number of contents (e.g., 6 patties of dog food), and the *common* names of ingredients in the products (so you need not be a chemist to shop well). If you find fault with how a product is labeled in regard to its true contents, write the FTC with all of the information pertinent to your complaint.

You will read over and over in this book about getting a warranty, shopping for warranties, keeping the receipt, and having warranty information on the receipt, if it is not written down anywhere else on the product or in accompanying literature. Warranties are part of your purchase — and you are paying for them. They are like an insurance policy included in the price of your purchase on many items. Your receipt (or receipt with separate written warranty) basically serves as a copy of the policy. Without this receipt, there is no proof of purchase, and this means that there is no proof that you are "insured".

The FTC enforces warranties with the Magnuson-Moss Warranty Act. This act defines a warranty as: any written proof of fact or promise in connection with a purchase which relates to the nature of the material or workmanship and assures that it is defect-free and/or will do its assigned job (in the case of something like a dishwasher) over a specified amount of time. The warranty, then, means that you are to believe that you are buying something that is the best it can be and will do the job for as long as promised by the manufacturers who sold it to you (or by the store, if they offer one).

The warranty means more to you — it also serves as a written promise or contract or provision to refund, repair, replace, or take other appropriate action to compensate you if the product fails to live up to the sellers' promises.

There are several types of written warranties:

Full warranties: these provide you with all of the same rights as mentioned above, but add to them. One of the additions is to protect you against damages that you may have suffered while using the product. These damages that arise during correct and prescribed use of the product can be recovered by bringing suit. These are called *consequential damages.* For example, imagine that you buy a hammer and use it to whack a nail into the wall to hang a picture. On the second or third stroke, the head of the hammer flies apart from the handle and hits you or your spouse in the face or the eye. If the hammer is warrantied, and you are using it correctly, you are entitled to recover the cost of:

- any emergency transportation to the doctor or hospital;
- any fuel used to go in your own car;
- the cost of treatment;
- the cost of hospital and/or doctor's fees;
- the cost of time which you might have lost from work;
- the cost of any correspondence with the company to rectify the situation;
- the cost of a lawyer if it goes to court;
- the cost of the trial;
- the cost of a new hammer.

To recover these costs, you are entitled to sue or recover from the manufacturer, the store, and sometimes even the salesperson who sold it to you.

Remember, though, that this provision of a full warranty is in effect only if there has been: no abuse of the product, no "buy at your own risk" disclaimer (which is not a valid defense against a full warranty in Maryland), no clause in the warranty which specifically excludes consequential and/or incidental damages. These do not defend the company against personal injury claims, but they may be cited if you try to recover property damages.

Remember that anything lost or damaged due to product failure under warranty is recoverable. Talk to your lawyer about this, or call the legal aid society if and when you need further information on it.

A **limited warranty** is one which does not go as far as the provisions of a full warranty do; it may even have conditions or restrictions on it which limit claims for anything above and beyond the principle of prescribed use — warranted to work only for the use for which it was intended.

When you shop, compare the warranties on the products which you are considering. If you get a twenty-dollar rebate or discount, but no warranty, will twenty dollars compensate you for sacrificing the full warranty? Think about it carefully — you may save now but pay in repair costs later on. A slightly higher-priced product which includes a longer or fuller warranty will likely be the better buy in the long run.

To learn about product warranties, you should obtain the following information when you are buying a product:

- the full name of the warrantor;
- the full address of the warrantor;
- the complete warranty in writing;
- any extra provisions written on the receipt;
- the duration of the warranty;
- approved service stores or servicemen and their locations.

By doing this and, should you have a problem, by keeping track of names and dates when you speak to people about it, you can cut through a lot of red tape and present yourself as a consumer with a formidable complaint. Your accurate records of problems you have and warranties to which you are entitled will be sure to speed the response of the warrantor; and, if that fails, will be of great help should you need to take the matter to court or arbitration.

But what if you don't get a warranty?

Maybe you were refused one when you asked for it, or you forgot, or there was not one available, according to the manufacturer or the store. You are still protected. Your rights are protected by an *Implied Warranty*, which indicates that just by the act of offering the product for sale, the manufacturer and seller are proclaiming that it is as good as it can be and that it will do its assigned task. This offers you protection (albeit not as complete protection as the warranties discussed above). For example, if you buy a garden hose, and that hose leaks, you are entitled, within a reasonable amount of time, to seek repair or replacement by the seller without charge to you. And if you give the manufacturer or seller a reasonable amount of time to take care of your problem, and you still are not satisfied, you are entitled to a refund of purchase price or a replacement.

If you feel that you have been charged a higher price than someone else for the same thing and by the same seller, you will be pleased to know that there is a law against the practice. The Clayton Act plainly says, "It shall be unlawful for any person engaged in commerce ... to discriminate in price between different purchasers of commodities of like grade and quality." This means a number of things to the consumer. First, if you are charged more for the same suit or dress than someone else is, for any reason (at the same time and store, of course), the seller is acting illegally. Secondly, if you are refused a sale which is granted to someone else, the seller is again in violation of federal law. Thirdly, if you attempt to buy a wholesale amount (a gross, a dozen, etc.) for a wholesale price which is charged to other wholesale purchasers, and you are refused or charged a higher price per item, the seller is in violation of federal law — even if that other purchaser is a regular wholesale account and you are not.

This last is very important, because it means that you can organize a buying club or neighborhood association, and then buy wholesale amounts at wholesale prices. You can also contract to buy a wholesale amount of almost anything — cars, building materials, home furnishings, food, etc. — and save on one-shot deals. For example, if you and some friends want to buy new cars, and can agree on the same make (and, sometimes, model), you can save some money by negotiating with the dealer to buy a "fleet" of, say, five cars. If you want to add a room onto your house, or better yet want to build an entire house with some friends, then you could request wholesale prices for all of the materials which you will use.

On the other hand, there are provisions enabling the seller to pick and choose his customers. He could refuse you, if he suspected that your purchases would be less in quantity or total cost than the usual wholesale customer's. To avoid this problem, award your buying group or your building crew a name. If you live on Elm Street, you could give yourself a name like Elm Associates. If you are building an addition with your friends from work, you could call your little group, "Fisher's Friendly Construction". In this way, you can get lower prices on the quantities which you would need. This is one of the principles behind co-ops and buying clubs, which are mentioned further on in this book in the chapter on food and drugs.

You can usually get discounts on large purchases just by asking store managers. Often the discounts are there for the asking. If you do a lot of business with a store in terms of high volume, make yourself known to the manager and, after he or she gets to know you and you are contemplating large quantity purchases, ask about discounts.

The Consumer Credit Protection Act was passed in 1968. It is commonly known as the Truth in Lending Law, and requires most lenders and lending institutions to make public their actual interest rates on loans and credit sales. In addition to this, the law stopped the cruel and deceptive lending method, while giving the public rights to cancel credit deals in which the home is put up as collateral.

Another provision makes it illegal for you to receive unsolicited credit cards, and also gives you protection against the use of stolen credit cards by the thief or someone to whom he could sell or give the cards.

The Fair Credit Reporting Act was passed in 1971 and gives you access to the sometimes mystical ways of credit and its effect on your name.

If you have ever bought insurance, applied for a job, or used a credit card, you have a file all about you somewhere in some credit bureau. You have the legal right to know the name and address of that bureau at any time you are refused credit, employment, or insurance based on a report about your creditworthiness. You can also find out who has seen the contents of that file, besides those who work in the credit bureau. You can help yourself out by limiting the access of people and organizations to that file. You can request a copy of the report that was made (for example) to the insurance company or credit card issuer, and you are entitled to change or correct inaccuracies of fact, as well as receiving a list of false reports which had also been sent out. This is free to you if you act within a specified period of time. You are also within your rights to sue anyone who keeps you from exercising these rights.

An amendment to this Act came in 1976, when the Fair Credit Billing Act was passed. The amendment protects against billing errors to charge accounts.

AT FIRST AMERICAN BANK YOU GET

BECAUSE YOU'RE SECOND TO NONE!

You do pay for the printing of your checks, but that's all!

FIRST AMERICAN BANK OF VIRGINIA

Full Service Bank
Member FDIC

Banking at its best at more than 40 Northern Virginia offices
ARLINGTON 827-8804 · FAIRFAX 821-7707 · ALEXANDRIA 827-8901

The Consumer Product Safety Act was passed in 1972. It set up a commission which collects, investigates, and distributes information concerning death, injury, illness, and damages caused by consumer products. It researches and develops new tests for products and enforces the new standards which it develops from the tests. It also sponsors and promotes product testing and works to make products safe and manufacturers responsive You can seek safety ratings and information on products which you are considering buying, by contacting the Consumer Product Safety Commission.

SOME LAWS TO BENEFIT CONSUMERS

	DC	Maryland	Virginia
Unit pricing of food	o	x	o
TV/Radio repair registration requirements	x	o	o
Tax incentives for solar energy	o	x	o
PUC passed accountability tests	x	o	o
Private trade schools are regulated	x	o	o
Loser in consumer case must pay attorney fees	o	o	o
Class action suits are allowed	o	o	o
Advertisements by optometrists are allowed	x	x	o
Open dating of food is required	x	x	x
No fault auto insurance	o	x	x
US-approved mobile home regulations are enforced	o	x	x
Rent deposits must be held in escrow	o	x	o
Landlord-tenants rights laws	o	x	x
Generic drug substitution allowed	o	x	x
Auto repair shop registration required	x	x	x

(From information derived from Help! The Useful Almanac, *1978, published by Consumer News.)*

WHEN ALL ELSE FAILS... SMALL CLAIMS COURT

If you get something repaired and it still doesn't work and you can't get your money back, if an iron doesn't work and you can't get a refund or a replacement — and you've written angry letters — then it may be time to go to Small Claims Court. Not only can you hope to get satisfaction, but you can also collect the costs you incur going to small claims court — and interest as well. Limits of judgements are up to $750 in the District of Columbia, $500 in Maryland, and up to $5000 in Virginia General District Court.

The concept of Small Claims Court was first instituted by the Massachusetts Legislature in 1920. This concept is meant to help people with relatively small civil problems — consumer problems, accidents, security deposit problems — collect recompense for damages suffered without undergoing an expensive and often time-consuming legal battle. It also helps to keep the courts clear of such small cases.

Small claims court should be used when all other avenues — such as the Better Business Bureau or the Consumer Fraud Division of the State's Attorney General's Office — have been exhausted. You have to make sure to file your claim in the appropriate court, which could be where the person you are suing lives, works, or conducts business, or, in the case of a corporation, anywhere they do business. In the case of an accident, the jurisdiction where the accident occured or where the defendent lives should be where the suit is filed.

You must sue the defendant under his proper name. If this is an individual, then you cannot sue him by a nickname. For a business, you should find out whether it is a sole proprietorship, in which case you can sue the owner; a partnership, in which case you name the partners; or a corporation, in which case you would address your suit to the registered agent of the corporation. With a corporation, you must be certain that the civil warrant is served *in person* to the registered agent. In order to find out what form a business takes, you can call the following offices:

DC Corporation Records: 347-0671, Extension 4

Virginia State Corporation Commission: (804) 786-3720 (Richmond)

Maryland State Department of Assessments and Taxation: (301) 383-2526 (Baltimore)

Make sure that your civil warrant is accompanied by an affidavit explaining your position. The clerk has the proper form for both the civil warrant and the affidavit. The clerks, particularly in Virginia, are quite friendly and helpful.

Going to Court:

First you assemble all of the relevant documents in an orderly fashion — bills, letters, receipts, guaranties, or any other relevant information. Make sure to bring witnesses if you need them. If they are unwilling to appear, you can ask the clerk to subpoena them: this runs $22 per person in DC, $5 in Maryland, and $1.25 in Virginia. Organize the facts in your mind, and write down some notes if necessary. Call the Clerk of Courts day before the trial to see if you are still scheduled to appear — if the other party did not receive notice, the date would have been changed.

When in court, arrive on time. If you are late, your claim could be dismissed. The clerk will call out the cases in order. You don't have to feel compelled to go through a trial -- if the defendant is willing to negotiate a settlement that is acceptable to you — go ahead and take it. But you don't have to take a settlement which you find undesirable — you are entitled to your time in court. In most cases, if the defendent has been served but neither he nor his representative shows up in court, then you can ask for a "default judgement".

When you are called you will be asked to present your side of the story first. You should be succinct, factual, and courteous while presenting your case. The American Bar Association suggests that you dress conservatively, not sloppily or flamboyantly, and that you avoid rambling testimony. The defendant is allowed to question you and your witnesses. Then the defendant is allowed to tell his or her side of the story, during which time you should not interrupt. The judge will declare the winner and the damages to be awarded. He may not do it immediately, but may think it over and notify both parties by mail.

One of the worst parts of the small claims process is attempting to collect your damages. After the judgment is made, you can request that it be paid in a single payment, or installments can be arranged if the defendant cannot accommodate one payment. But no matter what the defendant said about paying your money, he may very well avoid paying you. If this happens, ask the Clerk of Courts to subpoena him or her for an "Oral Examination", where you or your attorney is allowed to question him to find out whether or not he can afford to pay, by asking questions about what real and personal property he has.

Should you find yourself as a defendant in a small claims proceeding, and you lose, you have a number of days after the decision to appeal. In the District, the application fee for this is $5; in Maryland it is $60; and in Virginia, it is left up to the discretion of the judge.

BASIC SMALL CLAIMS INFORMATION

COURT	HOURS	FEES

District of Columbia Courthouse
500 Indiana Avenue, NW,
Room JM-260
Washington, DC
727-1760
	Monday-Friday 9-4
	Saturday 9-11:30
	Wednesday 6-8 pm
		$1 filing fee/claim
		$1.40 certified mail fee
		  to notify each defendent
		OR $1 US Marshall's fee
		  for personal delivery

District Court of Maryland, Dist. No. 6 15825 Shady Grove Road Rockville, MD 20850 977-3225	Monday-Friday 8:30-4:30	$5 filing fee/claim $2 certified mail fee OR $5 sheriff's fee

BASIC SMALL CLAIMS INFORMATION

COURT	HOURS	FEES
In Montgomery County: 801 Sligo Avenue Silver Spring, Maryland 20510 589-4084		
7359 Wisconsin Avenue Bethesda, Maryland 20014 652-7745		
In Prince George's County District Court of Maryland, Dist. No. 5 14757 Main Street Upper Marlboro, Maryland 20870 952-4070	Monday-Friday 8:30-4:30	same as in Montgomery County
County Service Building 5012 Rhode Island Avenue Hyattsville, Maryland 20781 779-4426		
Lucente Building 6188 Oxon Hill Road, Oxon Hill, Maryland 20021 567-2113		
Arlington County General District Court 1400 N. Courthouse Road Arlington, Virginia 22201 558-2446	Monday-Friday 8-5	$5 filing fee includes notification
Fairfax County General District Court 4000 Chain Bridge Road Fairfax City Courthouse Fairfax, Virginia 22030 691-2157	Monday-Friday 8-3	$6 filing fee includes notification
Alexandria General District Court 130 North Fairfax St. Room 218 Alexandria, VA 22314 750-6331	Monday-Friday: 7:30-4	$6 filing fee includes notification

CONSUMER ORIENTED GROUPS AND RESOURCES

American Civil Liberties Union
22 East 40th Street,
New York, NY 10016

Associated Credit Bureaus, Inc.
6767 Southwest Freeway,
Houston, Texas 77036

Auto Owners Action Council
1411 K Street NW
Washington, DC 20005
638-5550

Bureau of Consumer Protection
Federal Trade Commission
Washington, D.C. 20580

Bureau of Operations,
Interstate Commerce Commission
Washington, D.C. 20423
343-4761
(for complaints concerning interstate movers).

Catalogue of Consumer Information
GSA
18th and E Streets, NW
Room G142
Washington, D.C. 20405
566-1794

Citizens Action Group
113 C Street, SE
Washington, D.C. 20003
Helps students and citizens organize local consumer groups and PIRGs.

Commodity Futures Trading Commission
(800) 424-9398

Consumer Action, Inc.
1625 Eye Street NW
Washington, DC 20006
872-8660
Information on labeling and drugs

Consumer Electronics Group
Electronic Industries Association
2001 Eye Street NW
Washington, DC 20006

Consumer Federation of America
Suite 406, 1012 14th Street NW
Washington DC 20005
737-3732
Helps consumer groups organize; also publishes consumer news.

Consumer Help Center
2000 H Street NW
100 Bacon Hall   676-7585
Washington, D.C. 20052

Consumer Product Safety Commission
(800) 638-2666
in Maryland (800) 492-2937

Consumers' Union
1714 Massachusetts Ave. NW
Washington, DC 20036
Works on a wide range of consumer protection matters.

Consumers' Union
256 Washington Street,
Mount Vernon, NY 10550
(914) 664-6400

Cooperative League of the USA (CLUSA)
1828 L Street NW
Washington, DC 20036
Publishes how-to materials on starting and running co-ops.

Council of Better Business Bureaus
1150 17th Street NW
Washington, DC 20036
Will put you in touch with the right business bureau for your area.

DC Consumers Association
440 Emerson Street NW
Washington, DC 20011
882-2230

Disabilities Rights Center
1346 Connecticut Ave., Suite 1124
Washington, D.C. 20036
Works in the area of employment for those with disabilities.

Federal Tax Information
(800) 555-1212

Flammable Products Hotline
Consumer Product Safety Commission
(800) 638-2666
To see if materials you have are highly flammable.

Furniture Industry Consumer Advisory Panel (FICAP)
P.O. Box 951,
High Point, North Carolina 27261
(919) 885-5065
For disputes with furniture dealers.

Health Insurance Institute
1850 K Street NW
Washington, DC 20006

Initiative America
1316 Independence Ave. S.E.
Washington, DC 20003
547-1569
Gives information on organizing and technical assistance to groups: rights of initiative, and recall, as well as referendum on local issues.

The Institute of Life Insurance and Health Insurance
277 Park Avenue
New York, NY 10017
For questions concerning insurance that aren't directed to the state insurance departments.

Lawyers Committee for Civil Rights Under the Law
733 15th Street NW
Washington, DC 20005
Represents disadvantaged minorities in areas of voting rights, employment discrimination, educational opportunities, and criminal justice reform.

Major Appliance Consumer Action Panel (MACAP)
Complaint Exchange
Room 1514, 20 North Wacker Drive
Chicago, Ill. 60606
Collect: (312) 236-3165

Maryland Citizens Consumer Council
Box 34526
Bethesda, MD 20034
(301) 229-5900

Maryland Developmental Disabilities Law Project
University of Maryland Law School
Baltimore, MD 21201
Works to eliminate barriers to buildings and transportation, and to create better employment and medical systems.

Medical Committee for Human Rights
P.O. Box 7155,
Pittsburgh, PA 15213
For complaints concerning medical care.

National Tire Dealers and Retreaders Assoc.
Field Operations Department
1343 L Street NW
Washington, DC 20005
(202) 638-6650
Clearinghouse for any complaints.

National Resource Center for Consumers of Legal Services
1302 18th Street, NW
Washington, DC 20036

Nutrition Action
1775 S Street NW
Washington, DC 20009
332-9110
Information on food content and hazards.

Office of Consumer Affairs
Washington, D.C. 20201
Complaints: 245-6093
State and local programs: 245-9890
A government agency concerned with all kinds of consumer problems.

OSHA
15220 Gateway Center
3535 Market Street
Philadelphia, PA 19104
(215) 597-1201
If you think you are working in an unsafe or unhealthy atmosphere.

Residential Utility Consumer Action Group
P.O. Box 19404
Washington, D.C. 20036
To voice your feelings on utility issues.

Tax Reform Research Group
P.O. Box 19404
Washington, D.C. 20036
Sample copy of Tax Reform Research Group's "People and Taxes" monthly newspaper.

Tenants Rights
National Tenants Organization
425 13th Street NW
Washington, DC 20004
If you have no lawyer, can't afford one, and face eviction.

Virginia Citizens Consumer Council
Box 777
Springfield, VA 22150
790-8296

Virginia Consumers Congress
900 S. Washington
Falls Church , VA 22046
(703) 536-7366

Women's Legal Defense Fund
1010 Vermont Avenue NW
Washington, DC 20005
Works on removing discriminatory practices in housing, employment, and the like.

RELATED PUBLICATIONS

Bulletin of the National Consumers' League, 1028 Connecticut Avenue, NW, Suite 522, Washington, D.C. 20036. Published every two months.

Changing Times, 1729 H Street NW Washington, D.C. 20006, 298-6400.

Common Sense, National Consumer Congress, 1346 Connecticut Ave., NW, Washington, DC 20036, 797-7600. Subscription $10.00 per year.

Consumer Digest Magazine, 6316 North Lincoln Avenue, Chicago, Illinois 60659

The Consumer Information Catalog, published quarterly by the Consumer Information Center of the U.S. General Services Administration, Pueblo, Colorado.

The Consumer Information Index (guide to almost every consumer pamphlet put out by the U.S. Government), available from: Consumer Information, Pueblo, Colorado 81009

Consumer Newsweek, 816 National Press Building, Washington, D.C. 20045, 737-1190. A weekly newsletter on consumer news; $15 a year.

Consumer Reports, 256 Washington Street, Mt. Vernon, New York 10550

Consumers' Research Magazine, Bowerstown Road, Washington, NJ 07882. Monthly publication on consumer goods; includes a "Handbook of Buying" as one of the monthly publications. Subscription $8 per year.

Critical Mass, P.O. Box 1538, Washington, D.C. 20013. For information on economic and technical pitfalls of nuclear energy.

Danforth, Art. *Time to Organize?* Washington, DC: The Cooperative League of the USA, 1974.

Facts and Comparisons. Facts and Comparisons, St. Louis, Missouri.

State and Local Consumer Offices

District of Columbia:

Office of Consumer Protection
1407 L Street, NW
Washington, D.C. 20005
659-2617

Office of the People's Counsel
1626 Eye Street, NW
Washington, DC 20006
727-3071

Maryland:

Office of the Attorney General
One South Calvert Street,
Baltimore, Maryland 21202
(301) 383-3717

There is also a branch at 5112 Berwyn Road,
Second Floor
College Park, Maryland 20740
474-3500

Dealer Licensing and Consumer Services
Motor Vehicle Administration
6601 Ritchie Highway NE
Glen Burnie, Maryland 21061
(301) 768-7420

Public Service Commission
301 W. Preston Street,
Baltimore, Maryland 21201
(301) 383-2375

Office of Consumer Credit
One South Calvert Street, Room 601
Baltimore, MD 21202
(301) 383-3656

Anne Arundel County Board of Consumer Affairs
Arundel Center, Room 403,
Annapolis, MD 21404
(301) 224-7300

Baltimore County Consumer Fraud Division
State's Attorney's Office
316 Equitable Building
Baltimore, MD 21202
(301) 396-4997

Howard County Office of Consumer Affairs
8950 Rte. 108
Columbia, MD 21045
(301) 997-7604

Montgomery County
Office of Consumer Affairs
24 Maryland Avenue
Rockville, MD 20850
(301) 340-1010

Prince George's County Consumer Protection Commission
County Administration Building
Upper Marlboro, MD 20870
(301) 952-4700

Virginia:

Attorney General
Suite 308, 11 South 12th Street,
Richmond, VA 23219
(804) 786-1348

Office of Consumer Affairs
Department of Agriculture and Commerce
825 E. Broad St.
Richmond, VA 23219
(804) 786-2042

also at: 3016 Williams Drive
Fairfax, VA 22030
573-1286

Alexandria Office of Consumer Affairs
405 Cameron Street,
Alexandria, VA 22314
750-6675

Prince William County Office of Consumer Affairs
15960 Cardinal Drive,
Woodbridge, VA 22191
221-4156

Arlington County Office of Consumer Affairs
2049 15th Street North,
Arlington, VA 22201
558-2142

Fairfax County Office of Consumer Affairs
4031 University Drive,
Fairfax, VA 22030
691-3214

Consumer Help

Freedom of Information Clearinghouse, P.O. Box 19367, Washington, DC 20036. Write to get a pamphlet on How to Use the Freedom of Information Act.

Help: The Useful Almanac. Consumer News, Inc., 813 National Press Building, Washington, DC 20045

Inflation Fighting Ideas. U.S. Office of Consumer Affairs. Published periodically.

Kramer, Nancy, and Stephen A. Newman. *Getting What You Deserve.* New York: Doubleday, 1979.

National Consumer Buying Alert, The White House, Office of the Special Assistant for Consumer Affairs.

One Way to Build a Consumer Cooperative Buying Group. Washington, DC: The Cooperative League of the USA, 1972.

Public Citizen Reports and Publications, P.O. Box 19404, Washington, DC 20036. Write for a complete list of reports and publications

Ross, Donald K. *A Public Citizen's Action Manual.* New York: Grossman Publishers, 1973. If you want to organize to get information or action on consumer issues, this book attacks a number of common problems, and tells you how to take citizen action as a group.

Stone, Alan. *Economic Regulation and the Public Interest.* London, England: Cornell University Press, 1977.

Uniform Tire Quality Grading. Washington, DC: US Department of Transportation, April, 1979.

"You've Got to Move", Consumer Federation of America, 1012 14th Street NW, Washington, DC 20005, 737-3732. This newsletter is published once every three weeks. It costs $1 a year and reports on the activities of state and local consumer groups.

Webb, Beatrice, *The Discovery of the Consumer.* Washington, DC: Cooperative League of the USA, 1947.

Jewelry Objects D'Art
Estate Jewelry, Diamonds and Precious Stones
Contemporary, 18th and 19th Century Paintings
Oriental Rugs

the Antique Guild

Estates and Individual Items Purchased, Traded and Sold

Art Search
113 N. Fairfax
Old Town Alexandria
Virginia 22314
(703) 836-1048

Duke St. Antique Center
4615 Duke St.
West End Shopping Plaza
Alexandria, VA 22304
(703) 370-2500

Food Drugs & Cosmetics

DRUGS

There are actually very few cures around today. A drug may relieve your symptoms, but it will rarely, if ever, cure you. It becomes obvious then that you understand what, indeed, a drug is: A working definition for "drug" would be "anything which you use to stem, heal, or prevent illness".

Let's look at one common scenario: You've just seen your doctor, and he has prescribed some medication. Now you're off to the drug store with the prescription in hand. If you're like most people, the rest is easy: present the slip to the druggist, get your medication, pay him, and prepare to feel better. And, if you're like most people, you won't think twice about the transaction. Why should you? You trust your doctor, and you trust your pharmacist to do their best on your behalf. This blind faith could cost you some extra money. Somebody may, in fact, be cheating or overcharging you. It may be deliberate, but, more likely, it has to do with the controversy over *generic* and *name-brand* drugs.

Generic Drugs

Americans spend about $10 billion annually on prescribed medications, and nearly $3 billion on non-prescription or over-the-counter (OTC) drugs. Of these billions of dollars spent on drugs, a majority is spent on brand name prescribed products. These are drugs given names by their manufacturer other than the chemical name which represents the ingredients. For example, Parke-Davis manufactures a drug called *phenytoin sodium*, but markets it as *Dilantin*. In this case, phenytoin sodium is the generic name and Dilantin is the brand name. Dilantin is the far more familiar name, and the one you will hear the doctor prescribing, but actually he's calling for the drug compound phenytoin sodium.

This knowledge may be very important to you. It is possible that your prescribing doctor either does not know the generic term for Dilantin, or, if he does, has never found any reason to investigate the comparative costs of the brand name drug and the generic form. But then, why should he? If the drug has the desired effects, both patient and doctor should be satisfied. Right?

This is correct only from the doctor's point of view: he does not pay for the patient's prescription. If he did, it would probably interest him to know that generic forms of many drugs are not only cheaper than brand names but, in many cases, astoundingly so. (If you, as a consumer, want to check the cost comparison between specific brand names and generics, you might find the book *Facts and Comparison* handy. You will be able to see just what ingredients you are buying in a brand name drug, and how much you are paying for it compared to the generic form of the same drug. There are some times when you and your doctor may prefer generic forms, as for example when:

- The generic form is widely thought to be equivalent to the brand name drug;
- The dosage and method of taking the generic form are consistent with your doctor's prescription;
- The generic form has no additives to supply or precipitate complications or side effects;
- The generic prescription is cheaper; and
- You plan to stay on the medication over a long period of time and wish to keep costs down.

All of this is not to imply that generics have all the advantages and brand names the disadvantages. Generics have a place in medical treatment, and in the consumer's budget, but there are times when they just will not fill the bill:

- Your doctor may prefer the brand name form for its added ingredients, or lack of added ingredients — for example, it could be buffered, flavored, or compounded;
- Your doctor may know that there is no generic form or equivalent to the drug prescribed (some new drugs have patents still in force, and only one company has manufacturing rights);
- Your doctor may feel that you could forget the generic name when you report your progress or complications with a drug (especially when you are taking more than one drug). The brand name may have a shorter name that you will pay more for — but you may be more likely to have accurate communication with your doctor;

- Your doctor may be new to you and may not want to change to a generic form of medication from a brand name which you are already taking. Drugs have slight differences from batch to batch, and from manufacturer to manufacturer. If your previous doctor had prescribed a drug regimen, or long term maintenance prescription, and your body had become accustomed to it, your new doctor might not want to risk changing manufacturers because it might upset the way in which your body reacts to the medicine;
- Some proponents of brand-name drugs feel that there may also be what doctors call a "placebo effect" with certain drugs. In many cases, drugs which you have asked about with interest, or well-known drugs with good public reputations, are better for you because of your psychological reaction. Even if the drug has nothing more than fancier packaging and better publicity, you may benefit from what you have been convinced is the better medicine. Many doctors take the placebo effect seriously and usually adhere to it with inexpensive medicines. They may mention, for example, that you should take Bayer aspirin, despite the fact that it is more expensive than generic aspirin, for they will hope that you will continue to take it as prescribed because of its name and reputation.

Regardless of any of these conditions for or against using generics, the U.S. Food and Drug Administration (FDA) assures consumers that "...all drug manufacturers are subject to FDA inspection and must follow the Agency's Current Good Manufacturing Practice Regulations." Because of this safeguard, the FDA believes that "...there is no significant difference in quality between generic and brand name drugs."

Former FDA Commissioner Donald Kennedy has said, "There is simply no evidence to support the notion of serious quality differences between generic and brand name drugs."

Despite this assertion by Kennedy, there are those who feel that all drugs are not created equal. One such body is the Pharmaceutical Manufacturers' Association (PMA). The PMA feels that, in some cases, lower costs reflect lower standards of production of generic drugs. In essence, the PMA feels some cheaper drugs are of poorer quality.

The PMA also claims that drugs can vary in performance, even though active ingredients are identical. This can happen with drugs manufactured by intrastate producers who are not subject to federal inspection.

PMA also makes a case for the larger and more expensive producers — they tend to be the "innovaters", rather than the "copiers". In other words, they claim that, when you buy from one of the larger companies, you are usually supporting innovative research. They go even further, stating that you are getting the peace of mind that comes with knowing that the company has a better than average track record in terms of drug recalls. On the other hand, there are those critics of pharmaceutical manufacturers who claim that more money from the higher prices is going, not into innovative *research*, but into innovative *advertising*.

One of the more serious issues in the drug field is the inability of the FDA to monitor the consistency of drugs. This consistency is known as *bioequivalence* and is a major bone of contention between the government and the drug producers. The PMA feels that the purity of ingredients varies, but that the larger companies can safeguard against variations in formula and consistency of batch.

Incidentally, there are relatively few manufacturers of certain drugs like aspirin in the United States. These firms may sell to over a hundred other firms who will then ask to have a certain size, brand imprint, color, or shape made from the basic medicine. The large manufacturer will produce to various specifications, but will still be responsible for the high quality of the basic medicine.

Another issue is that of *bioavailability*. Bioavailability describes that fraction of the pill or medicine which you take that actually gets to where it will do its job. In the past, and in limited cases now, the varied ability of medicines depends on production technique. For example, a pill that is otherwise correct might fail to do its job because it does not dissolve fast enough. This failure to dissolve might be happening because the pill was too densely packed in the factory. Other factors — in and out of the manufacturer's plant — affect bioavailability.

State Laws

Are there any laws concerning generic drug prescriptions? Each state in the U.S. takes some kind of legal stand on this issue. Washington, DC, enacted its law in 1976. This law does not require a consumer to sign anything to receive generic drugs as substitutes for brand name drugs. There is also no requirement that your pharmacist notify the doctor of the generic substitution. And, unless the doctor writes the phrase "disperse as written", the pharmacist may fill the prescription generically without your consent, and without liability on the doctor's part. Nor is the pharmacist required to pass on to you the difference in cost between the brand name and the generic.

Maryland's law has been on the books since 1972 and is identical to the District of Columbia's — with one exception. In Maryland, if the prescription is filled with the generic, and the doctor has prescribed brand name, the difference in cost is returned to the consumer — clearly a better deal than you get in the District.

Virginia's law was passed in 1977 and is different from the two laws above, in that the physician is required to give prior written approval before the druggist can sell you a generic. The doctor is also liable for the medication prescribed. Cost savings, as in Maryland, are passed on.

The Good Patient

Being a good patient means asking the right questions and following the doctor's instructions. Being a good patient can also save you time and money — as well as make you healthier.

Smoking and Prescription Drugs: Ask your doctor about the effects of smoking on the drugs which he prescribes. This includes all forms of cigarettes, cigars, pipes, and even marijuana! Be particularly certain to ask this question if you smoke and are using contraceptives, darvon, asthma medication, and certain estrogens. The FDA article, "Drug Effects Can Go Up in Smoke" gives more information on smoking and drugs, of which the following is typical:

> Smoking also appears to interact with a number of other drugs such as imipramine, an antidepressant; glutethimide, a sedative; furosemide, a diuretic; and propranolol, a beta blocker.
>
> Further complicating the picture is the fact that smokers tend to consume other drugs and chemicals more frequently than nonsmokers. They take more cough medicine, aspirin-containing drugs, pain medicine, sleeping pills, tranquilizers, diuretics, hormones, iron medicine, amphetamines, antibiotics, stomach medicine, and laxatives than nonsmokers.

Drug Interactions: Smoking isn't the only thing that might cause a reaction or complication when you take drugs. How can you protect against inadvertent and often harmful drug interactions? There are some hints:

- When your doctor prescribes medication, remind him of other drugs you are using, including over-the-counter treatments, such as vitamins and sleeping pills. He should be aware of *all* of them — nothing is too insignificant or minor. Keep in mind, too, that alcohol is a drug — no matter what the volume — and will react with everything which you eat. If you plan to drink alcoholic beverages while on medication (at parties or at home, for example), tell your doctor.

- When your pharmacist fills your prescription, you may want to tell him what you had been taking in the past. Keep him abreast of what you are currently taking so that he can keep a record of your medications and can tell at a glance if you are in any danger of harmful drug reactions.

- When your friend suggests or gives you a drug prescribed for his own pain or disorder, decline. The drug which he might give you could accidentally harm you — and only your doctor or pharmacist may know that. But it will be too late if the doctor arrives on the scene *after* you take it. As a general rule, you should politely refuse the offer of someone else's medication or even over-the-counter drug without first consulting your doctor.

- When you get a drug prescription from your doctor or pharmacist, ask the generic name, no matter what the drug. Do this because many drug warnings have the generic name throughout the warning. For example, certain antacids warn about interactions with the antibiotic *tetracycline*, which is marketed under a number of different names. If you know only the generic name of your antibiotic, and took both it and the antacid, you could wind up a victim of a drug interaction.

- If you're a woman who is pregnant, or even just interested in getting pregnant, be sure your "other" doctor knows this as well as your obstetrician. Certain drugs which are routinely prescribed for common ailments should be avoided during the early stages of pregnancy, and this means that your doctor won't want to prescribe them if there's any chance you will become pregnant during the time you are taking them.

- They haven't finished writing the book on drug interaction effects yet. So, if you experience any persistent seemingly drug-related side effects which neither the pharmacist nor doctor mentioned ... ask about it! Remember that you pay them to help you.

Non-prescription Drugs — Over the Counter (OTC)

As the name implies, non-prescription drugs are those for which you need no prescription and thus which are commonly sold over-the-counter. That is how they get the name, which is abbreviated OTC. There are several basic categories of OTC drugs, each of which has basic characteristics, as discussed below:

Aspirin may be a true "wonder drug", because, while it is quite effective in relieving pain, doctors don't really know how it works. The chemical name is acetylsalicylic acid, and this is the active ingredient in aspirin. Aspirin is used as the generic name for this basic ingredient, which goes into hundreds of non-prescription medicines.

Aspirin is effective in numerous ways: it will aid in lowering your temperature, reducing inflammations, and easing various pains. There are many other things it can do which are not as pleasant: it can cause slight blood loss, stomach upset, and ulcers. For these reasons you should always take aspirin with a drink of water, or preferably milk. You would do this not only to protect your stomach in case the aspirin lodges against your stomach's lining, but also to insure the aspirin's dissolving. Aspirin has been known to wear away the mucus which lines your stomach. This will happen if you take too much aspirin and neglect to drink something with it. The resulting stomach sore is commonly known as an ulcer.

When you hear that an aspirin product is buffered, the manufacturer is telling you that the aspirin's inherent acidity has been reduced. This means that the risk of ulcer is reduced if not eliminated. But some tests refute the buffering process' power to reduce the aspirin's acidic nature.

There are relatively few aspirin makers in the United States compared to the number of firms who color it, buffer it, advertise it, package it, and market it. For this reason, the cheaper generic aspirins are usually a better value.

A popular alternative to aspirin as acetaminophen (which many people know by a brand name, "Tylenol"). Acetominophen is popular because it has less of a tendency to cause bleeding than aspirin, but, in large doses can cause liver damage. Acetominophen, according to the FDA, is really no safer than aspirin. In fact, in 1977, and FDA advisory panel recommended that warnings be put on aspirin and acetominophen labels. The warnings explain that prolonged use of these drugs could result in prolonged labor or bleeding for pregnant women, and, for those not pregnant, stomach distress, ulcers, and assorted complications arising from simultaneous administration of drugs prescribed for blood thinning, diabetes, gout, or arthritis. This, whenever you are taking prescription drugs, you should consult your doctor about the advisability of taking aspirin or acetominophen.

Antacids are supposed to settle your stomach when you have either eaten too much, or gotten heartburn, sour stomach, or acid indigestion. They do just that — usually no more and (you hope) no less. But the same FDA panel mentioned above warns against claims by some manufacturers that their products will also relieve: "nervous emotional disturbances", "nervous tension headaches", "cold symptoms", "overconsumption of alcoholic beverages", and "food intolerance".

Some antacids contain aspirin, which can further upset the stomach, but there are some newer products on the market which contain no aspirin. Look carefully at the ingredients listed on the label, and consult with your doctor whenever you are also taking other drugs.

Anti-acne preparations that you buy over the counter do not really claim any ability beyond cleansing and "fighting" acne and its spread. If you look closely at some of their ingredients, you will find water prominently listed. And, when you read their directions and promotional materials, you will also find that these preparations work by your scrubbing action. The anti-bacterial agents in the acne preparations do kill more bacteria than soap and water, but doctors say that surface bacteria are probably not the cause of the acne. Acne starts deep within the skin, and you cannot really deal with anything but the symptoms by using these medicines. So, for what the OTC acne preparations do for your skin, you may want to try soap and water, and save yourself some money. And, if you decide that the OTC preparation is worth the expense, keep your doctor informed on which one you use and how often. If the acne is bad enough, or acts up for unknown reasons, you may want to ask your doctor to recommend a dermatologist.

Antibacterials are usually found in ointments for minor cuts and burns. In 1977, the FDA advisory panel reported that five antibiotics used in non-prescription first aid ointments are safe and effective for keeping foreign substances and bacteria out of minor cuts. But the same panel said that there was no proof that the ointments promoted faster healing than ordinary body functions would.

The five substances okayed by the panel were: bacitracin, polymixin B sulfate (when added to another antibiotic), and three varieties of tetracycline.

The panel also concluded that antibacterial ointments should not be used for serious wounds if itching, redness, swelling, or pain develops or increases while using these products.

Antiseptics are used to kill bacteria in minor cuts and contain many of the same ingredients which antibacterials have. The same five ingredients recommended in antibacterials are also recommended in antiseptics. But, as with antibacterials, the panel warns that antiseptics do not speed the healing process and should not be used for more than a week or for continuing skin conditions.

Antiperspirants are thought to be drugs because they are intended to stop the body's perspiration process. In other words, they stop your body's sweat glands from their lubrication function, and, consequently, the sometimes objectionable odor which results. Deodorants will *not* stop the perspiring, but they will cover the smell. Many products are both antiperspirants and deodorants, but remember the difference when you shop.

The FDA found fault with one ingredient of many antiperspirants: Zirconium is an ingredient which, when inhaled, can cause lung disease and has therefore been removed from the market.

Cough and cold cures are really meant to treat only symptoms of coughs and colds. *There is no cure for the common cold.* And, of the 50,000 products which you could buy over the counter, not one will even shorten the life of your cold. Or, so says an FDA panel report which was published in 1976. The products you can get will drain your sinuses, stop your running nose, and clear up the gunk in the back of your throat, but they are not cold cures. Colds will run their course in your body. The best you can do is to relieve some of their symptoms.

Antihistamines will treat your allergic reactions to numerous things in the air or on your skin, and vitamins will help you some, but neither will stop a cold or cure it, according to that same FDA panel.

Laxatives are supposed to relieve your constipation. They are a big business — almost $300 million per year. But, for all of the television ads and written claims, the FDA rules them a big waste. According to a report released in 1975, only 45 of 81 laxative ingredients were both safe and effective. The rest? The rest were either unsafe, ineffective, or of indeterminant qualities. And, of all the people who use laxatives, the FDA panel said that 98 per cent were using them needlessly. As a matter of fact, your doctor may have a safe, cheap, and effective way of helping you merely by changing a few dietary habits.

Not only do folks take laxatives needlessly, they take them to excess, and this can cause damage. According to the FDA panel, "Prolonged laxative use can in some instances seriously impair normal bowel function. Use of laxatives for acute abdominal pain, vomiting, and other digestive tract symptoms and lead to serious life-threatening situations."

Those ingredients found safe and effective by the FDA panel can be purchased in Ex-Lax, Correctol, Milk of Magnesia, Haley's M-O, Serutan, and Feen-a-mint.

Those considered by the FDA panel to be unsafe and ineffective are calomel, jalap, and podophyllum.

Mouthwashes draw a lot of fire from the medical profession. Doctors have overwhelmingly refuted the worth of mouthwashes in testimony before the Select Senate Committee on Small Business.

If the products did not claim to be antiseptic, they were dismissed as worthless, if pleasant-tasting, rinses with no medicinal effect. And if they were antiseptic, they were either too strong or too weak for the doctors' liking. A mouthwash could upset the bacterial balance in your mouth and lead to further problems.

You may have noticed that mouthwash commercials lately have disclaimers against curing or lessening the severity of colds. This is happening because they indeed have no power to prevent or cure colds and yet had, up until recently, made such claims.

Sedatives are supposed sleep aids or sleep inducers. Their contents and effectiveness have been questioned by doctors who testified before the Select Senate Committee on Small Business. Testimony revealed that some who took over-the-counter sleeping pills were actually kept awake. Others who overdosed on non-prescription sedatives experienced hallucinations, headaches, and certain eye disease (precipitate glaucoma). Ninety-five percent of the advertisements for sleeping pills were said to be false. The panel convened by the FDA concluded that OTC sedatives may help "occasional simple nervous tension". For any prolonged problem with sleep or nervousness, see your doctor.

What to Do to Insure Your Responsible Use of Medicines

When you consult a physician, remember:

WHAT TO TELL THE DOCTOR:
1. Full details of all your symptoms.
2. Other doctors, including non-MDs, currently treating you.
3. Other medicines you take, including non-prescription products such as aspirin or laxatives.
4. Any allergic reactions you have to specific medicines, or side-effects that regularly occur when you take certain medicines.

WHAT TO ASK THE DOCTOR* ABOUT THE PRESCRIPTION HE GIVES YOU:
1. What *is* the medicine (type and name)?
2. What results are expected from your taking it?
3. How will you know if the medicine does *not* work as expected?
4. How long should you wait before reporting if there is no change in your symptoms?
5. Are there any side-effects you are expected to notice?

6. What side-effects (if any) are you to report?
7. Are there any cautions you should observe while taking the medicine? (Any foods or beverages you should avoid, other medicines you should not take, limitations on driving vehicles).
8. Are there any specific instructions about how and when to take the medicine?
9. How long should you continue to take the medicine?
10. Can the prescription be refilled? If it can, are you to check with the doctor before having it refilled?
11. Has a particular manufacturing source been specified on the prescription for the medicine — one the doctor is confident produces a reliable quality product, and, when possible, one whose product may cost less than other manufacturers' versions of the medicine?

FACTS YOU SHOULD KNOW ABOUT PRESCRIPTION MEDICINES:
1. Your condition may not require use of any medicine; don't insist on a prescription if the doctor says none is needed.
2. *No* medicine is expected by medical science to be effective for 100% of the people who use it; or even 100% of the times it is used by those for whom it *is* effective.
3. The medicine prescribed is a part of your medical *treatment;* it is not a consumer product for you to choose. It is, as much as a scalpel, a medical tool your doctor uses to help you regain, or retain, your health. Only your doctor should choose the medicines you receive.
4. When you receive a prescription for a medicine, get it filled; the success of your medical treatment depends on it.
5. After you have a prescription filled, take the medicine. Again, the success of your medical treatment depends on it.
6. When you take your prescription medicine, follow your doctor's instructions to the letter? If you do not remember or understand them, call the doctor's office.
7. You have the right to receive a written prescription that you may take to the pharmacy of your choice; or, if you asked for a phoned prescription, you have the right to specify which pharmacy you want the doctor to call.
8. Choose your pharmacy in advance of any illness, on the basis of any services you do or do not need (free home delivery, 24-hour availablilty, charge accounts), convenience, and reliability, as well as economy.

*Chances are the doctor will give you the answers to all of these questions without your having to ask, or you may already know the answers to some of them.

Courtesy of Consumer Affairs, Pharmaceutical Manufacturers Association, 1155 Fifteenth Street, NW, Washington, DC 20005.

FOOD

More and more of the money you make goes for less and less food nearly every trip to the market. The following tips will help you to cut your food bills and get more for the same money. You may need to change your habits or style somewhat, but the savings will be worth it. If you follow some of the more interesting and unusual suggestions below, you may have to do something totally new (like starting a buying club or co-op), and it might feel a bit uncomfortable. But the quicker you take some action, the sooner you will see benefits. This list of ideas starts with the simpler ones and works up to the bigger savings.

Good Ideas for Food Shoppers

- Plan your list before you shop. There is nothing old-fashioned about a shopping list. And there is nothing suave or cool about going list-less and carefree. Make a list by writing down all of the staples you have or are going to run out of soon and foods you will need for meals you are planning; then ask the other members of the family or household what other items they would like. Don't waste cash on an item that is cheap yet unwanted — there's no bargain on stale-this or rotten-that because no one ate it. Lists avoid waste.

- Keep the food section of the newspaper or local shopping circular around to consult while you make up your list. This way, you can shop the sales and compare stores in advance of your trip to the grocery store.

- Buy in case lots when it is cheaper. Always ask the store manager about this. Sometimes stores have periodic case specials, and some stores always give discounts when you buy a case.

- Cut convenience foods — unless you absolutely have no time to cook. They cost more and often have many empty calories of refined starches and sugar. If you make the same things yourself, it will not only cost less, but will probably also taste better. Also, having to cook may deter you from an extra dessert or late-night snack, because it would not be readily available.

- Snacks can make up as much as 10% of your weekly food bill. Train yourself to either cut down on costly snacks with low nutritional value; or go out and spend your snack allocation more wisely on healthier foods. You don't have to think like a nutritionist, but remember how much those flavored potato chips cost and how many you have to eat to satisfy that hungry feeling. You might as well have some carrots and celery with sour cream or yoghurt dip. It is better for you and more filling.
- Keep in mind the wealth of food you have in leftovers. True, it isn't a new idea, but don't forget to consider it when you go food shopping. What will make good leftovers? If you plan to buy a roast on Thursday, buy anything you need to make extra gravy for roast beef sandwiches in following days. And don't throw out the little bits and pieces of things that go well in chef's salads and omelettes. These things also make great spur-of-the-moment hors d'oeuvres and TV snacks.
- Consider buying a freezer. Studies have shown that it is probably worth it to you only in convenience, and particularly if you don't use it for storage -- for then you are just paying a lot more for the food you keep in it — but for rotating foods through it. Freezers do help you take advantage of meat specials. Of interest here might be a government booklet, "How to Buy Meat for Your Freezer", US Government Printing Office, Washington, DC, 20452, available at a small charge.
- Shop alone, and particularly avoid going to the store with inexperienced shoppers. These people are notorious for their expensive impulses and unnecessary purchases. Also, pay in cash; you will better see what you pay for and what the cost really is. Avoid telephone shopping, and credit card purchasing. The delivery and/or interest charges add up over a year and the money is better of spent elsewhere.
- Don't shop on an empty stomach — impulse buying is sure to follow;
- Keep records of prices which you pay for major food items and shift your purchases to substitute brands or goods as prices indicate better buys.
- Buy up things you like when they are on special and freeze or store them. Some forethought now will save you time and money in the future.
- Seriously consider the in-house or local brands. Each store may have more than one in-house brand name, each representing a different grade or quality of merchandise. You can save on comparable quality goods because you will not be paying for the national advertising or transportation costs. Buy what pleases you, but give the house labels a try.
- If a food is frozen, make sure it is not covered with frost. If the can is supposed to be round, make sure there are no bulges. Spoiled food is no

bargain, whatever the price. If you discover that food you've just bought is spoiled when you return home from the store, take it back. They should gladly refund the cost. If you live a long way from the store, call the manager immediately. He may be able to make an arrangement to refund your money on your next trip to the store.

- Buy your bulk items — like flour and sugar — in large bags and save money. Then, if you want, put them in containers of your own. Buying in large bags saves about 20% of costs. Also, if you want a convenience container (for food, cleaning products, etc.), buy it the first time around and save it; the next time you buy the product, buy the large or refill size, and refill the container you saved.

- Realize how much you can use before spoilage. The "economy size" is no bargain if you end up throwing away the excess. Buy what you can use.

- Watch out for the marked "pull date". These dates are often artificial and illogical, and the food is still good after they have come and gone. There are usually ample supplies of bakery goods, particularly day-old bread, but day-old meat is in short supply most of the time. Note also what doesn't seem to move in the stores at which you usually shop. If certain items on the shelves have outlived their pull dates, but you're sure they're still wholesome, ask for a discount on them. It doesn't hurt to bargain.

- Watch the checker carefully — inadvertent errors in punching in the numbers can cost you money. Also, he or she may not be aware of the sale prices or half-price marked-down items like day-old merchandise.

- Comparison shop — don't stick to one store. The time you spend checking out a variety of stores may will pay off in terms of dollars saved.

- You can save money by buying the cheaper form of a food: fresh, canned, dried, frozen, depending on availability and the time of the year. Decide what you want to do with the food, and see if a cheaper form fits the bill.

- Plan meals around weekly specials as much as possible.

- Shop the seasonal specials. Fruits and vegetables in season can save you a fair amount. Bake or can these things for future use. Avoid buying the first shipment of anything, though, for it will be the most expensive.

- If you are bold, ask the manager if he will meet the prices of competitive stores in the area. If there is, for example, only a few cents difference per pound between his price and the other store's, it may be worth it to him to keep you shopping at his store.

- Avoid doing food shopping at small convenience stores. You will pay a lot for the convenience, and, in the final analysis, is higher price a convenience?

- Proteins are important, but red meats are expensive. Try these substitutes: chicken, eggs, cottage cheese, peanut butter, dry beans, cheese. These are good for lunches and occasional dinners (chicken is an all-purpose quality dinner protein).

- When something new is on special, buy one unit of it the first day of the sale. If you don't like it, you are not stuck with more. And, if you do like it, you can return on following days and stock up on it while it is still on special.

- Always ask for a raincheck or out-of-stock slip on an advertised special if the store has run out. Most stores will gladly give them to you unless they specify otherwise. This helps to build good will for their stores, instead of sending you away grumbling about phony advertised specials.

- Consider using coupons — more on this will follow below.

- Look at tips and recipes offered by the US Department of Agriculture, your local Cooperative Extension Services, and the newspaper and magazines' food editors. These folks specialize in foods and have good insights.

Some other insights for you . . .

- Under federal law, the contents of a packaged product will appear in order of weight, the heaviest ingredient listed first. So, if you are stumped about which beef soup to buy, choose the one with more beef, all other things being equal, and get a better buy. Conversely, if you want less sugar in your cookies or cereal, consult the ingredient list to buy the one where sugar is further down the list.

- Did you know that the word "burgers" signifies more actual meat by volume than "patties"? If a hamburger contains anything besides meat, it is a patty. Patties will cost you less, but you are buying some cereal (like soy extender) and filler (who knows what?).

- If you are buying an imitation (like bacon bits), the label must say "imitation" — look for this. It frequently is true with flavoring found in sweets.

- Any product which has extra added vitamins and minerals, or claims special nutritional value, must show you the amounts and contents of these additives.

- And almost every food that you can buy has federal requirements on what percentage of primary ingredients it must contain. For example, canned hash must have 35% meat. The point is, Uncle Sam is trying to help keep you on a healthy diet.

- Open dating means that you are told the date on which the product must come off the shelves or be reduced in price. As mentioned before, these pull dates are sometimes arbitrary. This means that if a can has been sitting around on a shelf past its pull date, you should get a break on the price. And if you discover that you've paid full price for food past its pull date, return it to the store for a refund or partial rebate.

- Shopping unit prices is a great value device. Unit pricing tells you how much you are paying for a specified quantity. For example, 8 ounces of one brand of cheese at $1.59 is about 20c per ounce, or $3.20 per pound (16 ounces times 20c). And another cheese at 6 ounces for $1.40 may look like a good buy, but it really costs you about 23c per ounce or $3.68 per pound. Thus, you should be able to decipher the better buys just by looking at the unit prices posted just above or below the products and comparing them. Usually, you will find that store brands will have lower unit prices. If you are not interested in store brands, the unit pricing will help you to compare "name" brands to each other.

- Ground beef should also be compared — don't be taken in by great low prices. Fat content is the issue here. In Virginia, "regular" ground beef is allowed to contain 28% fat, "lean" may have up to 23%, and "extra lean", 18% fat. The District of Columbia has similar rules; and Maryland makes no restrictions on fat in meat sold in that state.

Buying Clubs and Cooperatives

Organize a buying club! It is really not very complicated, and it is usually fun. In fact, you probably would not have to go very far to find enough people to form a club from among your friends, associates, or relatives.

The whole club can consist of ten to twelve families. Since your group will be small, you can eliminate overhead like trucks, storage centers, and hired help.

In recruiting families and individual members, make sure that you have compatible eating habits (vegetarians won't always fit well with meat lovers). Also make sure that the commitments are strong enough so that people can be expected to help out when scheduled to and also in cases of emergency. Members should be willing to do as much shopping as possible through the club.

Agree on a common list and suppliers (which can be found in the telephone books). Also agree on a rotation list for food pick-up. A rotation of homes to use as distribution centers is also necessary. No one car should make all the deliveries. Food is "sold" to members on a per-unit basis, or bought with enough pooled money to cover all costs. There is no profit, for profit pushes up the price.

By cooperating with other clubs you can learn of new tips and suppliers. You can also pre-arrange large purchases like sides of beef.

Leftovers, though unusual, can be a problem, so work up a list of people who would be willing to buy up those surpluses at a savings. Or decide what charitable organization or other group you would donate the excess to. Work out agreements for prompt payment and conditions for entering and leaving the group. Members who are chronically late on payments and buy small amounts are best left out of future purchases.

Get to know each others' preferences and tastes — and be willing to experiment. The person doing the buying often has to make on-the-spot decisions for the group, particularly when buying fresh produce and meats. The member who refuses to try anything new complicates this process; but on the other hand, you shouldn't be expected to take part of a case of okra every week if you just can't stand okra.

Technically speaking, a cooperative (often called a "co-op") is the buying club taken one step further. A co-op is an entity which requires a larger permanent space and some investment. You would need a storefront or converted garage to shelve the foods, and some capital invested to cover the costs of running a co-op. Costs may include a rented or purchased freezer or refrigerator, a telephone line, and costs of paying employees who will move stock and operate the co-op when inconvenient to members. There are countless variables, but the principle works. For information on starting your own co-op, you can write to the Cooperative League of the United States at 1828 L St., NW. Washington, DC 20036.

There are many, many local small food co-ops and buying clubs in the area. One co-op, the Bethesda Avenue Co-op, is profiled later on in this section. Another, the Uncommon Market at 1311 North Troy Street in Arlington, VA (telephone 528-4806), operates in much the same manner as the Bethesda Store. The Community Warehouse at 2010 Kendall Street NE in the District of Columbia (832-4517) urges people to organize buying clubs, and can help to supply groups with food and ideas. On a recent visit there, we were treated to a rather "laid-back" philosophy — so if you are in a hurry to get started, need more information, or just basically prefer more conservative associates, you might want to consult with the co-ops listed above instead of the Community Warehouse. Also, the Greenbelt Cooperative Association, which operates the Coop and Consumer Food Marts, puts out a monthly cooperative newsletter. For further information on the Greenbelt operation, and other cooperatives in the area, you could consult with Don Cooper at the Potomac Cooperative Federation at 953-2770, extension 312.

WHERE TO FIND GOOD FOOD AND DRUG BUYS

Arnold Bakery Thrift Shop
Brookfield Plaza
Springfield, VA
569-1046

The best buys in this shop are the Arnold brand breads which are past the pull date marked on the package, but are still saleable. Although they will remain fresh in your freezer or refrigerator, they will not last as long as fresh-baked goods. The other items here are mainly for convenience and to round out what would otherwise be a limited selection. These items include Burh health food grains, which sell just at suggested retail prices. The Penn Dutch cookies, Herr's potato chips, and Drake's boxed cakes sell a few cents below what you would find them at in a supermarket — so it isn't worth coming here just to find them. The bread, however, as mentioned before, is an *excellent* bargain, and if you do come for bread, you won't lose any money by buying any of the other items. They also feature a selection of bagged candies, nuts, and crackers.

Hours are from 10 am to 7 pm, Monday through Friday, and Saturday from 10 am to 6 pm. Ample parking in the shopping center lot.

The Bethesda Avenue Coop
4949 Bethesda Avenue,
Bethesda, MD
986-0796

This is a worker-managed, community board-run co-op, carrying mostly bulk items. They carry some prepackaged goods. The shelves are stocked with bread, produce, cheese (imported and domestic), dairy goods, bulk grain, seeds, nuts, and spices. They also carry natural cosmetics. There are no rules which exclude anyone here. Rather, if you are willing to volunteer for three hours a week, you can get a 20% discount on your shopping. Next door, there is a cafe and bookshop affiliated with the co-op; crafts are also sold there. These two shops may jointly offer courses in nutrition, natural cooking, and like subjects — call for further information on this.

Checks are accepted, as are cash and food stamps (10% discount with food stamps). They say that they expect to have special treatment for senior citizens. There are a small number of allocated parking spaces in front of the store, and a larger number in lots up the street.

Box and Bag
8541 Piney Branch Road
Silver Spring, MD
589-8224

You can buy dry food, boxed food, canned food, paper goods, and cleaning products, as well as Sunbeam Bread and Entenmann pastries and cakes here. They carry Green Giant and Del Monte, as well as many other popular brands. They also have a second label, which is less well known, called Pride of Farm. All merchandise is first quality. Discounts vary by item, from a few cents to up to 30¢ or 40¢ per item. They provide boxes free but charge 2¢ per bag — or you can bring your own. They will reduce prices even further when manufacturers offer them a special allowance.

Other addresses:
Also in Upper Marlboro, Maryland, and Glen Burnie, Maryland.

Hours are from 10 am to 6 pm on Tuesday through Thursday, Friday from 10 am to 8 pm, and Sunday from 10 am to 2 pm. They accept cash and food stamps, and no travelers' checks. They take money-back and money-off coupons. All merchandise is 100% guaranteed. Parking in shopping center lots.

Budget Foods
8550 Laureldale Road
Laurel, MD
953-3053

Budget Foods is a warehouse-type operation, located in a small commercial area in Laurel. They stock dry groceries, canned goods, and paper goods. Bring your own bags and boxes, and bag your own sales — that is one way that they help the consumer to save money. Cartons are arranged in rows, stacked up to form aisles. Major labels of canned goods include Green Giant, Delmonte, and Libby's, and they also offer a second, lesser-known label, called Pride of Farm. Boxes are provided free, and all merchandise is first quality. They say that the distributor from whom they purchase their stock (who also operates the Box and Bag operations) has conducted studies which indicate that the consumer can save from 16% to 20% of his or her food bill by shopping at this type of outlet.

Hours are from 10 am to 6 pm on Tuesday and Wednesday, until 8 pm on Thursday and Friday, from 9 am to 6 pm on Saturday, and Sunday from 10 am to 2 pm. They accept cash and food stamps only. They will take money-off and money-back coupons. Parking is ample.

Discount Food Outlet
1011 E. Gude Drive
Rockville, Maryland
424-0997

An unusual food store, in a warehouse environment, the Discount Food Outlet offers about 40% salvage merchandise (things that were damaged in the warehouse or in trucking) which are not cosmetically intact; and 60% perfect merchandise, which comes from factory buying deals. There are always a number of packaged cereals, canned vegetables, and pet foods. Food brands include major companies like Progresso, General Foods, and Hunt's. Staples are always available at the same price. You can also find factory seconds of paper goods here, in which the perforations are not consistent. Some cans may be dented or boxes crushed, but they still met federal health standards. Other seconds are on items whose weight might be slightly short. Irregulars and seconds are labelled. The discount on perfect merchandise runs an average of 10% to 15% and you can get 20% to 50% off on salvage merchandise. You can get an additional 10% discount on case salvage goods. Other available items include luncheon meats, bacon, sausage, milk, butter, eggs, chicken — and a complete line of frozen foods. The atmosphere might put you off a bit, but for canned and packaged goods, you can get quite a good bargain here. Their advertisements usually appear in the Thursday Food section of the *Washington Post.*

Monday-Wednesday, they are open from 9 am to 5 pm; Thursday and Friday from 9 to 8 pm; and from 9 am to 6 pm on Saturday. Only cash and checks with proper identification are accepted payment. They accept food stamps, and also cents-off coupons. Satisfaction is guaranteed.

Division Medical Supplies
615 Division Ave., NE
Washington, DC
396-5555

Division Medical supplies mostly hospitals and nursing homes, with equipment ranging from surgical supplies to band-aids to hospital beds, all at warehouse prices. They also make these products available to the individual consumer, at a slightly higher price. They carry major brands, like Everest and Jennings wheelchairs, Edco, and a variety of others. All merchandise is first quality. The average discount here is about 10%, but as with all stores, it varies depending on the item — often you can get a better deal. Free delivery is available within a radius, including Maryland, Virginia, and DC. The customer can also order from manufacturers' catalogues anything that is not in stock. A store catalogue is available, starting the first of January, 1980. Manufacturers' guaranties or warranties are backed up by the company, and repairs, when necessary, are done here. The store also has licensed fitters for prosthetics.

Personal checks are accepted with proper identification, as are Master Charge, VISA, and Central Charge. At the time of publication, the management was considering offering American Express and NAC as well. There is a rent with option to buy plan, or customary rentals. They do accept third party Medicare/Medicaid payments. Parking is shared with the service station lot next door to the store.

For Eyes
809 West Broad St.
Falls Church, VA
241-0778/0779

Although many optical shops are offering special deals on a variety of eyeglasses, For Eyes was probably the first to open up this area's market in discount eyewear. Available are a wide selection of designer frames, as well as more conservative styles. Everything is guaranteed — if the frames break within a year's time, they will replace them free of charge. Single vision eyeglasses in plastic — tinted or clear — cost $29. Bifocals run from $35 for glass to $45 for plastic, and trifocals are priced at $45 for glass, and $55 for plastic. The prices of cataract glasses depend on the specific prescription. Trained opticians work at each store.

Other addresses:
1829 M St. NW, Washington, DC, 659-0777/0778.
1666 33rd St., NW, Washington, DC, 333-1120 or 222-2340.
8407 Georgia Avenue, Silver Spring, MD, 588-8407 or 588-8462.

Marketplace Foods
6801 Bland Street
Springfield, VA

The advantage of a no-frills warehouse style operation like this one is obvious: lower prices. You pay by getting a limited selection — in this case, from 750 to 1,000 items that are regularly stocked. Major brands are carried here, and produce is also available, delivered fresh daily from DC markets. This is a nicely arranged food store, with some stacked boxes, and some aisles with shelf space. There is a variety of packaged and canned foods, including major national brands, and some house brands of local and not-so-local stores. The store is large and roomy, and very neat. You bag (or box) your own goods. If you buy a case, you get an additional few percent off on your purchases. And your satisfaction is guaranteed, so you can return defective or unsatisfactory merchandise, as long as you have your receipt.

They prefer that you don't phone in to see what they have — again, a measure to help keep the costs down. The store is open from Monday through Saturday from 10 am to 7 pm, and Sunday from 11 am to 5 pm. Personal checks with proper identification are accepted. They are located in a shopping center, and parking is ample. Advertisements in small local papers will tell you about available specials. The store is closed on major holidays — Christmas, New Year's, and Thanksgiving.

Marlin Sales Annex
1415 Okie Street, NE
Washington, DC
526-1700

In the summertime, when we visited the Marlin Sales Annex, it had almost the air of an old-time street market. This is located in a warehouse, as an annex to a wholesale food operation. We considered it an exciting find — for both price and availability of items. Again, in this type of operation, there is a very limited selection of perishables, and the emphasis is on grocery lines of canned and packaged goods, as well as related items, like paper goods and pet food. The warehouse is organized roughly by aisles, with some cartons stacked up in displays, and some food displayed on counters as in a conventional grocery store. Large signs sit atop the displays of cartoned items, giving a price per unit as well as a case price — which gives you another 8% off the already discounted price. Marlin receives merchandise that may have been dented, or surplus deliveries, and goes through each case with a fine-tooth comb, eliminating what is dented or even cosmetically imperfect. What reaches the shelves should be in near-perfect condition — if it is not, the management asks that you tell them about it. Satisfaction is guaranteed 100% — and they take pains to emphasize this.

The average discount which you can expect is about 25% off grocery prices, sometimes below cost. They will supply bags or boxes to you if you don't bring your own.

Hours are Monday through Friday from 8 am to 4 pm, and Saturday from 9 am to 2:15 pm. This is basically a cash and carry operation, accepting personal checks with sufficient identification, with a minimum limit on check size. They do not accept any charge cards, but do accept food stamps. The store has its own parking lot — this is a relief, for the street outside is narrow, and can literally become stuffed with double-parked cars. They are less than a block from a bus stop on the Ivy City line.

MEDCO/Standard Drugs/Standard Discount
914 F Street NW
Washington, DC
737-4991

This is a chain of neatly-organized discount stores carrying primarily health and beauty aids, over-the-counter drugs, film, and a small line of sundries, as well as tobacco and cigarettes. They all sell Hanes underwear and socks, some convenience foods, and pet and school supplies. Generally, the merchandise brands, some nationally known and some lesss-well-known, are of a medium quality. Most merchandise is first quality, but, if not, it is labeled to the contrary. This is often true with items like T-shirts and linens. Special merchandise like this is displayed in sale bins. Prices are competitive with other similar stores, including larger full line chain discount stores, and you can expect to save 15% to 35% on your purchases. The difference in the three types of stores are slight. Most Standard stores have prescription counters, but Medco stores do not.

Other addresses:
Medco, 605 King Street, Alexandria, VA, 549-4289
Medco, 812 18th Street, NW, Washington, DC
Medco, 1107 Pennsylvania Avenue, NW, Washington, DC, 783-3510
Medco, 1113 G Street NW, Washington, DC
Medco, 717 11th Street, NW, Washington, DC, 737-4833.
Standard Drug, 1805 Columbia Road, NW, Washington, DC, 667-3237
Standard Drug, 1125 H Street, NE, Washington, DC, 397-4600.
Standard Drug, 3929 Minnesota Avenue, NE, Washington, DC, 396-1152
Standard Discount, 8670 Colesville Road, Silver Spring, MD 585-7846
Standard Discount, 1500 University Boulevard East, Langley Park, MD, 439-1300

Personal checks are accepted to a limit of $15. No credit cards are accepted. For returns, you can get cash back or credit, provided you have your receipt. At the Alexandria and downtown store locations, parking is on-street and limited. Hours vary, usually from 9:30 am to about 6 pm. Medco stores are closed on Sundays, but Standard stores are open. The Pennsylvania Avenue store is closed on Saturday.

Muehly's Thrift Bakery
1115 S. Charles St.
Baltimore, MD
(301) 539-1034

When we were researching some of the stores in the inner harbor section of Baltimore, we came across this discount store, selling day-old bread and cakes, and overbakes from Muehly's bakery. They also sell special orders which weren't picked up. What we particularly like about Muehly's — and what many commercial bakeries lack — is that they sell "real" bread and cakes, not prepackaged. In fact, the regular retail store is right around the corner. Its unprepossessing exterior is no indication of what is to be found inside. We bought two different types of cake, both of which were fresh — and remained that way for quite a while in our refrigerator, despite the claim that they were a day old. The cakes also tasted quite good. So, if you are shopping or visiting in the area, a stop here is probably worthwhile. The shop is actually around the corner south of the address given above, which is for the retail store.

They open at 9 am on weekdays. Beware: they say that they close up at 4 pm, but we found that they might close sooner than that, depending on business.

Pepperidge Farm Thrift Store
6554 Backlick Road
Springfield, VA
451-6979

This store sells mostly Pepperidge Farm products that are "not up to quality standards", which means that they might be a bit short on weight, overweight, or in a package that's a little irregular. There is a wide variety of items, including cookies, crackers, frozen cakes, turnovers, stuffing mixes, dumplings and relishes, and dressings. Sometimes they have case specials, and, on the whole, you can expect to save 20% to 30% off the customary retail price of the goods. They also carry Debbie's and Drake's cookies and cakes, and Charles' Potato Chips. The store is neatly organized and very clean.

Other address:
15513 New Hampshire Avenue, Cloverly Shopping Center, Silver Spring, MD, 384-4420, where the hours are Monday through Friday from 10 am to 6 pm, and Saturday until 5.

Hours at Springfield store: Monday through Friday, 10 am to 6 pm; Saturday from 10 am to 5 pm, and closed Sunday. Personal checks are accepted with proper identification. If merchandise is defective, they will give you a replacement, but this is basically an as-is operation.

Rodman's Discount Drugs
7723 Georgia Avenue NW
Washington, DC
723-5200

Rodman's may be the best-known discount druggist in this area. In addition to prescription and over-the-counter drugs, they also sell small appliances, cosmetics, food, sundries, photography equipment and film, tobacco products, and much more. Discounts vary, averaging about 10% to 60%, depending on the product. Most items are in stock, but, if necessary, the store personnel will special order for you. There are no deliveries. They usually run weekly sales, beginning on Wednesdays and lasting for a week; and monthly sales which begin on Sundays and last for 12 days. These are advertised in the *Washington Post*. Most of the stores are quite large and present a wide variety of merchandise.

Other addresses:
6305 Allentown Road, Camp Springs, MD, 449-4402
10362 Lee Highway, Fairfax, VA, 273-5996
5100 Wisconsin Avenue NW, Washington, DC 363-3466
3839 Alabama Avenue, SE, Washington, DC, 584-9000
Randolph Road, and Veirs Mill Road, Wheaton, MD, 946-3100
218 N. Frederick St., Gaithersburg, MD, 869-7900

Hours at the Georgia Avenue store are Monday through Saturday from 8 am to 10 pm, and on Sundays from 9 am to 7 pm. Hours at the other stores vary. Personal checks with proper identification are accepted, as are Master Charge, VISA, and NAC. Return policy is relatively flexible — with a receipt, you can usually make a return for cash or credit if you act within two weeks (or a month at the most).

Russell Stover Factory Outlet
Riverdale Plaza,
Riverdale, MD
779-2849

As the manager of this Russell Stover store explained, there are three levels of candy which are sold here: "full" — which is usually what you would buy in a retail store; "intermediate" — which would mean that the assortment is different that it would be in a full-priced box; and "seconds" — which are mis-shaped, mis-covered, and/or mis-marked (wrongly labeled). Intermediates are usually in their original boxes and are marked "intermediate". Seconds do not always appear in these attractive decorator boxes. The discount on seconds runs 50%; intermediates cost about 62% of the usual retail price. They can order first quality merchandise for you if you wish, with no deposit required. You can also taste samples here. The prices are the same year-round, and there are no special sales.

Hours at this store are from Monday through Saturday from 10 am to 9 pm. While personal checks are accepted, no credit cards are. They will hold items for you, upon request. But there are no exchanges or returns, as merchandise is sold "as is". The shop is at the intersection of Kenilworth Avenue and Riverdale Road.

Schmidt's Sunbeam Bakery
8008 Cryden Way
Forestville, MD
420-2400

Schmidt's is a family-owned business which sells surplus Sunbeam baked goods like bread, rolls, and cakes, as well as Mrs. Smith's restaurant pies, and other sweet goods, cola drinks, and potato chips. The average discount off retail is about 50%, and senior citizens get 10% off of that. Wednesdays are bargain days, when you can get even better buys.

Hours at Forestville are Monday through Saturday, from 9 am to 5 pm, and on Sunday from 8 am to 4 pm. Personal checks are accepted with identification. The nearest intersection is at Forestville Road.

Universal Beauty Supply Co., Inc.
Main Warehouse
2800-A Dorr Avenue,
Fairfax, VA
573-5500

The warehouse store on Dorr Avenue carries a smaller selection than the other stores, which are located in shopping centers. But the selection includes L'Oreal and Revlon cosmetics; Bel and Hairmate curling irons; Conair and J.R. dryers; and brushes by Denman, Scalpmaster, and Conair. Makeup is by Dermetics. They also sell beauty shop items like setting gels, shampoos, and hair coloring. In Springfield, they have a full range of perfumes, from drugstore brands to the fanciest French names. All stores carry Revlon and Dermetics nail polish. On special orders (which they do take), a partial or full deposit is required. You can save an average of 10% to 30% off usual retail prices by buying at Universal.

Other addresses and hours:
1055 W. Broad Street, Falls Church, VA; hours here are from Monday through Friday from 9:30 am to 6 pm, and Saturday from 9 am to 5:30 pm.
6773 Wilson Blvd., Zayre/Plaza 7; hours here are the same as at Broad Street.
5255 Duke Street, Alexandria, where the hours are Monday, Thursday, and Friday from 9 am to 5:30 pm, Tuesday and Wednesday from 9:30 am to 6 pm, and Saturday from 9 am to 5:30 pm.
2120 Veirs Mill Road, Rockville, MD; hours are the same as at the Broad Street and Wilson Blvd. locations.
Also part of the Universal Beauty Supply operation is Perfumes International at 6809 Springfield Plaza, which specializes in perfumes and cosmetics. The hours at Springfield are from Monday through Saturday from 9:30 am to 6 pm, Thursday until 9 pm, and Saturday from 9 am to 5:30 pm.

Washington Beef Company
1240 Fourth Street, NE
Washington, DC
547-8721

The Washington Beef Company has been purveying the finest in beef to well-known and lesser-known restaurants and hotels throughout the Washington area since 1932. Tired of having individual customers come to the door and ask if they could buy some, the management decided to do the public a favor, and open a retail outlet. This outlet is located right next to the warehouse, and in it they sell the highest quality finely trimmed beef, Empire kosher poultry and other ready-to-eat products, and other meats, such as bacon — which we noticed at a good price at our last visit there. The store's owners say that they offer a good value for your money — not a discount. If you are looking for fine cuts — or cuts you cannot even find in the supermarket — this is the place to come. On some of the packaged items, like bacon, you do get a bargain. Delivery is available free on orders of a minimum of $75 throughout a wide radius around the District. They also make available a product list, so you can see what they carry. Freezer specials are a particularly good buy. These are offered when they buy surplus from other stores, such as Giant and Safeway, and it is past the pull date marked on the surplus package. However, as long as it is kept frozen — which it is, in the large commercial lockers at WBC — it can be sold to the public without any worry. The WBC also has store specials weekly and daily. Weekly specials are advertised in the large newspapers in the area.

Hours are from Tuesday to Friday, from 8 am to 6 pm; Saturday, from 9 am to 4 pm and on Sunday from 8 am to 2 pm. The shop is closed on Mondays. Personal checks are accepted with proper identification, but no charge cards are taken. If there is any problem with the merchandise, they will gladly exchange it for you — but there are no returns. Parking is available in a small lot at the front of the store, or on the street, or — if nowhere else — at a fast food joint's parking lot nearby.

Wonder Bread Thrift Shop
5820 Seminary Road
Baileys Crossroads, VA
820-2746

These shops carry Wonder Bread and Hostess baked goods, including breads and cakes. They also carry candies, cookies, and pies from an assortment of manufacturers. Most items are a day old or surplus, and satisfaction is guaranteed. You can save an average of 40% by buying here. Each day there is a special, called a Superbargain, on a selected item.

Other addresses:
8522 Lee Highway, Merrifield, VA, 560-7878; Monday-Saturday, 9 am to 6 pm.
2301 Georgia Avenue NW, Washington, DC, 462-0990.
11290 Route 1, Beltsville, MD, (301) 937-8080; Monday through Friday from 8 am to 7 pm, Wednesday until 8, Saturday until 6 pm.
1175 Taft Street, Rockville, MD, off Gude Road, 424-4901; Monday through Saturday from 9 am to 6 pm.
Route 5, Waldorf, Maryland, (301) 645-1139; Monday through Saturday, 8 am to 9 pm.
7166 Burance Branch Road, Glen Burnie, MD, (301) 261-1588.
6550 Moravia Park Drive, Moravia Park, Baltimore, MD, (301) 483-2050; Monday through Saturday from 9 am to 6 pm.

LATE ADDITIONS:

Susan Kay Cosmetics
10551 Ewing Road
Beltsville, MD
937-4546

The small front entryway is deceptive: Susan Kay's is a large cosmetic store carrying cosmetics and accessories for men, women, and children. They feature well-known names of beauty products and perfumes, such as Orlane, Arden, Lancome, Ultima, and Revlon; a full line of men's and women's accessories; designer handbags by such names as Cardin, Gucci, Anne Klein, and Dior; watches; 14 karat gold jewelry; appliances of home and professional quality (e.g. hairdryers, curling irons); children's personal care items; salon quality supplies; and more. Discounts range by manufacturer, but you get 15% on Arden, 10% on Lancome, and 20% on Ultima and Revlon. Most non-cosmetic items are discounted 20% across-the-board. They also frequently bring in special purchase items where discounts can be up to 50% off comparable retail prices and will attempt to get items which they don't stock. There is a mailing list, and they send out flyers and brochures for periodic special purchases.

This store is open from Monday through Friday from 9 am to 6 pm, Thursday until 8 pm, and Saturday until 5 pm. Personal checks are accepted, as are Master Charge and VISA. There are no layaways or holds. There is a seven day return policy for credit, for merchandise returned intact with receipt. Ample parking out front and around the corner.

Discount Beauty Supply Inc./Craft House
3115 Hamilton St.
Hyattsville, MD
559-0058

You can purchase professional beauty supplies and craft supplies here. Brands of beauty supplies include Revlon, Wella, Clairol, Fermodyl, and Pantene. Everything is first quality. You can save from 15% to 20% as an individual, and more than that if you are a licensed beautician. Most items are in stock. On special orders, it takes a week to get them in stock. Special sales are held occasionally.

The store is open from 9:30 am to 6 pm on Monday through Saturday. Personal checks are accepted with proper identification, as are Master Charge and VISA. You can return items for cash or for credit.

The Pop Shoppe
6412 Brandon Avenue
Springfield, VA

This store sells primarily Po p Shoppe brand soda at reasonable costs. As of this writing, you can get 24 10-ounce bottles for $3.39 or 12 one-quart bottles for $3.79. If you buy at least cases in two months, you get one case free.

Hours are from noon to 5 pm on Sunday and from 10 am to 7 pm the rest of the week.

Other address:
7802 Richmond Hwy., Alexandria, VA.
This store is open from 10 am to 9 pm Monday through Sunday.

Plus Discount Foods
10700 Lee Highway
Fairfax, VA

A new chain of no-frills discount food stores selling canned, boxed, and other dried foods.

Other addresses:
610 Ritchie Highway, Severna Park, MD
New Silver Hill Road, Suitland, MD
Branch Road, Vienna, VA
14440 Jefferson Davis Hwy., Woodbridge, VA.

Discount Mail Order Drug Houses

NRTA/AARP
1909 K Street NW
Washington, DC

Membership in these groups is open to retired teachers and individuals over 55 years of age. A membership fee is required. They have seven regional offices with walk-in service, located in Long Beach, CA; St. Petersburg, FL; E. Hartford, Connecticut; Kansas City, MO; Washington, DC; and Indianapolis, IN.

Getz Prescription Company
916 Walnut Street
Kansas City, MO 64199
(816) 471-5466

There is no postage charge for mail order drugs from this company, but, on small orders, there is a nominal service charge.

Pharmaceutical Services
6427 Prospect Avenue
Kansas City, MO 64127

There is a $1 fee for orders under $8, but no postage charge at the time of this book's publication. An additional 10% discount is given to National Education Association members.

We suggest that you request price lists from these companies and compare the prices — or ask them what they charge for the prescriptions you usually get, if price lists are unavailable.

Pick Your Own Fruits and Vegetables

If you like to take long drives in the countries, but just cannot justify them because of the expense and shortage of gasoline, try combining these drives with picking your own produce. The money you save on the produce may compensate you for the gas... but, even if it doesn't, you will enjoy a pleasant ride and get some exercise too. The orchards and farms listed below are within a rough 80-mile radius of the District of Columbia. (There are others, but these are still further away. If you are interested in these, contact your local cooperative extension service. They will have complete lists; and, in Virginia, maps are available.) The ripening dates below (provided by the Maryland Cooperative Extension Service) are approximate and may differ slightly in the southern parts of Virginia, and depend on the weather. Always be sure to call ahead to get specific information.

MARYLAND: There are a number of counties which have here been eliminated from the comprehensive list, primarily those in the far northwestern section of the state, and on the Delmarva penninsula. While, geographically, those counties in Delmarva are within an 80 mile radius of the District, access to them is limited, and, because of this, the actual driving distance is excessive. What follows are the closer-in Maryland orchards and fields, listed in alphabetical order by county. Note that area codes are not included in the phone numbers below — if it's outside of your calling area, the area code is 301 anywhere in Maryland.

VIRGINIA: The following are arranged alphabetically rather than by county. Note that many feature products or services in addition to their pick-your-own operations.

Approximate Harvest Dates

FRUITS

Apples	August 15	— November 5
Blackberries	July 5	— August 1
Blackberries (Thornless)	August 1	— September 10
Black Raspberries	June 15	— July 10
Red Raspberries	June 15	— July 10
Blueberries	June 20	— August 1
Cider	July 21	— September 20
Grapes	August 15	— September 20
Nectarines	July 25	— August 25
Peaches	July 5	— September 20
Pears	August 15	— October 15
Plums	July 15	— September 15
Strawberries	May 15	— June 20
Sour Cherries	June 15	— July 15
Sweet Cherries	June 10	— July 10

VEGETABLES

Asparagus	April 25	— June 15
Beans (Green)	June 10	— September 15
Beans (Lima)	July 20	— September 1
Beans (Pole)	June 24	— August 30
Beets	July 4	— September 1
Broccoli	July 10	— September 1
Cabbage	June 1	— September 15
Cantaloupes	July 15	— September 15
Carrots	July 10	— September 15
Corn (Sweet)	July 4	— September 15
Cucumbers	July 1	— September 1
Cucumbers (Pickles)	July 1	— August 1
Eggplant	July 25	— September 10
Gourds	August 15	— October 30
Okra	July 15	— August 30
Peas (Green)	June 10	— July 1
Peas (Blackeye)	July 20	— August 30
Peppers	July 25	— September 15
Potatoes	July 1	— September 30
Potatoes (Sweet)	September 5	— December 15
Pumpkins	September 10	— November 30
Spinach (spring season)	May 1	— May 30
Spinach (fall season)	October 1	— October 30
Squash (Summer)	June 25	— September 1
Squash (Winter)	August 1	— September 30
Tomatoes	July 4	— September 15
Turnips	August 15	— November 1

Food, Drugs & Cosmetics

ANNE ARUNDEL COUNTY

Howard Gordon, Jr.
287 Sansbury Road,
Friendship, MD 20758
855-7309

Fruits; French hybrid wine grapes.

Pleasant Hill Farm
927 St. George Barber Rd.
Davidsonville, MD 21035

Fruits: Strawberries

Pettebone Brothers
1576-1578 Bay Head Road
Annapolis, MD 21401
757-2117/757-3128

Fruits: Strawberries

Pumphrey's Homegrown Veg.
10 Md. Rt. 3 South
Millersville, MD 21108
987-0669

Vegetables: Green peas, green beans, snap beans, blackeye peas, lima beans.

Belvoir Farm
1489 General's Highway
Crownsville, MD 21032
923-2107/923-6848

Fruits: S rawberries

BALTIMORE COUNTY

Eurice Farms
6250 Ebenezer Road,
Baltimore, MD 21220
335-4273

Fruits: Strawberries. Vegetables: Green beans, lima beans, green peas.

Hoffman's Farm
2038 Powers Lane
Baltimore, MD 21228
747-6957

Fruits: Grapes.

Huber's PYO Farm
12010 Philadelphia Road,
Bradshaw, MD 21021
679-1941/679-1948

Fruits: Strawberries. Vegetables: Green peas, green beans, tomatoes, cabbage, lima beans, blackeye peas, yellow wax beans, italian beans, spinach, peppers, cucumbers, okra, turnips, pumpkins, greens.

Arrowhead Farm
Offutt Road (South)
Randallstown, MD 21133
922-5465/(301) 464-2277

Fruits: Strawberries, peaches, thornless blackberries.

Esdraelon Vineyard
10618 St. Paul Avenue
Woodstock, MD 21163
328-2432

Fruits: Grapes.

Moore's Orchard
5242 E. Joppa Road,
Perry Hall, MD 21128
256-5982

Fruits: Apples, peaches. Vegetables: Snap beans.

Parker Farm Enterprises
43 W. Cherry Hill Road
Reisterstown, MD 21136
833-2447

Fruits: Strawberries. Vegetables: Green peas, sweet corn, lima beans.

Rutkowski & Taylor Farm
11211 Raphel Road
Upper Falls, MD 21156
592-8785/592-8764

Vegetables: Spinach, kale, cabbage, peppers, collards, cucumbers, green peas, mustard greens, beets, turnip tops, green beans, sweet corn, okra, tomatoes, squash, blackeye peas, broccoli, turnips.

CALVERT COUNTY

Stanley A. Ashmore
Route 1, Box 164
Huntingtown, MD 20639
257-6727

Fruits: Wine grapes.

Four Winds Farm
RR1, Box 721
Chesapeake Beach, MD 20732
257-6380

Fruits: Plums. Vegetables: Green beans, okra, tomatoes.

Calvert Produce
Box 30
Owings, MD 20836
257-2696

Vegetables: Green beans, tomatoes.

Neeld Orchard
Box 248
Plum Point, MD 20639
535-1655

Fruits: Peaches.

Strawberry Hill
Route 2, Box 15A,
Dunkirk, MD 20754
257-6463

Fruits: Strawberries

Josef & Donna Seidel
Box 233A
Huntingtown, MD 20639
535-2128

Fruits: Wine grapes, dessert grapes, peaches, thornless blackberries, red raspberries.

CARROLL COUNTY

Dale Aukerman
Stem Road
Linwood, MD 21764
775-2254

Fruits: Strawberries (organically grown)

Baugher Enterprises, Inc.
1236 Baugher Road
Westminster, MD 21157
848-5541

Fruits: Sweet cherries, sour cherries, red and black raspberries. Vegetables: Green peas, green beans.

Black Rock Orchard
Route 2, Box 33
Lineboro, MD 21088
374-9719

Fruits: Sour cherries, apples.

CHARLES COUNTY

Blythe Vineyards
Woodhaven Park
La Plata, MD 20646
934-4047

Fruits: Apples, wine grapes.

Mount Pisgah Berry Farm
Star Route 1, Box 1201A
LaPlata, MD 20646
743-3909

Fruits: Strawberries, blueberries (limited).

Stanley Farm
Route 484
Marbury, MD 20658
753-6229

Fruits: Strawberries.

FREDERICK COUNTY

Catoctin Mt. Orchard
Route 2, Box 364,
Thurmont, MD 21788
271-2737

Fruits: Strawberries, peaches, black raspberries.

Bountiful Acres
Route 2, Box 66
New Windsor, MD 21776
775-7475

Fruits: Strawberries.

Glade Link Farm
9332 Links Bridge Road,
Walkersville, MD 21793
898-7131

Fruits: Strawberries.

Zimmerman's Farm Market
Route 1, Box 42A
Adamstown, MD 21710

Vegetables: English peas, sugar peas, green beans, lima beans.

HOWARD COUNTY

Larriland Farm
2525 Florence Road,
Woodbine, MD 21797
442-2605

Fruits: Strawberries, peaches, apples. Vegetables: Tomatoes, green peas, broccoli, beets, spinach, snap beans, cauliflower, lima beans, sugar corn, squash, potatoes, pumpkins, cut flowers.

Sewell's Orchards
6233 Oakland Mills Road
Columbia, MD 21045
730-8910

Fruits: Strawberries, peaches, apples, blackberries, black raspberries. Vegetables: Green peas, green beans.

MONTGOMERY COUNTY

Homestead Farm
15600 Sugarland Road
Poolesville, MD 20837
948-5045

Fruits: Strawberries. Vegetables: Tomatoes, green peas, pumpkins.

Butler's Orchard
22200 Davis Mill Road,
Germantown, MD 20767
972-3299 (recorded)

Fruits: Strawberries, black raspberries, thornless blackberries. Vegetables: Green beans, green peas, tomatoes, pumpkins.

Fulks Farm Market
18849 Laytonsville Road,
Gaithersburg, MD 20760
Phone unlisted

Fruits: Strawberries. Vegetables: Pumpkins.

Hough's Orchard
20001 Peach Tree Road,
Dickerson, MD 20753
349-5330

Fruits: Peaches

Lewis Orchard
18900 Peachtree Road,
Dickerson, MD 20753
349-8555

Fruits: Fall apples

Neal's Orchard
21511 Peach Tree Road,
Barnesville, MD 20703
972-8555

Fruits: Peaches, cherries, plums, nectarines.

The Innstead Farm
18020 Edwards Ferry Rd.
Poolesville, MD 20837
972-7248/972-8092

Fruits: Strawberries. Vegetables: Snow peas, snap beans, lima beans, tomatoes, greens, Chinese cabbage.

Thompson's Farm Produce
14722 New Hampshire Ave.
Silver Spring, MD 20904
384-9177

Vegetables: Green peas, lima beans, green and yellow beans, tomatoes, pumpkins.

PRINCE GEORGE'S COUNTY

Cherry Hill Produce
Route 1, Box 484
Gallahan Road,
Clinton, MD 20735
292-4642/292-1928

Fruits: Strawberries. Vegetables: Cucumbers, green beans, broccoli, beets, blackeye peas, cranberry beans, cabbage, greens, lima beans, turnips, eggplant, June peas, lettuce, okra, peppers, wax beans, squash, tomatoes.

Hare's Berry Farm
7806 Colonial Lane,
Clinton, MD
868-4755

Fruits: Strawberries.

Renee M. Johnson Family
Swanson Road,
Upper Marlboro, MD 20870
552-2459

Fruits: Strawberries, thornless blackberries. Vegetables: Green peas, snap beans.

Kerby's Farm Market
8407 Indian Head Highway,
Oxon Hill, MD 20022
567-4375

Vegetables: Tomatoes, green beans, lima beans, summer squash, kale, mustard, rape, spinach, collards, turnip salad, sweet peppers.

Miller's Farm
Route 1, Box 649,
Clinton, MD 20735

Fruits: Strawberries, blueberries, blackberries, red and black raspberries, concord grapes. Vegetables: Tomatoes, green beans, lima beans, cucumbers, pickling cucumbers, okra, squash, peppers, sweet corn.

E. A. Parker & Sons
Route 1, Box 515,
Clinton, MD 20735
292-3940

Fruits: Strawberries, blackberries, red and black raspberries. Vegetables: Green peas, sweet corn, grean beans, lima beans, squash, greens, okra, tomatoes, blackeye peas.

Kenneth Simpson
10803 Annapolis Road
Mitchelville, MD 20716
390-6097

Fruits: Strawberries, blackberries. Vegetables: Corn.

Robin Hill Farm Nursery
Route 3, Box 366
Brandywine, MD 20613
579-6844

Vegetables: Pumpkins, kale, turnips.

QUEEN ANNE'S COUNTY

George H. Godfrey Farms
Route 1, Box 17
Sudlersville, MD 21668
438-3501

Fruits: Strawberries.

McGinnis Market
Rt. 544, ¼ mile from 290
Crumpton, MD 21628
778-4724

Fruits: Strawberries. Vegetables: Green peas, green beans, tomatoes.

Deer Track Farm
RD No. 1, Box 248
Chestertown, MD 21620
779-2963

Vegetables: Tomatoes.

Food, Drugs & Cosmetics

ST. MARY'S COUNTY

Cain's Farm
Route 1, Box 279,
Mechanicsville, MD 20659
373-5316

Vegetables: Green beans, sweet corn, lima beans

VIRGINIA

Barboursville Vineyard
P.O. Box 4,
Barboursville, VA 22923
(703) 83203824

Products: Grafted 1 and 2 year old vinafera vines dormant rooted: Carbernet Sauvignon, Chardonnay, Pinot Noir, White Riesling, Merlot, Gewurztraminer, and several other select varieties. Place your order early. Supply limited.

Belvedere Farm
Star Route TWT, Box 125
Fredericksburg, VA 22401
(703) 371-8494

Product: Strawberries in the early summer. Containers are furnished. Supervise your children.

Cherry Grove Farm
Bell Creek Rd. (Rte. 642)
Mechanicsville, VA 23111
(804) 746-3947

Product: Strawberries.

No minimum sale. No children under 12 allowed in picking field. Containers furnished, free with purchase of 5 lbs. or more. Play area provided. Customers supervise their own children.

Chiles Peach Orchard
Crozet, VA
Mailing address: Box 97, Batesville, VA 22924
(804) 823-5710 or 823-5511

Products: Pick-your-own peaches and nectarines. Pre-picked summer apples, peaches, and nectarines.

Bring your own containers. Call for harvest information.

Cochran's Vegetable Farms
Box 3
Lincoln, VA 22078
(703) 338-7248

Products: Green peas, sugar snaps, squash, green beans, beets, cabbage, sweet corn, green peppers, lima beans, tomatoes, Irish potatoes, eggplant, cantaloupes, watermelons, honeydew melons, pumpkins, cauliflower.

Bring your own containers.

Double "B" Farm
Box 154 C
Rhoadesville, VA 22542
(703) 854-4550

Product: Strawberries.

Containers furnished.

Edgeworth Farm
Route 1, Box 241
Gordonsville, VA 22942
(703) 832-2127

Product: Strawberries

Children under 10 allowed only under strict supervision of parents.

Fletcher's Orchard
Box 234-A
Manakin, VA 23103
(804) 749-3631

Product: Thorn-free blackberries.

Bring own take-home containers. Supply limited.

Gentle Giant Farm
Route 1, Box 170E
Port Republic, VA 24471
(703) 234-8827

Products: Summer squash, peas, cucumbers, zucchini, tomatoes, green beans, cabbage, broccoli, onions, peppers, and lima beans.

Children welcome when supervised by adults. Bring your own containers.

Gladden Fields
Route 1, Box 647
North Garden, VA 22959
(804 295-0329 or 296-1172

Products: Oregano, dill, green beans, lima beans, tomatoes, green peppers, beets, green peas, onions, cucumbers, okra, squash, carrots, and strawberries.

Bring your own containers.

Guilford Farm Vineyard
Rt. 2, Box 51, Stanley, VA 22851
(703) 778-3853
(202) 554-0333

Product: Grapes — White (Seyval Blanc, Rayon d'Or, Floretal Vignoles); Red (Foch, Chelois, Chambourcin, Leon Millot); other varieties in limited quantities. Apples (Winesap, R.I., Greening, Red & Golden Delicious)

Pick-your-own by appointment only 4 bushels of grapes minimum. Picked-to-order: Orders taken for pickup at vineyard or at 261 G Street SW (close to EPA, HUD, DOT, HEW, L'Enfant Plaza). Crusher-stemmer available for use at vineyard: bring lead-proof containers with tight fitting covers. Sold in bushel lots or bulk only. Priced by weight. Bring your own containers. Discounts on large quantities. Send for harvest notice.

H.H. Perry Canning Co., Inc.
Montrose, VA 22520
(804) 244-0440 or 493-4291

Product: Blueberries in mid-summer

Bring your own containers.

Harmony Hollow Orchard
P.O. Box 1454
Arco Star Route,
Front Royal, VA 22630
(703) 636-2009

Products: Peaches, raspberries, sweet corn, green beans, peppers, pumpkins, and popcorn.

Bring your own containers. Children and pets supervised by parents.

Hartland Orchard
Markham, VA 22643
(703) 364-2316

Products: Tree-ripened peaches, nectarines, and summer apples.

Heston's Farm
RFD No. 2, Box 404
Waynesboro, VA 22980
(703) 943-9657

Products: Peas, green beans, october beans, tomatoes, and lima beans.

Hill High Orchards
Route 1, Box 14
Round Hill, VA 22141
Metro Area: 471-1447

Products: Strawberries, raspberries, and blackberries.

Containers furnished by grower. Also country store featuring pre-picked fruit, jelly, honey, cider, fresh-baked pies, bedding plants, etc. Chidren allowed if kept under strict supervision.

Jordan River Farm
Huntly, VA 22640
(703) 636-9388

Product: Snow peas.

Manor Lane Farm
Route 2,
Warrenton, VA 22186
(703) 347-7267

Products: Sween corn, cantalopes, watermelons, zucchini, butternut squash, pumpkins, ornamental squash, popcorn, indian corn, and black walnuts.

Bring your own containers.

Inflation Fighter's Guide

Mason Reger, Inc.
P.O. Box 5
Mt. Jackson, VA 22842
(703) 896-7423

Product: Strawberries

Moormont Orchard & Rapidan Berry Garden
Rt. 1, Box 233,
Rapidan, VA 22733
(703) 672-2730 or 672-4235

Products: Table grapes (blue, red, and white), peaches, vegetables (including string beans, sweet corn, tomatoes, lima beans), damsons, watermelons, strawberries, summer and fall apples.

Moorland Vineyards
Off Rt. 641,
King George, VA 22485
(703) 775-3655 or 775-7062

Products: Grapes. Concord & Niagara (table use and jelly); Cascade (juice and rose wine); Villard Noir, Chancellor, Chelois (red wine); Villard Blanc, Seyval Blanc (white wine).

Bring your own containers. Group instruction session on vineyard management and home wine-making available. Wine making supplies for sale. Crusher-steamer and press available.

Oasis Vineyard
Hume, VA
(703) 635-7627 or 549-9182

Product: Grapes — French hybrids & Vinifera (Cabernet Sauvignon, Foch, Chelois, Chancellor, Sauvignon Blanc, Ryon D'or).

Bring your own containers. Will press.

Patterson Farms Inc.
Thornburg, VA 22565
(703) 582-5241

Products: Strawberries in early summer.

Ample parking. Shaded picnic and play area. Containers furnished. Children under 12 are not allowed in the picking area.

Potomac Vegetable Farm
9627 Leesburg Pike,
Vienna, VA
759-2119

Products: Strawberries, peas, lettuce, spinach, broccoli, cabbage, cauliflower, string beans, Italian tomatoes, okra, pumpkins.

Rick and Van's
Route 4, Box 95B
Fredericksburg, VA 22401
(703) 775-7890

Products: Squash, beets, peas, string beans, cabbage, tomatoes, and strawberries.

Bring your own containers.

Riverbend Farm
Route 3, Box 384-A
Rochelle, VA 22738
(703) 672-5311

Products: Peas, broccoli, cabbage, beans, beets, summer squash, sweet corn, tomatoes, okra, peppers, eggplant, cucumbers, potatoes.

Bring your own containers.

Shenandoah Valley Academy
Route 1
New Market, VA 22844
(703) 740-3161

Product: Strawberries.

Bring your own take-home containers. No children under 12 allowed in main patch.

W. S. Winfrey
Mechanicsville, VA 23111
(804) 746-5984

Product: Strawberries.

Strawberry Acres
Route 1, Box 248
Mt. Crawford, VA 22841
(703) 434-6008 (no Sunday calls)

Product: Strawberries.

Containers provided. No children under 12. Eat all you want as you pick.

Sweet Hall Landscape Nursery
Route 1, Box 154 A-1
West Point, VA 23181
(804) 843-3504

Product: Strawberries.

No minimum sale. Bring own take-home containers. Children permitted under parental supervision.

W. S. Winfrey
Mechanicsville, VA 23111
(804) 746-5984

Product: Strawberries.

Ward H. Kipps
Rt. 3, Box 422,
Rochelle, VA 22738
(703) 948-4171

Product: Grapes — Concord and others.

Bring your own containers. Grapes sold by weight. They also sell natural unheated honey.

Wenger Grape Farms
Rt. 2, Box 277
Waynesboro, VA
(703) 943-3751

Product: Dual-purpose grapes — Concord and Niagara.

Truck loads available. Packages for resale available.

MAIL ORDER

Grillot
10, Rue Cambon
Paris, France

Discounts of up to 60% on name brand perfumes. Write for free price list.

Cheeselovers International
Cheeselovers International Building
Box 1200,
Westbury, New York 11590

For $3, you get a membership and a certificate for $6 worth of free cheese. Cheeses sell at 3c to 7c/lb. above wholesale, and you can cancel your membership at any time.

Charles Loeb
615 Palmer Road
Yonkers, New York 10701
(914) 961-7776

Discounts to 96% on herbs and spices. Price list sent free.

Star Professional Pharmaceuticals
11 Basin Street
Plainview, New York 11803
(516) 822-4621

Vitamins and health aids for up to 60% less than comparable. Free catalogue.

Stechers Ltd.
62 Independence Square
Port-of-Spain
Trinidad, West Indies

Perfumes from famous French makers at 30% to 50% off.

Sunburst Biorganics, Inc.
838 Merrick Road,
Baldwin, New York 11510
(516) 623-8478

Vitamins, supplements and beauty aids, up to 60% off of retail. Free catalogue.

Vitamin Quota
14 E. 38th Street,
New York, New York 10016
(212) 685-7026

Vitamins, minerals, dietary supplements, and pet vitamins at half the usual price for name brands or less. Catalogue is free.

Western Natural Products
P.O. Box 284-W
South Pasadena, CA 91030
(213) 441-1458

Natural vitamins and health supplements. Send for free catalogue.

RELATED PUBLICATIONS

Burrack, Dr. Richard. *The New Handbook of Prescription Drugs*. Ballantine Books, New York, 1975.

The Co-Op Handbook Collective. *The Food Co-Op Handbook*. Houghton-Mifflin of Boston.

Eichenlaub, Dr. John E. *A Minnesota Doctor's Home Remedies for Common and Uncommon Ailments*, Second Edition. Prentice-Hall Reward Books, Englewood Cliffs, NJ.

"Food Co-Op Nooz." Food Co-Op Project Newsletter, 64 E. Lake St., Chicago, Illinois 60611.

Gaffin, Jean. *How I Feed My Family of Five on $135 a Month*. Creation House, Carol Stream, Illinois.

Graedon, Joe. *The People's Pharmacy*. Avon Press, New York, 1976. $4.95. 401 pp. This book is truly excellent — cram-packed with information on diseases, the body, prescription drugs, home remedies, etc. Its explanations are clear and interesting. For example it discusses what an allergy is ... and how to save money on prescription drugs. One chapter even lists prices of common drugs at chain drug stores. Truly worth keeping as a family reference book.

Graffenhagen, George B. and Linda L. Hawkins (eds). *Handbook of Non-Prescription Drugs*. American Pharmaceutical Association, Washington, DC

Holney, David N. (ed.). *The Merck Manual of Diagnosis and Therapy*. Merck & Co., Inc. Rahway, NJ.

Hurdle, Dr. J. Frank. *A Country Doctor's Common Sense Health Manual*. Parker Publishing, West Nyack, NY.

Kaysin, Bill and Ruth. *Eat Well on a Dollar a Day*. Chronicle Books, San Francisco.

Kratz, Carole, and Albert Lee. *The Coupon Way to Lower Food Prices*. New York, Workman Publishing Company, no date.

Sophie Leavitt's *Penny Pincher's Cookbook*. Sophie Leavitt, Hanover, PA, 1978, $5.95. 415 pp. Starts with shopping hints, equivalents, and substitutes. There is a chapter on penny pinching mixes. The casually conversational recipes (there are no ingredient lists) are not difficult to follow. She gives very commonsense directions (e.g., on serving size, "as many pork chops as there are mouths to feed"). As the title would imply, the author avoids expensive, rare, or fancy ingredients.

Long, Dr. James W. *The Essential Guide to Prescription Drugs*. Harper & Row, New York, 1977.

McCully, Helen. *The Waste Not, Want Not Cookbook*. Random House, New York.

The Medicine Show: Consumers Union's Practical Guide to Some Everyday Health Problems and Health Products, by the Editors of Consumer Reports, Consumers Union, Orangeburg, NY.

Martin, Eric W. *Hazards of Medication: A Manual on Drug Interactions, Incompatibilities, Contraindications, and Adverse Effects*. J. B. Lippincott, Philadelphia, PA.

Madell, Walter. *Drugs of Choice*. C.V. Mosby Co., St. Louis, Mo.

"Report to Consumers." Washington, DC: U.S. Department of Agriculture (call 447-5437 for free copies).

Rothenberg, Robert E. *The New American Medical Dictionary and Health Manual*. New American Library, Bergenfield, NJ.

Sehnert, Dr. Keith W. *How to Be Your Own Doctor (Sometimes)*. Grosset and Dunlap, New York.

Self-Help Action Center, 111013 S. Indiana Avenue, Chicago, Illinois 60628 — forms and aids for setting up your own co-op.

Stern. *How to Start Your Own Coop*. Walker Publishing Co.

Sue Jackson Shops Co-Op. Washington, DC: The Cooperative League of the USA.

Vickery, Dr. Donald M. and James F. Fries. *Take Care of Yourself — A Consumer's Guide to Medical Care*. Addison-Wesley, Reading, Mass.

Velella, Tony. *Food Co-Ops for Small Groups*. Workman Publishing Co., New York.

York, Jo Ann. *How I Feed My Family on $16 a Week*.

Clothing & Shoes

CLOTHING

No matter what your clothing tastes or needs — from work clothes to designer boutique items — you've probably noticed that you're paying more for everything than you had in the past. Inflation has been particularly noticeable in the clothing industry, with increases in costs due to items like increased costs of labor and transportation, the increased expense of petrochemicals (from which many synthetic fabrics are made), and the greater demand for natural fibers — and, consequently, their increased price.

Clothing prices can be particularly vexing when you are aware that if you wait only a few weeks, you can probably shave anywhere from 20% to 50% off your expenses. Seasonality and fashionability are key factors in the price of clothing. But there are ways to get around the high price of clothing.

The stores which are listed in this section all claim to offer prices below comparable full-price values in retail stores. In order for you to best benefit from shopping in these stores, there are a number of techniques you should learn. These appear in the following pages — and bear in mind that they apply not only to discount shopping, but to choosing and buying clothing anywhere.

FINDING YOURSELF A BARGAIN

The most important step toward getting clothing bargains is to become aware — of local shops near you which offer reduced prices; of local specialty and department stores' prices and how frequently these stores have sales, as well as how good their sales are; and of the going retail prices of a variety of goods. A number of resources can be useful in this undertaking — the maps in this book illustrate the location of all of the stores listed in this book throughout the metropolitan Washington area; display advertisements in local and area papers list prices of various items, and often illustrate the item; fashion magazines as well as fashion columns keep you informed of what's new, and often of how much these items cost. You should also familiarize yourself with the times when clothing stores traditionally offer good buys. Because the retailer's selling season precedes the wearing season by about three months, you can find the best buys late in the selling season, but still within the wearing season. You should wait for the "End of Season" sales, rather than jumping at merchandise the very first time it is reduced — unless you really want it and it is one-of-a-kind. Often, if you buy totally out of season, you can get tremendous buys on items that have been marked down four or five times, sometimes up to 75% off the original retail price. Use the sales shopping calendar on the following page as a guide to buying seasons.

Your knowledge should also be complete as to the needs of yourself and your family: you should keep a list of what sizes each wears in various items — a size reminder sheet — a sample of which is included later in this chapter. Don't forget wool or other allergies of the people for whom you are buying. You should also keep a list of clothing needs, much as you would keep a grocery list. While this sounds like a lot of work, it actually helps you to avoid making extra purchases, which are a waste of money. And if you can do it for food — why not for clothing?

You should also have a pretty good idea of your entire wardrobe — or that of anyone else for whom you shop. When buying, you should look for items which complement and enhance your existing wardrobe.

Know labels and brands. This is important for two reasons. If you buy at a place where the labels are cut out, you might still be able to figure out the brand from the remnant of the label. Also, you should know which brands are of a consistently high quality — and so, when you find these on sale or at discount houses, you will know when you are getting a good product.

Go for the classics — in clothing, as in furniture and other consumer items, faddish styles tend to date themselves quickly. If you feel compelled to be at the height of style, but cannot afford it, supplement a wardrobe of good classics with faddish accessories, which take a smaller outlay of cash. You could consider buying a cheap item of lesser quality, if you know it is going to be worn only a couple of times or for one season and then discarded. Take comfort in the hope that, since clothing has become so expensive, the styles are likely to change a little less rapidly. Mix and match pieces from different suits or outfits for new combinations. Also, you should stick to two or three basic color groups, so there is greater interchangeability between pieces, allowing you a greater number of outfits.

Clothing & Shoes 63

SALES SHOPPING CALENDAR FOR BUYING CLOTHING

December	January	February	March	April	May	June	July	August	September	October	November
Child's clothes	Infant's clothes	Millinery	Hosiery	Millinery	Purses	Dresses	Bathing suits — 7/5-8/30	Back to school clothing	Child's clothing	Back to school clothes	Child's clothes
Women's and child's coats	Men's Hats	Men's shirts	Infants' clothing	Infants' clothing	Lingerie	Bathrobes & Housecoats	Child's clothes	Women's and child's coats		Hosiery	Women's & kids' coats
Child's hats	Men's coats		Child's shoes	Women's and child's coats	Sportswear		Child's & Men's hats	Men's coats		Housecoats, etc.	Housecoats, etc.
Men's & boys' suits	Costume jewelry			Bathrobes & Housecoats etc.	Bathrobes & Housecoats etc.		Infants' wear	Furs			Dresses
Adults' shoes	Dresses			Men's suits			Purses				Men's & boys' suits
	Furs			Women's dresses			Lingerie				Adults' shoes
	Handbags						Millinery				
	Lingerie						Men's shirts				
	Men's shirts						Child's shoes				
	Child's shoes						Sportswear				

Cheaper doesn't always mean a better buy. Experts in food buying make a point of telling the consumer to buy items like beef not on a cost per pound basis, but on a cost per meal basis, which is more realistic. The same thing is applicable to purchasing clothing. An expensive suit may cost you more than a cheap one, but it is generally made better and lasts longer. But if you buy something that you really like, despite the fact that it costs more, you will not only tend to wear it more frequently, but it will probably outlast a more cheaply made garment. For example, a suit purchased for $185 may last three seasons, while a cheaper suit may begin to fall apart after one — and not be worth wearing. Thus, the cheaper suit cost you $120 for only one season, whereas the more expensive one wound up costing only $62.67 per season. As a rule, it makes sense to spend more on items which you wear frequently. Also, special features, like reinforced toes on socks, are often worth paying for.

A $100 dress for only $6 — sounds good, doesn't it? But don't let initial price be your only guide to buying. If a style or color doesn't suit you, you've wasted your money — unless you're smart enough to return your mistake quickly. Let's say that the $100 dress looks wonderful on the rack, or on the mannequin, but when you put it on it just doesn't hang right on you. You might tell yourself that with just a slight alteration, it will fit perfectly. But, despite all your good intentions, you may not really have the time to make those alterations — and the dress will hang in the closet unworn until you finally give it away to your niece, next-door neighbor, or local charity. Or, if you actually do get around to taking care of the alterations, you may well have underestimated the amount of time necessary to make the repair. And your time is worth money — or can be used in more pleasurable pursuits. For example, even if you are making only $3 per hour, and it takes you four hours to make a repair — you have already spent $12 which you thought you had saved. This is fine if you are unemployed and not looking for a job, because then your time is effectively worthless. But if you are looking for a job, you may be delaying the point when you will start making income — and thus costing yourself future income. Or you may merely be cutting into that free time which you have worked so hard to be able to enjoy. And that's not the only problem — you may have underestimated the skill necessary to make the alterations — and by doing a lousy job you have reduced the value of your "bargain" to just what you paid for it — it winds up looking cheap and/or homemade — and you are out not only $6 and your time, but you have suffered a lot of aggravation in the process. Finally, if you've decided to give the job to a professional, you are already adding substantially to the cost. All of this is not to say that buying something which needs alterations is to be ruled out — rather, that such an action be taken cautiously.

Since many people cannot make even the simplest repair, most stores offer damaged merchandise at substantial discounts. If you are really handy, or if the repair is relatively minor, damaged clothing can be a great buy. If you find an item that is missing a button or with a broken zipper, be sure to ask if you can get a discount if you purchase it. Usually the owner or manager in smaller stores, and buyers in larger stores make these decisions. Some items can be returned to the factory, but the stores are stuck with others, and they may be happy to have you take them off their hands.

Another hidden cost in clothing purchasing is the cost of cleaning. Along with everything else, the cost of dry cleaning has risen substantially over the last several years. And, for a garment made of leather, or another material which requires special handling, these costs can mount up to where you can buy back the items after only a few cleanings. Read labels carefully before you buy. Knowing fabrics and their wear characteristics, as well as how to clean them, can help you to save money. And you should also be aware that fabric manufacturers have traditionally been conservative in giving cleaning instructions — for example, that item which says "dry clean only" may be safely washed by hand in some cases. Ask the salesperson, experiment with other items you have, and use helpful hints in home sections of newspapers and magazines. You can also buy books which give hints on cleaning; some of these books are listed at the end of this chapter. Buying machine-washable clothes is probably the best idea, for it not only saves you money on dry cleaning bills, but saves you time on handwashing as well. You should also be concerned about colorfastness — not just of the body fabric, but of any related trimmings that are attached. Sometimes trims or such need to be dry cleaned even though the fabric could be machine washed. Try to avoid these garments.

Buying at retail specialty or department stores can yield as much of a bargain as can shopping at the stores which are listed in this section. You can increase your chances of getting a reduction by buying at the end of the season. It is worth remembering that the end of the selling season is quite often only the beginning of the wearing season. And many stores maintain a rack or area in the store where out-of-season, one-of-a-kind, damaged, and other merchandise is regularly displayed. Knowing about these can further your ability to buy below "the usual retail" price. And going to a regular retail store — even if you don't buy anything — is useful, because you get to see what the going rate is. Then, when you shop at a discount store or factory outlet, you can be assured of whether you are getting a good buy, or whether you can do better shopping elsewhere.

Wherever you shop, there are some basic rules to follow which can help you save money, time, and aggravation: Shopping at quiet times — like the dinner hour — is recommended. Then you will not feel rushed, and can think more clearly about your purchases. Barring the availability of such time to shop, the next best thing is to make sure that whatever you get is returnable — either for a refund or for merchandise credit. In many places, sale merchandise or "as is" merchandise is a "final sale", and no returns are allowed.

When buying at a factory outlet or store which offers irregulars or seconds, beware. These may not run true to size, and you ought to try them on. And if you are buying for other people, you should carry a tape measure with you — as well as a comprehensive list of all their measurements. Make sure that the irregularities are really minor, and that they don't affect wear. Scrutinize the garment to make sure you have found the flaw, especially if it is not labelled.

BUYING GOOD QUALITY

We all think that we pretty well know clothing — what you see is what you get. What could be simpler? If it fits, the color is right, the weight is right, and the price is right — what more could you do to ensure yourself a good buy?

But in clothing, you really must develop a trained eye to discriminate a good value. You should familiarize yourself with commonly used fabrics, as well as some major construction details, so that you can learn to recognize the indicators of quality merchandise

Buy clothes for comfort. No matter how stylish you want to appear — or how little money you have to spend, it is always a good practice to consider how you will *feel* wearing a garment. All the money in the world cannot compensate you for a day spent in a suit which is too tight under the arms, and chafes and binds you all day long.

The best kind of mirror to use is a three-way mirror because it allows you to see how the clothing fits you from many directions. While looking at yourself in the mirror, bend and stretch, and do whatever movements you commonly do in the course of a normal day. Watch how the item responds — or fails to respond — to these tests. Pay particular attention to the points of stress — seams which tend to split or places where you've noticed too small or poorly constructed garments you've owned have ripped apart. In a suit jacket, across the back is one of these places.

Fibers & Fabrics

Labels not only provide you with information on care instructions, but also tell you about the fiber content of the garment. The characteristics of each fiber are worth knowing, because the life — due to both wearability and care factors — of the garment depends in great part upon the *fiber* used as well as the *fabric* — the way in which the fibers are woven or knitted to create the piece of material from which the garment is made.

As for fabric, in general it is better to buy a firm, tightly-woven one. This is more advantageous for you as it will not snag easily and will provide better wear. In other words, it is just not as fragile as a more loosely woven piece of goods.

Fibers are divided into two groups — natural and manmade. Natural fibers include cotton, linen, silk, and wool — all of which usually cost more than synthetics. The following information comes from the U.S. National Bureau of Standards.

Cotton is a natural plant fiber, and is soft but strong. It is colorfast and heat- and moth-resistant. Unfortunately, it wrinkles and mildews easily, has poor crease retention, and is easily aged when exposed to sunlight.

Linen, a product of the flax plant, has a rough uneven texture. It does not produce lint. Its characteristics are quite similar to those of cotton, except that it will not hold a crease at all, and wrinkles very easily.

Silk comes from unwrapping the silkworm cocoon — and is therefore a continuous filament fiber. If a piece of apparel is labeled "all silk" or "pure silk", USDA regulations provide that it cannot have more than 10% by weight of dyes or other components. It is absorbent, wrinkle-resistant, and colorfast. Like cotton and linen, it also has poor crease retention. Its durability is limited, as it is yellowed by age, strong soap, and sunlight.

Wool comes from the hair of sheep, lamb, angora or cashmere goats, alpacas, and/or llamas. "Virgin wool" refers to new wool; "reprocessed" can contain fibers from unused wool products, e.g. remnants; and "reused" utilizes fiber from a previously used piece of goods. These distinctions are mandated by Federal law. A "worsted" wool is superior to other varieties in that it contains longer and smoother fibers that crease more readily than the others. Wool in general, is absorbent, warm, colorfast and wrinkle-resistant. Unfortunately, moths like to eat it, many people are allergic to it, it pills (forms fuzzy little balls) easily, and can be easily damaged by bleach, perspiration, and strong soap.

There are a large variety of brand names for a relatively limited number of manmade fibers. Below are listed some of the most common — and the characteristics of each.

Acetate comes from a plant fiber — celluose — and has been chemically converted to one of two forms: long continuous filaments or short spun fibers. Acetate is found in taffeta, satin, crepe, and brocade. Acetates can be soft or firm, look silky, and resist moths and mildew. Acetates are neither absorbent nor strong, wrinkle easily — but don't hold a crease well.

Triacetate is quite similar to acetate, but is usually soft and resistant to wrinkles. It also is neither absorbent nor durable.

Acrylic is very much like wool, and can be used in a variety of fabrics. It improves on wool, as it is moth, mildew and sun-resistant. However, like wool, it pills and holds static. Unlike wool, it is not absorbent.

Metallic fibers are either all metal, or other fibers treated with a metallic coating. They are quite brittle, lustrous, and resistant to sweat, chlorine bleach, and salt water. These fibers are non-absorbent.

Nylon is an extremely strong manmade fiber and is lightweight. It can and has been used in a variety of ways. It is colorfast, shape retentive, and resists moths, mildew, and perspiration. On the negative side, it pills and wrinkles, is non-absorbent, and can be damaged by sunlight.

Polyester is frequently used alone or in combination with other fibers. A 65% cotton, 35% polyester blend keeps the best features of both -- it is wrinkle-resistant, lightweight, and absorbent. Polyesters are colorfast and resist moths, wrinkles, perspiration, and mildew. Polyester, like nylon, pills. It is also difficult to remove oily stains from it. By itself, polyester is not absorbent.

Rayon was probably the first manmade fiber and is still among the least expensive. It combines well with other fibers and is absorbent and colorfast. Negatives include its failure to hold shape well, and lack of resistance to mildew and wrinkles.

Construction

Once you are aware of fabrics and of their qualities, the next area is that of *quality of construction*. Signs of good workmanship are easy to detect, once you have made an effort to learn about them. While examining a coat, a sports jacket, or a suit jacket you now have, you can apply the following questions to determine its quality, and use these questions later to help you assess the quality of a garment which you are interested in purchasing:

- Are the stitches small or large? It may not be obvious, but there are several advantages to small stitches — the pieces of fabric are bound more tightly together and the garment has a finer look. Also, large stitching is used on cheaper apparel because it takes both less labor and less thread.

- Are the edges of the fabric in the seams finished? Raw edges tend to ravel, and can even destroy the garment from the inside out. Examples of finished seams include those bound with seam binding; turned under and stitched; or overcast edges. Seam allowances are ample on more expensive clothing and better made, providing room to let out a garment if need be.

- Are the seams smooth, with no fabric puckering? It is important that the pieces of material are connected smoothly for both looks and wear. If there is any puckering when the clothing is on the hanger, you can be assured that there will be puckering — probably more — when it's on you.

- Are the linings made of a quality fabric? Many people have had the experience of the fabric just wearing away inside a coat or jacket — while the outside was still good. A cheap, thin material with no strength will not hold up very long.

- On something that is patterned, do the patterns match up across the garment? Checks, stripes, and plaids particularly should line up across the clothing.
- Buttonholes are another area of concern. The best buttonhole is *bound* — this is created with separate pieces of material sealing the sides of the hole. Next best is handsewn. The handsewn buttonhole uses more threads to cover the edges. Machine sewn buttonholes can be of varying quality — the best use a lot of thread — and no fabric edges should peek through the edges of the buttonhole.
- Buttons should be of good quality. Bone and mother-of-pearl are nice, but plastic is commonly used these days — and it comes in a variety of grades;
- Finally, zippers, if they exist, should be easy to work. If there is any difficulty with a zipper (barring threads or fabric being caught in it), this usually indicates a poorer quality garment.

On specific items, there are specific details to watch out for. In a winter coat, for example, wool is preferable. Look for the wool mark and corresponding fabric names, such as homespun, genuine Harris Tweed, melton, and Cheviot — which are of fine quality. A zipper or button-in lining enhances the value of a coat, since it makes it useful for all seasons.

In suits, the amount of hand tailoring correlates to the value of the suit, as well as to the price. Hand tailoring is expensive, and it also improves the wearability and look of the garment. To determine whether or not a jacket has certain handwork in it, roll the lapel tip. If it springs back quickly, it has been handstitched. Linings should fit perfectly, and have no puckering, either in the seams or where attached to the body of the garment. As with anything else, all patterns should match. If the garment wrinkles in certain areas on you, but not on the hanger, it indicates a need for alterations. As with anything else, when buying a suit, think of how often you'll wear it, and how often it needs to be pressed and cleaned. Usually a moderately priced suit is a blend — the higher priced suits are all wool — worsted.

Traditional Clothing for Women

NANCYE FLEMING SHOP

325 SO. WASHINGTON STREET
ALEXANDRIA, VIRGINIA 22314

(703) 683-3910

When buying men's shirts and pants, there are several things worth knowing. Concerning fabric, something that is sanforized is preferred, since this guarantees you that shrinkage will be no more than 1%. When stitch gauge is given, 118-20 stitches per inch is desirable, and the most desirable combination (as it wears the best) is a poly-cotton combination, which is more durable than a treated cotton, such as a permanent press fabric. Poly-cotton combinations are practically wrinkle free, when laundering directions are followed, and when they are hung up immediately after coming from the dryer. For measuring a man's shirt: the neck size, such as 16", refers to the measurement from the center of the top button to the farthest edge of the buttonhole; and sleeve length, e.g. 32½", is the measurement from the edge of the shoulder down to the wrist bone. If you fall between sizes, it is recommended that you go to the next size larger: i.e., the 32½" arm would take a size 33. Some shirts come in sizes which are combinations, e.g. 32-33. In measuring men's trousers, the length is properly measured from the top of the inseam at the crotch to the bottom of the hem — where the hem is desired. For a good fit, there should be no pinching or binding. Fullness is desirable, but it should not be obtained by piecing together of fabrics. This is something to look for, particularly in the crotch.

Children's clothing should be selected on the basis of durability, utility, comfort, and growth potential. Are there ample seams and hems? Because children have more sensitive skin, inside seams should be soft and lie flat — not be puckered, because this is an area where continuous rubbing can cause skin irritations. Of particular importance is buying clothing which fits well and has a minimum of features prone to snagging or catching. In addition to catching and snagging, too-loose clothing can be a fire hazard. Avoid buying fancy dress-up clothing for children, since they will get little wear out of it, and, when you do, don't spend a lot — from the first to the second wearing, your child might have grown two sizes. And, finally, let a child help in decision-making about the clothes he or she will wear — because the child will probably like it better, wear it more often — and take care of it.

CONSUMER PROTECTION FOR THE CLOTHING BUYER

When it comes to buying clothes, consumers are not unprotected. Not only do you have recourse to the store when something doesn't wear as it says it should under an implied warranty, but you can also expect to get what you pay for in terms of fabric or fur, to learn about how to take care of your purchase, and to be protected from fire hazards to a certain extent.

Laws protecting clothing purchasers include the Wool Products Labeling Act of 1940, which requires a garment label to state the type of wool or other fibers which make up 5% or more of the fabric. The Federal Trade Commission provides standardized definitions of these fibers. The Fur Products Labeling Act, passed in 1951, requires that a garment must be labeled as to type of animal fur, country of origin, whether imported or domestic, and whether or not the fur has been dyed or colored. The label must also disclose whether the garment is made from scraps or from whole pelts. The Textile Fiber Products Identification Act of 1960 is also under FTC jurisdiction. It established 17 generic groups of fibers — including but not limited to those listed in the text above. Manufacturers must label garments by fiber content in terms of percent, except, as in the wool products act, where a fiber comprises less than 5% of the fabric. The Permanent Care Labeling Act of 1972 is also executed by the FTC, requiring that "normal care" instructions be put on labels attached to the garment.

In addition to these labeling requirements, flammability has been a major area of action for the federal government. It started with the Flammable Fabrics Act of 1953, when the Departments of Commerce and Health, Education and Welfare were instructed to set up standards of flammability. (In 1973, the Consumer Product Safety Act delegated the responsibility to the Consumer Product Safety Commission.) The General Wearing Apparel Standard was adopted in 1954 and was effective in keeping extremely flammable items off the market, including, for example, items such as rayon sweaters. And, since 1973, children's sleepwear from size 0 to size 6X (excluding underwear and diapers) had to be fire retardant — meaning that it won't ignite if it comes in contact with a match or flame. This code was expanded in 1975 to include sizes 7 to 14.

OTHER SUGGESTIONS FOR SAVING MONEY

For high quality clothing at low prices, besides looking at discount stores and factory outlets, there are a number of things you can do. If you are the type of person who always wants brand new, then many of these ideas won't appeal to you. If, however, you are part of the growing legion believing that saving money is the major objective, and are willing to try a number of different, or even outlandish ways to do so, the following suggestions may be of value to you.

- Does your union or firm deal with certain businesses which offer special discounts to your members? If so, make use of them.

- A common idea, but one that pays off for many people, is buying in a thrift or secondhand shop. If you're very picky, you can find things that are brand new — that the donor or consignor just never got around to wearing — or you can get a good buy on something really expensive that someone with a lot of money decided to cast off — like a fur coat or a designer dress worn only once or twice. For children, thrift shops are ideal, since kids grow so fast. For accessories, or things like ice skates, thrift shops are really the best.

- Trading clothing takes many forms: A swapmeet of the neighborhood, block, or PTA can be an effective way not only to get rid of your old things, but to meet some of your needs as well. A PTA swapmeet can be especially good for getting children's clothes. Or you can trade clothes with a friend the same size or a next-door neighbor.
- If all else fails, consider giving your cast-offs to charity in order to get a tax deduction. Make sure you get a receipt.
- Buy classics for women in the men's, boys', or even girls' departments.
- Learn how to make repairs on something you already own that is in basically good condition but may be marred by a rip or a tear.
- Sew your own clothing — but be sure that you do it well. Homemade clothing which looks bad is no bargain. Also, even if you already sew, you should compare your costs for fabrics and notions with the cost of buying new — preferably on sale or at a discount store. If you find the difference minimal, it may not pay to make something. And you should count your time for something when making this comparison. A $10 difference between homemade and store-bought may not be worth saving if it would take you an entire day to make it.
- Recycle fabric from old clothes if you're a sewer. Restyle a dress... much as Scarlett O'Hara did in *Gone with the Wind*... with her mother's living room curtains.
- Experiment with dying fabrics, particularly natural fibers, to give them new appeal.
- Have good footwear repaired — rather than replaced.
- BUY LESS. More is not always better. Having a few good things is preferable to having many cheap or uncomfortable items. Good things last longer, and you are usually more satisfied with them.
- Finally, maintaining your clothing well helps to prolong its life. Allow clothes, natural fibers particularly, to relax and breathe. Don't wear them day after day. When they need dry cleaning, you can save yourself money by using a self-serve drycleaning machine, which is considerably cheaper than going to a dry cleaner. Such shops are listed in the Yellow Pages of local telephone directories. When storing wools, make sure they are well-cleaned, because moths prefer dirty and spotted clothes. Also, when clothing is hung up or neatly folded, you are giving it a longer life expectancy.

SHOES, BOOTS, AND PURSES

SHOES AND BOOTS

When you are shopping for shoes and boots, there are a number of tips which can help you to save money and avoid aggravation. The most important thing is to get the proper fit — as simple and obvious as this sounds, it is not as easy in reality. Many people just don't know what to look for — or some are buying for fashion and not for comfort. Footwear should be sufficiently roomy — traditional wisdom indicating a distance of ½" from the toe to the end of the shoe as sufficient. All toes should rest on the sole, not turning out to the sides. The ball of the foot and the widest part of the shoe should match up — this is where support is needed. And, of major importance is the heel, which should not slip when you are walking. While it should fit firmly, it should not pinch.

It is not enough just to try on the right shoe — most people's right and left feet are not the same size. Therefore, it is important to try on both shoes before buying. Leather is the material of choice, since synthetics are not absorbent enough to let your feet breathe. And shoes should be purchased near the end of the day, when feet are most swollen.

When it comes to style, as with clothing, don't make your choice on the basis of a passing fad. Neutral colors are most useful. Saving money on footwear: shop end of season sales and the bargain stores listed here, and take care of your footwear to extend its life — a minor replacement of a heel can save a lot of money. With children's shoes, however, periodic checking is necessary to make sure their feet haven't grown so much as to be cramped in their shoes.

Buying boots takes a little more knowledge than buying shoes. Because you look at a winter boot for warmth and support on cold and icy or wet streets, there are a number of factors to examine. Pile: the best pile is wool, because it is most absorbent. Manmade fibers, such as acrylic, polyester and nylon are durable. Thicker pile keeps your feet warmer. The size of the pile, however, should not be forgotten when choosing for size and comfort — you may need to go up a half-size to account for the pile.

Wrinkles or bulkiness around the ankles can cause discomfort. Low heels, while less atractive than high ones, give better traction on ice, as do rubber soles.

Worried about water? The best choice if you want something waterproof is to look for a boot made of one piece of rubber or vinyl — this is the only truly waterproof item. Others are merely water-resistant.

As with any other item, the signs of quality are in the craftsmanship. These signs can include centered back seams, buckles and other ornamentation that are securely affixed, and a zipper which works smoothly.

PURSES, POCKETS, HANDBAGS

Need and frequency and type of usage determine whether you should buy a leather or vinyl handbag. Leather carries more of a cachet and has more status, but is often more delicate than vinyl. An exception to this in both price and wearability is cowhide. Although more expensive than vinyl, it is the least expensive leather available, and wears well because it is heavy. For everyday use, cheap bags are worthless, because they fall apart easily — stitching, as in good clothing, should be small and tight. In cheaper bags, it is large and loose and prone to falling apart. A good bag in a neutral color will wear well and be versatile in use with many items from your wardrobe.

Areas of concern in buying a handbag start from the inside out. The storage space should be ample, and inside pockets with zippers are useful. Linings, like the outside of the bag, should be well made — cheap ones just fall apart, getting things like pencils and keys stuck in them, and hiding items like small change. The lining should be colorfast so that it does not discolor items — your wallet, for example — that are put inside it.

On the outside, the bag should be well-proportioned to your size — a small person with a large bag looks ungainly. The color should be fast on the outside as well, so that a bag rubbing against your coat doesn't leave a line of color. The handle should be well-anchored, since it is a point of maximum stress. The closure should be tight and effective to deter possible pickpockets and to avoid having the bag open accidentally, letting things fall out without your knowledge. Small metal feet on the bottom are excellent for protecting the bag from abrasion, and help it to wear longer.

Nat Lewis INC.
Feminine Fashions

All leading labels, all great savings

20-50% Off

1731 Eye St., NW — Marlow Heights Shopping Center — Iverson Mall

SEE WRITE-UP ON PAGE 379

FINDING CLOTHING & SHOE BARGAINS

Note: In this section, we include a much higher proportion of Baltimore stores than in other parts of the book. We did this because we felt that some truly excellent buys — as to both price and selection — were available there.

Anders of Timonium
2145 Green Spring Road
Timonium, Maryland
(301) 252-9555

Anders sells a full line of men's clothing. Although they do sell some of the better quality designer suits, such as Cardin and Kupenhaver, you would probably think of this warehouse-style operation as a place to get clothes of a medium quality for an inexpensive price. They also carry accessories like socks, ties, and belts. The clothing is neatly arranged, either hanging up or on tables, in a vast warehouse area. There are special sale tables, on which (at the time of our visit) you could find shirts at 3 for $12, trousers at 3 for $10, and a variety of odds and ends at greatly reduced rates. In general, though, you can expect to save 40% of the retail cost on a line of clothes ranging from low quality on up. There were eight separate dressing rooms here with curtains. Alterations are available, and the charges are clearly posted. Satisfaction is guaranteed on all sales, and you can return unsatisfactory merchandise for your money back. For big sales, there is a mailing list, and weekly featured items are advertised in the Baltimore area papers. Anders is part of a national chain which appears under different names in different parts of the country.

Other addresses:
Anders of Baltimore, 821 Oregon Avenue, Linthicum Heights, MD (301) 636-3700
Anders of East Point, 7930 E. Baltimore St., East Point, MD (301) 282-2800

Hours at the Timonium store are from Monday through Saturday, from 10 am to 9 pm, and on Sunday, from noon to 5. Summer hours are Saturday from 10 am to 6 pm. The other stores should have the same hours. Personal checks are accepted with valid identification as are Master Charge, VISA, and NAC. They discourage layaways, but will hold an item for you for up to a week without a deposit. The store policy is that, with a receipt, merchandise may be returned for cash (if you paid cash) within 7 days, and after that for store credit or an exchange. As this is a warehouse setting, there is a good amount of parking available.

Baby Products
2731 Wilson Blvd.
Arlington, VA
525-2972

See listing in the Furniture section for further details.

The Back Door/David's Village Store
4047 28th Street South
Arlington/Shirlington, VA
820-1327

David's Village Store is well-known for its high quality, usually conservative junior and misses wear. At David's Back Door, you can find a mixture of some of that same high quality merchandise out-of-season, samples, and some special purchase merchandise. The Back Door, which is a good-sized back room off their Arlington Store and is nicely arranged, features misses, women's and junior dresses, some skirts, and jeans. They display closeouts of Etienne Aigner shoes and bags, and sell Levi and Tami brands, as well as a size 9/10 sample line of Villager and Lanz. Out of season items from David's comprise part of the stock here. Most of the items, though, are off-brands, bought at special purchase. You can expect to get a discount of from 30% to 50% on these things. You can really get a good deal at their end-of-season sales, when they want to clear out the old merchandise. They have special bins where you can get items for $1, $2, and $3 that would normally run up to 10 to 12 times the price. And they also have a rack of hanging dresses that are similarly discounted, sometimes with special "two-for" prices. The dressing rooms are quite nice, much as you would expect from a regular retail store. No alterations are available.

Hours here are Monday through Saturday, from 10 am to 6 pm, and Thursday, from 10 am to 8 pm. In addition to personal checks with proper identification, they also accept Master Charge, VISA, American Express, and Central Charge. There is no layaway policy, but they will hold an item for one day. All sales are final, and there are no returns or exchanges. Parking is available in a large free lot behind the store. The store is located at the corner of 28th Street and Randolph Street in the Shirlington Shopping Center.

Bata Shoe Warehouse/Batco Shoes
6677 Moravia Park Drive
Moravia Park/Baltimore, MD
488-6363

We found the shoe warehouse that we visited really exciting. Not that they had the finest or most up-to-date merchandise, but they had a large selection, at substantially marked-down prices, and in a variety of sizes. Bata Shoe Warehouse is part of Batco Shoes, which manufactures its own line of shoes for its own stores. At their warehouses, they sell men's, women's, and children's shoes, as well as related accessories like socks, pantyhose, and handbags. Besides carrying their own stock, which includes seconds, they carry closeouts from other stores, and we noticed labels like Lifestride, Naturalizers, Jarman's, and Cobbies. The store is organized by size, but it also has things like sneakers and inexpensive shoes in bins. Also, terrifically reduced shoes can be found in these bins. At the time we were there, they had a big sale going on, and reductions were fantastic, but usually reductions run an average of 30%. They hold two major seasonal sales per year, and advertise in the radio and newspapers in the Baltimore area. They do not have a mailing list.

Other addresses:
125 Penrod Court, (Glen Burnie Business Center) Glen Burnie, MD (301) 766-5436
2207 Green Spring Drive, Timonium, MD (301) 252-6891

Hours at the Moravia Park location were Monday through Friday, from 9 am to 5 pm, and Saturday from 9 am to 1 pm.

Some of the other locations have later hours on Thursday nights. They accept personal checks with proper identification, including a driver's license, and also take Master Charge, VISA, and NAC. There are no layaways, but they usually will hold merchandise for you for a short time, depending on the store. Returns can be made for cash, usually within a month of purchase, providing, of course, that the merchandise has not been used. There is ample parking.

Hours for the stores are from Monday through Friday, from 10 am to 9 pm, and Saturday and Sunday, from 10 am to 6 pm. Checks, Master Charge, VISA, Central Charge, and NAC are accepted payments. 30%-50% is required on layaways, with pickup and final payment due within 30 days. They will hold items for a couple of days without a deposit. They do not give cash refunds, but will exchange unused merchandise accompanied by a sales receipt for up to one year. There is ample parking at both locations, with a lot across from the Silver Spring store.

Beltsville Men's Clothing Warehouse
Powder Mill Road and New Hampshire Avenue
Beltsville, MD
937-8999

Beltsville and Fenton Menswear shops carry a large line of men's clothing, including suits, shirts, ties, slacks, belts and overcoats, with blue jeans and other casual wear as well. Some well-known brands include Pierre Cardin, Givenchy shirts, and other similar designer names. Some come with the labels in; labels have been removed from others. All merchandise is fresh, in season, and first quality. The typical discount is from 30% to 40%. Large orders, as for groups, are done as special orders. Tailoring services are available. There is one large dressing room in Beltsville, and two individual units in Silver Spring. If merchandise is defective or doesn't wear well, they will replace or repair it. And they stand behind their work. Advertisements for selected items appear every two to three weeks in the *Washington Star* and *Post* newspapers.

Other Address:
Fenton Menswear Discount Store, 8484 Fenton Place, Silver Spring, MD, 587-2250: a smaller stock of goods is found here.

The Blouse House
8563 Georgia Avenue
Silver Spring, MD
589-4442

The Blouse House discounts a large quantity of blouses for women and children and sells them in a small, well-organized store, with everything on hangers. The garments come from one manufacturer and are made to sell at department stores; the labels have been removed from them. All are first quality, and there are no seconds. Some are samples, which come in size "medium" and are usually one of a kind. Blouses here are available in sizes up to 46. A typical value found here might be a blouse which normally retails for $18-$20 for only $6. But the management would not name an average figure, for the discount varies according to the blouse and the season. They are willing to fill large orders, but it takes a short wait. There are no dressing rooms in the store. All blouses are checked for flaws before they are sold, but, should you find something wrong with one, bring it back for a replacement or repair. They regularly put advertisements in the *Washington Post*.

Hours here are Monday through Wednesday, and Friday, from 9:30 am to 7 pm, Thursday to 9 pm, and Saturday from 9:30 am to 6 pm. Personal checks are accepted, as are Master Charge, VISA, Central Charge and NAC. There are no layaways. They will hold merchandise for only an hour or two. A Park and Shop lot is located in front of the store, and they will stamp your ticket so that you can park free for the first hour.

day from 10 am to 6 pm, Thursday and Friday to 8:30 pm, and Sunday from noon to 5 pm. Personal checks are accepted with proper identification, as are Master Charge, VISA, and Central Charge. 1/3 down on layaway, with 30 days to pick up your merchandise. They will hold items for 2 days. There are exchanges or store credit only on returns, and only within 7 days. The Rockville shop is located near the intersection of Randolph Road and Rockville Pike.

The Children's Wear Market
5556 Randolph Road
Rockville, MD
881-5131

In a well-organized shop with attractively displayed merchandise, just as in a traditional children's clothing store, you can find great buys on a wide range of children's clothing. Popular and designer labels are found here in infants' to girls' size 14, and to boys' size 16, and you can also get seasonal imports of European children's clothing. All merchandise is first quality, with some manufacturers' closeouts. The discount you can expect is an average of 33% off comparable retail prices, but can range widely, from 20% to 50% off. There are four individual dressing rooms. They stand behind the manufacturer's warranty, so, if anything should be defective about the merchandise, you can bring it back and expect satisfaction. They hold four major sales here per year, and discounts during these sales can run as high as 70% off the manufacturer's suggested retail prices.

Other address:
2173 Defense Highway, Crofton, MD 21114. Washington Metro Number: 261-0949; Local number: (301) 721-7818.

Hours are Monday-Wednesday and Satur-

Christina's
10251 Old Georgetown Road
Wildwood Shopping Center
Bethesda, MD
530-8677

Christina's is a long, narrow store, packed with merchandise ranging from jeans, pants and T-shirts to skirts, blouses, jackets and suits. At discounts of 20% to 50%, you can find names like SWI for blouses and T-shirts; Paula Saker; Kasper, Halston, and Anne Klein for New Aspects; Halston for blouses; Stewart Lang, Calvin Klein, Gloria Vanderbilt, and Charlotte Ford for jeans, jean skirts, and trousers; and TWCC and Dudley for suits and separates. All merchandise is first quality. There are separate dressing stalls, without curtains, but located along a closed-off corridor. For alterations, they will refer you to someone who does good work. There is a mailing list, and if you get on it you will be notified about their special sales, which include seasonal clearances, and a variety of ongoing specials.

Hours are Monday-Friday, from 10 am to 9 pm, Saturday from 10 am to 6 pm, and Sunday from noon to 5 pm. Personal checks are accepted with proper identification, as are Master Charge, VISA, Central Charge, and NAC. There are no layaways, but they will hold merchandise for 24 hours without a deposit. All sales are final, except in the case of manufacturer's defects, when merchandise will be replaced. There are, however, exchanges and credits given during the Christmas season on gift merchandise. They are located in a shopping center with ample parking.

The Clothes Connection
16 Normandy Shopping Center
Off Catskill State Parkway, from Belmont National Pike northeast of Ellicott City center
Ellicott City, MD
(301) 461-9533

If you really are averse to shopping clearance and discount stores, you will probably find this shop a satisfying surprise. Despite the average savings of from 30% to 50%, the management strives to maintain a shop that varies not at all from a fine quality ladieswear store. It has nice merchandise, a good, open layout, and excellent service. They sell misses and juniors clothing, including sportswear, some dressy wear, lingerie and a small assortment of accessories. We also noticed a selection of Jantzen merchandise when we were there. Quality ranges from medium to high, and all items are handpicked in New York by the buyer. Everything is first quality. They will recommend someone to do alterations. The Clothes Connection advertises its seasonal clearances and holiday sales in local papers, such as the *Ellicott City Times*, and the Columbia and Howard County papers.

Other stores:
New Hampshire Avenue, Colesville, MD, (301) 384-2977
Race Track Road, Bowie, MD, (301) 262-1526

Hours are from 10 am to 5:30 pm on Monday, Tuesday and Saturday; Wednesday through Friday, from 10 am to 9 pm. Personal checks are accepted, as are Master Charge, VISA, and NAC. You can lay items away with 25% down, providing you pick them up within 30 days. They will hold items without a deposit for up to 24 hours. There are no cash refunds, and you have five days to return unworn merchandise for credit. On special sale merchandise, all sales are final. There is ample parking in the large shopping center lot.

The Clothes Outlet
22-A Church Lane
Cockeysville, MD
(301) 628-1020

If you are looking for good, traditional style clothes, this small store, jam-packed with fine quality merchandise, is the place for you. They feature men's and women's clothing — sportswear and dressy. For women, purses and gowns are also stocked. Also available are boys' blazers and button-down preppy dress shirts. For men, they sell ties, shirts, and slacks. You can find here a large assortment of sweaters for the whole family, including many shetland wools. They sell no double knits. Except for a very small part of the stock, everything is first quality: there are two corners with irregular merchandise, marked as such. But this composes less than 3% of the total stock of the Clothes Outlet. You can save at least 30% here, with many items at 40% off and some at 25% off — and some are priced below wholesale. Most of their items are made by leading American manufacturers. There are four separate dressing rooms with doors. The tags show both the retail price and the selling price. Labels are cut out of most of the leading brands, at the request of the manufacturers and/or distributors, to avoid antagonizing retailers who sell at full price. For alterations, they will recommend a tailor, who will give you a discount. There is a mailing list, and there are seasonal clearances where prices are reduced even more.

Hours here are Monday, Tuesday, Friday, and Saturday from 10 am to 6 pm, with Wednesday and Thursday hours until 9 pm. Personal checks are accepted with proper identification, as are Master Charge and VISA. The layaway policy is lenient: with a reasonable down payment, they will hold items as long as payments are made every few weeks. They will also hold items for a day or two without a deposit. There are no cash refunds — exchanges or store credit only. While they prefer that you return merchandise with receipt within 7 days, they do give you some leeway on this. There is a small lot in front and to the side of the store. The shop is located right off of York Road near W. Bell and Co. in Cockeysville.

Crazy Sally's
2309 University Boulevard West
Wheaton, MD
933-6688

For name brands in children's clothing, from infants to size 14, Crazy Sally's has the total clothing picture. In a well-organized, well-displayed store, with all prices clearly marked, you can save 20%-40% on brands like Izod, Billy the Kid, Roy Roy, Oshkosh, Luvit, Lee, Levi, Danskin, Trimfit, Loungees, Little World, Bruxton, Nanette, Ruth Scharf, and Little Topsy. In some items, like jeans, they have both slims and regulars. All items are first quality and there are no closeouts. There are 6 separate dressing rooms, and service is personalized. Special sales are held periodically, and you can get on a mailing list for notification.

Hours are Monday through Saturday, from 9:45 am to 5:45 pm. Personal checks are accepted, as are Master Charge and VISA. They have no layaway and no holds. Merchandise can be returned for in-store merchandise credit only; no cash refunds.

Dan Brothers Discount Men's Shoes
1016 Light Street
Baltimore, MD
(301) 752-8175

Dan Brothers sells men's footwear. The Light Street store is the smaller of their two stores and is a rack store selling cancellations, job lots, and other shoes they want to move quickly. They always have special 2 for 1 sales here — so the price is always at least 50% off comparable retail. The Charles Street store is much larger, and has finer quality merchandise which is also more up-to-date. Typical brands include Bally, Freeman, Jarmans', and Clark's Wallabees. The Charles Street store has a selection of ladies' boots and Clark's Wallabees. You can special order shoes also at a discount. Shoe repair clinics are on the premises. Satisfaction is guaranteed. There are seasonal specials on selected items.

Other address:
1032 S. Charles, Baltimore, MD, (301) 727-9436

Hours are from Monday through Thursday from 9 am to 6 pm, and on Friday and Saturday from 9 am to 7 pm. Personal checks are accepted with proper identification. So is the American Express card. Layaways require a $5 minimum deposit, and pickup within 30 to 60 days. They will hold merchandise for you, and the return policy is liberal — check with the manager if you have a question. Parking is on-street and somewhat limited. But there are a number of other shops in this vicinity, so it is worth looking for a parking space.

Danielle's Ladies Sportswear Factory Outlet
22 South Howard St.
Baltimore, MD
(301) 752-0032

This is a true factory outlet. You enter an old building in the warehouse district of Baltimore and go up the stairs to a factory. You go through the workroom to a small, walled-off display area, crowded with a limited number of good quality items that are made here. The focus is on ladies' sportswear, and the price you can expect to pay is 50% of the comparable retail. Danielle fashions are sold at good retail stores across the country, frequently as store brands. They have new merchandise every day. When we were there, we found velvet blazers, fine wool separates, and a number of dresses, suits, jackets, and coats in season. All work is well-tailored, and the regular customer can get alterations done here. Seasonal reductions are often put on top of the already-discounted prices. The management is quite friendly here, and more than compensates for the factory atmosphere. The advantage of this kind of outlet is that you can often find things here in advance of the wearing season as you would in a retail store.

Open Monday through Saturday from 8 am to 5 pm. Personal checks are accepted with proper identification, as are Master Charge and VISA. A reasonable deposit is accepted on a layaway, and pickup should be within 2 weeks. All sales are final.

Dash's Designer
8133 Watson Street
Tysons Corner, VA
893-9225

Menswear is found at Dash's designer. Dash's attempts to offer high quality merchandise at a good discount — from 20% to 50% off retail — in a setting that is as good as, if not better than, fine quality retail stores. They carry sports jackets, suits, dress shirts, dress pants, and shoes, ranging from medium to high quality. You can find brands such as Givenchy, Cardin, Botany 500 and Eagle. All merchandise is first quality and in stock. At this branch, there were 12 separate dressing rooms. They charge for delivery. Alterations are available. There is a mailing list, and special sales are held once or twice a year, with special purchase items featured at other times.

Other Addresses:
3229 M Street NW, Washington, DC, 338-4050. Hours are Monday through Saturday from 10 am to 9 pm, and Sunday, noon to 6 pm.
1308 F Street NW, Washington, DC, 347-3303, Open Monday through Saturday from 10 am to 8 pm.
New stores opening at 19th and L in Washington, DC, and in Rockville, MD.

Hours here are from Monday through Saturday, from 10 am to 10 pm, and Sunday, from noon to 6 pm. Personal checks are accepted with proper identification, as are Master Charge, VISA, Carte Blanche, Central Charge, and NAC. They will hold merchandise for 48 hours.

Fashion Action
6840 Franconia Road
Springfield, VA

You can get some really good buys at Fashion Action on mostly medium quality merchandise — ladies' sportswear and casual wear. They also carry name brand jeans by Calvin Klein, Cacharel, and Anne Klein, and Try One tops, as well as Chego tops, shorts and sportswear. Discounts run 30% to 50%, and, when they have special sales, you can save a lot more. Everything irregular is so marked, but most merchandise is first quality. They have separate dressing rooms.

Other addresses:
6770 Richmond Hwy., Alexandria, VA
Congressional Plaza, Rockville, MD
Free State Mall, Bowie, MD
5831 Riverdale Rd., Riverdale, MD
3924 Donnell Drive, Forestville, MD
3672 King Street, Alexandria, VA
Gordon Plaza, Woodbridge, VA

Hours are generally from 10 am to 9 pm Monday through Friday, Saturday from 10 am to 7 pm, and Sunday from noon to 5 pm. They accept personal checks, VISA, Master Charge, Central Charge, and NAC. Returns can be made within 14 days with receipt. On layaways, they ask 10% or $3 down, whichever is greater.

Fashion Factory
9586 Old Keene Mill Road,
Burke, VA
455-4141

Fashion Factory is one of a number of stores discounting ladies', misses', and juniors' moderately-priced sportswear and other casual clothing. They also carry dressy clothes during the holidays. Some commonly found brands include Breckenridge, Act III, Pant-Her, Elles Belles, Anne Klein, Evan Picone, College-Town, and others. All merchandise is first quality, and you can save from 30% to 50% off retail on it here. There are no special orders, but if they don't have your size in, they will try to get it either from one of the other stores or from the warehouse. All the dressing rooms are booths with doors. While there is no mailing list, if you request notification about a specific item, they will call you when it comes in. They have two half-price sales, usually around April and November, and other clearance sales as they deem necessary. You can find their ads in the *Washington Post* and *Star* newspapers.

Other addresses:
785 Rockville Pike, Rockville, MD, 424-7141. Hours are Monday through Saturday from 10 am to 9 pm.
Beltway Plaza Mall, Greenbelt Road at Beltway exit 28, 345-6141, Monday through Saturday, 10 am to 9:30 pm.

Hours at the Burke location are Monday through Friday from 10 am to 9 pm, and Saturday from 10 am to 6 pm. Personal checks are accepted, and so are Master Charge, VISA, Central Charge, and NAC. There are no layaways, but they will hold non-sale merchandise for you for up to 5 days. Refunds are given if merchandise is returned within 7 days. Sale merchandise can only be exchanged or returned for credit — no cash refunds. There are free mall parking lots at all locations.

The Fashion Tree
Wildwood Manor Center
10231 Old Georgetown Road
Bethesda, MD
530-4423

The Fashion Tree is another of a string of smallish shops discounting middle level misses' and juniors' sportswear, dresses, and coats. We noted average savings of about 20% — a smaller average discount than the other similar stores offer. They do, however, carry a good selection of well-known brands, including Sir for Her suits, Danielle, Breckenridge, Sasson jeans, Calvin Klein jeans, Coscob, Fay's Closet, Eccobay, and Huckapoo. They also stock Fox Run coats and suits. Everything is first quality. It is a medium-sized shop, fairly crowded with racks of clothing, yet well-organized.

They also carry costume jewelry, belts, scarves and pocketbooks. They usually have big clearance sales at the end of the summer and during the winter, where they go down to 2 for the price of 1.

Other addresses:
Gaitherstown Plaza, 230 N. Frederick, Gaithersburg, MD, 926-5200
Village Mart Drive, Olney, MD, 774-2131

Hours at the Wildwood store are Monday through Friday from 10 am to 9 pm, Saturday to 6 pm, and Sunday from noon to 5 pm. They accept personal checks with identification, and also Master Charge, VISA, and Central Charge. No layaways are available at Bethesda. They will hold merchandise for you for 2 days without a deposit. Returns must be made with receipt within five days, for merchandise credit only. Sale merchandise is not at all returnable. Ample parking.

Frocks at the Docks
5 Prince Street
Alexandria, Virginia
548-7325

Frocks at the Docks is a tiny little place, almost hidden near a riverfront park in Old Town Alexandria, with fine quality designer dresses, slacks, shorts, and some coats in season. You will recognize brands here like Cacharel, Givenchy, Adolfo (hats), and de la Renta. Everything is first quality and in season. Discounts run 50% on the average, with 80% off comparable retail during markdowns. There are no special orders. There is one large dressing room to be shared by all the customers. No alterations are available, and there is no mailing list. Despite its small size and limited selection, you are likely to find items here, in very good condition, that most DC area discounters don't regularly carry.

Hours here are Saturday through Wednesday from 11 am to 6 pm, and Thursday & Friday from 11 am to 8 pm. Personal checks are accepted, as are Master Charge and VISA. All sales are final. Parking is limited — on street in often crowded Old Town Alexandria, or in a pay lot nearby.

The General Store
7688 Richmond Highway
Alexandria, VA
765-8600

There's an oft-repeated saying that goes "You get what you pay for" — but at the General Store you might get a little more. Instead of going to a discount department store and getting lower quality merchandise -- made of less expensive fabrics and not as well-constructed — for a low price, you could spend the same money getting good quality, yet still inexpensive clothing at the General Store. The management appears to have carefully chosen items not only for price, but for durability and looks as well. They feature jeans, shirts, India cloth dresses and shirts, T-shirts, and a variety of accessories, including a good selection of low-heeled sensible and inexpensive shoes for women, and comfortable shoes for men. Commonly found here are brands like Lee, Levi, and Hukapoo. Unless otherwise marked, all merchandise is first quality, and can always be found here at a price lower than at a department store or other retailer. Some of the stores, particularly 7th Street, have bargain basements, where they sell irregulars at a lower price. If an item is not in stock at the store nearest you, they will try to locate it from another branch or from their warehouse. For men, women, and children, there is an extensive selection of casual and work clothes. The stores are large, clean, and well-organized, with separate booths closed with doors and full-length mirrors. They advertise frequently in local papers.

Other addresses:
2834 Alabama Avenue SE, Washington, DC, 584-0700
18th Street and Columbia Rd., NW, Washington, DC, 234-2245
810 Seventh Street, NW, Washington, DC, 628-2700
1488 Rockville Pike, Rockville, MD, 881-1958
2800 So. Quincy Street, Arlington/Shirlington, VA, 820-2200
Landover/K-Mart Plaza, Landover, MD, 322-4747
7645 New Hampshire Avenue, Langley Park, MD, 431-4545

Hours at all stores are Monday through Friday from 11:30 am to 8:30 pm, Saturday from 10 am to 6 pm, and Sunday from noon to 5 pm. Personal checks are accepted with proper identification, as are Master Charge, VISA, Central Charge, and NAC. They will hold items for you for 24 hours without a deposit. There are no cash refunds, but exchanges can be made within 30 days of purchase. On sale merchandise, all sales are final. Parking is ample at all but the DC locations, where on-street parking is the rule. This is a local chain of stores.

Glenbrook Coat Company
333 West Baltimore Street
Fourth Floor
Baltimore, MD
(301) 752-6052

If you're looking for fine classic, extraordinarily well-made clothing, this shop is a true find. In the warehouse downtown district of Baltimore, you take a rickety freight elevator up to a factory workroom, and you will be let into another world — a fresh and comfortable showroom with some of the finest women's merchandise available in the area. You can save from 25% to 50% off the cost of these goods, which are sold in the best stores in major cities in the U.S. Wool dresses start at $325, ultrasuede at $350, and rainwear at $225, depending on the lining material. This is a strictly made to order business, and on the few racks there can be found samples of the various styles, materials and linings available. All of these are limited, but these are classic items that you would buy as an investment. Many of the linings and other print textiles are designed by the owner himself, who is also the chief designer for the firm.

The clothing here is especially useful for the career or traveling woman. Basically, each piece in the collection can fit with many others for an all-year-round ensemble. For example, you can buy a basic silk coat, have a Qiana lining in it, add a button-in fur or cashmere lining, and, for dress, add a fur collar. Or you can buy a suit, with a shirt dress, and wear the dress by itself or under the skirt. The lining on your coat could match the dress. Also, they have a wide selection of ultrasuede dresses, which are washable. They emphasize that the fabrics and the craftsmanship are both of the highest quality, and that the reason they can offer such inexpensive prices is that, by selling from the factory, they are avoiding the middleman's markup.

Hours are Monday through Saturday, from 9 am to 3 pm. Checks with proper identification are accepted. On layaway, a $50 to $100 deposit is required, and the rest is due when the garment is completed. Parking is found on the street, and is often difficult to come by, but there are municipal lots nearby.

Greenbaum's
104 N. Howard Street
Baltimore, MD
(301) 727-4544

Greenbaum's is a well-known jewelry store in the Baltimore area, selling gold and silver jewelry, watches, and some audio equipment. Most major brands are carried, including Seiko and Bulova watches. Occasionally they have seconds, and these are marked as such. National brand watches are discounted 25% off the list price, and other items vary in discount from 10% to 50%, depending on the item. On special orders, a deposit of ½ of the sale price is requested. They will modify designs for you if they can, and they also take special orders. There is a jewelry and watch repair shop on the premises. A store catalog is available, and manufacturer's warranties are offered. Sales usually occur either on major holidays, or in conjunction with other stores in the downtown area. They also sell a few small appliances. Greenbaum's makes you a "lowest price" promise — details of which are posted on the wall. They also take mail orders. And, finally, while you are at the Howard Street store, you should take note of a fantastic collection of silver miniatures of exquisite craftsmanship and beauty.

Other address:
2200 E. Monument St., Baltimore, MD, (301) 732-0523

Hours are 10 am to 5 pm on Monday through Saturday, and Thursday to 8 pm at both stores. Personal checks are accepted with proper identification, as are Master Charge, VISA, American Express, Central Charge and NAC. The layaway policy is liberal, based on the amount of the purchase, and you can pick your purchase up to a year after laying it away. Cash refunds are given up to 7 days after the date of the sale. There is limited street parking, but they do participate in Park and Shop with local lots nearby.

Harford Men's Shop
6818 Harford Road
Baltimore, MD
254-1717

This is basically a nice little neighborhood shop, worth going to if you are shopping in the Baltimore area, have some time, or just want to drive around to get a feel for the town. It's quite a little hole-in-the-wall, but service is friendly, and you might find a bargain. Cluttered with merchandise, it does carry a full line of raincoats year-round — which is the store's major asset — and menswear, including such brands as Glen Eagle, Rainfair, and Clipper Mist. Pants are by such names as Leeds and Kuppenheimmer. They also have a small selection of women's coats and suits by Misty Harbor and Boston Forecaster. Most merchandise is first quality, but irregulars are marked as such. You can hope for savings of 30% to 35% by shopping here. They will try to get special orders for you, and on these you can expect a 20% discount on the average. There is just one dressing room. Alterations are available at the shop. If merchandise is defective, they will exchange it for you. Special sales are held at the end of the season.

Hours here are Monday through Saturday, from 10 am to 6 pm. Personal checks are accepted, but no credit cards are taken. The layaway policy is flexible, generally requiring pickup within 30 days. All sales are final. The only parking is on-street, but it is usually sufficient.

Heel N Toe
Ravensworth Shopping Center
Braddock Rd. at Port Royal Rd.
Springfield, VA
321-8281

Heel and Toe sells ladies' shoes, accessories, handbags, jewelry, stockings and scarves — the amount and sophistication depending on the management of each store. The quality of the footwear runs from medium to high; included are such names as Pappagallo, Naturalizer, Air Step, Bartolini, and Cobbies. All merchandise is first quality, with some manufacturers' closeouts. The discount usually runs about 30%, or $10 per pair of shoes. Everything is in stock — no special orders — but they can check with the warehouse if a shoe is not in stock in your size. They receive new shipments of merchandise once a week. Minor repairs can be done here. The Marlow Heights store has a mailing list for special sales. They usually hold these sales twice a year — the end of December to the beginning of January, and sometime in the summer, around the Fourth of July. They display the shoes in boxes on shelves, organized by size. Boots are available in the fall and throughout the winter.

Other addresses:
1327 Connecticut Avenue, NW, Washington, DC, 223-4242
2368 Hunter's Wood Plaza, Reston, VA, 620-4319
6178 Arlington Blvd., Falls Church, VA, 534-3101
6414 Brandon Avenue, Springfield, VA, 569-4212
4313 St. Barnabas Road, Marlow Heights, MD, 423-9337
8638 Colesville Road, Silver Spring, 585-3200
7982 New Hampshire Avenue, Langley Park, 434-6900

Hours at Ravensworth Shopping Center are Monday through Friday from 10 am to 9 pm, and Saturday from 10 am to 6 pm. Many of the stores do not have evening hours. Personal checks are accepted, as are Master Charge, VISA, Central Charge, and NAC. As long as shoes are unworn and you have your receipt, the return policy is liberal. Parking at the shopping center locations is ample. These shops are part of a national franchise.

Hess Shoe Bargain Box
318 North Howard Street
Baltimore, MD
(301) 752-0698

These stores serve as the outlet for the women's shoes sold in the Hess Shoe Company stores. They stock surplus from the retail stores, as well as closeouts and end-of-season shoes. Brand names include Andrew Geller, Grasshopper, Selby, Bandolinos, Browsabouts, and Naturalizer, to name only a few. You can usually save about 25% to 40% off the retail price of these shoes, and, when they have special sales, the reductions are even greater. They also carry slippers, hose, and some handbags and dressier evening bags. The merchandise is all good quality, and the store is nicely arranged.

Other addresses:
Ridgely Plaza at York and Ridgely Roads, Timonium, MD, (301) 252-6518. Hours are Monday through Friday from 10 am to 9 pm, and Saturday until 6 pm.
Severna Park Mall, Route 2 at McKinsey Road, Severna Park, MD, (301) 647-2116.
Other locations throughout the Baltimore area.

Hours are Monday through Saturday from 10 am to 9 pm. Checks are accepted with 2 forms of identification. All branches accept VISA, Master Charge, American Express, and NAC. Parking is limited at the downtown store. There are no layaways.

Hit or Miss
1667 Rockville Pike
Rockville, Maryland
881-9777

Hit or Miss is a ladies' sportswear discounter which offers a variety of popular labels as well as designer names. The goods range in quality from medium to high. Names like Kasper, Givenchy, Landlubber, Diane Von Furstenburg, and College Campus are commonly found there, carrying with them discounts of an average of 25% to 50%. All merchandise is first quality, with some manufacturers' closeouts. When they have irregulars, they are so marked. They have a variety of accessories such as hats, underwear, belts, and pocketbooks. Dressing rooms are separate, and there are full length mirrors. If one store doesn't have what you want in your size, they will attempt to obtain it for you from another of the local stores. Should you find merchandise defective, they will take care of the defect or replace the item. There are usually three large sales annually, and a number of small ones, advertised in newspapers and on the radio, usually on holidays.

Other addresses:
7668 Richmond Highway, Alexandria, VA, 765-9765
6305 Leesburg Pike, Falls Church, VA, 998-9363
8393 Leesburg Pike, McLean, VA, 931-9328
10710 Lee Highway, Fairfax, VA, 691-9617
5232 Port Royal Road, Springfield, VA, 321-9844
3915 Branch Avenue, Marlow Heights, MD, 899-9895
9139 Central Avenue, Capitol Heights, MD, 336-9665
Forestville Plaza Shopping Center, Forestville, MD, 568-9810
Laurel Plaza Shopping Center, Laurel, MD, 725-8703
Route 450, Lanham, MD, 577-9520

Hours are Monday through Saturday from 10 am to 9 pm, and Sunday from noon to 5 pm. They accept personal checks with proper identification, Master Charge, VISA, and Central Charge. They usually ask 1/3 down on layaways, and final payment within 21 days. They will hold non-sale merchandise for 24 hours without a deposit. There are no cash refunds, but merchandise credit or an exchange can be made within 7 days of purchase, providing you have your receipt. This is a subsidiary of the Zayre Company, and is part of a national chain of stores.

House of Shoes
7822 Richmond Highway
Alexandria, VA
780-1197

A women's footwear store, the House of Shoes has an original concept which we didn't notice in use anywhere else in the area — it is a one price store. All of their shoes cost a maximum of $8 per pair, and all of their handbags a maximum of $10 each. Some prices are lower when they have their clearance sales, usually once or twice a year. They sell a hodgepodge of brands and styles, featuring Pappagallo, Kinney, Sears brand, shoes from stores which have overstocks or have gone out of business, some irregulars, and their own House of Shoes brand, which appears to be inferior to most of the other brands carried. Many imports were noticed on our last visit there, and we saw supplies of Bandolino, El Greco, Delmar, Solos, and Candies, in addition to the brands mentioned above. Styles ranged widely, including sandals and evening shoes; some were made of cloth, some of leather, and some vinyl. Most of the shoes were casuals, but the stock changes rapidly. The store is organized by size and is clean, but not terribly neat. Defective merchandise will be repaired if possible, or replaced.

Other address:
7432 Annapolis Road, Landover Hills, MD, 459-4404

Hours here are Monday through Saturday from 9:30 am to 9 pm, and Sunday from 11 am to 5 pm. They accept personal checks but no credit cards. Exchanges are made cheerfully in season, but there are no cash refunds. Parking is ample. This is a regional Atlantic coast chain of stores.

The In Outlet Shop
Falls Village
5730 Falls Road
Baltimore, Maryland 21209
(301) 323-6911

The In Outlet Shop specializes in handbags and shoes. They carry some of the best names, like Andrew Geller, Bally, and Charles Jourdain. They are first quality and from the current year. The discounts can average about 30%-50% off the comparable retail. There are no special orders. The Baltimore location is a rather strange old store, with the shoes arranged by size around a smallish room, and the large selection of leather handbags, including Coach brand, in a separate room. During seasonal clearances, you can expect even greater savings.

Other location:
Randolph Center, 12223 Nebel Street, Rockville, MD 20852, 468-0044. Hours here are weekdays from 10 to 6 pm, and Thursdays from 10 am to 8 pm.

Hours at the Baltimore store are Monday through Friday from 10:30 to 4:30 pm, Thursday to 8 pm, and Saturday to 5 pm. Personal checks are accepted, as are Master Charge, VISA, and NAC. Layaways require 20% down and 2 weeks to pick up or to make another payment. There are no returns or exchanges. Parking at Baltimore is in a small gravel lot; at Rockville, the shopping center lot is ample.

Jay's Designer Discounts
6535 Arlington Boulevard
Falls Church, Virginia

Jay's stores are nicely arranged, with a wide selection of merchandise and a wide variety of styles, sizes, and quality. They also have clothing for a large range of uses, from sportswear and active sportswear to clothes for the career woman and evening wear. They feature brands such as Kasper, Pierre Cardin, Sasson jeans, Beene Bag, Geoffrey Beene, Calvin Klein, Liz Claiborne, Jones of New York, and less expensive brands such as Bodin, Branch, Century, SWI, Tami, Stuart Lang, Fay's Closet, and She. All merchandise is first quality. The store is basically split into two sections, with the more casual and less expensive merchandise is one, and the dressier and better lines in the other. They advertise special sales regularly in the *Washington Star* and *Post* newspapers. They also sell shoes, lingerie and outerwear here. At the Falls Church store, the dressing rooms are separate booths within a larger area, but there are no curtains on individual booths.

Other locations:
7750 Woodmont Avenue, Bethesda: weekdays from 10 am to 6 pm, Thursday until 9 pm, closed Sunday.
Congressional Center, Rockville, MD: open Monday, Thursday, and Friday from 10 am to 9 pm, Tuesday, Wednesday, and Saturday from 10 am to 6 pm, Sunday from noon to 5 pm.
1404 Reisterstown Road, Pikesville, MD: open Monday, Thursday, and Friday from 10 am to 9 pm, Tuesday, Wednesday, and Saturday fro 10 am to 6 pm, Sunday from 11 am to 5 pm.
Old Keene Mill and Rolling Roads, Springfield, VA

Hours at Falls Church are Monday through Friday from 10 am to 9 pm, Saturday from 10 am to 6 pm, and Sunday from noon to 5 pm. Personal charges are accepted, and on charges there is a $10 minimum — with Master Charge, VISA, Central Charge and NAC accepted. Sale merchandise is not returnable, but regular priced merchandise is, within 7 days, as long as you have a receipt. Ample parking in Falls Church and Rockville. Bethesda is mostly on-street parking, but there are lots nearby. For layaway, you must put 1/3 down, and pay every two weeks, with pickup in 30 days. There is no service charge, and a notice is sent if you miss a payment.

Joseph A. Bank Clothiers
7237 Arlington Boulevard
Loehman's Plaza
Falls Church, VA
573-2800

Joseph A. Bank is a family-owned business, in existence in the Washington and Baltimore area for 75 years. They do almost all of their own manufacturing, and guarantee it to be high quality. They claim that, in season, you can save 30% off the cost of comparable garments in other retail establishments. Because they are the manufacturer, they can special order anything that you would want. All merchandise is first quality. Tailoring is available at a nominal fee. They do not sacrifice looks of the store or service — it appears much as any retail men's clothing store would. They have ample parking available, except for the downtown Washington store. Dressing rooms are separate. There is a mailing list, and an extensive well-illustrated catalogue which you can have sent out to you when you get on the mailing list.

In addition to the suits, coats, and jackets sold here, they carry a large assortment of good sweaters for both men and women. Hanes underwear is featured. They also stock a full line of accessories, including ties, socks, hats, and shirts.

Other addresses:
1015 18th Street NW, Washington, DC, 466-2282: open Monday through Friday from 9 am to 5:45 pm and Saturday from 9:30 am to 5:45 pm.
5222 Randolph Road, Rockville, MD, 770-3330, Monday through Friday from 10 am to 9 pm, and Saturday from 9:30 am to 5:45 pm

Hours at the Falls Church store are Monday through Friday, from 10 am to 9 pm, and Saturday, from 9:30 am to 5:45 pm. Cash, checks, VISA, Master Charge, or NAC are accepted. There is a 100% satisfaction guaranteed policy.

Returns for refunds or exchanges are liberal, and can be made within a year from the date of purchase. Layaway merchandise is held for one week without a deposit, or for 30 days with one.

Kidswear Outlet
9540 B Main Street
Fairfax, VA
323-1127

All the children's clothing at these shops is top quality and from well-known manufacturers like Levi, RobRoy, Tulip Top, Peaches and Cream, Rosebud Duds, Carter's, Vanilla, and Pantsmaker. These are neat shops, very well-organized, with a good selection of merchandise and sizes. In season, you can save 20% to 50%. You can save more during their seasonal closeouts, and you can get on the mailing list to get a notice of the special sales. There are separate booths with doors for dressing rooms. If they do not have a size in a desired item at one store, they will gladly order it from another of their branches for you.

Other addresses:
9558 Livingston Road, Oxon Hill, MD, 248-1288
Diamond Square Center, Gaithersburg, MD, 840-1410
Cabin John Shopping Center, Tuckerman Lane at Seven Locks Road, 299-6727
Route 40 West at Rolling Road, Baltimore, MD, (301) 747-7240

Summer hours are from 10 am to 9 pm Monday, Thursday, and Friday, and from 10 am to 6 pm on Tuesday, Wednesday, and Saturday. During the school season, hours are from 10 am to 9 pm Monday through Friday, and Saturday from 10 am to 6 pm. Open Sundays during the Christmas season. Exchanges or credits are given, but no refunds. Returns on defective merchandise are accepted. Personal checks are accepted with proper identification, as are Master Charge and VISA. Ample parking is available at the shopping center locations.

Linn's Maternity/Linn's Uniform
513 11th Street, NW
Washington, DC
737-0132

This is one of only two shops we found that deals specifically in maternity clothes discounting, and the only one which sells men's and women's uniforms at discounts to individuals. It is a small shop with two floors, in the heart of the Washington F Street shopping area. It is neatly organized by size and style of merchandise, and service is friendly. They say that all are famous brands. The grade of merchandise is generally medium quality, with some cheaper brands. Labels are cut out of the garments. They carry overalls, uniforms, and smocks upstairs, and a collection of maternitywear downstairs. Discounts average from 20% to 40% off comparable retail. Some are manufacturers' closeouts, and some are irregulars and seconds, but they are labelled. Most items are in stock, and if they're not, Linn's will try to order special items for you. The dressing rooms are separate booths. There is a mailing list, and special sales depend on what items the management wants to clear.

Personal checks are accepted. Layaway policy is such that the deposit depends on the amount of the purchase, with a minimum of $2 down on each item, and there is no set pickup time limit. Unless otherwise marked, returns can be made for cash within 5 days with a receipt, and you can make an exchange during a longer period after purchase. You can park free in the nearby Park and Shop lot with a minimum purchase of $25. This is part of an East Coast chain, which claims to be the largest uniform discounter on the East Coast.

Loehmann's
7241 Arlington Boulevard
Falls Church, VA
573-1510

Loehmann's is probably one of the best known, oldest, and largest women's wear discounters in this area. It is an extraordinarily large store, with rack upon rack of sports clothes, separates, and dressy wear. Quality is generally medium to high, with a few cheaper-made items. They also carry accessories, such as belts and hats. Coats are sold in season, as are bathing suits for the summer season. In the Back Room, the finest designer items are stocked. Labels are cut out of all garments — but sometimes you can recognize what brand it is from remaining fragments. The dressing rooms here are large open rooms — definitely not for the modest. There is no mailing list. The management refused to tell us their discount policy. They do get frequent deliveries and mark down items to clear quite often, so you might find it worth visiting a few times to see if they carry the type of items in which you are interested.

Other address:
Randolph Road at Nicholson Lane, Rockville, MD 770-0030

Hours at Falls Church store are from 10 am to 5:30 pm on Monday through Saturday, and Wednesday until 9:30 pm. Personal checks are accepted, but credit cards are not. All sales are final. For layaway, you must put 1/3 down, and you have 7 days to pay off the balance. Parking is ample, because these are both shopping center locations.

Lowenthal & Hess
Third Floor
34 S. Howard St.
Baltimore, Maryland
539-5650

They say that hats are making a comeback. If you're one of these women who want to stay on top of fashion — or if you just happen to be lucky enough to look good in hats — you'll be interested in knowing about Lowenthal and Hess. Another shop located in the old garment warehouse district of Baltimore, this firm is basically a hat distributor. The hats are arranged on top of cartons, roughly in aisle form, with a sample style on top of the boxes, or hanging above. One advantage of this shop is that you can buy hats ahead of the season, and not have to look at picked-over merchandise either at retail store sales, or at discount stores (which also happen to have more limited selections). The quality is from medium to high, and styles from conservative to more exotic. Prices are not marked on the hats; you have to ask the friendly proprietor. He says that prices range an average to 10% to 20% below comparable retail, but some savings are even greater, especially on out-of-season hats. There is also a small selection of handbags, in vinyls and fabrics.

The store is open 9:30 am to 4 pm on Monday through Friday. No credit cards are accepted, but personal checks are, when accompanied by proper identification. Layaway deposits are a minimum of 1/3, with pickup desired within 2 weeks. While there are generally no returns or exchanges, if you really have a problem the manager is flexible about it. Parking is on-street, and quite limited. However, there are a number of other shops in the nearby vicinity, making it worth finding a parking space here. There are also a number of lots at which you pay to park.

Max Rubin Factory Outlet
113 W. North Avenue
Baltimore, MD
(301) 837-8883

Men's clothing, suits and sportcoats, pants, and some accessories are stocked. This is a real factory outlet, and is one large room on the second floor of the Max Rubin factory. The merchandise here is generally low to middle quality, and is sold in such places as Hecht's basement store. They have a very large collection of polyester suits, and will have some wool blends for winter. 90% of the merchandise is first quality, and any irregulars are so labelled. The average discount is 25% to 30% off comparable retail, and they do take special orders, which they get directly from the factory downstairs when available. Separate dressing rooms are provided.

Hours are Monday through Friday, from 9 am to 4:45 pm, Saturday from 9 am to 3 pm, and, during July and August, on Saturday from 9 am to 1 pm. Personal checks are accepted with proper identification. Master Charge, VISA, and NAC are also valid here. For layaways, you put down either $10 per unit or 10% of the total as a minimum down payment, with payments every thirty days. They will hold items for you for a day or two. Seasonal merchandise is not returnable. But on most items, you can make an exchange, as long as you bring in your receipt. Cash refunds are generally not given, unless you inquire of the management in advance. There are large parking lots on either side of the building.

Off the Rax
8355 Leesburg Pike/Woolco Center
Tysons Corner, VA
821-9322

Women's sportswear and dresses are offered by this well-organized and inviting store. They carry many well-known designer labels in season, and these are left in the garments; but, at the request of the management, these cannot be mentioned in this publication. Most merchandise is first quality, with a rare 2-3% being irregular and marked as such. You can count on an average discount of from 30% to 50%, and more when they have special sales. Dressing rooms are separate. They try to stay current with the fashion trends, and buy as they see a style become fashionable — not committing themselves way in advance to one or two styles, but varying their items greatly. In addition to skirts, blouses, dresses and slacks, they carry bathing suits in season, and good quality socks, and a small number of other accessories.

Other locations are in Baltimore, Towson, and Cockeysville.

Hours at Tyson's Corner are Monday through Friday from 10 am to 9 pm, Saturday from 10 am to 6 pm, and Sunday from noon to 5 pm. Personal checks are accepted with proper identification, and Master Charge and VISA are also accepted. There is no layaway policy, but they will hold items for up to 24 hours without a deposit. Exchanges can be made within 7 days with receipt. If there has been only one markdown on sale merchandise, it too can be exchanged; but after two markdowns, all sales are final. There is a large parking lot in this Woolco Center shop.

Olde Towne Gemstones
2 Prince Street
Alexandria, VA
836-1377

While in this area there are probably a number of shops which discount gold and silver jewelry, we have found one where you can consistently get a good buy on gold and silver chains, and antique oriental jewelry. Olde Towne Gemstones is basically a rockhound's shop, but also carries a variety of jewelry made from semi-precious stones, and the already-mentioned gold and sterling silver chains. The chains are sold by weight by the metric system. These people buy from importers, not from distributors, so they are avoiding the markup. They claim that their prices reflect less than 50% of the usual retail price of these items. Having compared prices, we have found them to be consistently lower; in addition, as the price of gold rises, they do not raise their prices to match until their costs actually rise. So, where some shops charge you the new rate despite the fact that they paid the old rate, Gemstones keeps the old price on the merchandise. They also do jewelry repairs here.

Hours are Tuesday through Saturday, 10 am to 5 pm, Sunday from noon to 5 pm, closed Monday. Personal checks, Master Charge, and VISA are accepted. Hold policy depends on the individual and the item. Exchanges for a refund or for credit must be made within 30 days of purchase. Limited parking is available on the street.

Once Is Not Enough
4830 MacArthur Boulevard NW
Washington, DC
337-3072

We visited Once... because we had heard it offered new maternity clothes at a discount; they are indeed found among the shop's carefully selected used clothing. We found, however, that the owners also get great buys on new children's clothing, and on many high quality articles of women's clothing, from store closings, close-outs, and the like. The children's clothing includes well-known brands like Florence Eisman, Health-Tex, Polly Flinders, and a French brand, "Absorba", and these come from fine children's stores all over the East Coast. Maternity clothing includes brands like Monday's Child, Fine Co., and Sweet Mama. Prices usually run from 1/3 to 1/2 of full retail. New clothing in the shop is clearly marked. There is one large

OUTERGEAR
WASHINGTON'S ONLY DOWN FACTORY OUTLET

An enormous selection of down — racks of parkas, jackets and vests — all in prime northern down, all priced way below retail.

A huge variety of styles and colors in a wide range of sizes for men, women, and children.

Bring in the whole family for rugged cold-weather gear. Outergear has chilling discounts . . . . toasty customers.

11136 Rockville Pike, across from White Flint. (301) 770-5420. Open seven days. All major credit cards accepted.

dressing room for all to share. If merchandise is found to be defective, they will repair or replace it. Other new items in evidence at the time of our visit included jewelry and scarves, women's trousers of high quality, and beautiful imported wool coats at prices up to 60% off of the comparable retail. The store owners will pick up fine quality used clothing for consignment on request.

Personal checks are accepted, as are Master Charge and VISA. Layaway terms are negotiable. They also have a 24 hour approval policy on children's clothing. Intact items can be returned when accompanied by receipt.

Outergear
11136 Rockville Pike
Rockville, MD
770-5420

Outergear claims to be the biggest seller of down goods in the Washington area, and says that they can save you from 25% to 40% on your purchases here. In this long narrow shop are from 3,000 to 5,000 pieces of down clothing: vests, parkas, and coats, wool and acrylic sweaters, ski clothing, and longjohns. During spring and summer, they stock sailing, running, and jogging gear. The merchandise is of the highest quality generally available, representing such brand names as Camel, Downeast, Snowbird, Aspen, and their own Outergear house line. All merchandise is top quality, with some manufacturer's closeouts. Deposits are required on special orders, which are rare. If merchandise is found to be defective, it should be returned within one week, accompanied by the receipt. No repairs are done here. There is a mailing list for special sales, which will occur about three times per year.

Hours are from 10 am to 7 pm Monday through Friday, 10 am to 9 pm on Thursday, and 10 am to 6 pm on Saturday. Summer hours are slightly different, so phone ahead. Personal checks, Master Charge, VISA, American Express, Bank of Virginia, and Central Charge are accepted forms of payment here. There is no layaway policy. There are no refunds, but there are exchanges. On sale merchandise, there are no returns. There is ample parking in a large lot.

Sam Glass and Sons
301 N. Gay Street
Baltimore, MD
(301) 727-1398

Sam Glass is a family business selling a full line of men's clothing, all name brands, and most with the labels in. This is a very large, well-organized shop, with separate areas for different types of items, which include vests, ties, lots of suits, jackets, formal wear, raincoats such as Harbormaster, and other outerwear. Typical brands found here are Cardin, St. Laurent, Hardy Ames, Botany 500, Italiana, and Givenchy. They also carry a line of finer merchandise, such as Rubin Brothers and Petrocelli, which are marked considerably down from their usual retail prices. All merchandise is first quality and in season. They close out and reduce their merchandise below their usual 40% discount when they feel it is either out of season or out of style. Service is excellent here, and they will help you find anything and match things up for you. There are separate dressing rooms with doors on them. The products are guaranteed against defects. There is a mailing list, by which they can inform you of end-of-season closeouts and other special sales, which occur about 4 or 5 times per year.

This store is open from Monday through Saturday from 9:30 am to 5:30 pm, and Thursday night until 8:30 pm. Personal checks, VISA, Master Charge and NAC are accepted. *There is a sliding scale for down payments on layaway merchandise, and payment is expected every two weeks. If no payment is received on schedule, a notice is mailed out, they wait one week, and, if nothing happens, refund your deposit. Layaways are kept a maximum of 60 days. They will hold items for a maximum of 2 days without deposit. Cash or credit refunds are given with merchandise returned with all of its tags attached and a receipt. Clothing is guaranteed returnable as long as unaltered — and you can always get cash back. Ample parking is available to one side of the building and across the street.*

Sam's Tailoring Co. Warehouse
6245 Little River Turnpike
Alexandria, VA
354-3636

Sam's sells men's clothing of their own, as well as better-known manufacturers. It is a local chain of stores in Virginia and West Virginia. Appearances must be deceptive in this case, for the store we visited is quite small, and stock appeared limited, but there seemed to be a number of contented customers happily browsing and buying. A casual glance through the racks indicated brands like Pierre Cardin, Lord Jeff, Jaymar, Glen Oaks, Tobias slacks, as well as Arrow and Gant shirts and Interwoven socks. Discounts run from 20% to 30%, and all merchandise is either first quality in season, or manufacturers' closeouts. They do alterations here — and service is one of the advantages of such a small place. Incidentally, they also tailor ladies' clothing bought elsewhere. Dressing rooms are separate. They hold at least two major sales a year, in January and after the Fourth of July.

Checks, Master Charge, VISA, American Express, Central Charge and NAC are all accepted *in payment. 20% down is required on layaways, with 30 days to pick up. They will hold items for up to 24 hours without a deposit. Merchandise can be returned for an exchange or for credit, as long as you have the receipt. There are no returns on sale merchandise. Ample parking is found in the shopping center lot in front of the store.*

Sam Oidick
413 W. Baltimore St.
Baltimore, MD
(301) 727-5777

This is a small jobber's shop, again in the downtown Baltimore warehouse district. It is a nice little store which carries men's clothing from which the brand names have been removed — but the garments are generally high quality. Suits are discounted up to 50% and shirts from 25% to 50%; and they also carry trousers and other items. Pierre Cardin ties, and Excello and John Weitz shirts are stocked. There are separate dressing rooms. Raincoats and outerwear are also offered.

Hours here are Monday through Friday from 9:15 to 4:45 pm, and Saturdays until 2 pm. Personal checks are accepted, either with ample identification or if the customer is known to the management. All sales are final, and there are no layaways. Park and shop lot is nearby.

Schwartz Tailors
4618 King Street
Alexandria, VA
931-0458

Schwartz (like Sam's above), is a small men's clothing store that benefits the customer not only by discounting good quality merchandise, but by offering service. If you're not a stock size, you have probably more than once had to pass up a good buy because tailoring services were not available on the premises. So places like Sam's or Schwartz's, despite more limited selections than the larger stores, may be of interest to you. Schwartz's sells a full range of men's clothing, including shirts, jackets, suits, pants, raincoats, belts, ties, and sports jackets. The quality is medium to high, as they buy from name brand manufacturers, such as Botany 500, slacks from John Weitz, Johnny Carson suits, Nino Cerruti, and Pierre Cardin, to name a few. All is first quality merchandise, and you save from 20% to 30% on the average. There are no special orders. There are separate dressing rooms, each with a door. Special sales are held roughly 2 or 3 times per year.

Monday and Tuesday, hours are from 10 am to 6:30 pm; Saturday, from 10 am to 6 pm; and Wednesday through Friday, from 10 am to 9 pm. Checks, Master Charge, VISA, Central Charge, and NAC are accepted. Put ¼ down on layaways, with 90 days to pick up the merchandise. They will hold items for you for up to 3 days without a deposit, and cite a liberal return/exchange policy, as long as you keep your receipts and the clothing has not been worn. There is a small free parking lot in front of the shop.

Seventh Heaven
F St. between 11th and 12th NW
Washington, DC
638-5263

Of all the places visited for this book, this one was the busiest and the wildest. Seventh Heaven is a huge discount department store selling women's sportswear and an extensive collection of infants' and children's clothing. What distinguishes it from its larger competition is that is sells well-known brands at discount prices, not merchandise of a lesser quality. It is housed on the first floor of one of the large older stores in downtown DC, and has huge stocks displayed on the selling floor. Typical items include Calvin Klein jeans, Pampers, Time & Place juniors' wear, Danskins, Gloria Vanderbilt jeans, and costume jewelry. They pride themselves on their huge stock of well-known children's manufacturers, including Underoos, sold regularly here at a price rarely if ever seen at other stores. Discounts usually average 30%, but they have ongoing promotions all of the time, and sometimes up to 40% or 50% off. For example, they will unload good items very cheaply at their "garage sales", which they hold on their loading docks. In March, 1979, they had one promotion during which they gave away balloons and popcorn; and once they gave out Metro coupons as return fare to customers using public transportation. Usually they have one promotion per month. They specialize in infant clothing and can get anything not found on the selling floor out of their warehouse right across the street. They advertise frequently on the radio, and less often in DC papers.

Hours are from 10:30 am to 6 pm Monday through Friday, Saturday from 10 am to 6 pm, and Thursday from 10:30 am to 7 pm. Personal checks are not accepted, but Master Charge, VISA, Central Charge and NAC are. Layaways are accepted only on purchases of $15 or more, and you have to pay on them every two weeks — there is a posted schedule for the amount of deposit, depending on the total size of the purchase — but a minimum of $7 down is required. Refunds are given with receipts within 7 days of purchase. Credit is given for sale merchandise when returned. There is on-street metered parking, which is limited, but public transportation — at the Metro Center subway stop, or via Metrobus — takes you right to the store.

There's No Inflation in 7th Heaven.

SAVE 20-40%

Spectacular savings on first quality merchandise for children, infants, & juniors. Top Brand-Name Merchandise Discounted 20 - 40% Everyday. Famous maker clothing you'll see in department stores at prices you'll see only at 7th Heaven. Come in and Save!

7th HEAVEN

"discount ladies & children's wear" between 11th and 12th on F St. at Metro Center Subway Stop. **638-5263**
Open M-T-W-F 10:30 - 6, Thurs. 10:30 - 7, Sat. 10 -6

(Sign reads: REPENT SAVE 20-40%)

Shane's Shoe Store
1200 S. Charles Street
Baltimore, MD
(301) 538-4709

From the outside, Shane's appears to be a very small store, but the secret is that the stock is displayed in the crowded windows, and on racks inside — and when it comes to sizes, the salesperson will go into the large back rooms to retrieve your size and desired style. Most of the shoes in stock are overstocks from other stores and are in season and in style. All of them are well-known American and imported name brands — from medium to high quality. There is no average discount, but discounts do range up to 60%. Shane's will take special orders on men's shoes and do not request a deposit. Defective merchandise will be repaired or replaced. There is no mailing list, but they hold seasonal sales, when prices are marked down even further. Shane's is a family business which has been in this area for more than 69 years. We found it to have a good selection.

Other address:
1814 Pennsylvania Avenue, Baltimore, MD, 728-8895.

Hours at Charles Street are Monday through Thursday from 9:30 am to 5:30 pm, and Friday and Saturday from 9:30 am to 7 pm. Checks with proper identification are accepted, as are Master Charge, VISA, and NAC, and they use Equitable Trust's Welcome Check. Layaways must have one half the amount of purchase put down, and pickup within 30 days. Unworn merchandise can be returned in a reasonable amount of time for cash or credit. Marked down merchandise is not subject to return or exchange. Public parking is available up the street, and they will reimburse you for your expense with a purchase. But there is also metered on-street parking.

The Shoe Box
2809 Columbia Pike
Arlington, VA
920-7778

This is a neat small store selling women's shoes of medium quality. Brands commonly found here include Naturalizer, Lifestride, Sebago, Dexter, and Hush-Puppy. All merchandise is first quality. Depending on the time of the year, they may have manufacturers' closeouts. Discounts average 30% to 50% off comparable retail merchandise. Special sales occur here on holidays. Shoes are set up on racks running the length of this 1600 square foot shop.

Monday through Friday, they are open from 9:30 am to 6 pm, and Saturday to 5 pm. They accept personal checks with appropriate identification, Master Charge, VISA, and Central Charge. There are no layaways or holds. Usually, merchandise can be exchanged or returned for credit, but not for cash, unless prearranged with the management. On-street metered parking is available, or in the shopping center lot down Columbia Pike.

Shoe Giant
7601 New Hampshire Avenue
Langley Park, MD
881-9778

Shoe Giant is a small and crowded store, with floor-to-ceiling racks of shoes organized by size. They carry a range of men's and women's shoes, from low quality on up. In this place, you really have to sift through the merchandise. But you can find such men's brands as Bally, Johnston & Murphy, and French Shriner; and women's manufacturers such as Naturalizer, Airstep, and Lifestride. Discounts usually range at about 25%, and 20% on manufacturers' closeouts. They stand behind their product, and, should you find it defective, they will try to deal with this problem to your satisfaction. During their seasonal sales, additional discounts are possible.

Open from 9 am to 9 pm from Monday through Saturday. Checks, Master Charge, VISA, Central Charge, and NAC are accepted. 1/3 down payment is required on layaways, with 60 days to pay the balance and pick up the shoes. They will hold items with a small deposit. The return and refund policy is liberal. There is a large parking lot in front of the store.

The Shoe Horn
7770 Woodmont Avenue
Bethesda, MD
656-7797

A refreshing change on the discount scene: The Shoe Horn is a really nice open and airy shoe store for women, with shoes, boots in season, pocketbooks, and stockings. Merchandise goes from medium up to the best brands available, and includes such designers as Howard Fox, Golo, Jack Rogers, Amalfi, and a variety of others. Most merchandise is current and first quality, but there are a few pairs of last year's merchandise, with no irregulars or seconds being offered. Discounts are usually 20%, but, on clearance, range from 30% to 50%. The shop is arranged by style, rather than by size. Some shoes are marked "net", and they cannot be sold at 20% discount, but are still priced substantially below those found in a retail shoe shop. Customer satisfaction is guaranteed, and if there is any defect or flaw, or if the shoe falls apart within a short period of time, they will have it fixed or replace it for you. There is a mailing list, by which you can be notified of the sales. Sales generally occur on big holidays at the end of summer, and at other seasons' ends — in late June and late December.

Store hours are Monday through Saturday, from 10 am to 5:30 pm, and Thursday, until 7 pm. Checks, Master Charge, VISA, Central Charge, and NAC are accepted. They have a liberal layaway program, requiring at least 1/3 down, and usually pickup within 10 days, but this is flexible. Unworn merchandise with register receipt can be returned for credit or exchange. Parking is available on the street at meters, and there is a public lot nearby.

Shoe Stop
Wildwood Shopping Center
Bethesda, MD
530-3400

The Shoe Stop is a pleasant place to save money on ladies' shoes. They carry many well-known brands, like Charles Jourdain, Nigani, Joan and David, Bruno Magli, and Anne Klein, offering discounts which run from 20% all the way up to 75%, depending on the item. They have end-of-season shoes, late deliveries to other stores, overstocks from other retail stores, and no irregulars. They also carry handbags and knee socks, which are not discounted. The do have a mailing list. At a recent visit there we saw a $10/pair table, with values ranging up to $50 per pair, and we were told there are always items on this table. There are also seasonal clearances where you can save even greater amounts. The store is arranged by size, and it is self-service. The people who run it are very friendly, and will help you find what you're looking for. We noticed some excellent buys, such as "disco" shoes for $5 a pair! There are several other good bargain shops in this shopping center, so it's definitely worth a visit.

Monday through Friday from 10 am to 8 pm, Saturday from 10 am to 5 pm, and from noon to 5 pm on Sunday, except during the summer, when they are closed on Sunday. Checks, Master Charge, and VISA are accepted. 50% is required as a deposit on layaways, with 2 weeks to pick up the items. They will hold merchandise for 24 hours without a deposit. Returns are for credit or exchanges only. There is a large parking lot in the shopping center in which this shop is located.

Show-Off
Loehmann's Plaza Shopping Center
Arlington Blvd. and Graham Rd.
Falls Church, VA 22042
560-0270

For casual sportswear, Show-Off offers hard-to-beat prices, especially when they are having a seasonal clearance sale, as they were when we last shopped this store. Brands such as Bobbie Brooks, College Town, Peerless of Boston — in a middle price range — were abundant. They carry skirts, blouses, slacks, and some dresses, and some outerwear, but no accessories. Most merchandise is for the current season, but a little past the time when it *first* appears in the retail stores, because of a dating process which a number of manufacturers use. You can definitely expect a minimum discount of 40%, and anywhere up to 70% is not uncommon. All merchandise is unflawed, and they have a very large selection. Dressing rooms are closed booths. There is also a mailing list for major sale notification.

Other address:
Glen Forest Shopping Center, 5900-B Leesburg Pike, Baileys Crossroads, VA, 820-3903

Hours here are Monday through Saturday from 10 am to 9:30 pm, and Sunday from noon to 5 pm. They accept Master Charge and VISA, as well as personal checks with proper identification. Merchandise can be returned within 7 days of purchase for a cash refund, and within 14 days for credit or exchange. Layaway is discouraged on small items. This is an affiliate of a national chain store.

Showroom
Intersection of Old Keene Mill and Rolling Roads
Springfield, VA
451-8562

Showroom stocks a good selection of women's wear, from less expensive dresses and sportswear and suits to some better labels. We noticed some of the brands which were well-known — John Meyer, Jonathan Logan, and Hukapoo — there were many others. Starting with the fall line, they will also stock complementary accessories. The store is large and well-organized, with very friendly service. They keep a customer book for sales — if you sign up, they will notify you when they are going to have a sale — or if you ask them to call you when a certain item comes in, they will try to do so. The discount runs anywhere from 30% to 60% off comparable retail merchandise, and they do have a number of big clearances each year. The dressing room is a large room, with booths on all four walls (only a few have curtains), and you walk outside your booth to look in the mirror. The Springfield location provides a playroom for customers with small children — which was the only such room we saw at any of the stores we visited.

Other addresses:
7542 Annapolis Road, Lanham, MD, 459-0885. Whiteflint Plaza, Rockville, MD, 468-0515

Hours here are from 10 am to 9 pm on Monday through Saturday, and on Sunday from noon to 5 pm. Personal checks with proper identification, Master Charge, and VISA are accepted. You can get a refund within 7 days with a receipt. If something was a gift or was on sale, you can get an exchange or merchandise credit, but no refund. Ample parking in shopping center lots. They do not take layaways in the Washington area, but they will hold items for you for a reasonable amount of time without deposit.

Stephen's Men's Clothing Manufacturer's Outlet
717 Ellsworth Drive
Silver Spring, MD
589-6667

This shop carries men's clothing, including suits, sportscoats, hose and shirts of medium quality. Typical brands include Geoffrey Beene, Eagle Clothes, and Arrow. Other information was unavailable at the time of the visit.

Open Monday through Saturday, from 10 am to 6 pm. They accept payment in cash, Master Charge, VISA, and Bank of Virginia. There are no layaways or holds. Returns can be made for cash or credit within 7 days with a receipt. Parking is available on the street or in parking lots.

Shoe Town
8430 Old Keene Mill Road
Springfield, VA 22150
451-9796

This is a large national chain store which sells women's shoes, socks, handbags, sunglasses, shoe polish, shoelaces, and other related items. A large store, Shoe Town has racks of shoes arranged by size. Examples of brands include Capezio, Lord and Taylor, Saks Fifth Avenue,

Nunn Bush, and Amalfi — all first quality. Some shoes might be out of season, but you can expect to save 20% to 40% on your purchases, and even more when they have seasonal clearances in mid-winter and mid-summer.

Other locations:
7329 Arlington Blvd., Falls Church, VA, 560-9648
13629 Connecticut Ave., Wheaton, MD, 871-9865
1665 Crofton Centre, Crofton, MD, (301) 721-9825
656 Quince Orchard Rd., Gaithersburg, MD, 977-9831
Randolph Road at Nicholson Lane, Rockville, MD, 770-9799
7804 Riverdale Rd., New Carrollton, MD, 577-9840

Hours here are from Monday through Saturday from 10 am to 9 pm, and Sunday from noon to 6 pm. They accept personal checks with proper identification, VISA, NAC, and Master Charge. Returns are made on unworn merchandise with a receipt. Ample parking is available. A 10% deposit is required on layaways, and they must be picked up within 15 days.

Status II
4405 Willard Avenue
Chevy Chase, MD
652-4540

For really fine quality dressy sportswear, dressy women's clothing, and accessories, Status II is a must. You can get top designer lines from Courreges, Yves St. Laurent, Valentino, Calvin Klein, and Anne Klein at prices ranging from 50% to 80% off the retail price — because the merchandise is one year old. There are two separate dressing rooms in this small but elegant shop. There is a mailing list, and seasonal sales are held. Any merchandise found to be defective will be repaired.

Open Monday through Saturday from 10 am to 6 pm and until 8 pm on Thursday. Personal checks are accepted, as are Master Charge, VISA, American Express, Central Charge, and Diner's Club. There are no layaways, but the hold policy is liberal. All sales are final. Parking in nearby lots.

The Store
White Oak Shopping Center
Rte. 29 at New Hampshire Ave.
Silver Spring, MD
681-7993

In a large facility, The Store sells women's apparel and junior and misses sizes. They also sell suits, accessories (like stockings and socks), and seasonal items (like bathing suits), with such brands here as Pandora, Liz Claiborne, Cardin, Amanda blouses, and designer label jeans. All merchandise is first quality, and you can save 50% off the designer labels, and from 35% to 40% off the other merchandise. There were at this location 18 individual dressing rooms. Should you find a flaw in anything you buy here, they will uphold the quality and replace it if necessary. There is a mailing list for notification of special sales or other events, which occur seasonally.

Other addresses:
Hub Plaza, Laurel, MD, interesction of Rtes. 197 and 198, 725-7133
Aspen Hill Shopping Center, Connecticut Avenue and Aspen Hill Rd., Aspen Hill, MD, 460-5533

Hours at The Store are from Monday through Friday from 10 am to 9 pm, to 7 pm on Saturday, and Sunday from noon to 5 pm. Payment can be in cash, by personal check with proper identification, or by Master Charge, VISA, Central Charge, or NAC. 20% down payment is required on layaway items, and they must be picked up within 30 days. There are no cash refunds, only merchandise credit, and no returns at all on items marked "final sale". This is a regional chain store, located on the East Coast from Massachusetts to North Carolina.

Sugar's
Congressional Plaza
Rockville, MD

Sugar's is a modern store, selling sportswear, some dresses, and a good selection of accessories and handbags. The quality of the goods is middling, with brands commonly found here such as Modern Juniors, Bronson, Pant-Her, Hukapoo, and Garland. Discounts of at least 20% can be obtained. All merchandise is first quality, and there are some manufacturers' closeouts. If you can't find something in your size, they will see if the other store has it. Dressing rooms are separate, and each has a door. Alterations are available. There is a manufacturer's warranty on most clothing sold here, and if anything is defective they will take care of it.

Other location:
Manassas Mall, Manassas, VA

Hours here are Monday through Friday from 10 am to 9 pm, Saturday from 10 am to 6 pm, and Sunday from noon to 5 pm. Checks, Master Charge, VISA, American Express, Central Charge, and NAC are accepted. Layaways require 1/3 down and 1 month to pay. Cash refunds will be given if merchandise is returned within 5 days of purchase, and credit or exchanges within 10 days. There are no refunds on sale merchandise. There is a large free parking lot at the Congressional Plaza location, and ample parking in Manassas.

Syms
1000 E. Broad Street
Falls Church, VA
241-8500

The main items sold here are men's and women's clothing, with some accessories as they are made available to the store. At Syms, they take care to mention that theirs is an off-price store, which means that they buy at off-price directly from the manufacturer, which allows them to sell at greatly reduced prices to the consumer. The usual discount is from 30% to 50%, and somewhat more during end of season clearances, or on clearance racks found in both the ladies' and men's sections of the store. Because of the discounts, and the terms under which they obtain the merchandise, Syms does not advertise the names of the brand which they carry. But they do carry top quality designer labels, both domestic and imported, as well as some slightly less expensive items. Downstairs on the main floor, you will find ladies dresses, pantsuits, and handbags — in wide selection. Also, a variety of items on which the management gets a good purchase — ranging from kitchen items to umbrellas to towels. Also on this floor is a selection of inexpensive but well-made softsided luggage and cases. Men's accessories, like shirts, ties, and socks, are found in quantity here. Upstairs, men's shoes, suits, slacks, and other items are found in vast array. There is also an automatic price reduction policy in effect here on women's clothing: an item is premarked with the price it will sell for at the time it first comes in (about 69% of retail price), as well as with several progressively greater discounts; if the item remains on the floor, the price is automatically lowered, reaching a final price of 29% if it's still in the store after a specified number of weeks. You may find this particularly good if you want to buy something, decide the price is a bit too high, and are willing to take a

THE MANDY

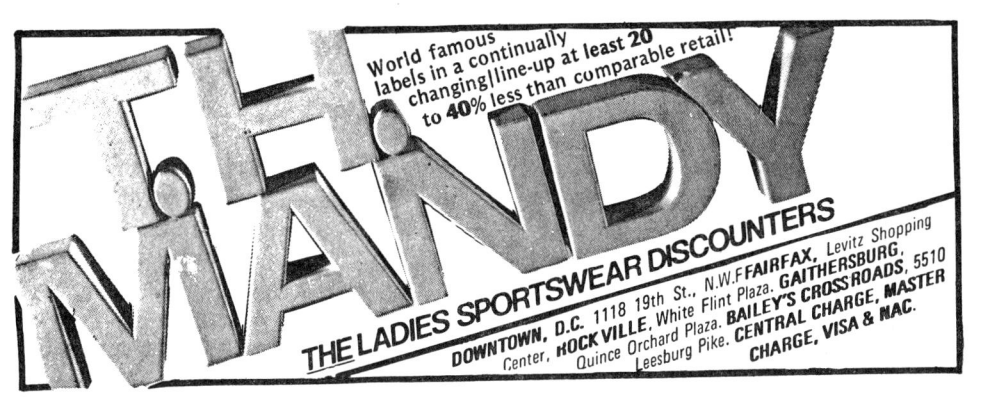

THE LADIES SPORTSWEAR DISCOUNTERS

World famous labels in a continually changing line-up at least 20 to 40% less than comparable retail!

DOWNTOWN, D.C. 1118 19th St., N.W. FAIRFAX, Levitz Shopping Center, ROCKVILLE, White Flint Plaza, GAITHERSBURG, Quince Orchard Plaza, BAILEY'S CROSSROADS, 5510 Leesburg Pike. CENTRAL CHARGE, MASTER CHARGE, VISA & NAC.

---

gamble that it won't be sold before the next price reduction. There are only two dressing rooms: one is for men, the other for women. They are large and open, and accommodate quite a few people at the same time.

Hours are from 10 am to 9 pm on Monday through Friday, and Saturday from 9 am to 6 pm. There are no cash refunds, and all sale merchandise is on final sale. Cash only or personal checks with proper identification are accepted. There is a huge parking lot. Syms is part of a privately owned East Coast chain of 8 stores, with others in Buffalo, Miami, Rosslyn, Westchester, and Long Island.

T. H. Mandy Co.
Levitz Plaza
Fairfax, VA
573-1184

I have always counted on Mandy's for fine quality in sportswear. They specialize in blouses and sweaters, slacks and skirts, and blazers. They also sell dresses in the summer. Mandy stores are large and well-stocked with good merchandise from designers such as Kasper, Paula Saker, Frederick Sport, St. Tropez, Sir for Her, and Pant-Her, to name just a few. The average discount is from 20% to 50%, and even more when they have their large seasonal clearance sales. In season, they have a limited amount of outerwear. If they do not have a size or color which you desire in stock at one store, they will be happy to call around for you and have it sent over from another. The dressing rooms here are large rooms, with booths on the four inside walls. The booths are open, and each has a mirror in it.

Other addresses:
5106 Nicholson Lane, White Flint Plaza, Rockville, MD, 881-1114
1118 19th Street NW, Washington, DC, 659-0025
658 Quince Orchard Plaza, Gaithersburg, MD, 840-9090
5510 Leesburg Pike, Baileys Crossroads, VA, 578-3737

Mandy's hours are from 10 am to 9 pm, Monday through Friday, and Saturday until 6 pm. The District of Columbia store has different hours. They accept personal checks with identification, VISA, Master Charge, Central Charge, and NAC. Returns or exchanges will be accepted on defective merchandise only. There is no layaway plan. Parking is ample at all but the downtown Washington location.

T. I. Swartz
Backlick and Keene Mill Roads,
Springfield, VA
569-0600

A menswear merchant, T. I. Swartz has made itself known for what they call Grade 4 suits. They say that, regardless of brands, all suits are graded; and, when you put a brand name on (depending of course on that name), you are automatically raising the price of the suit. So they manufacture their own suits, which are of the same high quality as most designer suits -- one grade below the highest grade — and sell them in season for 40% off comparably priced items. In addition to suits, they sell ties, shirts, overcoats, and slacks. Complete alteration services are available, and they can also make you a made-to-measure suit. There are separate dressing rooms.

Other locations:
Congressional Plaza South, Rockville, MD, 770-3566, Monday through Friday from 10 am to 9 pm, Saturday to 6 pm. 600 So. Pulaski Street, Baltimore, MD, (301) 233-6400, open Monday through Wednesday and Saturday from 8:30 to 5 pm, Thursday and Friday from 8:30 to 9 pm.

You can pay with checks or credit cards — American Express, Central Charge, NAC, VISA, or Master Charge. There is no layaway policy, but they will hold items for up to 2 days. Ample parking is available.

Ted Louis Clearance Center
Shirlington Shopping Center
Arlington/Shirlington, VA
578-4100

Ted Louis sells menswear like underwear, slacks, suits, belts, shirts, socks, shorts, and outerwear at a discount usually from 30% to 35%. Their merchandise comes from their full price store, end of season, manufacturers' closeouts, and some regular first quality merchandise. They carry brands such as Botany, Cricketeer, Chaps, Damon, Izod, Arrow, Jaymar, and Jockey. An example of a recent good buy there was a table full of trousers which normally retail from $30 to $40 per pair, reduced to $16.90 each. You can also find large sizes — up to 50 extra long — but no "portlys". Dressing rooms are separate booths with doors. Alterations are available, and there is a mailing list. Special sales events are held four times a year, and reductions are even greater than during the rest of the year.

Hours are Monday through Saturday from 10 am to 6 pm, and Thursday night until 9 pm. Personal checks are accepted, as are Master Charge, VISA, American Express, and Central Charge. Layaways require a 25% deposit and pickup within 30 days. They will hold items upon request. Returns can be made within 30 days. On sale merchandise, there are exchanges only — no cash refunds. Ample parking is available on the street and in a large free lot in back of the store.

Tyson's Clothes-Out
1524 Springhill Road
McLean, VA
821-0792

Coming Attractions brand warehouses its merchandise in this complex. A new feature of the warehouse is a small retail store which calls itself Tyson's Clothes-Out, and is located at the front of one section of the warehouse. They feature active sportswear, with women's items, and a predominance of menswear. This includes shorts, pants, and jackets; and chamois, wool, and corduroy shirts. Nine-tenths of the garments are irregulars or seconds, and they sell for 40% to 60% less than at normal retail. You can

Clothing & Shoes 105

also buy first quality merchandise here, but at the regular retail price. The dressing room is just a curtained-off area big enough for only one person. Everything is sold as is.

Hours here are Monday through Friday from 9 am to 4 pm. They may be open some weekends, so call to find out. They accept personal checks, Master Charge, and VISA. There are no layaways or holds, no returns or exchanges — all sales are final. The parking lot is large — but, as this is a warehouse area, it is often quite crowded.

Urdong's Outlet
1305 E. Gude Road,
Rockville, MD
279-9650

This warehouse outlet for Urdong's does not carry all of the same high quality merchandise that the retail store carries, but everything is first quality, at a discount of 20% to 50% on the average. The space is small, and the selection is limited, with a predominance of T-shirts and jeans. But they do also carry over items by such manufacturers as Young Edwardians, Tracy Petites, Starship, and Heidi. There are four individual dressing rooms at the Gude Road address. All sales are final. We did not visit the other two locations.

Other addresses:
1222 F Street, NW, Washington, DC, 628-9586: offers some discounts, but is a full service store.
3436 Donnell Drive, Forestville, MD, 736-3100

This store is open from 9:30 am to 5:30 pm on Monday through Saturday. Checks, Master Charge, VISA, American Express, Central Charge and NAC are accepted. They do not have layaways, but they will hold merchandise for 24 hours. Parking is available, except at the F Street store, where on-street parking or pay lots are the only alternatives.

Wall Street Clothing
932 S. Walter Reed Drive
Second Floor
Arlington, VA
920-0800

Wall Street Clothing claims that you can save up to 40% on the average on your clothes by buying at this store. They do carry men's clothing, including brands like College Hall, Browning, King and Co., and Yves St. Laurent shirts, some Pierre Cardin, Dior — but not at all times — Givenchy, Van Gil, and Von Furstenberg. Their merchandise is out-of-season and manufacturers' closeouts, but no irregulars. There are three dressing rooms with curtains across the front. They carry sizes to size 66 and have some accessories. Alterations are available.

Other address:
5560 Randolph Road at Nebel Street, Rockville, MD, 770-4984. Parking in Montrose Shopping Center.

Hours are Monday through Friday from 10 am to 8:30 pm, Saturday from 10 am to 5:30 pm, and Sunday from 10 am to 5 pm. They take personal checks with identification as well as Master Charge, Central Charge, and VISA. There are no returns, exchanges only. Parking at the Arlington store is in the parking lot in back. Alterations must be paid for in cash.

Wearhouse, Inc.
10768 Tucker Street
Beltsville, MD
937-4843

This is a warehouse outlet for T-shirts for children and adults. What they sell are overruns and misprints of their regular items at low prices. For example, they may be printing a custom job of gym shorts for a school, but the ink splotches -- these would be sold in this shop. Or a T-shirt may not have been evenly printed. They sell T-shirts, plain and printed, gym shorts, and three styles of nylon shell coats — with a pile lining, with a flannel lining, or unlined. All merchandise is first quality and domestically made. Misprinted T-shirts are charged at $1.99 each, and you can order a custom transfer T-shirt for only $2.50. They have a chart on display which shows the designs from which you can choose. There are no dressing rooms. The shop is very small, and in it are usually three bins. In one, you will find children's sizes; in the second, adults' sizes; and in the third, a variety of accessories, such as visors and bags, which are also marked down. In addition to their regular low prices, they have clearance sales, usually around major holidays, like Easter.

Hours are from 10 am to 4:30 pm, Monday through Friday. Personal checks are acceptable, as long as you have two forms of identification. No credit cards can be used here. All sales are final. There is a small parking lot. This is a privately owned corporation, of which this is the only retail outlet.

Wholesale Clothing Distributors
Village Square
Waldorf, MD
843-2172

This is a medium-sized store, with clothing on racks, which sells men's and women's jeans, tops, and other related items. They carry a wide range of brands and styles, including Faded Glory, Levi, McMuffin, Pilot blouses, and Eccobay. Merchandise, which is mostly first quality and only occasionally manufacturers' closeouts, is of a medium to high grade. The usual discount is 30% to 50%. Since they are a wholesaler, much of their business is in large quantities, which have to be ordered, and require a deposit of 1/3. There are two separate dressing rooms. Manufacturers' warranties come with the garments. Special sales are frequent.

Hours here are from 10 am to 7 pm Monday through Friday, and from 10 am to 7 pm on Saturday. Personal checks, Master Charge, VISA, Central Charge, and NAC are accepted forms of payment. There is no layaway, but they will hold items for you with a deposit. All sales are final. There is a large parking lot. The nearest major street is Route 5.

Zippers
7514 Leesburg Pike
Falls Church, VA
821-0490

Zippers specializes in Levi products — 95% of their sales are in Levis. In addition, they feature painters' pants and other types of work clothes. All merchandise is first quality, yet is discounted anywhere from 15% to 35% every day, and even more during sales. They have 80 sizes in stock and have a large warehouse stock if you cannot find your size and desired color when there. Each store has about 39 separate dressing rooms. They offer a money back guarantee — if you are not satisfied with the way the pants or shirts wear, bring them back for a replacement or refund. Selected items are featured during weekly sales all year round, but there is a big sale in the fall directed towards the back-to-school crowd, and at other major events during the year. They advertise mostly in the newspaper and on local radio stations.

Other addresses:
8430 Old Keene Mill Road, Springfield, VA
Congressional Plaza, Rockville, MD, 770-1650

The stores are open from Monday through Saturday from 10 am to 9:30 pm and Sunday from 11 am to 6 pm. They average 12,000 square feet. They accept personal checks with identification, Master Charge, VISA, Bank of VA, Central Charge, and NAC. They have a flexible layaway program. Refunds are made usually within ten days of purchase, and always with receipt, but the policy can be stretched. There is ample parking at all locations. This is part of a growing national chain of stores, which also includes Country Legend Stores.

Open from 10 am to 6 pm Monday through Saturday, and until 8 on Thursday. They accept personal checks, Master Charge, Visa, American Express, Central Charge, and NAC. They have layaway terms of 20% down and 60 days to pick up for coats. Merchandise can be returned with sales receipt for a cash or charge refund. If you lose your receipt, you get merchandise credit. On-street metered parking or pay lots.

LATE ADDITION:

The Attic
Philipsborn Retail Outlet
1201 F Street NW
Washington, DC

If you don't mind having misses and juniors clothing from last season and want truly good bargains, this is definitely the place to come. This is where the 33 stores in the Philipsborn chain send their merchandise after it has reached a 60% markdown and stayed at that level for 3 weeks in those stores. From the 60% they start at, they are gradually reduced first to 67½%, to 75%, and to 82½%, after which they are given to a charity. Their merchandise is generally of medium quality brands, such as Jantzen, Bobbie Brooks, Personal, and Cole of California. All merchandise is first quality. There are six separate dressing rooms. Typical buys when we visited included jogging shorts for 99c, costume jewelry from under $1 and up, sweaters for $5 to $8, and slacks for $8 on the average. This third-floor shop is loaded with everything to outfit a woman, from dresses to slacks to sweaters to blouses to outerwear.

MAIL ORDER:

Andean Products
Apartado 472
Cuenca, Ecuador
South America

Imported heavy sweaters of thick wool for about half as much as retail.

Budget Uniform Center, Inc.
941 Mill Road,
Cornwell Heights, PA 19020
(800) 523-6582

Free medical and restaurant uniform catalogues published three times and two times a year, respectively. Discounts of up to 35% on clothing, and 25% to 35% on related jewelry and pins.

I. Buss and Co.
50 West 17th Street
New York, New York 10011
(212) 242-3338

Discounts of up to 30% on surplus clothing and camping goods. Write with idea of what you want, as there is no catalogue.

Cambridge Wools, Ltd.
P.O. Box 2572
16-22 Anzac Avenue
Aukland, New Zealand

Sweaters of natural New Zealand wool for $35 to $45 (to order).

V. Juul Christensen and Son
17 Livjaegergade
DK-2100 Copenhagen
Denmark

Discounts of 30% to 50% and more on Icelandic sweaters in all designs. Ask for free catalogues.

Eileen's Handknits
Ardara, Donegal,
Ireland

Get a free brochure on cottage sweaters of Ireland, tams, and mittens at 30% less than comparable retail.

Eisner's Brothers
76 Orchard Street
New York, New York 10002
(212) 475-6868

Men's and boys' underwear and T-shirts at discounts up to 75%. Brochure is free.

Gohn Brothers
Middlebury, Indiana 46540
(219) 825-2400

Free catalogue of Amish clothing, at discounts of 20% to 70% off retail. Includes a lot of common clothing and accessories (like socks, handkerchiefs, shirts, etc.).

Goldberg's Marine
202 Market Street
Philadelphia, PA 19106
(800) 523-2926

Breton sweaters, French fishermen's striped sweaters, and waterproof slickers and boots at a good discount. Catalogue costs $2.

Hudson's
105 Third Avenue
New York, New York 10003
(212) 475-9568

Catalogue for $1 on brand name clothing for casual and camping wear. Discounts up to 40%.

Icemart
P.O. Box 23
Keflavik International Airport
Iceland

Sweaters and accessories by the Icelanders at prices at least 30% less than comparable retail. Catalogue costs $1 by air mail and is published in September.

Kennedy's of Ardara
Ardara County Donegal
Ireland

A free catalogue for sweaters and accessories of pure Aran wool in unique designs. Discounts up to 80% off comparable retail.

Laurence Corner
62-64 Hampstead Road,
London, NW 2 NU
England

From a catalogue costing $2.50, you can learn about all kinds of surplus goods varying discounts.

Clothing & Shoes

**The Nepal Craft Emporium
G.P.O. Box 1443
Katmandu, Nepal**

Nepalese handcrafts, clothing, and accessories at fantastic prices. Catalogue for $3.00.

**The Tibetan Refugee Self Help Center
Havelock Villa
65 Ghandi Road,
Darjeeling, India**

Discounts to 80% on Tibetan clothes, shawls, and soldiers' caps. Catalogue costs $1.00.

Additions to the Second Edition:

**Antique Guild
133 N. Fairfax St.
Alexandria, VA
836-1048**

Here you will find antiques, ivory pieces, oriental carpets, lamps, *objets d'art*, Erte prints, other interesting items, orientalia, small collectibles like snuff bottles, and a fine selection of jewelry gold, and silver. You can get particularly good buys on gold and silver items. They will also make trades, and buy as well.

Other location:
4615 Duke St., Alexandria, VA, 370-2500

**Molline's Boutique
10506 Connecticut Avenue
Wheaton, MD
949-1205**

Molline's is small and cluttered, absolutely jammed with women's clothing, some gifts, many accessories, lingerie, costume jewelry, raincoats, sandals, and more. Molline carries contemporary clothing by makers such as Act II, Lillyette, Goddess, Exquisite Form, Kollection, Scene II by Act III, and Jonathan Logan, which she marks up to prices about 10% to 15% below normal retail. She also gives additional discounts to those who pay cash, and quantity discounts on weddings or other large orders, such as for a choral group. Everything she sells is first quality — but it isn't all current, and therein lies the charm of Molline's. What she calls "leftovers" can range from 50% off of retail on one-year-old merchandise to giveaway prices on items that look to be 10 years out of style. There are three separate dressing rooms.

Hours are 10ish to 6ish Monday through Saturday. Personal checks are accepted, as are Master Charge and VISA. Layaway terms are negotiable. Items will be held up to 2 or 3 days without a deposit, and return policy is liberal. Ample parking.

**Webster's Menswear
4013 Branch Avenue
Marlow Heights, MD
423-3362**

For casual and dressy menswear, Webster's is an outlet store for its own Webster's brand merchandise — generally of a medium grade — and also carries some suits and shirts by designers like YSL, Don Robbie, Givenchy. The average discount is 40%. All merchandise is first quality. There are 6 separate dressing rooms. Seasonal and after-holiday special sales are held.

Other location:
Greenbelt Plaza, Greenbelt, MD

Hours are the same at both stores: Monday through Saturday from 10 am to 9:30 pm, Sunday from noon to 5 pm. Personal checks are accepted, as are American Express, Master Charge, VISA, Carte Blanche, Central Charge, and NAC.

Linens & More for the Home

Ace Restaurant Equipment
1917 New York Avenue, NE
Washington, DC
635-8132

Ace Restaurant Equipment sells restaurant equipment, cookware, flatware and dishes, and other products used in the food service industry. Everything is first quality, and discounts run from 10% to 40%. On used equipment, they offer a 30 day warranty. This is a warehouse setting, catering mainly to commercial accounts, but open to individuals.

Hours are from 8 am to 5 pm. Personal checks are accepted, and so are Master Charge and Visa. Layaway policy depends on discussion with the manager. Returns and exchanges depend on the item size and the way in which payment was made. There is a small parking lot.

Ambach Mill Outlet
York Road at Church Lane
Cockeysville, MD
(301) 666-7737

Ambach's is a very large store, containing everything for the bath, kitchen, and bedroom in the way of linens and accessories. They carry sheets made by Springmaid, Martex, and J.P. Stevens; towels by Cannon, Bathworks, and Springmaid. Most items are first quality, but they place lower prices on irregulars, which are marked. The discount averages from 20% to 30% off comparable retail. They do special order items, and on these require a 50% deposit. If merchandise is found to be defective, it will be replaced. Major sales are held all of the time on featured brands or items. The store is large and well-organized. Besides the linens, we noted bath accessories, brass bathroom accessories, placemats, soaps, and other merchandise, all by top name brand manufacturers.

Other addresses:
Glen Burnie Business Center, Glen Burnie, MD, (301) 768-8841
Also in Severna Park, MD

Personal checks are accepted, as are Master Charge, VISA, and NAC charge cards. Hours are Monday through Friday from 10 am to 9 pm, Saturday from 10 am to 6 pm, and Sunday from 11 am to 4 pm. The Severna Park store is closed on Sunday. On layaways, they generally ask for 20% down, and have a liberal amount of time for final payment.

THE CHINA CLOSET

Always the finest selection and price in china, glassware, stainless, linens, and gourmet accoutrements.

Chevy Chase
6807 Wisconsin Ave.
656-5400

Loehmann's Plaza
Arlington Blvd.
698-9236

White Flint Mall
468-2130

Baths Etcetera Value Center
7356 Little River Turnpike
Annandale, VA
750-2102

Baths Etcetera Value Center is a very large store with fine quality merchandise for far more rooms than just the bath: They sell shades at 20% off list, custom draperies, woven woods, tablecloths, throw pillows, bedspreads, Levolor blinds, and a large selection of accessories. The quality of their merchandise ranges from medium to the highest, as they market items by such manufacturers as Fieldcrest, Wamsutta, Nettlecreek, Bramson House, and Bean Ideal. The discount is 20% off list on Levolor blinds, 50% off on bedspreads, 50% on shower curtains, and 40% to 50% off on towels. On special orders, they ask a deposit of 1/3. The price on the special orders is also 20% to 30% less than retail. Monthly promotions are held on featured items. You can look forward not only to saving money here, but to enjoying browsing as well.

Personal checks are accepted, and so are Master Charge, VISA, American Express, Central Charge, and NAC credit cards. There are no layaways. They do have a liberal hold policy. Ample parking.

China Closet
6807 Wisconsin Avenue
Bethesda, MD
656-5400

China Closet stores are absolute treasure troves of kitchen and dining room accessories, tableware, and gadgets — all of fine quality and in varying price ranges. They carry gadgets, earthenware, silver-plated merchandise, baskets, aprons, stainless steel, knives, food processors, glassware, and (of course) china. They have a large and extensive gourmet section in each shop. Names commonly found here include Iron Mountain, Langenthal, Arabia, Franciscan, Bing and Grondahl, and Sabatier. They carry 200 patterns of china dinnerware and 100 varieties of glassware, with discounts ranging 10% to 50% off comparable retail. They specialize in close-outs and seconds, and claim the largest selection in the area. They will take special orders, particularly on Wedgewood, Noritake, and Bloch. They usually advertise special items in the Thursday *Washington Post*. Among other things, they present cooking demonstrations, frequently of Chinese cooking. Usually their demonstrations start in the fall, so you should call for further information if you are interested.

Other addresses:
Loehmann's Plaza Shopping Center, Arlington Blvd., Falls Church, VA, 820-1900

White Flint Mall, Rockville, MD: Hours are from 10 am to 9:30 pm Monday through Saturday and from noon to 5 pm on Sunday — these are the mall hours as well. Phone 468-2130.

The store hours are from 9:30 am to 6 pm, Monday through Saturday, Thursday night until 9 pm, and Sunday from noon to 5 pm. They accept VISA and Master Charge credit cards, as well as checks with proper identification. There are no layaways. They have a flexible return policy and will take anything back with a receipt. Without a receipt, you get merchandise credit. In Bethesda, on-street parking or public lots; in White Flint and Virginia, ample parking.

Debois Textile Mill Outlet
1835 Washington Blvd.
Baltimore, MD
(301) 837-8081

Filled with fabrics, some children's clothing, sheets, bedspreads, curtains, comforters, kitchen towels & cloths, patterns, and notions in a comfortable disarray, Debois Textile is an exciting place to visit. They carry brands such as Buster Brown children's clothes, J.P. Stevens, and Bates bedspreads. No merchandise is first run, first quality — everything is closeouts, irregulars and seconds, and is so labeled. Discounts average from 30% to 50%. They will take special orders on custom draperies, with a 50% deposit. They hold special seasonal sales or special purchase sales, where discounts run to 75% off. There is also a special back room with great buys on beautiful designer upholstery fabric.

This factory outlet is open from 10 am to 5 pm on Monday through Saturday. They accept VISA, NAC, and Master Charge, but no personal checks. All sales are final. They have no official layaway policy. Exchanges can be made within 7 to 10 days of purchase. Ample parking.

Discount Mart
Eastover Shopping Center
Oxon Hill, MD
583-3180

The Discount Mart carries a variety of low to medium quality goods, including linens, jeans, mirror tiles, paintings, lamps, sheets, spreads with matching draperies and curtains. About 40% of their merchandise is first quality, and the remaining 60% consists of irregulars or seconds, both so marked. The discount off retail averages 50%. There is one individual dressing room. They hold two sales yearly. Everything is set up on shelves, tables, and racks, and each item is individually priced.

Other address:
2824 Alabama Avenue, SE, Washington, DC, 583-3180

Hours at this store are from 10 am to 9 pm, Monday through Saturday. Personal checks are accepted with proper identification, as are Master Charge, VISA, and Central Charge credit cards. No layaway policy. Exchanges must be made within 7 days of date of purchase. Ample parking at Eastover Shopping Center location.

Fabric Man
11760 Parklawn Drive
Rockville, MD

Refer to Fabric & Yarn section (following) for complete discussion of this store, which also sells a full line of items for bed and bath.

Foam Fabricators
5560 Randolph Road,
Rockville, MD
770-6770

The name says it all — for high density foam cushions, this is the place to go. Everything is first quality, less 1/3 off retail. The staff at this tiny store can cut or make anything you want out of foam for furniture, pillows, and cushions.

Other address:
3211 Brinkley, Temple Hills, MD, 630-4800

Hours are Monday through Saturday from 10 am to 6 pm, and Thursday until 8 pm. Personal checks with identification, Master Charge, and VISA are accepted. There are no layaways, holds, returns, or exchanges. There is a large parking lot at the store.

Giovanni's Bed Bath & Table
80 Halpine Court
near Congressional Plaza
Rockville, MD
770-4343

Giovanni's looks crowded even though merchandise is shelved and organized on display tables and is of a fine quality. In this warehouse-style setting, you can find good buys on linens, bed, bath, and kitchen accessories, and pillows and sheets. The quality goes from medium to high. 90% of the merchandise is first quality, by such manufacturers as Fieldcrest, J.P. Stevens, Wamsutta, and Bloomcraft. The seconds and irregulars — comprising about 10% of the stock — are so marked. Discounts start at a minimum of 25% off retail and average up to 35%. They take special orders on custom-made spreads, asking for a 20% deposit and a wait of from 3 days to 4 weeks.

DISCOUNT BED AND BATH

HUGE SELECTIONS! ALL FAMOUS LABELS! SAVE 20% TO 50% OFF REGULAR RETAIL PRICES!

★ OPEN MONDAY — SATURDAY 9:30 to 9; SUNDAY 12 to 5 ★

SEE US FOR THESE
AND MANY MORE
DOMESTIC ITEMS
FOR YOUR HOME!

- SHEETS
- PILLOWS
- TOWELS
- BATH SETS
- COMFORTERS
- BEDSPREADS
- BLANKETS
- AREA RUGS
- PILLOW CASES
- SHOWER CURTAINS
- KITCHEN TOWELS
- CAFE CURTAINS

THE **fabric man**

SATISFACTION GUARANTEED!
Oxon Hill, Maryland 5000 Indian Head Hwy
Opposite Eastover Shopping Center
Lanham, Maryland 7401 Annapolis Road
Silver Hill, Maryland 3120 Branch Avenue
Rockville, Maryland 11760 Parklawn Drive
Bailey's Xrds, Virginia 5524 Leesburg Pike
MAJOR CREDIT CARDS!

The store is open from 10 am to 6 pm on Tuesday through Friday, and Saturday from 9:30 am to 5:30 pm. They accept personal checks with identification, and Master Charge and VISA charge cards. There are no layaways, but they will hold items for 24 hours. All sales are final.

Graham Van Leer and Elmore Co. Inc.
8453-A Tyco Road,
Tysons Corner, VA
891-8992

This store, primarily geared to the contractor and construction professional, sells Naturalite skylights at 10% off regular retail prices. The skylights come in a variety of sizes — most are double bubble — in choices of clear or tint. The more you buy, the bigger the discount that you get. It's just a small warehouse, but you can definitely get a good buy on skylights.

They are open weekdays from 8 am to 5 pm, and Saturday from 12:30 to 4 pm. Checks or cash are accepted. They will take returns.

Kitchen Bazaar
Seven Corners Shopping Center
Seven Corners, VA
534-0220

Kitchen Bazaar is a great place to look for items for your kitchen and dining room — they carry a vast assortment of gadgets and the newest things in cooking and gourmet-dom. But let me stress that they are not really a discount store — rather, their sales are so good and so frequent that they are worth mentioning in this book. They carry everything for the kitchen for the gourmet, including stainless flatware, dinnerware, COPCO, Le Creuset, Cousance, HOAN, Foley, and Tuscany brands. Almost everything is first quality, other than special purchases, which are marked. Mailers are sent out five times a year for sales — and they are long booklets — so extensive are the lists of specials. The average savings on sale merchandise is 20% to 50%. The life of the mailer savings is usually 6 weeks. They also hold other special sales on merchandise, with ads in the newspapers announcing these. Food processor demonstrations are held once a week, as are maximoven — a hot air circulating fan line of ovens — demos. They also have special classes to go with featured merchandise.

Other address:
4455 Connecticut Avenue, NW, Washington, DC, 244-1550

The Seven Corners store is open Monday through Friday from 10 am to 9:30 pm, Saturday from 10 am to 6 pm, and Sunday from noon to 5 pm. They accept personal checks with identification, and also Master Charge, VISA, Central Charge, and NAC credit cards. They will make refunds or exchanges any time if you are not satisfied with your purchase, as long as you have your receipt. Ample parking in Virginia, limited parking in Washington.

Linen Loft
11134 Rockville Pike
Rockville, MD
468-0444

At the Linen Loft, you can find items for the bed, bath, and kitchen, of the highest quality. 85% of merchandise is first quality, with the remaining 15% irregulars and seconds, so marked. On brands such as Springmaid, Stevens, YSL, Calvin Klein, Halston, Wamsutta, Utica, and Fieldcrest, you can expect savings of 25% to 60%. They also carry toilet seats, linens, towels, potholders, dish towels, placemats, bath mats, and bathroom accessories. On special orders, there is usually a wait of from 4 to 6 weeks, with a 50% deposit requested. The stores are clean and well-organized, with attractive displays and well-marked merchandise. They advertise their special sales in the newspapers.

Other address:
5900-A Leesburg Pike, Baileys Crossroads, VA, 820-7260

The Linen Loft is open from Monday through Saturday from 10 am to 6 pm, and on Sundays in winter from noon to 5 pm. They accept personal checks with identification, Master Charge, VISA, and Central Charge credit cards. They will hold items for up to one week. There are no refunds, but store credit is given on unopened merchandise within two weeks of purchase. There are no exchanges on irregulars or closeouts.

Linens N Spreads
6230 Rolling Road
Springfield, VA
569-0566

This is a large, very attractive, and well-laid-out shop which has a beautiful selection of towels, bedspreads, comforters, and decorator throw pillows. They concentrate on items for the bedroom and bathroom, and some for the dining room; but they did not carry sheets at the time of this writing, although they planned on having them soon. Also carried here are shower curtains, custom draperies, blankets, mattress pads, miniblinds, shades, shutters, woven woods, and bath accessories. Brand names found here include Kirsch, Wear-Ever, Avanti, Bloomcraft, Fieldcrest, J.P. Stevens, and Countess York. They carry many closeouts and about 20% of stock is seconds or "if perfects", which are labelled. The discount varies by item, but you can expect from 20% to 60% on most items. Most items are in stock, and the deposit required for special orders (such as draperies) depends on the manufacturer. They were starting a mailing list when we talked to them, and they plan to send out informational flyers.

Open Monday and Thursday from 10 am to 9 pm; Tuesday, Wednesday, and Friday to 7 pm; and Saturday until 6 pm. Personal checks are accepted, as are Master Charge and VISA. There are no layaways, but they will hold merchandise for up to 24 hours. There are no returns on towels, mattress pads, and other such items which are marked "irregular" or "if perfect". There is a 72-hour return period on other regularly-priced merchandise. Defective merchandise can be returned for credit or an exchange. Parking is ample in shopping center lot.

Paper Mart
5540-A Randolph Road,
Rockville, MD
881-5282

The two locations of Paper Mart have different faces: the Rockville store is well-organized, with merchandise attractively displayed, and has a great selection of party goods and novelty items. The Hyattsville store is oriented more toward an institutional line and is used as an outlet store. Both carry items like party and dinnerware; decorations; and things like heavy duty disposable dinnerware are found in the institutional line. Popular brands sold here include Chinette, Silent Service, Paper Art, and Contempo. All merchandise is first quality, and discounts run from 10% to 45%. Everything is in stock. If you desire custom printing on napkins, they require a 50% deposit and three days wait for your order.

Other address:
5214 Monroe Place, Hyattsville, MD, 277-8989: open Monday through Friday from 9 am to 4 pm.

The Rockville store is open from 10 am to 6 pm on Monday through Saturday, and Thursday night until 8 pm. *Personal checks are accepted with proper identification, as are Master Charge and VISA credit cards. Returns on unopened merchandise only.*

Place Setting Outlet
112 W. Padonia Road,
Padonia Park Shopping Center
Cockeysville, MD
(301) 252-7944

This small store is worth stopping in if you happen to be in the Cockeysville area, but the selection is more limited than in comparable stores closer to the Washington area. They sell china, stoneware, flatware, gourmet kitchen items, many glasses, and mugs. Brands range from medium to high and include such well-known names as Noritake, Rosenthal, Arabia, Villeroy and Boch, Oxford Hall, and Dalia. They carry Sabatier knives and many gadgets. All merchandise is first quality or first quality discontinued. Discounts average 20%. You can get the same discount on special orders, with a 50% deposit. They have special sales on their store's anniversary, and on holidays. You can get on their mailing list, or read ads in the *Sun* and *Baltimore* magazine for these specials.

The Place Setting Outlet is open from Monday through Saturday from 10 am to 5 pm, and Thursday to 9 pm. Personal checks are accepted with proper identification, as are Master Charge and VISA. They rarely do layaways, but they will hold merchandise for up to 24 hours without a deposit. Exchanges can be made, with no set time limit. There is adequate parking in the shopping center lot.

Pottery Fair
7273 Arlington Blvd.,
Falls Church, VA
560-5118

Pottery Fair shops are small, but crammed full of all kinds of tableware, kitchen gadgets, and cookware. You will recognize such well-known names as Villeroy and Boch, Block, Arabia, Iron Mountain, Denby, Wedgewood, Royal Doulton, Copenhagen, Marshall Studios, and Lenox. You can save 10% to 40% off of comparable retail prices on these items. Everything is first quality, and they do take special orders. They also feature stainless steel flatware and accessories, glassware, tablecloths, and placemats and Sabatier knives.

Other address:
5534 Connecticut Avenue NW, Washington, D.C. (near Chevy Chase Circle), 363-4498

The Virginia store is open Monday, Thursday, and Friday from 9:30 am to 9 pm, and Tuesday, Wednesday, and Saturday to 6 pm. They accept personal checks with identification, VISA, Central Charge, and Master Charge. They will make exchanges on sale items. Layaway is available, and there is ample parking in Virginia, but more limited parking at the Connecticut Avenue location.

Read Plastics
12331 Wilkins Avenue
Rockville, MD
881-7900

Visiting Read Plastics is an experience. It actually consists of two retail outlets — one of which is aimed at the contractor and the other at everyone. In this second place, called the Plastics Place, they sell plastic, plexiglas, and lucite materials for making things; they sell adhesives, ceiling panels, plastic bags, bookends of lucite, table tops, cutting boards for $1.75

(plastic, of course), Micarta sheets for counter tops — and many more plastic materials. Materials are sold by the pound — and you can get all types of plastic scraps cheaply this way for home projects. They have free instruction sheets for making and installing plastic storm windows, and other free information.

Open from Monday through Friday from 8 am to 4 pm. They accept personal checks with valid identification, VISA, and Master Charge. There is a $15 minimum on checks and charges. All sales are final. There is ample parking.

Spreads and Things
1327 Rockville Pike
Rockville, MD
340-6622

This is a small, well-organized shop, with samples attractively displayed. You can find savings of from 20% to 50% on such items as bedspreads, custom window shades, Levolor blinds, and woven woods, all in high to medium quality merchandise. You will recognize such brand names as Fieldcrest, Bates, Dakota, Waverly, Bloomcraft, and Burlington. Everything is first quality or first quality discontinued merchandise, with these latter comprising 80% of the stock. On special orders, they ask a 50% deposit, and a wait of 4 to 10 weeks. They have a mailing list for the Virginia store only. They claim the largest selection of spreads in this area.

Other address:
Pan-Am Center, Fairfax, VA

Hours at both stores are Monday through Saturday from 10 am to 5:30 pm, and Thursday nights until 9 pm. They accept personal checks with identification and VISA credit cards. Their layaway policy is liberal. They will hold items for up to 24 hours. You can get a refund within two days of purchase and merchandise credit within 10 days.

Designer Linen Outlet
Bed Bath & Kitchen

30 to 60% SAVINGS EVERYDAY

Major credit cards accepted

11134 Rockville Pike
Across from White Flint next to Luskins
468-0444

Bailey's Crossroads
5900 A Leesburg Pike
Rt. 7 between Columbia Pike & Rt. 50
820-7260

Linen Loft, Inc.

"Brand Name Quality for Less Everyday"

Fabrics & Yarn

Arnold Hurt Fabrics
3420 Wisconsin Avenue NW
Washington, DC
363-1771

Arnold Hurt's is a small store crowded with shelves filled with bolts of upholstery and drapery fabrics. They may have dress goods at the Annapolis store, but not at the DC location. Discounts average 50% and sometimes run as high as 60% on the fabrics. Merchandise is good quality, and many fabrics are on full bolts. Many remnants and other special items are found in large bins and are sold at lower prices. You can special order from the books, but at the book price. They also carry Kirsch hardware, thread, and other related items.

Other address:
1505 Forest Drive, Annapolis, MD, (301) 263-3093

Hours are from 10 am to 6 pm, Monday through Saturday. Personal checks are accepted with proper identification. There are no returns or exchanges. There is a parking lot nearby and on-street parking at the Wisconsin Avenue address.

Bazaar Knitting
9543 Braddock Road
Fairfax, VA
978-1211

Bazaar Knitting is a small store that looks like a conventional retail knitting shop. They carry needlework and needlepoint accessories, kits, yarn, embroidery materials, and books. The books and accessories are not discounted. The discounts on materials run from 15% to a high of 40%. Brand names commonly found here include Brunswick, Reynolds, Bernat, and a fine selection of imports, including Royal Paris. Most merchandise is first quality, and closeouts are found marked down in a bin. They also have materials for quilting. While most items are in stock, they still discount special orders. Satisfaction is guaranteed. Every brand is tried by the management before they sell it to make sure it lives up to its promises. There is a mailing list, and every couple of months they have special sales on featured items.

The store is open Monday through Wednesday from 10 am to 6 pm, and Thursday and Friday to 8:30 pm. Saturday, they close at 5:30 pm. These are summer hours, in the winter, the store is open until 8:30 pm from Monday through Friday, Saturday hours are unchanged, and they are also open from 10 am to 3 pm on Sunday. Personal checks are accepted with proper identification, as are Master Charge and VISA. There are no layaways, but they will hold items without a deposit for up to a week. They give cash refunds. Ample parking in Twinbrook Mall.

Calico Corner
6400 Williamsburg Blvd.
Arlington, VA
536-5488

Calico Corner is a beautifully-designed shop, filled with bolts of upholstery, drapery, and slipcover material, all seconds of fine and designer quality merchandise. Although the names of the brands cannot be mentioned in print, you can find them on the selvages of the fabrics. There is always a special sale corner, where prices per yard are marked well below the usual discounted price. On regular merchandise, they offer discounts of 50% and more off comparable retail prices, and knowledgeable personnel are eager to help you out with your sewing projects and give you hints on creating better products. They also have handy giveaway pamphlets, which go into some detail about fabrics and sewing techniques, as well as new ideas in the field.

They are open from Monday through Saturday from 9:30 am to 5:30 pm. They accept VISA and Master Charge. There are no returns, so they give you swatches to take home to be sure you want the material; or, by leaving a deposit, you can take the whole bolt home on approval. Parking available in a medium-sized lot.

DeVaris Fabrics
3104 Duke Street
Alexandria, VA 22314
751-9193

Devaris Fabrics features upholstery, slipcover, and drapery material, and all of the necessary notions in a medium-sized, well-organized shop, stuffed with goods. They will also make your needlepoint into custom pillows. Fabric prices run from a special 99c per yard to $20 per yard for the finest fabrics. The average discount is 60%. Curtain rods and wallpaper are discounted 10%, and sometimes more. Depending on the quantity you buy, you could save up to 25% on these items. Merchandise is first quality, with a large number of closeouts and some irregulars, which are labeled. They will also special order merchandise for you, and you can save about 25% off comparable retail on these items. They frequently put ads in the newspaper, noting their 99c special and other featured buys.

This store is open from 9:30 am to 6 pm Monday through Friday and Saturday from 10 am to 5 pm. Some evenings, they may have later hours. They accept personal checks with identification, as well as Master Charge and VISA. Layaway: the amount down depends on the customer, but pickup should be within 30 days. All sales are final; there are no returns. Parking is available in a small lot.

Discount Fabrics
2219 N. Glebe Road
Arlington, VA
528-6834

Discount Fabrics is a medium-sized neatly organized shop, selling upholstery fabrics, dress goods, trims, patterns and buttons, and other notions by name brand manufacturers. Patterns are by Simplicity, Butterick, and McCalls. They offer you savings of from 30% to 50% on manufacturers' closeouts and seconds, and fabric from furniture manufacturers' overstocks. Personnel are knowledgeable about sewing and are happy to give you any tips that they can. At the time of our visit, buttons were on special and were ½ off the marked price.

This store is open from 9:30 am to 5:30 pm Monday through Saturday. They accept personal checks with proper identification. There is no time limit on returns, but no cut fabrics can be returned. Ample parking available in store lot.

Danneman's
6150 Franconia Road
Alexandria, VA
971-2771

At Everfast they carry such brands as Everfast, Wamsutta, Dan River, and Burlington. They give you an average discount of 10% on dress goods, and from 30% to 40% on drapery fabrics. They will also send out for labor on bedspreads and quilts for custom orders. Drapery fabric irregulars ran a special 98¢ to $1.49 a yard at the time we visited. They will hold items for 1-3 days, unless they are on sale. This is a nice store, neatly organized with a good selection of fabrics. They also have a children's play area. You can sign up for the mailing list.

Other locations:
2970 Gallows Road, Falls Church, VA
573-0440
5041 Nicholson Lane, Rockville, MD,
770-3580

The stores are open Monday, Thursday and Friday from 9:30 am to 9 pm; and Tuesday, Wednesday and Saturday to 6 pm. They accept personal checks, Master Charge, and VISA. Refunds or exchanges are given on merchandise returned with receipt. They will hold non-sale items for up to 3 days. Ample parking available at all locations.

Fabrics Unlimited
5015 Columbia Pike
Arlington, VA

If you really want designer quality dress goods, you must visit Fabrics Unlimited. They buy from cutting rooms and from manufacturers. They frequently have brands like Liberty, Oscar de la Renta, tweeds used by Adele Simpson, and suitings used by John Anthony. They carry some imports and a large selection of ultrasuede. Every piece of fabric is hand selected and is inspected before it goes on the shelf. Everything is first quality, and the discounts run from 25% to 45%. 90% of merchandise is in stock, but there are special orders on the 35 colors of ultrasuede. They also specialize in natural fabrics and carry a selection of beautiful trims and notions, which are arranged by color. Sales are mostly seasonal and occur four or five times a year. They will also fill mail orders by request and will happily supply you with information on good dressmakers. Salespeople are extraordinarily well-trained and friendly — also, for such a small shop, there is plenty of help. They will all give you any advice you need on sewing. A unique aspect of this shop is the sample store displays, which give you an idea of what the pattern and fabric look like put together. They have developed for their displays a capsule wardrobe which is easy to sew and features copies of designer originals, for which they will give you a free set of instructions.

Store hours are from 10 am to 6 pm on Monday through Saturday, and until 9 on Thursday. Personal checks are accepted with proper identification, as are Master Charge and VISA. If you put down a deposit, they will guarantee to hold an item for you. Returns are flexible and handled to the advantage of the customer. Parking is available in mid-sized shopping center lot.

DISCOUNT FABRICS & NOTIONS

OPEN MONDAY — SATURDAY 9:30 to 9; SUNDAY 12 to 5

The Fabric Man Discounts everyday! Special promotions every week! We buy right so you can too! We're Washington's famous Discount Fabric Supermarkets always offering gigantic selections of up-to-date dress fabrics and decorator fabrics for the home. Complete notions and patterns departments. Professional sales help. Open 7 days a week for your convenience.

THE fabric man

SATISFACTION GUARANTEED!

Oxon Hill, Maryland 5000 Indian Head Hwy
Opposite Eastover Shopping Center
Lanham, Maryland 7401 Annapolis Road
Silver Hill, Maryland 3120 Branch Avenue
Rockville, Maryland 11760 Parklawn Drive
Bailey's Xrds, Virginia 5524 Leesburg Pike

MAJOR CREDIT CARDS!

Fabric Man
11760 Southlawn Lane
Rockville, MD
881-2232

The Fabric Man offers a good selection of dress materials and upholstery fabrics, as well as a complete bed, bath, and kitchen shop for linens and accessories. They feature bedspreads, comforters, towels, and sheets by such manufacturers as Cannon, Fieldcrest, Martex, Wamsutta, J.P. Stevens, and Dan River. Fabric, while not designer goods, comes from all major mills. Firsts predominate, with seconds brought in occasionally for special promotions. Patterns and notions are also sold here. The average discount runs from 20% to 50% on everything. Special orders are also discounted. There is a money-back guarantee on your satisfaction. Sales are held irregularly, with ads in the *Washington Post* Sunday Style section most frequent. The stores are large and neatly organized.

Other addresses:
5000 Indian Head Highway, Oxon Hill, MD, 567-6500
7401 Annapolis Road, Lanham, MD, 459-1666
3120 Branch Avenue, Silver Hill, MD, 894-1100
5524 Leesburg Pike, Baileys Crossroads, VA, 671-0600

Hours are 9:30 am to 9 pm, Monday through Saturday, and from noon to 5 pm on Sunday for all stores. Personal checks are accepted with proper identification, as are Master Charge, VISA, Central Charge, and NAC. On layaways, they require 25% down and pickup and final payment within 30 days. They will hold items without a deposit. Return policy is reasonable — if you have questions about it, check first with the management. There is ample parking at all locations.

G Street Remnant Shop
805 G Street, NW
Washington, DC
393-7892

If you really love fabrics, you could go into the G Street Remnant Shop and not come out for a week. They carry such a huge selection of decorator and designer fabrics, fittings, notions, patterns, and trims that the problem is usually not finding what you want, but trying to decide from among the many alternatives. Merchandise is all first quality and end-of-roll designer goods. On the fifth floor, they feature all of the patterns, silk thread, and trims in a turn-of-the-century decorated boutique, where they also sell Bernina sewing machines. Patterns are by Vogue, Butterick, and Folkwear. They also feature antique buttons and buckles, threads and ribbons, notions, and other sewing needs, including important aids, some of which are rarely found in this area. The sixth and seventh floors are literally stuffed with a wide variety of dress fabrics and men's suitings. Among these items are a big supply of ultrasuede, a $1.77 table always filled with cottons, a bridal boutique, a silk boutique, endless varieties of wools, and new merchandise daily. Out-of-season goods are generally marked down below their usual prices. They have seasonal sales. And they will mail samples all over the United States. About 1/2 of the clientele here is in the professional trades related to fabrics, clothing design, or other types of design. On the first floor, at 801 G Street, there is also a Decorator Shop, in which they feature beautiful upholstery, drapery, and slipcover fabrics.

The store is open from 9 am to 7 pm Monday and Friday, from 9 am to 8 pm on Thursday, and from 9 am to 6 pm on Tuesday, Wednesday, and Saturday. Personal checks are accepted with proper identification, as are Master Charge,

G Street Remnant Shop / Couture Fabrics

The World's Most
Unusual Fabric & Trim
Source!

805 G Street NW
5th, 6th, 7th Floors
Metro Red Line Exit:
Gallery Place

Fabrics: 393-7892
Patterns, Notions: 393-7896

Hours: Mon, Fri 9-7;
Thurs 9-8; Tues, Weds, Sat 9-6

Major Credit Cards
Free Parking In Rear
With Minimum Purchase

VISA, American Express, and Central Charge cards. There are no returns or exchanges. They will give you park and shop credit with a minimum $5 purchase. Otherwise, there is limited on-street parking.

Honeycutt's Fabrics
5866 Leesburg Pike
Baileys Crossroads, VA
820-2882

Honeycutt's is basically a large retail store selling upholstery, slipcover, and drapery fabrics; but, because the store is so large, and specializes in custom draperies and slipcovers, they generate a large number of closeouts and remnants, which are placed in a special back room: folded pieces are on tables, and bolts line the walls and fill bins. They also feature specials out of their warehouse, which is at the back of the store. The fabrics range in quality from low to the highest quality. They give discounts on short pieces and on big remnants, the remnants running ½ of the usual price. They also give discounts on quantity buying on their regular merchandise. They hold a big sale on George Washington's Birthday. We found a superspecial here in the remnant room: cotton sheers for 29¢ a yard. While this bargain is not the norm here, it just goes to show how low the prices are on some items.

Open Monday, Thursday, and Friday from 10 am to 9 pm, and Tuesday, Wednesday, and Saturday from 10 am to 6 pm. They accept personal checks with proper identification and Master Charge, VISA, Central Charge, and NAC credit cards. On layaways, they ask for 1/3 down. They will hold items for one week with a deposit, and for 24 hours without a deposit. Return policy is flexible. There is a small lot here.

Minnesota Fabrics
6702 Richmond Highway
Beacon Mall
Alexandria, VA
765-4440

Minnesota Fabrics doesn't really bill itself as a discount store. It is a national chain of stores operating efficiently via centralized buying. They feature different merchandise for different audiences in each store, depending on the volume of business in the area and the affluence of the local people. Why are we including this store in the book? Because Minnesota Fabrics has outstanding buys on their weekly sale tables, especially toward the end of the season, and even better buys on their clearance tables, which can go as low as 3 or even 4 yards for $1. They carry both dress and upholstery goods, and the basics year round. They also sell all kinds of notions and threads. They have many manufacturers' closeouts, irregulars, and seconds. Savings on the basics run from 10% to 15%, and an average of 40% on special sales. They can also special order and give you the same special sale prices as on in-stock merchandise.

Other addresses:
9650 Main Street, Fairfax, VA, 323-1311
5100 Nicholson Lane, White Flint Plaza, 468-0228
Penn Mar Shopping Center, Pennsylvania Avenue and Donnell Drive, Forestville, MD, 568-8890
Reston Avenue and Lawyer's Road, Herndon, VA, 620-9330
8575 Landover Road, Landover Plaza, Landover, MD, 772-2888
6343 Columbia Pike, Barcroft Dart Shopping Center, Lincolnia, VA, 941-1994
1173 University Blvd., Langley Park, MD, 439-3100
3042 Rolling Road, Springfield, VA, 569-3232

Store hours are from Monday through Friday, from 10 am to 9 pm, and Saturday, from 10 am to 6 pm. They accept personal checks with identification, VISA, NAC, Central Charge, and Master Charge credit cards. There are no layaways, but they will hold items for up to 24 hours. Return policy is liberal. Patterns can be returned with receipts as long as unopened and current. They take special orders on ultrasuede, but generally they do not carry any real designer fabrics. You can also have upholstery buttons covered here.

Triple S Discount Fabric Center
Perring Parkway Shopping Center
Baltimore, MD
(301) 665-1700

If you really love sorting through huge piles of bargain fabrics and looking for great finds, this is a perfect place to shop. They carry mill ends, closeouts, towels, and other domestics, at prices averaging 30% to 40% below comparable retail. They also give you a discount of 10% on notions. They carry fabrics from major mills, bedspreads by Martex, and sewing patterns as well. On flawed merchandise, they will make fair exchanges. They hold sales quite often, distributing circulars every 6-8 weeks and putting ads in the *Baltimore Sun*. They do have mailing lists and often feature special drawings from those on the mailing list, with prizes of $25 gift certificates. Personnel are quite friendly.

Other addresses:
4701 O'Donnell, Baltimore, MD, (301) 675-7800
8090 Ritchie Highway, Glen Burnie, MD, (301) 761-3300

The Perring Parkway store is open from Monday through Saturday from 10 am to 9 pm. The O'Donnell Street store opens earlier and closes at 6 pm. Personal checks are accepted, as are Master Charge and VISA. They will hold items for you for up to about 10 days without a deposit. Return policy is liberal, but they prefer that exchanges be made within a maximum of 7 days. Ample parking at Perring Parkway store.

VIP Yarns
Springfield Mall
Springfield, VA
971-0053

VIP is not really a discount store *per se*, rather they carry some good buys on their own brand of yarns and threads. They stock yarn and needlepoint materials and accessories, as well as crewel, canvas, needles, and crochet hooks. They also sell instruction and pattern books, and all types of macrame accessories. Their house brand yarn is Caron, which is sold at a lower price than comparable brand-named materials. They also carry manufacturers' closeouts and seconds, which can be found on special bargain tables. Discounts range from 20% to 35% below the usual retail price. They can special order large quantities and other brands which are not displayed. With proof of age, they will give senior citizens a 10% discount. They advertise in the *Washington Post*, usually twice a month.

Other address:
Loehmann's Plaza, Rockville, MD, 770-9710

The store is open from Monday through Saturday from 10 am to 9:30 pm, and on Sunday from noon to 5 pm. The Rockville store has different hours. Personal checks are accepted, as are Master Charge, VISA, and NAC credit cards.

MAIL ORDER

Down Home Comforts
P.O. Box 281
West Brattleboro, VT 05301
(802) 348-7944

Small occasional pillows at 30% below retail. Catalogue/retail brochure costs 40c.

MacGillivray and Coy
Muir of Aird
Benbecula
Western Isles, Scotland
PA88 5NA

Tartan travel rugs at $8 (depending on exchange rate), and other rugs and covers for very reasonable prices.

Walter Drake Silver Exchange
5902 Drake Building
Colorado Springs, CO 80940
(303) 596-3140

Silverware at 40% to 75% discount on brand names. Price list comes free.

Some Notes on Purchasing Window Coverings

If you are in the market for window coverings — curtains or draperies in particular — the first thing to do is to consider how much money you want to spend. Once having figured this out, determine the style in which you're interested, preferred color, and type of use which these window coverings will get. Then measure the exact dimensions of the window(s) before you start shopping — so you don't have to guesstimate when you get to the store. Remember that floor length curtains are measured from the ceiling to ½" above the floor.

Experts suggest that certain items and extras can be useful and helpful — Linings are effective in helping to prevent fading of the curtain materials from the action of the sun. On the other hand, some materials are treated to be fade-resistant. Sanforized materials are also recommended, since this reduces the risk of shrinkage — and a consequently ill-fitting window treatment. As in clothing, neat stitching and well-made pleats are at a premium — the finer it is made, the better it will look and last on your windows.

Polyester is the fabric of choice for many, as it resists fading, abrasion, and wrinkles; and also washes easily and well. Curtains backed with acrylic foam have proven easy to care for. Layered window treatments, such as a set of draperies over sheers, provide insulation. Insulated linings and drapery fabric are also available, if heat loss or penetration is a problem.

There are basically four cost levels for curtains and draperies, depending on what you choose to do: If you sew your own, you can save substantial amounts of money over comparable retail items; ready-made curtains are the cheapest, but size and style are limited; made-to-measure curtains and draperies are good when you want to spend in the mid-range. The shop provides the fabric, and you give them the window measurements. Sales on these are usually held twice a year, and you can save substantial amounts by taking advantage of these sales.

The most expensive, but most flexible alternative is to have custom-made draperies. There are no limits on style, color, fabric — or anything. Needless to say, the cost goes up with your imagination.

As with clothing, the fiber composition is essential to the way the curtains wear and look. Important concerns are how well the fabric drapes; durability and resistance to abrasion (rubbing) is particularly worth noting on draw panels, which will move back and forth against each other; how resistant to sun fading; and size stability — when the drapery is washed or cleaned, or when humidity changes, does the size of the drape also change? Open weaves tend to be less stable. Final considerations are care, and flame resistance.

This is how the fibers stack up on the important factors:

Acetate:
- Fair durability and abrasion resistance
- Quite good on stability
- Fair to good on sunfastness
- Fair on fire resistance
- Cleaning — some are washable, some dry clean only

Cotton
- Very durable
- Stable
- Resists abrasion well
- Burns easily
- Fair on sunfading
- Easy to wash

Acrylics and Modacrylics:
- Fine for durability, abrasion, humidity-stability
- BUT, acrylics may darken in the sun
- Good in flame resistance
- Some are washable, others are "dry clean only"

Fibreglass: Great at everything except abrasion

Nylon:
- Durable, resists abrasion and humidity
- Light colored nylon fades in sun
- Melts before it burns
- Washable

Polyester: Same qualities as nylon, with greater resistance to sun fading

Rayon:
- Fair in durability and stability
- Fair to good in sun and abrasion resistance
- Burns quickly
- Safest to dry clean — best results

Appliances & Electronics

APPLIANCES

Appliances, especially large ones, are not cheap. In fact, the consumer in this country spends $11 billion annually on appliances, large and small. Yet we really know little about buying appliances beyond that first, sometimes steep, purchase price. Things like maintenance, cost of operations (usually electricity and sometimes gas), and warranties are critical to our longterm satisfaction with the product. Energy efficiency, another aspect of major appliances, is often overlooked, but it is beginning to be of great importance to the individual consumer, whose way of life is constantly being threatened by energy shortages.

So, while price is important, the difference between a good buy and a good appliance could be great. But you could get both, if you know how to analyze both your needs and the advantages of various appliance models.

What is a good appliance?

Simply put, a good appliance is one which is affordable and does what it says it will do for a minimum period of time. The consumer is ultimately the best judge of just which brand or model of appliance is best for his or her household. Because you as the consumer are familiar not only with your needs, but with your budget, you can determine what features you are looking for in an appliance, and how much you are willing to pay for it.

What are you paying for?

In an appliance purchase, you are paying for far more than just the basic unit which cools your food, bakes your bread, or mixes the dough. You are paying for energy or time saving features, as well as warranties.

For example, when shopping for a new refrigerator, you should consider whether you are always opening your refrigerator for a cold drink, and thus wasting that energy meant to cool the food by letting the refrigerator cool your kitchen. If so, it may very well be a good idea to buy that new refrigerator with an ice and ice-water dispenser on the door. While you will initially pay extra for this convenience, it may save you energy costs in the long run.

The same holds true for a time-saving feature: It is likely that very busy refrigerator owners have not got the time to defrost their freezers. In this case, a frost-free refrigerator, although it uses more energy, may be more effective for your needs.

There are trade-offs of initial cost and operating expenses upon which you, as the consumer, must decide. The trick is to avoid buying an extra feature that will not be used in your household. Therefore, before you start shopping, it is a good idea to list the requirements of the appliance which you want.

It is also a good idea to shop warranties. To recapitulate the discussion found in an earlier chapter of this book, there are two basic types of written warranties which you will encounter: full and limited. The full warranty assures you that: 1) the defective product will be fixed or replaced free of any charges including removal and installation; b) the necessary repairs will be done in a reasonable amount of time after you complain; c) you are not responsible for anything unreasonable to get warranty service (such as shipping a freezer back to the factory); d) the warranty is good for anyone who owns the product during the warranty period; e) if the necessary repairs have not been made after a reasonable amount of time, you get your choice of a replacement or refund.

This is a good package, but it has one condition: A full warranty does not necessarily cover the entire product. It is not unusual for a television set to have a full warranty on the picture tube only.

The Magnuson-Moss Warranty Act requires any consumer product that costs more than $15 to have a warranty card available to the consumer to look at as an aid to comparison shopping. It could be worth the higher price of a fully warrantied product to know that you are somewhat insured against high repair costs in the future.

After you have purchased an appliance, make sure that any additions to the manufacturer's warranty made by the salesperson or store are written down on the warranty card or receipt. If these things are not written down, they cannot be enforced. The same goes for any provisions of a guarantee, which functions as a warranty.

What happens after the warranty expires?

"Authorized service is very important, especially in the post-warranty period," says Sally Browne, Director of Consumer Affairs for the Electronic Industries Association. Unauthorized service dealers may have a problem in getting parts. Browne explains that "in-warranty repairs are less expensive, but people often pay higher prices for parts and service that would have been unnecessary had they read the product's accompanying operations manual" — and either used the appliance correctly, followed maintenance instructions, or gone to an authorized repair shop when malfunctions occurred.

What is energy efficiency in an appliance?

Just as auto manufacturers are trying to squeeze more miles out of a gallon of gas, so the appliance manufacturers are trying to make their appliances run on less energy. "The biggest area of concern to the manufacturers is energy efficiency," reports Marion Johnson, speaking for the Association of Home Appliance Manufacturers (AHAM).

In December of 1975, under provisions of the Energy Policy and Conservation Act, manufacturers of such appliances as refrigerators, refrigerator-freezers, freezers, dishwashers, water heaters, clothes washers, and central and room air conditioners must label their products with estimated annual operating costs. This new provision can be helpful to the consumer in appliance shopping. The Department of Energy is also running consumer seminars across the nation on energy usage of appliances.

Amendments made in 1978 to the 1975 Act provide minimum efficiency standards for appliances and manufacturer compliance with these standards.

Currently, the Potomac Electric Power Company (PEPCO) reports that the approximate charge for one kilowatt hour (kWh) is $.05. Although this seems insignificant, the figures increase dramatically when you consider how many hours you actually run a light bulb or dishwasher.

In fact, it is estimated that 10% of your electric bill goes for powering small appliances, lighting, and cooking. This figure can be trimmed by judicious use of appliances, particularly those which take an initial big draw on electricity — for example, those which create heat, including irons, hotplates, and electric rollers.

Who makes appliances?

Major laundry appliance makers are: Norge, General Electric, Whirlpool, Maytag, White Consolidated Industries, Borg-Warner, and McGraw-Edison. Major heat pump and air conditioner makers are: General Electric, Carrier, Borg-Warner, Fedders, McGraw-Edison, White Consolidated Industries, Trane and Company, and Whirlpool.

While these names are almost certainly familiar to you, what is probably less familiar is that house brands of such well-known retailers as Sears and Montgomery Ward are often "ghost-manufacturered" by the same big names. These products are made to the retailer's specifications, with the retailer's logo affixed to them. Whirlpool makes Kenmore refrigerators for Sears, Hobart (a big industrial manufacturer) makes the Kitchen Aid brand, Design and Manufacturing Corporation makes dishwashers for Sears. (Design and Manufacturing Corporation is the largest private producer of dishwashers in the United States.) General Electric is also currently making all Montgomery Ward brand television sets.

As for small appliances, Presto and Waring are two of the largest makers of such products as mini-fryers, slow cookers, and popcorn, yogurt, hamburger, and coffee makers. These are trendy products which seem to come and go in terms of mass appeal and sales. The design, advertising, and packaging for these products seems to change from Christmas to Christmas.

Large appliances maintain their timeliness for a longer period of time. Unlike the auto industry, the appliance industry puts out new models of most appliances only once every three years. "The inner workings are usually the same from year to year," assures AHAM's Johnson. Small refinements are made in new models, but the consumer can be assured that the product purchased a few years back will not become obsolete and require hard-to-find parts. The United States Department of Agriculture puts the average life expectancy for a new refrigerator at 16 years. A freezer which you buy in 1980 will supposedly last you until the year 1995. The Association of Home Appliance Manufacturers refuses to publish similar statistics due to the great variance in average usage across the country. ". . . But," Johnson assures us, "parts should be available to consumers, through reputable dealers, for as long as the product is in general use." The Association has also recommended voluntary guidelines which allow for prompt delivery (within two working days) on replacement part requests.

USDA findings indicate these to be the average life expectancies of major appliances:

Sewing machine	24 years	Vacuum cleaner	15 years
Upright vacuum cleaner	18 years	Clothes dryer	14 years
Ranges	16 years	Clothes washer	11 years
Refrigerator	16 years	Television set	11 years
Toaster	15 years	Spin-dry washer	10 years
Freezer	15 years		

The following hints can be useful when shopping for an appliance:
- Think of the addition to your utility bill each appliance will make.
- Consider name brands first. Although they are more expensive, you will usually have less trouble finding replacement parts and service on them than for off brands. The next best is a house brand of a large national store, like Sears Roebuck and Co., which maintains a stockpile of parts for all of its products, and service departments all over the country.

- Consult *Consumers' Reports* and other such publications for comparisons of current brands and models. They will not only rate each unit on important qualities, but will give you an idea of the overall value of each.
- Start by looking at a no-frills model, then decide how many of the refinements you need — and what they are worth to you.
- Look for model clearance sales, for example, at the end of a model year.
- Make sure that the appliance will be neither too large nor too small for your needs. Particularly when buying a clothes washer or dryer, make sure that the dryer will accommodate all that the washer will produce.
- Make sure that the appliance will fit the space which you have available for it without causing you discomfort and potential safety hazards.
- Comparison shop — of course. But look not only for price, but for a dealer with a good reputation as to service. Check with the Better Business Bureau, the local Chamber of Commerce, or the local Consumer Protection Office to see if there have been any complaints about the dealer in the past and, if so, if they have been satisfactorily resolved.
- Make sure you know what the price includes — delivery? installation? warranty?
- Look for the UL (Underwriters' Laboratories) seal on the body of all electrical appliances. If it is only on the wire, then it means that only the wire is so approved.
- Make sure that your electrical current can handle the new appliance, and that your outlets are sufficient.
- Find out where repairs are available.
- When getting repairs for which you are liable, compare the costs in advance by telephone shopping the repair departments of the appliance stores, as well as independent repair people.

The Federal Trade Commission guidelines for energy cost labels on appliances went into effect May 19, 1980. Manufacturers are required to affix to appliances labels which inform consumers about annual energy costs for each product. The law covers refrigerator-freezers, freezers, dishwashers, clothes washers, water heaters, room air conditioners, and furnaces.

For room air conditioners and furnaces the information on the labels emphasized the Energy Efficiency Ratio (EER), which is the number of British Thermal Units (BTUs) per watt of electricity used. For other appliances, the labels will indicate estimated annual operating costs.

The appearance of the labels will be consistent throughout the industry, with a yellow background and black lettering, and will be identified with the words "Energy Guide" at the top. In addition to operating costs, the labels will also have information which indicates how the specific appliance rates against comparable models.

Because operating costs vary with the cost per unit of gas and electricity, thy label will not only include an estimate based on the average national cost of energy but will also include a range of costs according to different energy prices. Remember, while the purchase price may be higher for a more efficient unit, in the long run that unit may well be a better buy.

ELECTRONICS

Electronic home entertainment systems are a very good value these days, offering initial affordability, low operating and maintenance costs, and versatility. For example, "The audio electronics industry estimated that consumers in this area, paying an average of .05c per kilowatt hour of electricity, will pay an average of $5.45 per year to run a stereo system," according to Sally Brown, Director of Consumer Affairs for the Electronics Industries Association.

Stereo systems are only one aspect of home entertainment systems: technical electronic advances have made it possible for consumers to purchase new and more versatile entertainment products. New types of television sets, projection television units, home computers, video cassette recorders and video games, and video disc recorders are all currently enjoying wide popularity.

To shop more intelligently for these items, you must examine the major elements of home electronics, as well as the purpose and uses of each of these devices.

STEREOS

One of the most popular electronic entertainment devices, second only to television, is the home stereo system. You can either shop for a system as a whole or purchase components as you need or can afford them.

The tuner or receiver allows you to select and receive the signal of one radio station at a time. The FCC permits AM broadcasts in this country to be received on the 55 to 160 kilohertz (kHz) band, and FM broadcasts on the 88 to 108 megahertz (mHz) band. The tuner allows you to pick out any station and, if you have bought a good tuner, it will block out the undesired static and other everyday interference.

The turntable, in its most basic form, will simply turn a record at a constant rate. The most popular rates are 33-1/3 and 45 rpm. (The initials *rpm* stand for "revolutions per minute" — the number of turns the platter will spin in one minute. The tone arm holds the stylus (needle), which rides between the grooves of the record, picking up the mechanical signals of the record and passing them to the cartridge. The cartridge translates this mechanical energy into electro-magnetic energy, which is then amplified (either in the tuner's built-in amplifier, or in an amplifier that is a separate component of the system). You can buy a turntable with or without a cartridge and needle.

There are some basic facts about the needle that you should understand. The stylus can be made of a number of materials, all of which will deteriorate with use — some faster than others. Since a stylus will deteriorate and loose its shape or smoothness, it is a common practice to change it an average of every twelve months. This maintenance will insure good sound and minimal damage to records.

The amplifier is currently built into most receivers; these built-in amplifiers will work with your turntable and/or tape deck. If, however, your receiver comes without one, or an extra amplifier is desired, a simple amplifier will do the trick. The purpose of an amplifier or "amp" is just what you would imagine: to boost the power of the signal that passes through it.

An amplifier in good working order will amplify the signal with a minimum of distortion (called harmonic distortion). The exact amount of distortion is rated and supplied to you on a tag accompanying the amplifier. You may wish to shop around with distortion rates in mind. The better models are very close in distortion rates. You may also want to ask the salesperson to let you hear a signal put through a particular amplifier which you are considering.

The amplifier must also be a consideration in choosing speakers. It takes a certain amount of power to push or drive sound through a speaker. Without enough power, the speakers will produce a weak sound. The amount of power your amplifier can achieve is described in RMS (root mean square). As long as the receiver or amplifier drives the speakers and supplies you with an acceptable sound quality, there is little more for the lay person to know about RMS. The acceptable sound produced by the system, without any strain, is called stereo component compatibility. A competent salesperson can help you to achieve this compatibility.

The amplifier also allows you to tailor recordings to your own taste. Most any amplifier will allow you to add or reduce the amount of bass, treble, and mid-range to the level which you enjoy. And the amplifier will also boost the volume of the signal clearly and cleanly.

The Speaker is to a stereo system's performance as a singer's throat is to a concert. It's just that simple — in theory . . .

Speakers come either built into enclosures, or by themselves, for custom installation. There are three basic types of speakers: woofers, tweeters, and mid-range. The woofer handles all of the low notes and bass tones. The tweeter handles the highest-pitched sounds. The mid-range handles anything in between. If you are listening to a symphony, the tuba will come through the woofer, the piccolo over the tweeter, and the violins through the mid-range speakers. A speaker enclosure having all three kinds of speakers is known as a "three-way" speaker system. In addition to these three diverse types, there are single speakers available which are versatile enough to provide three types of sound in one enclosure.

Although speakers are supposed to give sound-for-sound reproduction of whatever you are listening to, experts in high fidelity agree that different speakers lend certain touches to the sound which they produce. In choosing a speaker, the size of the room and the particular sound desired are both important. For someone who loves rock music and bass guitars, a speaker with a 'bassy" sound is desirable. Speakers for the bedroom usually ought to be smaller than the ones for the living room. A word of caution from the experts: Bigger isn't always better! You can, at the least, begin to get headaches from four-foot-high speakers in a small den. In short, you should buy the speaker that's right forthe job. Some of the latest developments in high fidelity electronics are in the area of smaller, space-efficient speakers.

Tapes

Some people prefer tape to records. Tape is re-usable and easy to care for. The basic tape recorder or tape player is only a mechanism for moving the tape at a constant speed past an electromagnetic receptor or "head". The head does the same job in a tape machine that a stylus/cartridge combination does on a turntable. One has a choice of three kinds of tape machines and at least five types of tape:

- *Open reel* or *reel-to-reel* tape recorders are considered by experts to offer the best quality sound, the widest frequency response, the quietest background (the least amount of background hiss), and the greatest versatility. All this can be attributed to the greater width of open reel tape, which affords a greater magnetic "palette" for the sound to be recorded. Open reel tape is also easily repaired.
- *Cassette recorders* are the most popular, according to industry estimates. The cassette type actually employs a small reel-to-reel version in miniature. A cassette is easily carried and requires less over-all care than open reel tape. However, the tape surface is less than half that of open reel — so you pay for convenience with less versatility. Cassettes are made with thinner tape, which precludes a long life and makes repair difficult.
- *8-Track recorders* use the same size tape as open reel (or reel-to-reel) models. The tape is contained in a plastic shell, like a cassette, yet offers you the option of eight continuous programs. The 8-Track cassette houses a single reel or loop of tape.

These are all only the basic parts and alternatives of stereo systems. Audiophiles often add more specialized equipment to augment their systems' versatility and capacity.

Shopping for Stereo Systems

With this background information, the informed purchaser can proceed in assessing what is needed for his home. Some good advice on this subject comes from Ms. Browne, who says, "Determine your needs *before* you shop." Stereo gadgetry abounds wherever you look for equipment. There are all kinds of refinements and extras available, but, as Ms. Browne warns, "The more advanced the technology, the more you'll pay." It is a good idea to keep in mind where the equipment will be listened to and how often. Many of the newest developments are mesmerizing: speakers smaller than shoe boxes that can fill an entire room with sound, digital tuning, remote control tuning, receivers with a memory which will play the appropriate song or songs from an album side, amplifiers that amplify sounds outside of the normal hearing range (like the second cello in the Boston Pops), tape recorders that can record an entire concert while reducing the noise level and cleaning the sound (this ability to reduce the noise and to cleanse the sound is due to a process called Dolby Noise Reduction).

When shopping for hi fi equipment, the consumer should, according to Ms. Browne and other experts, test drive the equipment; many reputable stereo dealers will allow you to try a component — or sometimes even an entire system — out at home. And, as is the case with most every consumer purchase, it is recommended that you read the operating instructions and manual thoroughly. These give you information about regular maintenance and repairs, warranty, and installation. Be particularly sure to send in the warranty card, and keep the receipt (showing the serial numbers) in your files.

Buying Televisions

Buying a television is pretty much a matter of budget, personal taste, and need. There are a number of things to bear in mind while shopping for a television. The owner of a large area chain of stores which specializes in televisions makes the following suggestions:

- Stick to name brands — these have been tested by groups such as the Consumers' Union; and results which appear in periodicals such as *Consumer Report* can give you a lot of information about how the sets compare. Further, parts are easier to find for standard brands.
- Service should be a major consideration. The machine should be easy to service, and it is usually desirable that the dealer from whom you bought it be able to service it — unless you know a particularly handy repairman. You will also save money in the long run by going to the dealer with problems — a warranty station, by nature, is not making much if any money, so they are not going to jump to fulfill your claim. So it would be penny smart and pound foolish to avoid paying a few extra dollars initially and not get a guarantee of good service.
- Call the Better Business Bureau, the Chamber of Commerce, or your local consumer protection agency to find out how dealers are rated by consumers — what complaints these agencies have had, and how satisfactorily they have been resolved.
- Remember that you are buying a package — the best deal is not necessarily in the lowest price.

FINDING APPLIANCE & ELECTRONIC BARGAINS

A & A Appliance
7614 Georgia Avenue
Washington, DC
723-3315

A & A claims to be Washington's most unusual discount store, selling appliances and housewares by all name-brand manufacturers, including G.E., Westinghouse, Sony, and Panasonic, among others. All merchandise is first quality, and prices average 10% to 40% less than comparable retail. Most items are in stock, but A & A will do special orders. Delivery is included in the cost of major appliances. They are an authorized warranty station for Eureka, Regina, and Sunbeam, as they also sell a wide variety of home care equipment, as well as small appliances, which are all warrantied.

Open from 9 am to 6 pm Monday through Friday, Saturday from 9 am to 4 pm, and closed Sundays and holidays. Personal checks or cash are accepted. 10% down is requested on layaways. They will hold items with a deposit. Damaged or defective merchandise can be replaced or returned.

Atlantis Sound
1528 Rockville Pike
Rockville, MD
770-4048

If you are looking for good quality car or home stereo components and accessories, you should check out Atlantis Sound. They carry components by Pioneer, AR, Onkyo, Kenwood, Acutex, Altec, Phase Linear, and SAE. They say that they will meet and beat all competitive prices, with discounts ranging from 10% to 40%. Most items are in stock. The Rockville store was small and crowded, but all merchandise was fresh. On purchases over $200, free delivery is offered. Warranties on receivers are extended one year beyond that offered by the manufacturers. And they service all merchandise. Sales personnel are quite knowledgeable. Special sales events are held frequently.

Other addresses:
7811 Old Georgetown Road, Bethesda, MD, 652-6462
4315 St. Barnabas Road, Marlow Heights, MD, 423-5020
3220 Old Lee Hwy, Fairfax, VA, 273-8634
5224 Port Royal Road, Springfield, VA, 321-9288
230 W. Broad Street, Falls Church, VA, 532-5500

All stores are open Monday through Thursday from 10 am to 7 pm, Friday to 9 pm, and Saturday to 6 pm. Rockville and Falls Church are open on Sunday as well. Personal checks, Master Charge, VISA, American Express, Central Charge, and NAC are accepted. Layaway terms are liberal, but there are no holds on merchandise. You have 3 days within which to return merchandise for a refund, after that for store credit or exchange. On special sale merchandise, there are no cash refunds. Adequate parking.

Belmont TV
4723 King Street
Alexandria, VA
671-8500

If you watch a lot of television, you probably have heard all about Belmont. If you don't know about it — here it is. They sell televisions, stereos, CBs, parts, accessories, car stereos, and videotape recorders. They market brands such as RCA, Zenith, Sanyo, and Sharp televisions, and Sansui, JVC, and Technics stereo equipment. All merchandise is first quality. The discount depends on the items, but runs 10% to 20% below suggested retail on televisions, 20% to 25% on stereos, and 50% on tubes. Most items are in stock. Free delivery is available on most large items. On televisions, they extend the warranty provided by the manufacturers, which is included in the price of the unit.

Other addresses:
12500 Layhill Road, Wheaton, MD, 942-1300
6179 Livingston Road, Oxon Hill, MD, 839-2300
Maryland City Plaza, Laurel, MD, 776-5330
8034 New Hampshire Avenue, Langley Park, MD, 434-7505

All stores have the same hours: from 10 am to 7 pm on Monday through Friday, and from 9 am to 6:30 pm on Saturday. Personal checks are accepted with proper identification, as are Master Charge, VISA, Central Charge, and NAC. Layaway terms are liberal, and so is the return policy. They will make exchanges on defective merchandise. Ample parking at all locations.

Chafitz
856 Rockville Pike
Rockville, MD
340-0200

For a really great selection of novelty and electronic items, go to Chafitz. The merchandise, which consists of calculators, electronic specialty products, video equipment, short wave radios, office equipment, electronic games, and car radios — is all well displayed for the customers' convenience. All merchandise — by such manufacturers as Texas Instruments, Sharp, Sony, Panasonic, and Sanyo — is first quality or manufacturers' closeouts. The average discount on all of these items is 15%. Most items are in stock. They will take phone and mail orders and ship merchandise at the customer's expense. They promulgate a "meet or beat" policy: that is, they will meet any verifiable price of a competitor. They are also the manufacturers of Boris, the electronic chess game.

Open from 10 am to 9 pm on Monday through Friday, until 6 pm on Saturday, and on Sunday from noon to 5 pm. Personal checks are accepted with proper identification, as are Master Charge, VISA, American Express, Central Charge, and NAC. There are no layaways, but they will hold some merchandise for up to 24 hours. Returns or exchanges can be made within 2 weeks of purchase, unless marked otherwise. Ample parking in a large lot.

Circuit City
6840 Franconia Road
Springfield, VA
569-0990

Discounts are offered on televisions, radios, tape decks, portable radios, car stereos, stereo components, video cassettes, cameras, and record and tape accessories. Brands commonly found here include Technic, Pioneer, Onkyo, Sanyo, Sharp, Sony televisions, Panasonic, RCA, Zenith, and Emerson. They do repairs, and they also take special orders. As far as the discount is concerned, they say, "The streets are paved with bargains."

Other addresses:
5520 A Leesburg Pike, Baileys Crossroads, VA, 671-2700
10140 Bacon Drive, Beltsville, MD. 937-2100
6932 Wisconsin Avenue, Bethesda, MD, 657-2044
10530 Detrick Avenue, Kensington, MD, 949-0898
4501 St. Barnabas Road, Marlow Heights, MD, 630-3500

Stores are open from Monday through Friday, from noon to 9 pm and from 10 am to 6 pm on Saturday. They accept personal checks with proper identification, VISA, Master Charge, and Central Charge. They offer a 30-day satisfaction guaranteed policy. Layaway terms are 1/3 down and 90 days to pay and pick up. Ample parking at most locations.

Contemporary Sound
666 S. Pickett St.
Alexandria, VA
370-4448

At this shop, not only do they stock over 150 brands of stereo components, by such manufacturers as Sherwood, Advent, and Directadisc, but they also have a fantastic collection of imitation wood stereo system cabinets — inexpensive, quite attractive, interesting to browse through. These are made by a number of manufacturers — Gusdorf, O'Sullivan, and Busch — and range in price from only $89 to $200. You can also order from the catalogue, in addition to buying in-stock models. Prices on the stereo systems run 20% to 50% less than comparable retail, depending on the brand. Most items are in stock. They will ship UPS on request. They do repairs here on speakers. Special sales events occur weekly and are advertised in the *Washington Post*.

Other address:
7418 Baltimore Blvd., College Park, MD, 699-9207

*Hours from 11 am to 7 pm Monday through Thursday, Friday until 8 pm, Saturday from 10 am to 7 pm, and Sunday from noon to 5 pm at all stores. Personal checks are accepted with local identification, as are Master Charge, VISA, and Central Charge. Layaway terms are 10% down and 30 days for final payment and pickup. They will hold items with a deposit for up to 30 days. Defective merchandise will be re-*placed. Returns can be made for merchandise credit or an exchange. There is ample parking.

Discount Sound
121 Maple Avenue
Vienna, VA
281-6370

The Rockville store is the main warehouse as well, and the Vienna store is a fairly small storefront. What they sell is audio components and accessories, by Kenwood, Akai, Pioneer, Technics — and just about every other brand on the market. All merchandise is first quality. Prices fluctuate with the market, but they say that they can meet any price in the area. Warranties are manufacturers' and are usually from 2 to 5 years. They send repair work under the warranty out to the Audio Clinic. You can order by telephone from the Rockville store, which has a toll-free number, and they will ship items to you. Special sales are held on holidays, and are usually advertised in the local newspapers.

Other address:
5618 Randolph Road, Rockville, MD, 881-8890

Hours are Monday, Thursday, and Friday from 11 am to 9 pm, Tuesday and Wednesday until 7 pm, and Saturday from 10 am to 6 pm. Personal checks, Master Charge, and VISA are accepted. Layaway and hold policy are negotiable. There are no cash refunds. A small parking lot in Vienna.

District Sound Inc.
2316 Rhode Island Avenue, NE
Washington, DC
832-1900

District Sound, with its sister store in New Jersey, claims to be the oldest mail order hi-fi store in the country. They operate mainly on a mail order basis, publishing an extensive selection in their catalogue. They sell good quality hi fi gear and car stereos, by Pioneer, Technics, and Betamax (VCRs). All merchandise is first quality, new. They say their prices are on the average 30% to 50% off list, and usually better than most of the large stereo discounters in the area. While you pay shipping on interstate sales, you avoid the sales tax. They offer manufacturers' warranties, but you are directed to trained local service agents for any warranty work. They have a mailing list of past customers to whom they send catalogues. They rarely have special sales, but sometimes a special purchase or discontinued item is offered in the catalogue at an extra savings.

Open from 9:30 am to 5:30 pm Monday through Friday and until 4 pm on Saturday (in summer, only until 1:30 pm). Personal checks are not accepted, but cashier's checks, Master Charge, VISA, and NAC are. There are no layaways or returns. If merchandise is found to be defective, it is repaired as per warranty terms. Parking is very limited on street.

Erol's
3610 Columbia Pike
Arlington, VA
521-3510

Erol's sells TVs and only TVs — and claims to be the largest exclusive TV dealer in the Washington metro area. They carry Zenith, RCA, and SONY equipment, including video equipment. Everything is in stock, and prices range at least 20% under so-called manufacturers' list. There is no charge for delivery of consoles, and complete installation. They are a factory authorized service center and do all warranty work here, as well as other repair work on RCA, Zenith, and Sony systems.

Other addresses:
2200 University Blvd. W., Wheaton, MD, 942-1322
4618 St. Barnabas Road, Marlow Heights, MD, 894-3000
15920 Shady Grove Road, Gaithersburg, MD, 840-5660
13648 Jeff. Davis Hwy., Woodbridge, VA, 494-8143 or 690-1127

Arlington, Wheaton, and Marlow Heights are open daily from 10 am to 9 pm and Saturday until 6 pm. Gaithersburg and Woodbridge are open from noon to 9 pm, and Saturdays from 10 am to 6 pm. They accept personal checks, VISA, Master Charge, and Central Charge. You can return or exchange within 30 days for any reason.

German HiFi
12350 Parklawn Drive
Rockville, MD
881-8830

However crowded and small the shop on Parklawn Drive is, the merchandise is well-displayed, and of a consistently high quality. This includes stereo components, radios, tape recorders, video recorders, television, and related accessories, by such makers as Sansui, Panasonic, TDK, Sanyo, Pioneer, and Sony. All merchandise is first quality, and discounts range from 20% to 50%. Most items are in stock. Manufacturers' warranties are offered, usually from 1 to 3 years. Holiday sales are frequent.

Other address:
930 9th St., NW, Washington, DC, 737-7728: open from 9:30 am to 6 pm daily.

The Rockville store is open Monday through Saturday from 9:30 am to 6 pm, on Monday and Friday until 9 pm, and on Sunday from 11 am to 5 pm. Personal checks are accepted with proper identification, as are Master Charge and

NO NEED TO SHOP FROM A CATALOG! AT GEORGE'S YOU CAN SEE 'N' TOUCH WHAT YOU WANT BECAUSE...

GEORGE'S CHAINWIDE SELECTION IS

*a smash!
WITH OVER 2,600 COLOR TVs ON DISPLAY!

dazzling!*
WITH OVER 1,000 BLACK 'N' WHITE TVs ON DISPLAY!

*spectacular
WITH OVER 1,400 AUDIO COMPONENTS AND STEREOS ON DISPLAY!

*marvelous!
WITH OVER 1,300 REFRIGERATORS AND FREEZERS ON DISPLAY!

*superb!
WITH OVER 1,000 MICROWAVES AND RANGES ON DISPLAY!

incredible!
WITH OVER 900 WASHERS AND DRYERS ON DISPLAY!

George's
THE LEADER-SINCE 1926

OVER A DOZEN LOCATIONS IN WASHINGTON, D.C., MARYLAND, AND VIRGINIA

VISA. Layaway terms are liberal. Merchandise which is defective can be exchanged within a week, but there are no refunds. Parking is limited at Washington and ample at Rockville.

George's
6400 Commerce Street
Springfield, VA
971-2002

Almost all major brands of appliances can be found at George's large stores, such as Caloric, GE, and Whirlpool. They carry everything from fans, through ovens and refrigerators, to speakers, radios, car speakers, televisions, and the full range of major appliances. They also carry furniture by Bassett and Armstrong — mostly a medium line of goods with simulated woodgrain. All merchandise is first quality. At the Springfield store, you can find bedding as well. They take special orders. The stores are well-organized and neat.

Other addresses:
2135 Queens Chapel Rd., NE, Washington, DC, 529-1692
816 F Street, Washington, DC, 347-2293
13534 Jeff. Davis Hwy., Woodbridge, VA, 690-1193 or 491-4151
6192 Greenbelt Road, Greenbelt, MD, 345-2500
Rte. 1, south of Alexandria, VA, 360-4600
3801 Branch Ave., Iverson Mall, Hillcrest Heights, MD, 423-8088
12125 Rockville Pike, Rockville, MD, 881-8570
3036 Annandale Road, Falls Church, VA, 532-3262
8387 Leesburg Pike, Falls Church, VA, 893-1750
3509 Connecticut Ave., NW, Washington, DC, 966-3530
8239 Georgia Ave., Silver Spring, MD, 588-4030
6200 Branch Avenue, Allentown Mall, Camp Springs, MD, 449-3450

Store hours vary somewhat but generally stick to a schedule of from 9:30 am to 9:30 pm Monday through Saturday and from noon to 5 pm on Sunday. They accept personal checks, Master Charge, VISA, NAC, and Central Charge. Returns can be made within 10 days of purchase with receipt. Delivery is free except on advertised specials. They may hold some merchandise for you. Ample parking.

HiFi Buys
1362 Holton Lane
Langley Park, MD
434-5330

For stereo equipment, auto stereos, video records, televisions, and accessories, our researcher found HiFi Buys to be a small and well-stocked store, comfortable and easy to browse and test equipment in. Brands carried include Pioneer, Kenwood, Marantz, Sony, and Technics, all first quality. Discounts run from 10% to 50% below comparable retail prices. Most items are in stock but they ask a 25% deposit on special order items. A store catalogue is available. They also offer plans to extend the manufacturers' warranties, but they do no repair work here. Sales are frequent, about once a month, and are advertised in the *Washington Star* and *Post*.

Hours are from 10 am to 6 pm on Tuesday, Wednesday, and Friday; until 8 pm on Monday and Thursday; and until 4 pm on Saturday. Personal checks are accepted, as are Master Charge, VISA, and NAC. Layaway policy is liberal. They will hold items with a deposit, but they evaluate each situation. There are no returns after 30 days, but they will exchange equipment for equipment of greater value. All sales are final.

Koko's
305 W. Broad Street
Falls Church, VA
534-4148

Koko's is a small shop staffed with friendly people, selling mostly televisions and a more limited stock of video cassette and tape recorders. Brands offered include only Zenith, RCA, Sony, and GE. All merchandise is first quality, and they work on a low markup, offering what they claim to be the lowest prices in the area. On special orders, they ask for a 10% deposit. At the Falls Church store, they have free delivery, but at the warehouse store, where the prices are somewhat cheaper, you take your purchase with you or pay $10 for delivery almost anywhere in the Washington metropolitan area. Most products are warrantied for 90 days on labor, 1 year on parts, and 2 years on the picture tube; and they will extend the warranty for a charge. Repairs are done here. They do not hold special sales.

Other address:
Warehouse store, 8455 Tyco Road, Tysons Corner, VA, 893-0344

Hours at the Falls Church store are from 7 am to 7:30 pm Monday through Thursday, until 9 pm on Friday, and until 6 pm on Saturday. Warehouse is open on Saturday and Sunday. They accept personal checks, Master Charge, and VISA. On layaways, a deposit of 30% is required, with payment and pickup within 30 days. They will hold items for you. Refunds or exchanges must be made within 7 days of purchase. There is adequate parking at both locations.

Luskin's
5150 Duke Street
Alexandria, VA
621-1600 X 330

Stereos, televisions, radios, and large kitchen applicances can all be purchased at Luskin's. Brands available include Sony, Zenith, RCA, GE, Toshiba, Sanyo, MGA, Westinghouse, and Frigidaire. All merchandise is first quality. The local manager said that they use a pricing firm, which prices all of the items and helps them to set the lowest prices in the area. Most merchandise is in stock. Delivery is free. They offer a 30-day price warranty, which is that they will meet any verifiable price of a competitor within 30 days after your purchase, and refund you the difference. Repairs are done at their own facilities. They do have a mailing list for special sales. Each store has these sales twice a year.

Other addresses:
2901 Wilson Blvd., Arlington, VA, X340
5023 Wisconsin Avenue, Washington, DC, X320
3171 Queens Chapel Rd., Hyattsville, MD, X305
11305 Georgia Avenue, Wheaton, MD, X300
Landover Mall, Landover, MD, X310
St. Barnabas Road near Branch Ave., Marlow Heights, MD, X314
Featherstone Square, Woodbridge, VA, 491-4141
11132 Rockville Pike, Rockville, MD, X325

Hours are from 10 am to 9:30 pm Monday through Saturday, and from noon to 5 pm on Sunday. They accept personal checks with proper identification, Master Charge, VISA, Central Charge, and NAC. Merchandise, except major appliances, can be returned with receipt within 7 days if unopened. All special sale merchandise is not returnable. Parking is adequate at all locations.

Marty's Electronics/Auto Radio
2412 University Blvd. West
Silver Spring, MD
933-6700

Car radios, CB speakers, and accessories, in a range of prices, are what you can find at Marty's Electronics. With brands like Sanyo, Clarion, Pioneer, Speak-a-matic, and Hi Gain, the store offers discounts of 30% on first quality merchandise. However, our researcher found it a rather disorganized place, with no displays as found in other similar shops. They do have a store catalogue available. Warranties are offered by the store: 30 days on labor and 90 days on parts. They have a full repair shop. Special sales are advertised weekly.

Open Monday and Tuesday from 9 am to 7 pm, Wednesday through Friday until 9 pm, Saturday until 6 pm, and Sunday from noon to 4 pm. Personal checks are accepted, as are Master Charge, VISA, American Express, Central Charge, and NAC. Layaway terms are liberal. Merchandise will be held with a deposit. There are no cash refunds, but there are exchanges with receipt within 90 days.

Math Box III
9650 Main Street
Fairfax, VA
978-5400

The Math Box is a local chain of very inviting stores at which to buy calculators, answering machines, minicomputers, electronic games, and SCM typewriters. They specialize in calculators, 5-foot TV screens, Omni VTRs, and programming books. The brands carried include Casio, Texas Instruments, and Hewlett Packard. The store at Fairfax is large and well-organized, with good displays that were conducive to testing and demonstration. All merchandise is first quality, except for very, very infrequent closeouts on inexpensive reconditioned merchandise. Discounts vary but average about 15% under list. They give 1-year factory warranties and 30-day store warranties. They also take phone and mail orders. Weekly advertisements are placed in the *Washington Post*, usually with a featured item in each.

Other addresses:
Math Box I, 4431 Lehigh Road, College Park, MD, 277-6828: open Monday through Saturday from 10 am to 6 pm, and Monday and Thursday until 8 pm. Math Box II, 2627 University Blvd. West, Wheaton, MD, 933-6555: open Monday through Saturday from 10 am to 6 pm, Tuesday and Friday nights until 8 pm.

The Fairfax store is open Monday through Saturday from 10 am to 6 pm, Tuesday and Friday until 8 pm. Personal checks are accepted, as are Master Charge and VISA. They will usually hold items for about 2 days. There are no refunds, but merchandise can be exchanged within 7 days. Ample parking at Fairfax, adequate at other locations.

Murrell's TV
2140 Wisconsin Avenue NW
Washington, DC
338-2915

Murrell's is basically a small shop specializing in servicing and selling televisions. They also carry antennas, some shortwave and multiband radios, and air conditioners in the summer. At the time of our visit, they also carried Sony and Panasonic turntables. Television brands usually found here include RCA, Zenith, Sony, Sylvania, and GE, with Philco sets more infrequently. They carry all first quality merchandise and some reconditioned sets. They also take trade-ins.

Discounts vary by season and with the demand for televisions but usually range from 20% to 25%. Everything is either in stock in the store or in their large warehouse. Delivery is available within the Northwest Washington area and to the northwest suburbs only, at a charge starting at $7.50. They usually warranty televisions for 1 year on parts and labor, and 2 years on the picture tube. A complete service shop is part of Murrell's.

This store is open from Monday through Friday from 9 am to 7:30 pm, and Saturday from 9 am to 6 pm. They accept Master Charge and VISA. Layaways are not encouraged. The official return policy states that there is a $15 restocking fee on exchanges, which must be made within 30 days of purchase. Parking is available on the side of the building and in back.

Myer Emco Inc.
11611 Old Georgetown Road
Rockville, MD
468-2000

Myer Emco concentrates on selling good quality stereo equipment at a moderate discount and giving high quality service to their customers. They carry stereo components, tapes, accessories, and "audiophile" records in their three large stores. Brands like Advent, Yamaha, Allison, Toshiba, and Phillips are commonly found here. All merchandise sold here is first quality. On larger orders, there is free delivery and installation. They also offer free turntable and stylus testing to anyone who comes in — whether the consumer purchases something or not. Trades are taken, and some used merchandise is carried. Myer-Emco has an extensive audio lab in each store, with highly trained technicians in each to do repairs and warranty work. There is a mailing list, and special sales are held periodically.

Other addresses:
Willston Shopping Center, Route 50, Falls Church, VA
1212 Connecticut Avenue NW, Washington, DC. Opens at 10 am Thursday and Friday.

Hours at the stores vary: Rockville store is open Monday through Wednesday and Saturday from 10 am to 7 pm, until 9 pm on Thursday, and from noon to 9 pm on Friday. They accept personal checks with proper identification, as well as Master Charge, VISA, Central Charge, and NAC. Layaway terms include a negotiable, usually 10%, deposit, and a liberal period of time in which to complete payments and pick up the merchandise. Returns depend on the individual circumstances (Returned merchandise is not sold as new). Parking is ample in shopping center lots in Virginia and Maryland, and there is a park and shop lot in D.C.

Reliable Home Appliance
7000 Spring Garden Drive
Brookfield Plaza
Springfield, VA
451-7686

Everything in the RHA we visited was stacked in cartons throughout the store. They sell washers, dryers, ovens and all major appliances, television sets, adding machines, radios, and toasters, by such names as Eureka, Sylvania, Kelvinator, Oster, Proctor, Sony, and Westinghouse. They work on a cost plus limited markup basis and invite comparison with others who discount the same merchandise. They charge for delivery. They will take special orders with a good-sized deposit.

Other addresses:
919 11th Street, NW, Washington, DC, 737-2537, closed Sunday.

Rte. 450 at Race Track Rd., Bowie, MD, 262-5800.
2986 Gallows Road, Falls Church, VA, 573-8081
4516 St. Barnabas Road, Marlow Heights, MD, 423-0200
Montrose Plaza Shopping Center, Rockville, MD, 770-2525

All stores are open from 9 am to 9 pm daily, and Sunday from noon to 5 pm. They accept personal checks and cash. Credit terms are available. Return policy is liberal, as long as you return the merchandise in fresh condition, with the receipt. Layaway terms are for 30 days, with a 10% deposit.

Royce's TV and Audio
7808 Georgia Avenue NW
Washington, DC.
723-5600

For television and audio equipment, you should shop at Royce's for Zenith, Sony, Sanyo, Pioneer, and Curtis Mathes. All merchandise is first quality, with competitive prices running 10% to 40% below comparable retail. Free delivery is available. Warranty repairs are done here, and they have full service repair and service facilities.

Open 9 am to 9 pm on Monday through Friday, and until 6 pm on Saturday. Personal checks are accepted with proper identification, as are Master Charge, VISA, Central Charge, and NAC. For layaways, they ask 10% down and pickup and final payment within 6 months. They will usually hold items with a deposit. Check with manager about exchanges or returns. There is a small parking lot.

Appliances & Electronics

St. Clair Kitchens
800 North Henry Street
Alexandria, VA
836-0020

St. Clair's offers everyone the opportunity to buy at low builders' prices. They carry a fantastic choice of kitchen cabinets, counter tops, sinks, and major appliances, from Frigidaire, Admiral, and Tappan. They carry cabinets from the least expensive — though still quite nice — to the very best, in brands like Borowood, Maryland Maid, Hagerstown, Less-Care, and Whitehall. All appliances are in stock, and so are most Borowood cabinets. You can look at the well-laid out showroom for ideas, all finishes and hardware being displayed in addition to quite a number of room displays. They ask 50% down on special orders, and the remainder on delivery. Everything is warrantied for at least one year. Free delivery is available on some items. Appliances are delivered and installed for a nominal fee.

Open Monday through Friday from 8:30 am to 5 pm, and Saturday from 9 am to 1 pm. They accept personal checks on deposits, and cash, certified check, Master Charge, or Visa on delivery. No merchandise can be returned unless defective. There is ample parking.

Saxitone Tape Sales
1776 Columbia Road NW
Washington, DC 20009
462-0800

Because they are specialists in tape and tape recorders and related accessories, Saxitone can offer substantial discounts on recording tape — 30% to 40% off the cost of tape, and 20% to 25% off the usual retail cost of the tape recorders. All merchandise is first quality. UPS delivery is available at a charge. They will take special orders, usually requesting a 25% down payment, depending on the item. A store catalogue is available, as are warranties. There is a mailing list, and they send out mailers for their frequent special sales. They also take mail and phone orders. The store is quite neat, clean, and well-organized, with well-trained personnel.

Open from 9 am to 6 pm on Monday through Friday, and until 6 pm on Saturday. Personal checks are accepted, as are VISA and Master Charge. There are no layaways. Unopened merchandise accompanied by the receipt is returnable within a reasonable period of time. On-street metered parking is limited.

Slattery's Appliances
4309 Wisconsin Avenue, NW
Washington, DC
363-8112

For over 44 years, Slattery's has been a family business that specializes in appliances — items for the kitchen, televisions, stereos, washers, dryers, and vacuum cleaners among the inventory. They carry major brands like GE, Maytag, Whirlpool, Kitchenaid, RCA, Zenith, Sylvania — all American makers. Most are first quality, but occasionally there are some that are scratched. They also carry used merchandise. The discount varies, but prices are usually in the range of 15% to 20% off comparable retail. Most items are in stock. Free delivery is available within the metropolitan area. They do all of their own service. They have special sales, with advertisements for them in the newspapers two or three times a year. The store is divided into two sections — one is for parts and service, the other for retail sales.

Hours are from 9 am to 6 pm on Monday through Saturday. Personal checks are accepted, as are Master

Charge, VISA, and Central Charge. Layaway terms are 1/3 down, with pickup and final payment within 60 days. They will hold the last of a given item for up to 24 hours. They give cash refunds or exchanges within a reasonable period of time. There is a small parking lot in back of the store.

Star Appliances/Star Radio
5560 Port Royal Road,
Springfield, VA
296-8046

The downtown and Springfield stores have different inventories — Springfield concentrates on appliances and televisions, with brands like GE, Frigidaire, Westinghouse, Jennair, Zenith, RCA, and Quasar at an average discount of 10% below suggested retail, and the downtown store is stocked with radios and stereos. Check with the Springfield store on the telephone — at the time of our interview, they were considering moving the store to Rockville.

Other address:
1220 Connecticut Avenue NW, Washington, DC, 296-8046

The Springfield store is open from 11 am to 5 pm on Monday through Saturday. The downtown DC store is open from 9:30 am to 6 pm Monday through Saturday. Personal checks are accepted, as are Master Charge and VISA. Check with manager about layaways and returns. Ample parking in Virginia, on-street or pay lot in DC.

Star Vacuum
4733 Silver Hill Drive
Suitland, MD
736-1308

As the name would suggest, Star Vacuum specializes in vacuum cleaners — bags and attachments. They carry a wide range of brands, including Eureka, Hoover, Mastercraft, and Premiere in new machines, and an assortment of used machines. All the new machines are first quality and are discounted an average of 20% to 25% off manufacturers' suggested retail prices. All merchandise is in stock. Within a limited delivery area, delivery is free. They are a factory-authorized service center for the brands which they sell. They also repair any brand of sewing machine.

Other address:
8815 Annapolis Road, Lanham, MD, 459-1813

Hours at both stores are Monday, Wednesday, Friday, and Saturday from 9 am to 6 pm, and Tuesday and Thursday from 9 am to 7 pm. Personal checks are accepted with proper identification, as are Master Charge, VISA, American Express, Central Charge, Diners Club, and NAC credit cards. Layaway policy is flexible, and they will hold items for up to 24 hours without a deposit. Merchandise can be returned for credit or for an exchange within 5 days of purchase. Adequate parking at both locations.

Stereo Discounters Warehouse
6730 Santa Barbara Court
Elkridge, MD
(301) 796-3996

If you are looking for a *really* good deal on a stereo system, tape deck (and accessories), car stereo, VCR, tapes, or speakers — and if you'd consider buying a closeout, refused delivery, repaired unit, damaged merchandise, or demonstrator — you should look here. They carry makers like Sherwood, Sansui, Technics, Kenwood, Pioneer, Scott, Sony, and JVC. Discounts on the slightly worn-out or damaged merchandise can be super — often below cost. You can also get new equipment here, which they also sell in their other Baltimore and

Pennsylvania locations, but the best deals are here at the warehouse. A store catalogue is available for first quality goods, and manufacturers' warranties are offered unless the merchandise is sold "as is". On warranties, they have their own service department to do the repair work. There are special sales held 4 to 6 times a year, to move out seasonal stock. They also have a mailing list.

Other address:
1220 Connecticut Avenue NW, Washington, D.C. 396-8046

Hours are from Monday through Friday from 11 am to 9 pm, and Saturday from 9:30 am to 5:30 pm. This is part of a large Baltimore and Pennsylvania chain. Personal checks are accepted with proper identification, as are Master Charge, VISA, Central Charge, and NAC credit cards. On layaways, they ask 20% to 25% down, and pickup must be within 60 days. They will give you a complete refund within 7 days, no questions asked. Adequate parking.

Suitland Electronics
4712 Suitland Road SE
Suitland, MD
735-4000

Here they sell CBs, auto radios, accessories, TVs, and electronic parts, by such makers as Cobra, President, GE, Bearcat, and Zenith. Most merchandise is first quality, with some dealer's closeouts. Discounts run from 10% to 50%. Most items are in stock. This is a full service store.

Other address:
1209 Taft Street, Rockville, MD, 762-8600

Hours are Monday through Friday from 9 am to 6 pm, Saturday from 8:30 am to 5 pm, and Sunday from 10 am to 2 pm. They accept personal checks, Master Charge, VISA, Central Charge, and NAC. Layaway policy is flexible. They will also hold items for several days without a deposit. Radios are not exchangeable. There is a small parking lot.

Surplus Electronics
9600 Baltimore Avenue
College Park, MD
441-9090

Surplus Electronics is an unusual store, with a large selection of surplus electronic parts, well-organized with rows of shelves and glass bottles containing all of the interesting and unusual little parts. They carry equipment for CBs and ham radios, as well as the new frequency counters. They say that, on the average, they offer a 45% discount. They can also order standard non-surplus items, with a 50% deposit and a wait of from 1 to 4 months. New parts only are guaranteed. They advertise specials frequently.

Open from noon to 9 pm on Monday, Tuesday, Thursday, and Friday; and from noon to 6:30 pm on Saturday. They accept personal checks, Master Charge, and VISA. Layaway terms are liberal. Items will be held for up to 24 hours with a 50% deposit. Return policy depends on the merchandise — whether it is new or surplus.

Tanen's
409 11th Street, NW
Washington, DC
783-0395

Tanen's is a small downtown store absolutely crowded with all kinds of large and small appliances, gold jewelry, watches, Kodak film, and CBs. It also has a watch and jewelry repair service. They carry major brands like RCA, Whirlpool, Seiko, Panasonic, Zenith, and

Sony. They work on a markup basis which is more limited than a regular retail store would be satisfied with. Most items are in stock, but they will special order that which is not. Delivery is available at a charge. They also do repair work on warrantied items, as well as watch and jewelry repair. They sell their gold jewelry at 30% below comparable prices in the area.

Tanen's is open from 9 am to 6 pm weekdays, until 7 pm on Monday, and until 5 pm on Saturday. They accept personal checks with proper identification. On layaways, they request 10% down and final payment and pickup within 60 to 90 days. Exchange policy is liberal — you can return or exchange items within a reasonable period of time, providing of course that you have the receipt. Metered on-street parking is available, or pay lots nearby.

antique phone repairs. Of interest to the browser is a display of an antique switchboard and phones; the operator is a mannequin dressed in a turn-of-the-century outfit. The store is small, but well-laid-out.

Open from 10 am to 7 pm Monday through Saturday, Thursday until 9 pm, and Sunday from 1 pm to 5 pm. They accept personal checks, Master Charge, VISA, American Express, Diners Club, Carte Blanche, Central Charge, and NAC. $10 to $20 is usually requested on layaways, with 60 days to pay, and they will also hold merchandise for up to 24 hours with a deposit. Any exchanges should be made within two weeks of purchase. There is metered parking; or you can have your ticket validated for the lot under the building with a purchase.

Telephone Warehouse of Georgetown
1055 Thomas Jefferson Street NW
Washington, DC
333-2900

Motto: "We meet all competitive prices" — and this means on telephones, answering machines, and all related equipment. Equipment comes from ITT, Stromberg-Carlson, GTE, and Northern Telecom, phone answering devices from Codeaphone, Recordacall, Phonemate, and Sanyo. Many items are manufacturers' closeouts. Discounts run 20% to 25% below comparable retail, and they take custom orders and special orders, deposit depending on the cost of the item. A store catalogue is available. They do warranty work on answering machines. They have a mailing list and do mail order shipments by UPS nationwide. One item is featured weekly at a special sale price. They claim the largest selection of antique telephones and also do

Vacuums Unlimited
311 N. Glebe Road
Arlington, VA
527-6600

The store which we visited was a teeny tiny little store with vacuum cleaners on shelves and on the floor, lining the two side walls. This store features sales and service on Kirby, Royal, Eureka, Hoover, Electrolux, Filter Queen, and Rainbow. The discount depends on the manufacturer — it ranges from a 10% discount to 40% with a trade-in. All machines are either first quality new, or rebuilt. Delivery is free within the immediate area. They all do warranty work for some of the brands and do mail order as well. All stores, the management stated, are the same size as this one.

Other addresses:
4229 Annandale Road, Annandale, VA, 354-4100
6041 Leesburg Pike, Falls Church, VA, 379-0500

Appliances & Electronics

They accept personal checks, Master Charge, VISA, NAC, Central Charge, and American Express, and they will give you instant financing with your charge card. Small parking lot at Arlington location.

Where to Complain about Appliances:

Major Appliance Consumers Action Panel (MACAP)
20 North Wacker Drive
Chicago, Illinois 60606
(312) 236-3165

Whirlpool Corporation
24 hour toll-free number
In Michigan: (800) 253-1301
Outside of Michigan: (800) 632-2243

Westinghouse Appliance Service
Toll free: (800) 245-0600
In Pennsylvania: (800) 242-0580

Maytag Corporation
In Iowa, Missouri, South Dakota, or Wyoming, call (800) 228-9445
Others, call your local representative or write to 403 West Fourth Street North, Newton, Iowa 50208, or call (515) 792-7000

Admiral Corporation
24 hour toll-free number
In Illinois: (800) 447-1305
Elsewhere, call collect: (309) 827-0002

General Electric Company
Major Appliance Group
Appliance Park
Louisville, Kentucky 40225
(502) 452-3248

Sears Roebuck
Service inquiries must be directed to the store nearest you, each of which has its own policy.

MAIL ORDER

Annex Outlet Ltd.
43 Warren Street
New York, New York 10007
(212) 964-8661

For discounts of 35% to 40% on blank tapes and video equipment, send for free tape catalogue.

Argus Radio & Appliances
507 East 80th Street
New York, New York 10021
(212) 794-1705

Ask for price quotes. Discounts run 20% to 30% off of retail on large appliances and televisions.

**Bloom and Krup
206 First Avenue
New York, NY 10009
(212) OR 3-2760**

Ask for price quotes. Discounts run 10% to 30% off of retail for appliances, televisions, and furniture.

Bondy Export Company
40 Canal Street
New York, New York 10002
(212) 925-7785

Call for price quotes. Discounts run a minimum of 30% on large appliances, audio equipment, cameras, luggate, televisions, and small appliances.

T. M. Chan & Co.
P.O. Box 33881
Sheung Wan Post Office
Hong Kong

Radios, cassette recorders, amplifiers, cassettes, tape decks, cameras, and clock radios, at a discount of 30% or more. Send for free catalogue.

EBA Associates
2329 Nostrand Avenue,
Brooklyn, New York 11210
(212) 252-3400

Call for price quote. Discounts run from 10% to 40% off list on major and small appliances, and audio and video equipment.

Far East Company
K.P.O. Box TST 7335
Kowloon, Hong Kong

Cameras, watches, and audio equipment at a discount of 50%. Send $1 to cover air mail postage on the free catalogue.

Flash Photo Electronics
1206 Avenue J
Brooklyn, New York 11230
(212) 253-7121

Call for price quote. Discount runs 10% to 30% on appliances; audio, television, and video equipment; and cameras.

Focus Electronics
4523 13th Avenue
Brooklyn, New York 11219

Ask for price quote. Discounts run 10% to 30% on large and small appliances, audio and video equipment, televisions, and cameras.

Foto Electric Supply
31 Essex Street
New York, New York 10002
(212) 673-5222

Ask for price quotes. Discounts at minimum of 30% on televisions, large appliances, and video equipment.

International Distributors of America
150 W. 28th Street,
New York, New York 10001
(212) 989-7162

Ask for price quotes. Discounts run 10% to 40% off retail on TV, audio, and video equipment.

International Solgo, Inc.
77 W. 23rd Street,
New York, New York 10010
(212) 895-6996

Ask for price quotes. Discounts run up to 40% on appliances, cameras, audio components, jewelry, luggage, televisions, and video equipment.

Jilor Discount
1177 Broadway
New York, New York 10001
(212) 683-1590

Ask for price quotes. Discounts run 5% to 50% on televisions and video equipment.

Kunst Sales
45 Canal Street
New York, New York 10002
(212) 966-1909

Ask for price quote. Discounts run 10% to 50% on small kitchen and personal care appliances.

Lewi Supply
15 Essex Street
New York, New York 10002
(212) 777-6910

Ask for price quote. Discounts run 20% to 40% off retail on sewing machines, cameras, typewriters, and Sony products.

Phantasmagoria
311 South 11th Street
Tacoma, Washington 98402
(206) 383-2041

Discounts run 20% to 25% off retail on Alladin lamps and Champion juicers. Write for catalogue, which costs 50c.

S & S Sound City
58 West 45th Street,
New York, New York 10036
(212) 575-0210

Call for price quote. Discounts run 10% to 40% on appliances, audio components, televisions, and video equipment.

Sound Machine
2836 Kennedy Blvd.,
Jersey City, New Jersey 07306
(800) 526-6070

Ask for price quote. They guarantee lowest prices on televisions, video equipment, and audio components.

Stereo Corporation of America
1629 Flatbush Avenue
Brooklyn, New York 11210
(800) 221-0974

Discounts of 30% to 70% on audio components. Send for free catalogue. Price quote also given by telephone.

Universal Suppliers
P.O. Box 14803
Hong Kong

Send for catalogue, which is free by surface mail, $2.50 by air mail. Save 30% to 60% on audio components, as well as cameras, jewelry, and more.

Warehouse Sound Co.
Railroad Square
Box S
San Luis Obispo, CA 93405
(805) 544-9700

Free catalogue published three times a year. Save 15% to 30% on anything in the way of audio equipment and supplies.

Wisan TV and Appliances
4085 Hylan Blvd.,
Staten Island, New York 10308
(212) 356-7700

Ask for price quote. Discounts of 10% to 40% on appliances, audio, and video equipment.

A RELATED PUBLICATION

Powell, Evan, with Robert P. Stevenson *Complete Guide to Home Appliance Repair. Popular Science*, Harper & Row, New York 1978. Rather technical. Illustrations sometimes do not relate well to text. Troubleshooter guides are good.

Furniture Bedding & Lighting

Singles buy furniture. Newlyweds buy furniture. Old people buy furniture. Almost everyone does it at least once, and often more. For at some time in your life, you will probably need, at the very least, a bed to sleep on and a table to eat off of. And whether you buy the cheapest or the most expensive merchandise available, the price will make it obvious that furniture is an investment. The scarcity and high cost of hard woods and the high price of skilled labor have worked together to put the finest wood furniture out of reach for most people, and to make other good quality furniture an expensive proposition.

Because it demands such an investment of money, you should budget your furniture purchases before you let your grandiose dreams and ideas take over and you start spending huge amounts of money. The first step in budgeting for furniture is establishing priorities — if you spend a large portion of your time in the bedroom, then perhaps you should spend a comparable proportion of your money on bedroom furniture (even though traditionalists recommend that more money be spent on formal public areas like the living room). And certain items are worth spending more on — generally case goods (wood items) — because they last and look good for a long time, and often become the family heirlooms.

If you're on a very tight budget, then you should determine what is essential and put off buying the less important things until you have more money. Furniture should not be bought on the spur of the moment, nor solely for its attractiveness. It should rather be bought to fit into the room for which it is intended — no matter how much a large mediterranean style dining room set might appeal to you, there's probably no way to make it fit into your 9x12 dining room!

In buying furniture, you should realize that neither price nor brand name are a guarantee of quality, so you should learn how to recognize the elements of quality and to recognize when a price is fair or even a bargain. The information below lays out some guidelines for assessing quality. You can add additional information to these basic points as you become more knowledgeable and interested in furniture, by reading about styles and construction, and by asking questions of salespeople and well-informed individuals. Reading trade journals like *Home Furnishings Daily* can help to familiarize you with brands, and to see at what quality level the manufacturers advertise and, thus, rate their own goods.

CASE GOODS

Case goods refer to non-upholstered furniture. Wood furniture can last a lifetime and more — because of its durability and beauty. However, the craftsmanship and materials which are used are expensive, making wood furniture the most expensive. You can combat this problem by buying simple styles, which require less handwork, and are thus less expensive. Wood used for furniture ranges from hard to soft, hardwood being preferred. Hardwood comes from leafbearing deciduous trees and includes birch, maple, mahogany, cherry, oak, walnut, and teak, and such exotic varieties as ebony, rosewood, and myrtle. Birch is very strong, cherry is expensive and solid, oak is durable, and walnut is expensive because it is rare. Softwoods come from coniferous, or needlebearing trees (evergreens), of which pine is an example. Pine and other softwoods tend to be used in more rustic styles of furniture. Further information on these woods can be obtained through the Fine Hardwood Association.

One of the advantages of solid wood is that refinishers can plane it without fearing peeling off, as would happen with a veneered piece. Also, solid wood can be glued together in blocks to form new shapes and allows great versatility in design. Solid wood is usually made from planks ½" to ¾" thick, and all exposed parts on a piece that claims to be solid wood must indeed be solid.

But solid wood is expensive, and it does have drawbacks. So *veneer* has become a common and quite acceptable substitute for solid. Veneer is basically a wood sandwich of from 5 to 7 thin layers of woods, with the inside of the sandwich being solid wood. There should always be an odd number of plies — 9, 7, and 5 indicate fine quality, and 3 plies are used in cheaper construction or for ornamentation. If a piece has only two plies, this means there is only one thin sheet facing the core on either side, which gives little strength or durability. While the core should be solid wood, on less expensive pieces it is sometimes composition or pressboard, both of which warp with time.

Veneers are formed by placing thin sheets or layers of fine hardwood at crossgrain to the core. Another layer is added on each side, again at crossgrain to the first layers. This process continues with additional layers, which adds stability and strength to the piece. All of the layers are put together with strong adhesives, and bonded under heat and pressure to form a strong finished product.

Advantages of veneers are many — economy, beauty of graining, and durability are foremost. New adhesives have made shrinking and cracking of the veneers a rare occurrence. Veneered pieces resist warping, changes in temperature, humidity, air conditioning and overheating — all of which solid woods fall prey to. Also, greater flexibility in design is possible with veneers — at a much lower cost than solids.

Besides solid woods and veneers, there are a number of less expensive forms for case goods, which include laminates (in which a core of wood or pressboard is covered with a plastic surface, which is bonded to it with an adhesive); chipped board and composition board (both of which are formed from wood fibers); and the least expensive, plastic panels printed to look like wood. These are found in lower-medium and lower priced furniture.

Finishes

Finishes vary from oil to paint to lacquer or wax — anything that will protect and enhance the surface. Clear finishes are usually applied to fine grains, so that the grain shows through. On cheaper materials, a tinted or opaque finish will be used to alter the color. Finishes produce many effects on wood surfaces. Depending on what is used and in what manner it is applied, a rough, rustic, warm, or smooth finish is achievable.

Finishes, no matter what type, should be matched, showing no drips, runs, streaks, or bubbles — surfaces should be smooth. Varnish gives a glossy finish, and oil a dry matte glow. So-called "super" finishes are chemical treatments which let the wood show through but give excellent protection under heavy usage. Distressed finishes are made to look as if they are old. Painted is just what the name implies.

Joints

Besides the quality of the wood itself, the next most important aspect of case goods is the sturdiness of the construction. One important indicator of quality of craftsmanship is seen when the joint is examined. For the stronger the joint, the better the construction.

The most common type is called a *dowel* joint: a wooden peg attached to one piece of the furniture is coated with glue and put into a hole in the corresponding section.

Usually considered the strongest joint is the *mortise and tenon*. In this variation, a square or rectangular slot is cut in one piece, and a projecting tongue of wood is cut from the other. Table tops are often put together like this, since a large piece of wood, such as is needed for a table, would probably warp if it were made from one solid piece.

A strong and attractive joint found on many old pieces is the *dovetail*. Also used for decorative purposes on some pieces, this type of joint is formed by notching two pieces of wood and interlocking them.

The cheapest and least effective joint is the *butt joint.* Two pieces of wood are merely butted together, and sometimes nailed, or nailed and glued.

You can also recognize quality construction when corner blocks or braces are added for strength at points of stress and are attached with glue. Drawer bottoms in particular should be blocked in this manner.

Drawers should have center guides, and all of their surfaces should be smooth. On better pieces, the inside will be made of wood, although not always of the same quality as the exterior. In some furniture made today, the insides of the drawers are molded plastic, which is attached to a wood or plastic front. Beware of these plastic drawers — they can crack and are almost impossible to fix.

On a case good, when you take the drawer out, look inside. There should be center and/or side guides for the drawer as well as reinforcing blocks. There should be a dust panel beneath the drawer separating it from the drawers below and preventing items from dropping out of one and falling into another. On a good piece, as you replace the drawer, it should not jiggle, but should fit well.

On the outside of the piece, all drawers should line up, and all hardware should be aligned. Hinges on doors should be invisible from the outside, unless part of the design. The heavier the hardware the better. Often, on special orders, you can ask to have the decorative hardware replaced if it is not to your liking.

Look at the backs of wood pieces before you buy. They should be hardwood or plywood, and should be set in grooves, glued and screwed (NOT nailed or stapled) to the frame of the piece.

On wooden chairs, corner block construction is desirable. Stretchers — those pieces of wood which connect between two legs — sometimes just across the front and the back, sometimes linking all four sides — add stability. If a chair is shaky in the store (unless the store's floor is not level), it will only get worse when you take it home.

When buying dining room furniture, make sure that all the leaves are included in the purchase, and that they are easy to insert and fit properly. They should match the table's grain and finish perfectly. If the leaf is a hinged section which rests on a leg or bracket, you should make sure it is secure when extended.

A table should be extremely stable. Lean on it. On level ground, it should neither rock from side to side nor move nor sway. As with other pieces, look for good joining and corner blocks. On large pieces, you should look for casters, which make it easier to move and to clean around the piece.

UPHOLSTERED FURNITURE

Upholstered furniture is assembled in steps. The outside fabric covering is probably the single most expensive part of the package. Despite this, there is no uniform system for grading fabrics and no government minimum quality standards for them. Each manufacturer does grade his own fabrics numerically or alphabetically. But this refers primarily to price, not to wearability. The best of one line may actually turn out to be the most delicate. In general, regardless of fabric grade, you should look for a tight weave and pay attention to the thickness of the fibers. The best weave is one which lets little light through it when held up to the light.

Woven fabrics come in two basic types: *flat* and *pile*.
Flat fabrics include:
- plain fabrics, such as satin, twill, denim, and homespun;
- jacquards, whose pattern is woven into the fabric, like brocades and damasks (which can appear sculptured or shimmery, but are not the most durable), brocatelles and matelasses (which are made of cotton or cotton blends, are quilted, and wear well), or tapestries (which are made in two or more colors, with a flat weave and design and are particularly durable in cotton); and
- novelty yarns, which are deliberately irregular in color or size, including broken weave patterns, like tweeds, shantungs, and bouclés.

Pile fabrics include:
- frieze, a hard-wearing fabric which periodically comes in and out of style, covered with surface loops of nylon or wool, which are dense, well-packed, and close to the surface;
- doeskin, which is a relatively inexpensive and light cotton pile fabric;
- velvets, in which the woven surface loops have been cut to form a thick, short pile (silks and manmade fabrics wear longer than cottons in velvet form). Variations of velvet include cut, crushed, pressed, and velour.
- plush, which is an overgrown velvet.

Vinyls are familiar to many, Naugahyde being a well-known brand name of vinyl upholstery. Vinyls come in graded weights, with or without a backing. In less expensive grades, vinyl tends to crack, discolor, and tear with age. Good vinyls are easy to clean and take hard use. However, they all feel clammy to your skin in humid weather.

Leather is a very expensive natural upholstery fabric which comes in a number of cuts and grades; among these, suede is the most fragile and least suited for upholstery.

Fibers

The fiber is as important to the durability of the piece of upholstered furniture as the weave. When you use natural fibers, stains, moth, and mildew can be problems. But cotton takes color well and blends easily. Linen wears quickly unless blended with other fibers. Wool pills and fuzzes easily, and silk is the most delicate fiber.

The manmade fibers are not liable to stains, moths, and mildews the way natural fibers are, except for rayon, which is susceptible to mildew. Acetates, like Celanese and Estron, are not strong enough for use in upholstered pieces, as they abrade and wrinkle easily. Acrylics, like Acrilan and Creslan, clean easily but have poor abrasion resistance, pill, and wear only moderately well. Nylons like Antron and Enkatron seem to have many things in their favor, as they clean easily, are abrasion-resistant, wear well, and take color well. But they also pill, stretch, and soil easily. Olefins, such as Herculon, are bulky tweedy fibers which currently enjoy wide use. They resist abrasion and stains, and clean easily, but they are highly heat sensitive. Rayon lacks dimensional stability, so it doesn't hold shape well, and it also wrinkles easily. However, when blended with another fiber like nylon, products like Tusson and Zantrel are formed, and the blend becomes soft and comfortable and takes dyes extremely well. Polyesters are usually made into thin fabrics and are, in general, inappropriate for upholstery.

Construction

While the appearance and wearability of the outside of an upholstered piece are important, the inside affects comfort and durability. The inside consists of cushions and/or padding, a frame and supporting foundation, and coils or springs for resilience.

Cushions can be made of down, feathers, latex foam rubber, polyurethane foam, hair, cotton, kapok, sisal, excelsior, or palm-leaf fibers — and that is also the order of expense.

Cushions filled with down or a combination of feathers and down offer the most seating comfort. However, they need frequent plumping up, and some people are allergic to feathers or down. When feather or down upholstery is used over springs, a firmer seat is provided, and less plumping is necessary. Latex foam rubber provides a comfortable but firm seating surface. Some manufacturers combine it with down to give extra surface softness. The density of the core determines its life, and a good grade will have a pincore — many tiny airholes close together. Polyurethane foam is lighter and cheaper than foam rubber, and it is both resilient and fungus resistant. It sits well, particularly when merged with polyester fibers to form polyurethane foam fiberfill, which (according to many) is the best buy on the market for comfort at a reasonable price. Polyurethane foam by itself is sometimes wrapped in a layer of cotton or other padding, or is even covered with muslin to prevent the covering fabric from sliding around on it. The best polyurethane foam has a high density, for low density materials "sit out" quickly. Hair padding is generally found in older pieces of upholstered furniture; it is expensive, firm to sit on, and allergenic. Cotton has no bounce, resilience, or firmness, and is mildew and moisture susceptible. At the bottom of the list are kapok, sisal, excelsior, and palm leaf fibers all of which are subject to mold and mildew, break down and crumble, and give no bounce.

The frame should be made of kiln-dried hardwood, such as ash, birch, or hard maple, which do not warp. Plywood and particleboard are not acceptable for frames. Joints on the frame should be double doweled, and not stapled or glued together. In modern furniture, steel or strong rigid plastics are sometimes used for the frame.

Attached to the frame is the supporting foundation, which can consist of webbing — jute, steel, nylon or other synthetic, or (in the least expensive furniture) even a board. The purpose of this foundation is to hold up the springs or cushions. In better pieces of furniture, it consists of jute webbing tightly woven in wide strips and closely interlaced across the frame. Above this foundation are located the springs, which come in two varieties: *coiled* and *flat*. Coils can be single or double cone, zig-zag, or s-shaped. A double cone is the most comfortable. In the best pieces of furniture, these coils are hand tied, but this is rare because of the expense. In the average upholstered chair, there should be 9 to 12 springs, placed where the webbing is crisscrossed.

The only way that you, as a consumer, have of knowing whether or not the construction is fine, and what the elements actually are, is by seeing a cross-section example of the construction of the piece. Sometimes, with finer furniture, such a cross-section will be available. Barring that example, however, you must rely on the attached tag that reads "Do Not Remove under Penalty of Law". Instead of joking about the tag, you should read it — it gives worthwhile information about the construction materials of the piece, and some manufacturers also include cleaning and care instructions.

SPECIALTY FURNITURE

The term "specialty furniture" is not one in common usage, but it describes many items which don't fall into the traditional categories outlined above. *Children's furniture* fits in here.

In children's furniture, look for mar-resistant tops and sturdy hardware. It doesn't make sense to buy much small-sized furniture for kids, because not only do they get bigger fast, but, unless they are extraordinarily well-trained, you will be spending a lot of time putting away clothes into their drawers — and you don't want to break your back doing it.

There is no economy in buying what is offered as *teen furniture* — once past the stage of children's furniture, teens are only around for a few years and have already started developing adult tastes. It makes more sense to buy them adult furniture which you or they can use in the future.

In October, 1972, *Consumer Reports* tested *recliners* and found that they all — regardless of price — came out to be reasonably sturdy and reliable. With that in mind, the recommendation was to go first for comfort, second for style, and, when all else is equal, to go for the lowest price.

Sleep sofas are usually not good to sleep on every night. If the mattress were fine enough for you to do so, the price would become prohibitive. While their value as couches has been recently improved, they still do not really qualify as everyday beds, unless you really are living in a cramped space and have no choice.

In an area as mobile as metropolitan Washington, *knockdown (KD) furniture*, which comes in a box and is assembled by the buyer, has been a real boon to peripatetic consumers. When first developed, KD furniture

Our Knock-Downs You Can Carry Out.

All Wood Storage Bed

You Can Take It With You!

That's the whole idea. You can take it with you right out of the store! From apartment to house! From city to county! From state to country! From here to eternity!

Knock-Down Outlet
Easy to assemble carry home **furniture.**

Our Prices: We Knock It Off!

We knock it off every day! You don't have to wait for a sale. Your Knock-Down Outlet has them on sale every day. Come in and you'll agree: our prices are a knock-out!

Tyson's Corner
Old Courthouse Rd. & Rt. 123
(703) 356-4245

Georgetown
On Wisconsin at P Street
(202) 333-3777

Gaithersburg
Walnut Hill Shopping Center
(301) 948-1828

was limited to certain plastics and metals, and was not considered anywhere near the quality of "real" furniture. But, as designers have gotten more interested in this medium, what was once considered cheap and inadequate has gotten more sophisticated, while retaining its economic qualities. Knockdown furniture can be made from many materials — wood, plastic, metals, and wood products among them. Its advantages include economy, the elimination of delivery charges and waiting periods, and easy portability from place to place. If evaluating

knockdown furniture, you should consider the same basic qualities that you would in more traditional furniture; but you should realize that because of the lower cost and the limitations of the genre, there will be some points of divergence from fine furniture. But, in general, no sharp edges should be exposed, and color or finish should be uniform throughout.

On *casual metal furniture,* look for neat joints, smooth edges, and an undercoating of paint several layers thick. *Wicker or rattan* furniture should have secure joints and smooth surfaces.

SOME SUGGESTIONS ON BUYING FURNITURE

- Watch for furniture sales — they generally occur in August and January.
- Good used furniture can be a good buy — as can seconds if the damage or flaw is barely noticeable.
- Mix and match styles to your taste.
- Always compare prices before buying.
- Ask for return policies in writing.
- On special orders, carefully read the terms concerning cancellations, returns, guarantees, and payment. Make sure that everything is correctly written down. Common abbreviations include: FOB (free on board — you pay the freight charges); COM (customer's own material — you provide material for the upholstery); and CBD (cash before delivery).
- Always get copies of all guarantees — from the manufacturer and the store.
- Avoid bait and switch operations. If some fantastic buy is offered, but when you walk in the salesperson tries to dissuade you from buying it, be wary, and examine his or her explanations.
- Wherever you are buying, if they say that they are offering you a fantastic discount, you can verify that discount by asking to see materials put out by the manufacturer, such as a catalogue or other type of price list, which clearly state the manufacturer's suggested retail price.
- There's nothing wrong with closeout merchandise. The term "closeout" merely refers to designs or patterns which are no longer being manufactured. Since upholstery fabrics are changed so frequently, you can often find an upholstered piece in a discontinued fabric that suits your fancy . . . and at a good price.

When you are buying a piece of upholstered furniture, keep the following points in mind:

- Check for your comfort: sit on it and bounce up and down — see how it reacts.
- Look at the sample construction model to see quality of construction.
- Read labels and look for how many times the springs have been tied. On better pieces, it will be eight; on lesser, four.
- Check padding for lumps and bumps, which are unacceptable.
- Run your hands over the piece. If it is well padded, you will feel no sharp edges or bumps.
- Make sure the frame feels secure and does not wobble.
- Watch someone else do these tests, and watch the reaction of the furniture.
- Cushions should fit snugly. Better ones are reversible to distribute wear. Zippers are used on cushions for a better fit — not for ease of cleaning.
- Seams, welts, or cording should be straight, buttons should be secure.
- Fabrics with patterns should be centered and match at the seams.

BEDDING

Buying bedding is likely to be the most important furniture purchase you will ever make, since the average person spends about one-third of his time sleeping. That time will be spent almost exclusively on bedding. Yet few people seem to give much thought to their bedding, which is a relatively expensive purchase with long-range ramifications. Your choice of bedding affects not only how you sleep every night, but how long the bedding itself will last. By spending a little more time and doing a little more research, you can profit by getting a great deal of better sleeping and relaxation. And you'll be spending a bit more money, too: cheap bedding is no bargain when it comes to comfort. If you can find the high quality bedding which you desire at a good low price at one of the stores listed in this chapter, then you've got a bargain. But if you settle for the cheapest price, regardless of make or line, then you're saving only in the very short run — and you could have a problem from the first night on. And you're stuck with your mistake, since health laws state that when bedding is delivered to the purchaser's home, it is automatically assumed to be used. The only valid reasons for returning a mattress are defects or flaws in manufacturing, or damage done by shipping. The only exception to this would be when the manufacturer or retailer made fantastic claims about the merchandise — and backed it up with a "you test it" guarantee.

Mattresses

There are two popular types of mattresses: *innerspring* and *foam*.

An innerspring mattress is constructed of a number of different elements. Consider first the steel springs or coils. These coils are enclosed by layers of padded upholstery; they could be open or cloth-pocketed. Steel wires hold the coils together and apart on a steel frame. Contrary to popular wisdom, the number of coils has relatively little to do with the product, although there should be a minimum of 200-300 in a twin bed, and at least 800 in that bed if they are cloth-pocketed. Comparing the number of coils is much like comparing a 4-cylinder car to an 8-cylinder. They both run, but they have different characteristics.

What is more important is the gauge and temper of the coil steel. Further, if coils are coated with latex, they become noiseless; and baked-on enamel rustproofs them. On top of the coils is placed a layer of cushioning, a layer of insulation, and finally the outer shell of ticking.

The cushioning material can be cotton, latex, urethane foam, wool, or polyester. The insulation layer gives buoyancy and can be wire, plastic, cotton net, hog hair, sisal, or cotton.

A cloth flange runs around the border of the mattress, anchoring the coils to the ticking, cushioning, and insulation materials. This flange should be tightly machine-sewn to withstand stress. In less expensive models, this edge is just rolled and stitched, and this technique detracts from the life of the bed.

This is true for a smooth top mattress. A quilted mattress is made in much the same way, except for the prequilting of the ticking.

Handles on the side of the mattress make it easier to move and should be cord, steel, or plastic, anchored by a metal plate. If they are cloth, or if handles are held in place with eyelets rather than by a plate, the handles may give way with repeated turnings.

Small ventilation holes, sometimes called *ports*, are desirable, as they allow air to circulate. Sometimes these ports are installed but do not really vent the inside — make sure they do.

Foam mattresses are produced in two materials — latex (rubber) or urethane (plastic), or sometimes in a combination of the two. Latex is better. It is molded to the shape, and can be pincore (with tiny holes throughout it) or honeycomb (with slightly larger holes). The larger the holes, the more prone to buckling is the mattress.

Urethane mattresses are cut from large blocks of urthane and are less resilient and firm than the latex. Both types are non-allergenic, mildew- and mold-proof, light, and flexible, and they do not need to be turned to distribute wear. They come in a variety of thicknesses, but a minimum of 4" is suggested.

For firmness in a foam mattress, a one-piece core is recommended, rather than many layers put together. Foam mattresses are also finished with a ticking, which is sometimes quilted to a thin layer of foam. When buying a foam mattress, you should be sure that the foam does not sink down with your body when you lie on it.

And there is one other type of foam mattress — shredded foam — but this is not recommended for comfort or for durability.

Foam tends to deteriorate with age, while wear on an innerspring mattress occurs on the sides and in the center, where it sags. In general, an innerspring mattress will usually last longer than a foam mattress of the same quality.

Foundations

While industry members may tell you that a foundation and mattress wear out at the same time, this is not generally true. If the mattress wears out first, it can be replaced and the new mattress used with the old foundation. On the other hand, one should never put a new mattress on an old worn-out foundation; this will just age the new mattress.

There are a number of different foundations: box springs are the most commonly known. Basically, these are constructed like innerspring mattresses, but with fewer, heavier coils than the mattress. These coils sit on a wood frame, on wood slats which should be firmly joined of good dry wood. A layer of padding or filler is placed on the top to protect the mattress; then the whole is covered with ticking on the top and the sides. A dust sheet covers the bottom; it is usually of a lighter weight material. Coil spring foundations can be purchased without the padding or ticking, but they are difficult to find. Though they are cheaper, they need more cleaning, and it is frequently necessary to place some protection for the mattress over them.

It is desirable to have plastic corner guards on the box spring; they protect the edges of the foundation when it is placed into the frame.

Another foundation, less popular and less expensive, is the *flat spring foundation*. This is basically a sheet of metal wires connected to all four sides of a frame. While less expensive than a box spring, this type of foundation tends to sag quickly and provides less bounce than the coil type of foundation.

Frames

Frames which support the mattress and foundation, should be strong and sturdy, with riveted legs. In the larger sizes, there should be an additional bar which runs lengthwise down the middle to give support to the center of the bed. The angle rails should be at least 1" by 1" to best support the foundation. Casters make it easier for you to move the bed to make it or to clean around and under it.

Comfort and Durability

Comfort is something which each individual must decide on for him or herself and can be determined only by trying out every prospective bed purchase. Firmnesses are *not* standard, so that the manufacturer's classification of "extra firm" may have little to do with your comfort. Therefore, a bedding purchaser should roll around a bit when trying out mattresses in the store, and bounce on them a little. You should try to give the bedding the same types of movement you would when you would use it at home. If the bedding is intended for a couple, both ought to try it out together, since the springs act differently with two people on the mattress. The springs should act independently, so that the lighter person doesn't wind up rolling into the middle!

Size is also a determinant of comfort — and sizes are standard. It is better to decide what size you are going to get before you buy. Remember that not only does larger bedding cost more initially, but buying sheets, pillows, and pillowcases will also be more expensive. For height, 6" to 10" of length should be added to the height of the tallest sleeper to insure his comfort. Width should be that which gives you the most comfort. A twin bed at 39" for one person actually gives the most sleeping room. A double gives two people 27" each, or one person 54". A queen increases that slightly but noticeably to 30" per individual, and a king goes to 38" per person, one inch smaller than the twin.

Besides giving room to the sleeper, the bed must also fit in the room. Remember that it must not only go in the room, but must first go through hallways and other rooms to get there. This is particularly important if you pick it up yourself. Also, a room whose dimensions are less than 12x15 is probably too small for a king size bed to fit in comfortably. On the other hand, a room that already has a double can usually comfortably accommodate the queen size.

Actual bed sizes:

Twin	39" wide x 75" long
Long Twin	39" wide x 80" long
Full/Double	54" wide x 75" long
Long Full	54" wide x 80" long
Queen	60" wide x 80" long
King	76" wide x 80" long
Long King	76" wide x 84" long

Speaking mostly about innerspring mattresses... Quality can be measured by five criteria: *durability* — how well the insides stand up to continued use; *conformity* — how well separate sections of the mattress act independently to conform to the contours of the body; *permeability* — how well the mattress allows the air to circulate around the body; *absorbency* — how quickly water is absorbed by the mattress; and *flammability*. The importance of this last is obvious, and under a 1973 law entitled the Federal Flammability Standards Act, new mattresses must be sufficiently fireproof to resist being ignited by a burning cigarette. (Remember, though, that blankets and sheets don't have similar restrictions, and thus you cannot rely on the Act to prevent accidents which occur from, among other things, smoking in bed.)

Consumer Reports simulated prolonged use on a variety of innerspring mattresses, testing for durability and other characteristics. They concluded that a mattress should be permeable enough to allow the air to circulate and body moisture to dissipate. They found damask ticking to be more effective in this regard than print ticking, which usually had a layer of plastic beneath it. Padding with polyurethane also detracted from permeability, while air ports helped. They concluded absorbency should be slow; it was found that damask was more absorbent.

For a mattress in everyday use, durability is a major concern, and you could check the brands recommended by *Consumer Reports*. But if you wish to use bedding only part of the time — for example, in a guest room or summer home — it makes sense to purchase a less expensive mattress, chosen according to comfort and price.

The mattress cover may be tufted quilted, or smooth-topped; damask or printed. Damask is more colorfast, more permeable, and more absorbent than printed. Printed ticking may in time discolor the bottom sheets.

Attractiveness

Mattresses should not be bought on the basis of looks — they will just be covered with sheets and blankets. So even a set of mismatched innerspring mattress and box spring is acceptable. You should be more concerned that the ticking be heavy, sturdy, and closewoven for best wear.

How Mattresses Are Sold

Most companies produce several quality and price ranges. Most make *premium* or *top-of-the-line* models, which come with 15-20 year guarantees. These are made the same in all factories which produce that brand of bedding, no matter where they are located. Then they also produce a less expensive *promotional* line, which may be made differently at each of the manufacturer's plants — the result being a product which varies by region. There are a few companies which manufacture the same promotional line throughout the country. Promotional units are manufactured to hit a popular price point, and usually vary from premium as to number and weight of coils, as well as layers of padding in the mattress.

Some Caveats on Buying Bedding

- Read labels to compare quality of construction.
- Realize that, although a mattress may be guaranteed, if you have a problem with it during the guarantee period, you may be responsible for the cost of shipping it back to the factory.
- Don't be taken in by companies that advertise a great buy on one item — and then don't have it when you get there — and don't let them switch you to another item.
- Be sure you get what you ordered and paid for. Make sure the model number and all other relevant information is down on your receipt.

Hubbard-Dale Inc.

317 S. Washington Street
Alexandria, Virginia 22314
836-1111

1511 Quaker Lane
Alexandria, Virginia 22302
379-7977

Licensed in Virginia, Maryland, District of Columbia and Delaware

Hubbard-Dale
REALTORS

SPECIALISTS IN FINE RESIDENTIAL PROPERTIES
IN OLD TOWN AND NORTHERN VIRGINIA

GETTING FURNITURE AND BEDDING BARGAINS

ABC Liquidators
3185 Wilson Blvd.
Arlington, VA
524-2244

ABC Liquidators runs a large store packed with used merchandise from hotels and other commercial sources, and new mattresses — some second and some first quality. The used furniture is from a middle-priced line, including some bedroom sets, some color televisions, and dinette sets. You can purchase new furniture by Clyde Gable, Conway, and Lane here, but these are not accompanied by warranties. You can save up to 70% off of some Simmons factory seconds on bedding; and from 10% to 15% on new beds by Eastern Sleep and Sleepwell, which do have warranties. New Simmons merchandise can also be special ordered.

Other address:
6419 Marlboro Pike, Great Eastern Plaza, MD, 735-1050

Hours are Monday through Friday, from 10 am to 9 pm; Saturday from 10 am to 6 pm, and Sunday from noon to 6 pm. They accept personal checks, Master Charge, VISA, Central Charge, and NAC. Returns for a cash refund or exchanges must be made within 7 days of purchase. On layaways, 25% deposit is required and 30 days for final payment and pickup. In Virginia, there is a parking lot to the side of the building, for which they will stamp your park-and-shop coupon; and in Maryland they have their own parking lot.

Abbington Design Associates
2709 S. Wakefield,
Arlington, VA
931-5602

Aimed at designers but also open to government and military personnel, Abbington Design Associates carries lines of medium to high quality residential furniture. Styles are both traditional and modern. Brands commonly found here include BB Continental, Wyman, Hickory Chair, and Tomlinson. All merchandise is first quality: about half is in-stock and the other half has to be ordered. On orders, you put 1/3 down when you place the order and the remaining 2/3 when the merchandise comes into their warehouse. They could not quote an average savings but said that you should be prepared to get a price close to what a designer would pay with a trade discount. You must pay your own delivery. This is a small shop with bedroom furniture and modern designs downstairs, and traditional furniture and accessories upstairs; some very elaborate designs are in evidence. You can also order carpeting here, as well as custom spreads and Lane bedroom sets.

Hours are from 10 am to 5 pm Tuesday through Saturday. Personal checks, Master Charge, and VISA are accepted, but cash is not. On layaways, they request 50% down, and there is a liberal time for final pickup and payment. There are no returns or exchanges; this is made very clear on the purchase contract.

Antiquities Brass Beds & Bedding
1114 N. Irving Street,
Arlington, VA
243-2929

This is a tiny little shop selling bedding, brass bedsteads, and a full line of brass accessories for what they claim to be somewhat below standard retail. Serta Bedding is offered at from $35 to $100 off list price and comes with the Serta warranty. The brass bedsteads and headboards are their own house brand, comparable to those found in department stores, and prices are supposed to run 15% to 45% below comparable retail prices. The brass accessories are priced at 10% to 20% off of comparable retail prices. Antique beds may be available — check with the owner for specifics.

Hours are from 10 am to 6 pm, 7 days a week. Layaways are to be picked up within 30 days, with a $25 to $50 deposit required. There are no returns. Metered on-street parking is available.

Baby Products
2731 Wilson Blvd.
Arlington, VA
525-2972

Baby Products is simply filled with everything for babies — furniture, clothes, toys, beds, and more. Brands commonly found here include Bassett, Simmons, Childcraft, and many brands of clothes. They also carry Basset adult furniture. Everything is first quality. There is no average discount — each item is priced depending on its cost to the store. On special orders, a minimum deposit of $10 is usually required. All pieces of clothing are handpicked, to avoid any flawed merchandise, and any problems are settled to the customer's satisfaction. Sales are held periodically.

Other location:
389 Main Street, Laurel, MD 674-4433

Hours are flexible and are about the same for both locations: Monday, Wednesday, and Friday from 10 am to 9 pm, and Tuesday, Thursday, and Saturday to 6 pm. Personal checks are accepted, as are Master Charge and VISA. On layaways, a $10 deposit is requested, and final payment and pickup dates are flexible — this applies to furniture only. Refunds are made within 7 days with a receipt. Store credit is given if you lose your receipt. On-street parking is available.

Bedding and Furniture Discount
6801 Richmond Highway
Alexandria, VA
765-5565

We found this to be a small and worn-out looking little building at the Richmond Highway location, covering three floors. They were selling low to medium quality bedding, sleep sofas, living room furniture, and bunk beds. Serta sleep sofas, Lane and Franklin recliners, Kroehler sleep sofas and living room furniture, Lane occasional tables and chests, Eastern Sleep and Kingsdown Posture bedding, as well as Re Li On foam mattresses were carried. Discounts average from 30% to 35%, and up to 50% on bedding. Almost all of the merchandise is in stock; on what is not, a 25% deposit on special orders is requested. All merchandise is warrantied.

Other address:
101 No. Frederick Avenue, Gaithersburg, MD, 840-8590

Monday through Friday from 10 am to 9 pm, Saturday from 10 am to 6 pm, and Sunday from noon to 6. Personal checks with proper identification, Master Charge, VISA, Central Charge, and NAC are accepted. Layaway policy depends on the item. Exchanges are offered on defective merchandise; otherwise all sales are final. Parking available on premises.

Bedding World
1304 E. Gude
Rockville, MD
279-2234

This small, well-organized store has a good selection of bedding, sleep sofas, bunk bends, and head and foot boards and is the only authorized Spring Air dealer in the area. They also carry Rowe sleep sofas and Swan brass products. All merchandise is first quality or manufacturers' closeouts. Discounts range from 15% to 30%. Most items are in stock, but on special orders they ask for a 15% to 20% deposit, and there is a wait of from a week to 10 days. Manufacturers' warranties are offered. They advertise special sales in the newspapers.

Open Monday through Wednesday from 10 am to 6 pm, Thursday and Friday until 8 pm, and Saturday until 5 pm. Personal checks with proper identification are accepted, as are Master Charge and VISA. Layaway policy varies with the item. On return policy, check with the management before you buy.

Better Homes Furniture
2844 Hartland Road, off Lee Hwy.
Falls Church, VA 22043
560-4044/4045

A large, neatly-organized store, Better Homes Furniture sells a wide range of solid cherry and mahogany furniture, both traditional and imported oriental. They feature such brands as Carrollcraft, American Drew, Sterlingworth, and Crawford, and they are constantly expanding the lines. They also import rattan furniture. Everything is first quality, with a few items of special purchase merchandise infrequently brought in on special sale. Discounts are said to average 40% to 60%. They back up the warranties with in-home repairs, and if an item is not repairable, they will replace it.

Specials are offered every week, and on most major national holidays. They also sell oriental gifts, handpainted ginger jars, and screens made of rattan and wood.

The store is open from 10 am to 9 pm on Monday through Friday, from 10 am to 6 pm on Saturday, and from noon to 6 pm on Sunday. Personal checks, VISA, and Master Charge are accepted. On layaways, a 1/3 deposit is requested, with 30 days for pickup and final payment. They will hold items for up to 24 hours without a deposit. Full refunds are given within 30 days of purchase, but there are no cancellations on special order. A large parking lot is available.

Bon Marché
1213 Banks Street NW
Washington, DC
338-4730

Bon Marché lives up to its name — in French, it means "good buy" — and that is what you get on modern furniture, primarily made of teak, or of chrome and glass, with some walnut and oak available. They carry European imports, Scandinavian imports, and Sealy sleep sofas in a large open showroom at one edge of Georgetown. All merchandise is first quality. While not discounted, their merchandise — tables, desks, sofas, lamps — runs 20% to 25% below comparable retail prices. Most items are in stock, and on those which aren't they ask a 1/3 deposit for a special order. Delivery is available at a charge. If merchandise is defective, they will replace it. They have just recently begun a mailing list and feature weekly sale items. They may have an extra discount program for those who purchase items and get on the mailing list, so ask about it. They also carry a large selection of decorative baskets. The chrome and glass furniture is manufactured for them in Italy. You

Furniture, Bedding & Lighting 169

can get good modern furniture at reasonable prices here.

The store is open from 11 am to 8 pm Monday through Friday (except Wednesday, when it closes at 6 pm), and Saturday from 10 am to 6 pm; it is closed on Sunday. Personal checks are accepted, as are Master Charge and VISA. On layaways, they request 1/3 down and 30 days for final payment and pickup. They will hold items up to 24 hours with a deposit. No cash refunds are given, and returns for credit or exchanges must be made within 10 days of purchase. There is a small parking lot in back — and a tortuous route to it.

C. L. Barnes Clearance Center
2525 Mount Vernon Avenue
Alexandria, VA
780-7444

The Manassas and Alexandria stores differ in that the first is a full-time operation, and the other is open only for special monthly sales, one weekend a month. The Alexandria location was once a retail store and has been converted to more of a warehouse type operation. The Manassas store is still full service, and offers furniture for the whole house, as well as carpeting and bedding. They carry La-Z-Boy recliners at both locations. Brands are generally medium quality, with some higher. The merchandise at the clearance centers consists of many closeouts, floor samples, special purchases, and such. They are by makers such as Bassett, King Koil, Serta, Simmons, Rowe, Hickory Frye, Trendline, and Singer. Savings on closeouts and special purchases range up to 50%. The average discount on other items is about 20% off comparable retail. They can also order from any of their stores at discounts of 20% off manufacturers' suggested list on Thomasville, Hickory Frye, and Pennsylvania House. Free delivery is available. All items come with a minimum store guarantee of one year, unless they are sold "as is". They will honor all manufacturers' warranties, no matter where the item was purchased. Complete repair services are available. There is a mailing list, which is composed mainly of names of prior purchasers and credit accounts. Preferred customers get a notice of sales in advance.

Other address:
8219 Centreville Road, Manassas, VA, 368-2147.

Store hours at Manassas are from 10 am to 9 pm Monday through Friday and until 6 pm on Saturday. Alexandria store is open one weekend a month for special sales. Personal checks are accepted, as are Master Charge and VISA. They also offer their own credit terms with a 90 day cash option — if you pay within 90 days, there is no finance charge. Layaway policy is negotiable. Defective merchandise will be repaired or replaced.

Carolina Furniture
4507 Jeff Davis Blvd.,
Fredericksburg, VA
(800) 549-3960

Carolina Furniture suggests that you make a local selection of furniture, then call them with the manufacturer and model number to order. The reason? They say that you will save from 25% to 35% in this manner. And the merchandise which they stock is made by what they consider to be the top 10% of furniture manufacturers — brands like Simmons, Thomasville, Stiffel, Henredon, and Hickory. All merchandise is first quality, with a concentration of traditional, transitional, and just a bit of contemporary furniture. They also sell carpeting and lamps. Delivery is free within a 100-mile radius, and they extend any factory warranties for an additional year. If merchandise is defective, it will be repaired or replaced. On major holidays, they have special sales. The store is nice, consisting of small rooms which are a bit crowded with furniture, most of which is very good-looking.

The store is open weekdays from 10 am to 7 pm, Monday and Friday until 9 pm, and Sunday from 1 pm to 6 pm. They accept personal checks, Master Charge, and VISA. With a 1/2 purchase price deposit, they will hold merchandise for up to 30 days. Returns are not accepted on special orders. A free medium-sized parking lot is available.

Cort Furniture Rental Clearance Center
3137 Pennsy Drive,
Landover, MD
773-3369

Using a clearance center concept — keep that merchandise moving — Cort eliminates the backlog of used furniture and manufacturers' closeouts, mostly of medium quality. Manufacturers represented here include Bassett, Lane, and Chrome Craft. About 30% to 40% of the merchandise is closeouts or irregulars, with the remainder composed of rental returns, with savings up to 70% possible. This all happens in a large warehouse, with a huge floor space, where the dinettes, bars, chairs, lamps, mirrors, sofas, and bedroom suites are displayed. Manufacturers' warranties are upheld, and they will do repairs on store merchandise if necessary. They advertise in the *Washington Post* classifieds.

The store is open from Monday through Friday from 10 am to 7 pm, and Saturday until 5 pm. They accept payment by personal check, Master Charge, VISA, and NAC. There are no layaways and no holds. Returns are accepted.

Custom Bedding
3554 Bladensburg Road,
Bladensburg, MD
699-1330

No frills atmosphere — it must mean a bargain. Well, at Custom Bedding the amount of the bargain depends on the manufacturer. They sell bedding, sleep sofas, and some dinettes, mostly by small local manufacturers. They carry primarily top lines of Simmons, Serta, and Sealy, with 30 different types. They also carry Eastern Sleep and Therapedics. Almost all merchandise is first quality, except some irregulars of some of the lesser known brands which they carry. Delivery is available at a charge. Manufacturers' warranties are upheld. Clearance sales are held from time to time.

Hours here are Monday through Friday from 10 am to 9 pm, Saturday until 7 pm, and Sunday from noon to 6 pm. Checks, Master Charge, VISA, American Express, Central Charge, and NAC are all accepted. Layaways are flexible on deposit; pickup is usually requested within 30 days. Merchandise is returnable only if defective. After 30 days, the customer must deal with the factory. The parking lot here will hold about 15 to 20 cars.

Backroom at Danker Furniture
120 Halpine Road
Congressional Plaza
Rockville, MD
881-6010

Danker's carries fine lines of furniture. In the Back Room, which is actually two rooms upstairs, they carry furniture which just has not sold well, and damaged furniture. All items are sold "as is", with no returns, so they ask that you examine all items closely. Discounts run 40% and up. Danker has also recently introduced a new "price beating" policy whereby they will beat any verifiable prices in the area on their regular merchandise.

Furniture, Bedding & Lighting

The store is open from Monday through Friday from 10 am to 9 pm, Saturday until 6 pm, and Sunday from noon to 5 pm. They accept personal checks with proper identification, as well as Master Charge and VISA. On layaways, 1/3 down is requested with two weeks to pick up and make the final payment. Items will be held up to two weeks. There are no returns or exchanges. Parking is ample.

Decor Furniture
6228 Richmond Hwy.
Alexandria, VA
765-5500

The Richmond Highway location of Decor Furniture has a deceptive exterior — it looks quite small, but the store extends well in back from the road. Traditional and some modern styles are presented in a nice range of medium furniture. Name brands include Broyhill, and Brookwood, which is said to be the house brand of upholstered furniture for major furniture and department stores in the area. Most merchandise is first quality, with a lot of special purchase items from manufacturers' closeouts and overstocks from other stores. Discounts run all the way up to 75%. Though most items are in stock, you can also expect to save money on special orders from catalogues, with a 20% deposit. Waiting period depends on the factory and trucking. All items are delivered free unless otherwise specified. The store has a nice display area, uncrowded and generally well laid out. First quality merchandise is warrantied for one year on materials. Should repairs be necessary under the warranty policy, they will attend to them with their own professional furniture refinisher.

Other locations:
6755 Wilson Boulevard, Falls Church, VA, 532-0838

4646 Suitland Rd., Suitland, MD, 735-1111
640 University Blvd., Langley Park, MD, 434-8700

All stores are open from 10 am to 9 pm on Monday through Friday, until 6 pm on Saturday, and from noon to 5 pm on Sunday. They accept personal checks with proper identification and all major credit cards. On layaways, they require at least 10% down, with a 30-day limit to pickup and final payment. Without a deposit, merchandise will be held for up to 24 hours. There is no set policy on returns and exchanges — they will work for the customer's satisfaction. Ample parking at all locations.

Denis Sleep Shop
7681 New Hampshire Avenue
Langley Park, MD 20783
434-0334

In this medium-sized store, many beds are displayed in a slightly but not too crowded display area. The brands they carry are from medium to high quality and include brands such as Serta, Simmons, Englander, and Eclipse bedding, and sleep sofas by Serta and Simmons. All merchandise is first quality, with discounts ranging from 15% to 20%. About 70% of the merchandise is in stock, and they ask for a 10% deposit on special orders, which usually can be delivered within a couple of days. Free delivery is offered on orders over $150.00. Premium brands of bedding come with 15-20 year guarantees, and promotional with 1-year warranties. They hold monthly sales. With a purchase, you are also entitled to buy a frame at half-price, which saves you another $15 to $20.

Monday through Friday, the store is open from 10 am to 9 pm, and until 6 pm on Saturday. Personal checks are accepted, as are Master Charge, VISA, Central Charge, and NAC. Layaways are made with a 10% down payment and up to 60 days for final payment. There are no exchanges, according to the health laws of the state. But defective merchandise under warranty will be replaced or repaired. Parking available.

Design East
151 Riggs Road NE
Washington, DC
882-2300

A large showroom filled with very modern furniture, of medium to high medium quality, with discounts ranging from 10% to 50%. They represent 350 manufacturers of quality furniture from the US and Canada, including Thayer Coggin, Dixie, ChromeCraft, Monarch carpets, Sunset lamps, Basset and Lane furniture, Levolor blinds. All is first quality or discontinued styles. About 40% of their trade is in special orders, and they usually request a deposit of about 35%. Delivery is available at a charge, which usually runs about 2-4% of the total cost of the package. Workmanship is usually guaranteed. They have a mailing list and conduct special sales seasonally. They are also a franchised dealer for Simmons bedding.

Open from 10 am to 7 pm Monday through Saturday. They accept personal checks with proper identification, Master Charge, VISA, American Express, Central Charge, and NAC. On layaways, they request 1/3 down and 60 days to pay. You should talk to the manager in advance about returns or exchanges. There is a large parking lot on one side of the building.

Design Resource
8455-B Tyco Road,
Tyson's Corner, VA
790-8080

The motto: "famous names at unheard-of prices" — on everything for the interior, including design services. Design Resource sells the best of everything -- all special orders. They declined to list name brands but suggested that those who were interested should call with desired brands and check prices with them. Everything is first quality, and the discounts vary with the merchandise. They require a 50% deposit on the orders, and delivery usually takes from 8 to 12 weeks. Installation is extra. Most of the furniture is modern, with a limited choice of traditional styles. They have bookfuls of fabric samples, and catalogues, with just a few furniture samples in the showroom. They do have a mailing list for special sales and plan on having at least one special a year.

The hours at this catalogue showroom are Monday through Wednesday from 10 am to 5 pm, Thursday and Friday to 9 pm, and Sunday from noon to 5. Personal checks, Master Charge, VISA, and American Express are accepted. Returns are subject to a 25% stocking charge. Adequate parking is available.

Designer Sales Showroom
5803 Rolling Road
Springfield, VA
451-9183

What started as a shop for licensed designers and has everything for decorating a home is also open to the individual consumer. Medium to high quality furniture by such names as Clyde Pearson, Selig, Baker, Burlington, and Greiff Fabrics are commonly found here, all first quality with discounts ranging from 20%

Furniture, Bedding & Lighting   173

to 45% off suggested retail prices. They also have miscellaneous accessories in the showroom, and a gallery of brass beds. Most merchandise has to be ordered and takes a 10% deposit. Delivery is free within 50 miles. All products are warrantied, and they offer complete service should something need repair. Advertisements for special sales are found in the *Washington Post*. The showroom basically operates on a cost-plus basis. They also provide interior design services, with a staff of designers readily available.

The showroom is open from 10 am to 8:30 pm on Monday through Friday, until 5 pm on Saturday, and from noon to 5 pm on Sunday. Personal checks are accepted, as are all credit cards, which are actually used to finance your purchase through GEAC at the rate of 1½% per month. On layaways, they request 10% down, and pickup and final payment within up to a year. With a small deposit, an item will be held for you.

NOW! G.E. 4,000 Air cond. $129. Also (5,000 & 6,000)
APPLIANCE WAREHOUSE BARGAIN ANNEX
MERCHANDISE MART
NEAR NEW WHITE FLINT MALL
Washington's Own
American Interior Design Centre
Features Decorator-Mode Service to Select the Exact Style & Fabric, Etc. That suits your home best — Select from large variety of Name Brand FURNITURE, CARPETS, BEDS, WALLCOVERINGS, FLOOR COVERINGS, LAMPS, DRAPES—Also TV, Washers, Dryers, Dishwashers, Refrigerators, Etc.
...AT BIG SAVINGS!
Price makes friends... Quality keeps them!
MAJOR APPLIANCES — LOW, LOW PRICES
BUY DIRECT FROM WAREHOUSE DISPLAY
SINCE 1949
MERCHANDISE MART
U.S. MERCHANDISE MART
NEAR NEW WHITE FLINT MALL ®
5055 NICHOLSON LANE
3 Min. N. OF BELTWAY EXIT 19
2 BLOCKS OFF ROCKVILLE PIKE
NON/AFFILIATION WITH U.S. GOV'T.
AMERICAN INTERIOR DESIGN CENTRE BUILDING
(Phone) 881-3050

See Writeup on Page 384

Design Store Warehouse Clearance Center
9201 Gaither Road
Gaithersburg, MD
869-6212

The regular Design Store shops are well-known for their fabulous modern furniture and gifts. Many of these same items can be seen at the Clearance Center in one of its two departments: In the gift department, they feature closeouts, returns, special purchases, bulky items, and Marimekko fabrics. In the furniture section, they have factory clearance, discontinued, floor sample, and special purchase items. All of the brands are high quality, including COPCO kitchenware and teak from Thailand. Discounts on the giftware run from at least 33% to 40%, and on the furniture are from a minimum of 40% up to 75%. Delivery is available for $20 no matter where in the metro area, and same day service is guaranteed on Saturday and Sunday. Upholstered furniture is warrantied for two years; other merchandise is sold as is. They put newspaper ads for special sales in frequently, the biggest ones being three times a year, Thanksgiving and a couple of other occasions. On special purchase sales, items are sometimes priced below the factory price. The warehouse is open a couple of days before the sale, so that customers can inspect the furniture and other merchandise, but markdowns are not actually made until the day the sale begins.

Open from 10 am to 9 pm Monday through Friday, until 6 pm on Saturday, and from noon to 5 pm on Sunday. Personal checks are accepted, as are Master Charge, VISA, American Express, Central Charge, and NAC. There are no layaways, holds, returns, or exchanges. Ample parking is available.

Dinette Distributors
8453 C Tyco Road,
Tysons Corner, VA
893-1630

This is a relatively small showroom in a warehouse shell, specializing in kitchen and dining room sets. These run the gamut from very casual and inexpensive to some of the most attractive and elegant available, with a large number in the middle range — some with butcher block tops and some of chrome with glass table tops. Brands found here include Blacksmith Shop, Chromecraft, and Daystrom. Most are first quality or manufacturers' closeouts. Discounts run from 10% to 63% on the closeouts. Most items are in stock. They have delivery, but there is a charge for it. On special orders, you cannot expect as great a discount as on in-stock merchandise. Items are usually warrantied for one year by the manufacturers. Repairs are done here for warranty work. They have special sales on holidays.

Other address:
12225 Nebel St., Rockville, MD, 770-1430

Both stores are open from 10 am to 9 pm on Monday through Friday, from 10 am to 6 pm on Saturday, and Sunday from 11 am to 5 pm. Personal checks, Master Charge, and VISA are accepted forms of payment. 10% to 15% down is requested on layaways, with final pickup and payment within up to 6 months. Ask in advance about returns and exchanges. Small parking lot.

Dinette Gallery
9213 Baltimore Blvd.
College Park, MD
474-1440

The Dinette Gallery is a fairly large store, well-lighted and with a good selection of dinettes on display. In addition to the dinettes, you can also find dining room furniture and accessories like lamps and pictures here. Quality is usually upper medium, with such brands as Blacksmith, Cal-Style, Chromecraft, and Douglas. Most of the merchandise is first quality, and about 20% is closeouts. Discounts average 20% to 30% off list price. Delivery service is available. On special orders, which are infrequent, they ask for 20% down, and delivery takes about 4 to 6 weeks. They uphold the manufacturers' warranties, which are usually good for one year. Special sales are held on holidays, and they put weekly ads in the paper.

Store hours are from 11 am to 9 pm on Monday through Friday and from 10 am to 5 pm on Saturday. Personal checks, Master Charge, and VISA are accepted in payment. 20% down is requested on layaways, with final pickup and payment within 90 days. Usually they will hold merchandise for up to a week with a small deposit. Deposits are accepted within a day or two of purchase. There is a small parking lot.

Top Drawer
8909 McGaw Court
Columbia, MD
730-0320

In this warehouse style store, you can find a full range of furniture for your home, from contemporary to traditional styles. There are no brand names on the furniture, but quality is medium and up. The average discount is 10% to 30% below retail, and 50% off in the large Clearance Center and on factory closeouts. Knockdown furniture is found in the "Furniture to Go" section at prices 30% below usual retail. All merchandise is first quality, and much is in stock. A deposit of 1/3 is required on spec orders. Catalogue items are discounted 10% to 30%. Wallpaper, carpets, and window products are discounted 10% to 30%, depending on quantity. They also sell custom draperies.

Store hours are Monday, Thursday, and Friday from 10 am to 9 pm; Tuesday and Saturday until 6 pm; and Sunday from noon to 5 pm. Closed Wednesday. Personal checks are accepted, as are American Express, Master Charge, and VISA. Layaway terms are negotiable. Items will be held from 2 to 3 days with a deposit. They also allow CODs. Special orders can be canceled at no charge with 7 days. But sales are final on clearance items and "Furniture to Go". Parking is ample.

Famous Furniture & Bedding Barn
Rte 5
Waldorf, MD
843-1747

You can find here a full range of furniture and bedding: furniture by such manufacturers as Bassett, Clayton, Marcus, and Standard; as well as bedding by Sleep Bedding, Eastern Sleep, and Therapedics. All merchandise is first quality and manufacturers' closeouts. Discounts run from 10% to 30% off retail. Most items are in stock, with a minimum of 10% required on special orders. Delivery is available at a charge. Manufacturers' warranties are backed up by in-store repair people. They advertise specials in the newspapers.

Other addresses:
4724 Suitland Road, Suitland, MD, 568-1818

Hours are the same at all stores, from 10 am to 8 pm on Monday through Friday, to 6 pm on Saturday, and from noon to 5 pm on Sunday. They accept personal checks with identification, Master Charge, VISA, Central Charge, and NAC. Layaway policy is liberal. All sales are final.

Furniture and Carpetland
1582 Rockville Pike
(across from Congressional Plaza)
Rockville, MD
468-2929

Sister to Carpetland stores located in Georgetown and Alexandria, Furniture and Carpetland goes them one better by carrying furniture from medium to high quality by such manufacturers as Bassett, Lane, Burlington, and Globe. All merchandise is first quality, with some closeouts and irregulars. Most items are in stock, and free delivery is available. They have a mailing list and say that special sales are conducted during the spring and fall.

Hours are from 10 am to 9 pm on Monday through Friday, until 8 pm on Saturday, and from 11 am to 6 pm on Sunday. They accept personal checks, Master Charge, VISA, American Express, Central Charge, and NAC credit cards. On layaways, a 10% deposit is requested, with final payment in up to 6 weeks. Items will be held for up to 2 days. Cash refunds are given.

Furniture Surplus
7313 Livingston Road,
Oxon Hill, MD
567-6400

The outside of this store may remind you of the Salvation Army store, but inside the displays are attractive despite the clutter, and the merchandise is of an average grade. Furniture and bedding by manufacturers such as Thomasville, American of Martinsville, Stanley, Simmons, Serta, Burlington House, and Bassett are all carried, all first quality or manufacturers' closeouts. On closeouts, you can save 50%, and from 20% to 30% on other items. Most merchandise is in stock, and on special orders a small deposit is requested, with a wait of about 6 weeks. Free delivery is available. Premium bedding is guaranteed for 15 to 20 years, and everything else carries a one-year guarantee. Repairs are done here. They hold no special sales.

Open from Monday through Friday from 10 am to 8 pm and Saturday to 5 pm. Personal checks are accepted, as are Master Charge, VISA, and Central Charge. Layaway terms are liberal. They will hold items up to 24 hours. There are no returns on special orders, but other returns and exchanges are circumstantial A small parking lot.

Furniture World Factory Outlet
7329 Landover Road
Landover, MD
341-9292

They take away the frills and commissioned salespeople in order to give you 35% to 60% savings on furniture, bedding, carpeting, dinettes, and living room suites, by such names as Bassett, Broyhill, Lane, and Englander. All merchandise is first quality, with no closeouts or irregulars. Most merchandise is in stock, and they request 1/3 down on special orders, with 2 to 6 weeks wait. Delivery is available at a charge. They back the manufacturers' warranties, but do no repairs here. A mailing list is compiled from the list of purchasers. Special sales are held on holidays.

The store is open from 10 am to 7 pm on Monday through Saturday, and Thursday and Friday until 9 pm. Personal checks are accepted, as are Master Charge, VISA, American Express, Central Charge, and NAC. Layaway terms require a 10% down payment; final pickup must be within 90 days (at the longest). They will hold items with a deposit. There are no refunds, only store exchanges and credit. The policy is the same for special sale merchandise, unless otherwise stated. Small parking lot.

Gaithersburg Warehouse
9107 C Gaither Road
Gaithersburg, MD
840-1182

If it's office furniture you want, the Gaithersburg warehouse — all 10,000 square feet of it — is one place to look. In addition to the office furniture, about 10% of their stock is residential items like tables and chairs. Typical brands include Directional, Steelcase, and General Fireproofing. Most of their merchandise is first quality discontinued showroom samples, and they have some used and irregulars as well. You save at least 50% off standard retail prices. They also carry antiques and do refinishing and cabinet making in their own shop. You can find many one-of-a-kind items here. Delivery is available at a charge. Most sales are on an "as is" basis, but you can get repairs done here. While there is no mailing list, they do keep a list of individuals who ask to be informed when specific items come in. Advertisements are run periodically in the *Washington Star* and *Washington Post* classified sections.

Personal checks are accepted, as are Master Charge and VISA. They will hold merchandise with a deposit for a week or two. Exchanges are more commonly offered than returns.

Galleries by Gallahan's Furniture
105 Old Greenwich Drive
Fredericksburg, VA
From Virginia: 1-800-572-2700
MD or DC: 1-800-336-2770

HUGE is the only word to describe Gallahan's stores. You can get practically everything that you need to decorate an entire home in medium to high quality merchandise — lamps, furniture, carpets, and accessories. Styles are both traditional and contemporary. Brands found here include Henredon, La-Z-Boy, Davis, Stanley, and Thomasville. Most merchandise is first quality. Average savings run from 20% to 30%. Merchandise is well-displayed in room set-ups in one half of the store, and nicely arranged in other sections. There is an area devoted to bedding, one to carpeting, and one to early American furnishings. They also sell appliances and paintings. They discontinue some of their own merchandise and floor samples, with savings on these in excess of 40%-60%. Most items are in stock, and on special orders they ask for a 50% deposit and the balance when the merchandise comes in; or, if you pay in full when the order is written, they will give you a 3% discount. Delivery is free within a 100-mile radius of their store. They also offer a unique "on-the-road" decorator service, which is free within just about the same radius as delivery: they will bring samples, etc., into you home to help you design it. If merchandise has no warranty, they will give their own one-year limited warranty. All repairs are taken care of here. They have a mailing list, but it is used less now than it used to be.

Hours are from 10 am to 5 pm on Monday through Thursday to 8 pm on Friday, to 5 pm on Saturday, and from noon to 5 pm on Sunday. Personal checks and cash are accepted. Layaways are discouraged, but you can put a small deposit down and they will hold an item for you. There are no returns, but they will make exchanges. Ample parking.

Hecht's Home Furnishings Clearance Center
Virginia Plaza Shopping Center
Rte. 236 and I-395
Alexandria, VA
524-5100

The Virginia Plaza store is large, with two floors — the upper floor in use usually during large sales events. Most of the items found are furniture and appliances .out of Hecht's retail stores, cancellations, discontinued models, floor samples, and returned merchandise. On every one-of-a-kind piece, they have an automatic price reduction policy: the price is reduced 5% every 30 days. In general, discounts here range from 20% to 60%. Delivery is available at a charge. The store offers warranties on just about everything sold, except "as-is" merchandise. Holders of Hecht's charge cards are automatically put on a mailing list and get brochures for the three major sales they hold annually — around Christmas through January, in April, and in August. At this time, they sell domestics and housewares upstairs. The Parkington store is much smaller, and in it they carry furniture and appliances.

Other address:
In-store clearance center, Parkington Store, Arlington, VA, 524-5100.

Hours are the same for both stores: from 10 am to 9:30 pm on Monday through Saturday, and from noon to 6 pm on Sunday. Personal checks are accepted, as are Master Charge, VISA, American Express, and Hecht's Charge or Washington Shopping Plate. There are no layaways, but they will hold items up to 24 hours. Most merchandise is sold as is, but returns policy should be checked with manager if there is any question. Ample parking.

Knock-Down Outlet
Old Courthouse Road and Rte. 123
Tysons Corner, VA
356-4245

Knock-Down Outlet offers quality furniture made of solid woods at reasonable prices. Since all the furniture is modular, it is very easy to transport. They carry couches as well as wooden furnishings for the entire home. They carry no brand names — rather, a product is made to their company's specifications, and everything is first quality. The concept is unusual — it works like this: There are seven basic units which come in two finishes (one finish looks rustic, the other somewhat modern). The units are all 30" wide across the bottom and are either 20" or 30" tall. These are drawer and door units, which can all be stacked or used separately to create an endless variety of pieces of furniture. There are also bookshelf-type library units in a choice of natural finish or walnut stain. A store catalogue is available. They carry a selection of sleep sofas, all of foam, and modular seating with a limited choice of fabrics. Wood furniture comes flat in a box, and you could put a whole roomful of furniture in a small station wagon. All merchandise is warrantied for a year. The owner claims that there is never a bad piece of furniture — "only a faulty part" — and that such faulty parts can be replaced the same day that you discover them.

Other addresses:
Wisconsin at P Streets, NW, Washington, DC, 333-3777
Walnut Hill Shopping Center, Gaithersburg, MD, 948-1828

Hours at all stores are from Monday through Wednesday and Saturday from 10 am to 6 pm, Thursday and Friday to 9 pm, and Sunday from noon to 5. Personal checks are accepted, as are Master Charge, VISA, Central Charge, and NAC.

Lee's Dinettes
11201 Grandview Avenue
Wheaton, MD
946-5590

In a relatively spacious store, with attractive displays of medium quality furniture, you can find not only dinettes, but bar stools, wall systems, buffets, china closets, and bookshelves, by such makers as Blacksmith, Daystrom, Cal-Style, and Chrome Craft. Merchandise is all first quality, and you can save from 20% to 45% off average retail prices. Most items are in stock, and they request 1/3 down on special orders, with delivery in 4 to 8 weeks. Delivery is available and may be free, depending on the distance of your home from the store. Merchandise all comes with a one-year full guarantee.

Other address:
586 S. Washington Street, Falls Church, VA, 533-1020

Hours are from 10 am to 9 pm Monday and Friday, until 6 pm other nights, and closed on Sunday. Master Charge and VISA are accepted in payment. Layaway terms are liberal. Items will be held with a deposit. Exchanges are made.

Lee Furniture Warehouse Showroom
4596 Eisenhower Avenue
Alexandria, VA
751-4747

Lee's is a medium sized furniture warehouse, crowded with good quality merchandise for living room, dining room, bedroom, and accessories. Manufacturers such as Thomasville, American of Martinsville, Stanley, Lane, Globe, Bassett, Kroehler, Burlington, and Rowe are commonly found here, at discounts of 25% off the average. 80% of their business consists of special orders, for which a 1/3 to 1/2 deposit is required. Furniture will be delivered anywhere in the area for 3% of the net sale. While there are manufacturers' warranties, this family-operated concern also tries to give you its own personal guarantee of satisfaction. They have been advertising mostly in local papers and are just setting up a mailing list. Most of the furniture is traditional, with some contemporary, and a few early American pieces. All pieces are marked with suggested retail prices, as well as store prices. For example, we were shown a Clyde Pearson chair marked at $519, which Lee was selling for $409.

Open Tuesday through Friday from 10 am to 8 pm, Saturday until 6 pm, and Sunday from noon to 5 pm. They accept personal checks with proper identification, VISA, Master Charge, Central Charge, and Bank of Virginia charge plans. Layaway terms depend on the individual and the merchandise, but they usually don't like to hold items for a long time. Returns are discouraged on special orders — but it depends on each case. There are no problems with refunds or exchanges on merchandise bought off the selling floor.

Lu Anne Warehouse
6930 Wisconsin Avenue, Rear
Bethesda, MD
986-0040

For bedding of high quality from such manufacturers as Sealy, Simmons, Therapedic, Sleepwell, Springair, and Eclipse, you can go to Lu Anne Warehouse and save an average of 25% off of retail. Most items are in stock, and on special orders they ask a 25% deposit. Delivery is free on better merchandise. All merchandise is warrantied at least a year, and they back up the warranty. Repairs are done here. Every 6 to 8 weeks, they advertise special sales in the *Washington Post*.

Open Monday through Saturday from 10 am to 5:30 pm, Thursday night to 8 pm.

Closed Monday in July and August. Personal checks are accepted, as are Master Charge and VISA. On layaways, they request 10% down and payment and pickup within 30 days. Exchanges must be made within 30 days. Parking for 5 cars in back.

Mastercraft Interiors
14650 Southlawn Lane
Rockville, MD
279-2664

Mastercraft advertises that they sell fine quality merchandise at ½ the usual markup of a retail furniture store. The store is crowded, but furniture is tastefully displayed. In addition to what they claim is the largest selection of 18th century cherry and mahogany Queen Anne and Chippendale style pieces in the area, they offer a complete design service and stock oriental rugs. Manufacturers found here include Pennsylvania House, Hickory Chairs, and Kittinger. All merchandise is first quality. 40% of the merchandise is in stock; the rest is special order. They ask for a 1/3 deposit, and there is a wait of from 4 to 16 weeks on these orders. Most of the special orders are on upholstered goods. Most manufacturers do not give specific warranties, except for Pennsylvania House; but Mastercraft gives its own warranty that all merchandise is free of structural defects for a year. Bedding is warrantied for 15 to 20 years. They hold seasonal sales, during which they pass on the manufacturers' added discounts to the customer.

Hours are from 10 am to 9 pm on Monday through Friday, Saturday until 6 pm, and Sunday from noon to 5 pm. They accept Master Charge and VISA. Layaway terms are 1/3 deposit, and pickup and payment within 90 days. They will hold items for a liberal amount of time. Returns are situational — check with manager before buying. There is a small parking lot.

Mattress Center
3451 N. Fairfax Drive, Arlington, VA
527-6777

Two light open rooms of mattresses and sleep sofas by Serta, Sealy, Simmons, and Sleepwell, with average savings of 10% to 50% — that's what you'll find at the Mattress Center. Better savings are found on the discontinued items which they carry. Everything is backed with a warranty. Free delivery service is available inside the beltway. They also sell anodized brass beds by Dresher, as well as Regent sleep sofas and bedding by Sleepwell, a local (Norfolk, Va.) firm.

Hours are from 9 am to 5 pm on Monday, Tuesday, and Saturday, and until 9 pm on Wednesday, Thursday, and Friday. They accept VISA, Master Charge, and personal checks with proper identification. Free delivery inside the beltway. Ample parking.

Mattress Discounters
3000 Duke Street, Alexandria, VA
370-0404

This store offers discounts on mattresses by Sealey, Thereapedic, and LeMoine and on anodized brass headboards. Most items are in stock. All merchandise has a one-year unlimited warranty. They hold special sales on weekends and holidays. Merchandise, policy, and hours are the same at all stores.

Other addresses:
7430 Annapolis Road, Landover Hills, Lanham, MD, 459-4450
Intersection of St. Barnabas Road and Branch Ave., Marlow Heights, MD, 899-3070
2831 Gallows Road, Fairfax, VA, 573-0104

Open Monday through Friday from 10 am to 9 pm, Saturday until 6 pm. Personal checks are accepted with proper identification, as are NAC, Central Charge, American Express, Master Charge, and VISA. Layaway terms are negotiable. Exchanges are possible. There is a free small lot at Duke Street.

Military Personnel Buying Service, Inc.
2516 Columbia Pike Arlington, VA
920-1400

Appropriately located just outside the walls of Fort Myer, the Military Personnel Buying Service is also open to government personnel. The showroom is small and cramped, with many appliances displayed and a very little residential furniture. However, they can order (at a price representing about 5% over their cost) appliances and televisions by manufacturers like Sylvania, Kitchen Aid, Jennair, Kelvinator, Maytag, and Speed Queen. Carpets by such names as Alden and Alexander Smith are also sold here. A vast array of sofas, tables, chairs, beds, and flooring can all be ordered from medium and better quality manufacturers' catalogues. Factory warranties are upheld. Delivery is built into the price of the merchandise.

Open Monday and Thursday from 10 am to 8 pm, Tuesday, Wednesday, and Friday from 10 am until 6 pm, and Saturday from 9 am to 5 pm. They accept cash and personal checks with proper identification. Returns can be made on in-stock merchandise. Limited parking available.

Modern Age of Maryland
5544 Nicholson Lane
Rockville, MD
881-4646

Modern Age has an inviting showroom full of moderately priced modern and contemporary furniture, mostly of teak and walnut, and much of chrome and glass. They carry paintings and accessories as well. Most merchandise is first quality, and there are some manufacturers' closeouts. Savings on most items are roughly 20% below comparable retail, with the exception of Frederick Cooper lamps, which are not discounted. Most items are in stock, with special orders taking from 3 weeks to 6 months; a 20% deposit is required. Delivery is available at a charge. Merchandise is warrantied for one year. If there are any problems, someone from their service department will make in-home corrections. There is a mailing list for special sales, which are held about 3 or 4 times a year.

Open Monday and Thursday from 10 am to 9 pm, Wednesday, Friday, and Saturday until 6 pm, and Sunday from 12 to 5 pm. Personal checks are accepted, as are Master Charge, VISA, and American Express. Layaway terms are 20% down and (depending on the item) from 7 to 30 days for pickup. No returns on special orders. Return for credit within 7 days of purchase. Ample parking available.

Modern Mart
8455 G Tyco Road
Tysons Corner, VA
893-9198

The names are similar — Modern Age and Modern Mart — and so are the furnishings. At Modern Mart, however, there is oak and rosewood in addition to the teak, walnut, and chrome-and-glass furniture, as well as more designer type accessories. Brands represented include Thayer Coggin, Brookwood upholstered pieces, Custom Craft, and Lane. All merchandise is first quality. The minimum savings you can expect is 20% off comparable retail. They require a deposit of 20% on special orders. Delivery is available for $20. Merchandise is warrantied for one year, and repairs are done by this company. They do have a mailing list, and they often feature advertised special items. The store is in a warehouse shell, but it is light and inviting, with furniture tastefully displayed.

Open Monday and Thursday from 10 am to 9 pm, Tuesday through Saturday until 6 pm, and Sunday from noon to 5 pm. Personal checks, Master Charge, and VISA are accepted in payment. Layaway terms are 20% down, with 90 days to pay and pick up your merchandise. Returns or exchanges should be discussed in advance with the manager. A good-sized but crowded parking lot is available.

Montgomery Ward's Bargain Room Sales
7100 Old Landover Road
Landover, MD
341-7848

This is where Montgomery Ward in this area gets rid of discontinued, scratched and damaged furniture and large appliances, all from the same sources as their retail stores use. 25% minimum is taken off the original price of the merchandise. Under $100, there is an $8.50 delivery charge; delivery is free on purchases over $100. All items are sold "as is". Special sales are advertised in the newspapers.

Hours here are from 9 am to 8:30 pm, Monday through Saturday. Personal checks with identification, and Ward's

P. J. NEE—Discount Furniture Showcase

You'll never pay list prices at P.J. Nee. We sell America's finest brand name furniture at North Carolina discount prices — 20-40% off every day. Our prices include home delivery and service... and a 99-Year Tradition of dependability and customer satisfaction.

- Henredon
- Thomasville
- Hickory
- Burlington
- Pearson
- Hibriton
- White
- Flair
- Simmons
- Sealy
- Serta
- Howard
- American
- Dixie
- Lane
- Jasper
- National
- Hickory Tavern
- Union-National
- Hammery
- Thayer Coggin
- Davis

Plus many more

7126 WISCONSIN AVE., BETHESDA, MD. — PHONE 652-7000

own credit card are accepted. There are no layaways or holds, and all sales are final, which is made clear to you when you buy here.

P. J. Nee Clearance Center
7126 Wisconsin Avenue
Bethesda, MD
652-7000 or
(800) 492-8364

P.J. Nee still looks like the fine quality, full service retail furniture store it started out as over 99 years ago, and it still acts like it, offering a full repair shop, delivery service, and phone orders — but it's changed its pricing policy. The management decided to help its customers cope with these inflationary times and now offers all merchandise at discounts ranging from 20% to 40% off comparable retail prices. Most furniture is traditional, with some contemporary items. Henredon, Thomasville, Schoonbeck, Baker, Thayer Coggin, Clyde Pearson, Flair, Davis Cabinet, Century, and American of Martinsville are all found here. Mattresses and sleep sofas are by such manufacturers as White Cross, Sealy, Simmons, and Serta. All merchandise is first quality and some items are discontinued. Delivery is free within a 50 mile radius of the store. On special order merchandise, which most sales are, the same discount is offered as for in-stock merchandise. A brochure should be available soon. Merchandise is serviced free of charge for the first 90 days in your home, and in-home repairs are made as provided by the warranties. There is a mailing list for those who have purchased items here, and they have holiday sales. The store is filled with room set-ups on three floors, with approximately 30 dining room and 30 bedroom sets on display. One section is devoted to teen furniture and one section to casual furniture. They also sell carpeting, accessories, and oil paintings.

Other address:
Warehouse District Center, 9128 Gaither Road, Gaithersburg, MD

Hours are Monday through Saturday from 10 am to 6 pm, Monday and Thursday until 9 pm, and Sunday from noon to 5 pm. They accept personal checks, Master Charge, VISA, and GEAC revolving charge accounts in payment. Layaways are not encouraged, but they will write up advance sales for later delivery. They will hold items with deposit, depending on the situation. Exchanges can be made within a week of purchase. They have a small lot, and there are big public lots nearby as well as on-street parking. They take phone orders.

SCAN Furniture
7311 Arlington Blvd.
Loehmann's Plaza
Falls Church, VA
573-0100

Most Scan stores are large and filled with teak, oak, rosewood, and walnut modern furniture, some veneered, and some solid, within a range from moderate to high prices. You can also find upholstered furniture in a comparable range of prices. Price does depend on the type of wood used, as rosewood and walnut cost considerably more than teak and oak. Scan carries fine furniture imported from Scandinavian countries, as well as a limited selection of housewares, which are also contemporary in style. Their room displays are exciting and well-done. The range of prices and compatibility of many pieces makes Scan a place to buy when you are planning ahead. You can buy less expensive pieces now, and then later buy better pieces of the same woods to fit in with the older pieces. They have dining room, living room, study, and adults and children's bedroom furniture. Prices are said to be so reasonable because this is a CO-OP store — part of the Greenbelt Consumer Services cooperative.

Other addresses:
1054 31st Street NW, Washington, DC, 333-5015
4301 Connecticut Avenue NW, Washington, DC, 966-1916
13701 Georgia Avenue, Silver Spring, MD, 942-0600
Columbia Mall, Columbia, MD, (301) 730-1606
Warehouse Store, Savage, MD, 953-2050
6871 New Hampshire Avenue, Takoma Park, MD. 270-1550

Open Monday through Friday from 10 am to 9 pm, and Saturday from 10 am to 6 pm. They accept personal checks, VISA, Master Charge, and COOP Credit plans. They will hold items for up to 30 days. A 25% deposit is requested on all orders. Except for small items, everything is delivered free.

Scherr Furniture
12340 Parklawn Drive
Rockville, MD
770-6892

Scherr carries used rental furniture as well as brand-new in-stock and custom order furniture. At the time of our visit, most was either contemporary or traditional. Brands are generally in the medium range, by makers such as Lane, American of Martinsville, Davis Cabinet, Basset, American Drew, and Bracewell. All merchandise is first quality. Discounts are 25% on new merchandise and usually over 50% on used merchandise. On special orders they request a 50% deposit. New merchandise is delivered free, and there is a $15 delivery charge on used items. They back up the manufacturers' warranties. They have a mailing list, and special sales every weekend.

They also feature a wide range of accessories, like lamps, mirrors, and other decorative items.

Open from Monday through Friday from 9 am to 6 pm, and from 9:30 am to 5 pm on Saturday. Personal checks are accepted, as are Master Charge, VISA, Central Charge, and NAC. They request 25% down on layaways, with 30 days to pickup and final payment. They will hold items for 24 hours. Check with manager in advance about returns. All used merchandise is sold "as is". Parking in medium-sized lot in front of store.

Sears Furniture and Appliance Clearance Center
911 Bladensburg Road, NE
Washington, DC
399-7500

For regular store brand appliances and furniture from Sears, but which have been discontinued, damaged, or used and reconditioned, this store offers discounts which run from 18% to 80%. The items are displayed in a warehouse fashion at the back of the Bladensburg Road Sears store. Delivery is available, cost depending on your distance from the store. Sears' regular "satisfaction guaranteed" policy applies here also; and if something goes wrong, they will arrange for repairs, or you will get your money back — as long as merchandise was not sold on an "as is" basis. They put advertisements in the *Washington Post* for the special sales. From the flyers which they print for these special sales, it appears that the best buys are on furniture and bedding; the bargains on appliances (which are all Kenmore) seem more limited.

Other address: Rte. 5, Waldorf, MD, (301) 645-3601

The store is open daily from 9:30 am to 6 pm, Monday and Friday to 8 pm, and closed on Sunday. Personal checks are accepted, as is the Sears charge card.

There are no layaways, but they will hold merchandise for you for up to 48 hours without a deposit. Return policy is flexible, and you should discuss it with the manager before buying. Parking lot in back and on-street parking in front.

Sleep King
7240 Arlington Blvd.
Falls Church, VA
573-5908

Sleep King is a small, but light and airy shop, crammed with bedding by such manufacturers as Serta, Reliance and Eclipse, and sleep sofas by Serta, Lambert, Brookwood, and Schweiger. All merchandise is first quality, and savings can range up to 50% off comparable retail. Delivery is free within a specified area. Most of the sleep sofas come with a 1-year guarantee, and bedding warranties run from 1 to 15 years. Most bedding is in stock for immediate delivery, but most sleep sofas have to be ordered, except for what is in stock.

Open Monday through Friday from 10 am to 9 pm, Saturday until 6 pm, and Sunday from noon to 5 pm. They accept personal checks, VISA, and Master Charge. They will replace or repair damaged merchandise. Delivery is free within immediate area. Layaways are 10% down, with payments every 2 weeks, up to 3 months. There is a medium-sized parking lot.

Slumberland
9608 Fort Meade Road
Laurel Plaza
Laurel, MD
498-7750

Slumberland sells bedding, sleep sofas, and brass beds by manufacturers such as Sealy, Serta, Englander, and King Koil, with discounts from comparable retail ranging from 15% to 25% on most first quality merchandise and some manufacturers' closeouts. Most merchandise is in stock, but upholstered pieces usually need to be special ordered. They also take telephone orders. Delivery is available at a charge. Special sales are held weekly.

Other address:
5620 Kenilworth Avenue, Riverdale, MD, 927-2466

Hours are from 10 am to 9 pm Monday through Friday and to 6 pm on Saturday. They take telephone orders. They accept personal checks, Master Charge, VISA, American Express, Central Charge, and NAC. They will hold items for up to 30 days. There are no returns or exchanges. There is a large free parking lot.

Southern Furniture Surplus
5522 Leesburg Pike
Baileys Crossroads, VA
671-3777

This is a "wonder" store — you'll wonder how they managed to get so much furniture into the space! The large store is jam-packed with merchandise throughout; it's even stacked up toward the back. The quality is mostly medium, with mostly first quality, some closeouts, and a few special purchase items. In-stock merchandise is usually cheaper than special orders, but the cost savings depends on the item. Delivery is available at a charge. Warranties are backed up by the store's own repairman, who takes care of any problems. Once in a while, an advertisement in their display window will announce an additional 10% off everything in the store.

The store is open from 10 am to 9 pm Monday through Friday, until 6 pm on Saturday, and from noon to 5 pm on Sunday. Personal checks are accepted, as are Master Charge, VISA, American Express, Central Charge, and NAC. Layaway terms are flexible. They will also hold items with a small deposit. Exchanges are handled on an individual basis, usually within 72 hours. Defective merchandise or freight-damaged merchandise will be repaired or replaced with no charge for redelivery.

Springfield Furniture
(Catalogue Furniture Sales)
7970 Forbes Place
Springfield, VA
321-8811

This large furniture warehouse yielded a pleasant surprise: though its ambiance is definitely "no frills", the merchandise turned out to be of medium and better quality. Such manufacturers as Thomasville and Baker are typical, and 200 brand names are carried. All merchandise is first quality, and they work on a cost-plus basis, saving the consumer from 20% to 30% on the average. About one half of their sales are from in-stock merchandise, and the other half from manufacturers' catalogues. On these special orders, they ask 50% deposit. Most furniture is traditional, with some very nice Victorian reproduction lines being carried here as well.

The store is open from 10 am to 9 pm from Monday through Friday, and until 6 pm on Saturday. Personal checks are accepted, as are Master Charge, VISA, and NAC. Items will be held for up to 24 hours. There are no returns or exchanges.

Stanis Furniture
2800 Dorr Avenue
Fairfax, VA
573-7082

Stanis Furniture is well-organized: in the front room, you can look through fabric samples and manufacturers' catalogues at comfortable tables with club-style chairs and consult with their sales personnel, or you can proceed to the small warehouse in back, where the traditional Queen Anne and other 18th century lines are displayed. Savings are substantial on such manufacturers as Serta, Flexsteel, Pearson, Jasper, Crawford, Reprodux, and Bernhardt. All merchandise is first quality, and all from fine woods. They do refinishing and make in-home service calls, and there is free delivery in the metro area. Much of their business is from special orders.

Open daily from 10 am to 9 pm, Saturday until 6 pm, and Sunday from noon to 5 pm. Monday holidays they are open from 10 am to 6 pm. They accept personal checks with proper identification, and VISA and Master Charge as well. Returns are accepted. Parking is limited.

Stofberg Brothers
2626 W. Patapsco
Baltimore, MD
(301) 644-1700

Stofberg Brothers' place is a large, large store filled with a full range of contemporary and traditional furniture by such well-known manufacturers as American of Martinsville, Beechley, Burlington, Thayer Coggin, Stiffel, Thomasville, Century, Hickory Manufacturing and Hickory Chairs, as well as Forecast custom-upholstered items, and Bennington pine furniture. Discounts on all merchandise, which is first quality, range from 20% to 35%. Delivery is free within the immediate Baltimore area. Deposits are taken on custom orders. All upholstered goods are on special orders. They back up manufacturers' warranties, and they service what they sell. There is a mailing list, and if you are on it you are invited to four special sales per year.

This store is open daily from 9 am to 5 pm, Monday and Thursday until 9 pm, *and Saturday until 3 pm. Personal checks are accepted, but no credit cards. There are no layaways, but they will hold items which are not being closed out, or which are not on special sale. All sales are final. Medium sized parking lot.*

Turnpike House Furniture
9960 Main Street
Fairfax, VA
691-1010

Turnpike House is an extremely large store, with average savings of 25% below manufacturers' retail prices. Concentrating on traditional styles, they carry such brands as Henredon, Hinkel Harris, Jasper, Thomasville, Schoonbeck — all in the middle to upper middle furniture quality range, and including about 200 brands altogether. All merchandise is guaranteed to be delivered in perfect condition. They also have four interior designers who will go out and help you in your home. All merchandise is first quality, and they claim that they will meet North Carolina or anyone's verifiable price (but will give only a limited warranty under those conditions).

Open daily from 9 am to 9 pm, Saturday until 6 pm. They offer 30, 60, and 90 day accounts. Ample parking.

Village Sleep Shop
15900 Shady Grove Road,
Gaithersburg, MD
948-8858, 8859

Furniture, bedding, brass beds, sleep sofas, wall units, brass pole lamps, and mirrors can all be purchased at the Village Sleep Shop. Brands include Brass Beds of America, Wesley-Allen, Swan, Sealy, Serta, Regents, Flexsteel, and Schweiger. All merchandise is first quality. Savings run 5% on the bedding and

Furniture, Bedding & Lighting

20% on other items. Most has to be ordered. You save about 5% to 10% on the promotional lines, 15% on premium top-of-the-line bedding, and 20% on items from other departments. Most merchandise has to be ordered, and they ask a 20% down payment with delivery within 6 weeks. Delivery is free within the local area. Bedding warranties vary, usually one year on promotional bedding and fifteen on premium. Sales are frequent. The store is large and well-lighted and has a particularly good selection of brass beds. Personnel are quite knowledgeable.

The store is open from 9 am to 9 pm on Monday through Friday, until 6 pm on Saturday, and from noon to 5 pm on Sunday. Personal checks are accepted, as are Master Charge, VISA, Central Charge, and NAC. Layaway terms vary with merchandise and purchaser. Return policy is liberal, but there are no cancellations on special orders. Ample parking

W. & J. Sloan Clearance Centers
4025 28th Street South
Arlington, VA
578-4885

Furniture for the living room, dining room, and bedroom — as well as some office and summer furniture — can be purchased at these stores. The emphasis is on good medium quality furniture, with such brands as Henredon, Jasper, and Baker represented here. Merchandise is first quality, closeouts, and some irregulars and seconds, which are labeled. The average savings are from 20% on some items to 40% off comparable retail on most. Most items are in stock, but there are some special orders. On special orders, you are asked to pay in full in advance. Delivery is available for a price. Only a few items can be special ordered — and these include upholstered pieces like chairs and couches. Furniture is warrantied. There is a mailing list, and

---

"For value, service and peace of mind shop Turnpike House"

Philadelphia High Boy
Circa 1740

Quality Furniture Brands
OVER 200 INCLUDING:

Henredon	Hickory Mfg.	Hitchcock Chair
Henkel Harris	Barcalounger	Vanguard
Stiffel Lamps	Weiman	Key City
Clyde Pearson	Gordon	Jasper
Thomasville	Sumter	Caro Craft
Kling	La-z-Boy	Dixie
Classic Leather	Burlington House	Lane
Gilliam	American Drew	Tell City
Wildwood	Brandt	Temple Stuart

PRICE AND SERVICE POLICIES

- EVERYDAY DISCOUNTS FROM MANUFACTURERS RETAIL PRICES, PLEASE CALL FOR PRICE QUOTES.
- WE WILL MEET ANY VERIFIABLE DELIVERED PRICE FROM ANY AUTHORIZED DEALER INCLUDING NORTH CAROLINA OUTLETS.
- NEVER A DELIVERY OR SET-UP CHARGE
- EXCELLENT STAFF OF INTERIOR DESIGNERS TO ASSIST YOU IN YOUR HOME OR IN OUR SHOWROOM
- LARGE DECORATED SHOWROOM FOR UNDISTURBED BROWSING AND DECORATING IDEAS
- EVERY PURCHASE CAREFULLY INSPECTED CLEANED AND POLISHED PRIOR TO DELIVERY
- EXCELLENT AFTER-THE-SALE SERVICE
- OUR 15TH YEAR OF SERVICE TO OUR CUSTOMERS

FAIRDALE FURNITURE'S

Turnpike House

9960 Main Street, Fairfax, VA
591-5882
"Your Quality Furniture Store in Fairfax"

Location: Fairview Plaza Shopping Ctr. on Rt. 236, 1 Mi. East of Fairfax Courthouse, Beltway Exit 6W, 4½ Mi.

special sales are held almost every week. This is part of Sloane's Furniture Store; it does not carry just closeouts on Sloane's merchandise, but also carries other lines at different price levels.

Other addresses:
4433 Connecticut Avenue, NW, Washington, DC, 363-1877
10400 Old Georgetown Road, Bethesda, MD, 530-7240
57 Monroe Street, Rockville, MD, 279-2400
9480 Main Street, Fairfax, VA, 978-2100

All stores have the same hours: Monday through Friday from 10 am to 9 pm, Saturday until 6 pm, and Sunday from noon to 5 pm. They accept payment by personal check, Master Charge, VISA, American Express, and Central Charge. They will accept deposits and hold merchandise for a limited time, but there are no layaways. All sales are final.

Warehouse Sleep Centers
9629 Lee Highway
Fairfax, VA
273-2228

Rowe, Sealy, Simmons, and King Koil bedding, Swan brass beds, and Bonderized Brass Beds — this is what you can find at the Warehouse Sleep Centers, all at discounts from 15% to 30%. The stores are large and modern, with merchandise neatly arranged. Most merchandise is in stock. While delivery is available, you can save an additional $20 by taking your purchase with you. They also carry folding cots and bunk beds. The salespeople seem quite knowledgeable.

Other address:
366 S. Pickett Street, Alexandria, VA, 751-3580

Hours here are from 10 am to 9 pm on Monday through Friday, until 6 pm on Saturday, and on Sunday from noon to 5 pm. They accept Master Charge, VISA, and Central Charge. Because of health laws, there are returns only on damaged or defective merchandise. There is no minimum deposit on layaways, but payments should be regular and completed within 4 to 6 months. Ample parking is available.

Woodward & Lothrop Shirley Retail Store
Edsall Road Exit, west off I-395
Springfield, VA
750-1600

Except when they have their special sales, which occur four times a year, this store serves as a clearance center for furniture and appliances of discontinued, closeouts, and damaged merchandise from Woodward and Lothrop stores. When they have the special sales, they also feature a wide range of housewares and accessories, which are also discontinued, etc. Discounts are good, but they declined to mention the average price. The store is basically a large room in the front of a huge warehouse, with furniture arranged neatly throughout. For the special sales, the warehouse is open to the public, with all of the goods displayed, carnival-like, between the massive aisles of stored furniture.

Open Monday through Saturday from 10 am to 9 pm, and Sunday from noon to 6 pm. Personal checks are accepted, as are Master Charge, VISA, American Express, and Woodies' or the Washington Shopping Plate. There are no layaways, but they will hold items for up to 24 hours. There are no firm rules for returns, but basically most merchandise is sold on an "as is" basis.

WHERE TO FIND LIGHTING BUYS

Alexandria Lighting Supply
701 N. Henry,
Alexandria, VA
548-2320

Cardinal Lighting
10358 Lee Highway
Fairfax, VA
591-8060

Cardinal Lighting carries lamps and chandeliers, as well as a line of energy-saving dimmers, gas detectors, fixtures, clocks, bulbs, track lighting, doorbells, and the expected table and floor lamps. Discounts range from 20% to 40% off of comparable retail prices. You can find well-known brands here like Lectrics, Kichler, Fine Art, Remington, and Sedgfield, as well as Casablanca ceiling fans. All merchandise is first quality. They do chandelier and lamp repairs, and they stand on their service, guaranteeing in-home service within 1 year of purchase on most items. They will also special order merchandise for you.

They accept VISA, NAC, and Master Charge, as well as personal checks with proper identification. Their layaway policy is liberal. Returns or exchanges can be made on unused items (with receipt) within a reasonable period of time. Ample parking is available in the shopping center lot.

Consolidated Electrical Distributors (previously Prince George's Electric)
4822 Lawrence Street
Bladensburg, MD
779-1000

This store is primarily geared to the contractor or building professional, but maintains a small shop, called the Chandelier Room, at which individuals are allowed to shop. The store stocks such items as fixtures, chandeliers, track lighting, intercoms, bells, doorbells, and bulbs. They carry a wide range of brands, including Progress and Forecast, and Nutone bells. Prices average below retail, but a bit above what the contractor pays. Delivery is available on very large orders. They will honor manufacturers' warranties, returning problem merchandise to the factory for repair or replacement. The manager here offered two hints for buying lighting: always inspect the contents of the carton before you leave the store to make sure nothing is broken, and always purchase your bulbs at the same time as the fixture to make sure you get the right size and type of bulb.

The store is open daily from 7:30 am to 5 pm, and on Saturday to 1 pm. Personal checks and VISA are accepted. There are no holds or layaways, and returns and exchanges are discouraged. There is a small crowded parking lot with adequate parking.

Dominion Electric Supply Co.
5053 Lee Hwy,
Arlington, VA
536-4400

Other address:
22 K Street, NE, Washington, DC,
789-0500

Eagle Electric
940 New York Ave. NW
Washington, DC
628-0950

Interstate Electric Supply Co.
8435 Lee Highway
Fairfax, VA
560-2500

You can expect to save an average of 33% on merchandise which you buy here, which includes chandeliers, fixtures, ceiling fans, and medicine cabinets. They also carry special dimmer switches, clocks, and doorbells, as well as Casablanca fans; and they feature Rittenhouse sound and security systems. The showroom is medium-sized and nicely organized, with all first quality merchandise. They have 36,000 square feet of warehouse space and usually have just about everything in stock. An illustrated color catalogue is also available.

Hours here are Monday through Friday from 8 am to 5 pm, Wednesday until 9 pm, and Saturday from 8 am to 1 pm. They accept charge cards with a minimum purchase of $5, including Central Charge, VISA, and Master Charge. There are no refunds or exchanges, but if you insist on a return, you must have the invoice and are subject to a 20% handling/restocking charge. Ample parking in their own lot.

Joseph M. Catalano Co., Inc.
929 W. Broad Street
Falls Church, VA
534-8400

Catalano's is a large showroom full of lamps, chandeliers, and other fixtures at discount prices. Discounts on lamps run 25%, and 40% on lighting fixtures. They carry such brand names as Rembrandt, Lightolier, Remington, and Frederick Cooper, and they also sell Nutone doorbells. All merchandise is first quality, and they do take special orders.

This store is open from 7:30 am to 5 pm on Monday through Friday, Thursday to 9 pm, and Saturday until 4 pm. They accept personal checks. Returns must be made within 10 days of purchase and are subject to a 20% restocking charge. Free delivery with a minimum purchase of $25.00. Ample parking in store lot.

Kole's Lighting Showroom
Shady Grove and Gaithersburg Rds.
Gaithersburg, MD
948-6434

Kole's sells traditional, contemporary, and colonial lighting fixtures, wall lamps, table lamps, and track lighting, as well as hand-leaded Tiffany-style lamps and Casablanca decorative ceiling fans. Popular brands usually found here include Halo Track, Georgian Art, Forecast, Schonbeck, Laurel, and Remington. All merchandise is first quality. 80% of merchandise is in stock, with a deposit of 1/3 requested on special orders. Repairs are done here. Sales are held frequently. They also give free lighting design consultation.

Open from 9 am to 6 pm Monday, Tuesday, Wednesday, and Saturday; and until 9 pm on Thursday and Friday. They accept personal checks, Master

Charge, and VISA. On layaways, they request 1/3 down, and final payment and pickup within a reasonable period of time. They will hold items with a deposit beyond 24 hours — without deposit, a maximum of 24 hours. In-stock merchandise can be returned for cash, credit, or other refund. There is a small parking lot.

Lamp & Shade Center
9691 Lee Highway
Fairfax, VA
691-0494

You can find table and standing lamps, chandeliers, and ceiling fixtures discounted at 35% to 40% off retail price here, with medium quality and some designer quality lines being carried. Some commonly found brands here include Westwood, Luxo, Toga, and Stiffel. All merchandise is first quality. All merchandise is in stock, but you can order from manufacturers' catalogs if you wish. They give guarantees on wiring and sockets and will do repairs on warranty work, as well as your own merchandise. Holiday special sales. The stores are very neat, medium-sized, and well-organized.

Other addresses:
7406 Little River Turnpike, Annandale, VA, 941-2966
5714 Connecticut Avenue, Washington, DC (Chevy Chase Circle), 362-4312. Free parking in rear.

Hours are Monday, Thursday, and Friday from 10 am to 9 pm, and Tuesday, Wednesday, and Saturday to 6 pm. They accept personal checks, VISA, Central Charge, and Master Charge. Refunds are given within seven days of purchase. Items can be held for 24 hours. There is ample parking at all locations.

Lamps Unlimited
Springfield Mall Shopping Center
Springfield, VA
971-7585

The best buys at this chain of stores can be found at the clearance centers. The shopping mall locations are long, narrow stores, each carrying a wide selection of lampshades, standing and table lamps, fixtures, wall lamps, Lightolier fittings, and Clover fixtures. You can expect to save 40% off list price on fixtures, including Lightolier. Well-known brands featured here include Stiffel, Murray Fais, Schonbeck, and Laurel Contemporary. They also take special orders. They do lamp repairs and will help to fit shades to specific lamps. At the clearance centers, they carry irregulars and manufacturers' closeouts.

Other addresses:
Tyson's Corner Center, VA, 893-3188
Seven Corners Shopping Center, Seven Corners, VA, 534-9440
1509 Rockville Pike, Rockville, MD, 881-5666
Riverdale and Annapolis Roads in Carrollton Mall, Carrollton, MD, 577-7177
Clearance centers at Shirlington Shopping Center, Arlington, VA, 578-0810, and 11610 Rockville Pike in Rockville, MD, 881-5623.

These stores are open from 10 am to 9:30 pm Monday through Saturday, and from noon to 5 pm on Sunday. They accept personal checks, VISA, Master Charge, and Central Charge credit cards. Ample parking at mall stores.

Lighting Gallery
6715 Backlick Road
Springfield, VA
451-3300

The Lighting Gallery stores are very attractive and neatly organized, selling chandeliers, fixtures, swags, lighting accessories, and wall brackets, with a few table and floor lamps in evidence at the Springfield store. They feature imported crystal lighting, handmade Tiffany-style shades, and track and recessed lighting. Brands are from medium to high quality, and all first quality merchandise, by such manufacturers as Lightolier, Sounamon, Kenroy, Halcolite, Progress, Juno, Weiss & Biheller, Forecast, and Georgian Art. Discounts are 40% off the retail price of fixtures. While roughly 80% of the merchandise is in stock, they will take special orders with a 50% deposit. The store stands by the manufacturer's warranty. Sales are held frequently.

Other address:
12340 Parklawn Drive, Rockville, MD, 881-9222

Hours here are Monday through Saturday from 9 am to 6 pm, Monday and Thursday to 9 pm, and (in summer only) Saturday until 2 pm. They accept VISA, Master Charge, and personal checks with proper identification. They ask for 50% down on most layaways, with 30-60 days for final payment and pickup. Ample parking in both locations.

Reed Electric Co.
1611 Wisconsin Avenue, NW
Washington, DC
338-7500

Reed Electric has just moved to new and larger headquarters in Georgetown and features a complete line of bulbs, fixtures, floor and table lamps, track lights, recessed lighting, Casablanca fans, and all related hardware items. Popular brands usually found here include Majestic, and Weiss & Biheller. All merchandise is first quality. While they take special orders, they prefer to minimize them. Also featured is an unusual collection of crystal chandeliers from Czechoslovakia and Austria. Delivery is available, as is installation at additional cost. There is a complete lamp repair shop downstairs on the lower level, where lamps can be made to your specifications. They advertise featured items weekly. The downstairs showroom features shades, as well as ceiling fans by such makers as Casablanca, Fasco, and Caribe.

This store is open from 8:30 am to 6 pm on Monday through Saturday. They accept in payment personal checks with proper identification, Master Charge, VISA, American Express, and Central Charge cards. They generally do not have layaways, but they will hold items for up to 24 hours. Exchanges are preferred — returns are subject to a 10% restocking charge. Bulb sales are final. There is a medium-sized free parking lot.

Sunlighting
6533 Arlington Blvd.
Falls Church, VA
534-1010

Sunlighting's largest store is at the Falls Church location — and it is quite large, featuring 119 brands of lamps, shades, and accessories in a complete lamp store on several levels. Merchandise is well-displayed. On chandeliers, you can expect to save 40%, and a minimum of 10% on other items. Name brands sold here include Stiffel, Westwood, Mobilite, Keystone, and others. They also carry a large selection of mirrors in modern and traditional styles. All lamps come with a lifetime guarantee.

Other addresses:
Congressional Plaza, Rockville, MD, 881-3433 (Lamp and Bath Center)
568 N. Frederick Avenue, Gaithersburg Square, Gaithersburg, MD, 926-2443
Marlow Heights Shopping Center, Marlow Heights, MD, 423-1662

The store is open from 10 am to 9 pm on Monday, Thursday, and Friday; and to 5:30 pm on Tuesday, Wednesday, and Saturday. The other addresses have different hours. There are Sunday hours in winter. They accept VISA, Master Charge, Central Charge, and personal checks with proper identification. Returns can be made within 10 days of purchase with receipt. On the layaways, they request 1/3 down with no maximum time to pay up the rest. Ample parking at all locations.

MAIL ORDER

Antique Export Establishment
P.O. Box 21 498
LF 9493
Mauren, Liechtenstein

Write about catalogue. Discounts up to 90% off comparable prices.

Lamp Warehouse
1073 39th Street,
Brooklyn, New York 11219

Any lamps by Stiffel, Fine Art, Westwood, or other brands — write for price quote and discount up to 30%.

National Furniture and Fabrics Sales
1949A W. Green Drive
P.O. Box 2314
High Point, North Carolina 27261
(800) 334-2509

Upholstered furniture by National Furniture and by well-known names. Catalogues are $2 for National's, $5 for brand names, or $5 for both. Discounts range up to 40%.

Plexi-Craft Quality Products Corporation
195 Chrystie Street,
New York, New York 10002

Plexiglas accessories for over 50% less than retail. Catalogue costs $1.00.

Sion Fuk Enterprises
125-2 Wu-Fu 2nd Rd.
Kaohsiung, Taiwan,
Republic of China

A small catalogue for $5.00 with well-designed pieces of furniture in rosewood, teak, and camphorwood. Prices run 30% to 70% below comparable. One problem: minimum US order is $5,000.

RELATED PUBLICATIONS

Aronson, Joseph, *Encyclopedia of Furniture*. New York: Crown Publishers, Inc., 1965.

Cannel, Elaine, *How to Invest in Beautiful Things Without Being a Millionaire*. New York: David McKay Company, 1971.

Grotz, George. *The Fun of Refinishing Furniture*. Dolphin Book, Doubleday & Co., Inc., Garden City, NY, 1979.

"Mattress Buymanship", *Better Homes and Gardens*, May, 1979.

Williams, Patricia M. *Buying Home Furnishings: Beating the Home Furnishings Experts at Their Own Game*. New York: St. Martin's Press, 1975.

Zakas, Spiros. *Furniture in 24 Hours* and *More Furniture in 24 Hours*. New York: St. Martin's Press, 1978, $5.95. Spiros Zakas and his students at the Parsons School of Design offer a variety of designs — some casual, some outlandish, and some elegant — that the do-it-yourselfer should not find too difficult to accomplish. Photos of each, list of tools, cost, time to make it, and detailed plans and sketches are provided for each.

For the Office

OFFICE SUPPLIES, MACHINES, AND FURNITURE

Even if you have never worked for a large company, you probably know that larger firms and commercial accounts usually get quantity discounts on their purchases. And you, as an individual or perhaps as the owner of a small business, probably wish that you could get that same preferential treatment. And you can — at many of the stores listed in this section. Although on many items the discount will not be as great as a large firm would receive, the prices should still fall substantially below current retail prices for the same items. Many of these stores have a sliding scale of charges, with price per unit declining as you buy more units. And, if you do choose to buy in quantity — either by organizing a group of friends for a single large purpose, or forming a buying club for continuing purchases - you should request an increased discount.

**Central Office Supply Co., a division of Central Business Machines
911 12th Street NW
Washington, DC
628-0800**

This store carries a full range of office supplies — from paper clips to furniture. And it is filled with practically every name brand, all of first quality. While this store isn't set up like a retail store, they also have catalogues from which you can order items they have in stock or will have to order specially for you. On special orders, a deposit of about 25% is usually required. But they have ample warehouse space, and most office supplies are in stock. They stand behind all of their merchandise and will replace defective items. If you get on the mailing list, you will be sent a "hot list", which is issued periodically and lists the featured items, the Central Office Supply price, and the customary list price. Discounts range widely, depending on the item, but we noted 40% and 50% discounts on some.

Hours are Monday through Friday from 8:30 am to 5:30 pm. Personal checks are accepted, but business checks are preferred. VISA and Central Charge are accepted. Merchandise can be returned within a liberal time range for credit to the account or exchange. On returns that were special orders, a 20% restocking fee is assessed. Telephone orders are taken, and there is a $20 minimum order for deliveries, which are then free within about a 20-25 mile radius of the District of Columbia.

MARK CENTER - 10 MINUTES FROM THE WHITE HOUSE

A campus-style office environment, unique in the Washington Metropolitan area, only 5 minutes from the Pentagon. One hundred thirty acres of wooded park with 3,000,000 square feet of quality office space under development. Project will include a luxury resort hotel and conference center. Join Prudential, CNA, Control Data, Potomac Research and our other tenants; they are our best references.

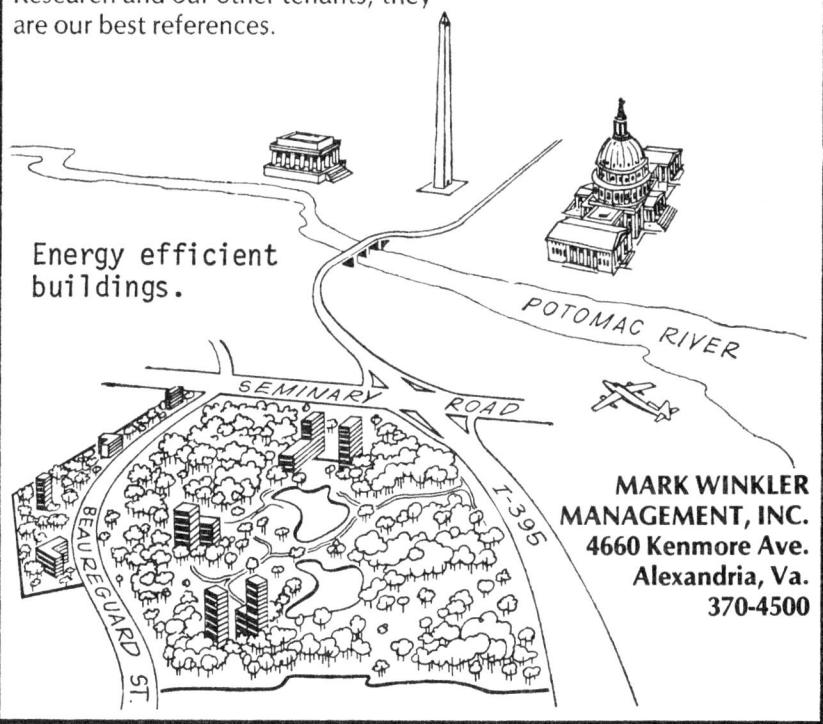

Energy efficient buildings.

MARK WINKLER MANAGEMENT, INC.
4660 Kenmore Ave.
Alexandria, Va.
370-4500

Desks and Furnishings Office Furniture Clearance Center
2810 S. Quincy Street
Shirlington/Arlington, VA
931-8550

Before saying anything else, please note that Desks and Furnishings (D&F) also discounts all of its first quality name brand merchandise at its regular retail stores — and there is a big color catalogue which you can obtain by asking for it or by being put on the mailing list. But, for the really good buys, you should shop their Clearance Centers. At these centers, they feature anything you could find in their retail stores — including office furniture and accessories. In the clearance stores, however, the quality is mostly medium, whereas the retail stores sell some very fine office furniture. At the retail store, everything is first quality. At the Centers, discontinued, used, and damaged goods, and clearance items make up the inventory. Discounts average up to 40% off retail. You can put in special orders for new merchandise at the retail stores. Also, on new catalogue/retail store items, you get a discount on delivery by paying cash or with a check; otherwise, there is a $10 minimum delivery charge, which goes up with your distance from the store. This Shirlington Center is very large and offers many choices to the prospective office furniture buyer.

Other addresses:
513 Rhode Island Avenue NE, Washington, DC, 832-0586
11850 Rockville Pike, Rockville, MD, 881-6950
There are also a number of retail stores, which are listed in your local telephone book.

Hours here are Monday through Friday from 10 am to 7 pm, Thursday to 9 pm, and Saturday from 10 am to 4 pm. Hours vary by store. Personal checks are accepted with proper identification, as are Master Charge, VISA, American Express, Central Charge, and NAC. 10% deposit is required on layaways, with liberal time for final payment and pickup. They will hold items for three days. There are no cash refunds — all sales are final, except for new merchandise, which can be returned if you are not satisfied or if it is defective. They have their own parking lot at the Shirlington location, and sufficient parking at the other stores.

Discount Typewriter
2758 S. Randolph Street
Shirlington/Arlington, VA
671-7503

The manager here was quick to stress the difference between two lines of typewriters: Most companies, he explained, manufacture a line for the consumer, and then they make a "quality" line, which is distributed through office machine dealers. It is the "quality" line which this store purveys, and that line is usually the more expensive one. They also carry calculators, computers, and a variety of minicomputers. They merchandise almost every brand of typewriter on the market (except for Hermes), and Sharp and Adler calculators. All merchandise is first quality. They claim that they are rarely undersold, and the discount is usually from 10% to 20% below comparable retail. Computers are not discounted. Most things are in stock, and special orders are rare. They do have free delivery, and guarantees are offered. Any repairs on merchandise you buy here or already own can be repaired here, and they do all repair service on Xerox equipment.

Hours are Monday through Friday from 9 am to 5:30 pm, Thursday to 8 pm, and Saturday from 10 am to 5 pm. Personal checks are accepted with proper identification, as are Master Charge and VISA, but there is a 3% surcharge on credit charges over $350. There are returns only in the case of defective merchandise, which should be promptly brought to the attention of the management. There are large parking lots nearby.

Estes Office Machines
8309 Fenton Street
Silver Spring, MD
589-1200

There may be many more office machine stores which give discounts to individuals — and we would like to hear about them. But this small, well-lighted store takes pains to advertise its competitive prices, particularly on used/reconditioned machines. They have a good selection of office machines and office supplies; and they also offer service and rentals. Typical brands found here include Victor Calculators; IBM, SMC, and Silver-Reed typewriters; and Rex-Rotary copiers. All merchandise is first quality. On special orders a 10% deposit is required. Delivery is available free on purchases. If they have no other warranty, new machines are guaranteed for 90 days, and service for 30 days. They do all types of service on typewriters and calculators. Estes Office Machines has seasonal sales on their merchandise.

Hours are from 8:30 am to 5:30 pm, Monday through Friday. Personal checks are accepted with proper identification, as are Master Charge, VISA, and NAC. They have a layaway policy and also make trades and exchanges. They will hold items with a deposit, and merchandise can be returned within 30 days. The store is located off Colesville Road.

Interstate Office Supply
1116 N. Fairfax Street
Alexandria, VA
683-5500

This is not a store for browsers. You go into a small no-nonsense office, where they have catalogues covering all of the supplies carried — brand names like Avery, Swingline, Liquid Paper, and more — all medium to high quality lines. You can expect a discount of from 30% to 40% off list prices, and everything is in stock. If you should require something which they do not normally carry, they will special order it for you, with advance payment required; there will be a restocking charge if you change your mind. There are no discounts on special orders, unless they are made in large quantities. Delivery is available free with minimum orders of $10 within the metropolitan area. A store catalogue is available. If merchandise should prove defective, they will return it to the manufacturer for a replacement. We have found the bargains substantial here — and, while they have been set up to cater to businesses, this is one good place that doesn't discourage private customers.

Hours are on Monday through Friday from 8:30 am to 6 pm. Personal checks are accepted with proper identification, and returns should be made within seven days of purchase. There is limited on-street parking in front of the store and across the street.

Lerner Law Book Co.
53 E Street NW
Washington, DC
628-5785

If you are in school yourself or if you have children, you will really appreciate Lerner's. Here they sell school supplies at discount prices. While this is essentially a law school book store, serving most of the law schools in the area, they carry a full line of school supplies — at excellent prices. And most of these supplies fill the bill in offices too — pens, refills, and pencils, pads of paper, spiral notebooks, typewriter paper and supplies, binders, folders, Whiteout, and more — all major brands. Most everything is first quality, and there are some overstocks and special purchases. Their system has three desirable facets. First, you get a 10% across-the-board reduction on all supplies. Then, when you buy $15 worth of merchandise (even if it's not all at one time), you get credit towards an additional $1.50 worth of goods; and, third, because the manager buys to fill a huge warehouse way in advance, he has certain items that are still marked with prices from one to three years ago — and he sells them at these prices. One thing he mentioned in particular was index cards going for an outrageously low price. There is no price list, because prices (especially of paper goods and pencils, which rely on wood supply) change so frequently.

The store is open from 9:30 am to 6 pm, Monday through Friday, and from 10 am to 2 pm on Saturday. Payment by personal check with identification or cash only. Return policy is liberal. Limited on-street parking, and some pay parking lots nearby.

Metropolitan Office Furniture
8344 Leesburg Pike
Tysons Corner, VA
734-9077

Metropolitan Office Furniture has made an effort to interest the small customer in its complete line of office furniture and lamps, both new and used. The merchandise here is of various quality levels, and includes such well-known names as High Point, Vanguard, Galaxy, and Cole. Many are manufacturers' closeouts, on which you can save 20% to 30%. They frequently run promotions on special purchase irregulars, on which savings average about 40% — usually on two-drawer files, which are ideal for a home office. They also carry used merchandise, which we have seen run for 50% of retail in near-perfect condition — but of course this varies with each item. Most items are in stock, and they ask for a deposit of from 25% to 50% on special orders. Delivery is provided free on new furniture. And the customer can order from the manufacturer's catalogue. A store catalogue is also available. Metropolitan offers a one-year guarantee on new merchandise, and they do repairs on merchandise which is under the guarantee or which you bought there. Periodically they feature certain items at greater than usual reductions — and these sales are advertised in the *Washington Post*, usually in the Sunday magazine section.

Metropolitan's hours are from 9 am to 6 pm Monday through Friday, and from 9 am to 4 pm on Saturday. They accept personal checks with proper identification, Master Charge, VISA, American Express, Central Charge, and NAC. They will hold items for up to a week. The return policy is liberal, and you can return items for cash, credit, or an exchange within a reasonable period of time if not satisfied. The nearest intersection is at Rte. 123.

Office Furniture Inc.
1206 K Street, NW
Washington, DC
737-8028

This is quite a large office furniture and accessory showroom, located in a quiet section of K Street, away from the major business district of the city. They sell furniture for both the office and the reception area, as well as lamps, accessories, pictures, and wastebaskets. The grades of merchandise range from low to high, and many well-known brands are carried — Jasper desks, Stovewall files, Bentson, Kimball, Anderson-Hickey, Taylor chair, and Kimball. All merchandise is first quality unless labeled otherwise. Discounts average 25% and up, but this varies by manufacturer. Most items are carried in stock. This store provides free delivery within the Washington metropolitan area. The customer can order from manufacturers' catalogues, and can also order by mail or by telephone. Manufacturers' warranties are offered, and the store will replace defective parts for you when the merchandise is still under warranty. They periodically have sales on selected items.

Open from Monday through Friday between the hours of 8:30 am and 5 pm, and closed on holidays. Business and personal checks are accepted with proper identification. No credit cards. Return policy depends on merchandise and circumstances. There is free parking in back.

are backed up by the store. They will send out their own repairman to take care of any work covered by the warranty. Customers' names are included on a mailing list. And sometimes you can get particularly good buys when the store makes special purchases.

Other addresses:
728 7th Street, NW, Washington, DC, 628-1990; 8:30 am to 5:30 pm, Monday through Friday.
1680 L Street, NW, Washington, DC, 466-2661: 9 am to 5 pm, Monday through Friday.
11534 Rockville Pike, Rockville, MD, 881-6050: 9:30 am to 6 pm Monday through Friday, 9:30 am to 4 pm Saturday.

Hours at the Falls Church store are Monday through Friday from 9:30 am to 6 pm, and Saturday from 9:30 am to 4 pm. Checks are accepted with identification, as are Master Charge, VISA, American Express, Central Charge, and Diners Club charge cards. Returns or exchanges depend on the merchandise. Ample parking at suburban locations.

Office Furniture Mart
6769 Wilson Blvd.
Plaza 7 Shopping Center
Falls Church, VA
534-4077

The Office Furniture Mart is a local chain for stores, selling files, desks, chairs, lamps, and some accessories in a complete line of mostly medium quality office furniture. Some of the brands include Kimball, Biltrite, and DFI. Everything at the retail stores is of first quality, and the average discount is about 30%, with some higher and some lower. Most items are in stock, but a deposit of about 20% is required on special orders. Free delivery is provided on new large items. A store catalogue is available, and manufacturers' warranties

Office Furniture Mart Clearance Center
2122 24th Place, NE
Washington, DC
832-2555

The Office Furniture Mart Clearance Center is a large, neatly-organized facility, stocked with factory returns, closeouts, damaged merchandise, and rental returns — all the same quality of goods offered by their retail stores. Discounts are usually about 50% of the retail price. Despite this being a clearance center, they will also order catalogue merchandise for you at this location. Delivery is free with orders over $50 in the metropolitan area. Most merchandise is sold as is, and there is no warranty, but on new merchandise the guarantee is for a year. There are mailing lists for special sales and events, most of which are held on major holidays. Large advertisements appear in the *Washington Star* and *Post* for these sales. There appeared to be many really good buys on furniture and accessories, and a wide selection of goods.

This store is open from 8 am to 4:30 pm from Monday through Friday, and (in the winter only) on Saturday from 9 am to 3 pm. Personal checks are accepted, as are Master Charge, VISA, American Express, and Central Charge credit cards. While there are no layaways, they will make an effort to hold items for you. Most sales are "as is", and exchanges or credits can be made on returned merchandise. There is a large parking lot.

S & S Office Supply, Inc.
711 G Street SE
Washington, DC
543-7112

This is a very small little office supply store in a basically residential neighborhood. Most of the merchandise is not on display — you just ask for it, and they will bring it out from the stockroom. They carry top quality brands of office supplies and have access to office furniture as well. All office supplies are first quality, and they give an across-the-board discount of 10% to individuals. Everything is in stock except for the furniture. Free delivery is available.

S & S Office Supply is open from 8 am to 6 pm Monday to Friday, and Saturday from 9 am to 2 pm. They accept personal checks with identification, and Master Charge and VISA credit cards. Cash refunds will be given on unused merchandise within 30 days of purchase. Parking is on street and limited, but if you live or work in the Capitol Hill area, you would probably just want to walk over.

Thrifty Business Supply Centers
151 Riggs Road, NE
Washington, DC
882-2300

Thrifty sells office furniture and supplies from this location, but most of its goods are in the warehouse and will be delivered to customers. They carry a complete line of general office supplies, data processing equipment, office space planning services, and most major brands of office furniture, including Burroughs and Fireproofing. The space is shared with a sister business that deals in residential furniture, which is displayed here, but most furniture orders in this location are placed from catalogues. As far as small office supplies are concerned, the store stock is extremely limited, and it is unlikely that they would be interested in ordering small quantities for an individual. But larger orders of office supplies will arrive from their warehouse within three working days after the order is placed. Thrifty offers free delivery on orders of $75 or more.

Office hours are from 9 am to 7 pm Monday through Saturday. Checks are accepted, as are Master Charge, VISA, American Express, Central Charge, and NAC Credit Cards

Washington Photocopy
4380 MacArthur Blvd.
Washington, DC
333-4585

A full-service store, Washington Photocopy sells a wide range of copying machines and supplies for an average discount of an amazing 50%, according to our researcher. These include brands like Royal, Toshiba, Mita, Olivetti, and SCM. They sell both new and used merchandise and take trade-ins. They also carry a small number of manufacturers' closeouts. Delivery is available for a price. Machines are fully warrantied up to 90 days, and repairs are done here.

Hours here are from 8:30 am to 5:30 pm, Monday through Friday. Personal checks are accepted with proper identification.

Office Furniture Outlet
411 New York Avenue NE
Washington, DC
546-8838

We can't guarantee that you will always find something unusual here, but there is a great likelihood that if you decorate your office or den with furniture from this store, it will surely be unique. This store's management buys used office furniture from liquidation and bankruptcy sales, and new items when really cheaply priced. They always seek the best quality items, and prices (while hard to compare, since many items are no longer made) run from 50% to 70% less than comparable new items. Prices for items in bad condition, or which need the handyman's touch, hit rock bottom. The store is large, crammed with the mundane (ordinary swivel chairs and metal files and desks) and graced with the unusual and sophisticated (partner's desks, leather upholstered chairs, oak filing cabinets, and even some desktop items from bygone eras).

Hours here are 9 am to 5 pm Monday through Friday, and from 10 am to 4 pm on Saturday. Personal checks are accepted, as are Master Charge and VISA. Items will be held with a deposit. They will take returns within a week. Parking is available in the lot to the east of the building.

MAIL ORDER

Adirondack Direct
219 E. 42nd Street,
New York, New York **10017**
(800) 221-2444

Office equipment and supplies, and a line of modern office furniture. Catalogue free, published 3 times a year. Discounts to 43%.

Buy Direct, Inc.
216 W. 18th Street,
New York, New York **10011**

Write for free catalogue to buy business forms, envelopes, and letterhead at about 30% less than comparable retail.

Frank Eastern Co.
625 Broadway,
New York, New York **10012**
(212) 677-9100

Everything for business or home office, at discounts up to 60%. Catalogue is free.

---

smARTen UP YOUR WALLS AND WALLET AT TRULY AFFORDABLE PRICES

prints, posters & custom framing for home & office

GRAPHICS OF OLD TOWN LIMITED	JUST GRAPHICS
315 Cameron St.	Skyline Mall
Alexandria, VA	5147 Leesburg Pike
836-5095	Baileys Crossroads
	931-5471
Springfield Mall	
Springfield, VA	
971-1332	

Carpeting Flooring & Wallpaper

CARPETING

If you're like most people who go out shopping for a carpet, color is probably the first thing on your list of priorities. And that's the way the industry wants it — for if you think color, and are swayed by fashion in carpeting, you will not only buy more often, but you will not question what you are buying. This will save the carpet dealer and salespeople time that would otherwise be "wasted" in explanations.

At some time or another, practically everyone in the DC area is forced to buy at least minimal carpeting — for most apartment buildings with wooden floors require that a sound-absorbent covering be placed over the floors for the protection of the wood and to absorb sound.

For most people, carpeting is a major purchase... yet most people shopping for carpeting tend to "buy blind". Perhaps it is the complexity of the field that leads many dealers to avoid explaining to the consumer the ins-and-outs of the product and the industry. Perhaps even some of the salespeople have not mastered the field! All available materials which could demystify this subject have, to a great extent, remained in the hands of the industry. In this section, we bring you some of the relevant facts about carpeting in a relatively non-technical manner. The following information should be read *before* you even begin to look for carpeting, so you will know what you are looking for. At the end of this article are hints to consider when you plan your purchase.

CARPET CONSTRUCTION

Until 1939, cotton flax, linen, wool, and silk were the fibers from which carpets were fabricated. Around 1939, manmade fibers began to become popular. Through 1960, however, these accounted for only about 20% of sales. Since that time, improvements in synthetic fibers have made them more acceptable, less expensive, and easier to maintain. They have become so fashionable and desirable that it is generally estimated by carpet industry experts that 98% of all carpets currently sold are made from synthetic fibers.

In general, synthetics — nylon, acrylic, polyester, olefin — are made from material which is liquid under heat. This material is blown through a perforated plate called a *spinnerette*. As it goes through the small perforations and then cools, a filament of fiber is formed. Varying shapes are created, depending on the shape of the spinnerette (just as the shape of cookies depends on which cookie cutter is used). Shapes help to determine much about the fiber — bulk, luster, and soil-hiding characteristics, among other things. After formation, the fiber is stretched, which adds to its strength. The fiber can then be combined or blended with natural fibers to achieve the best qualities of both, just as polyester and cotton are combined in clothing fabrics.

Perhaps the subject about which least is known to the carpet buyer is that of the characteristics of the many fibers from which carpeting can be created. The chart on the following page lays out the advantages and disadvantages of each.

While type of fiber used plays a significant part in the way a carpet wears, construction also plays a role in wear, and an even more important role in looks. There are three major types of construction: *tufted*, which as of this writing has garnered from 95% to 98% of the market; *needlepunch*, which is generally utilized for less expensive and flat carpets; and *woven*, which used to be the standard, but the cost of which has put it out of reach for the vast majority of carpet purchasers.

Tufted carpets can be maufactured about 25 times as fast as woven carpets. Tufting is a process of stitching the fiber (which then becomes the pile) to the carpet backing. The final look of the carpet depends on the shearing process.

Pile density is of major importance in the quality of a carpet. It is a function of gauge and stitch rate. *Gauge* is the distance between the crosswise needles which attach the yarn to the backing, and *stitch rate* is the number of stitches each of these needles makes per inch. *Pile height* is just what it sounds like: the height of the pile as attached to the backing. Quality control is important in the production of a carpet, since this ensures that the density is well-maintained. The super-wearability of commercial carpeting is attributable to a low pile, high stitch rate, and tight gauge. Incidentally, the term *broadloom* merely refers to the width of the carpet — broadloom is at least 54" wide.

CHARACTERISTICS OF FIBERS USED IN CARPETING
WOOL:
Characteristics: The best carpet wool comes from sheep in the roughest climates. Pleasing to sight and touch. Rough surface diffuses soil visibility. Good cleanability. Solvent-resistant. Scaly, doesn't hold dirt. Resilient.

Disadvantages: High cost. High static, Fuzzes. Bad moth resistance. Poor abrasion resistance Allergenic. Hard to remove stains.

NYLON:
Characteristics: Developed in 1938 by du Pont, nylon is technically a thermoplastic polyamide resin made from a base of coal tar and water. Good bulk and cover. Crush resistant. Good wearability. Clear color. Good dye depth. Good lustre range. Abrasion resistant. Soil resistant. Can be static resistant. Non allergenic. Easy to clean. Mildew resistant. Good light scattering.

Disadvantages: High static if untreated. Sun fades. Reflects soiling faster because of luster (new nylons don't have this problem).

POLYESTERS:
Characteristics: Look like a combination of nylon and acrylic. Polyesters were first used in the carpet industry about 1954. Technically, a polyester is a complex ester formed by polymerization. Fiber has an internal cross section which hides dirt well. High bulk and good hand. Good color and luster, particularly in brights. Abrasion resistant. Low cost. Cleans well. Mildew and moth resistant. Non-allergenic.

Disadvantages: Because of its high bulk and good hand, some manufacturers put in less than acceptable pile — which crushes down and looks bad.

POLYPROPYLENES (OLEFINS):
Characteristics: Technically a petrochemical fiber derived from petroleum oil. Manmade grass is one form of this fiber. Non-allergenic. Good cover and bulk. Abrasion resistant. Most are stain resistant. Low static. Mildew and moth resistant. Outstanding wearability. Least static build-up — which makes it quite soil resistant.

Disadvantages: Low resilience. Fair color clarity. Low melting point. Poor solvent resistance.

ACRYLICS:
Characteristics: Acrylics were developed in 1957 by Monsanto. They must contain at least 85% acrylonite units. Usually used in luxurious textured rugs. Acrylics have good wear qualities but are less durable than nylon. They resemble wool more than any other manmade fiber. Low static level. Excellent cover and bulk. Good apperance retention. Wide color range. Non-allergenic. Moisture resistant. Good resilience. Mildew resistant. Easy to clean. Mothproof.

Disadvantages: Low abrasion resistance. Poor alkali resistance. Fuzzes.

MODACRYLIC
Characteristics: Modacrylics are like acrylics, but have 85% acrylonitrile Units. This is a modified acrylic. Not as resistant or reslient as acrylic. But it has better fire resistance.

Blends of fibers give the resulting carpet characteristics of both fibers used. These are not common, but the following are sometimes used:

NYLON & OLEFIN:
Static is reduced by the addition of separate olefin yarns to nylon.

ACRYLIC & MODACRYLIC:
Because of superior flame resistance of modacrylic, a blend of 70% acrylic, 30% modacrylic is sometimes used.

Needlepunch carpeting appears flat. In this process, the primary backing is sandwiched between the yarn. This is a particularly useful carpeting outdoors and in schools, since it is dense and will bear heavy traffic. The backing for a needlepunch carpet is usually olefin, a synthetic. While it has excellent wear characteristics, it tends to attract lint.

There are three main varieties of *woven carpets:* Wilton, Axminster, and velvet.

Wilton is made on a jacquard loom and uses pattern cards which allow this process to form intricate patterns. As it is made, some of the pile fiber appears on the back. Wiltons can be sculptured or embossed, or level pile.

In *Axminsters,* almost all of the yarn appears on the surface. Axminsters can be produced in an almost endless variety of patterns. Axminsters most closely approximate the effects of handweaving, as each tuft is individually set into the pile. Thus, each tuft could theoretically be a different color than the others. Axminsters are easily recognized by the back of the carpet, which has a ribbed appearance along the width and cannot be rolled widthwise. This is a cut pile at an even height and evidences excellent crush resistance. It is cheaper to construct than a wilton.

Velvets are the simplest woven carpets and are usually found in solid colors. But a wide variety of texture and color effects is possible. In the velvet, all of the yarn is used for the pile. Twice as many velvets are sold as Axminster and Wiltons put together. When closely woven, these carpets are long-wearing and rich looking.

Texture

Shearing to form texture is the next step in the manufacturing process. Three basic texture groups can be created, and these define a wide number of texture choices offered to the carpet consumer: Loop Pile, Cut Pile, or Selectively Sheared are the alternatives.

Level loop (round wire) can be tufted or woven. The words *round wire* apply to the looped pile, which is woven on a loom. This is usually a tweed or print. In general, this subcategory has excellent crush resistance, easy maintenance, and good wearability. When low, it is excellent for the kitchen or family room, especially when the tufted variety has a rubber backing. This is the only construction commonly sold by gauge.

High-low and patterned loop round wire refers to a multilevel carpet which has a sculptured effect.

Velva Loop texture is made with the tufting process, but it has the smooth appearance of a woven velvet.

Selectively sheared styles include *Level loop, random shear*, which is variously referred to as patterned, sculptured, carved, or embossed. Some loops are sheared and others are not. This is considered to be a very durable carpet. This also fits into the cut pile family and is called "cut and loop". This category includes "tip shears".

In the cut pile group, *smooth cut pile* or *plush* is considered the luxury texture. Its great density makes it desirable for formal areas (such as dining rooms and living rooms) and places where you might want "nothing but the best" (such as master bedrooms). However, it shows footprints and other furniture marks. This is where yarn is sheared at a single level so it appears smooth. The density is great. When acrylic is used in a plush, it is generally untwisted; nylon in a plush is usually twisted, which gives a nubbier look and feel to the carpet. Plush is not recommended for high traffic areas because of its tendency to show marks.

Multi-level and *patterned* are usually found in the lower price ranges, and here the tufts are cut to a variety of heights. This texture is easy to maintain and suffers little crushing.

Shag and mini-shag are usually preferable in low traffic areas. These are made from a long cut pile, whose yarns are twisted to hold texture. They hide dirt well — so well, in fact, that is is very easy to lose things in them. Shags are not effective as a long-time investment, despite their luxurious look. Not only might you tire of the look (and of losing things in them), but keeping them clean is a great deal of work: they must be not only vacuumed, but *raked*, much as you rake leaves, in order to retain the best appearance.

Saxony is similar to a plush, but uses a heavier yarn. It is plied (meaning it uses a number of threads of yarn to form one), and heat set. Each tuft is individually distinguishable in a saxony

Frieze and *twist* are similar cut textures. Both are tightly twisted and heat set, usually not in a very high density pile. The finish is even, but the surface is rough. Frieze is usually longer and shaggier than twist.

Backing

Tufted carpeting is affixed to a primary backing as it is produced. This backing can be *jute*, a natural fiber found in Bangladesh, India, and only a few other locations, or a synthetic, such as an *olefin*. A secondary backing is attached to the rug, with a layer of latex adhesive or thermosetting plastic to hold the two backings together. This adds dimensional stability to the carpet. This secondary backing can also be either synthetic or natural.

Synthetic backings can be woven or nonwoven. The advantage of a synthetic is its immunity to rot and mildew retention; it is also non-allergenic. Unwoven synthetic backings are superior in that they cannot unravel.

Jute is sometimes unavailable in quantity, depending on world markets. Since jute is a rougher fiber, the carpeting adheres better to it. It offers greater dimensional stability than synthetics.

Foam rubber can also be used as a secondary backing, and when it is it provides a built-in cushioning. Often cheaper carpets have foam backings.

Cushion or Padding

Whatever you call it, cushioning adds immensely to the wearability and value of a carpet, despite its additional cost. It increases carpet resilience, increases comfort, assures longer carpet life, increases the insulation factor, aids sound absorption, helps the pile to retain its shape, increases the effectiveness of cleaning; and reduces the impact of the floor on the foot while walking. However, if it is too thick and soft, it is easy to accidentally punch holes through the carpet with thin high heels (such as are often fashionable in women's shoe styles).

Padding can be separate from or bonded to the carpet. Commonly used cushions include foam rubber, sponge rubber, urethane foam, polyesters, and felt.

Foam rubber has a latex rubber base and often comes in flat sheets from 1/8" to 5/8" thick. A medium weight would be 28 to 56 ounces per square yard. Foam rubber is denser than sponge rubber.

Sponge rubber is usually from 3/16" to 5/16" thick, and provides excellent resilience and the most softness. Sponge rubbers are heavier than foam, but this can sometimes be misleading: the extra heaviness can be caused by filler, and that filler can sometimes speed deterioration of the pad. Sponge rubber pads come with a flat surface or waffled (rippled) surface. This may be cured onto the back of the carpet.

Urethane foam is usually ¼" to ¾" wide, and comes in three varieties: bonded, prime, and densified prime. Bonded urethane is foam which is ground into particles and compressed to the desired density; prime is excellent because it has the highest density, and densified prime is better than plain prime.

Polyester is used as a backing, and in this role it demonstrates flexibility and firmness; it also has the smallest number of producers.

Felt were traditionally used, and can be found in variety: hair felt (becoming scarcer), a combination of animal hair and fiber, fiber felt, or rubberized felt. Felts act as a dense cushioning material with a firm feel — and, the more hair, the better the cushion. Rubberized felt is the cushion recommended for oriental rugs.

How to Determine Fibers by Touch, Look, or Smell:

Acrylic & Modacrylic:
Clear colors.
Not glossy.
Fuzzes easily, especially in cut pile textures.
Not slick feeling like nylon.
Forms crystalline lumps when burned.

Nylon
Shiny, hard, and slick usually.
If you rub your hand back and forth on it, it makes the skin raw.
Melts to a hard bead.

Olefin: It is sometimes difficult to tell the new ones from nylon. Has a low melting point.
If you pull the side of the sole of your shoe across it rapidly, a melt mark will be left.

Polyester: Usually soft and slick, and has a waxy, almost silky feel. Comes in bright colors.
Displays little or no fuzzing.
Burns to hard, crystalline lumps.

Wool: Similar in looks to acrylic.
Fuzzes easily, especially in plush form.
Burns slowly and extinguishes quickly, leaving a crusty ash.

Installation

Installation can be done three ways. Direct glue-down, where the carpet is glued directly to the floor, has a major drawback — floors must be sanded when the carpet is removed. Carpet with cushioning can be put down over tackless strips, or a carpet can be installed over a separate cushion.

TIPS ON BUYING CARPETING

- Decide on how much you want to spend.

- Decide if you want wall-to-wall, an area rug, or a room-size rug. Area rugs are used to highlight a conversation or activity area. The advantage to them is that they are pick-up-and-go, have no installation costs or problems, and can resist wear easily, since they can be turned so that wear is distributed evenly over the surface. Area rugs can even be hung on the wall. They are also useful over carpeting to conceal badly worn areas. Using an area rug does leave exposed your carpeting or flooring, which must also be cared for. Area rugs can be made from remnants, but the remnant should be "honest" — that is, left over from a first-run carpet; sometimes seconds are offered as remnants, but aren't labelled as such. Make sure to ask about this.

Room size rugs are advantageous in that they roll and move easily, cut and bind easily, and are portable. This last will save you money if you plan to move in a few years. Beware machine-washable 9x12s. Not only are they usually cheap, but how many people have washing machines large enough to accommodate them? Room size rugs can also be cut from remnants. Both room-size rugs and area rugs should be finished all of the way around. They can be *bound* — that is, have cloth tape sewn along the edges. This is the best way to finish a rug and is second in expense only to *fringing*. Fringing means that a fringe is applied all around the rug, or perhaps just to the two widthwise edges, for a decorative effect. The 4" knotted fringe is the most popular. Remnants can also be finished by *serging*, in which the carpet is stitched all along the side. *Sealing* is the cheapest way, but the raw edges are left exposed with this technique. A latex rubber cement is applied in a bead all along the carpet. This is particularly preferred for foam-backed carpets, but no technique is guaranteed on a foam-backed carpet.

Wall-to-wall carpets are luxurious and create an illusion of space. They also eliminate the necessity to clean or wax exposed edges of the floor. On the other hand, they are not portable, nor can they be turned to redistribute wear.

- Carpet tiles have been considered an inferior alternative, used to save on carpeting. They can be priced as high as or even higher than wall-to-wall — and you save only on installation. These usually come in 12" squares, which have a tendency to curl up at the corners with age. Manufacturers have been working at improving them.

- Look for carpeting in January and February OR July and August — that's when it goes on sale.

- Assess the way in which you live, as well as the function of the area to be carpeted. Consider who will be using the room — children or adults?; the function of the room — eating, entertaining, sleeping; household pets who could dirty it up; the type of traffic through the room — from the outside directly?; and what kinds of dirt are likely to enter it. Using this information helps to make a decision about color. There are many arguments in favor of buying a neutral or a medium tone — light colors or pastels tend to show dirt and stains, very dark colors show lint. Neutrals are the most versatile and give you the option of switching the carpet to another room as your tastes change. Buying a bright pink carpet for the living room — even if you love bright pink — limits what you can do with that carpet when you redecorate. Also, odd colors tend to go out of style — no matter how luscious they looked when your bought them — since your tastes are probably influenced by current trends and styles. If you must buy a weird or difficult-to-match color, recognize this as a whim and act accordingly. If you consider that the carpet you buy will probably have a short life, you may decide not to invest in high quality.

- Know the *exact* dimensions of your rooms. This will help you to avoid buying either too much or too little. You can get locked into a contract of, say, 10 square yards for 12 dollars a yard, but find out later you need 12 square yards — and the price for these additional two yards may then be considerably more than the $12 for the first 10 yards. Yardage can be estimated by multiplying the width of the room in feet by the length in feet and dividing by 9. Plan to buy extra for stairs. This can be folded up against the risers at the top of the stairs, and unfolded downward as the carpet on the treads wears away. Nylon with jute backing is suggested for stairs.

- Be aware of what your room looks like, and have a good idea of the colors in it. Take color shapshots of the room(s) to be carpeted, if possible. Assemble swatches of fabrics and wall coverings which you are using or going to use in these rooms.

- Compare dealers, in terms of both prices and services. Check with friends to find out where they bought carpeting, and remember to find out if they are satisfied with their purchase.

- Don't expect the retailer to tell you everything about the carpet. He should be knowledgeable as to the various fibers, the need for padding, and what's most soil resistant. You should, however, take responsibility for carefully checking the back of the dealer's sample (assuming you're not buying remnants), to see what it says about cleaning, flammability, wear, light and color fastness, and fiber content.

- Look for quality by giving the carpeting a test for "grinning". Bend the carpet face side out. If it grins at you, don't grin back! Grinning means that the backing shows between the rows of tufts. Grinning means that there is not the desired amount of tufting and the pile will crush or mat easily. Some manufacturers have tried to cover this up by matching the backing — dyeing it to "erase" the grinning. This doesn't work — and don't be fooled by it.

- Ask that prices for installation, padding, and carpeting be itemized. That way, you will know what you are paying for — and it makes it easier to compare dealers. Package pricing can be deceptive. In a $10-per-square-yard package, the carpet could be worth only $5 a yard, the rest being charged for padding; or the carpeting could be worth $7 a yard, with only the remaining $4 going for padding.

- Installation — This is not a do-it-yourself job, except in a small square room. Many consumers are surprised at the cost of wall-to-wall installation, but there is little question that it is worth it. There is no point in buying a quality carpet, perhaps getting a great bargain — then ruining it by a botched home done job. Spend time looking for an installer if the dealer doesn't have his own. Be sure to ask for references, and check one or two of the actual installations. You may be able to save money by contracting the installation out yourself, and not using the dealer's services.

   Make sure to ask *exactly* what you get — is it glue down, tackless strips? Are all extras — such as below-grade installation, stairs, etc. — included in the price?

Some Caveats:

- Beware of commercial carpeting advertised at prices of regular residential. The work *commercial* can be misleading. True commercial carpeting is extremely heavy duty and usually costs from 2 to 3 times that of comparable residential.

- Beware of rayon — it doesn't wear well.
- Beware of companies that advertise in such places as the TV schedule — and give a phone number, but no address.
- Avoid such things as "three full rooms of carpeting" for a wonderful price. If what they have is good quality, it will be such a weird color that you probably won't want it. And, if you do, they will try to dissuade you from buying it and instead talk you into something of a higher price and quality.
- Make sure you get a sample of the carpet you finally purchase to take home — so you will know if the right thing is delivered.
- In buying carpeting, awareness of your needs and informed questioning and research are an absolute necessity. Don't buy until *all* of your questions have been answered.

Government Intervention

There have been some attempts on the part of the federal government to help you the carpeting consumer. Major efforts include the 1971 ruling that large and small carpets and rugs must be flame-retardant — that is, they must restrict and extinguish flames from a match dropped on them. If they are flame-retardant, they must be labeled with a "T". If they are not, they must have a warning to that effect.

Carpeting is one industry which has resisted grading or standardizing, making it more difficult for the consumer to compare goods. Most carpets offer no manufacturers' guarantees. However, there is some help for the consumer which resulted from government involvement. Since 1975, in FHA-mortgaged homes, carpet to be used is subject to a testing and certification program. This carepting must meet standards of wear for both fibers and backing, resistance to fading, flammability, and static.

Directories which list certified manufacturers and their styles of carpeting are available from:

>Electrical Testing Laboratory, Inc.
>2 East End Avenue
>New York, New York 10021

>Associated Dallas Laboratories
>P.O. Box 15705
>Dallas, Texas 75215

>Metallurgical Engineers of Atlanta, Inc.
>3480 Oak Cliff Road,
>Atlanta, Georgia 30340

Note also that approved carpeting must be retested annually.

RESILIENT FLOORING

Resilient flooring is just what the name implies — and a bit more: a smooth-surfaced tile or sheet goods with a bit of bounce — the ability to recover from impact or pressure. What they all have in common: they are usually fastened with an adhesive to the surface of the floor, but the softer materials are more sensitive to continued impact, for example — a desk on a floor will gradually wear down the spot where the leg touches the floor. Sheet goods are easier to maintain, as there are few if any exposed seams (which could catch and hold dirt and grime).

Resilience is where the similarity ends between members of this tile and sheet goods family. The material of manufacturer, the method of placing a design on the tile, and the grade or quality separate them into a number of categories:

Types of Resilient Flooring

Tiles include solid vinyl and vinyl asbestos, as well as three materials which are losing in popularity or are preferred for commercial installations only: asphalt tile, rubber tile, and cork tile.

Solid vinyl flooring is considered the best and most expensive. A greater variety of patterns and colors are offered in it. Solid vinyl demonstrates considerable resilience and good acoustic properties. It wears well and resists oil and grease; it is thus excellent for use in kitchens. Disadvantages of solid vinyl include high initial cost, low resistance to solvent-base cleaning materials, and dullness caused by continuing foot traffic (lustre can be replaced by using steel wool buffing, or an acrylic based compound).

Vinyl asbestos is the most popular today. It is resistant to oil, grease, acids and alkalis (which means that strong cleaning fluids can be used on it, and it can be installed below grade). This vinyl is available in several thicknesses, 1/8" being recommended for commercial or hard use. The decoration is provided by an embossing process. Now "indexed" embossing makes it easy to match up and have the look of one piece. Some have semi-translucent chips embedded in them. Designs may or may not go through the whole thickness.

Asphalt has generally been replaced in popularity by vinyl asbestos tile because of its inability to resist grease, and because it came in a limited variety of colors and styles. Asphalt is the hardest wearing and the least expensive — both to buy and to maintain. However, it tends to crack and to show dents and burn marks; and it can be softened by high temperatures or cracked by low temperatures.

Rubber is an expensive flooring which is usually installed commercially. It has a long life expectancy, the exact life depeding on its thickness. Its appearance is good, it is comfortable to walk on, and it has good acoustic capabilities. It is also easy to maintain. On the negative side, it shows a sensitivity to cleaning compounds and is not resistant to fatty acids, solvents, oil, or grease. Also, ultraviolet light (sun) affects it negatively. Synthetic rubber products show better performance on oil and grease resistance and age better.

Cork is one of the earliest of the resilient floorings, and it is still the most resilient. It comes in both sheets and tile. It is extremely porous, which is a disadvantage. Because of its superb resilience, however, it is very comfortable to walk on, shows good acoustical properties, and displays a rich appearance. Four types of cork flooring are available: natural unfinished, waxed (at the factory), resin-reinforced (which gets rid of some of the porosity), and vinyl cork tile (which is highly impervious to staining).

There are two main types of sheet vinyl flooring — inlaid or rotovinyl.

Inlaid vinyl is considered the top of the line. It is made up of thousands of tiny vinyl granules, which are built up layer by layer, then fused with heat and pressure, resulting in a rich look and a noticeable depth of color. Inlaid vinyl is particularly durable, resistant to gouges and chips. And even if it does chip, this is unlikely to show, since the pattern goes through the piece of goods. Because of its weight, it is generally recommended that this be professionally installed.

Rotovinyls are also called rotogravure vinyls. These are decorated by a rotogravure process, which combines photography and printing. This process was developed after World War II (inlaid vinyl was available before rotovinyl). It allows great variety and clarity in printed designs. The printed design is protected by a topping of clear vinyl or polyurethane, called the "wearlayer". The desired thickness of the wearlayer is a minimum of ten mils, the best having a wearlayer of 25 mils. All rotovinyls are made with an inner core of foamed or expanded vinyl, which cushions them. Price of the merchandise does have a relationship to cushioning — the greater the price, generally the greater the cushioning. Below they cushion, they have a mineral fiber layer for dimensional stability, and for moisture and alkali resistance.

Other Types of Flooring

Ceramic Tile is made from clay or a mixture of organic materials, and finished by kiln firing. It can be used both indoors and out, the most common types in use being quarry and ceramic mosaic tiles. Quarry tile is larger than others, usually 6" x 6", and up to 1½" thick. The earthy colors are natural. The tiles themselves are easy to maintain; however, some types of grout (the substance used to fill the spaces between tiles) are porous and retain dirt. A new type of grout — silicone based — has been developed and is said to avoid some of the problems of ordinary grout. Ceramic tiles are oil, grease, and moisture resistant. When you are selecting ceramic tiles, important things for you to consider include wear, slip resistance, and acoustic properties of the tiles, as well as fire resistance of the installation materials. Unglazed tile holds up best to heavy-duty use.

Slate is a brittle flooring, with low abrasion resistance to metal scratches. Slate is made from stratified rock, its thickness depending on the quality of the rock. Available natural colors include red, blue, green, grey, black, and purple. Slate must be laid over a cement base.

Marble is considered to be the aristocrat of stone floors, and it is usually installed for special effects — for example, in a foyer. The finest marble is imported from Greece, Italy, and Central Africa. Marble consists of limestone with grains of dolomite and/or calcite running through it.

Terrazzo tile is excellent for heavy traffic areas both inside and out. It is as strong as concrete. It comes in several ways: Usually it is 70% or more of crushed waste marble and granite chips, the other 30% being composed of Portland cement with pigments added. Terazzo is poured and set on site, and also available in precast tiles in a variety of sizes and types. Terrazzo is *not* suggested as a do-it-yourself flooring.

Brick used as a flooring resists abrasion, and has a long life and low maintenance costs. It may be sealed and polished in order to avoid the porosity it naturally exhibits.

Wood is a popular flooring and is offered in a variety of woods and units. Pecan is the hardest hardwood commonly used for floors; maple is hard, close-grained, strong, and arrasion and wear resistant; red and white oak provide different grains, depending on how they are sawed. Wood floors are usually made of planks, strips, or blocks (like parquet). There are many variations in materials: you can obtain further information from the National Oak Flooring Manufacture Association and the Maple Flooring Manufacturers Association, who set standards for wood floors.

Regardless of what flooring you choose, if you do not install it yourself, remember that installation charges are usually not included in your purchase. These can run anywhere from $3/sq yd up. And this does not usually include preparation of the floor. If any other old floors have to be ripped out, or irregularities covered by an underlayment — another layer of floor — it can run substantially more. Be sure that you ask about all these charges and get the total price in writing when buying the flooring.

FINDING BARGAINS IN CARPETING, FLOORING, AND OTHER DECORATING AIDS:

There is such a plethora of stores selling flooring and carpeting at a discount in this metropolitan area that we found it impossible to discriminate between them, except by noting whether they concentrated selling remnants, closeouts, or custom orders. There are hundreds of carpet brands, and many stores carry most of them. So we suggest that you use the following guidelines for finding carpet bargains:

- All of these stores fall into about three basic categories: those which sell primarily remnants, closeouts, roll ends, and such; those that sell primarily wall-to-wall goods; and those which sell a combination of these two. We have provided you with this information about each store. In order for you to make the best use of this information, you should determine what your needs and budget are.
- All other things being equal, you should consider location — how near a store is to where you work or live (preferably, where you live). This is important, just in terms of saving you gas and driving time. Also, should you have any problems with the goods or installation, this makes servicing easier.
- Shop warranties — in the case of the carpeting, installation is guaranteed anywhere from one year to the life of the carpet;
- Use the preceding information provided in this chapter to decide what kind of carpeting or flooring you want and use it to help you judge quality;
- Try to compare prices between the same goods at different stores. Be sure you understand what manufacturer, what line of carpeting or flooring, and what material is meant in each quotation you get. This information helps you to compare stores and prices.

Alexander Wallpaper
2964 Gallows Road
Falls Church, VA
560-5524

Alexander's is a large wallpaper store with an extensive selection of almost every brand available, including names such as Schumacher and General Tire. They take special orders on such custom brands as Royaleigh Designs. All merchandise is first quality, unless otherwise marked. You can expect to save from 10% to 50% on the wallpaper, depending on the maker. The store is well stocked, with stacked bins containing each design: A large number of designs are hanging up to show the wide range available.

Other address:
12221 Nebel St., Rockville, MD, 770-5014

Hours are Monday through Saturday from 10 am to 5 pm, and Thursday until 9 pm. They take personal checks with proper identification, Central Charge, VISA, Master Charge, and maybe American Express. There are no returns or exchanges. Ample parking is available.

Allstate Carpet
1019 Cameron Street
Alexandria, VA
549-6363

Allstate primarily does commercial work, like offices. But they do have fine quality remnants left over from their jobs — carpeting, sheet vinyl, and padding. The discount is at least 30% off the retail price. And if you do buy large quantities on special order, you get additional discounts, which vary by manufacturer. Free delivery is available in the immediate area. There are three main areas to this store: the front room, with carpet samples and the office; the "Armstrong room" for sheet vinyl and tile; and the back warehouse area, where they have the remnants of carpeting, sheet vinyl, and padding. They feature a "carpet of the month" special.

Hours are 8:30 am to 5 pm weekdays, and Saturday from 10 am to 3 pm (except in July and August). Personal checks are accepted with proper identification, as are Master Charge and VISA. Carpets are rarely held. All sales are final, but they will rollout remnants to check for flaws before you leave the store. There is usually adequate on-street parking in front of the store.

Arlandria Carpet
3825 Mt. Vernon Avenue
Alexandria, VA
548-8299

Arlandria Carpet is a friendly neighborhood carpet store in a good-sized facility, carrying carpet, sheet vinyl, tile, wallpaper, wood flooring, and all related sundries. They stock a wide range of brands, with such well-known names as Mohawk, West Point Pepperell, Monarch, Barwick, Congoleum, GAF, Bennington, Amtico, and Nafco. Most merchandise is first quality, with some remnants and some closeouts. The prices are considered competitive with the market, and you can expect to save the most on closeouts and remnants. On special orders, they usually ask for a deposit of about 50%. Free delivery is available within the immediate area. They will do installation, and this is guaranteed for two years. They also do repairs, cleaning, binding, and fringing. And if you need any help, they will be happy to give you free instruction in using the materials and tools which you purchase.

Hours here are Monday through Friday from 9 am to 8 pm, and Saturday from 9 am to 5:30 pm. Personal checks are accepted with proper identification, as are Master Charge, VISA, American Express, Central Charge, and NAC. On layaways, they require 1/3 deposit and pickup usually within 30 days. They will usually hold merchandise for up to 24 hours. There are no returns or exchanges of ordered or cut goods, but remnants can be exchanged. There is a small parking lot in front, and additional parking in back.

Associated Carpets and Interiors
2630 Columbia Pike
Arlington, VA
521-6911

Like some of the other stores in this section, this is primarily commercially oriented but has in stock a number of remnants and rolls for the individual consumer. They carry brands like Berman, Burlington, and McGee — about ten to fifteen major mills, whose products run the gamut from low to high quality. You can also special order the carpets from sample swatches. Discounts on these carpets run from 10% to 30% off. They have many first quality mill ends and rolls. The store also stocks Belgian wool oriental-style carpets, and hand hooked rugs from India and Pakistan. You can also expect a 10% to 30% discount on vinyl flooring brands like Armstrong, Congoleum, and GAF. They do steam cleaning, sell wallpaper at a

10% discount, and have drapery samples for special order draperies.

Hours are Monday and Tuesday from 9 am to 8:30 pm, Wednesday through Friday from 9 am to 5 pm, Saturday from 10 am to 5 pm. They accept personal checks and (with a minimum of $50) Master Charge and VISA. There is delivery, which is not free. Free parking is available across the street in the Filmore lot.

Bill's Carpet
**10980 Lee Highway
Fairfax, VA
691-1664**

Bill's advertises a lot — but that doesn't mean you can't get a good buy there. Bargains at Bill's — like anywhere else — depend on your being discriminating. But also, they depend on which store you shop in — as each is geared in quality and style to the neighborhood in which it is located. They carry brands like World, Cabincraft, Monarch, Coronet, Lees, Salem, and Congoleum (for sheet vinyl) and four grades of carpet padding. In stock they have mill trials, irregulars, odd rolls, overstocks, closeouts, and special purchase carpets. But you can also special order, and on special order items you also get a discounted price. They buy Hoover vacuum cleaners by the truckload and have them available regularly at a good price. Bill's carries a line of wool rugs from Belgium, which they claim to market at $25 to $50 below the retail sales price. Delivery is available for a fee.

Other addresses:
Rte 1, opposite Laurel Shopping Center, Laurel, MD, 498-4400
Korvette Shopping Center on Rockville Pike at Randolph Road, Rockville, MD, 468-5858.
7812 Richmond Highway, Alexandria, VA, 360-3900
3914 Bexley Place, off St. Barnabas Road, Marlow Heights, MD, 432-4060
134 W. Broad Street, Falls Church, VA, 536-3544
Also in Timonium, Owings Mills, and Glen Burnie, MD.

Hours at the Fairfax store are Monday through Friday from 10 am to 9 pm, Wednesday and Saturday from 10 am to 6 pm, and Sunday from noon to 5 pm. They accept checks with proper identification, Master Charge, Central Charge, and VISA. There are no layaways. Ample parking available. Returns are accepted on defective merchandise.

Carpeteria
**7422 Little River Turnpike
Annandale, VA
256-4885**

The store we visited was a nice, neat, but small store. Although they do carry remnants and rolls, the store was not filled with piles of them. They specialize in wall-to-wall carpeting, remnants of carpeting, a few oriental-style rugs, and sheet vinyl. Quality in general is medium, but it depends on which store you are looking at. They carry brands like Masland, Philadelphia, Lees, and Evans and Black, as well as Excelon floor tile and Congoleum sheet vinyl. All merchandise is first quality, but they do have some mill trials, and remnants from local distributors. The discount depends on the manufacturer, and on whether you are buying from in-stock rolls — in which case you get a better buy — or special ordering. Delivery is available, but it is not free. The store offers a one-year warranty on installation. They have special sales about once every two weeks, and holiday sales.

Other addresses:
8035 Sudley Road, Manassas, VA, 631-0519
9542 Arlington Blvd., Fairfax, VA,

591-9280
and in Woodbridge

Hours are the same for all stores: Monday through Friday from 10 am to 9 pm, Saturday from 10 am to 6 pm, and Sunday, usually from noon to 5 pm. They accept personal checks with proper identification, Master Charge, VISA. Their layaway policy is flexible. Returns on defective merchandise. Ample parking. This is a local chain.

Carpet Barn
Route 355
Rockville, MD.
948-7111

Not only can you find carpets in the Carpet Barn stores, but you can also buy sheet vinyl, custom draperies, wallpaper, wood flooring, tiles and area rugs. These come in a range of grades — from low to high quality, with brands like Lees, Trend, Milliken, CabinCraft, Armstrong, Congoleum, and GAF commonly found here. About 35% of their carpet business is in remnants, and the remainder in wall-to-wall carpeting. Saleable irregulars comprise about 20% of their business, and these are labelled. They call their prices competitive and say they undercut those of a department store by about 20% to 30%. There are special orders, and delivery is available at a fee. They say that the labor (on installation) is guaranteed on the carpet for the duration of the carpet's life in the house. They also do repairs.

Other addresses:
Jeff Davis Highway, Woodbridge, VA, 550-9734 or 494-2101
Marlboro Pike and Forestville Road, Forestville, MD, 736-5800
As Colonial Carpets and Interiors, Mc Lean, VA, 356-1000
Korvette's Shopping Center, Baileys Crossroads, VA
7423 Annapolis Road, Landover Hills, 459-1950

303 Mill Street, Vienna, VA, 938-8900

Hours are the same for all stores: Monday through Friday from 9 am to 9 pm, Saturday from 9 am to 6 pm, and Sunday from noon to 5 pm. There are no remnants at the McLean store. Checks are accepted with identification, and so are Master Charge, VISA, and NAC. There are no cash refunds — store credit only. Sale items are not returnable.

Carpet Carnival
1506 University Blvd.
Langley Park, MD
434-1160

Carpet Carnival has a large supply of remnants, roll ends, and discontinued carpets, which they say they sell at competitive prices. Carpet brands include Monarch, Trend, and Galaxy, tile is by manufacturers such as Armstrong and Congoleum. All merchandise is first quality. There are special orders, and they offer a shop-at-home service. Installation is guaranteed for one year. Sales are frequently held.

Other address:
6304 Allentown Road, Camp Springs, MD, 449-3300

Hours at these stores are from 10 am to 9 pm on Monday through Friday, and from 10 am to 6 pm on Saturday. Personal checks are accepted, as are Master Charge, VISA, Central Charge, and NAC. Layaways must be picked up and paid in full within 90 days. They will hold items with a small deposit for up to 3 days. There is a small lot at the Langley Park location.

Carpet House of Maryland
5544 Nicholson Lane
Rockville, MD
770-4045

This was really one of the nicest carpet

and decorating stores which we saw throughout the area. Besides carpet remnants, they offer bedspreads, drapes, and wallpaper. They sell Kirsch woven woods, 7 or 8 lines of wallpaper, many custom-made drapes from about 100 different manufacturers, Armstrong sheet vinyl, many remnants of commercial carpeting, and wall-to-wall special order carpeting by such manufacturers as Bigelow, Coronet, Columbia, and Maslan. All merchandise is first quality, with a few manufacturers' closeouts. Discounts run about 20% to 25% below comparable retail prices. Most everything except the carpet remnants have to be special ordered, but there are some popular styles and color carpet rolls in stock. Delivery depends on the size of the order, and on whether they are doing the installation. They guarantee the padding and installation for the life of the carpet. Sales are held about once a month. They also do cleaning and patching, and they use their own installers. This store attempts to specialize in designer lines — and seems to be succeeding.

Other location:
Route 1 at 198, Laurel, MD, 953-2525

Hours here are Monday, Thursday, and Friday from 10 am to 9 pm, and Tuesday, Wednesday, and Saturday from 10 am to 6 pm. Personal checks are accepted with proper identification. Master Charge, VISA, and Central Charge are also accepted. Layaways require 20% down. Returns can be made on in-stock merchandise within 7 days of purchase. There is a large parking lot in front of the store.

Carpet House
Central Plaza Shopping Center
Route 1 at Route 198
Laurel, MD
Toll-free from Washington: 953-2525; toll-free from Baltimore: 792-4343

Carpet House offers the consumer a large selection of carpets, draperies, wallpaper, and tile. These range in quality from low to the very highest, with such popular brands as Lees, Mohawk, Bigelow, Masland, Philadelphia, Horizon, and Monarch. Everything is first quality. The owner claims to give you about 20% discount. About half of the merchandise is in stock, including some remnants, and the other half is on special orders for which he requires a 50% deposit. Free delivery is available. Labor, including installation, is guaranteed as long as the customer owns the carpet. Specials are held here on holidays.

Hours at this store are from 10 am to 9 pm, Monday through Friday, and Saturday from 10 am to 6 pm. Personal checks are accepted with proper identification, as are Master Charge, VISA, Central Charge, and NAC. Layaway and hold policies are flexible.

Carpetland
3240 Duke Street
Alexandria, VA

At Carpetland, they carry a large selection of remnants, wall-to-wall carpeting, and a variety of oriental-style and genuine oriental rugs. At the Rockville store, they also carry furniture. some sheet vinyl, and tile. The quality is generally medium, and they represent such brands as Georgian, Monarch, Burlington, and Masland. Most everything is first quality. Discounts depend on the carpet. On special order items, you receive a discount of 10% off list price, and a 30% deposit is required. Delivery is available at a charge. Installation is guaranteed for one year. The Duke Street store is crowded but well-organized, and the orientals are hanging up in rows, so you can get a good idea of what they will look like on your floor.

Other address:
3273 M Street, NW, Washington, DC

333-3612
Furniture and Carpetland, Across from Congressional Plaza, Rockville, MD.

Hours are Monday through Friday from 10 am to 9 pm, Saturday until 8 pm, and Sunday from 11 am to 6 pm. Personal checks are accepted with proper identification, as are Master Charge, VISA, Central Charge, and NAC. Layaways are made at the discretion of the salesperson or manager. Return and exchange policies are liberal. There is a small lot at Duke Street, and limited on-street or pay parking in Georgetown.

C. D. Majors Carpet Mart
6928 Braddock Road,
Annandale, VA
256-1701

C. D. Majors is attempting to create a major brand discount carpet and drapery showroom, offering good design services, without effecting the "discount store" look. The store is extremely well-organized and very clean. Merchandise, which ranges from medium to the more expensive lines, is well-displayed. They carry fifty mills, including Roxbury, McGee, and Americana. Sheet vinyl is by manufacturers like Kentile, Flintkote, GAF, Congoleum, and Amtico. Everything is first quality, and all must be special ordered. Discounts range from 15% to 25%, depending on the manufacturer and the item. One-third deposit is required. Labor, particularly installation, is guaranteed for two years. If you want to get a good buy on your carpeting and draperies, but don't want to sacrifice service or quality, this is definitely one place to shop.

Personal checks are accepted with identification, as are Master Charge and VISA. There is a large free parking lot.

Carpets USA
2810 Graham Road,
Falls Church, VA
573-4888

This store is neatly arranged, but stock looks limited, and policies seem inflexible. They deal with local suppliers and carry a line of mostly mid-quality remnants, with all wall-to-wall being special order. They claim to give you a price which is $1 a yard over wholesale price.

Hours are 10 am to 9 pm Monday through Friday, and Saturday from 10 am to 6 pm. Payment can be made with cash or with personal checks with proper identification. There are no returns or exchanges. They will hold items for 2 weeks with ½ of the cost as a deposit. Ample parking in shopping center.

Catalogues Unlimited
11151 Georgia Avenue
Wheaton, MD
946-4224

Catalogues Unlimited sounds like a fascinating place from our researcher's account. She says that they carry catalogues from which you can order a full range of items, including furniture, carpeting, wallpaper, tile, office furniture, restaurant equipment, and more. And you can choose from a low quality up to the highest avaailable, mostly from well-known brand names. Discounts run from 20% to 40% on all first quality merchandise. This is a showroom where they have samples of the carpet, tiles, and wallpaper which they can get for you on special orders in a very short period of time. Furniture takes from 4 to 12 weeks wait. Free delivery is available. They uphold the manufacturers' warranties.

Hours here are from 10 am to 6 pm on Monday through Friday, and from 10 am to 4 pm on Saturday. Personal checks are accepted with proper identifi-

cation, as are Master Charge and VISA. There are no layaways, but they will hold items for 2 weeks with a deposit. There is a large parking lot.

Ceramic Tile
**12240 Wilkins
Rockville, MD
881-2520**

This shop carries a wide range of tile, plastic laminates, bathroom vanities, counter tops, faucets, shower doors, marble, slate, and many related accessories. Well-known brands, in a standard grade, include Robertsons, American Tile, Dupont, Corian, and Wilson Arts Plastic Laminates. Most merchandise is first quality, with some irregulars. Prices are said to be competitive. Most items have to be ordered, and you must wait an average of 2 to 3 weeks, putting one-third deposit on the merchandise. You can order from manufacturers' catalogues.

Personal checks are accepted with proper identification. There are no layaways, but they will hold items for you for up to a week. Tile can be returned (if in full cartons) within 10 days of purchase, but there is a 20% handling charge in most cases. There is ample parking.

Colesville Hardware and Wallpaper
**13423 New Hampshire Avenue
(at Randolph Road)
Silver Spring, MD
384-5673 or 0606**

Colesville Hardware is a small "country" style hardware store, crowded with tons of gadgets and merchandise stashed in every available nook and cranny. You can save from 10% to 50% on all first quality wall coverings by Sanitas, Walltex, Imperial, Schumacher, Van Luitt, Grieff, and other manufacturers. Everything is by order; you must put down a 1/3 deposit, and there is a wait of 2 or 3 days. Orders can be shipped UPS. On holidays, they take additional discounts off the merchandise, and occasionally they have special featured items.

Hours are Monday through Friday from 8 am to 7 pm, Saturday from 8 am to 6 pm, and Sunday from 9 am to 2 pm. Personal checks are accepted with identification, and so are Master Charge and VISA. There are no layaways or holds. There is ample parking. Returns depend on the distributors' policies, usualy within 30 days if in original package. Cut rolls, or single rolls, cannot be returned. Usually, there is a 20% handling charge on returns.

Color Tile
**7500 Richmond Highway
Alexandria, VA
768-5651**

Color Tile sells ceramic tile, vinyl tile and sheet vinyl, carpet squares, wallpaper, mirror squares, caulking, and a variety of related tools. The wallpaper is usually of medium grade and below and is quite inexpensive. The tiles and sheet vinyl are such major brands as GAF, Armstrong, and Amtico. The adhesives and sealers are all the Color Tile brand. Everything is first quality. They do not give a discount *per se* except to contractors, but the prices are, on most items, lower than usual retail. Everything is available in stock, and what is not comes from their warehouse. They ask for 100% of cost in advance on items that are ordered from the warehouse.

Other locations:
315 Ritchie Highway, Glen Burnie, MD, (301) 768-3112
6600 Arlington Blvd., Falls Church, VA, 241-TILE
8410 Sudley Road, Manassas, VA, (703) 369-7070
2012 University Blvd., Hyattsville, MD, 439-1692

Hours here are from 9 am to 9 pm Monday through Friday, Saturday from 9 am to 5:30 pm, and Sunday from 11 am to 5 pm at all store. Personal checks are accepted, as are Master Charge and VISA. Returns are made for credit or for cash refunds. Parking is available at all locations. This is part of a national chain.

Custom Carpets
Turnpike Pickett Shopping Center
Fairfax, VA
323-1333

Custom Carpets stores are neat and well-organized, with many items in stock. They often have extra-special buys on discontinued colors. You can special order brands like Milliken, David, Philadelphia, Columbus, Alden, Majestic, Alexander Smith, and Burlington — in fact, they market every brand in the country except for two. Most prices are quoted with the padding and installation included. There appeared to be no price tags on the merchandise, and it was explained that the salespeople know all of the prices.

Other locations
111 Maple Avenue, Vienna, VA, 938-7400
7301 Little River Turnpike, Annandale, VA, 256-1000

Open Monday and Tuesday from 10 am to 9 pm, Wednesday through Saturday from 10 am to 5 pm. The Vienna store is open from 9:30 am to 9:30 pm from Monday through Friday, and Saturday from 9:30 am to 6 pm, as the Annandale location. Cash is accepted, and they have terms.

Decorative Rugs and Carpets
3230 Duke Street
Alexandria, VA
751-4100

Decorative concentrates on selling the medium to high lines of such manufacturers as West Point Pepperell, Burlington, Lees, Trend, Philadlephia, Masland, and Milliken. They feature wall-to-wall carpeting, remnants, imported area rugs, hardwood flooring, sheet vinyl, and tile — by Congoleum, GAF, Solarium, and Mannington. Everything is first quality, and the true discount ranges from 10% to 20%. About half the items are in stock, and the other half have to be special ordered (they ask a deposit of from 1/2 to 1/3, and there is a wait of 10 to 14 days). Installation is guaranteed for 1 year. There is a mailing list for special sales, which usually occur sometime in the spring and the fall.

Other location:
6198 Arlington Blvd., Falls Church, VA, 241-1133
White Flint Plaza, Rockville, MD
1200 N. Henry Street, Alexandria, VA (warehouse outlet)

Personal checks are accepted, as are Master Charge, VISA, and NAC. On layaways, they require 1/3 down and pickup within 30 days. They will hold items for 24 hours. Returns depend on prearrangements with salesperson or manager. No sale merchandise is returnable. Parking in a small lot at the Duke Street location.

Dennis Tile Sales
6775 Wilson Blvd.,
Falls Church, VA
532-2337

The Wilson Boulevard location of Dennis Tile seems like a really nice place to look for tile. They have a good selection, well-displayed, and friendly personnel. The selection ranges from ceramic tile to marble, to other decorative floor and wall tile treatments. The quality starts at the high side of medium and goes to the finest decorator merchandise. Most are imported, from all over the globe — Italy, Japan, France, Germany, and other places. The discounts run 10% to 30% off comparable retail stores, at what they say are generally the lowest prices in the area. Prices run from $1.26 to $6 per square foot on tile, and $10 per square foot on marble. Most merchandise is in stock, but they ask for 1/2 down on special orders. On large orders (like 300-400 feet) they will deliver. They have designers on the staff who will help you and give you a free estimate if desired. If you wish to take one of their sample boards home, you must leave a deposit. Installation is guaranteed for one year. On installations, they will send out an estimator and give you a written proposal (signed), with everything costed-out. They also sell appropriate setting materials, tools, and tile cutters. All merchandise is priced per square foot, not per piece of tile.

Other locations:
1215 Kenilworth Avenue NE, Washington, DC, 397-2400, open until 5 pm on Thursday night.
1057 Gude Drive, Rockville, MD, 340-7580, open until 8 pm on Thursday night.

Personal checks or cash are accepted. As for holds, they will work with you and hold merchandise if (for example) you are working on remodeling or building your house and you don't have a place to store everything. Refunds are made only on full cartons, and then there is a 20% return charge. They always request ½ of the total cost on orders, and the remainder when you pick up the tiles. They have adequate parking at all locations.

Discount Rugs
6600 New Hampshire Avenue
Takoma Park, MD
270-2212

Discount Rugs sells carpeting from manufacturers like Barwick, Monarch, McGee, Aladdin, and Chandelle. About half of their merchandise is first quality, and the other half is composed of closeouts and remnants. On in-stock merchandise, you save from 40% to 50% off retail; and on special orders you save about 20% off retail, with a 25%-33% down payment and a waiting period of four business days. The store is medium-sized and well-organized, and it has a huge remnant selection. There are free deliveries within the immediate area. Labor is guaranteed for one year. And they hold sales on major holidays.

Hours are Monday through Friday from 10 am to 9 pm, and Saturday from 10 am to 6 pm. Checks are accepted with identification, as are Master Charge, VISA, and Central Charge cards. On layaways, they require 25% down, and pickup and final payment within 30 days. They will hold items for 24 hours without a deposit. Returns made the same day get refunds in the manner in which they paid — i.e., cash, credit card. Exchanges can be made within 2 or 3 days.

Discount Rugs and Carpets
6222 Baltimore Boulevard
Riverdale, MD
927-7585

This is a small shop chock-full of remnants. Their brands vary from medium quality on up. On remnants, you can save 1/3 off comparable retail prices. They will custom order just about any carpet you want. Warranties are those offered by the manufacturer, and installation is guaranteed for one year. They have special sales on major holidays.

They are open from 10 am to 9 pm on Monday through Friday and until 6 pm on Saturday. They accept payment by personal check, Master Charge, VISA, and Central Charge. On layaways, they request 25% down and 30 days for final payment. They will hold items for up to 24 hours without a deposit.

End of Roll Carpets
7500 Richmond Highway
Alexandria, VA
765-1900

End of Roll carries mostly medium quality wall-to-wall carpeting and remnants, from 80 different manufacturerrs. Almost everything is irregulars, manufacturers' closeouts, and seconds. Discounts run up to ½ the retail cost. If you special order first quality merchandise, they give you a 20% savings. On wall-to-wall, they say that they give you a 5-year warranty on the carpet and 2 years on installation. They hold sales once or twice a month.

Other locations:
Shirlington Road, Arlington, VA, 521-2225
2010 University Blvd., Adelphi, Md. 434-3553

Hours are Monday through Friday from 10 am to 9 pm, Saturday from 9 am to 9 pm, and Sunday from 11 am to 70m. Checks are accepted with proper identification as are Master Charge, VISA, American Express, Bank of VA, Central Charge, and NAC charge cards. Layaways require one-half down and pickup within 30-60 days. No refunds or returns on "as is" merchandise, and merchandise credit or cash (check) refunds through the bookkeeper on other purchases. Parking is available at all locations in lots.

Fred O. Harris & Sons
1315 E. Gude Drive
Rockville, MD
762-1192

Fred Harris & Sons sell medium and high quality carpeting by Coronet, Philadelphia, Horizon, Georgian, World Carpets, and others. Remnants account for about 40% of their stock, about 10% is manufacturers' closeouts, and the rest is first quality wall-to-wall. The discount is around 35% to 40%. Most items are in stock, but on special orders, they ask a 50% deposit and 6-8 weeks for delivery. Installation is guaranteed for one year. The store is small and crowded, but the samples are well-displayed.

Hours are Monday through Saturday from 10 am to 5 pm, and on Thursday night until 9 pm. Personal checks are accepted with adequate identification, as are Master Charge and VISA. There are no layaways, but they will hold merchandise for 24 hours. There are no returns or exchanges on remnants.

Georgetown Carpet
Columbia Pike and Glebe Road
Arlington, VA
892-4411

Georgetown Carpets has a lovely showroom, with neatly organized sample books and many oriental carpets hanging on the walls. They allow you to special-order oriental and oriental-style carpets from a catalog, and from samples on wall-to-wall merchandise. They carry almost all mills and give a 20% average discount on these goods. They also carry some remnants left over from their own large jobs, and some mill trials, both of which they discount further. They give a 5-year guarantee on wall-to-wall carpeting. The largest part of their business is in oriental and oriental-style rugs, of which they have a dazzling variety of fine quality from China, India, Persia, and Belgium. This store has special sales about once every two weeks.

Open daily from 10 am to 9 pm, Saturday from 10 am to 7 pm, and Sunday from noon to 5 pm. They accept Master Charge, VISA, American Express, Central Charge, and NAC charge cards, as well as personal checks with proper identification. They allow a one-week approval period on orientals. Parking is available in the small shopping center's lot.

Home Tile
3409 Wilson Blvd.
Arlington, VA
528-9289

Home Tile stores are set up much like warehouses, stacked cartons creating aisles, with samples of each pattern on top of each stack of cartons. They carry a lot of ceramic tile, marble tile, sheet vinyl to order, parquets, bathroom fixtures, grout, grouting tools, ceiling tile, and all kinds of adhesive. The discount depends on what you are buying and the amount of the purchase. They seem to have a good selection of tiles, but we were not impressed with the prices, which are marked on the cartons. The best buys here appeared to be on remnants.

Other addresses:
779 Hungerford Drive, Rockville, MD, 762-0066
9350 Lanham-Severn Road, Seabrook, MD, 459-2233
7641 New Hampshire Avenue, Langley Park, MD, 434-1444
6433 Marlboro Pike, District Heights, MD 736-4563
7684-A Richmond Highway, Alexandria, VA, 768-4722
8104 Sudley Road, Manassas, VA, 361-3717
14402 Jeff. Davis Highway, Woodbridge, VA, 494-3743
3903 Mt. Vernon Avenue, Alexandria, VA, 549-2280

Hours are Monday through Friday from 9 am to 8 pm, and Saturday from 9 am to 5:30 pm. There are no charges under $10 on Master Charge, Central Charge, and Bank of Virginia cards. Checks are accepted with identification. They will hold items up to 45 days with 50% deposit. You can return any unused portions within a reasonable period of time with receipt. Special orders are on a minimum purchase or $5, payment in advance, and no returns.

Hollywood Carpets/Budget Carpets
10212 Southard Drive
Beltsville, MD
937-5595

Hollywood specializes in carpets and also carries custom draperies and vacuum cleaners. Carpet brands are from medium to high quality, mostly by Philadelphia, Coronet, and Cabin Craft. They buy many full rolls and about 15% to 20% of their merchandise consists of remnants, which they purchase in large quantity. They have solids, some printed rugs, and a limited amount of imitation oriental carpets. The Budget side of this large store features carpets at $6.99 and under a yard, and the drapery samples. The other section is devoted to carpets which sell for over $6.99 square yard. Custom orders make up a very small proportion of this business. They guarantee everything to be first quality, and guarantee installation for one year. They also bind carpets. Special sales are rare, usually held once a year — around inventory time.

Open from 9 am to 8:45 pm on Monday through Friday, until 5:45 pm on Saturday, and sometimes open on Sunday. Personal checks are accepted, as are Master Charge and VISA. Layaway terms are negotiable. They will hold items for a day or two. Uncut merchandise can be returned. Parking is ample.

Interior Wall
5542 Randolph Road
Montrose Center
Rockville, MD
881-8255

The Interior Wall carries wallcoverings, draperies, blinds, shades, and paint, mostly from medium to high quality. They also offer free design service. All merchandise is first quality, and you can expect to save from 10% to 50% off comparable retail. About 85% of the merchandise has to be ordered; the rest is in stock. The usual wait is from 2 to 3 days, but is from 2 to 3 weeks on custom orders. A deposit of 1/3 is required. They back the manufacturers' warranties. They advertise weekly and have special sales on holidays.

Hours are Monday through Wednesday from 9:30 am to 6 pm, Thursday and Friday from 9:30 am to 9 pm, and Saturday from 9 am to 6 pm. Personal checks are accepted with proper identification, as are Master Charge and VISA charge cards. There are no layaways or holds.

Karpet King
5600 Randolph Road
Rockville, MD
770-4110

This is a small store, partly organized and partly cluttered, where they sell oriental, wall-to-wall, and area carpets, as well as tile and linoleum. The quality runs from medium up to the highest. Representative manufacturers and lines include Burlington, Philadelphia, Coronet, Armstrong, Galaxy, Monticello, Lees, and Venture. 50% of the merchandise is first-run and first-quality, and the other 50% consists of manufacturers' closeouts, irregulars, and seconds. Savings average from 25% to 35%.

Other address:
15551 Frederick Road, Rockville, MD, 424-7333

Hours are 10 am to 9 pm Monday through Friday, 10 am to 7 pm on Saturday, and on Sunday from noon to 5 pm. Personal checks are accepted with identification, as are Master Charge, VISA, Central Charge, and NAC. Layaway policy is flexible, and there are holds for up to 24 hours. Carpets can be exchanged within 24 hours, but for cash refunds prior arrangements should be made. Ample parking.

Kings's Smarten-Up
2808 Graham Road at Lee Highway
Falls Church, VA
560-4700

King's carries most major brands of wallcoverings, with 1000 patterns in stock (those which have proven to be the most popular with the local clientele. The discount. which runs from 10% to 50%, depends on the manufacturer and the popularity of the design. They do not sell irregulars, but they do generate their own closeouts, which are patterns which they decide to discontinue. Everything is guaranteed against defects, except discontinued patterns or grasscloth. With any pattern in stock, they allow you to take it home, hang two strips, and, if you are dissatisfied, take it down, bring everything back — and receive a full refund! They will also cut large enough samples for you to take home and decide what you want. About every three weeks, they give free paper hanging classes, and they will put on special demonstrations and classes for groups upon request.

Other stores:
Penn Daw Plaza, Alexandria, VA, 765-0800
13289 Gordon, Woodbridge, VA, 491-6900

Hours are from 9:30 am to 9 pm Monday and Friday, from 9:30 am to 5:30 pm on Tuesday through Thursday, and Saturday from 9:30 am to 5 pm. Personal checks are accepted, as are VISA, Master Charge, and Bank of Virginia credit plans. Returns can be made within 30 days in general.

Macon Tile
12201 Nebel Street,
Rockville, MD
881-2616

Macon tile deals in imported and commercial decorative tiles and claims the largest showroom in the area. They sell a range of items from the lowest to the highest quality, including names such as Franciscan, Latco, London Tile, Gail, and imports from Italy, Japan, South Africa, and Amsterdam. They do not really give a discount, but they have good everyday prices on stock items. Most merchandise is first run, first quality, with some manufacturers' closeouts. About 75% of the merchandise has to be ordered. Sales are usually held only to reduce stock, and this happens infrequently. Discounts are offered to builders, designers, and architects — and for other very large orders.

Personal checks are accepted. Returns are accepted on stock items with a 20% charge. There are no refunds on special orders.

Mr. Sunshine
1119 W. Broad Street
Falls Church
241-2929

Mr. Sunshine has a very small showroom, crowded with samples of a wide range of first quality and roll-end carpets from Mohawk and McGee, and some Burlington lines. They also sell Belgian wools, and handwoven rugs from Packistan and Persia. Most items must be special ordered, and the quoted price includes installation and padding. Savings range from 10% to 40%, They also display designer Solarian, on which they give discounts of 30% to 40% off retail. There is a five-year wear guarantee on carpeting, and a 10-year guarantee on installation, providing any steam cleaning is done by them. There is a five-year installation guarantee on sheet vinyl.

Hours are Monday through Friday from 10 am to 7 pm, and Saturday from 10 am to 5:30 pm. They accept VISA, Master Charge, and Central Charge cards. Returns or exchanges should be made within three days.

Plymouth Wallpaper
720 Frederick Road,
Catonsville, MD
(301) 788-8500

Definitely an exciting place to look for wallpaper, and one of the best finds in this book! Plymouth carries a huge collection of papers in two separate stores. Their regular store is organized with rows of bins, and all the tools which you need to install the wallpaper. They also have books from almost every manufacturer, from which you can order. If they have these patterns in stock, you get a better buy than special ordering. In the store they regularly carry loads of seconds and closeouts from major manufactuers, on which you can get particularly good buys. They claim the largest selection in the country, with 1 million rolls in stock, as they service many wallpaper stores throughout the nation. They also have trained salespeople who can give you decorating advice. But wait — you can get really rock-bottom prices in the surplus store, where they sell room-size bundles of wallpaper for outrageously low prices. They have two-for-one sales two times a year, and sales on most major holidays. For these sales, they advertise in the *Baltimore Sun*, and also regularly advertise in it two times a week. They give clinics and demonstrations, in which they teach you how to hang your wallpaper.

Other address:
1100 N. Chester Street in East Baltimore, New warehouse.

Hours are 9 am to 9 pm on weekdays, 9 am to 5 pm on Saturday, and Sunday from 11 am to 5 pm. Personal checks are accepted with proper identification. They also accept all charge cards. They request 1/3 cown on layaways, and pickup within 30 days. Sample rolls can be returned for credit. Liberal exchange and return policy — all double rolls can be returned if left over from a job.

Price Right
11910 Parklawn Drive
Rockville, MD
881-5595

Their motto is "If you haven't shopped Price-Right — you haven't got the right price". They try to uphold this policy on carpet and linoleum, claiming to be able to beat anyone else's price by about 25%. They say that they carry every mill in the world, including Lee, Bigelow, Coronet, Philadelphia, and Mohawk. No merchandise is first quality, according to our researcher — everything is manufacturers' closeouts, and seconds, and all are so labeled. As to discounts, they say that carpeting usually selling for $15 a yard runs $7.50 here, and that they limit their mark-ups to a very small amount. While most items are in stock, they do order first quality, well-to-wall if you desire. They offer Saturday specials with coupons. Free delivery is available. Materials are backed by the manufactuer, and this is put in the store's contract. They give you a free yardstick with every purchase.

Hours are from 9:30 am to 9 pm on Monday through Friday, 9 am to 6 pm on Saturday, and until 5 pm on Sunday. Personal checks are accepted, as are Master Charge, VISA, Central Charge, and NAC charge cards. On layaways they request 10% down, and pickup within 90 days maximum. They will hold items for several days. Exchanges on uncut merchandise may be made withing 48 hours of purchase. A small parking oot is available.

Rug Man
648 S. Pickett Street
Alexandria, VA
370-4558

The Rug Man sells wall-to-wall carpeting and remnants, ranging from the lowest to the highest quality, with such names represented as Barwick, Trend, and Gulistan by Stevens. Their stock is made up of first quality merchandise, manufacturers' closeouts, irregulars, and seconds. The discount is about 50% off list price on remnants. On special orders, they give the manufacturer's list price. Most items are in stock. The facility is a very large warehouse, with many large rolls to choose from. Their specialty is remnants s (at very low prices for good quality), mill overruns, and closeouts; and they also offer a competitive price for an installation and padding package.

Other location:
11501 Rockville Pike, Rockville, MD, 770-5695

Hours are Monday through Friday from 9 am to 9 pm, Saturday from 9 am to 7 pm, and Sunday from 11 am to 6 pm. Personal checks are accepted with proper identification, as are Master Charge, VISA, and NAC charge cards. They ask for 30% down on layaways, and payment and pickup within two weeks. Holds are worked out with the salesperson, as are returns and exchanges. Ample parking available.

Shamrock Supply Co.
10226 Southard Drive
Beltsville, MD
937-1966

Shamrock has two large fresh-looking rooms in a row of warehouse-type stores. In the first room, you can find Muralo paint, a wide range of wallpaper sample books, samples for custom louver blinds and woven woods, and all kinds of painters' tools and accessories. In the second room are racks filled with in-stock wallpaper. You save 30% to 40% off the retail prices of in-stock wallpaper here, and get discounts on quantity lots — such as room lots — of about 10% on special orders. They hold six major sales a year, but they always have a featured item at a special price. Brand names found here include Sanitas and David and Dash wallpapers, Muralo paints, as well as a fine selection of Spanish and other imported papers. All merchandise is first quality. They ask a deposit of 50% down on most special orders. Shamrock can also special order murals and carpeting for you. Any merchandise found to be defective will be replaced, or you can have your money refunded.

Hours are from 9 am to 5 pm on Monday through Friday, and from 10 am to 4 pm on Saturday. Personal checks are accepted, as are Master Charge, VISA, and Central Charge. Sales on in-stock merchandise are final. Special order merchandise can be returned, subject to a 20% handling charge, no more than 30 days after purchase. Parking is adequate.

United Floor and Wallcoverings, Inc.
3923 Plyers Mill Road,
Kensington, MD
942-5677

This is a small, attractive store offering a large selection of carpeting, with attractively displayed samples. They carry carpeting, Armstrong and Congoleum floorings, and wall coverings, ranging in quality from the lowest to the highest. Carpet brands found here are Williamsburg, West Point Pepperell, and Monarch (among others), and they also market Fashion-Styletex wall coverings. Discounts average 20% off comparable retail prices. 100% of their sales are special order merchandise. You put down 50% and usually wait from 2 to 3 days for flooring, one week for carpeting, and two days for wallcovering. They guarantee labor for one year. And special sales are held on holidays.

Open Monday through Friday from 9 am to 5 pm. Personal checks, Master Charge, VISA, and Central Charge are accepted forms of payment. There are no layaways, but they will hold merchandise for up to a week. There is a 20% handling charge on returns. Sale merchandise is final sale.

Walls by Daizee
5414 Randolph Road
Rockville, MD
881-4620

This shop sells draperies, slipcovers, wallpaper, shades, blinds, and custom draperies and fabrics. Typical brands here are of medium to finest quality and include Kirsch, Bob Burger, DelMar, Levolor, Van Luitt, and Schumacher. All merchandise is first quality. The discount ranges from 25% to 30% on the average, depending on the item and the manufacturer. About 90% of their business is on special orders, for which there is a 2 to 3 day wait and a 25% deposit required. They take telephone orders, and you can also order in the store from the sample books and swatches. They hold sales here on major holidays. They also offer interior design services.

This store is open from 10 am to 9 pm on Monday, Thursday, and Friday, and until 6 pm on Tuesday and Wednesday. Saturday, they are open from 10 am to 5 pm, and Sunday from noon to 4 pm. Personal checks, Master Charge, and VISA are accepted. Layaway policy varies, but usually they request 25% down and payment within 2 to 3 weeks. You can return extra rolls, but you pay the shipping fee. Cash refunds or exchanges will be made within a week of purchase. There is a small parking lot.

Wholesale Carpet
6604 Old Landover Road
Landover Hills, MD
322-5799

Wholesale Carpet carries a wide range of carpeting and floor coverings. About fifty percent of their trade is in remnants, 10% in closeouts, and another 10% in irregulars and seconds, with the remainder in first quality, first run merchandise. The average discount runs 20% off comparable retail. Special orders can be made from manufacturers' catalogues.

They hold weekly sales, advertise major sales one or two times a year, and put out flyers monthly.

This shop is open from Monday through Friday from 10 am to 9 pm, Tuesday until 7 pm, Saturday to 6 pm, and Sunday from noon to 5 pm. Personal checks are accepted with proper identification, as are Master Charge, VISA, American Express, Central Charge, and NAC. Layaway policy is liberal, with pickup to 8 months from date of deposit. They will hold merchandise with a deposit. There are no refunds — merchandise credit only. All sale merchandise is final sale. There is a small parking lot.

Woodmont Carpet Co.
11712 Parklawn Drive,
Rockville, MD
770-4555

Woodmont carpet has just begun to set aside a bargain room, selling first quality and manufacturers' closeouts from their usual retail store. Their merchandise is usually of the highest quality: they represent manufacturers and names like Cabin Craft, Barwick, Milliken, Matrrix, Lees, Oleg Cassini, and Galaxy for carpeting; Amtico, Armstrong, Vinylcraft, GAFSTAR, Mannington, and Kentile tiles and sheet vinyl; and Schumacher fabrics. The discount depends on the quality, but averages from 15% to 40% below comparable retail. Installation is guaranteed for one year. They run newspaper ads weekly and have special sales on holidays. The store is well-organized, with large spaces and attractive displays. They carry a huge assortment of merchandise, all non-discount in appearance.

This store is open from 9 am to 5:30 pm Tuesday through Saturday, and is open until 9 pm on Monday and Thursday. Personal checks are accepted, and so are Master Charge and Visa charge cards. There is no layaway policy. Refunds are made on stock merchandise, but not on special orders — unless arranged beforehand, in which case there might be a handling charge. There is a medium-sized parking lot.

Post Wallcoverings
(800) 521-8750
P.O. Box 411
Royal Oak, Michigan 48068

The concept of Post Wallcoverings sounds really good — it is a mail order wallcovering business from which you can purchase any wallpaper available. The discount is a consistent 27% off retail price, and you pay no sales tax. Delivery is also free. They have a mailing list and, once a year, they send out basic information about their operations and pricing policies to everyone on the list, or to anyone who calls in. You call them and tell them the name of the book, the pattern number, the manufacturer's suggested retail price, and the number of rolls desired. There is no minimum purchase requirement, and no deposit. Post requires no payment until the wallpaper is delivered. They also discount all lines of Levolor blinds and woven woods at 27% off the suggested retail price.

Hours are 9 am to 5 pm Monday through Friday. Personal checks are accepted. There are no returns, but defective merchandise will be replaced.

RELATED PUBLICATIONS

Annual Handbook of Contract Floor Covering. Floor Covering Weekly Publications, 1977-1978.

Carpet Specifiers' Handbook. Second Edition. Dalton, Georgia: Carpet and Rug Institute, 1976.

Floor Products Technical Manual. GAF, 1976.

"Resilient Floor Coverings." *Better Homes and Gardens,* July 1979, pp. 28-30.

Tires & Auto Parts

TIRES

You kick them, but do you really know what you are kicking? You ride around on them all the time and entrust yourself to their ability, but do you know how to take care of them? Did you know that they could kill you if you push them too hard or neglect them too often?

They are your car's tires.

They are treated like slaves and are rarely given much more respect. You could save a few dollars, and you can save your life if you learn the proper care and feeding of your car's tires. Many people buy one or two or even a whole set, install them, forget they exist, and keep on driving. No matter what driving habits you have, you owe it to yourself to keep a watchful eye on your tires from the time you purchase them to the time you finally have to replace them.

What is a tire anyway?

A tire has a number of parts. The part outside you see is the heavy rubber tread. Any symptom of illness will usually appear here first. The tread is made of rubber that has been conceived with both traction and a smooth ride in mind. Except for specialty models, the rubber is a blend of toughness and resiliency. This is important to remember, because if you tend to abuse one characteristic, like toughness, by overinflating, you will notice that you get a harder ride because you've lost some pliability.

There are also parts that you don't see: underneath the heavy tread are any number of tread reinforcements. Steel, polyester, and nylon belts and cords bolster the strength and resiliency. Under this there is the inner tube, which does double duty in the summertime at many beaches and pools. The inner tube actually holds the air and expands the tread shell. It is important that you keep the inner tube valve (the stem that protrudes through the hub cap) from rubbing against the hub cap. It is also important that it be kept free from any blockage which could make filling the tire difficult.

Most radials are tubeless. Also, most tires which are steel-belted are tubeless, because the strength of the steel makes them puncture-resistant.

How do tires differ?

The grade of rubber, the traction quality, and temperature tolerance are all variants. These are so important to the consumer that the manufacturers are required to list, *on their tires*, the quality grading for each category. This is designed to assist the consumer in buying the right tire for the right job at the right price.

The Uniform Tire Quality Grading System, established in 1979, is the name of the program which requires tire manufacturers to list the three vital grades on the side of the tire. The listing will either be in the form of a sticker on the tread, or as raised lettering on the side of the tread:

Treadwear will appear as a number in a multiple of ten. The higher the number, the better the expected mileage. A tire graded at 80 will be expected to give you somewhat less mileage than one graded at 150. The grade of 100 represents 30,000 miles (the number of miles that type of tire lasted on a government track). The mileage you get should be in line with the government's rating if you keep the tires properly inflated, aligned, and balanced. Any number other than 100 means life expectancy is either reduced or increased in a proportionate manner. A grade of 140 would then mean the tire would be expected to give you 40% more, or 42,000 miles — under test conditions.

Traction is graded in three categories: A, B, C. The tire's traction capacity is figured in terms of friction with the road.

Grade A is achieved when the friction level produced (or the tire's ability to grab the road surface) exceeds an arbitrary number set by the Department of Transportation for traction on two kinds of test courses. Grade A is the best and safest.

A grade of B signifies smaller traction capacity than grade A. If the tire is graded C, you can be sure of only one thing: that the tire has significantly reduced traction compared to grade A; there is no minimum requirement for grade C. This means a tire could meet no traction requirements and still be rated grade C.

Temperature resistance is also graded A, B, C. In this case the grade measures the heat resistance of the tire and the tire's capacity to stay relatively cool at high speeds. A rating of A assures you that the tire can run at temperatures of up to 115 degrees for a sustained period without severe consequences (like a blowout or tread separation). A tread separation would mean that the seam between the tread shell and the rest of the tire has begun to come apart. The grade B means the tire can sustain itself at a running temperature of 100 degrees. The grade C tire will run hotter than both A and B; aside from this, little is known. There *are* minimum requirements for tires graded C, however, so you do have some modicum of assurance.

There are four basic tire constructions:
1. **Bias ply tires** are the simplest which you can buy. They consist of either nylon, rayon, or polyester cords grouped together in belts, running on an angle under the tread. In a 2-ply construction there are two belts crisscrossing each other, and in a 4-ply, four belts. Since the cords run angle, or on the bias, they are called bias ply. But one problem with this type of construction is the friction between the cords when they rub together.

2. **Bias belted tires** are an improvement over regular bias ply tires. In this type of construction, the cords are covered with a layer of belts just below the tread. This cuts down wear and tear to some extent, but it is only another step on the road to tire excellence.

3. **Radial tires** include almost every improvement in the tire to date. With the radial construction, cords that run on an angle in the bias ply tires are nearly parallel, and run from side to side of the tire. This means that no scissoring friction will age the tire. Radials are also belted for toughness and flexibility. And, because more of the tire surface meets the road, the water chanelling grooves are more efficient, which means that they are safer on wet surfaces.

4. **Elliptical construction tires** are the most advanced of tire constructions. They improve on the radial concept by allowing higher inflation pressure. The higher the pressure, the better the tire's shock absorbing capacity. Yet they still save you gas. One minor drawback is the new rim needed by many cars in order to accept the newer elliptical construction.

What Is a Retread?

A retread is a tire remade by attaching a new layer of tread to a used tire casing (or shell). Retreads can be excellent values when they are of high quality, because all retreads sell for less than new tires. A spokesman for a local tire chain store (along with other experts) cautions that retreads are better used in the fall and winter. This is due to occasional tread separation at high temperatures. It is recommended that you keep a retread as a spare and use retreads in the winter months to cut the costs of new snow tires. It is also important to remember that retreaded tires are recommended for use only on the rear wheels — and this rule should be strictly followed. Retreaded tires must (by requirement) have information regarding their component parts and load capabilities as well as ply content. If a dealer hedges on any of this information, shop elsewhere, no matter how irresistible the deal may seem. It is of paramount importance that the retread be as trustworthy as a new tire — its responsibilities are just as great.

One final point on tire installation. The Department of Transportation (DOT) advises you to avoid mixing tires of different construction types on your car at one time. You should either have five (including the spare) bias plys or five radial tires at all times. In case you must mix tire types on your car, it is important that each axle have the same type of tire. This means that you might have radials on the front and bias ply on the rear axle, for example.

Shopping for Tires and Extending Tire Life

Usually you have a choice of the tire size for your car, van, or truck. It may be that you can use a radial or an oversized tire, which can afford you a greater load capacity. If you tow or carry heavy loads you'll want a tire capable of the work load. Using the grade system, you can shop around for a larger tread size and better traction.

And remember to comparison shop with the tire grade in mind. An appreciable difference in the treadwear grade may justify a higher price, but try not to trade too much treadwear capacity for traction, as you may feel the loss of traction at an inconvenient time. You would be well advised to sit down and figure out your tire needs realistically, and then seek the proper tire ratings when comparison shopping for price and warranty. Your driving needs and habits should dictate the desired ratings.

United States Department of Transportation (DOT) figures show a great disparity in tire life depending on the owner. An owner who often makes jack-rabbit starts and "tire screeching turns" will get as low as 14,000 miles on a tire that another driver might get 30,000 miles on in the same city.

DOT reports that every year consumers in this country throw away millions of dollars in unnecessarily junked tires. These are tires discarded mostly due to consumer ignorance and abuse.

Here is a list of very simple steps which will maximize your tire life and thus save you money on replacement tires:

- Don't overload or underinflate the tires. Either of these can put undue pressure on the tire and force it to work under the worst circumstances. Think of it this way: you couldn't carry a heavy load on the run for very long... so why make your tires do it? You also wouldn't want to carry anything heavy while squatting down; your legs would weaken. The same holds true for your tires: If underinflated, a tire will begin to weaken around the sidewalls and under the tread. Any kind of weakening will reduce tire life.
- Become familiar with your tires' capabilities. The tire will have on its side the maximum load and pressure capacities. Adhere to these recommendations, and the tire will remain healthy and able.

WE WILL NOT BE UNDERSOLD!

SEE OUR LISTING IN THE TIRE SECTION...
How to buy a tire for less without getting less tire!

- DELCO BATTERIES
- GENERIC BATTERIES
- ORIGINAL EQUIPMENT WHEELS
- SUPERIOR, ROCKET, APPLIANCE & AMERICAN RACING CUSTOM WHEELS

Anyone can sell you a cheap tire. The trick is to get a good tire at the lowest possible price. That isn't as simple as it sounds either. Most tire manufacturers make several grades of tires and there is a substantial difference in terms of manufacturing costs, materials, and life expectancy from one grade level to another. So even if you buy a name brand you aren't assured that you got your money's worth.

We sell quality tires at the lowest possible price. That way if you get good value for your money, you'll come back and buy from us again. In fact, you might even tell a friend about us. And that's important. Our advertising budget is very small relative to the number of tires we sell. That's part of how we keep our overhead down so we can keep prices down. Other ways we keep overhead down is by locating in industrial parks where rent is cheap and by getting tires by the tractor-trailer load direct from the factory.

Just remember, at Universal Tire Warehouses our tires aren't cheap they're just inexpensive.

Mon. & Thurs. 10 to 8; Tues., Wed., Fri. 8 to 6; Saturday 8 to 1

GOODYEAR
MICHELIN
B.F.Goodrich
GENERAL TIRE
SEMPERIT
GENERIC

Tires mounted free on most cars

Universal Tire WAREHOUSES

VISA, MASTER CHARGE, CENTRAL CHARGE, NAC

- Strive for more miles when you drive. Don't feel you can drive over chuck holes or make screeching turns and stops without sacrificing future miles. When you hear a squeal going around a tight corner, realize you've aged your tires a good couple of miles more than was necessary. And those long black skid marks you may occasionally leave behind represent upwards of 100 miles or more you won't get in the future.

Some more tips for extending tire life:
- Buy a good tire pressure gauge to check your pressure often.
- Check your tires (cold, never warm) for tire pressure at least once a month.
- On a long trip inflate the tire pressure to four or five pounds more than average (but never more than the maximum). The ride may be a bit harder, but the tires will run cooler.
- If tires seem overinflated when hot, *don't* bleed the "extra" air out. Later, when tires cool, the pressure will be too low. Some expansion due to heat is expected.
- A tire which seems chronically low should be checked often and then probably replaced. The leak could be due to anything from a slow leak to a bent valve.

- Check old air valve stems when replacing old or winter tires. A cracked valve stem can be replaced for a fraction of the cost of an entire tire. But, if neglected, the cracked valve can render a tire useless over time.
- Check your spare tire pressure as often as you check your other tires.
- Rotate your tires every 6,000 miles, including your spare, to a new position on your car. The owner's manual diagrams the best method. Examine each tire while it is off the car for signs of uneven tread wear. You may need to replace a tire or shock or simply realign the tire.
- Make it a habit to check over your tires' looks as often as you get into your car.
- Don't bounce over barriers (such as curbs or parking blocks) if you must cross them.
- Be attentive to your tires pulling the steering wheel to one side. If this happens, it may be due to an over- or under-inflated tire. Rear pulling or swaying may be due to inflation problems in rear tires. A thump-thump noise made during hard braking may indicate breakdown problems — get it looked at soon.
- Store tires in a cool place, lying flat and away from any motors. Motors tend to emit ozone, which can break down rubber.

Excessive heat is a real problem to be avoided. Heat can separate the ply section in the tire (see diagram) to the point of a gap which leads to the tread wearing off the tire or the tire blowing out while in use. This can be quite hazardous under highway conditions. Retreaded tires are especially susceptible to this.

AUTO PARTS

Americans spend a total of $50 billion dollars a year on assorted maintenance expenditures for their cars and light trucks. The average American spends $380 in repair and maintenance costs for each automobile in his household.

These figures come from a report issued in May, 1978 by the Department of Transportation. Included in the costs are allowances for: repairs, maintenance, tires, batteries, oil and accessories, accidents, fuel waste, pollution, and reduced vehicle life due to improper repairs and maintenance. Of the total expenditure for auto maintenance the DOT study shows $6 billion was spent on maintenance-related accidents. A total of $47 billion was spent on all repairs and maintenance.

The auto repair industry is big business. It may seem confusing to the average car owner when repairs are needed. But there are some principles to keep in mind: familiarizing yourself with your car's owner's manual will make you more aware of what to expect of maintenance costs, and it will also show you what to do to keep down costs by keeping the car in good working order. This manual belongs within easy reach for consultation — not buried "somewhere" in the glove compartment.

You would also do well to talk to a licensed mechanic, have him do your repair work, and advise you on which car repairs can be done by the do-it-yourselfer, and with which parts. For some repairs you will be able to make a small investment in special tools for standard maintenance (such as spark plug changes) and cut your repair costs over the years. Also find out where your mechanic gets his parts, and compare prices and quality of those parts with a car catalogue, such as Chilton's. With this information you can learn basic repairs and valuable information concerning quality parts.

When major repairs crop up it is best to see the dealer first while shopping around for repair estimates. This is especially true if your car is currently under warranty by a dealer.

Whether or not you are doing the actual work yourself, it is wise to inquire about rebuilt parts. These parts, when applicable and available, can save you up to a third or even half of new part prices. And, if you need a part you just can't afford, take a chance on area junkyards. Often a part can be taken intact from a junk car; this will give you great savings over new parts.

Finally, it is very important to get a receipt for any work done, and to investigate labor and part warranties before you sign or agree to any work.

MORRIS KATZ & SONS
CAR RADIO AND STEREO CENTER, INC.

Selling, Servicing & Installing Car Radios...
Ever Since There Were Car Radios!

CAR **RADIOS**

CAR RADIO REPAIRS

Corner Prince & S. Peyton Sts.　　　　　　　　　　683-5670
Alexandria, VA　　　　　　　　　　　　　　Ample Free Parking

AUTO PARTS AND TIRE BARGAINS

Stores selling auto parts and tires look pretty much alike — so in the following pages we have concentrated on providing you with information about what brands they carry and what kind of discounts they offer. In the course of our research, we found that all of these stores could be roughly split into about four different groups, which reflect pricing and merchandising policy. Usually, at an automobile dealership or gas station, you will pay full price on parts and tires. Then there are large chains of auto parts stores, which carry many house brand parts and some better known brands at discount. The next level is that of the smaller independents or chains, which usually offer high quality merchandise at prices below list, and are frequented by mechanics and hot shot do-it-yourselfers. For lower prices, you can look for used parts at salvage shops or shops which specialize in used auto parts, or junkyards, where you can often get really inexpensive parts.

Most tire shops carry most major manufacturers, and some carry a limited selection of major manufacturers as well as a selection of house or lesser-known brands. Use the free services available through tire dealers as a point of comparison — some offer free mounting. Compare the costs of balancing as well. When buying tires, be sure to get the whole package price.

You should use information from friends as well as from mechanics and trade publications to help you decide what auto parts and tires you want to buy. When you decide what you want, use the telephone to compare prices of the same product at a number of the stores listed below. Again, all other things being equal, you should stick with the shop closest to you, as this saves you gas and makes getting service more convenient. And, as always, compare warranties.

Amp Auto Parts
8655 Richmond Highway
Alexandria, VA
780-7477

This privately-owned chain of three local stores sells American and foreign car and light truck parts. They carry all name brands. All items are first quality and rebuilt, with discounts averaging 20% to 40%. Most items are in stock. They offer a 90 day warranty on parts and will replace defective electrical parts. Once in a while they have sales, which they advertise in local papers. Sometimes they offer 10% off coupons.

Other address:
431 S. Maple Avenue, Falls Church, VA, 534-8863

Stores are open from 8 am to 7 pm Monday through Friday and until 5 pm on Saturday. Personal checks, Master Charge, and VISA are accepted. Returns are usually no problem, but they are not accepted on electrical parts. There are small but ample parking lots at both locations.

Angel's Car Radio
2900 Jefferson Davis Highway
Alexandria, VA
548-0776

Angel's sells car radios, tape decks, and speakers, with name brands like Pioneer, Audiovox, Craig, Sanyo, Tenna, and Blaupunkt. All merchandise is first quality, and you can save at least 20% and up to 50% depending on the merchandise. They claim the largest selection in the area, with all major brands and up-to-date models. They warranty all merchandise and do repairs. Sales are held here on major holidays.

Other address:
800 South Washington Street, Falls Church, VA 22046, 532-0300

Hours are Monday through Friday from 8:30 am to 6 pm, and Saturday to 4 pm. Personal checks, Master Charge, VISA, and Central Charge are accepted. All sales are final. But satisfaction is guaranteed. If you have a problem within the warranty period, they will remove the unit and give you full credit, with no charge for removal. They always give advance estimates, even on the smallest jobs.

Bargain Tire Co.
8217 Lee Highway
Merrifield, Fairfax, VA
280-4110

Bargain Tire features Goodyear, Goodrich, and Lee of Conshohocton (a division of Goodyear) tires. They sell new, used, and retreads. Free mounting is offered. Repairs are available. All manufacturers' warranties are backed up, regardless of point of purchase. Goodyear tires are sold at 20% less than list/advertised prices. They also carry Best batteries. This company is locally-owned.

Other address:
2245 Huntington Avenue, Alexandria, VA, 960-4420

Open 8 am to 5:30 pm daily and until 1 pm on Saturday. They accept personal checks with proper identification, Master Charge, VISA, Central Charge, NAC, and American Express. Returns will be accepted on all but special orders.

Beck Arnley Auto Parts
2740-A Gallows Road
Vienna, VA
573-9204

Beck Arnley carries foreign car parts, 99% of which are new. They carry brands such as Castrol, Lucas, and Bosch, as well as OEM — original equipment manufacturers. The management quoted a typical example of their pricing policy: a $99 retail British Leyland TR-6 rear muffler can be obtained here for $45. But the average discount is around 25%. On special orders, the amount of deposit varies with the item and its cost. On most merchandise, they back up the manufacturers' warranties, or offer a 90-day courtesy guarantee of their own. Only 15% to 20% of their business is retail. Advertisements for the Beck Arnley independent distributors appear in the *Washington Post*. They will also ship merchandise as desired.

Other addresses:
4469 Beech Drive, Marlow Heights, MD, 899-3770
1321 Gude Drive, Rockville, MD, 424-4600.

All stores are open from 8 am to 6 pm on Monday through Friday, and Saturday from 9 am to 3 pm. No personal checks are accepted, but Master Charge, Visa, Central Charge, and NAC are. There is a 10% handling charge on all returns, unless they gave you the wrong part. Returns must be made within 30 days. Electrical parts are non-returnable. Ample parking is available.

B & S Auto Supply
302 Riggs Road NE
Washington, DC
526-6366

B & S sells auto parts and accessories, new and rebuilt, foreign and American, from a medium-sized, cluttered shop. They sell major brands, all first quality, with average discounts of 30% to 40% off list price. Most items are in stock. They back up the manufacturers' warranties, and will replace defective merchandise.

This store is open from 8 am to 5:30 pm on Monday through Saturday. Master Charge and VISA are accepted forms of payment. There are no returns on electrical parts, no refunds on tools, and a 10% handling charge on merchandise returned for credit. Returns must be made within a reasonable period of time. Ample parking in shopping center lot.

Beltway Kawasaki
8807 Annapolis Road
Lanham, MD
577-8883

You can find motorcycles, parts, accessories, service, insurance, and trailers for motorcycles at this store, all first quality. They claim that they will meet any deal. Everything is in stock, but if you ask for a special order, they ask for a 50% deposit, and there is a wait of one to two weeks. They back up the manufacturers' warranties and will do repairs on Kawasakis.

Store hours vary by season. At the time of the interview, they were open from Monday through Friday from noon to 9 pm, and Saturday from 9 am to 6 pm. They accept personal checks, Master Charge, VISA, Central Charge, and NAC. Layaway policy is flexible, as are holds. Returns are made for cash or credit on parts and accessories. Ample parking in Lanham Shopping Center area lot.

Capital Cycle Corporation-BMW
2328 Champlain Street, NW
Washington, DC
387-7360

This store carries BMW parts only, and they are factory originals. The discounts average 20% but often go to about 50% of the dealer's price. On special orders, they ask for full payment in advance. This shop does a huge mail order business and ships items UPS. There is a free store catalogue available, and a mailing list you can have your name put on. They offer a warranty for 6 months against defective merchandise. About every other month, they usually have special sales on overstock merchandise. They do work on BMW's at $15 an hour; they claim this is among the cheapest rates in the city.

Personal checks are accepted, but credit cards are not. There is a 15% restocking charge if the customer made a mistake in choosing a part. Returns can be made, usually within 30 days of purchase. There is a medium-sized free parking lot on the side of the building.

Carolina Auto Parts & Supplies
6213 Georgia Avenue NW
Washington, DC
723-1993

Carolina sells auto parts: foreign and American, rebuilt and new. They feature brands including TRW, Everhot, SMS, Cayco, Gates, and Bendix. All is first quality merchandise with a 10% discount off list price. 90% of their merchandise is in stock, with only a short wait on special orders. Free delivery is available. Electrical parts are returnable only if defective. On heavy parts, there is a 90 day warranty, for which you must keep your receipt.

Hours here are from 8 am to 11 pm Monday through Saturday, and until 9 pm on Sunday. They accept personal checks with proper identification, Master Charge, VISA, American Express, Central Charge, and NAC. There are no layaways. Electrical parts are not returnable. On other returned items, there is a 20% handling fee. There is parking in a small free lot.

Consumer Discount Tire
273 Derwood Circle
East off Gude Drive
Rockville, MD

At these facilities, they sell tires and provide mounting and balancing services. All tires are first quality, of brands such as Michelin, B.F. Goodrich, Centennial, and Firestone. The general public discount is 25% off retail prices. If you are a government or military employee, or belong to a member buying group, like certain businesses in the vicinity, construction groups, etc., you can get an additional 5% to 8% off the already-discounted prices. 90% of merchandise is in stock. Usually there is a 3-day wait for special order merchandise, with an average 20% deposit requested. Some tires carry warranties based on mileage. They offer free mounting on standard wheels. They hold special sales on a weekly basis and advertise in the newspapers.

Other addresses:
9176 Red Branch Road, Columbia, MD
309 Ritchie Road, Capitol Heights, MD
6407 Industrial Road, Springfield, VA
8524 Tyco Road, Vienna, VA
13900 Lee Highway, Centerville, VA
9412 Grant Avenue, Manassas, VA

All stores are open Monday through Friday from 8 am to 6 pm, and on Saturday until 3 pm. Personal checks with proper identification, Master Charge, VISA, American Express, Carte Blanche, Central Charge, and NAC are all accepted. They will hold items for up to 24 hours. Unused merchandise can be exchanged or money refunded as long as you have a receipt. Adequate parking at all locations.

Douglas Speed Sport Center
8205 Fenton Street
Silver Spring
589-2000

At Douglas Speed Sport, they sell automotive parts and accessories, and custom and high performance parts, all of high quality, from such manufacturers as Accel, Carter, Edelbrock, Hurst, Holly, and Isky. All merchandise is first quality, and they give discounts ranging from 10% to 50%. About one-half of the merchandise is in stock, and the other half has to be special ordered, which takes about a day.

This store is open from 10 am to 6 pm weekdays, until 7 pm on Tuesday and Thursday, and from 10 am to 3 pm on Saturday. Personal checks are accepted, as are Master Charge, VISA, and NAC charge cards. Layaway policy is liberal, with a final payment and pickup due within 45 days of purchase. They will hold items up to two days. There are no cash refunds. Items can be returned within 5 days, subject to a 10% handling charge. Metered on-street parking is nearby.

D & R Tire Wholesalers, Inc.
1301 E. Gude
Rockville, MD
424-4585

At D&R, they sell tires, original equipment wheels, custom wheels, shocks, and brake and alignment work. Quality of merchandise runs the gamut as to price and quality. Brands seen here include

Dunlop, Michelin, Goodyear, Semperit, Saxon (which is their house brand), and Encore. Most merchandise is first quality. A very small percent is manufacturers' closeouts, and some blemished tires. The average discount here is from 30% to 40% off retail list. Most merchandise is in stock. Alignments are guaranteed for one year. Sales are held on an irregular basis.

Other address:
10112 Bacon Drive, Beltsville, MD, 937-4437

Hours are Monday and Thursday from 9 am to 8 pm, Tuesday, Wednesday, and Friday to 6:30 pm, and Saturday from 9 am to 2 pm at both stores. Personal checks are accepted, as are Master Charge, VISA, American Express, Central Charge, and NAC credit cards. There are no layaways or holds. Cash refunds are not given on special order merchandise.

Factory New Car Buying Service
114 Essenton Drive
Upper Marlboro
249-9179

These people offer you the chance to buy an American car at the lowest price without haggling with the dealer. They suggest that you check with the dealer first, look at the car you want and get his best price, and then give them a call including all of the details about the vehicle which you desire. They will then quote you the actual dealer invoice cost, including options you desire. They claim to save you up to $750 on a car — less on the larger, luxury models. They can also obtain trucks up to one ton. Delivery is made either from a local dealer or from Detroit. If it is from the local dealer, you are informed which one just prior to delivery. You have a factory warranty, which will be honored by any authorized dealership, as long as you follow all of the usual rules and such about keeping records, etc. The reason that dealers are willing to participate is that they are dealing with this service basically under a fleet purchase mentality, which minimizes their sales time investment, as well as their paperwork. Call for brochures and other information.

Fairfax Auto Parts/Economy Auto Parts
8701 Lee Highway
Fairfax, VA
560-1560

For most major lines of auto parts, both new and rebuilt, you can come to Fairfax or Economy Auto Parts. They say that they can save you 15% to 45% off manufacturers' list prices.

Other addresses:
10912 Lee Highway, Fairfax, VA, 591-6500
7809 Centreville Road, Manassas, VA, (703) 368-7191
Economy Auto Parts, 3855 Pickett Street, Fairfax, VA, 978-4500

All stores are open from 8 am to 9 pm Monday through Friday, Saturday until 4 pm, and Sunday from 10 am to 4 pm. They accept payment in personal checks, VISA, and Master Charge. There are no returns on electrical parts, and exchanges are allowed on everything else. Parking is available at all locations.

G. W. Imirie, Inc.
4948 Fairmont Avenue
Bethesda, MD
654-8316

G. W. Imirie sells auto parts for foreign and American cars and trucks, and numerous tools, wrenches, and accessories as well. Most items are from major manufacturers and first quality new merchandise, but they do sell some rebuilt items, which carry a 90-day warranty.

The discount to the general public is an average of 20%. They have several lines of tools, from the less expensive for the do-it-yourselfer to professional level equipment. If you are a member of their club, you obtain an additional discount of about 15%. Special orders must be paid in full in advance. They will replace defective parts and back up all warranties to the customer's satisfaction. Club members get on the mailing list and get periodical notices of special sales. The Wheaton store also has a complete machine shop for customizing engines.

Other address:
11322 Fern Street, Wheaton, MD, 949-0112

All stores are open from 8 am to 6 pm on Monday through Friday, and from 8:30 am to 3 pm on Saturday. They accept personal checks with identification, and all major credit cards except Diners Club. Electrical parts sales are final. Items with receipt can be returned, subject to a 10% restocking charge. Parking is ample.

Greg's Auto Radio
554 N. Washington Street
Falls Church, VA
532-0612

Greg's sells CBs, auto radios, and the like, by makers such as Panasonic, Motorola, Sanyo, and Pace, at an average discount of 10% to 30%. Installation costs extra. Most merchandise is first quality, with irregulars and closeouts marked. They have a display board, from which you can choose the items you want and then place your order at the counter. They back all manufacturers' warranties and give a 6 month warranty on repairs. They also sell and install Phonemate equipment.

Other address:
8455 Tyco Road, Vienna, VA, 893-2236

Hours are from 9 am to 6 pm on Monday through Friday, and on Saturday until 4 pm. There are no returns after 30 days. They accept VISA, Master Charge, and NAC credit cards. Ample parking is available.

Hi Gear Auto Parts
7034 Backlick Road
Springfield, VA
451-5055

Hi Gear sells not only auto parts, but bicycles, tools and accessories as well. They do not usually sell large parts, like engines or carburetors, but they can special order them for you. They sell some smaller rebuilt parts. Hi Gear advertises weekly specials in the newspapers.

Other addresses:
Andrews Shopping Center, MD, 736-0880
4731 Marlboro Pike, Coral Hills, MD, 736-6200
Eastover Shopping Center, Eastover, MD, 839-3100
Belair Shopping Center, Bowie, MD (closed Sunday), 262-9100
Chillum Terrace Shopping Center, Hyattsville, MD, 559-4141
Dodge Park Shopping Center, Landover, MD, 772-1111
7665 New Hampshire Avenue, Langley Park, MD, 434-0844
7454 Annapolis Road, Lanham, MD, 577-2722
Laurel Shopping Center, Laurel, MD, 725-4888
Penn-Mar Shopping Center, Forestville, MD, 420-3444
Waldorf Shoppers World, Waldorf, MD, 843-6200
Mt. Vernon Plaza Center, Alexandria, VA, 765-7600
Shirley Duke Shopping Center, Alexandria, VA, 751-3333
Baileys Crossroads Shopping Center,

Baileys Crossroads, VA, 820-5151
11002 Lee Highway, Fairfax, VA, 273-7171
1118 W. Broad St., Falls Church, VA, 533-0600
Manassas Mall, Manassas, VA, 361-5550
128 Branch Road, Vienna, VA, 938-0404
Featherstone Mall, Woodbridge, VA, 491-3443

Hours are from Monday through Friday from 9 am to 9 pm, Saturday until 6 pm, and Sunday from 10 am to 4 pm. They accept personal checks with identification, VISA, Master Charge, NAC, and Central Charge. There are no refunds on electrical parts.

Market Tire
3300 Jeff. Davis Highway
Alexandria, VA
836-6807

Market Tires specializes in tires and shocks and sells a complete package of exhaust and brake work. They sell Michelin and Goodyear tires (which are the only two major tire brands they stock), Sturdy front end parts, Monroe shocks, and Bendix brakes, all first quality. The average price is 15% below retail, less during sales — and sales occur frequently. Most items are in stock; on special orders they ask for 20% down. Warranties are offered by the store on service. Special sales are held twice monthly.

Other addresses:
2214 University Blvd. E., Langley Park, MD, 439-6565
6105 Livingston Road, Oxon Hill, MD, 839-5100
4410 Suitland Road, Suitland, MD, 736-1700
Rte. 1 and Bowie Road, Laurel, MD, 776-5560
Hampton Mall, Central Avenue at I-495, 336-3330
8801 Annapolis Road, Lanham, MD, 459-5110
6609 Backlick Road, Springfield, VA, 451-5200
10784 Lee Highway, Fairfax, VA, 273-5311
8397 Leesburg Pike, Tysons Corner, VA, 893-3530
4125 Wilson Blvd., Arlington, VA, 527-8000
Manaport Plaza, Manassas, VA, 361-8206
3526 S. Jefferson St., Baileys Crossroads, VA, 820-5873
8010 Fenton Street (at Sligo Avenue), Silver Spring, MD. 589-5650
457 N. Frederick Road, Gaithersburg, MD, 948-8660
4725 Cheltenham Drive, Bethesda, MD, 656-5200
11800 Rockville Pike, Rockville/Wheaton, MD, 881-8440
3156 Bladensburg Road NE, Washington, DC, 526-3885
114 M Street SE, Washington, DC, 488-7234

Hours at the DC stores are from 7:30 am to 7 pm Monday through Friday. At the other stores, they are open from 7:30 am to 8:30 pm Monday through Friday, and Saturday to 5:30 pm. Personal checks are accepted with proper identification, as are most major credit cards. Adequate parking in DC, ample parking at other locations.

Merchants Tire and Auto
6620 Backlick Road
Springfield, VA
451-4970

Merchants takes care of tires, engine work, and everything except bodywork. The major tire brands that they carry are Michelin and Firestone, and all parts are first quality. Discounts vary from manufacturer to manufacturer, but they average 15%, and you can get an extra discount if you belong to any of the member buying groups. Most items are in stock, but there are special orders on large items. Customer satisfaction is guaranteed, and they offer their own warranty in addition to any offered by the manufacturer. They place ads in the newspapers on a daily basis. Merchants is affiliated with Consumer Discount Tire, which sells only tires. Three of their units also sell gasoline, including this one at Springfield.

Other addresses:
5220 Duke Street, Alexandria, VA 751-6363
9210 Livingston Road (near Livingston Mall Shopping Center), Oxon Hill, MD, 248-1595
3130 Branch Avenue (at Suitland Parkway), Marlow Heights, MD, 894-1888
909 Chillum Road (at Riggs Road), Hyattsville, MD, 559-6100
Laurel Shopping Center, Rte 1, Laurel, MD, 725-7575
3306 Indian Head Highway, Forest Heights, MD, 567-2105
7911 Annapolis Road, Lanham, MD, 459-4974
Rolling Road at Bauer Drive, West Springfield/Burke, VA
4206 John Marr Drive, Annandale, VA, 256-4102
1431 Chain Bridge Road, McLean, VA, 893-3830
8350 Leesburg Pike, Tysons Corner, VA, 893-1515
13980 Jeff Davis Highway, Woodbridge, VA, 494-7166
1503 Lee Highway, Rosslyn, Arlington, VA, 524-6323
4801 Lee Highway, Arlington, VA, 525-5550
6680 Arlington Blvd., Falls Church, VA 534-1636
7860 Sudley Road, Manassas, VA, 368-3159
7851 Old Georgetown Road, Bethesda, MD, 652-9590
379 Hungerford Drive, Rockville, MD, 424-3245
4471 Willard Street, Chevy Chase, MD, 986-9060
1141 Bladensburg Road, NE, Washington, DC, 396-3502

Hours at most locations are from 7 am to 8 pm Monday through Friday, and Saturday until 5 pm. Personal checks with proper identification, Master Charge, VISA, American Express, Central Charge, Carte Blanche, NAC, Diners Club, and Firestone credit cards are all accepted. Defective merchandise can be returned.

Morris Katz and Sons
Prince and S. Peyton Sts.,
Alexandria, VA
683-5670

Morris Katz and Sons sell car radios, speakers, a few tapes, cassette players, and car seats made to order, and they do installation and repairs on all of these. They carry only Audiovox equipment and custom-made seat covers. All merchandise is first quality, unless labeled otherwise. On the average, you save 25% off of retail prices. Most items are in stock. They guarantee parts and labor for 90 days. They have Sunday sales every week, and are members of all local Chambers of Commerce.

Hours here are Monday through Saturday from 8 am to 6 pm. Personal checks with proper identification are accepted, as are Master Charge and VISA. There are no layaways. Exchanges can be made to upgrade the merchandise, but there are no cash refunds. There are parking lots in front and in back of the store.

Nationwide Tire
1121 W. Broad Street,
Falls Church, VA
533-2800

At Nationwide Tire, they sell tires at substantial discounts to the public. Members of large groups — including government, military, and many credit unions — receive even greater discounts. Manufacturers' warranties come with the tires, but there is no mileage guarantee unless noted on the receipt. They advertise their sales regularly in the newspapers.

Other addresses:
Old Georgetown Road & Cordell Ave., Bethesda, MD, 656-9200
3550 Bladensburg Road, Cottage City, MD, 779-8545
2074 University Blvd., Langley Park, MD, 434-9200
8511 Annapolis Road, Lanham, MD, 577-2100
706 Washington Blvd., Laurel, MD, 776-4131
6101 Livingston Road, Oxon Hill, MD, 839-4777
12103 Rockville Pike, Rockville, MD, 881-1916
4412 Suitland Road, Suitland, MD, 736-1332
11149 Veirs Mill Road, Wheaton, MD, 942-0550
5709 Leesburg Pike, Bailey's Crossroads, VA, 820-6770
9580 Main Street, Fairfax, VA, 323-1044
7800 Richmond Highway, Hybla Valley, Alexandria, VA 360-4344

Hours are Monday through Friday from 7:30 am to 6 pm (Falls Church and Laurel open 8 am to 6 pm), and Saturday from 7:30 am to 4 pm. They accept personal checks, Central Charge, NAC, Master Charge, American Express, and VISA. Ample parking available.

The Parts Place
5408 Eisenhower Avenue
Alexandria, VA
370-0610

At the Parts Place, they sell new and some rebuilt foreign car parts, including those distributed by Beck-Arnley. They claim discounts of 15% on all first quality merchandise. They will special order items for you; they ask a 50% deposit on big items, and there is usually a wait of from 2 to 3 days. All parts, except electrical, are guaranteed. Sales are held occasionally, but on no regular basis.

Hours are Monday through Friday from 8 am to 6 pm, on Saturday from 9 am to 3 pm. They accept Master Charge, VISA, and personal checks. Returns can be made within 30 days of purchase if unused and accompanied by receipt. There are no returns on electrical parts. There is adequate parking in front of the shop.

Penn Jersey Auto Parts
1501 Mt. Vernon Avenue
Alexandria, VA
548-0866

Penn Jersey is a chain of independently owned franchises, selling new and rebuilt auto parts — mostly American, mostly name brands. These brands include Prestone and DuPont products, as well as their own shocks, which are manufactured by Monroe. Their merchandise is all first quality, and they say that their prices are competitive. A 50% deposit is usually requested on special orders. They offer their own warranties and have special sale items each week.

Other addresses:
7511 Landover Road, Landover, MD, 772-1122
4823 Silver Hill Road, Suitland, MD, 736-2664
5407 Ager Road, W. Hyattsville, MD, 559-8104
5614 Kenilworth Avenue, Riverdale, MD, 864-6761
8853 Richmond Highway, Alexandria, VA, 780-3455
114 W. Broad Street, Falls Church, VA, 532-4842
8637 Flower Avenue, Silver Spring, MD, 587-3848

2655 University Blvd., W., Wheaton, MD, 942-9224
Walnut Hill Shopping Center, Gaithersburg, MD, 948-2733
1614 Rockville Pike, Rockville, MD, 881-2330

Hours are pretty much the same for all stores, some having late evening hours. Most are open from 9 am to 6 pm Monday through Saturday. Some, but not all, take personal checks. They also take Master Charge, VISA, Central Charge, and NAC credit cards. They request a 10% down payment on layaways, with pickup and final payment within 90 days. Return policy is liberal. Each has ample parking. Each store is independently owned, part of an East Coast franchise.

Performance Discount Tire
5426 Eisenhower Avenue
Alexandria, VA
823-2666

They sell tires here — and tires only. This includes brands like Metzler, Continentals, Michelin, Dunlop, Goodrich, and Goodyear. Everything is first quality, and they give fifty percent off list prices! Special orders can be filled, usually in one day, and they request a $5 or $10 deposit. A store catalog is available. And they stand behind manufacturers' warranties, doing repairs here when necessary. Sales are usually held here about twice a month. Balancing is done in all stores, but front end alignment is done only at some.

Other addresses:
7816 Parston Drive, Forestville, MD, 735-6400
8509 Grovemont Circle, Gaithersburg, MD, 948-1090
5103 College Ave., College Park, MD, 277-1888
11910 Parklawn Drive, Rockville, MD, 770-4320

Store hours are from 9 am to 6 pm on Monday through Friday, and until 2 pm on Saturday. Personal checks are accepted, as are Master Charge, VISA, Central Charge, and NAC. On layaways, they ask for $25 down and $25 per month on large items. No returns on used merchandise.

Tire Man
5854 Leesburg Pike
Baileys Crossroads, VA
820-5700

The Tire Man claims to sell name brands at discount prices and sells stock and custom wheels, as well as medium to high quality tires. All merchandise is first quality, with discounts ranging from 20% to 25%. Most merchandise is in stock. Some tires have extended warranties. Sales are held once or twice per week. Free mounting is offered on stock wheels.

Other addresses:
4863 Marlboro Pike, Coral Hills, MD, 568-6700
2901 Hamilton Street, Hyattsville, MD, 559-3200

Hours are from Monday through Friday from 8:30 am to 7 pm, and Saturday from 9 am to 5 pm. Personal checks are accepted with proper identification, as are Master Charge, VISA, Central Charge, and NAC credit cards. There is adequate parking at all locations. No returns or exchanges.

Tires by NTW
7890 Backlick Road,
Newington, VA
451-7610

NTW works on two price bases: for club members, like government or military personnel or member corporations, they publish a discount catalog, which varies from 10% to 40% off of list price, depending on the tire and the manufacturer. Non-members pay 10% above the discount catalog prices. They do not carry Firestone, but they carry Pirelli, Michelin, Goodyear, and Continental. They also sell mag wheels, and cycle tires. There is no charge for mounting on regular wheels, but there is an extra charge on mags. Work is guaranteed.

Other addresses:
9025 Comprint Court, Gaithersburg, MD, 948-3050
12174 Nebel St., Rockville, MD, 881-6134
10745 Tucker St., Beltsville, MD, 937-4655
7701 Penn Belt Dr., Forestville, MD, 420-1155
5258 Port Royal Rd., Springfield, VA, 321-7811
1524 Springhill Rd., Tysons Corner, VA, 893-4210
67 K St. SW, Washington, DC, 554-4605

Hours are from 9 am to 9 pm on Monday, until 6:30 pm on Tuesday through Friday, and Saturday from 9 am to 1 pm. (DC store is open until 6:30 pm on Monday.) They accept personal checks, Master Charge, NAC, VISA, and Central Charge. Exchanges with receipt. Ample parking at all locations.

Total Auto Parts
7890-D Backlick Road,
Springfield, VA
569-5850

A complete auto supply store, carrying major brands and rebuilt or new parts like engines and carburetors. Discounts run 30% and up.

They accept Master Charge and VISA. A small parking lot is available. Liberal return policy, with no returns on electrical parts.

Universal Tire
7234 Fullerton Road
Springfield, VA
451-3390

You can buy tires, batteries, and wheels at Universal Tire. They carry such brands as Michelin, Goodyear, General, Semperit, Superior, and Delco. Discounts run differently for different brands, but samples given include an approximate 38% on Michelins and 25% on Goodyears. They give extra discounts to member groups. They carry a very few closeouts and irregulars, but these are labeled. Although most things are in stock, they will do special orders, asking for 10% down and with a wait of usually three days. A catalogue of their goods is available. In addition to the manufacturer's warranties, they offer a complete road hazard insurance policy at a small additional charge. Tires are mounted free on most cars, except mags. They also provide you with a free Comprehensive Tire Buying Guide, which is full of consumer tire information. In addition to mounting and balancing, they have a complete under-car and front end alignment services available.

Other addresses:
Surplus Center, 14628 Southlawn Drive, Rockville, MD, 762-7506
10714 Hanna Street, Beltsville, MD, 937-4770
2509 Schuster Drive, Cheverly, MD, 773-5900
5008 Beech Place, Marlow Heights, MD, 899-6680
866 Rockville Pike, Rockville, MD, 424-1200
15615 Frederick Road, Gaithersburg, MD, 424-4770
8825 Brookville Road, Silver Spring, MD, 585-7690
8304 Merrifield Ave., Merrifield, VA, 573-8100
3850 S. 4 Mile Run Dr., Shirlington, VA, 931-6400

Stores are open from 8 am to 6 pm Monday to Friday, and until 2 pm on Saturday. They accept personal checks, Master Charge, VISA, Central Charge, and NAC. Satisfaction is guaranteed within the first 500 miles. Free parking lots available at all locations. This is a local chain.

LATE ADDITION:

New Town Auto Parts Inc.
3170 Bladensburg Rd. NE
Washington, DC
526-1885

You can buy new and rebuilt, foreign and American, auto parts at New Town Auto Parts. Brands they carry include Bendix, Gabriel, Monroe, and Moog. Discounts range from 25% to 35%. On special orders, they ask a 1/3 deposit, and no returns are possible. They offer a 90 day warranty on rebuilt parts, and new parts come with manufacturers' warranties. They have special sales on closeouts and overstocks. They will help you out with parts as much as they can, but they are not mechanics. The store is large and clean.

The store is open from 8 am to 8 pm on Monday through Friday, from 8 am to 6 pm on Saturday, and from 9 am to 4 pm on Sunday. They accept personal checks, Master Charge, VISA, Central Charge, and NAC. There are no layaways or holds. There are no returns on merchandise in good condition, but defective merchandise can be exchanged. Ample parking is available.

RELATED PUBLICATIONS

Cutter, R.A. "Sorting Out Imported Tires." *Mechanics Illustrated*, Fall, 1979, pages 52-54.

Ethridge, J. "Uniform Tire Quality." *Motor Trend Magazine.* Fall, 1978, pages 38-41.

"New Ways to Compare Tires." *Consumer Reports.* April, 1979, pages 198-199.

"Tire Buying Guide: How to Buy Tires and Where." Gaithersburg, MD: Universal Tire Warehouses, Group Sales Corporation, 1979.

Catalog & Surplus Stores

There are many stores, such as catalogue showrooms, of which the merchandise defies classification into any of the categories used elsewhere in this book. Surplus stores also fit no specific classification. Thus, this section is devoted to those and other stores which sell more than one type of merchandise.

Most additional and detailed information about local catalogue stores is repeated in their catalogues. These publications are usually in full color and feature just about every item in their inventory. Prices in print may vary from the time the catalogue was printed, especially on items like gold and silver, whose prices are volatile. Most of these catalogues also list a comparison "retail price" next to their price, to give you an idea of what kind of savings you are getting by buying from their stores.

Best Products
2800 S. Randolph St.
Arlington, VA
578-4600

Best Products showroom stores are very large and well-laid-out. They carry sports equipment, china, silver, crystal, home appliances, calculators, cameras, kitchenware, and a large supply of interesting gift items. In season, they stock gardening products and lawn furniture. Catalogues are available, and they print special flyers for special sales. Flyers and catalogues are sent to those on the mailing list. They have periodic clearance sales and advertise special sales in the newspapers.

Other addresses:
12345 Parklawn Drive, Rockville, MD, 881-8422
2982 Gallows Road, Falls Church, VA, 573-7150
7710 Riverdale Road, New Carrollton, MD, 459-7400

All four area stores are open from 10 am to 9 pm Monday through Friday, from 10 am to 6 pm on Saturday, and from noon to 5 pm on Sunday. They accept cash and personal checks with proper identification. There are no layaways. Returns are accepted with the sales receipt as long as merchandise is in its original packaging.

Evans Distributors and Jewelers
6200 Little River Turnpike
Alexandria, VA
256-6700

Evans is basically a catalogue store which sells a wide variety of merchandise, including jewelry, clocks, lamps, watches, silver, televisions, stereos, radios, cameras, appliances, luggage, housewares, giftware, toys, lawnmowers and lawn furniture (in season) and sporting goods. Compared to suggested retail, you can save from 15% to 50% on this wide array of items. The Alexandria and Rockville stores are large, with most merchandise on the shelves for direct pickup, but at the Arlington store you have to place your order at a counter and wait for the personnel to retrieve it from the stockroom. They have specials on featured items about once a month.

Other addresses:
5060 Nicholson Lane, Rockville, MD, 770-6400
Rte. 50 at Glebe Road, Arlington, VA, 892-2800

Store hours are usually Monday through Saturday from 10 am to 9 pm, and Sunday until 6 pm, except for Christmas hours, which are until 10 pm Monday through Saturday, and Sunday from 10 am to 6 pm. Personal checks are accepted with proper identification. There are layaways only on jewelry worth over $100, for which a 20% deposit is requested and pickup and final payment

---

Washington's favorite savings book. It's here. It's free.

The new 1980 Evans catalog is in. 450 pages in color. 6,000 items—appliances, jewelry, tv's, sporting goods, hardware, toys, luggage, stereos, cameras. Everything's in the book. And it's all in stock. Pick your catalog up now.

Evans
DISTRIBUTORS & JEWELERS, INC.

ARLINGTON BLVD.
& GLEBE ROAD
ARLINGTON, VIRGINIA 22204
PHONE: (703) 892-2800

5060 NICHOLSON LANE
ROCKVILLE, MARYLAND 20852
(Near White Flint Mall)
PHONE: (301) 770-6400

6200 LITTLE RIVER TURNPIKE
ALEXANDRIA, VIRGINIA 22312
(Near Landmark)
PHONE: (703) 256-6700

within 60 days. All stores have their own parking lots. Cash refunds are given up to 14 days from the date of the purchase. After that period, you can return merchandise for an exchange. They will repair or replace defective items within 30 days of purchase.

John Greenan & Sons, Inc.
6320 Backlick Road
Springfield, VA
451-6000, 6001, 6002, 6003

John Greenan's is one of the smaller area catalogue stores. Items stocked include diamonds and jewelry, clocks and watches, luggage, housewares, small appliances, and gift items. In addition to selling these products, they do engraving and jewelry and watch repair; and they will design or redesign jewelry. They also give 50% off on Kodak photo developing. They publish flyers for special sales.

Other address:
1314 Fenwick Lane, Silver Spring, MD
587-2717, 2718, 2719

Hours are Monday through Friday from 10 am to 9 pm and Saturday until 7 pm at the Springfield store. Hours at Silver Spring are on Monday, Thursday, and Friday from 9 am to 9 pm, and Tuesday, Wednesday, and Saturday from 9 am to 6 pm. Christmas hours for both stores are Monday through Friday from 9 am to 9 pm, Saturday until 6 pm, and Sunday from 10 am to 4 pm. Personal checks are accepted, as are VISA and Master Charge. 10% is requested on layaways. Merchandise can be returned within 10 days of purchase.

J. C. Penney Clearance Center
Eastover Shopping Center
Indian Head Highway
567-4773

At this clearance center, you can find furniture, console TVs, appliances, carpeting, and bedding, all J.C. Penney brand. Some of these items are actually made by top manufacturers, who also market under their own labels. There is no first quality merchandise here: everything is scratched, dented, or discontinued; and everything is sold "as is". You can save from 30% to 50% off the regular price. Delivery is available for $20 within the delivery area. There are no warranties on furniture, but appliances and TVs are generally warrantied for 1 year on parts and labor, unless sold without a warranty. They occasionally conduct tent sales. The clearance center is located next door to a retail Penney's department store.

Regular hours are Monday through Friday from 11 am to 8 pm, Saturday from 10 am to 7 pm, and Sunday from 11 am to 4 pm. They accept personal checks with proper identification and J.C. Penney credit cards. There are no layaways. There are no returns, except on appliances which are not economically repairable; for these you may get a refund or exchange. Large parking lot available.

Marshall's
Rtes. 236 and 395
Alexandria, VA

Marshall's is a discount department store that does not sell cheap merchandise; rather, it puts good merchandise within reach of a modest budget. The way in which this is accomplished is through selling out-of-season merchandise, irregulars, and closeouts. They carry clothing for the whole family (this is the largest part of their inventory), linens, shoes, and a limited but good selection of china and giftwares. The discount ranges from 30% to 50% off comparable prices. There are plenty of dressing rooms, all with curtains. There are often special racks with things that are very out-of-season or which need mending. These can provide you with some great buys. We have found the best buys here to be on men's shirts, pajamas, underwear, and accessories; on children's clothing; and on women's lingerie, accessories, and underwear. There is also a good selection of shoes for the whole family. Many designer brands are in evidence, especially in the accessories section.

Hours are Monday through Saturday from 9:30 am to 9:30 pm, and Sunday from noon to 5 pm. Personal checks are accepted with proper identification, as are Master Charge, VISA, and Central Charge. Layaways require 10% down with pickup and final payment within 30 days. They will hold items for up to 24 hours. You can get a refund with your receipt within 7 days of purchase, and an exchange within 30 days. Ample parking in free large lot. This is part of a national chain.

Metro Discount Club
P.O. Box 12
Olde Towne Station
Alexandria, VA 22313

What this club offers for a membership fee of $25 is the opportunity to save 10% at a limited number of participating merchants in the Northern Virginia area, as well as four issues of their *Consumer's Guide to Daily Discounts*. The idea seems good, and you would probably benefit if you already use or are planning to patronize the merchants who are participating, and if you would spend $250 or more at their establishments. The club claims that they are expanding their network of retailers along with their membership. Consider looking into it.

Montgomery Ward Catalog Surplus Store
Fleet and South Haven Sts.
Baltimore, MD
(301) 563-1682

This store sells catalogue overstock, with some current first-quality merchandise and a very few irregulars, as well as out-of-season merchandise. You can expect a discount of at least 25% and often more. Prices are marked down as merchandise continues to sit on the shelves. The inventory consisted mostly of clothing, with some furniture, several shelves full of housewares and kitchenware, and a corner devoted to children's toys. There appeared to be some quite good buys, particularly on the kitchen items and other gadgets.

The store is open from 9:30 am to 9 pm on Monday, Thursday, and Friday, from 9:30 am to 6 pm on Tuesday and Wednesday, and is closed Sunday. They accept personal checks with proper identification and Montgomery Ward's credit cards. There are no layaways. There are returns and exchanges with a receipt, and on everything with proof of purchase. Ward's maintains its "satisfaction guaranteed" policy at this store as it does at its retail outlets. Ample parking available.

Sears Surplus Store
Maryland City Plaza
Rte. 198
Laurel, MD
498-5587

This store is separated into two sections. In both sections they sell merchandise from Sears catalogues that is either "distressed" or no longer listed, and some special purchases. In the larger section, they sell domestics, housewares, clothing, tape players, and costume jewelry. In the smaller section, they feature wood and metal furniture, some appliances, rugs, and sporting goods. Discounts run 35% to 50% off usual retail price. They give the Sears "satisfaction guaranteed" promise with all merchandise sold here. For special clearance sales, they advertise in small local newspapers.

Other address:
Waldorf Shopping Mall, Waldorf, MD, 645-2765

Hours are Monday and Wednesday through Friday from 10 am to 9 pm, Tuesday until 5:30 pm, and Saturday to 6 pm. They accept personal checks with identification, and Sears credit cards. There are no layaways, but they will hold merchandise for up to 24 hours. Returns are allowed when merchandise is accompanied by the receipt.

Springfield Surplus
6530 Backlick Road
Springfield, VA
451-5687

Springfield Surplus is a huge jumble of all kinds of sports, camping, and work clothes, and accessories. They carry Levi and Lee jeans, painters' pants, Hagar pants, Carolina shoes, army combat boots and other army surplus, flies and lures for fishing, backpacks by Himalayan and others, camping gear, fishing gear, boots, lifejackets, and a weird assortment of used odds and ends. While some things are not discounted, many are sold at 10% to 25% below retail. Wear blue jeans to the Springfield store.

Other address:
4220 Annandale Road, Annandale, VA, 256-9467

Hours are Monday, Wednesday, and Friday from 9 am to 9 pm, Tuesday and Thursday from 9 am to 7 pm, and Saturday from 9 am to 6 pm. They accept personal checks with proper identification, VISA, and Master Charge. Returns can be made within 7 days with receipt. Adequate parking available.

Sunny's Surplus
14th & H Streets NW
Washington, DC
347-2744

You get the real bargains here on closeouts and surplus, because some things are sold at the premarked manufacturers' prices. They carry Lee and Levi products, sweat shirts and pants, hats, pea coats, combat boots, bags, camping gear, air mattresses, underwear, blankets, and all kinds of casual shoes, socks, and other clothing. The store is packed with items, and there are a variety of interesting little gadgets which they also stock.

Other addresses:
9th and E NW, Washington, DC, 737-2032
3342 M Street NW, Washington, DC, 333-8550

Hours are from 9 am to 6:45 pm Monday through Saturday, and until 8:45 pm on Monday and Thursday for the downtown stores. They accept personal checks with proper identification, Master Charge, VISA, and Central Charge. There are no layaways or holds. You can return unused merchandise with a receipt for a refund or exchange within 30 days of purchase.

Super Surplus Centers, Inc.
8008 Wisconsin Avenue
Bethesda, MD
652-7050

This store is a very neatly organized surplus store, consisting of four basic merchandise areas — one for luggage, one for camping equipment, one for general merchandise (like sporting goods and caps), and one which is filled with workclothes and shoes. Luggage comprises about 10% of their stock. They carry name brands like Himalayan and Antler. They also carry seconds of certain items. You can also have foam cushions (e.g.

We are all that our name implies...

- Appliances
- Audio
- Cameras
- Diamonds
- Giftware
- Jewelry
- Luggage
- Silver
- Sporting Goods
- Toys
- TV
- Watches

Best Products is America's leading catalog showroom merchandiser. Best offers brand name merchandise at remarkably low prices. In the showroom or in our giant catalog, one look at our merchandise and your cost will convince you that we are BEST.

2800 S. Randolph St.
Arlington, Va.
703/578-4600

2982 Gallows Rd.
Falls Church, Va.
703/573-7150

7710 Riverdale Rd.
New Carrollton, Md.
301/459-7400

1701 Whitehead Rd.
Baltimore, Md.
301/265-6900

8432 Pulaski Hwy.
Baltimore, Md. (Golden Ring)
301/574-2700

1245 Eudowood Plaza
Baltimore, Md. (Towson)
301/296-6100

12345 Parklawn Dr.
Rockville, Md.
301/881-8422

BEST™

for a van or camper) made to order at this store.

The store is open from 9 am to 6 pm on Monday through Saturday. Personal checks are accepted, but they do not take credit cards, and there are no layaways. They will hold merchandise for a number of days without a deposit. There are no cash refunds, but returns can be made within a reasonable period of time. Small parking lot in back.

Surplus Centers
3451 N. Washington Blvd.
Arlington, VA
527-0600

This store sells not so much surplus as first quality merchandise for camping and sports, by such makers as Camptrails, Levis, Herman boots, Timberland, Redwing, and Nike shoes. They also carry tents, which are sold at 10% to 15% below retail. They carry a large variety of camping gear, which is generally 5% below comparable retail. They do carry some Levi irregulars and some army surplus merchandise. Manufacturers' warranties are honored. From time to time, you can save money at their special sales.

Other address:
2094 Veirs Mill Road, Rockville, MD

Hours are from 9 am to 9 pm Monday through Friday, and to 6 pm on Saturday. Personal checks, VISA, Master Charge, Central Charge, and American Express cards are all accepted forms of payment. Returns or exchanges should be made within 5 days of purchase, but this policy is liberalized at Christmas time. Adequate parking at both locations.

Surplus Center/Luggage Sales
714 12th Street, NW
Washington, DC
737-2545

In this large store packed with surplus work clothes and shoes, uniforms, umbrellas, sportswear, and luggage, you can find such brand names as Lee, Camptrails, Academy, and American Tourister at prices which average about 20% below comparable retail. There are separate booths for dressing rooms. Alterations are available, and manufacturers' warranties are offered. They give an across-the-board discount of 30% on American Tourister soft side luggage. And you can find a wide selection of luggage and attache cases on the upper level.

Other address:
8701 Flower Avenue, Silver Spring, MD, 589-2676

The store is open from 9 am to 6 pm on Monday through Saturday. Personal checks are accepted with proper identification. Master Charge, VISA, Central Charge, and NAC are also accepted. On layaways, they ask for a deposit of 10% and pickup within 30 to 60 days. Refunds are given on merchandise returned within 7 days of purchase with receipt. There are no returns on luggage. They will stamp your park-and-shop coupon with a purchase.

W. Bell and Co.
1991 Chain Bridge Road,
Tysons Corner, VA
881-2000 (all stores)

Most W. Bell and Co. stores are large and well-organized, with merchandise attractively displayed. They sell fine and less expensive jewelry, watches, cameras, small appliances, luggage and attache cases, silver, crystal and china, and a wide range of gift ideas and housewares. Discounts are substantial on most items. An attractive store catalogue is available.

W. Bell & Co.

JEWELRY AND FINE GIFTS AT LOW CATALOG PRICES

ROCKVILLE • DOWNTOWN • TYSON'S CORNER • SPRINGFIELD • FALLS CHURCH

Other locations:
Springfield Mall, Springfield, VA: Monday-Saturday from 10 am to 9:30 pm
435 S. Washington St., Falls Church, VA: Monday-Friday from 10 am to 9 pm, and Saturday from 9:30 am to 6 pm
12401 Twinbrook Parkway, Rockville, MD: hours same as Falls Church
7933 Annapolis Road, Lanham, MD: hours same as Falls Church
19th and L Streets, NW, Washington, DC; Monday through Saturday from 9:30 am to 6 pm

All showrooms are open Sunday from noon to 5 pm. The Washington showroom is open Thursday night until 8 pm. Christmas hours are later. Special sales are advertised periodically in the Washington Post. They accept personal checks, Master Charge, and VISA. Merchandise can be returned within 10 days of purchase when accompanied by sales receipt and in original package.

MAIL ORDER

The Airborne Sales Co.
P.O. Box 2727,
Culver City, California 90230
(213) 870-4687

Catalogue costs 50c and contains a selection of government surplus at great discounts.

Alden's
5000 Roosevelt Road
Chicago, Illinois 60607
(312) 854-4141

A mail order store with particularly good buys on sale merchandise. Catalogue is sent free.

Madison Square Park Distributors
19 East 26th Street
New York, NY 10010
(212) 889-7700

Discounts of from 30% to 65% on appliances, cameras, jewelry, and luggage. Catalogue is free.

MESHNA
P.O. Box 62
East Lynn, MA 01904
(617) 595-2275

Electronics surplus at great prices. 25c catalogue.

A new name in the business — The name in professionalism!

Member
National Association of Realtors

VICKI·BAGLEY REALTY INCORPORATED

2201 MT. VERNON AVENUE
ALEXANDRIA, VIRGINIA
549-7100

3015 M STREET, N.W.
WASHINGTON, D.C.
333-8020

Laurence Corner
62/64 Hampstead Road
London NW 2 2NU
England

Deals mainly in clothing, but also has art materials, camping stuff, hardware, and some lab equipment.

Ruvel
3037 North Clark Street
Chicago, IL 60657
(312) 248-1922

U.S. Army and Navy surplus goods at discounts up to 60%. Catalogue costs $1.

Service Merchandise Co., Inc.
P.O. Box 40818
Nashville, TN 37204
(800) 251-1212

Cameras, audio equipment, tools, jewelry, leather goods, silver, televisions, and camping goods at discounts up to 40%. Catalogue is free.

Unity Buying Service Co., Inc.
810 South Broadway
Hicksville, NY 11802
(516) 433-9100 X80

Up to 50% discount. You must buy a membership for $6 a year. Name brand items like those found in a catalogue store.

Late Addition:
BASCO, Inc.
Beltway Plaza
6000 Greenbelt Road,
Greenbelt, MD

A new catalogue store accepting VISA and Master Charge. Open daily and Saturday from 10 am to 9 pm, and Sunday from noon to 5 pm.

Entertainment & Leisure

There are many ways to entertain yourself and to enjoy your leisure time without spending a small fortune in the Washington Metropolitan Area. This chapter introduces a melange of ideas on saving money on books, records, toys, games, and other leisure and hobby items, and places at which to buy them. It also offers a list of movie theaters and film groups which offer reduced price or free tickets, and low-priced theater performances throughout the area.

THEATER AND FILM

Maybe you have seen everything that is playing at the Kennedy Center, Arena Stage, the National Theater, and any of the other major sources for plays and other special events, as well as all of the first-run movies in town. Maybe you are on such a tight budget that you simply cannot afford to do those things. In either case, you're probably wondering what you could do for a little entertainment outside of your home.

There are a large number of moderately-priced and inexpensive entertainment alternatives. There are drama societies of colleges and universities in the area, cinema societies which charge cheap admission for classics or two or three year old features, movie theaters which offer discounts for buying a subscription or for coming at dinnertime (twilight shows), and repertory movie theaters. All of these charge less for an evening of entertainment than the big name theaters, yet still offer the variety and interest. And you can even get some discounts at the big name theaters.

Professional Theater

Arena Stage
6th and M Streets SW
Washington, DC
488-3300
554-9066 for group rates.

Senior citizens and students pay only $4.50 for all shows, as long as they order tickets within 48 hours of the performance. Groups of from 20 to 249 get a 15% discount on the price of the ticket.

Folger Theater
201 4th Street SE
Washington, DC
546-4000

Students and senior citizens pay $5 for all tickets, except for Friday and Saturday performances.

Ford's Theater
511 10th Street NW
Washington, DC
347-4833

Students get a discount price of $6 per evening performance from Tuesday through Sunday, but are only allowed to purchase tickets during the half-hour immediately preceding the show. They pay $4.00 for matinees. Students should get a "Matinee Club Card", which is free, just by filling out an application; or bring valid student identification.

Kreeger Theater
6th and M Streets SW
Washington, DC
488-3300

Senior citizens and students can pay $4.50 per performance for any show, subject to available seating. Students under 25 and with valid identification can make reservations 2 days before the performance. Groups of 20 or more are offered a 15% discount on tickets.

Kennedy Center
Washington, DC
634-7201
Children's programs: 254-3600
Other programs: 254-3718

For activities at the Kennedy Center, excluding Saturday evening performances, there is an allotment of tickets set aside for full-time students, handicapped individuals, senior citizens, and military personnel from E1 to E4. These tickets are sold for 50% of the face value. These go fast, so it is suggested you go to the box office to buy them 2 weeks in advance of the performance. You must buy these tickets in person. Groups of 10 or more with advance reservations can also get a discount.

Free progams include:

Fine Arts Symposium on Thursday from noon to 1 pm. Features various actors and actresses connected with shows appearing in the area.

National Town Meeting, sponsored by Mobil Oil Corporation, occurs about once a month during the day, with panel discussions of contemporary issues by well-known personalities.

Organ Recitals on Wednesday at 1 pm at varying locations — either at the AFI facilities with accompanying silent film clips, or in the Concert Hall.

Programs for Children and Youth, in the fall through the spring. On Wednesday through Friday, there are programs for school children, who come in classes. On Saturday, these programs are open to the public on a first-come, first-served basis, starting at 11 am. Professional groups touch all areas, such as puppetry, music, opera, folk dancing, magic, and children's radio theatres.

Imagination Celebrations, a festival for children and youth for two weeks in early April.

Lisner Auditorium
George Washington University
Corner of 21st and H Sts. NW
Washington, DC
676-6800

A variety of performances are sponsored by individual groups, which include the Washington Ballet, the Washington Civic Opera, and the Washington Performing Arts Society. Ticket prices vary and can be as high as for other professional shows, such as those at the Kennedy Center or National Theater. There is a general admission ceiling of $7 or $8. But some sponsors offer discounts to students. Tickets can be obtained, not at Lisner, but from the event sponsor. Advertisements are placed in the *Washington Star* and *Post*. Mailing lists are kept by individual sponsors.

Considered by the critics to be one of the top restaurants in the Washington area

La Bergerie

FRENCH CUISINE
BANQUET FACILITIES
220 NORTH LEE STREET
OLD TOWN ALEXANDRIA, VA
683-1007
Ample parking across the street
Open 7 days a week — Closed Sundays from Memorial Day to Labor Day.

University, Community College, and College Drama Groups

American University
Kreeger Music Building
Washington, DC
Box office: 686-2317

Performances are under the supervision of the Performing Arts Group. A variety of experiences is offered. Most tickets cost less than $5.00; students are offered discounts, and there is usually one free show for students. They advertise these shows in the school paper and in the *Post* and *Star*. Performances, which are held in several different theatres on campus, usually begin at 8:30 pm. You can get on the mailing list by placing your name on the list at the box office.

Catholic University Hartke Theater
Corner of 4th Street and Michigan Avenue NE
Washington, DC
635-5367

Through the Performing Arts group here, drama and musicals, as well as Shakespearean productions, are presented during the school year from October through May at the Hartke Theater. Evening performances start at 8 pm and matinees at 2:30 pm on Sunday. Subject to change with inflation: $5.00 general admission, $4.00 for senior citizens, and $3.00 for groups and students. They advertise in the school papers, as well as in the *Post* and *Star*. There is a mailing list.

George Mason University
Fairfax, VA
691-7950

The performing arts groups here sponsor a variety of performances of dance, drama, and music, with admission usually free. These performances usually take place at 8 pm, in the Auditorium of the North Campus, at 10675 Lee Highway, Fairfax. You can phone in or present your name at the box office to get on the mailing list. They advertise in the campus newspaper and on bulletin boards.

George Washington University
Marvin Theater
800 21st Street NW
Washington, DC
676-6305

For student productions, $5 general admission to a selection of current and classic dramas. Senior citizens pay the faculty-alumni rate, which is $2.50 per performance or $12.50 for a five-performance season ticket. Students pay $5 for the whole series. Groups of 20 or more pay $2.00 each per performance.

Georgetown University

All year round on Wednesday evenings, the Healy Program Room hosts a Coffee House free. On Tuesday from 5 pm to 7 pm, there is a mid-evening Arts Series on the Healy Lawn free during the summer. These include a variety of performances, such as jazz and rock groups. There is also Summer Theater, which consists of Evenings of One Acts; these cost $3.00 for general admission and $2.00 for students. They take place on alternate weekends. Musicals usually cost $1.00 more for admission. The Mask and Bauble Society (625-4960), located at Poulton Hall, Stage III, at 37th and P Streets NW, puts on a range of dramatic productions. Hours vary, and tickets usually cost $3.00 for general admission and $2.00 for students.

Howard University
Cramton Auditorium
6th and Fairmont Sts. NW
Washington, DC
636-7198

Various organizations bring shows in here. You must call the sponsoring organizations for information.

University of Maryland
College Park, Maryland

Student performances are staged at the Tawes Theater, for which the box office number is 454-2201. These performances can be dramas, musicals, or comedies. Evening shows generally start at 8 pm, and tickets cost $4.00 for general admission, $3.00 for senior citizens, students, and children, and $2.00 for full-time University of Maryland students. Groups of more than 20 pay $3.00 each, except for Friday and Saturday evenings. There is a subscription rate, the "standard" rate being $10.50 for four productions if you go on Thursday evenings, or to Sunday matinees. A "special" subscription rate is $8.00 for four productions, extended to students and to senior citizens, for Thursday evening and Sunday matinee performances. The standard subscription for Friday and Saturday evenings is $13.25; and for students and senior citizens, this costs $10.50. There is a mailing list, and they advertise in community papers, on campus, and in the *Washington Post*. The Tawes Theater also hosts professional performances as well. Tickets are offered at half price to senior citizens and to University of Maryland students. Other students can obtain discounts for some performances. Also check with the Hoff Theater for other student-involved drama activities: 454-2803.

Montgomery College Rockville Campus
Box office: **279-5253**

Performances are put on by the Student Experimental Theater, four times annually: two are drama, one is a musical, and one is an opera. They take place at the Campus Center Building. Prices are $3.50 for general admission ($4.50 for musicals), and students and senior citizens receive a $1 discount. They generally advertise in the *Post* and around campus. There is a mailing list, and there are also subscriptions.

Montgomery College Takoma Park Campus
587-4090 ext. 273

This campus usually presents only two performances a year. These take place at the Commons Edition, Drama Department, New York Avenue and Takoma Avenue. During the school year, they start at 7 pm and are free. There is a mailing list, which you can place your name on by calling 587-4090, extension 282 or 248. They advertise in the student paper and around campus.

There are no performances at the Germantown Campus.

Northern Virginia Community College

At the Alexandria Campus, the Speech and Drama Department sponsors several performances per year. These are offered in the Multipurpose Room on evenings and weekends. They advertise in the newspapers in the area and around campus. The phone number is 323-4241.

At the Annandale Campus, the Novan Theater Players usually present three performances a year, on Fridays during the spring and summer. These are free. They take place at CC 106 on the Annandale Campus. They advertise in local newspapers and around campus. Contact Muriel Hanson at 323-2272 for details.

Prince George's Community College

At the Largo Campus, they present four productions a year, two in the fall and two in the spring, of Shakespeare, musicals, or whatever. These take place in the Queens Fine Arts Theater. Faculty, students, and staff are admitted free, with general admission at $2.00 and senior citizens at $1.00. Performances run over a two week period, beginning at 8 pm on Thursday, Friday, and Saturday. Call the box office at 322-0444. There is also a mailing list, and performances are advertised in local newspapers and on the radio.

Trinity College
269-2303

The drama club puts on two productions annually, one in late fall and one in the spring. Admission is $2. These take place at O'Connor Auditorium. They advertise at their own and at other campuses.

Experimental and Community Theater

One alternative to the high price of a professional theater is the experimental and community theater experience. Those listed below represent only a sampling of some of the better known local groups! These can be found in almost every community. For example, in Alexandria, there is the Little Theater of Alexandria. And don't forget productions by high school drama departments as well as church groups for fundraisers. While the quality of the casts and production sets may not be anywhere near as sophisticated as even those of community theaters, they are inexpensive and can be a lot of fun — particularly if your child or his or her friends is in the show, or if you support the cause for which money is being raised.

DC Space
443 7th Street NW
347-4960

They present a range of experiences, including dance, music, drama, and film. All tickets cost from $2 to $5. Performances occur throughout the year on evenings and weekends. There is a mailing list which you can get on to receive copies of their schedule and information about other activities.

Mt. Vernon Church
Undercroft Auditorium
900 Massachusetts Ave. NW
Washington, DC
347-9620

This church put on 4 plays a year, generally asking for contributions of $2.50. These are put on on Friday, Saturday, and Sunday evenings. They advertise these shows and also have a mailing list.

Port City Playhouse
3801 W. Braddock Road,
Alexandria, VA
549-8492

This group produces six performances a year of musicals and other plays. Students and senior citizens pay $3.75 for the musicals, and $2.50 for the non-musicals, a reduction of $1.50 from the customary general admission charge.

National Presbyterian Church
4101 Nebraska Avenue NW
Washington, DC
537-2800

There is a free Vesper Concert Series with musical events, which occur about once a month.

New Playwrights' Theater
1742 Church Street NW
Washington, DC
232-1122

This group stages new plays, staged readings, and small cabaret productions. Six full productions are presented per year, on Wednesday through Sunday at 8:00 pm. Admission is $7.00 on weekends, and $6.00 on weekdays. Senior citizens, students, unemployed people, and children get discounts. They advertise their shows in the paper and also have a mailing list.

Prism
2412 18th Street NW
Washington, DC
232-4286

This group puts on dramatic productions four times a year, charging $4.00 general admission and $3.00 for students and senior citizens. Shows start at 8:30 pm on Wednesday through Sunday. They advertise in small local papers and have a mailing list.

Chez Andrée
RESTAURANT FRANÇAIS
THE "BOURGEOIS" FRENCH RESTAURANT

- Award winning cuisine
- Wide-ranged menu
- Comprehensive wine list
- Plenty of free parking
- Major credit cards accepted
- Coat & tie **not** required

OVER 15 YEARS OF SERVICE

10 East Glebe Road, Alexandria, Virginia

call 836-1404

Sylvan Theater
Washington Monument Grounds
484-8138

Often called the Shakespeare Summer Festival, this group also puts on several other types of productions during its run at the Monument Grounds during June and July. They offer free admission and quality performances.

Trapier Theater
St. Alban's School
Washington, DC
537-6537

This group puts on three performances during the summer, including drama and comedy. Shows start at 8:00 pm, with admission $5.00 general, and $4.00 for students and senior citizens. They have a mailing list and advertise in the *Washington Star* and *Post*, and on radio and television.

The REP, Inc.
3710 Georgia Avenue
291-3903

This group puts on dramatic productions year-round, advertising them in the *Washington Post* and on the radio. The performances are scheduled for 8 pm on Friday and Saturday, and for Saturday and Sunday matinees. The cost for evening performances is $6.00 and for afternoon, $5.00.

Movie Theaters: Special Discounts

The following theaters all offer special discount rates at certain times, or to certain qualified groups or individuals. Most theaters that offer twilight shows limit ticket sales to a short time before the show, which means you may have to wait in line to get tickets. At some theaters, admission prices are higher on weekends.

DISTRICT OF COLUMBIA:

Inner Circle Theater
2105 Pennsylvania Ave. NW
331-7480

Admission is $1.75 before 5 pm, and $3.50 after 5 pm and on weekends.

Jenifer Cinema I and II
5252 Wisconsin Ave.
244-5703

The theater opens at noon, and the charge for admission for the earliest show daily is $1.50.

K-B Cerberus
3040 M Street NW
337-1311

Special reduced admission of $2 on weekdays for the show which begins around 5:30 or 6:00 pm, marked with an asterisk in the newspaper listings. Admission for senior citizens is $2 Monday-Saturday until 6 pm (except for X-rated movies or if otherwise specified). Adults $2.50 for shows between 1 and 3 pm on Monday through Thursday.

K-B Janus
1660 Connecticut Ave. NW
232-8900

Bargain prices are in force Monday through Friday for the show which goes on about 5 pm at both cinemas A and B; at those shows, the prices for adults are about those for children under 11, which are $2.00. Senior citizens pay only $2.00 for matinees on Monday through Saturday.

Lincoln Twins 1-2
1215 U Street NW
667-3000

Adults pay only $2.00 from 2 pm to 5:30 pm instead of the usual $3.00 fee.

Ontario
1700 Columbia Rd. NW
462-7118

This is a repertory theater, charging $2.50 for adults and $1.50 for childen under 12 for all shows except Saturday matinees from 1-6 pm, when it is $1.50 for adults and $1.00 for children.

Outer Circle 1 & 2
4849 Wisconsin Avenue NW
244-3116

Adults pay only $2.00 on Monday through Friday before 5 pm, instead of the usual $3.50.

MARYLAND:

AMC's Academy 6
Beltway Plaza Mall
Greenbelt
474-7700

A lot of different discounts here: senior citizens pay $2.50 per show with an AMC Senior Citizen Cards; students do also, with a discount card. The twilight show, usually between 5 and 6 pm, costs $1.50, and on Wednesday morning they show a "dollar" movie, which comes with complimentary coffee.

AMC's Carrollton 6
7828 Riverdale Rd.
New Carrollton
459-7130

More AMC discounts: same as AMC's Academy, with the exception of the Wednesday morning dollar show.

Beltway Plaza
6000 Greenbelt Road,
Greenbelt
474-2636

The show which starts between 1 and 2 pm is discounted every day, with admission at $2 for everyone. Senior citizen admission is $2 all of the time.

Key College Park
7242 Baltimore Blvd. (Rte. 1)
College Park
927-4848

You can buy a passbook of 10 admissions to this repertory theatre for $15.00. They charge $2.50 for a double feature.

Village Mall III
19236 Montgomery Village Ave.
Gaithersburg
948-9200

The show which starts between 5 and 6 pm on Tuesday and Wednesday costs $1.50, and senior citizen admission is $1.50 all of the time.

VIRGINIA

AMC's Skyline 6
Rte. 7 — Skyline Mall
Baileys Crossroads   931-3600

The twilight show, around 4:30 on Tuesday and Wednesday, costs only $1.50 admission. Students and senior citizens pay $2.50 general admission other times (a 50c reduction from the general admission), providing they pay 50c for a membership card and full admission the first time.

Beacon Hill
6738 Richmond Hwy
Alexandria
768-7612

The first show costs $2.00 for everyone. Senior citizens pay only $2.00 at all times.

Fair City 3
9650 Main St.
Fairfax
978-7591

The first show of the day costs $2.00 for everyone. Senior citizens pay $2.00 admission at all times.

Roth's Tyson Corner 5
Tyson's Corner Center
McLean
790-1007

The show which starts at about 5 pm on Monday through Friday costs $1.75 admission for all.

Shirley Duke 3
Shirley Duke Shopping Ctr.
Alexandria
370-5565

You can buy a book of 10 tickets for $15.00, and use two passes per couple at a time.

Springfield 1, 2, 3, 4, 5, 6
Springfield Mall
971-3991

The first show every day costs only $1.50 for all.

Movie Theaters: Senior Discounts

In addition to those with special lower admissions at specific time or with coupon books, some theaters offer reduced rates for senior citizens. (Note that some senior citizen discounts are also listed in the preceding section, and in the section on repertory theaters.)

DISTRICT OF COLUMBIA:

Avalon 1 and 2
5612 Connecticut Ave. NW
966-2600

Seniors pay $2.50 admission from Monday through Thursday and $3.00 on Friday and Saturday.

K-B Cinema
5120 Wisconsin Avenue NW
363-1875

Seniors usually pay $1.50, depending on the show.

K-B MacArthur
4859 MacArthur Boulevard
337-1700

Seniors pay $1.50 for Saturday matinees.

K-B Studio
4600 Wisconsin Avenue NW
686-1700

Seniors pay $1.50 on Saturday afternoon.

Uptown Theater
3426 Connecticut Avenue, NW
966-5400

Seniors pay $3 instead of the customary $4 adult admission.

MARYLAND:

Andrews
4801 Allentown Road
Camp Springs
736-6373

Senior citizens are admitted for $2.00.

Aspen Hill 1 and 2
13729 Connecticut Ave.
Wheaton
460-3010

Monday through Thursday, they give senior citizens a 50c discount, except on Disney movies.

K-B Baronet West
7651 Old Georgetown Rd.
Bethesda
986-0500

Seniors are charged $1.50 for the Saturday matinees.

K-B Georgetown Square
14300 Old Georgetown Rd.
Bethesda, MD
530-7500

Saturday and Sunday matinees, senior citizens are charged $2.00.

K-B. Langley
8014 N.H. Ave.
Silver Spring
434-5700

For the Saturday matinee, senior citizens usually pay $1.50.

K-B Silver Spring
8619 Colesville Rd.
Silver Spring
585-4100

Senior citizens pay $1.50 admission on Saturday for the matinee.

Landover 6 Theaters
Landover Shopping Mall
Landover
341-9100, 9101

Senior citizens pay $1.75 admission with identification.

Marlow I-II
3899 Branch Ave.
Marlow Heights
423-6363

Senior citizens pay $1.50.

Mercado
2285 Bel Pre Rd.
Wheaton
598-7730

Senior citizens pay $2.00 admission.

New Carrollton
8301 Annapolis Rd.
New Carrollton
459-5666

Seniors pay $1.50.

Oxon Hill
Oxon Hill Shopping Ctr.
Oxon Hill
839-2525

Seniors pay $2 admission.

Rockville Shopping Mall
Courthouse Square
Rockville
340-0282

Seniors pay $2.00 admission.

Roth's Manor
5544 Norbeck Road
Rockville
460-1222

Seniors pay $1.50 admission.

Wheaton Plaza-3
Wheaton Plaza Shopping Ctr.
Wheaton
949-8120

Seniors usually pay the same admission as children do.

White Flint Movies
11301 Rockville Pike
Rockville
881-5207

Seniors pay children's rates on Sunday through Thursday.

VIRGINIA:

Annandale
7039 Little River Turnpike
Annandale
256-7600

Senior citizens pay $1.50.

Bradlick
Braddock & Backlick Rds.,
Annandale
256-1471

Senior citizens pay $2.00 admission.

Buckingham Theatre
231 N. Glebe Road
527-0444

Seniors pay $1.50

Centre
1513 N. Quaker Lane
Alexandria
836-1000

Senior citizens pay $1.50 admission.

Fairfax Circle
Arlington Blvd. & Lee Hwy.
Fairfax
591-5110

Senior citizens pay $2.00, the same as children's admission.

Hybla Twin
7846 Richmond Hwy.
Alexandria
780-8181

Seniors pay $2.00 admission.

Jefferson
2936 Annandale Rd.
Falls Church
532-8040

Senior citizens pay $1.50.

Springfield Cinema I & II
7039 Old Keene Mill Rd.
Springfield 451-7505

Senior citizens pay $1.50 admission.

State Theater
220 N. Washington St.
Falls Church
532-1555

Senior citizens pay $1.50.

KB Cinema 7
Leesburg Pike Plaza
Baileys Crossroads
931-7171

Senior citizens pay $2.00 admission.

KB Crystal
1811 Jefferson Davis Hwy.
Crystal Plaza, Arlington
521-6464

Senior citizens pay $1.50 admission.

McLean Theater
6657 Old Dominion Drive
McLean, VA
356-7444

Senior citizens pay $1.75 from Monday through Thursday.

Reston Twin Cinemas
11840 Sunrise Valley Drive
Reston
620-9590

Senior citizens pay $1.75 admission.

Rosslyn Chinese Theater
1601 N. Kent Street
Arlington
522-2009

Seniors pay $2.00 admission.

Roth's Mount Vernon
8644 Richmond Hwy.
Alexandria
780-3380

Senior citizens pay $1.50 admission.

Towncenter 3
Sterling
430-8380

Senior citizens pay $1.50. Occasionally they have $1.75 matinees for everyone on Saturday and Sunday.

Pickett Shopping Ctr.
Fairfax
323-0461

Senior citizens pay $2.00 admission.

Tyson's Cinema
8371 Leesburg Pike
Vienna
893-3616

They play R-rated films. Senior admission is $1.50.

Tyson's Twin Theaters
Tyson's Corner Ctr.
McLean
893-7368

Senior citizens pay $1.50 until 6 pm.

University 3
10659 Braddock Rd.
Fairfax
591-1990

Senior citizens pay $2.00 admission.

FILMS AT LOCAL COLLEGES & UNIVERSITIES

Information About	Phone	Days Films Are Shown	Admission Charge	Type of Films	Eligibility	What Number to Call for Information	Where are Films Shown?
University of Maryland	454-2801	Tuesday, Wednesday, & Thursday-Sunday	$1.75	Collectors & Contemporary	anyone	454-2801	Hall Theater Student Union
Georgetown University	625-4866	Friday & Saturday	$2.00	Recent	anyone	625-3181	Medical Center Auditorium on Reservoir Rd.
George Washington University	676-7312	Thursday, Friday, and Saturday 8 pm to 10 pm		Feature: full length, recent, oldies	anyone	676-7312	Marvin Center 800 21st NW, or Lisner Auditorium 21st & H NW
Catholic University	635-5777	Wednesday & Friday	$1 or $1.50	recent at charge; oldies free	anyone	635-5777	Nursing Auditorium, Michigan Ave. & Brookland St.
George Mason U.	323-2196	Friday & Saturday 7:30 & 9:45	$1 adults	Recent	anyone	323-2196	Lecture Hall, 4400 Univ. Dr.
American University	686-2070	Friday nights in academic year, 8 pm & 10 pm	usually free or $1	Current in last 2-3 years, some classics	anyone	244-5340	Ward Circle Bldg., Lecture Room 1
Montgomery College	279-5093	Friday at noon, 3 pm, & 8 pm	Free	Current in last 2-3 years	Because seating is limited, prefer public at 3 pm. Try to limit, but sr. citizens welcome	279-5293	Humanities Bldg., Lecture Aud.
Howard University	636-7007 636-7008	Throughout the week, a couple per month	Free	Documentaries on current topics	anyone	636-7007 636-7008	University Center Auditorium
No. Va. Comm. Coll. Annandale	323-3466	Friday nights at 8 pm			anyone	323-3466	
No. Va. Comm. Coll. Alexandria	323-4207	Friday Nights at 8 pm	Free	Cultural, on a theme (like Shakespeare or Oscar winners)	anyone	323-4207	Room 120 Campus Bldg.

Repertory Film Groups

The American Film Institute
Kennedy Center
Washington, DC
785-4600

A repertory theater showing American classics as well as interesting foreign films, with a somewhat complicated admission system. Usually, general admission is $3.50, children pay $1.75 and senior citizens pay $2.50. For a membership fee ($15.00 a year for individuals and $25 for a double), general admission is reduced to $1.75 for members and $2.50 for guests. Military, senior citizens, and students pay $2.50 at most times. The midday feature is often priced at $3.00 until the show which begins about 5:00 p.m. On special series, they frequently offer reduced rates on series tickets. Members are offered tickets ahead of time, which means that some shows are sold out in advance.

Air & Space Theater
Air & Space Museum
7th St. & Independence Ave. SW
381-6264 (call to check film)

Between the hours of 10:15 and 8:15 pm daily, they show the film "To Fly" and other films every 40 minutes. The charge is 50c per adult and 25c for senior citizens, students, and children under 16.

Circle Theater
2105 Pennsylvania Ave NW
331-7480

For a repertory of older American films and a collection of interesting foreign films, the Circle charges $1 admission before 5 pm and $2 per person after 5 pm and on weekends. You can also buy a book of 10 tickets for $10, which can be used at all times.

Anacostia Park Pavilion
472-3869

General films are shown here on Tuesday and Wednesday at 7:30 from June through August — free.

Biograph
2819 M Street NW
333-2696

Though admission is usually $3 for adults and $1.50 for children under 12 and senior citizens, you can also buy a book of ten tickets for $15. But these cannot be used on Friday, Saturday, or Sunday between the hours of 5 pm and midnight. Also, you can use only two of them at a time. They provide a repertory of old films, and some newer classics.

Black Film Institute
University of the District of Columbia
425 2nd St. NW
Washington, DC 20001
727-2396

They have seasonal repertories: films are shown free within 10 to 16 week blocks, with one month vacation in between. These are scheduled for Thursday at 7:30 pm. Several films can be presented during one evening. Write above address for the current season's schedule.

Community Cafe
4949 Bethesda Ave.
Bethesda, MD
986-0848

At 9:00 pm, documentary and entertaining films are often shown free.

DC Recreation Department

Monday through Friday during the summer months, films are shown free at different locations in each of the various wards. For information call — Ward 1: 673-7611; Ward 2: 673-7009; Ward 3: 282-2201; Ward 4: 576-6878; Ward 5: 576-6874; Ward 6: 767-8086; Ward 7: 767-7470; and Ward 8: 767-7210.

Georgetown Theater
1351 Wisconsin Avenue NW
Washington, DC
333-5555

This is a repertory theater, showing mostly American films. The usual admission is $3.50 per adult and $1.50 per child and senior citizen. But you can purchase a book of ten admissions for $22.50, which are good at any time.

Ontario
1700 Columbia Road NW
Washington, DC
462-7118

General admission is only $2.50 (children $1.50) for a very varied repertory, including Spanish language films. There is a 1 am show on Friday and Saturday nights for $2.50 admission. They frequently have triple features.

Smithsonian Institution
381-5157

At any of the museums or other Smithsonian facilities, they frequently offer shows free or at a reduced rate to Resident Associate members. Call for further information.

BOOKS, RECORDS, AND MAGAZINES

In this chapter, we list a number of places to shop for records and books at reduced prices. In addition to shopping at these locations, you should also consider the following hints to help you save:

- Buy paperback books — they're cheaper than hardbound. The only time you really would want to buy a hardbound book is for reference, for a book that you might expect to read many times, or if you like to see the fancy binding or dust cover on your shelf. After all, if you are reading a book only once, why bother buying the sturdier form?
- Used books can also be an excellent buy — expecially used hardback books. You usually get about 25% to 50% off — and more for older or more arcane books.
- Publishers' closeouts — remainders — are another good source for inexpensive books. University presses frequently publish catalogues of books which they wish to clear. You can get on one of these mailing lists — usually presses of major universities like Harvard University and the University of Michigan — and learn about all of the great buys on interesting subjects. Other stores deal in remainders constantly, and also periodically publish booklets listing those which they wish to get rid of — Marboro books is one of these.
- If you decide to join a book club, choose carefully, and retain membership only until you have fulfilled your obligation. By doing this, you can usually save half the retail price. However, the major

- drawback of book clubs is that you pay postage and handling. But if gas gets too expensive or if your time is worth a great deal, it may be worth paying for the convenience.
- Don't overlook your public library. You'll save a lot if you borrow instead of buy — especially on books that you expect to read only once. And if you patronize the public library, you'll find out about a lot of other free things that go on there.

There are two major ways to save money on magazines:

- Borrow or read them at the public library;
- Subscribe when they are offered to you at a special price. If you are already receiving a certain magazine, the publishers may offer you a special price to extend your subscription. Many magazines have Christmas specials, through which you buy one subscription and get a second at a reduced rate. Or you can go through organizations which wholesale magazine subscriptions, such as Publishers' Clearinghouse, at 382 Main Street, Port Washington, New York 11050. But even if you don't find a reduced subscription rate, you'll find that almost all regular subscriptions offer a discount off the newsstand price.

There are several ways to save on records:

- Comparison shop the stores which are listed below, as their specials and everyday prices vary.
- Look for clearances, or bins with "cutouts". Cutouts are basically discontinued records, which you can purchase generally for $1.99 to $3.99, depending on the record.
- You can also buy from record clubs, which function pretty much the same way that book clubs do. Usually they will offer you a promotional package of from 6 to 14 records for a nominal fee of 1c or $1.00, and then require that you buy a like number of records. This can be an effective way of saving money if you fulfill your obligation, then quit the club. That way, you will have paid about half price for the albums, plus postage.
- On classics and standards, it is also worth looking for a rendition on a less-expensive label. This is particularly effective for children's recordings, which are going to be battered around pretty badly.
- And you can borrow records from the library, just as you would books.

HOME AND COMMUNITY RECREATION

Besides the obvious things that you dan do around the house with your family or friends, like playing games, watching television, and just entertaining, there are a multitude of activities and resources which are provided free for the taking, with just the expense of gasoline, in most cases.

Public libraries not only lend books, but often lend records. And in the Washington area, the Suburban Washington Library Film Service lends movies to responsible adults for a period of 24 hours. Participating libraries include Alexandria, Arlington County, Fairfax County, Loudoun County, and Montgomery County public library systems. catalogues of all the films, with descriptions and running times, are available at all local libraries in the participating systems. The films cannot be lent to public schools for curricular use; may not be used for fundraising events, commercial purposes, or anywhere that admission will be charged; cannot be used on television transmission, and cannot be copied. You must make reservations in person, on the telephone, or in writing, as far in advance, stating the date which you wish to use it. You must have a competent projectionist, and only a 16mm sound projector in good working condition can be used. Besides this film service, the libraries often present free films during the evenings, sponsor lectures, and conduct reading programs.

Community recreation programs are an excellent source of inexpensive entertainment. Besides the parks, pools, and skating rinks for which they are usually responsible, the Recreation Departments sponsor special programs (such as the Alexandria Ethnic Festivals), maintain small museums, and sponsor band concerts as well as a variety of other programs.

LOCAL RECREATION DEPARTMENTS

Jurisdiction	Telephone	Address	Further Information
Alexandria	750-6325	115 N. Patrick St. Alexandria, VA 22314	Brochures available at courthouse, recreation centers, and libraries.
Arlington County	558-7000	300 N. Park Drive Arlington, VA 22203	Available at libraries. Mailed only to county residents.
Fairfax County	691-3291	3949 Chain Bridge Rd. Fairfax, VA 22030	
District of Columbia	673-7660	3149 16th St. NW Washington, DC	You can get a *Recreation Guidebook*, is comprehensive and great . . . a bi-monthly "Do You Know", complete calendars of DC events for 2-month periods.

Howard County	(301) 992-2483	George Howard Bldg. 3430 Courthouse Dr. Ellicott City, MD	
Montgomery County	468-4176	12210 Bushey Dr. Silver Spring, Md. 20902	Call 468-4320 to be put on mailing list for free county concerts. These occur indoors in autumn through spring, and outdoors in summer. Also call Cultural Arts at 468-4172 for other activities.
Prince George's County	277-2200 Ext. 257	6600 Kenilworth Ave. Riverdale, MD 20840	Calendar of Activities, can also be picked up at County Libraries. At Ext. 342, you can get Dimensions In Music, about ongoing musical affairs.

Other numbers:
```
DC Recreation Department ...................... 629-7211
National Park Service ............................. 426-6700
Northern Virginia Regional Park Authority ............ 278-8880
Maryland National Capital Park and Planning Commission . 277-2200
Zoo ........................................... 628-4422
```

Local colleges and universities, aside from the plays and movies mentioned elsewhere in this chapter, sponsor a host of free lectures and films. You can find out about these by subscribing to the school paper, which is usually quite inexpensive, or by calling the department which covers the programs in which you would be interested. It is also a good idea to just check around with a number of departments. Sometimes they run free lecture or film series, or demonstrations. You can also get on mailing lists, which would provide you with an ongoing source of information on programs of interest to you.

Some less expensive alternatives inside the home include using family games that are not only fun, but teach or stretch the intellect. Many of these are gaining in popularity now, including the omnipresent chess, backgammon, go, Scrabble, and others.

Build your own play equipment — but only if you are handy. You can get patterns from women's and family magazines free or at a small fee by mail. Materials may wind up costing as much as prefabricated equipment (this is rare), but the final product, such as a sandbox or merely a hopscotch pattern on the driveway, is worth the effort. Not only do you or the children have the play facilities, but your time was well-spent developing new skills or brushing up on old ones while creating the product, not to mention the sense of pride of creation.

Read books from the library. Use them in your projects. Use them in your hobbies. Hobbies are another source of fun at home. These can range from quite inexpensive to very expensive, depending on the degree of sophistication. A coin collector can spend vast amounts of money on his hobby, for example. But that money is almost always seen as an investment, since collections over the last decade or so have continued to increase in value if the collector uses a little forethought.

SAVINGS ON TRIPS AND VACATIONS

While trips and vacations usually wind up costing you a small fortune, mostly because of gasoline and the cost of accommodations (unless you camp or just choose the cheapest motel available), you can get free planning help from many sources. And sometimes the planning of a trip — real or imaginary — is just as enjoyable as the actual trip. Chambers of Commerce for the areas or cities to which you are going provide a wealth of information. Visitors' Bureaus provide similar information and are usually located in large cities. Counties often have tourist bureaus. Airline brochures, as well as travel folders (available from travel clubs and travel agencies in great profusion), can be a fantastic and colorful source of information about an area. In fact, last year, the Society of Travel Agents opened its convention for one day to the general public. For a modest admission fee (which was donated to a charity), you could go through about 75 exhibits from different countries and pick up all manner of articles, brochures, and promotional items. Railroad and ship lines also make similar literature available. Travel books from the library can help you out tremendously in planning your trip. Even though you will probably want to buy one or two books when you actually go on the trip, you will have a better idea of what books to purchase. Travel magazines give you many ideas. Use the small mail-in ads at the back of the magazines to send away for other free information.

And, when it comes to actually saving money on the trip, you can plan your trip in the low or off season, especially to places where the weather doesn't make too much of a difference. And to save money on accommodations, you can take a camping trip, if you also have a fondness for the outdoors.

Travel groups, charters, and such have become increasingly popular, and this is one way in which you can save money, particularly on European, African, or South American destinations. You can buy a land package for a reasonable cost and get excursion fares for lower than customary prices. Because airlines and charter groups change prices and itineraries frequently, according to demand and availability, the best thing to do is to check with travel clubs and airline representatives for the most up-to-date fare and destination information.

Special rate breaks are worth evaluating, particularly when you are travelling with children. For example, one airline offered a second adult fare free, providing that the first adult meet certain restrictions. Most airlines reduce the price of a ticket for a child traveling with one or two adults. You should *add up* the total fare for your family or group, based on these fee schedules, rather than just looking at the individual fares. Also check Amtrak, which has a number of special fares for certain routes on round-trip travel. Also note that on Amtrak, children under 5 travel free, but for airlines, children between 2 and 12 years of age travel at half price.

It may be obvious, but remember that car rental firms which are further away from the airport and have a bus ferry service to their facility, often offer a better buy on rental car rates.

Room rate structures may vary in a town by location — sometimes to an extreme. For example, in a beach community, the hotels located on the beach may charge considerably more than those across the street, whose guests must use a public beach. Assuming that the public beach is not objectionalbe, take the room across the street, and use the difference saved for a night out! Also, when traveling with children, look for motels and hotels which allow children to sleep free with adults.

MUSEUMS

Washington, DC and its environs are home to many, many museums, which variously commemorate the history of the country, of wars, and of the nation's presidents, and which act as the storehouse of the nation's treasures, and as presentor of the science, technology, and industry of the nation. Many of the museums are part of the Smithsonian Institution; some are run by the U.S. Park Service, some by the National Trust for Historic Preservation, and some by private foundations or owners.

The largest collection of museums in this area falls under the jurisdiction of the Smithsonian Institution. Created by an Act of Congress in 1846, the Smithsonian was established to carry out the terms of the will of James Smithson, an Englishman, who bequeathed his entire estate to the United States, for this express purpose: "to found at Washington, under the name of the Smithsonian Institution, an establishment for the increase and diffusion of knowledge among men."

Subsequently, Congress vested responsibility for administering this trust in the Smithsonian Board of Regents, which is composed of the Chief Justice of the Supreme Court, the Vice President, three members of the Senate, three members of the House of Representatives, and nine citizen members.

The resulting institution is the Smithsonian, an independent trust establishment, which conducts scientific and scholarly research, administers the national collections, and performs other educational public service functions, supported by its trust endowments and gifts, grants and contracts, and by funds appropriated to it by Congress.

The Center of Activity for the Smithsonian is the Smithsonian Institution Building at 900 Jefferson Drive, SW, Washington. This building is open from 9 am to 5 pm Monday through Sunday, except for Christmas. Hours for all of the Smithsonian museums between Memorial Day and Labor Day are from 9 am to 9 pm, 7 days a week. The Smithsonian Institution is composed of 12 museums and the National Zoo. Seven of the museums are located on the National Mall between the Washington Monument and the Capitol Buildings: The Freer Gallery of Art. the National Museum of History and Technology, the National Museum of Natural History, the National Air and Space Museum, the Hirshhorn Museum and Sculpture Garden, the Arts and Industries Building, and the National Gallery of Art. These museums, as well as the four located in other sections of the city, are discussed below.

The Smithsonian Institution offers tours of many of these galleries, demonstrations, movies, and lectures, and even concerts — most of them free of charge. For general information on the galleries, you can telephone "Dial-a-Museum" at 737-8811, which connects you to a 24-hour recorded message giving daily announcements on new exhibitions and special events at the Smithsonian; Dial-a-Phenomenon at 737-8855, also a 24-hour recorded message, giving weekly announcements on sky and natural earth activities; and General Visitor Information at 381-6264, from 9 am to 5 pm daily (with TTY equipment provided for the deaf by dialing 381-4411 TTY).

The Smithsonian Calendar of Events appears monthly in both the *Washington Post* and *Washington Star*. Monthly calendars can also be obtained at the museums, or, if you are a member "resident associate", you will receive such information in the mail. Further information can be obtained from the Visitor Information and Associates' Reception Center, Smithsonian Institution, Washington, DC 20560, which prepares a list of ongoing exhibits for your information.

Most of the museums of the Smithsonian have libraries and study rooms in which to work or study. You should inquire at each of these facilities for details.

Two excellent brochures are available which discuss in some detail the museums in the area. One — entitled "Smithsonian Institution" — is available from the Institution itself. The other encompasses more than just the Smithsonian museums, and is called "Washington: The National Mall", available through the Government Printing Office (Publication No. 1978-0-247-802), or at many of the museums and public buildings on the Mall.

Anacostia Neighborhood Museum
2405 Martin Luther King Jr. Ave. SE
Washington, DC

Part of the Smithsonian Institution. A center for black heritage, with constantly changing exhibits.

Arts and Industries Building
On the Mall
At Jefferson Drive, SE
Washington, DC

Part of the Smithsonian Institution.

Corcoran Gallery
17th Street at New York Avenue, NW
Washington, DC
638-3211

Open from 10 am to 4:30 pm on Tuesday through Sunday. The Education Department of the Corcoran Gallery prearranges tours for children and adults. Tour subjects include American and European works of art, photography exhibits, and current works by Washington area residents. Tours for children include "Architecture is Elementary" and "The Design Game", developed to teach children to perceive color, design, and architecture. The Corcoran also sponsors special exhibitions, and a series of talks at noon. They are host to the Contemporary Music Forum the third Monday of each month at 8 pm, which presents music of modern and avant-garde composers. The Friday Evening Series is a monthly performance, usually of solo artists or string quartets, at 8:30 pm, with $5.00 tickets to Corcoran members (the usual general admission price is $8.00). They also show films, at a nominal charge to the public and free to members, usually on weekends.

The Hirshhorn Museum and Sculpture Garden
8th Street and Independence Avenue, SW
Washington, DC

This is a gallery of modern sculpture and other modern art, part of the Smithsonian Institution. Free films and lectures related to the permanent collection and to the periodic special exhibits are offered. Call 381-6264 for details. Free museum tours are also offered. Sculpture tours for the blind can be scheduled by calling 381-6713 weekdays from 10 am to 4 pm.

do it yourself framing at...

gallery one

no appointment necessary

metal moulding cut while you wait

quality custom framing also available

Old Town Alexandria
823 King St.
683-3022
Hours: Tue-Fri 10-9
Sat 10-6, Sun 1-5, Closed Mon

Loehmann's Plaza
7307 Arlington Blvd.
573-2157

Fairfax Circle
3222 Pickett Road
Across from Memco
273-1590

The Freer Gallery of Art
Jefferson Drive at 12th Street SW
Washington, DC

This museum has an excellent and extensive collection of oriental art, and the best collection of paintings by Whistler in the area.

National Museum of History and Technology
12th Street and Constitution Avenue NW
Washington, DC

Tours are available, as are demonstrations on spinning and weaving, printing and typefounding, musical instruments, and machine tools. Films on popular subjects are frequently scheduled, as are concerts (sometimes using the old instruments from the museum's collection). Call 381-6264 for details.

The Library of Congress
1st Street at East Capitol
(across from the Capitol building)
Washington, DC

The Library of Congress has exhibits of books and documents on the main floor, of photographs, drawings, posters, and other graphic items on the floor below, and of musical instruments, scores, etc. in the corridor leading to the Music Division. These exhibits change several times a year. The main reading room (which visitors can view from above) is also interesting, as are the architecture and decoration of the building. A fine series of chamber concerts (free to the public except for a 25c handling charge for tickets) is held in the Coolidge Auditorium, and there are free lectures and other events from time to time.

Museum of African Art
316 A Street NE
Washington, DC
547-6222

Open from 11 am to 5 pm on weekdays, and from noon to 5 pm on weekends, they offer lectures, films, musical performances, public forums, and demonstration themes. There is a Kwanza celebration each December. And, of course, exhibits of African art at all times.

National Air and Space Museum
7th Street and Independence Ave. SW
Washington, D.C.

This division of the Smithsonian offers free public tours at 10 am and 1 pm, and they have school tours, lectures, and teacher workshops. Call 381-4056. The Albert Einstein Spacearium simulation of heavens and space travel carries a nominal charge. In the theater there are special films, also at a nominal charge.

The National Archives
Pennsylvania Avenue at 7th Street NW
Washington, DC

The National Archives preserves and makes available for reference the permanently valuable records of the U.S. government — including the Constitution and the Declaration of Independence. It has an Exhibition Hall, which is open from 9 am to 10 pm on weekdays and from 1 pm to 10 pm on Sundays and holidays from March through October, closing at 6 pm in the winter, and closed on Christmas. Access to the Research Rooms is controlled and limited to those who have passes, which can be easily obtained by students, scholars, researchers and the like. Guided tours are available for special groups.

The National Collection of Fine Arts
8th and G Streets NW,
Washington, DC

Tours by appointment. Special events include films, concerts, seminars, and lectures. To receive monthly calendars of events, send name and address to: National Collection of Fine Arts, Smithsonian Institution, Washington, DC 20560, Attention: Public Affairs.

National Gallery of Art
10th Street and Constitution Avenue, NW
Washington, DC

Tours are free. In the new East Wing, lectures by visiting art authorities and staff are given at 4 pm on Sunday afternoon. Free films are presented on a varying schedule. Free concerts in the West building's East Garden Court every Sunday evening at 7 pm, except for late June to late September.

National Museum of Natural History
10th Street and Constitution Avenue, NW
Washington, DC

Tours are available. Part of the Smithsonian Institution.

National Zoological Park
Main entrance in the 3000 block of Connecticut Avenue, NW
Washington, DC

Not really a museum, but part of the Smithsonian. The Friends of the National Zoo sponsor free and moderately priced events (including some trips) related to zoo activities.

The Renwick Gallery
17th Street and Pennsylvania Avenue, NW
Washington, DC

"The Creative Screen" is a film program which takes place twice a month on Tuesday during lunchtime. Concerts and other musical events, lectures, and craft demonstrations at varying times.

National Portrait Gallery
8th and F Streets, NW
Washington, DC

Gallery tours free from 10 am to 3 pm.

The Phillips Collection
1600-1612 21st St. NW
Washington, DC

This is called "a gallery of modern art and its sources" and consists almost entirely of the collecting efforts of its founder, the late Duncan Phillips. The main part of the gallery is the original Phillips home. The atmosphere is comfortable and relaxed — you can sit in a comfortable chair and gaze at a painting at your leisure, and no one will rush you along. Distinguished recitals are presented here every Sunday at 5 pm from September through May (except Easter); they are free, and early arrival is recommended. Tours are available to groups by appointment. The Collection is open from 10 am to 5 pm on Tuesday through Saturday, and from 2 pm to 7 pm on Sunday.

FREE ENTERTAINMENT AND INFORMATION

Industry Tours can be a good source of free entertainment. However, Washington itself is rather short on industry other than the government. But tours of government buildings are numerous, including that of the Bureau of Printing and Engraving, and, of course, of the White House. In Baltimore, the following factories offer tours and some samples of their wares:

- Coca-Cola Bottling Co. of Baltimore, 2525 Kirk Avenue, 245-9000 for children.
- General Motors Assembly Division, 2122 Browning Highway, Baltimore, 276-6000.
- McCormick & Co., 414 Light St., Baltimore, 639-6460. House of Spices tea house and museum. Friendship Court for tea time, 10 am to 4 pm, Monday-Friday. Tours by appointment.

If you want to see great current shows, but just can't afford the tickets, you can often gain entrance to dress rehearsals for nothing or for a nominal charge. Policy on this varies not only by the facility, but also by production and by sponsor. Dance rehearsals at the Kennedy Center have been opened to dance groups, for example. Similarly, sports fans who can't afford the great games may be able to attend practice games.

It's just a little thing, but if you are shopping, you could time your trip to coincide with a cooking or kitchenware demonstration at a mall specialty shop or department store. Many of these are by the finest area cooks, and you can learn a cooking hint or two and enjoy the experience. Also, modeling and fashion shows are advertised in the papers, and you could also time your store visits to take advantage of these events.

Pamphlets, leaflets, booklets — paper, paper everywhere. This area houses so many trade groups and membership associations that you can learn everything about almost anything you are interested in — and get absolutely tons of free information. For example, the Insurance Information Institute offers excellent booklets on buying casualty, auto, and life insurance — pamphlets that add up to a small book. The American Institute of Architects offers advice to people considering careers in architecture. American Bar Association makes information available, some at a small fee, on choosing a lawyer. Groups directed at consumer aid, as mentioned in another chapter of this book, have loads of information on how to protect yourself as a consumer, and often on buying and using specific products or services. Just look under the words "National Association", "Association", "American Association", or anything similar in the Washington, DC and other local area telephone books. Even if the people who answer cannot help you, they will be sure to refer you to someone who can.

Use school and recreation department sports facilities when you can, instead of paying extra for private facilities. Some indoor swimming pools are open to the public at no charge or for a small fee. Check with your local recreation department or high school for specific information.

Many organizations hold conventions in the Washington area, and often they open the convention center with its exhibits to the public, usually for a nominal charge. In 1979, for example, the American Society of Travel Agents opened up its convention for a day, donating the admission proceeds to a charity. The exhibits and demonstrations can be quite interesting.

Create your own amateur theater group, music club, readings club, or any other type of club you want, with your friends, neighbors, and/or family. View the club meeting as a break from your routine.

Have pot luck suppers regularly with a dining club of friends. These can range from the most planned and sophisticated dinners, around exotic themes like Moroccan cooking — for the most advanced and/or interested participants — to the most mundane meat loaf, mashed potatoes, and jello dinners. It beats the high cost of dining out, you enjoy the company of others, and you don't do all of the cooking or cleaning up. Wild variations on these can include costumed renaissance suppers, biblical feasts, or futuristic fantasies.

WHERE TO GET GOOD BUYS

American Physical Fitness Co., Inc.
8524 Tyco Road
Tysons Corner, VA
821-2766

This warehouse-type store sells professional-quality physical fitness equipment, a good selection of exercise bikes, weightlifting apparati, and things for gymnastics — nothing for team sports, though. The quality is the best, as they sell the benches and exercise machines which they manufacture for schools and other institutions, York weights, and Tintori exercise bicycles, as well as American-made running shoes by Ambi. All merchandise is first quality, and you pay 1/3 less than list prices. Most items are in stock, except for special-order items like saunas. Delivery is free on orders over $300, and cost $10 for smaller orders. All merchandise carries at least a one-year guarantee. Defective merchandise can be replaced. Special sales will be held on holidays.

Other address:
14650 Southlawn Lane, Rockville, MD, 340-0001

Open from Monday through Friday from 10 am to 9 pm and Saturday until 6 pm. Personal checks are accepted with proper identification, as are Master Charge, VISA, American Express, and Central Charge credit cards. Returns can be made within 10 days of purchase, subject to a 15% restocking fee on refunds. Adequate parking is available.

Attic Books
2442 Ennals
Wheaton, MD
949-1007

This small shop specializes in used and out-of-print books. It is small, orderly, and crowded with an interesting selection of popular paperbacks, as well as a good choice of older hardbacks The prices are ½ the cover price on paperbacks, with a minimum of 25c, except for science fiction books, which carry a minimum of 50c. The savings on hardbacks range from 40% to 60% off the original list price. This shop will also take books in trade.

Other address:
Under same ownership, Bibliotheque, 8305 Fenton Street, Silver Spring, MD, 585-7373

Hours are Monday through Friday from noon to 8 pm and Saturday from 10 am to 8 pm. Personal checks and cash are accepted. Layaways and holds are up to the discretion of the owner. Books are not returnable for cash, but for trades and other store merchandise.

Bicycle Village
6184A Arlington Boulevard
Falls Church, VA
534-7370

This is a large bicycle store selling men's, women's, and children's bicycles with 3,

5, and 10 speeds, for the purposes of racing, touring, track riding, or just playing around. They also carry accessories. Bicycles range in price from some at the low end for $90-$100, up to the highest quality available. Brands carried include Zebra, Kenko, Gitane, Sentinel, Randar, Kent, and Urago Pinto. All merchandise is first quality, and the prices run from 10% to 20% under list price. They have a large warehouse, so just about everything is either in stock or can be obtained within a day. They also sell Campagnolo parts and other items for those who wish to build bikes. Warranties depend on the bike, but are usually lifetime warranties on the frame, and one to two years on parts, with a 60-day free adjustment warranty. Repairs are done here. Special sales are held on holidays.

Other address:
Bicycle Pro Shop, 3405 M Street, NW, Washington, DC, 337-0311

At the Falls Church store, hours are from 11 am to 7 pm on Tuesday, Wednesday, and Friday; from noon to 7 pm on Monday; from noon to 9 pm on Thursday; and Saturday from 9 am to 6 pm. Georgetown store hours are different. Personal checks are accepted, as are Master Charge, VISA, American Express, Central Charge, and NAC. Layaway terms require from 10% to 20% down, with 90 days to pickup and final payment. Returns or exchanges must be made with receipt. Ample parking at Falls Church location.

Crown Books
Backlick and Old Keene Mill Roads
Springfield Plaza, Springfield, VA
569-6666

Crown Books specializes in best sellers, offering a discount of 35% on hardback *New York Times* bestsellers, 25% on *New York Times* paperback bestsellers, 20% on all regular issue hardbacks, and 10% on all regular issue paperbacks. Remainders range in discount from 20% to 80%. The stores vary in size, all well-organized. They also carry a full line of children's books.

Other addresses:
7271 Arlington Blvd., Falls Church, 573-3500
14567 Jefferson Davis Hwy., Woodbridge, 491-2124
9622 Main Street, Fair City Shopping Center, Fairfax, 425-9188
352 Domer Avenue, Laurel Shopping Center, Laurel, MD, 953-9663
4400 Jenifer Street NW, Washington, DC, 966-8784
8365 Leesburg Pike, Pike 7 Shopping Center, Vienna, VA, 442-0133
2924 Chain Bridge Rd., Oakton, VA, 281-0829
8339 Sudley Road, Manassas, VA, 369-5741
21st and K Streets, NW, Washington, DC, 659-2030
12111 Rockville Pike, Rockville, MD, 881-6113
East West Highway and Wisconsin Ave., Bethesda, MD, 656-5775
6828 Race Track Road, Bowie, MD, 262-4101
11181 Veirs Mill Road, Wheaton, MD, 942-7995
17th and G Streets, NW, Washington, DC, 789-2277. Closed Sundays.
6222 Little River Turnpike, Virginia Plaza, Alexandria, VA, 750-3553
602 Quince Orchard Road, Gaithersburg, MD, 258-9330
1449 Chain Bridge Road, McLean, VA, 893-7540

Discount Musical Instruments
1015 Noyes Avenue
Silver Spring, MD
565-2054

This is a guitar and accordion shop which is an adjunct to a school of music instruction. The shop is located in the home of the owner of the school, who sells Yamaha guitars at a discount of 30% off comparable retail prices, with 20% off on special orders (i.e., instruments he does not have in stock). He also buys, sells, and reconditions accordions. Part of this operation is a repair business, and all instruments are guaranteed.

Hours are usually from 9 am to 1 pm on weekdays or by appointment — all in advance. He accepts personal checks. Returns are subject to a rental fee after a certain period of time. There is ample parking in a long driveway to the home.

Special sales are advertised in the Washington Post classified advertisements.

Discount Records and Books
1340 Connecticut Avenue NW
Washington, DC
Books: 785-1133
Records: 785-2662

On the record side, this shop is stocked with tapes and records, budget classics, and imports. They feature weekly specials with popular records at special prices. Usually a record listing at $7.98 is sold here for $6.99 if popular and $6.79 if classical, except when on special sale. Cutouts and used records are sold at prices ranging from 59c to $4.99. Most of the cutouts are in classical, popular and jazz. To get used records, they will occasionally find a large collection which contains a lot of out-of-print records in good condition. They can offer these at much cheaper prices than standard new records. They will also do special orders without a deposit. Defective records will be replaced.

On the book side, they carry all American publishers, and some literary journals. Many books are classics, many from the best seller list; and they also have an extensive back list. Most books are first quality, some are "hurt" books, and some are remainders. Paper and hardback books over $3 are discounted 15% off list price, and 20% off is given on those on the *New York Times* and *Washington Post* Best Seller lists. Some books are not discounted, particularly special orders, which must be paid for in full when you order them.

Other addresses:
5454 Wisconsin Avenue, Bethesda, MD. Books: 656-6605; Records: 657-8822
White Flint Mall, Rockville, MD. Books: 881-8075; Records: 881-5670

They accept personal checks with proper identification, Master Charge, VISA, Central Charge, and NAC. With receipts you can return merchandise within 7 days for store credit or an exchange. There are no exchanges on paperback books. Spines on books must be unbroken, or they will not accept returns. Hours vary slightly from store to store.

Giant Music Centers
9416 Main Street
Fairfax, VA
323-1528

Giant carries the top brands of musical instruments like guitars, amplifiers, organs, PA systems, microphones and drums. Most equipment is sold at 10% off and some up to 40%. A uniform discount is given on drums of 33% off. Records and tapes which are in the sale bins went for 40% off list at the time of our visit. Records which list for $7.99 or $8.98 are sold for $6.99 and $6.38 from the regular stock. Discounts on instruments generally depend on the manufacturer.

Other addresses:
2615 Columbia Pike, Arlington, VA, 920-5420
109 E. Broad Street, Falls Church, VA, 532-0884

Open from 10 am to 9 pm on Monday through Saturday, and noon to 5 pm on Sunday. They accept personal checks with identification, and Master Charge and Visa on a minimum purchase of $5. Returns are made for a credit slip or exchange. Layaway terms usually require a 20% deposit with 3 months preferred period for final pickup and payment. Parking is ample.

Gordon Miller Music
8802 Orchard Tree Lane
Baltimore, MD
(301) 825-7333

Gordon Miller sells rock music equipment, including electric guitars, acoustical guitars, drums, amplifiers, PA systems, and related accessories. Brands carried include Fender, Gibson Guitars, Peavey, Acoustic Amps, and drums by Yamaha and others. All merchandise is first quality, and the average discount is 30%. 90% of merchandise is in stock, and on the items for which they take special orders, they request ½ deposit. Guarantees are offered, and repair work is done here.

Open from 10 am to 9 pm on Monday, Tuesday, Thursday, and Friday; and until 6 pm on Wednesday and Saturday. Personal checks are accepted with proper identification, as are Master Charge, VISA, and NAC charge cards. Layaway terms require a 25% deposit, with pickup and final payment within 30 days. They will hold items for about 2 days. Cash refunds are given on merchandise returned within 30 days with receipt. Exchange policy is flexible and depends on the brands. Ample parking is available.

Juvenile Sales
6612 Richmond Highway
Alexandria, VA
768-7500

This is a very large store selling children's toys and furniture, baby food, Johnson and Johnson baby products, Pampers, swing sets, pools, party goods, bicycles, and other related merchandise for children. All brands are medium to high quality, representing such names as Lego, Fisher-Price, Playschool, and Milton Bradley. All except red tag merchandise is first quality. Discounts range from 15% to 25%, depending on the manufacturer. For example, an item which was premarked $1.09 was selling here for 84c. All merchandise is in stock, and all items carry a 30 day warranty. If anything is defective, it will be replaced. They hold special sales, usually every other week, which are advertised in the Wednesday *Washington Post*. Sales at Christmas time are held two times a week.

Other addresses:
2321 University Blvd. West, Wheaton, MD, 949-5157
4415 John Marr Drive, Annandale, VA, 941-5200
6824 New Hampshire Avenue, Takoma Park, MD, 829-0879

Hours are from 10 am to 9 pm on Monday and Friday, and until 6 pm on other days. They accept Master Charge, Central Charge, and VISA. On layaways, they request a 10% deposit for in-stock merchandise, and 20% for in-warehouse merchandise, with final pickup within 30 days. This applies to certain items, like bicycles and juvenile furniture, and not to special sale items. Refunds or exchanges will be made within 30 days of purchase with appropriate receipt. Ample parking in large lot at Richmond Highway and Annandale locations.

Kemp Mill Records
Loehmann's Plaza
Falls Church, VA
573-1668

At Kemp Mill Record stores they sell singles and albums of soul, rock, jazz, and blues of all major labels — RCA, Motown, Gordy, etc. They usually have special sales on weekends. They can special order from any catalogue unless the record is a cutout. Average discount is about 25% off list price.

Other addresses:
6177 Livingston Road, Oxon Hill, MD, 567-2980
6707 Annapolis Road, Landover Hills,

MD, 772-0399
1331 F Street, NW, Washington, DC, 638-5153
7417 Baltimore Blvd., College Park, MD, 699-9550
7728 Old Marlboro Pike, Forestville, MD, 568-9521
9709 Fort Meade Road, Laurel, MD, 498-2120
1351 Lamberton, Wheaton, MD, 649-1595
6912 Braddock Road, Annandale, VA, 354-3117

Hours are from Monday through Friday from 11 am to 9 pm and Saturday from 10 am to 8 pm. They do not accept personal checks, and they accept Master Charge and VISA only on purchases of $15 and over. Items can be returned within 7 days of purchase as long as you have a receipt. Ample parking is available.

Kramerbooks
1347 Connecticut Avenue NW
Washington, DC
293-2072

One of the best attractions of Kramerbooks stores are the cafes and restaurants which are incorporated into the stores. Of their stores, only one carries remainders in bulk, which are tremendously discounted. The 1347 Connecticut Avenue location carries many trade hardbacks from University presses, imports, some textbooks, and a good selection of arts, crafts, and other interesting remainders. Almost all merchandise is manufacturers' closeouts, on which you can get excellent buys — even up to 80% off. Outside, in nice weather, there is a book stand with a selection of books for $1. There are special promotional sales, for which they produce a catalogue. Get on the mailing list to become a recipient of one of their mailers. There is a cafe upstairs. They publish a list of suggested summer reading and also carry some reference books.

This store is open from 9 am to 8 pm on Monday through Thursday, from 9 am to 11 pm on Friday, from 11 am to 11 pm on Saturday, and from 11 am to 6 pm on Sunday. They accept personal checks, Master Charge, VISA, American Express, and Central Charge. Most items can be exchanged. On-street parking at pay meters.

Marboro Books
601 King Street
Alexandria, VA
683-3081

Marboro Books carries primarily remainders of hardbound and paperback books, as well as a lot of new and popular books. They have special sale tables with books ranging from 49c each and up, including a variety of remainders and "hurt" books. The discount on non-remainders or non-special sales runs 20% on hardbound books and 10% on paperbacks. They will try to give the same discount on special orders. About four times a year, they produce a catalogue for special sale books, for which there is a mailing list.

Other addresses:
National Airport, Washington, DC, 684-8118. Hours are from 8 am to 9 pm daily.
3131 M Street NW, Washington, DC, 965-8865
1832 M Street NW, Washington, DC, 223-3755

Hours at the Alexandria store are from Monday through Wednesday from 9:30 am to 6 pm, Thursday and Friday until 9 pm, Saturday until 6 pm, and Sunday from 11 am to 6 pm. Personal checks are accepted with proper identification, as is VISA. Books can be held for up to one month without a deposit. Returns are made for exact exchange or for credit. Metered parking available at all locations (at airport, parking in pay lot).

Marvin's Sport City
Iverson Mall
Hillcrest Heights, MD
423-6336

This sports equipment store is clean, well-lighted, and attractive. Located in a shopping mall, it features attractive displays and attentive salespeople. They carry a line of general sporting goods, mostly high quality, with brands such as Nike, Converse, Wilson, Puma, Bancroft, and Davis. Most merchandise is first quality, but there are some seconds, which are marked. The average discount here is 20% off list price. Most items are in stock, and they ask a 50% deposit if they have to special order from a factory.

Open Monday through Saturday from 10 am to 9:30 pm, and Sunday from noon to 5 pm. Personal checks are accepted, as are Master Charge, VISA, American Express, Central Charge, and NAC. Layaway terms are liberal, with up to 90 days for final payment and pickup. They will hold items for up to a day. Refunds are given within 7 days of purchase with a receipt. Parking in shopping center lot.

Melody Record Shop
1529 Connecticut Avenue, NW
Washington, DC
232-4002

A medium-sized and very neat record shop, Melody Records is fully stocked with American and imported records. Discounts depend on the type of record. In general, most albums which sell for $7.98 or $8.98 list go here for $5.99. Jazz records of $7.98 list are priced at $4.99 or $5.29 here. They have some cutouts and out-of-print records, which are priced from $1.99. They also feature weekly specials and put new releases on special prices. They usually ask for a 25% deposit on special orders. They put advertisements in the window or in the newspaper. Sometimes they carry specials on all records of one label. They sell mail order; you pay the postage, but no tax out-of-state.

The store is open from Monday through Saturday from 10 am to 9 pm. Personal checks are accepted with proper identification, as are Master Charge, VISA, American Express, and Central Charge. There are no refunds, but they will replace defective merchandise, and will exchange unopened items. Parking is limited to on-street metered spaces.

Modern Photographic Supply
The Shutter Bug
140 Chartley Road
Reisterstown, MD
(301) 833-2112 or 2600

This is a small store absolutely stuffed with camera equipment, accessories, film, and more. Used cameras and equipment are a specialty here. Merchandise ranges from low to high quality, with such brands as Kodak, Polaroid, Pentax, Nikon, Minolta, and more. They also carry used Leicas. Most merchandise is first quality, unless otherwise marked. They do carry some special purchase items, which are marked down considerably. The discount varies by item and manufacturer, from 15% to 50%. Most items are in stock or in the warehouse. Special orders depend on the supplier, and the volatility of the exchange rates at the time of the order. The store is service-oriented, with all repairs done here. But they are not an authorized warranty dealer. They were developing a mailing list at the time of publication of this book, and they have special sales on featured items such as overstock. Personnel are well-trained and can give expert instruction on use of the equipment that they sell. They will also send manufacturers' reps to give training demonstrations or classes to qualified groups, such as a photo department in a university, or a club.

Hours are from 10 am to 9 pm on Monday through Friday, and until 6 pm on Saturday. During the holiday season from Thanksgiving until Christmas, they are open from 10 am to 9 pm on Saturday as well, and Sunday from 11 am to 4 pm. Personal checks are accepted with proper identification, as are Master Charge, VISA, American Express, Central Charge, and NAC. They also give instant credit through the MFC state credit agency. They will try to hold items. Cash refunds are given within 3 days of purchase, and credit up to 7 days of purchase. After 7 days, a minimum 10% usage charge is assessed on returned merchandise.

The Music Box
8006 New Hampshire Avenue
Langley Park Shopping Center
Langley Park, MD
434-9728

This is a small neighborhood store, selling mostly records. The type of music includes soul, jazz, and disco, as well as one of the largest selection of country and western music in the area, and some big band music. Typical prices are $5.99 for those records listed at $7.99, and many new releases in that price range are sold for $4.99. 45s which list at $1.49 are usually sold here for $1.09. On special orders, they ask $1 down per record, and full payment in advance for 45s. Defective merchandise will be replaced. They will also send records mail order, with a charge for postage.

Open from 9:30 am to 9:30 pm from Monday through Saturday, and Sundays from fall through spring from 11 am to 4 pm. Master Charge, VISA, Central Charge, and NAC are accepted. They will usually hold items for up to a week without a deposit. Returns and exchange policy is flexible — check with the manager if you have questions about anything. Parking is sufficient.

Orpheus Discount Records
1024 Connecticut Avenue NW
Washington, DC
785-5558

The inventories of the two stores differ. The Georgetown store carries a lot of classical music in addition to the rock, jazz, disco, reggae, and folk sold at the downtown store. Both stores carry records and tapes, all first quality. They usually give about $2 off the label price, and $3 off on special sales. Cutouts usually are priced at $1.99 to $2.99. They will take special orders. They have periodic storewide sales.

Other address:
3225 M Street NW, Washington, DC, 965-3302

Open Monday through Friday from 10 am to 7 pm, and until 6 pm on Saturday. Georgetown store is open from 10 am to midnight on Monday through Thursday, until 2 pm on Friday and Saturday night, and from noon to midnight on Sunday. Personal checks are not accepted, but Master Charge, VISA, Central Charge and NAC are. Defective merchandise can be exchanged. Parking is on-street at both locations.

Penguin Feathers
5850 Leesburg Pike
Baileys Crossroads, VA
379-7677

Rock, jazz, some folk and country, and imported copies of lesser known European labels are sold here. The Vienna store sells classical records as well. The prices run as follows: $7.98 label-price records for $5.99, and $8.98 for $6.99. They also carry cutouts for $2.99 or $3.99. Cassettes and tapes are priced much the same way the records are. They will take special orders. They have promotional specials all of the time.

They engage in contests, in cooperation with record companies and with WAVA and WPGC radio stations.

Other addresses:
521 Maple Avenue East, Vienna, VA, 938-0110
691 Monroe Street, Herndon, VA, 471-1600
7345 Little River Turnpike, Annandale, VA, 354-5310
7116 Richmond Highway, Alexandria, VA, 660-6888

All stores are open from 10 am to 10 pm Monday through Sunday, except for the Herndon store, which opens at 11 am. Albums and tapes can be returned for credit or exchanged within a 2-week period after purchase. They accept personal checks with two forms of identification, Master Charge, VISA, Central Charge, and NAC.

Penn Camera
414 10th Street NW
Washington, DC
347-5777

A small shop jammed full of cameras and equipment, the Penn Camera store has well-trained personnel and fine quality merchandise. They feature such manufacturers as Nikon, Cannon, Olympus, Konika, Minolta, Pentax, Leica, Fujica, Vivitar, Ricoh, and Yashika at discounts of 10% to 30% off list price. Most merchandise is first quality, with a small percentage of manufacturers' closeouts. Most merchandise is in stock; on special orders they request a 10% deposit and note that there is wait of 2 to 8 weeks for the order to arrive at the store. Free delivery is available. They will take used cameras in trade. There is a store catalog available. Repairs are done here, particularly on slide and movie projectors. Special sales are held.

Open Monday through Saturday from 9 am to 6 pm, except until 3 pm on Saturday in July and August. Personal checks are accepted, as are Master Charge, VISA, American Express, Central Charge, and NAC. They request 20% down on layaways, and will also hold items for several days. Cash or exchanges are given for returns. There is a small parking lot available.

Professional Bookcenter
226 South Washington St.
Alexandria, VA
549-8025

This is a really unusual store — it provides a full range of professional technical and scientific books, which are the cream of the crop of the newest published books. These are available in limited quantity, from 1 to 6 of any specific book. The reason that the merchandise is limited in this way is that the store is basically an outlet for a company which deals in promoting and displaying these publishers' books — and finds that it is cheaper to sell them than to pay return freight to the publisher. Just about every major American publishing company is represented here, including many small scholarly and University presses, as well as some foreign works. All merchandise is first quality, and you get a minimum of 40% off the list price of the book. They have 20,000 to 25,000 books in stock, and they specialize in psychology, computer science, natural and environmental studies, the arts, education, law, criminology, and related subjects. They will take mail orders for an extra $1 per title, up to a maximum of $3 charge for postage and handling. They are also starting a mailing list; they emphasize that they encourage browsing, preferably by serious book buyers.

Open Saturday from 10 am to 6 pm, Sunday from 1 pm to 6 pm, on selected holidays from 11 am to 5 pm, and during the week by appointment.

Personal checks or cash are accepted payment. They will hold items for up to 2 weeks on the reserve shelf without a deposit. Books are not returnable. Parking is on-street and metered, but free on Sundays.

Pro Golf Discount
15811 Frederick Road
Rockville, MD
279-7444

At Pro Golf you can, not surprisingly, buy golf equipment, such as clubs and accessories of a high quality, including such brands as PGA, Power Belt, Browning, Confidence, Dunlop, First Flight, Hogan, Links, and McGregor. All merchandise is first quality, with discounts ranging from 30% to 40%. For example, one advertised sale offered $17.50 umbrellas for $6.50. Most items have to be ordered, for which a deposit and a wait of from 30 to 90 days is necessary. Manufacturers' warranties accompany most merchandise for one year at least. They do repairs here. Specials are advertised every two weeks, and they have big sales on holidays.

Open from 10 am to 9 pm on Monday through Friday, until 6 pm on Saturday, and from noon to 5 pm on Sunday. Personal checks are accepted, as are Master Charge and VISA. Layaway terms are very liberal, with 5% deposit and pickup within 90 days. They will hold items for up to one week. Exchange policy is flexible. Small parking lot.

Record and Tape Ltd./Book Annex
1900 L St. NW and
1022 19th St. NW
Records: 785-5037
Books: 296-1296

In downtown Washington, this concern sells its records from one store, and the books from a store practically next door to it. In Georgetown, the two departments are merged into one extremely long store. At these stores, they sell a full line of records, including classics, jazz, rock, country, and oldies. Books are both hard and paperback. A record which lists at $7.98 costs $6.49 here. Cutouts run $1.99 and up. They take special orders on both books and records. The personnel are knowledgeable. They usually have a classical label on sale every week, jazz sale one week, etc. They offer a discount of 20% off hardback best sellers, 15% on books over $4 in value, and 10% on books under $4 in value.

Other address:
Georgetown, 1239 Wisconsin Avenue NW, Washington, DC, 338-6712

Local checks are accepted with proper identification, as are Master Charge, VISA, Central Charge, and NAC. Everything is guaranteed. They will exchange records unopened within a reasonable period of time. There are no returns on books.

Record Works
2916 Chain Bridge Road,
Oakton, VA
281-9220

At the Oakton location, Record Works shares a medium-sized store with another operation. It features classical, rock, and other records. They price $7.99-label records at $5.99, and 45s at 99¢. They will take used records in trade. They do take special orders. Used records and cutouts cost from $1 to $3.

Other address:
1392 Chain Bridge Road, McLean, VA, 356-2344

Open from 10 am to 9 pm on Monday through Saturday, and on Friday until 8 pm. They accept personal checks, Master

Charge, and VISA. *Exchanges are made on defective records or on unopened merchandise within 7 days of purchase. Ample parking at both locations.*

Rolls Music Center
1065 W. Broad Street,
Falls Church, VA
533-9500, 9511

For electric and acoustical guitars, amplifiers, PA systems, and other equipment for making and producing rock music, you could go to Rolls Music Center. They carry brands like Ludwig drums, Marshal, Sunn, JBL, Fendex and Ampex, all first quality. The discount is almost always 40% or more. On special orders they request a 10% to 15% deposit. New equipment comes with manufacturers' warranties, and they guarantee parts and labor for 6 months on used equipment. They will repair anything which they sell. Sales are held periodically. The store is large, and the personnel are quite friendly and informative.

Open Monday through Friday from 11 am to 9 pm, and Saturday until 6 pm. They accept personal checks with identification, Master Charge, VISA, Central Charge, and NAC. Layaway terms are 10% to 15% down, with pickup within 90 days on new merchandise and 30 days on used merchandise. They also do their own financing at 18% a year. Merchandise can usually be returned within 7 days of purchase for credit. Ample parking in shopping center lot.

Second Story Books
816 N. Fairfax Street,
Alexandria, VA
548-4373

The Second Story Books Warehouse has an absolutely huge collection of books — hardbound and paperback, from used to remainders. Average discounts run 50% off list price, more or less on hardbacks depending on the condition of the edition. They will buy books 7 days a week, will search for books for you, will mail items, and can do rebinding here. They feature continuous sales of remainders and damaged merchandise. They also sell used and remaindered records. The price of books ranges from 25c to $5 on the average.

Other addresses:
5017 Connecticut Avenue NW, Washington, DC, 244-5550
3236 P Street NW, Washington, DC, 338-6860
2000 P Street NW, Washington, DC, 659-8884

The Fairfax Street Warehouse Store is open from 10 am to 6 pm on Monday through Sunday. Hours differ at other locations. Personal checks are accepted, as are Master Charge, VISA, and American Express. Merchandise will be held up to one week without a deposit. All sales are final. Limited parking at Alexandria and downtown locations.

Simon Harris Sporting Goods
220 N. Gay Street,
Baltimore, MD
(301) 685-1815

You may need help from the personnel here to find things — but they'll help you find anything you need in the way of sporting goods. They carry major brands like Adidas, Wilson, Chris Evert shoes, and many other manufacturers. Most merchandise is first quality, with some few discontinued items. Discounts run from 25% to 60% on the average. They might have a mailing list, and they advertise their special sales in the Baltimore area papers.

Open Monday through Saturday from 9:30 am to 6 pm. They accept personal checks and no credit cards. There are no layaways or holds. On-street parking and some lots nearby.

Tee to Green Shop
582 Cranbrook,
Cranbrook Shopping Center
Cockeysville, MD
(301) 667-GOLF

Tee to Green is a large, neatly-organized and well-stocked store, specializing in everything for the golfer: clubs, clothes, and accessories. All are top pro lines, including shoes by Footjoy, Dexter, and Hushpuppy, and clubs by Wilson, Spaulding, and others. They carry only first quality merchandise. Discounts run from a minimum of 20% to an average of 40% off list prices. They also give discounts of 20% on special order merchandise, for which they usually ask a 25% deposit. Dressing rooms are separate booths with doors. Guaranties are offered, and they do club repairs here. Special sales occur at the end of the season, or when they want to close out a line. They also offer a full line of teaching, including individual lessons with videotaping of your swing, etc., for $10 per half hour.

Open from 9 am to 11 pm, 7 days a week, except in the summer. Summer hours are from 9 am to 9 pm, Monday through Saturday, and from 10 am to 5 pm on Sunday, from April through the beginning of October. Personal checks are accepted with proper identification, as are Master Charge, VISA, and NAC. Layaway terms require a 25% deposit; the period of time until final payment and pickup is negotiable. They will hold items for up to 24 hours. Exchanges only can be made within 14 days of purchase — no refunds. Any final sale merchandise is marked as such. Ample parking in shopping center lot.

Tennis Warehouse
1131 Taft
Rockville, MD
762-2863

Despite the small warehouse, the store is neatly organized, with clothes hung on racks and rackets well-displayed. They carry tennis equipment and accessories, including rackets, and a selection of clothing, shoes, and balls. Their merchandise is top quality "pro merchandise" by such names as Head, Wilson, TopSeed, Fred Perry, Loomtog, and Tretorn. Everything is first quality, and discounts run 10% off list on rackets, and 20% to 50% off list on clothing. Everything is in stock. They have one dressing room. There is a mailing list, and special sales are offered periodically, depending on their stock. They will mail orders if the customer pays freight. Inventory fluctuates seasonally.

Open Monday through Friday from 9 am to 5 pm. Personal checks are accepted, as are Master Charge and VISA. There are no layaways, but the hold policy is liberal. Exchanges can be made, but there are no refunds. There is a small parking lot.

3Rs Book Store
5111 Backlick Road
Annandale, VA
750-2300

This small bookstore provides a wider selection of books than you might imagine possible: they have a giant warehouse in Maryland, and a microfiche system to determine immediately whether any book is in stock. They carry a selection of best sellers, and a large choice of Victorian Gothic romances, among other things. They discount hardbacks 25%, and 15% is given off the retail price of paperbacks. There are no discounts on orders which they must submit to the publisher.

Open from 10 am to 9 pm on Monday through Saturday, and from noon to 5 pm on Sunday. Personal checks are accepted, as are Master Charge and VISA. They will hold items for up to 24 hours. Return and exchange policy is liberal. Ample parking in large shopping center lot.

Toys by Garrison
11130 Rockville Pike
Rockville, MD
881-5530

This warehouse-like store carries mostly novelty items, inexpensive toys, gag gifts, and party goods. Some name brands include Fisher Price, Milton Bradley, and Parker. Most merchandise is first quality, and the discount depends on the item — on some there is no discount. They will special-order merchandise for you, asking a 50% deposit first. They hold occasional sales.

Open Monday through Saturday from 9:30 am to 6 pm. Personal checks are accepted, and so are Master Charge, VISA, Central Charge, and NAC. There are no layaways, but they might hold merchandise. No returns are accepted after 15 days from date of purchase. There is a small parking lot.

Toys R Us
5521 Leesburg Pike
Baileys Crossroads, VA
820-2428

The Toys R Us stores are large, almost barnlike, affairs, filled with school supplies, toys, children's furniture, books, TV games, and sporting goods, ranging in quality from the less expensive to the better brands. Marx, Mattel, Hasbro, and Kenner are representative of the name brands which they carry. All merchandise is first quality.

Other addresses:
4444 St. Barnabas Road, Marlow Heights, MD, 423-6614
8201 Annapolis Road, Lanham, MD, 459-6070
11800 Rockville Pike, Rockville, MD, 770-3376
11151 Lee Highway, Fairfax, VA, 273-0444

Open from 10 am to 9:30 pm on Monday through Saturday, and from 11 am to 6 pm on Sunday. They accept personal checks, Master Charge, VISA, and NAC. There are usually no holds or layaways. Returns and exchanges depend on the item and the season. Ample parking is available at all locations.

Tunz-a-Fun
7844 Richmond Highway
Alexandria, VA
360-3400

Another large toy store, Tunz-A-Fun carries children's toys, furniture, bicycles, sporting goods, infant paraphernalia (such as cribs), and games and hobby items as well. They carry brands like Mattel, Koliko, Parker Brothers, and all other major name brands. They sell first quality as well as discontinued items. They claim their prices to be lowest in the metro area, as supported by a 1978 survey by the Americans for Democratic Action. They also have a "reduced rack", which is an aisle where they put damaged, discontinued, or other clearance merchandise at much lower-than-ordinary prices. On special orders, they ask that you pay in advance and will order from the manufacturer when they can. They will back manufacturers' warranties. They were working on a mailing list at the time of the interview. Schools can be put on a list, by sending a letter on their letterhead, and will then get a 5% discount on their purchases.

Hours are from Monday through Saturday from 9:30 am to 9 pm, and 11 am to 6 pm on Sunday. Personal checks are accepted, as are Master Charge and Visa. On layaways, they request a down payment of 10% or $5.00, whichever is greater, with final payment and pickup within three months. They will hold items for up to 24 hours. Return policy is liberal, and you are guaranteed a refund with the receipt, as long as the merchandise is intact in the original package. Ample parking in large lot.

Veneman Music
**6319-21 Amherst Avenue, Springfield, VA
451-8970**

The store sells a large selection of musical instruments, sound systems, and related accessories. Veneman's stores are large and spacious, with instruments well-displayed. They carry a selection of student as well as professional level equipment, with such names as Fender, Gibson, Yamaha, Music Man, JBL, Guild, Dean, Rogers, Ludwig, Pearl, and Bundy at discounts from 30% to 40% off manufacturers' list prices. They also carry PA equipment. Most merchandise is first quality, with some seconds, which are marked. They will do special orders for you. They back up manufacturers' warranties, and are an authorized service center for 90% of the equipment which they sell. Special sales are held once a year, usually in June. They do have a mailing list.

Other addresses:
6000 Greenbelt Road, Greenbelt, MD, 474-0002, also visited by researcher
1150 Rockville Pike, Rockville, MD, 762-5100

Springfield store is open from 10 am to 9 pm on Monday through Friday, and until 6 pm on Saturday. Greenbelt store opens at 9:30 am Monday through Friday. They accept personal checks with proper identification, Master Charge, VISA, Central Charge, NAC, and American Express cards. Layaways require 10% down and maximum 90 days for pickup and final payment (20% down on used merchandise). At the Springfield store, equipment could be exchanged for merchandise or a credit slip within 7 days of purchase, but at the Greenbelt store, we were told that all sales were final.

Walmer's Doll House Factory
**2100 Jeff Davis Highway, Alexandria, VA
548-8804**

Walmer's is a true factory outlet, where they sell irregulars or seconds of their dollhouses, and a few firsts. They also sell first quality doll furniture for the convenience of the consumer. There are no structural flaws in the seconds, only flaws in the wood, which are usually quite minor. The houses are offered at a price easily 1/3 off the usual retail price. Everything is sold "as is". Once a year, on a Saturday, they have a warehouse sale, with returned merchandise as well as seconds at good prices.

Open from 8 am to noon and from 1 pm to 5 pm on Monday through Friday, and Saturday once a year for the special warehouse sale, usually in August. Personal checks are accepted with proper identification. 25% down is requested on layaways, with 30 days to pay and pick up merchandise. Hold policy is flexible. There is a small lot and on-street parking nearby.

Waxie Maxie's
**1613 Montgomery Avenue
Congressional Plaza
Rockville, MD
881-5464**

Waxie Maxie's sells records, tapes,

phonograph needles, and other accessories. They carry major labels, such as Columbia, RCA, Warner, Electra, and Atlantic. Merchandise is all first quality, with some manufacturers' closeouts. Records which list at $7.99 cost $5.99 here; $8.99 list records cost $6.99. All 45s cost $1.09 here. They often have special values on records and charge from $1.99 to $3.27 on these items. Sales are held at traditional holiday times, such as Christmas, Washington's Birthday, July 4th, Labor Day. There are weekly sales in the stores, as well as a special sale every two weeks.

Other addresses:
721 H Street, NW, Washington, DC, 543-2134
5807 Eastern Avenue, Chillum, MD,
3933 South Capitol Street, Washington, DC, 561-1343
7515 Landover Road, Landover, MD, 773-7006
13963 Connecticut Avenue, Silver Spring, MD, 460-3133
11201 New Hampshire Avenue, Silver Spring, MD
4554 Duke Street, Alexandria, VA,
6208 Greenbelt Road, Greenbelt, MD, 474-0040
1159 University Blvd., Hyattsville, MD, 439-0606
13981 Jefferson Davis Hwy., Woodbridge, VA, 491-6518
4115 Branch Avenue, Marlow Heights, MD, 899-6636
9109 Central Avenue, Capitol Heights, MD, 350-1116
107 Monroe Street, Rockville, MD,
111 Harry Flood Byrd Highway, Sterling, VA, 430-6500

Open Monday through Saturday from 10 am to 9 pm, and on Sunday from noon to 5 pm. They might accept personal checks with identification; they definitely do accept Master Charge, VISA, and Central Charge. There are no layaways. They will hold items for a few days without a deposit. Exchanges must be made within 2 weeks Ample parking

---

The best does not always cost the most: the Potomac Gallery of old town ...is proof.

fine art
picture framing
art instruction

201 king st., alexandria, 683-1133

MAIL ORDER
Art Supplies

Ashley Isles, Ltd.
Fenside
East Kirkby,
Spelsby, Lincs, England

Write for free catalogue. Savings of 30% to 60% on woodworking tools.

Dick Blick
Box 1267
Galesburg, Illinois 61401
(800) 477-8192

Art supplies at discounts of up to 25%. Send $2 for catalogue.

Drown Art Products
840 Broadway
New York, NY 10003
(212) 673-0150

Save 55% on metal frame parts. Send for free price list.

Inflation Fighter's Guide

Karl Heidtman
563 Remscheid 14
Postfach 140 309
West Germany

For wood carving tools, at 30% to 50% off comparable retail prices, send for price lists and catalogues.

Frank Mittermeier, Inc.
3577 E. Tremont Avenue,
Bronx, New York 10465
(212) 828-3843

For discounts on engraving, carving, and other tools, with savings up to 30%, write for free catalogue.

Polyart Products Co.
1199 East 12th Street
Oakland, California 94606
(415) 451-1048

For acrylic artist paints at 50% to 80% off list, send for free price list.

Stu-Art Products, Inc.
2045 Grand Avenue,
Baldwin, New York 11510
(800) 645-2855

Send for free catalogue and samples of metal frames. Discounts run up to 50%.

Utrecht Linens Co.
33 35th Street,
Brooklyn, New York 11232

Professional art supplies and equipment at a 20% to 50% discount. Ask for free catalogue.

Books and Records

American Education Services
University House
419 Lentz Court
Lansing, Michigan 48917
(517) 371-5550

Discounts on magazines of up to 50% for students or educators.

Chesterfield Music Shops, Inc.
12 Warren Street,
New York, New York 10007
(212) 964-3380

Records and tapes at up to 70% off of comparable retail prices. Catalogue published free 3 or 4 times a year.

Defender Industries
255 Main Street,
P.O. Box 820,
New Rochelle, New York 10801

Books on sailing and boating at a discount.

Freedom Press
In Angel Alley
84 Whitechapel High Street
London E 1
England

Books about freedom and anarchy at discounts of up to 30%. Send for free catalogue.

Golden Earth Wholesale
512 E. Lambert
Brea, California 92621
(714) 990-0681

20% off list price on books about practical topics, including farming and gardening.

Hacker Art Books, Inc.
54 W. 57th Street
New York, New York 10019
(212) 757-1450

Hacker Art Books for 30% to 40% under retail. Free catalogues are published in March and October.

Ken Lange
6031 N. 7th Street
Phoenix, Arizona 85014
(602) 266-5637

Books on American Indians and Western Americana at discounts of 40% off retail prices.

Literary Mart
1261 Broadway,
New York, New York 10001
(212) 684-0588

Free price lists for major encyclopedias — current and old — at 10% to 75% off list.

Magazines at Discount
P.O. Box 601
Broomall, Pennsylvania 19008

Discounts of up to 50% on magazines for everyone. Write for further information.

Mohr WF-78
24725 Butler Road,
Junction City, Oregon 97448
(503) 998-8233

Books on saving and making money, and erotic literature, at discounts of up to 70%. Ask for free catalogues.

The Pendleton Shop
P.O. Box 233
407 Jordan Road,
Sedona, Arizona 86336
(602) 282-3671

Books on crafts and hobbies at a discount of 30%. Price list available for 65c (refundable).

Publishers Central Bureau
Dept. WBM
1 Champion Avenue
Avenel, New Jersey 07131

Overstock books and records, with discounts up to 83%. Catalogue is free.

S & C Huber, Accoutrements
82 Plants Dam Road
East Lyme, Connecticut 06333

Country crafts and craft supplies at a discount of 20% and more. Catalogue costs 75c.

S & P of New York Budo, Inc.
P.O. Box 2
Depew, New York 14043

Books on martial arts and related accessories of martial arts at discounts of 30% to 40%. Catalogue costs $1.

The Strand Bookstore
828 Broadway
New York, New York 10003
(212) GR 3-1452

Out of print books, reviewers' copies, all 50% off list. Send for free catalogues.

Watkins & Doncaster
Four Throws
Hawkhurst, Kent
England

Books on naturalistic topics from fungi to fossils, at good prices, at a minimum discount of 30%. Catalogue is free.

Cameras

Ashreh Supply Corporation
473 Broadway
New York, New York 10013
(212) 925-9507

Top brands in cameras for up to 50% off. Ask for free catalogue.

Bona Fide Novelties
Photographic Division
1123 Broadway
New York, New York 10010
(212) 242-5442

Camera film and developing paper at up to 70% of list. Ask for free catalogue.

T.M. Chan & Co.
P.O. Box 33881
Sheung Wan Post Office
Hong Kong

Send for free catalogue on cameras and accessories at discounts of 30% and more.

Entertainment & Leisure

Dignan Photographic, Inc.
Box 4338
12304 Erwin Street,
North Hollywood, California 91607
(213) 762-7139

Kits and information on developing your own photos at 40% to 50% below retail laboratories. Price list is free.

Executive Photo
884 Sixth Avenue
New York, New York 10001
(212) 532-1277

Discounts of up to 50% on cameras and accessories. Catalogue costs $3.

Far East Co.
K.P.O. Box TST 7335,
Kowloon, Hong Kong

Save 30% to 50% on cameras and accessories. Catalogue is free, or $1 by air mail.

Flash Photo Electronics
1206 Avenue J.
Brooklyn, New York 11230
(212) 253-7121

Cameras and film at 10% to 30% off comparable retail.

Focus Electronics
4523 13th Avenue
Brooklyn, New York 11219
(212) 871-7600

10% to 30% off on cameras and film.

Foto Electric Supply
31 Essex Street,
New York, New York 10002

Minimum of 30% discount on cameras and photographic supplies.

Garden Camera
345 Seventh Avenue
New York, New York 10001
(212) 868-1420

Cameras, film, calculators, and darkroom equipment and supplies at 30% to 50% off comparable retail. Catalogue costs $1.00.

International Solgo, Inc.
77 West 23rd Street,
New York, New York 10010
(212) 895-6996

Discounts of 25% to 40% on a full line of cameras.

Minifilm Photo
167 West 32nd Street
New York, New York 10001
(212) 695-8100

Discounts of 25% to 40% on top names in cameras, as well as darkroom equipment and supplies. Catalogue costs 50c.

Oriental Films
P.O. Box 5784 TST
Kowloon, Hong Kong

Brand name cameras, lenses, accessories, and projectors at a minimum discount of 30%. Price list is free.

Solar Cine Products, Inc.
4247-49 South Kedzie Avenue
Chicago, Illinois 60632
(312) 254-8310

Photographic equipment and accessories at up to 40% off of comparable retail prices. Free catalogue published twice yearly.

Stereo Discounters
6730 Santa Barbara Court
Baltimore, MD 21227
(301) 796-5810 or
(800) 638-3920 except in Md.

Yashica cameras at savings of 30% off retail.

Universal Suppliers
P.O. Box 14803
Hong Kong

Free price list, or $1.80 by air mail, for savings on cameras, binoculars, telescopes, and other optics.

Crafts

America's Hobby Center, Inc.
146 West 22nd Street,
New York, New York 10011
(212) 675-8922

Discounts are from 10% to 40% on all kinds of hobby items, like boat, airplane, and train models. Catalogue for each type of model costs about $1.50.

Cambridge Wools, Ltd.
P.O. Box 2572
16-22 Anzac Avenue
Aukland, New Zealand

Discounts of from 30% to 70% on wool, yarn, and spinning wheels. Free leaflet and samples.

Empire Models
Dept. C
P.O. Box 42287
Tucson, Arizona 85733
(602) 881-1257

Model airplanes, accessories, and tools at discounts of 10% to 40%. Catalogue costs $1.50.

Fabric Cutaways
Darlene's Originals
P.O. Box 424-7
Arcadia, South Carolina 29320
(803) 579-2033

Leftovers and seconds of fabric sold by the pound. Catalogue costs 35c. Discounts range up to 80% off comparable retail.

Fort Crailo Yarns
2 Green Street
Department 3
Rensselaer, New York 12144
(518) 465-2371

Yarns for handweaving and rugmaking, as well as novelty yarns. Discount is usually 30%. Sample cards available at a charge.

Gohn Brothers
Middlebury, Indiana 46540

All kinds of sewing notions and goods at very cheap prices.

Kasuri Dye Works
P.O. Box 7101
1959 Shattuck Avenue
Berkeley, California 94704
(415) 841-4509

Supplies for Ikat, a form of Japanese weaving, and all necessary supplies, probably can be used for other crafts as well. Catalogue costs 75c.

Kohlman's Miniatures Shop
33 Newton Road
Rochester, New York 14626
(716) 225-0754

Dolls, books, dollhouses, and the rest at a good discount. Write for catalogue.

Stavros Kouyoumoutzakis
Workshop Spun Wools
166 Kalokerinou Avenue
Iraklion, Crete, Greece

Yarn at good discounts, up to 60%. Free price list and samples available.

Leathercrafters Supply Company, Inc.
Dept. WM
25 Great Jones Street
New York, New York 10012
(212) 673-5460

Leatherworking tools, equipment, and supplies at discounts up to 40%. Catalogue and price list for $1.50.

D. MacGillivray and Co.
Muir of Aird
Benbecula
Western Isles, Scotland
PA 88-5NA

Shetland wool, yarn, and fabrics, as well as cashmere and lambswool at discounts of 30% to 70%. Brochure and price list free, swatches and samples for $1.00.

National Handicraft Co., Inc.
337 Lincoln Road,
Miami Beach, Florida 33139
(305) 534-7314

All kinds of craft materials at discounts to 30%. Free catalogue upon request.

Natural Craft, Inc.
2199 Bancroft Way
Berkeley, California 94704
(415) 841-4909

Dyes, inks, paints, jewelry findings, etc. at discounts of 25% to 33%. Catalogue is $1.00 (refundable).

New England Earth Crafts
882 Massachusetts Avenue
Arlington, MA 02174
(617) 646-2450

Materials, equipment, and supplies for spinning, weaving, pottery, etc., at discounts of 40% and more. Catalogue is $1 (refundable).

Test Fabrics, Inc.
P.O. Drawer O
200 Blackford Avenue
Middlesex, New Jersey 08846
(201) 467-6446

You can buy 1 yard and more of natural and synthetic fabrics for good prices. The price list is free, and the swatch booklet costs $4.50.

Sports

Berman's Racquets
17065 West Dixie Highway
North Miami Beach, FL 33166
(305) 949-2722

Tennis racquets of professional quality at savings up to 30%. Free catalogue.

Custom Golf Clubs, Inc.
10206 Interregional Hwy.
Austin, Texas 78763
(512) 837-4810

Equipment and supplies for golf and tennis, as well as fishing. Catalogues each cost $1 (per sport). Discounts run 30% to 50%.

Golf Haus
700 N. Pennsylvania
Lansing, Michigan 48906

They say they have the lowest prices on pro golf clubs anywhere, at discounts of 20% to 60%. Catalogue is free.

Las Vegas Discount Golf and Tennis
4813 Paradise Road,
Las Vegas, Nevada 89109
(800) 634-6745

Golf and tennis items at 25% to 60% off comparable retail. Brochure and price list are free.

Toys

G. Henke and Co.
3530 Warburg
West Germany —RFA

Board games at prices to 50% of retail. Catalogue costs $2.00.

Auctions

To the discriminating consumer with an eye for price, auctions and sales of used items can be a fantastic source of fine quality furniture, jewelry, or housewares. To the consumer who wants to save by buying surplus or in bulk, surplus and salvage operations offer a variety of goods at sometimes fantastically low prices.

But most of the consumers really don't know where to look for these buys, maybe stumbling on an advertisement in the newspaper for a government surplus auction or for a bankruptcy sale, and wondering if it would be worth going to. Usually the lack of time or inclination — or the apprehension that it probably would be a waste of time — prevents the interested consumer from following through on the idea of going to a surplus sale, bankruptcy auction, or salvage operation.

If you have ever considered one of these sources as a place to find something for yourself, your home, your boat, or your business — but ignorance of what was available, what they offered, and how they operated back; or if you have become interested in these sales as a way to save money and maybe have an interesting time doing it, this chapter is for you. It introduces you to a wide range of resources for used, surplus, salvage, and other kinds of merchandise which sell at prices usually well below retail.

Adam Weschler & Son, Inc.
905 E Street NW
Washington, DC
628-1281

Auction Frequency, Dates, and Time: Every Tuesday from 9:30 on, for general household furniture and fixtures, and a variety of miscellaneous items. Inspection for these sales is on the day before the sale from 9 am to 5 pm; during the auction, you are free to wander around and inspect anything not yet sold (except jewelry, which is locked up in glass cases). Catalogue sales for fine art, antiques, and oriental rugs occur four times a year in February, May, September, and December. These are three-day sales (Friday through Sunday), each preceded by a four day exhibition period (usually the previous weekend). The catalogue costs $10, or $13 by mail, with a $1 exhibition donation turned over to a local charitable fund.

Notification: Catalogue sales notification is placed in *Antiques Monthly*, in trade publications, and in New York, Richmond, Philadelphia, and Washington newspapers. General household auctions are advertised in the *Washington Star* and *Washington Post*. There is a mailing list for catalogue sales and specialty sales; call or write to be put on the list.

Types of Merchandise: At the weekly auctions, they sell all sorts of general furniture, furnishings, bric-a-brac, office furniture (not at every sale), jewelry, and odds and ends. The merchandise for these sales comes from a variety of sources — estates, unclaimed storage items, bankruptcy, consignments, etc. — and the selection varies widely from week to week (although there is always household furniture). The prices also vary greatly. At the catalogue sales, they sell fine art, fine furniture, oriental rugs, and collectibles; prices average about $300 to $500 per item, though some are higher and a few are lower. Weschler's makes available a sheet showing their "guesstimates" on each item, and many of these are surprisingly accurate.

Condition of Merchandise: Merchandise at the weekly sales is all sold "as is". (When the auctioneer wishes to point out an obvious defect, he mentions that the item is "as is". When the defect is slight, he may say "slightly as is". But all merchandise is sold the way you find it.) Catalogue items are as specified in catalogue.

Terms: Cash; or you may pay by check if you have previously applied for approval. They will store your purchase up to 3 days after the catalogue sales; items bought at the weekly sales should be removed the same day. And at the weekly sales, once you've bought an item, you are responsible for it; they encourage you to box up small items immediately to avoid loss or breakage.

Alex Cooper Auctioneers, Inc.
345 N. Charles Street,
Baltimore, MD 21201
(301) 752-4868

Auction Frequency, Dates, and Time: There is no set time; auctions are usually held every 3 to 4 weeks, for one day.

Notification: There is a mailing list; write or call to be put on it. They advertise in local newspapers and in the *New York Times*, usually 2 to 3 weeks prior to the sale.

Type of merchandise: Fine antiques, collectibles, and turn-of-the-century pieces.

Condition of items: Inspection is held the day before the sale. Condition of items varies.

Price Range: Varies from $1 to $10,000.

Terms: Cash or certified check only.

Allgood Used Equipment
636 S. Pickett Street,
Alexandria, VA 22304
823-2303

Auction Frequency, Dates, and Time: Held twice a month; no definite time, but they try to schedule them during the day on Tuesday, about 10 am.

Notification: They normally advertise in the Sunday *Washington Post* on two consecutive Sundays before the auction. To get on the mailing list you must attend an auction and register for it.

Type of merchandise: Usually comes from businesses that have just closed. May include truck fleets, construction steel, restaurant equipment, tools, business inventory, and business furnishings.

Condition of Merchandise: Good. Inspection held 2 days before auction.

Price Range: from $10 to $10,000.

Terms: Depends on auction — usually cash, personal checks or credit cards.

Atlantic Auction Inc.
3420 Reisterstown Road,
Baltimore, MD 21215
(301) 542-9300

There are two types of auctions held through this concern:

1. Automobiles:

    Auction Frequency, Dates, and Time: Every other Saturday from 10 am on.

    Type of Merchandise: All kinds of trucks, cars, and boats.

    Price Range: Variable.

2. General Auctioneering — through bankruptcy or real estate foreclosures.

Terms: Cash or certified check only. There is no financing available.

LEBWOHL STUDIO

conservation of

art on paper

411 Cameron St. Old Town

836-3339

Alexandria

C. G. Sloan & Co.
715 13th Street NW
Washington, DC
628-1468

Auction Frequency, Dates, and Time: General household sales are held every three weeks on weekends, from 10 am to 5 pm. Catalogue sales are held six times a year: in early November, middle December, February, April, June, and September, usually from 10 am to 5 pm on Thursday through Sunday.

Notification: They advertise in the *Post* classifieds for a few days before the sale, in the *Baltimore Sun*, and in antique journals and tabloids. Catalogues cost $15 by mail and $12 at the door.

Type of Merchandise: Household items are usually used furniture, as well as crystal, china, paintings, old appliances, bicycles, and other such items, at prices ranging from $2 to $200. Catalogue items include fine antiques, porcelain, fine crystal, paintings, oriental antiques, and china, at prices ranging from $100 to $100,000.

Condition of Merchandise: Most household items are used, and catalogue items are generally in good condition. Inspection for the household items occurs on Thursday or Friday before the auction weekend, from 9 am to 5 pm. The catalogue sales inspection occurs the week before the sale, from 9 am to 5 pm.

Terms: Cash or personal checks only. There are no deliveries. They will store purchases for up to 3 days. Call in advance about consignments. You are responsible for bringing your items there. They will give a rough appraisal free when you are consigning merchandise to them. Commission to buyer and seller is 10% of selling price, so that on a $100 sale, the seller receives $90, the buyer pays $110, and Sloane's gets $20.

Colonel James Auction
13718 Baltimore Boulevard
Laurel, MD 20810
(301) 953-9492

Auction Frequency, Dates, and Time: Every Friday night at 7 pm.

Notification: Advertisement in the *Washington Post* on Friday, under "Auctions"

Type of Merchandise: Furniture, utensils, toys, once in a while a car, and mostly oak antiques.

Condition of Items. Usually good. Inspection occurs all day on Friday before 9 am until the beginning of the auction. Everything is sold "as is".

Price Range: Generally from 50c to $300.

Terms: Cash, personal check, VISA, and Master Charge are accepted for purchases of $15 and more. They take consignments, taking a cut of 25% from an individual with a tax number and 30% from one without.

George's Auction
7618 Centreville Road
Manassas, Virginia 22110

Auction Frequency, Dates, and Time: First Sunday of each month at 1 pm, held outside.

Notification: There is no mailing list. They advertise in the *Journal* newspapers, Potomac local newspapers the week before the auction.

Type of Merchandise: Primitive pieces, glassware, and furniture.

Price Range: 50c and up.

Terms: Cash or personal check.

Harris Auction Galleries, Inc.
875 No. Howard Street,
Baltimore, MD 21201

Auction Frequency, Dates, and Time: Auction takes place every other Wednesday at 10:30 am.

Notification: They have a mailing list for collectors of books, graphics, paper, and Americana. Collectibles auctions take place approximately 10 times a year. They send catalogues out at varying prices (depending on the type of postage requested). Call for more information on this type of auction. They advertise in the *Baltimore Sun* for both the collectibles and the regular Wednesday sales.

Type of merchandise: On Wednesday, they have antiques, household items, and turn-of-the-century furniture.

Condition of Items: Wednesday merchandise is good, as are collectibles. Inspections are held Tuesday from 9 am to 5 pm prior to the sale and Wednesday prior to the sale's beginning.

Price Range: Varies.

Terms: Cash, or personal check with proper identification. No out-of-state checks accepted.

Law's Auction
P.O. Box 675,
7209 Centerville Road
Manassas, Virginia 22110
Metro number: 631-0590
Local number: 361-3148

Auction Frequency, Dates, and Time: General auctions held Friday night at 6:30 pm. Antique and estate auctions are held the first Sunday of every month and the preceding Saturday. Starts at 11:00 am on Saturday and noon on Sunday. Other catalogue sales of period furniture are held in January, April, July, and October, starting at noon on Saturday and Sunday. Sometimes they have special auctions on Tuesdays, which they advertise in the paper. They also have a flea market every second and fourth Sunday, with 70 to 80 exhibitors, from 8 am to 5 pm, all the year round.

Call Ms. Walters for information on renting space.

Notification: Call or write for inclusion on mailing list for catalogue and antique auctions. Catalogues cost $4 by mail and $3 at the door. There is no admission charge for other items. Every sale is advertised in the *Washington Post* and *Washington Star*.

Type of Merchandise: They sell box lots. Items at general auction go from 25¢ up and include used and household items, some needing repair, and a lot of oak furniture. At the antique and estate auctions, they feature a lot of Victorian furniture of good quality, primitives, and country items that do not need repairing. These items go for $4 to $5000. Catalogue sales of English and American period furniture and accessories of very good quality are also held; prices range from $50 to $20,000. The very best items are seen at these sales.

Condition of Items: For general auctions, inspection starts at 8:30 the morning of the sale. For antique, estate, and catalogue sales, inspection is held from 1 pm to 9 pm on Friday, and from 9 am to the time the sale starts on both days.

Terms: Cash, VISA, or personal checks are accepted. They will store merchandise for up to five days.

Len's Country Barn
9929 Rhode Island Avenue
College Park, MD 20740
441-2546

Auction Frequency, Dates, & Time: Once or twice a year, at above address, in spring and fall. Estate sales would be conducted at the estate.

Notification: You can get on a mailing list by calling or writing. They advertise in all major and most local newspapers.

Type of Merchandise: Antique furniture, oak-walnut/Victorian mostly; clocks, jewelry, household items, and sometimes cars.

Condition of Goods: Sold "as is". Inspection several days in advance and the morning of the sale.

Price range: Varies, depends on interest and crowd.

Terms: Cash, personal checks with identification, sometimes credit cards — Master Charge and VISA.

M & H Auction Service Inc.
8660 Cherry Lane
Laurel, MD 20810
(301) 725-6777

Auction Frequency, Dates, and Time: Every Saturday night at 7 pm.

Notification: There is no mailing list. They advertise in the *Washington Post* and other newspapers on Saturday.

Type of Merchandise: They deal in a lot of oak furniture, none of it modern.

They also sell glassware, pictures, primitives, and anything in the antique line, usually from the 1850's to the 1940's.

Condition of Merchandise. They sell refinished furniture, usually in good condition. Inspection is held from noon to the beginning of the auction on Saturday.

Price Range: Average, from $150 to $350 for a round oak table, and from $250 to $600 for a china cabinet.

Terms: Cash, check, VISA, or Master Charge

Rogers Auction Gallery
12101 Nebel Street,
Rockville, MD
881-5544

Auction Frequency, Dates, and Time: Every Friday at 7:30 pm. They also do special catalogue sales.

Notification: There is no mailing list for the Friday auctions, but there is one for the catalogue sales. Auctions are advertised in the *Post*, *Baltimore Sun*, *Journal* newspapers, and antique magazines.

Type of Merchandise: Furniture from 1900-1940, paintings, rugs, and glassware generally. Three times a year they hold special antique and jewelry auctions.

Condition of Merchandise: Usually good condition. Inspection is possible up to the day before the auction.

Price range: $1 to $5,000.

Terms: Cash, personal checks, VISA, or NAC. They take very little consignment; depending on what is put on sale, the consignment fee averages 20%.

Samuel Yudkin & Associates
1125 King Street,
Alexandria, VA 22314
(703) 549-9330

Auction Frequency, Dates, and Time: They have three types of auction: Stamps and First Day Covers, which occur about thrice a year (inspection for these is by appointment three days prior to sale); Books and prints, a monthly catalogue sale, usually beginning at 11 or noon; and spot auctions, in which they liquidate store or household goods (these occur infrequently, and inspection is one or two days before the sale).

Operations: This is an open auction, but not an absolute auction. Sometimes the owner of an item places a reserve price on the item.

Notification: There are three separate mailing lists. For the stamps and first day covers, you can subscribe to notices at $1 a year, or, for an additional $1.50, get lists of the prices at which items sold at previous auctions. For the books and prints auction, a subscription is $15.00 a year, or $25 with a price list from previous auctions. The spot auctions occur so infrequently that there is no fee for being placed on the mailing list. They also advertise in the *Washington Post*, in the book section and under "auctions" or "antiques and collectibles". In addition, they advertise in trade journals, such as *Antique Trader*. These advertisements appear for several weeks prior to the sale. For spot auctions, they run only for a week prior to the sale.

Type of Merchandise: Stamps and first day covers are international, mint, air mail, and UN Canal Zone. Books are first editions, illustrated books, original graphics, comic books, and a good selection of Hogarth prints. For spot auctions, merchandise usually consists of furniture, hardware store contents, storage van cubicle contents, cars, and items from pawn shops.

Condition of merchandise: Varies; usually very good, unless otherwise noted.

Price Range: On stamps, the minimum bid is $1, and they go as high as $500. On books, the minimum bid is $5, and they have gone as high as $1400.00

Terms: Master Charge, VISA, personal checks. Items are returnable if the buyer has not been able to inspect the item — primarily in long distance or mail orders, or if there was a major error in the catalogues. The buyer pays a 10% premium to Yudkin on everything but spot auction merchandise. The consignor pays 15% of sale price to Yudkin. The price charged the consignor depends on the amount of sales, and is negotiable at $100 worth of merchandise or more.

Sam W. Patterson & Co., Inc.
407 N. Howard Street,
Baltimore, MD 21201
(301) 685-1320

Auction Frequency, Dates, and Time: Every Thursday from 10:30 am.

Notification: No mailing list, but advertisements in classified section of the *Baltimore Sun*.

Type of Merchandise: Old and new furniture, household items like china, silver, books, and coins.

Price Range: Varies.

Terms: Cash or personal check if drawn on local bank, with proper identification. Immediate removal of purchase required. They handle property and estate sales also.

Thieves Market
7704 Richmond Highway
Alexandria, VA 22306
360-4200

Auction Frequency, Dates, and Time: Major auctions are held on six occasions: New Year's Day, George Washington's Birthday, Memorial Day, July 4th, Labor Day, and Thanksgiving. Auctions begin at 10 am. Inspection can be made three days before the sale from 10 am to 5 pm. There is no consignment. Everything is owned by the Thieves' Market and sold with reserve to the highest bidder at open auction.

Notification: Write or call to be put on mailing list. Advertisements in *Washington Post*, *Washington Star*, local papers, and antique tabloids.

Type of Merchandise: Eighteenth and nineteenth century furniture, paintings, oriental rugs, bric-a-brac, jewelry, as well as silver and bronzes.

Condition of Items: Sold "as is". Any imperfections are specified.

Price Range: $50 to $5,000

Terms: Cash or check with approved credit card.

Thomas J. Owen & Son, Inc.
1111 E Street, NW
Washington, DC 20004
628-3090

Auction Frequency, Dates, and Time: Vary.

Eligibility: Open to public.

Notification: They advertise in the *Washington Star* in the classified section under "auctions".

Inspection of Items: None. Everything is bought "as is".

Type of merchandise: Real estate and homes from foreclosures.

Condition of items: Varies.

SCRAP AND SALVAGE OPERATIONS

ABC
65 N Street NE
Washington, DC
488-7850

This operation recycles newspaper, rolls of paper, and old publications. Paper is sold by weight, depending on what kind it is: $20 a ton for newspaper and $100 a ton for blank white paper. The only way to get a real bargain is to buy wholesale quantities.

Ace Wrecking and Building
516 Kennedy Street NW
Washington, DC
882-8620

You can buy pieces from homes that have been torn down or remodeled. Typical items include doors, windows, bathtubs, trim, plumbing and heating plants, used brick, and other building materials. They have even had paneling from the Jockey Club. Prices run less than 50% of new. They will deliver for a nominal fee. A move to 1810 13th Street was in the planning stage as this book went to press. They are open from 8 am to 4 pm on Monday through Saturday; and there is an answering service to take calls at other times.

Georgetown Junk
3256 M Street
Washington, DC
333-1900

Open from 7 am to 2:45 pm Monday through Friday, and from 8 am to 1 pm on Saturday, this firm buys recycled papers, including newspapers, corrugated stock, and all types of ledgers. They sell paper by weight, the price varying with what the market will bear. Usually, they get 30c per 100 pounds of newspaper, and $4.00 per 100 pounds of blank white paper.

Montgomery Scrap Corporation
15000 Southlawn Lane
Rockville, MD
424-3000

They buy high grade waste paper, like tabulating cards, computer paper, and white bond, as well as printers' waste. They will sell to the public, depending on what people want. Open Monday through Friday from 7 am to 5 pm, and Saturday until 3 pm.

Tertel Salvage Company
488-7178

This is a paper company which buys and sells office waste, including typing paper, tab cards, high grade paper, etc. Prices depend on the product. At the time of our interview, you could get 100 pounds of white ledger paper for $4.00, hard white paper for $6.50 to $7.00 per hundred pounds, colored ledger paper for $3.00 per pound, printout paper for $5.00 per 100 pounds, and manilla tab cards for $7.00 per 100 pounds. They usually sell to paper mills.

SHERIFFS' SALES

Arlington County
Police and County Vehicles:

Auction Frequency, Dates, and Time: Auction held once a year, usually in fall or early spring, starting at about 10 am.

Eligibility: Anyone over 18 years of age is eligible at open auction.

Notification: They advertise in all major newspapers, including the *Washington Post*, the *Washington Star*, the *Journal* newspapers, and in supermarket newspapers, as well as with a postcard campaign. To be put on the mailing list, send a self-addressed postcard to:

> Equipment Division
> Department of Public Works
> 4251 S. 28th Street
> Arlington, VA 22206

Type of Merchandise: Police and administrative vehicles, construction equipment, air compressors, sedans, motorcycles, vans, fire trucks, school buses, platform trucks, and some wreckers. Not all vehicles are in condition to be driven off the lot. There is no guarantee or warranty. You are allowed to start the vehicle, but not drive it around, because most vehicles are not inspected or certified. They will tell you if a major component is not functioning.

Condition of Merchandise: As is. Inspection is held 3 days prior to the auction, from 9 am to 4 or 5 pm each day. Price is based on replacement criteria: cost of replacement, condition of vehicle, cost of repairs, mileage (usually from 60,000 to 100,000) and age of vehicle (usually 5 to 7 years.)

Price Range: Varies. Large sedans go for from $100 to $1000. Trucks go for much more than sedans, motorcycles for $1500 to $1800. A 1950 GMC wrecker went for $1250 at a recent auction, a 1974 dump truck for $670, and a Dodge van for $650. An externally damaged police car went for $110, and a pickup for $750.

Where auction is held: Arlington County Property Yard, off Arlington Mill Drive and Shirlington Road, next to Police Impoundment Lot.

Terms: Complete payment in cash or guaranteed certified check. $100 deposit required at each sale. 48 hours to remove vehicle from lot.

Abandoned, Confiscated or Impounded Vehicles:

Auction Frequency, Dates, and Time: Held periodically, about once every two months.

Notification: They advertise 10 days in advance in the *Northern Virginia Sun*, with notices posted in libraries, courthouse, and police headquarters.

Eligibility: Anyone over 18 years of age.

Condition of Merchandise: Poor to good.

Price Range: $50.00 and up — anything under that price is junked.

Auctions are Held: Police Impoundment Lot, 2720 S. Taylor Street, Shirlington/Arlington

Information: 558-2393

Sheriff's Department:

Auction Frequency, Times, and Dates: Usually about once a month.

Notification: Courthouse bulletin board, on property for sale, at nearest post office bulletin board. Foreclosure sales usually advertised in the paper.

Type of merchandise: Non-necessities, like cooking utensils, radios, televisions, furniture, and bicycles.

Montgomery County

Liens and Judgments:

Frequency of Auction: 12 per year. Can be held any day.

Notification: Advertised in county-published newspaper only.

Type of merchandise: Household goods, vehicles, homes — any personal or real property.

Condition of Merchandise: Varies. Inspection for ½ hour prior to sale.

Price Range: Varies, usually good buys.

Terms: Cash, certified check, or money order.

Information: Call 279-8286

Abandoned Vehicles:

Frequency of Auction: Every other month, the first Saturday, usually open at 8 am, with auction beginning at 10 am.

Notification: There is a mailing list to let you know the date of the auction. They advertise in county newspapers at least 21 days prior to auction.

Type of Merchandise: 225 vehicles per auction, with a minimum bid of $21. All kinds of cars, sometimes trucks.

Condition: 95% of merchandise is junk. Inspection is 2 hours prior to sale beginning.

Price Range: Best cars bring $700 to $800, junk brings $35 to $60.

Terms: Cash or personal checks.

Prince George's County

Liens, Judgements, and Foreclosures:

Auction frequency: Almost every day. They place a legal ad in the County newspaper. Auctions are held wherever the County Attorney's office chooses to hold them.

Notification: Notices published in legal newspapers, local Prince George's newspapers. There is no mailing list.

Condition of Merchandise: Varies.

Type of Merchandise: Homes, townhouses, condominiums. Whatever is mortgaged and the payments were not kept up.

Price Range: Varies.

Terms: Up to County Attorney's Office.

Liens and Judgements: Personal Property and Vehicles

Auction Frequency: Whenever the County Attorney's office decides that things should be going up for sale.

Notification: Publish notice in the *Enquirer Gazette*, which is printed in Upper Marlboro once a week.

Type of Merchandise: Homes, cars, and other personal property.

Condition of Merchandise: Varies. Inspection of vehicles is up to the discretion of the towing station. There is no inspection of personal property.

Price Range: Varies.

Terms: Cash or certified check.

Where Sales Are Held: Vehicles sold at towing stations. Real property sold at court house door at Upper Marlboro, with a description being read. Personal property would be sold wherever it was located.

Information: 952-4696.

County and Police Vehicles
ADB Auction Systems
P.O. Box 158
Brandywine, MD 20613
372-8876

This firm handles disposition for Prince George's, Montgomery, Charles, and St. Mary's Counties, and for PEPCO and the Chesapeake and Potomac Phone Company surplus vehicles.

Auction Frequency: Held once every two months on no fixed date, Fridays at noon.

Eligibility: Open to all auto dealers, but only to out-of-state individuals. This occurs because of Maryland state law, which requires that vehicles pass inspection before being sold. These vehicles have not been inspected; therefore Marylanders cannot purchase them.

Notification: They advertise in the *Washington Post*, *Baltimore Sun*, and *Richmond Times*, and they put flyers in local stores. There is no mailing list, but they will send you a flyer if you call in.

Type of Merchandise: Ex-police cars, including Plymouths and Ford Falcons, dump trucks, fork lifts, front end loaders, C&P vans, PEPCO Valiants and Mavericks.

Condition of Merchandise: Vehicles from 1967 to 1977, from very poor to good condition. Inspection on day of sale from 9 am to the time of the auction.

Price Range: Varies from $50 to $5000.

Terms: Cash or certified check the same day as the sale.

Where held: Intersection of Route 301 and Cedarville Road, Brandywine, MD.

Information: (301) 372-8876. They also sell miscellaneous items such as jewelry and bicycles for Prince George's County, which are from unclaimed merchandise. These auctions occur once every three months and are open to the public.

Arcade Auctions
733 15th Street NW
Washington, DC 20005
393-3480

Auction Frequency, Dates, and Time: Held every Thursday at 11 am.

Notification: Mailing list is available. Send them your name and address on a postcard if you want to be included. They advertise in the *Washington Post* every Sunday of the week of the sale.

Type of Merchandise: They handle forfeited items from Washington area pawnbrokers. This includes jewelry, radios, and cameras, with a strong emphasis on jewelry. Arcade Auctions also represents the DC Government on items abandoned, stolen, or siezed.

Condition of Items: Pawnbroker items are guaranteed to operate. Items from Police Department and government are sold "as is". Inspection is held the Wednesday before the auction from 11 am to 3 pm.

Prices: From $5 to a couple of thousand dollars (particularly on jewelry).

Terms: Cash; checks are sometimes accepted.

FEDERAL GOVERNMENT AUCTIONS

General Services Administration — Carson City Silver Dollar

This is a public auction with a fixed price for silver dollars minted in Carson City. Tentatively, at the time of this publication, the 1883 CC was to go for $30 plus postage, uncirculated, on an "as is" basis. The 1884 CC was also going for $30. 90% silver coins from 1879-1885, and 1890-1 cost about $20.00. They also have an auction by mail bid, shortly after the first auction ends. On 1880, 1881, and 1885 coins, they request a minimum bid of $100 per coin plus postage, by registered mail. There is a limit of 5 coins per category per bidder. For more information, send a postcard with your name, address, and zip code on it to Carson City Silver Dollars, San Francisco, California 94170.

Department of Commerce — Fleet Disposal Branch

For that large merchant vessel you've always wanted, this is the place. The Division of the Fleet Reserve of the Maritime Administration, Washington, D.C. 20230, sells ships on sealed competitive bids, which are opened in the Office of the Secretary of Maritime Administration. They sell merchant vessels of 1500 tons or more.

Condition: World War II vintage ships. Inspection for a month before bids are opened.

Eligibility: Restricted to US citizens.

Notification: There is a mailing list, obtained by writing the above address or by calling 377-4416. They advertise in the *Chicago Commerce Journal,* the *Commerce Business Daily,* and other papers.

Terms: 10% of bid enclosed bid; balance within 25 days of date of award. You must scrap the ship within 24 months of date of delivery. These ships are to be used as scrap, not for transportation purposes. During the 24 month period prior to scrapping, they can be used as schools, storage, or standing/exhibition ships. There are three reserve fleet locations — East Coast, West Coast, and Gulf Coast; ships may be offered from any of these locations. They have not offered any ships for sale since March 1978 because of the asbestos problem — there will not be any sales until this is cleared up.

US Customs Service Auction

Auction Frequency: Auctions are held once a year, about mid-October, beginning at 9 am.

Eligibility: Anyone is eligible; there is no age requirement. However, when alcoholic beverages are auctioned, you must be a licensed importer to bid.

Notification: You can be put on a mailing list; a catalog is usually sent a month before the auction. Send your name to the District Director of Customs, 103 S. Gay Street, Baltimore, MD 21202, or call (301) 962-2762; or you can send your name and address for the mailing list to Dulles International Airport, P.O. Box 17423, Washington, DC 20041, or call 566-5242 or 566-8511. They advertise in the Washington-Baltimore area on television, radio, and newspapers three weeks prior to the sale.

Type of Merchandise: Anything and everything that has been abandoned or seized by the US Customs in the Washington-Baltimore Districts. Much of this is merchandise which was abandoned because the individual or company to whom it was addressed did not act within 5 days of entry of the merchandise into the US; it was then transferred to a government warehouse and left unclaimed for a year. Merchandise at the most recent sale included 384 mopeds, 500 pounds of frozen fish, cars, jewelry, camp trailers — just about everything except real property.

Condition of Merchandise: Inspection is held the day before the auction.

Price Range: Fluctuates.

Department of Defense - - Defense Property Disposal Offices

FORT BELVOIR:

Auction Frequency: Once every month or 6 weeks on a Wednesday, with registration beginning at 8 am and sale beginning at 9 am. They no longer have live auctions. You still bid, but you do so by filling in a card and submitting it; the manager of the sale reads the high bid.

Notification: There is a mailing list, which you will be placed on if you call or write. They advertise only in army post bulletins.

Type of Merchandise: Office machines and furniture, hand tools, electronic and test equipment, buffets, dressers, filing cabinets, a few vehicles — around 250 items per sale.

Condition of Merchandise: Fair to poor — all used property. Machines usually need repairs. Inspection 5 working days prior to sale date, from 8 am to 3 pm.

Price Range: Varies.

Terms: Cash or personal checks.

Where held: Fort Belvoir
 Meade Road, Building S 1976
 North Post (opposite main gate on Rte. 1)

Information: 664-1090

BRANDYWINE:

Auction Frequency: About every two months, probably on a Tuesday. Local spot bid procedure for which the bidder has to be present. You fill out a card, and the top bid wins. Registration usually at 8 am, with sale starting at 9 am.

Eligibility: Open to general public, except employees of Property Disposal Office.

Notification: There is a mailing list available; call or write for inclusion on it: Defense Property Disposal Office, P.O. Box 147, Brandywine, MD 20613, or call 372-8844. They also advertise on the local radio and in the local newspaper.

Type of Merchandise: Vehicles such as pickups, sedans, vans, station wagons from late 60's to early 70's; office furniture, machines, and equipment; bicycles.

Condition of Merchandise: Fair to poor.

Price Range: Varies.

Terms: Cash, certified check, or registered check. 5 day free storage.

Where Held: Brandywine, MD
 Along Rte. 381 South
 Property Disposal Office

FORT MEADE:

Auction Frequency: There is no set time for these spot bid sales — usually they occur once every two months, with registration at 8 am and sale beginning at 9 am.

Notification: There is a mailing list. To get on it, call or write Defense Property Disposal Office, Building T 6297, Fort Meade, MD 20755 or (301) 677-6366. They also advertise in the Fort Meade papers, daily bulletins, and local area newspapers.

Eligibility: Open to general public.

Type of Merchandise: Office equipment, electronics equipment, clothing, and vehicles — limited to 1 ton trucks or pickup at maximum size.

Condition of merchandise: Varies. Inspection five working days before sale.

Price Range: Varies.

Terms: Cash or personal checks. Five working days to pay and remove before items go into storage, for which you are charged.

NATIONAL:

There is also a national auction for larger items, such as large 2½ ton trucks, buses, generator sets, automatic data processing equipment, and defense industrial plant equipment. This is a sealed bid auction. To inquire about the mailing list for it, write to: Department of Defense, Surplus Sales, P.O. Box 1370, Battle Creek, Michigan 49016.

General Services Administration

For all GSA Auctions in this category, information can be obtained by writing:

> Surplus Sales Center
> Building 197, Navy Yard Annex
> Washington, D.C. 20468
>
> Or by calling: 472-2190

VEHICLES:

Auction frequency: Held once a month, usually the second Wednesday, in the early afternoon.

Notification: They have a mailing list but prefer telephone inquiries. They will advertise vehicles in the *Washington Post* the Sunday before the sale; in the *Washington Star's* Wheels section the Friday before the sale; and in the *Journal* newspapers the Friday before the sale.

Eligibility: Anyone over 18, except for GSA employees.

Type of Merchandise: Four-door sedans, some test cars, some smaller cars like AMC Hornets, '74 Valiants, park police motorcycles, and cruisers — all five years old or with 60,000 miles minimum on them.

Condition of Merchandise: Inspection on day of sale from 11 am to time of sale.

Price Range: Competitive billing — usually high, but there are some good buys.

OFFICE MACHINES AND FURNITURE:

Auction Frequency: Auction held twice a month until the end of the year. Spot bid sale, but you don't have to be there in person — you can find out if you won by writing or calling GSA. Sale is at 10 am on Thursday.

Type of Merchandise: Metal furniture predominates — desks, chairs, and bookcases. Occasionally they have wooden furniture, but file cabinets are scarce. All makes of machines such as typewriters and calculators, adding machines, and IBM Selectrics from time to time.

Condition of Merchandise: Inspection prior to bidding from Monday through Wednesday, 8:30 am to 3:30 pm, and Thursday until 10 am.

MISCELLANEOUS:

Auction Frequency: Usually held on a monthly basis, but there is no set schedule. Spot bid sale.

Notification: Mailer for miscellaneous items gives partial listing, but they suggest you come down and look at what they have.

Type of Merchandise: Televisions, clothing, computer equipment and electronic equipment, medical items, shop items such as drills, presses, and saws. All merchandise sold "as is".

OTHER:

There is also a mailing list of property outside of the Washington, D.C. area. This would cover Virginia, West Virginia, Maryland, Pennsylvania, and Delaware. Items are sold by sealed bids. Send request for information to address above. Specify area of interest — what kind of commodities — and state what you want information about.

Internal Revenue Service

Auction Frequency: No regularity.

Eligibility: Anyone other than IRS employees or close family.

Procedure: 50% are sealed bid, 50% are open bid. This is explained in the notice of the auction, with all of the other information. They take bids for individual items and bids for the whole lot — and take the best option.

Notification: Advertising is done by each of the different offices which hold these sales. The Wheaton office advertises in the *Washington Post* or *Washington Star* in the Sunday editions as well as the *Montgomery Sentinel* and *Prince George's Post* on occasion. The E Street office advertises in the *Post* or *Star* on Sunday; the Suitland office in the *Prince George's Sentinel* or *Enquirer Gazette*; the Annapolis office in the *Annapolis Evening Capitol*; the Frederick office in the *Frederick Post* and/or the *Carroll County Times*; the Baltimore office in the Sunday *Baltimore Sun*; and the Baileys Crossroads office in the *Journal* newspapers and the *Northern Virginia Sun*. These are one-time ads which would appear no less than 10 days prior to the sale. In addition, notice of the sales are posted in the county courthouses and also in local post offices.

Type of Merchandise: Business property, sometimes household items, occasionally cars, boats, furniture, or building materials.

Condition of Merchandise: As is, with inspection before the sale.

Terms: Cash or certified check at the time of the sale. Deferred payment is sometimes an option in the case of real property.

Baltimore:
   Chief of Collection Division
   Internal Revenue Service
   P.O. Box 538,
   Baltimore, MD 21203
   (301) 962-3151

Frederick:
   Group Manager
   Internal Revenue Service
   Collection Division
   922 East Street
   Frederick, MD 21701
   (301) 663-9245

Annapolis:
   Group Manager
   Internal Revenue Service
   1419 Forest Drive
   Annapolis, MD 21403
   (301) 268-0840

Wheaton:
   Internal Revenue Service
   South Wheaton Shopping Plaza
   Wheaton, MD 20902
   427-7020

Suitland:
   Internal Revenue Service
   5408 Silver Hill Road,
   Suitland, MD 20028
   763-1920

Washington:
   Internal Revenue Service
   1201 E Street NW
   Washington, DC
   376-0231

Baileys Crossroads:
   Internal Revenue Service
   One Skyline Place
   5205 Leesburg Pike
   Room 602
   Baileys Crossroads, VA 22041
   577-0200

U.S. Postal Service

Auction Frequency: Sales are held as damaged and unclaimed articles accumulate, usually twice a year. Auctions always occur on Wednesdays, beginning at 9 am.

Eligibility: Anyone, with the exception of Postal Service Employees.

Notification: Mailing list for upcoming auctions: notices are sent two weeks in advance of the auction. Direct requests to the Postmaster, Parcel Post Branch, Washington, D.C. 20013, or call 523-2043

Type of Merchandise: Anything that people could send through the mail, including televisions, books, records, jewelry, and household items. Also in auction are excess postal equipment such as floor waxers, adding machines, and other equipment that could be unserviceable, over a certain age, or sometimes even brand new.

Condition of Merchandise: Varies, with much damaged merchandise. They highly recommend inspection. Inspection is held the Tuesday before the auction, from 8 am to 4 pm that day. There is no review of the merchandise the day of the sale, but you can get a catalogue the day of the inspection. Nothing is guaranteed, and everything is sold as is. They are not responsible for quality or quantity of the merchandise.

Price Range: From $10 to $400, with better jewelry going up even higher.

Terms: People who are interested in large quantities put up an advance deposit prior to the sale; they can then wait until the end of the sale to pay the remainder. People interested in only two or three items pay cash immediately as they buy it. It is better to put a deposit down rather than have to pay for each item separately. They accept cash, travelers' checks, and money orders — but no personal checks.

Operation: This is an open auction in which the auctioneer continues to up the price as long as there are paddles or hands up in the air, until one bidder is left. The action is very fast-paced.

Where Held:
United States Postal Service
3070 V Street NE
Washington, DC 20018
523-2043

Small Business Administration:

Auction Frequency: There is no set date — it depends on whether they have to foreclose on businesses or not.

Eligibility: General public except for employees of the SBA.

Notification: There is no mailing list, but they advertise in the *Washington Post*, *Washington Star*, and sometimes in local newspapers. These ads appear 10 days prior to the sale, under the heading of "auction sales" or "public sales"; they run two or three times in each paper.

Type of Merchandise: Wide variety, always depending on who was foreclosed upon: equipment from a grocery store, such as freezers, cash registers, inventory; radios; records; clothing; ceramic furnaces; restaurant equipment; or showcases.

Condition of Merchandise: Varies. Inspection the day before the auction if there is a large amount of goods; otherwise, on the day of the auction, an hour or two before it begins.

Price Range: Varies.

Terms: Most auctions require cash, certified check, or bank check.

Information:
Small Business Administration
Washington District Office
1030 15th Street NW
Suite 250
Washington, DC 20417
Attention: Liquidation Section
Or call: 653-6960

Energy

The cost of living is rising dramatically, with fuel costs contributing a large part of the increase each year. In the face of impending fuel shortages and consequent price hikes, it makes good sense to take some positive action to reduce the costs of heating, cooling, and otherwise powering your home.

There are numerous ways to fight the huge budget bite energy can make. The tried and true methods include weatherization, insulation, and conservation. You might have scoffed at these methods in the past, or not realized how valuable they could be, but these days it is hard to ignore how effective any or all of these three approaches can be.

WEATHERIZING

Weatherizing your home means keeping the weather you want in while keeping the undesirable weather out. If you don't want to wind up paying to heat or cool the neighborhood, you should make sure that your house holds in the hot or cool air for which you pay. You will use less energy by weatherizing, and your heating and cooling bills will reflect this saving.

Weatherization is also an umbrella term for procedures like caulking and weatherstripping. Chances are that, when you bought your house, it had some caulking or weatherstripping, or you might have taken care of these things yourself years ago. Whether your house has old weatherization or none at all, it is probably in need of some help. If you can stay on top of your house's weatherization needs, you can stay on top of a good part of your energy costs.

Caulking

Caulking is sealing up any thin area where air can penetrate. Wherever air can come from the outside into your home, you can be losing heat in winter and cooled air in summer. This is called *infiltration* and usually occurs around doors, windows, floors and walls. Other common areas of leakage include:

- where door and window frames meet the structure of your house;
- corners of the house where siding meets;
- where wood sills meet the house foundations, as in the basement;
- special openings on the outside of your home where you have water faucets, outlets, vents, gas or oil lines, etc.;
- where chimney or masonry butts up against siding;
- where pipes and wires penetrate the ceiling below and unheated attic into your house;
- around the furnace flue, plumbing vents, pipes, and attic air ducts;
- between heated and unheated areas like your garage, attached tool shed, etc.;
- around skylight frames;
- around window-mounted air conditioners.

These areas require inspection to determine whether they need new sealant. Caulking sealant comes in three varieties, and you may want to consult the dealer to determine which one best suits your needs.

Two points to remember when buying caulking: a) the higher the performance of the caulking, the longer it will last. The higher quality material will also probably be the more expensive one; and b) examine the contents label on the caulking container for lead base compounds. The U.S. Department of Housing and Urban Development recommends avoiding these, as they are poisonous.

To do the caulking you will need a caulking gun, caulking cartridges, putty knife or large screwdriver, a good steady ladder, and a sharp knife or scissors.

In using caulking, read the manufacturer's instructions and recommendations. Adhere to them for best product performance. Caulking is meant for use in depths from ¼" to ½". If you have deeper gaps, fill them in with filler material like oakum, glass fiber, mineral wool, or sponge rubber, to within ¼ to ½ inch of the surface. Then caulk over the filler. For long cracks or seams you can use caulking compound that comes in rope form. To use this, just unwind it and force it into the crack with your fingers or any thin blunt tool handle.

Weatherstripping

Weatherstripping is used where caulking is inappropriate. It consists of strips of vinyl, metal, felt, or foam rubber. The characteristics of each kind suit each one for certain jobs. For example, metal-backed vinyl is good for the space between the door and the door jamb. Felt would be almost worthless here, because it is not durable. In fact, felt and foam rubber tend to shrink over time and should not be used where friction can wear them down.

Weatherstripping entails nailing or tacking the material to wood and metal edges in your house. You will need a hammer, nails, screwdriver, tin snips, tape measure, ladder and/or hacksaw, depending on where you are weatherstripping and what material you are using. You can buy weatherstripping by the foot or in kits to finish doors and windows. How well the stripping works depends on the tightness of the seal.

INSULATION

New homes are often underinsulated to save the builder money on construction costs — although this is becoming less true as buyers are demanding more insulation. But it was especially true of homes built in the days when energy was cheap and plentiful. If your home fits this category, or you merely want to increase its energy-use efficiency, you can add new insulation. Any home can be insulated, and you can also add to already-existing insulation for increased energy efficiency.

Choose your insulation carefully. Check the combustibility and fire-retardant properties (some fireproof insulation materials come with combustible backings and adhesives — which should not be left exposed) and attractiveness to rodents or termites, as well as the cost of materials and labor.

Most important, choose the insulation you want by its "R-value". The R-value is an indication of insulating ability. The higher the R-value, the better the insulating power. Wherever possible, avoid leaving insulation vulnerable to moisture. Moisture will significantly lower the R-value of the insulation material.

Where to insulate:

- ceilings with uncoated, unprotected, or unconditioned spaces above;
- exterior walls, walls between living spaces and unheated garages or storage rooms;
- floors above cold spaces, vented crawl spaces, garages, open porches;
- between sloping rafters;
- between the studs of the kneewalls in the attic;
- between the joists of the floor below the living space;
- in dormer walls and dormer ceilings.

When you shop for insulation, make sure that you inquire about installation precautions and safety measures if you intend to do the work yourself.

CONSERVATION

Conservation can be the simplest energy-saving method. By slightly altering your energy use, you can still be comfortable while saving money. Energy conservation entails:

- setting your thermostats at a maximum of 68° in winter and a minimum of 78° in the summer, according to U.S. government suggestions;
- keeping doors and windows closed when either heating or cooling your home with energy-using systems;
- getting the most out of appliances through conserving use — like operating dishwashers only when full; and
- buying energy-efficient appliances.

Learn to shop for energy efficiency by comparing EERs (energy efficiency ratios). The higher the EER, the more efficient the product. Products with high EERs may cost you more initially, but save you money in energy costs — over the long haul.

After you have taken any or all of the preceding steps (insulation, conservation, and weatherization), you may want to examine the cost of the existing way in which you heat and cool your house and water. There may be some savings in either switching to, or augmenting your present heating/cooling system with another form of energy.

ENERGY-SAVING TIPS

Products to Cut Heating Costs
- Window quilts, which act much like shades inside the house, fitting onto a track on the sides of the window frames.
- Automatic thermostat timers, which turn heat up and down automatically so that energy isn't wasted by heating the house, for example, when no one is at home all day.
- Flue Dampers, which automatically close the flue when the burner is not running, preventing heat loss up the chimney.
- Radiator and baseboard reflectors, which consist of reflective material placed behind the heat source to reflect the heat back into the house, instead of letting it dissipate out through the walls.
- Oil burner with a high-speed flame retention head, which is more efficient than older burners.
- Storm windows made of heavy duty polyvinyl plastic, which mount inside the home like shades for extra insulation on the windows.
- Chimney-top dampers, which eliminate heat loss up the chimney when there is no fire in the fireplace and you have no damper (or only a poorly-fitted one).
- Electrical-outlet draft sealers are installed around cover plates of switches and outlets, to prevent heat loss through these sources.
- Clogged filter indicator tells you when the furnace filter needs to be changed. A dirty filter makes your furnace function less efficiently.
- Plastic foam pipe insulation cuts heat loss on heating and hot water pipes that go through unheated areas of the house.

Improve your H.P.G.*

(with Long & Foster)

House hunting can be fun—if you have all the time and money in the world. But if you're like us, you have to make the most out of both your time *and* money. Driving endless neighborhoods is a house-hunting luxury most people can no longer afford.

From Frederick to Fredericksburg and Annapolis to Leesburg, Long & Foster has more than 1,000 sales associates and 31 offices. We know your neighborhoods. And that knowledge can improve your *Houses Per Gallon.* Here's how.

Walk into the Long & Foster office nearest you. Tell us the type of home you want. We'll screen the thousands of homes currently listed and select only those which meet your specific requirements. You'll review the listings and pinpoint the houses you want us to show you in the neighborhoods you prefer. You're halfway home.

Then we'll visit those houses (gas is on us) until you find the right one, plus we'll coordinate all the contract details and help you shop for the best financing. You've saved time and money *and* found your dream home.

The best of both worlds. Long & Foster.

*Houses Per Gallon

LONG FOSTER
REALTORS®

Executive offices: 3918 Prosperity Ave., Fairfax, VA 22031
For our office nearest you, call
573-2290

Saving Heat in the Home
- Close off unused rooms;
- Close doors and windows. If you want to sleep in a cool room, close the register or radiator;
- Check room thermostat — it may be in error;
- Pull drapes across windows at night for insulation;
- Open drapes on bright sunny days to let the sun warm the house;
- Add a radiant panel or heat lamp to the bathroom for extra heat only when you need it;
- Turn the thermostat down to 55° when you are going to be away a day or more.

Keeping Cool
- Keep storm windows and doors installed when using your air conditioner;
- Install an attic fan to cool the whole house;
- Shade windows with trees, blinds, or screens;
- Exhaust cooking heat and shower or dryer steam with a ceiling fan;
- Schedule moisture-releasing housecleaning chores early in the morning or on cool days;
- Begin air conditioning early on days forecast to be very hot;
- Close the duct system where room air conditioners are located.

ALTERNATIVE ENERGY SOURCES

If you currently use conventional oil, electric, or gas heat, you may want to explore some cheaper alternative or supplements to your system.

Heat Pumps

The heat pump is not really a new idea, but in recent years a lot of improvements have been made on it — enough to make heat pumps worth a second thought. The principle behind them is really kind of simple: To heat your home, heat is sucked into your home from the air outside (no matter what its temperature), and, to cool your home, air is cooled by refrigeration coolant as it is sucked into your home. This works because there is always heat in the air — no matter how "cold" the air seems to your skin. A heat pump is designed to draw this heat out and circulate it in your home. It can be used as effectively in winter as in summer. New developments have made the heat pump at least as reliable as any other popular energy source used today.

The improvements in heat pumps have really come in the energy efficiency area. Now, most heat pumps will give you one-and-one-half times the heat for every unit of energy you expend than they did before. This means more heat for your money — or the same amount of heat for less money. And one advantage of the heat pump is that a single unit will both heat and cool, so that your electricity bill stays relatively constant (assuming that rates do) in both winter and summer. You have a control which allows the unit to change from the heating to cooling system and back again, as you wish.

According to PEPCO, you can save up to 35% of your energy costs (compared to an *electric* furnace) by using a heat pump.

Wood-burning Stoves

The wood-burning stove has made quite a comeback. Once used for both cooking and heating, later often used as a romantic centerpiece, it is being rediscovered as an effective alternative to oil and electricity as a primary source of heating your home. But, as with any other energy form, you should realize that wood rises in price from season to season, and also, as more people use wood stoves and the demand for wood increases. Wood stoves are being made to function more efficiently these days, and provide dependable constant heat. You can also get models that can be cooked on or used just to heat your home. The range in price varies from design to design and also depends heavily on purpose.

There are two types of wood-burning stoves: *radiant* and *forced* air. The radiant is the old-fashioned design, which is used to heat either a room or a large open building. In this type, the heat literally radiates from the stove. The problem with this type is that the room temperature is inconsistent, getting cooler the further away you get from the stove. For that reason, these are preferred for use in heating separate rooms, summer homes (as they are used infrequently); and as a secondary source of heat in a home.

The better wood stove, which can be used as a primary source of heat, is the forced air variety. This stove utilizes a blower system to circulate the air around the whole house. These can be installed in an existing fireplace and hooked up to the flue, or can be freestanding. With these, a back-up system is recommended — for when you are away, in case your electricity is cut off and the blower won't operate, or if you forgot to stock up on wood. The surface can still be used to cook on, and, with the doors removed, it can still be used as an open fireplace if that is where it is installed.

If you use a radiant heat stove, you will want to surround it with a screen to protect unwary pets and small children from burning themselves. With either kind, you will want to protect the surrounding floor with a fireproof flooring material within a certain distance of the stove. In most local jurisdictions, this is dictated by the housing codes.

You will also need a good dependable supplier of wood. Hard woods are recommended (like oak); but, in a pinch, some stoves can burn a variety of wood and wood products, or even coal. If you are not proud in energy matters, you may be able to augment your wood supply by picking up chopped wood and/or wood chips from telephone and electric line maintenance crews. Your wood stove dealer should be able to estimate your seasonal wood use when you choose a particular model and describe its intended use (many people get by on 2-3 cords [128 cubic feet/cord] of wood a season). Use depends on whether you leave the doors open or shut on the front of the stove. In case your dealer doesn't stress it — keep your chimney or stovepipe clean with a professional cleaning at least once a year. A clogged or dirty pipe is a hazard as well as a pollutant.

Here are some of the features for which to look when purchasing a wood stove, as suggested by the North Carolina Agricultural Extension Service:

- Examine wood capacity of the stove;
- Remember to ask the method by which the stove is loaded (from the front, the side), what kind of wood, how it should be cut, etc.
- The maximum length of the wood which the stove can accommodate and burn well;
- How easy it is to remove the ash, and how frequently this should be done;
- The type and thickness of the materials used to construct the stove;
- What type of material is used to line the firebox;
- What are the terms of the warranty, and how easy is it to obtain parts should you need them;
- How flexible is the stove for heating water and cooking food;
- How is air circulated around the stove;
- How is the door handle or knob protected when the stove is in use, so that the user doesn't get burnt. Also, how safe is the unit around children or pets?

Solar Power

Solar power is not just for long-haired dreamers or rich eccentrics — it works.

Solar power or solar energy is an umbrella term for a number of methods for putting the sun's heat to work in your home. The two main kinds of solar energy systems (systems being those set-ups for capturing the sun's energy and turning it into useful home-heating energy) are *active* and *passive* solar energy systems.

Passive solar is by far the easier and less costly version of solar heating. And *heating* here means both for hot water and for home heating use. Strictly defined, passive solar means "a solar system which uses no mechanical assistance to move or regulate the release of collected energy". Obviously there is less expense when you have no mechanisms, but there is also less energy at your disposal. Because of this you should consider passive solar as only one part of your home's comprehensive energy system. Also, the more passive the system the less of a role it will play as a year-round energy source. You already use passive solar energy in its most basic form – pure sunlight. You can alter or build to better use solar power. Your windows can gather heat in the winter when oriented toward the sun. To avoid having these same windows overheating your house in

Q. WHAT'S THE ANSWER TO HOME HEATING COSTS?

A. BUCK STOVE™

UL Listed

The Alternative
Primary Heating System
convert your home to wood heat and eliminate 60 - 80% of your current heating costs

THE BUCK STOVE COMPANY OF OLD TOWN
109 South Alfred Street
Alexandria, Virginia 22313   Phone: 703/683-4886

the summer, clever landscaping would place deciduous trees in front of the windows, shading them and screening them from the sun. This is just one example of passive solar design.

These simple measures will help heat your home, but you can also heat water with passive solar power. This system will be more costly to install than others, but will yield a better return on the investment.

Solar water heating can be used for two different purposes: hot water for personal use, and home heating use. Personal use means hot water for bathing, washing, cooking, etc. Home heating with passive solar means heating the water without any added machinery and circulating it around your home the same way.

The passive system for space and water heating works on an easy principle: let the sun shine on. But how well the sun can do this, and your ability to hold that energy, is a tricky proposition depending on your geographical location. Certainly a sunny area would be good, but if your house isn't made of a dense enough material, you'll lose the heat soon after your house collects it. Stone, brick and concrete are all good for heat retention because they all store it quickly and hold it long enough to warm the house.

By erecting a tank over your house (or at least above its highest point), whether attached or freestanding, and by painting it black, you will have a ready supply of solar heated water. But this is risky, and you should not depend on this method for long-term needs. A cloudy day or a few cloudy days could leave you without a good supply — you might instead have a useless tub of lukewarm water.

Rather than being stuck with lukewarm water and a house that's hotter on one side than the other, you may want to opt for an *active*, mechanically-assisted solar system. In many cases "mechanically-assisted" simply means using a pump.

Strictly defined, an active solar system includes: equipment to trap the sun's energy (using a collection panel) and move it (the energy) to its intended point of use (your bathtub, furnace, or sink) for water heating, space heating, and possibly space cooling. And if you are doing any of these things, you may want a storage system, too. This storage system would ostensibly be a tank to store the heated water or air.

Equipment to trap the sun's energy usually is a solar collection plate. The plate consists of a sandwich construction with glass on the top facing the sun, and a black backing to attract and hold the sun's heat. Liquid flows between these two sides and heats on its way to the pumping mechanism. This mechanism moves the liquid to either its heating destination or a storage tank for later use. If, however, you opt for air-to-air heating, you would substitute the air for liquid and storage would be a bit different.

Collecting the solar energy is really quite straightforward and can be done in a variety of ways.

There are three types of solar heat-delivery systems. These are methods to distribute the heat from the panels to your home where you can use it.

A **Liquid-to-Air** system can work in one of two ways: either by using an existing hot air circulating furnace; or by using an installed room-type liquid-to-air heat exchanger (a more practical idea if your home has no ductwork).

In the first system, using a furnace already in place, you can have a fan coil for a liquid-to-air heat exchange installed in the ductwork. And a heat sensor placed in the duct will be able to "kick-on" the oil furnace when auxiliary power is necessary. However, if you have no ducts in your home, you should consider the room heat exchangers. These exchangers come in various sizes, with self-contained blowers or fans to circulate the heated air.

Air-to-Air systems use only one type of delivery method. The heat is drawn from the collector panels and moved along to a storage tank of pebbles. From the storage bed of pebbles, the hot air is moved around the house through ducts. This method requires larger ducts than many homes have — so new ducts may need to be installed — and an air purifier may also be needed to keep pollen and other impurities out of your home.

Liquid-to-Liquid systems entail baseboard radiators. Heated water (or other appropriate liquid) is circulated from the solar collector panels around your home, in the baseboard radiators. The problem with this system is that it provides diminishing returns as the outside temperature drops below 20° F. When this happens, the effectiveness of the solar collector in keeping the liquid running through it drops with the air temperature. It is a good idea to have a solar fan coil connected with your system to "kick-in" and provide added heat. The solar fan coil will act as a liquid-to-air heat exchanger, as explained above.

These are the main types of delivery systems, simplified without the extensive explanations needed to install any of the systems. We assume that knowing the logic of the systems and the way the "solar heat loop" works will be sufficient to whet your appetite for knowledge about other solar energy systems.

It is a good idea to seek out the advice of a solar engineer and have him or her estimate your home's solar needs. If you can't find a solar engineer or architect in the Yellow Pages of the telephone book, contact the National Solar Heating and Cooling Information Center for a referral.

If indeed you do decide to use solar power, shop around for your equipment the way you would for any other major purchase:

- Ask for proof of the product's advertised claims. The proof should come from independent testing result by either a laboratory or a university. Get the test results themselves — not the manufacturer's report.

- As with any purchase, examine the warranty very carefully. Is it full or limited? What are the limitations? How long is the warranty for? Are parts, labor, and service covered? Who will do the actual servicing? Ask about where the repairs will be done and what financial arrangements are to be made in honoring warranties.
- Solar systems are made up of component parts. Not all components work well together. If you buy a system which is incomplete, make sure that the seller is knowledgeable about choosing compatible components.
- Get the name of the firm which will expertly service your system. Don't settle for the line: "Oh, any plumber or handyman can fix it . . ." And, unless you are very knowledgeable about solar energy yourself, don't attempt to service the system. There are two reasons for this. First, you may unknowingly damage the system, and, secondly, by not using an authorized serviceman, you could violate the warranty terms.
- Unless you are very familiar with solar components — don't try to use a do-it-yourself kit. One mistake could ruin your investment.
- Before you buy a solar energy system, check with the Better Business Bureau and any local citizens' solar organization on the seller's reputation, and ask for tips concerning your purchase.
- Make sure that any verbal claims concerning your purchase are written down and signed, accompanying your receipt. And save both.
- If you do have any legitimate complaints, get in touch with the local district attorney's office, the Better Business Bureau, and the local consumer protection agency. Make sure that your complaint is specific and well-documented.

SAVE MONEY ON GASOLINE

Driving and Car Maintenance

Here are some bearable ways to improve your gas mileage and save on fuel costs. Many of these suggestions deal with increasing your car's performance through better maintenance. This makes sense because, after all, increasing your fuel efficiency depends greatly on the efficiency of your engine.

- Consider buying your next car with a manual transmission;
- Get the model's standard engine on your car, not a luxury 8-cylinder engine;
- Consider, even, a diesel engine, which gets good mileage and doesn't need tune-ups — but consider also that, in the event of a serious energy shortage, diesel fuel may be hard to find, since truckers and farmers will undoubtedly have their needs met before those of ordinary drivers. The diesel fuel is vital to the farmers' and truckers' livelihoods, which in turn are vital to the country's economic well-being;

Energy

- Do without power brakes, steering, and anything else on your car that would add weight or limit your control of gasoline consumption;
- Don't get air conditioning for the same reason — it weighs a lot and uses extra energy when it is operating;
- Buy the lighter car if you are torn between two models;
- Get the car with the smaller front end — this helps to cut wind resistance.
- Look for a streamlined design to cut excess wind resistance;
- Buy a roof rack that is removable and use it only when necessary.
- Buy radial tires — they are said to give better mileage and to last longer;
- Buy bias ply if you cannot afford radials;
- Avoid buying a trailer towing rig or package which means using a higher axle ratio on your car;
- Use the engine's prescribed octane gasoline — it should be most efficient at that level;
- Don't fill up the tank to capacity — gasoline is heavy and it could also overflow as you make sharp turns;
- Use a good motor oil of correct viscosity for greater engine performance;
- Add some antifriction compound to the motor oil;
- Consider an electronic ignition system if you don't intend to keep your car tuned with regular tune-ups because you are lazy or don't have the time;
- Replace your worn-out exhaust system with a free-flow type;
- Put in a temperature-controlled or variable pitch radiator fan;
- Put in a vacuum gauge or miles-per-gallon meter — devices commonly available which help you to monitor your driving habits;
- Maintain steady speeds — rapid acceleration and constant braking waste gas;
- Don't brake uphill — ease off the gas instead;
- Accelerate gradually;
- Pass and merge smoothly
- Don't oversteer — many people drive their cars as if they were in a desert race. All that side to side movement is hard on your gas mileage;
- Never pump the gas pedal!
- Watch out for sudden accelerations, which shoot excess gas into the carburetor;
- Use your air conditioner sparingly;
- Avoid prolonged warm-ups; they just waste gas — instead, drive slowly and evenly for the first few blocks, and the car will warm itself up;
- Turn the engine off at long red lights and during highway delays — but only if the gas wasted idling will be more than the gas used to turn the engine back on;

- Avoid overusing electrical accessories, which use up energy;
- Use your brakes, not gears, to slow down or stop during braking maneuvers in a standard transmission car;
- If you have a manual transmission, skip a gear during downhill starts;
- Don't accelerate uphill unless it is necessary, as this uses more gas up than normal and gradual acceleration;
- If your car has an automatic transmission, conquer hills with gradually increasing speed through gradually pressing the accelerator;
- After cresting a hill in a small car, ease off the gas and let momentum increase your speed;
- Read signs and maps to anticipate your terrain and road conditions, so that you don't have to employ wasteful driving maneuvers;
- Read traffic signals and anticipate the changes from red to green;
- Change lanes smoothly in traffic;
- Use the inside track — this is shorter — in driving around curves, and stay in your lane;
- Never tailgate — it just leads to stop and start driving;
- Don't let yourself get boxed in;
- Keep an eye on cars two ahead of you to gauge stops and starts;
- Don't speed into a headwind — you're just using up excess energy;
- As you drive, think about the extra money you could save with these methods and how you might spend it;
- Check the accuracy of your speedometer;
- Check to be sure that the automatic choke isn't stuck;
- Replace dirty oil and air filters;
- Change the engine's oil less often than every three months, but not longer than 3,000 miles;
- Change your oil and air filters on schedule;
- Keep an eye on your PCV valve and replace it when necessary;
- Keep your spark plugs and ignition points clean, gapped, and replaced at recommended times, for greater engine efficiency;
- Learn how to "read" spark plugs for wear and gas mileage;
- Have your ignition timing kept to specifications;
- Check your distributor cap and rotor for signs of wear and corrosion;
- Keep your car properly lubricated;
- Have the car checked for faulty bearings and brakes that drag;
- Check the weatherstripping for insulation damage;
- Wax the car to lessen wind resistance — dirt and mud add extra drag;
- Plan your trip routes;
- Avoid high speeds on rainy or snowy roads;
- Travel during the off-season and stop for meals at off-peak hours — less idling and waiting in lines, and smoother traffic at these times;
- Calculate your route in gallons, not miles;
- Combine your errands when you use your car, and do your errands in an efficient manner, using gas logically;
- Have a knowledge of secondary routes for times when the traffic is tied up, or for an emergency;

HOW CAN YOU SAVE MONEY BY SPENDING MONEY?

ALEXANDRIA TOYOTA

- LOW COST
- GAS ECONOMY
- HIGH TRADE-IN VALUE

SUPRA • CORONA • COROLLA • CELICA
LAND CRUISERS • HALFTON TRUCKS

ALEXANDRIA TOYOTA

1707 MT. VERNON AVE.
ALEXANDRIA, VIRGINIA
836-2700

- Park with foresight — consider how easily you can exit the parking space;
- Minimize heater use in the car by dressing warmly to drive on cold days, and similarly dress down to drive in the summer;
- Go over your car for excess weight and remove it, e.g. those barbells you carry around in your trunk;
- Don't carry a full tank around on local driving routes. You don't need it (except for security in times of gasoline shortages), and the gas is heavy;
- Don't keep your snow tires on longer than necessary: they just drive your mileage down;
- Clean the snow off your car in winter; and get snow and slush out of the fender walls;
- Arrange to start and end your work day to avoid peak hour crowded roads and stop-and-go traffic conditions;
- Use the telephone and mail service to replace short trips;
- Consolidate the errands you can't avoid: make one large errand run instead of many small ones;
- If you are not particular about the direction in which you are driving — for example, when you go for a ride in the country — go with the wind.
- Keep some change around for tolls so you can have shorter stops at the tollbooth;
- Drive more slowly and at an even pace;
- Keep your tires properly inflated;

If you are really interested in learning more about gasoline-saving energy tips, there is an excellent book available from Chilton Books entitled *The More Miles Per Gallon Handbook*, written by Ronald Weiers and published in 1974. It lists more tips than the preceding and gives clear explanations of them. Also, the U.S. Government makes available a number of gas and energy-saving publications, as do major oil companies.

Gasohol

Many folks are wondering about gasohol. While it may lessen our dependence on foreign oil supplies, the liberation will be slow in coming.

Gasohol is a mixture of mostly gasoline with some alcohol. The alcohol stretches the gasoline supplies. The mixture can usually serve as well as pure gasoline, depending on the tuning of the engine. And, since alcohol is fairly plentiful, it should be cheaper than pure gasoline.

Gasohol can be made with many different types of alcohol. These alcohols are made from a recipe which can combine a variety of source materials: grass, garbage, fecal matter, etc. Many of these sources can come from your own back yard. But if you are fantasizing about a marriage of Rover's droppings, raked-up leaves, and a gallon of premium, realize before you start stockpiling the waste products that there is the problem of distilling the alcohol. Your compost pile will yield some alcohol, but without some distillation it will be watery and in too small a quantity, anyway, to make a dent in your fuel bills.

Some good old boys who already had stills for making illegal moonshine are now getting government subsidies to make alcohol for gasohol mixtures, and there are also a number of farmers and large companies experimenting with sources and refining techniques. But unless you've inherited a still (which you couldn't operate legally without a permit) or have access to highly refined alcohol, making gasohol is a task best left to others. In coming months, you will see it popping up more and more — it will give just as good service as premium gas — and will cost you just as much too.

On the local and state level, gasohol has elicited some interest. In Prince George's County, the County Council resolved on March 27, 1979, to have the County Executive work with The Cooperative Extension Service to develop programs to teach local farmers to produce alcohol through the use of solar stills and other means, and to make instruction plans for these available; to conduct research and to make available procedures to obtain required or necessary permits for such alcohol production; and to develop the best methods for marketing and distributing alcohol and to help out the farming community in using these techniques.

RELATED PUBLICATIONS

Alternative Sources of Energy. Alternate Sources of Energy, Inc., Route 2, Box 90A, Milaca, MN. Quarterly. $10.00/yr.

Anderson, Bruce, and Michael Riordan. *The Solar Home Book: Heating, Cooling and Designing with the Sun.* Brick House Publishing Co., Harrisville, NH 03450. $8.50 (soft cover).

Apies, Henry R., Seichi Konzo, Jean Calvin, and Wayne Thomas. *350 Ways to Save Energy (and Money) in Your Home and Car.* Crown Publishers, New York.

Baker, Bill. *How to Beat the Energy Crisis and Still Live in Style.* G. P. Putnam's Sons, New York.

"Basics of Solar Heating and Hot Water Systems." Washington, D.C. AIA Research Corporation, 1977.

Buying Solar. Washington, DC: Federal Energy Administration, Superintendent of Documents, U.S. G.P.O.

Daniels, G. *Solar Homes and Sun Heating.* New York: Harper & Row, 1976.

"Design Manual for Solar Water Heaters." North Hollywood, California, Horizon Industries, 1977.

"A Do-It-Yourself Insulation Guide for an Energy-Wise Home." Washington, DC: Potomac Electric Power Company.

"Do-It-Yourself Weatherization Guide for an Energy-Wise Home." Washington, DC: Potomac Electric Power Company.

Eccli, Eugene E. (ed.). *Low-Cost Energy-Efficient Shelter for the Owner and Builder.* Emmaus, PA: Rodale Press, 1976. Covers financing, lowering costs when building, lowering operating expenses, solar power. Each chapter by one of a group of authors. List of where to get equipment and information — places and books are listed. Excellent Bibliography.

"Energy in the Home — Changing Your Habits." HE 407, Cooperative Extension Service, Purdue University, West Lafayette, Indiana

Felton, Vi Bradley. *150 Ways to Save Energy and Money*. Pilot Books, 347 Fifth Avenue, New York, NY 10016.

Fisher, R., and B. Yanda. *Solar Greenhouse: Design, Construction, and Operation*. Santa Fe, New Mexico: John Muir Publications.

Foster, W.M. *Homeowner's Guide to Solar Heating and Cooling*. Blue Ridge Summit, Pennsylvania: Tab Books, 1976.

Hand, A. J. *Home Energy How-To*. New York: Harper & Row, 1977.

Hickok, I. *The Buy Wise Guide to Solar Heat*. Hour House, P.O. Box 40082, St. Petersburg, Florida, 33473, 1976.

"How to Improve the Efficiency of Your Oil-Fired Furnace." LC 1085, US Department of Commerce, Washington DC 20230.

How to Save Gasoline and Money. Washington, DC: U.S. Department of Energy, May, 1979. For this and another pamphlet, *Tips for Energy Savers*, write to: Energy, Box 62, Oak Ridge, Tenn. 37830.

"How to Save Gasoline . . . and Money." Washington, DC: U.S. Department of Energy, 1979. Lucas, T. *How to Use Solar Energy in Your Home and Business*. Pasadena, California, Ward Ritchie Press, 1977.

Martz, C.W. (ed.). *Solar Energy Sourcebook*. Washington, DC: Solar Energy Institute of America, 1977.

Mazria, E. *The Passive Solar Energy Book*. Rodale Press, Inc., Emmaus, PA 18049, $10.95.

Meador, R. *Future Energy Alternatives*. Ann Arbor, Michigan: Ann Arbor Science Publishers, Inc., 1978.

Merrill, R., and T. Gage (eds.) *Energy Primer*. New York: Dell Publishing Co., 1978.

Money Saving Guide to Energy in the Home. Doubleday and Co. ($3.50 softbound), *Consumer Reports*.

Montgomery, Richard with Jim Budnick. *The Solar Decision Book*. Dow Corning Corp., Midland, Michigan 48640.

Murphy, J.A. *Homeowner's Energy Guide*. New York, Thomas Y. Crowell Co., 1976.

National Solar Heating and Cooling Information Center, PO Box 1607, Rockville, MD 20850, (800) 523-2929.

Oddo, S. (ed.). *Solar Age Catalogue*. Church Hill, Harrisville, New Hampshire: Solar Age Publishing.

"101 Ways to Cut Home Energy Costs — Right Now!" *Popular Mechanics*, September, 1977.

PEPCO (Potomac Electric Power Company), 1900 Pennsylvania Ave., NW, Washington, DC 20068, 833-7500.

"Save Energy, Save Money." Washington, DC: Potomac Electric Power Company, 1978.

Shelton, Jan, and Andrew B. Shapiro. *The Wood Burner's Encyclopedia*. Waitsfield, Vermont: Vermont Crossroads Press.

Solar Age. Solar Vision, Church Hill, Harrisville, NH 03450. Monthly. $20.00/yr.

Solar Energy. Pergamon Presss Ltd., Maxwell House, Fairview Park, Elmsford NY 10523. Monthly, $140.00/yr.

Solar Heating and Cooling. Gordon Publications, P.O. Box 2126-R, Morristown, NJ 07960. Bimonthly, $6.00/yr.

Solar Industry Index. Washington, DC: Solar Energy Industries Association, 1977.

Sunset Homeowners Guide to Solar Heating. Lane Publishing Co., Menlo Park, California 94025. $2.95.

Twitchell, Mary. *Wood Energy, A Practical Guide to Heating with Wood*. Charlotte, Vermont: Garden Way Publishing.

Weiers, Ronald M. *Chilton's More Miles Per Gallon*. Radnor, PA: Chilton Book Co., $2.95 (soft cover).

Legal & Medical Services

LEGAL SERVICES

Power and intrigue are often conjured up by the words "Washington lawyer". You might imagine corporate cases involving millions of dollars, litigation before the Supreme Court, lobbyists, or even Congressmen and Senators. But those words also conjure up fear in some people's minds — fear of legal problems and fear of exorbitant legal fees.

It is just this slanted picture of what a lawyer does — and how much he charges to do it — that intimidates most people — and often prevents them from finding a lawyer except in times of dire emergency. Many people do not even realize when a problem can be solved through legal means. And there are a large number of issues that surface in just about everyone's life — from real estate settlements to will writing to reading over contracts for hidden strings — that could be handled using the routine services of a lawyer.

The American Bar Association in its 1978 booklet *The American Lawyer: How to Choose and Use One* stresses the need for a legal checkup or "preventive law" and the concomitant need for a family lawyer. The ABA suggests that a lawyer can be helpful with a full range of issues: wills, real estate settlements, buying a home, marriage and divorce, bankruptcy, and more. While of course it is in the best interests of the bar association to say this — since they are representing a constituency of lawyers — there also a great deal of truth in what they say. Many times, just having a lawyer look over a lease or purchase contract can save you far more than he or she costs you in the long run.

But because most people would prefer not to have to think about these things in advance — nor deal with legal fees — until they find themselves in a critical situation without a lawyer, only at that point do they develop an interest in finding someone to represent them and provide them with legal counsel. But a high-priced lawyer is not the only alternative - it is just one of many. From Legal Aid Societies at the lowest economic level to prepaid legal plans, the variety of legal resources is great, and fee schedules range proportionately.

FINDING A LAWYER

If you have a case for which you really need an attorney, especially where you stand to lose a lot of money, it doesn't make any sense to shop price alone. And it doesn't make any sense to take the first person you happen upon — whether recommended by a friend or relative, or merely picked at random out of the Yellow Pages. The little extra amount of time spent conducting a well-organized and thorough search for an attorney is a small price to pay for being well-represented. A number of resources list the names of practicing attornies and their specialties. At public libraries and bookstores, you can find the *Martindale-Hubbell Lawyer Directory*. The *Lawyer Register* also gives similar information. You can inquire of friends, other professionals that you know, or even your clergyman or social worker. When asking these people about lawyers, it's not enough just to get the name of someone — anyone; you should ask them if they or anyone they know has taken a similar problem to this lawyer, and how happy that person was with the outcome of the case and the lawyer. Other places to get names of lawyers include your local Bar Association, law schools, public interest organizations which deal with civil rights or class action suits, prepaid legal services plans, or advertisements.

Referral Services are usually functions of the local Bar Associations. The DC Bar, also known as the Unified Bar, is the largest bar organization in Washington, to which every licensed District of Columbia attorney must belong. It manages the Lawyer Referral and Information Service, about which more will be said later. The Bar Association of Washington is a voluntary organization, and it also offers a Referral Service. The *Lawyer Register*, at the DC Bar (1426 H St NW, Suite 840), which gives information on member lawyers, can be viewed without charge from Monday through Friday, 9 am to 5 pm, or by calling 683-1509. Using a law school clinic as a referral service also has merit: the director, or other individual responsible for referrals, may be useful in giving you the names of graduates of that law school who deal in your type of problem, or of other attorneys he or she has seen in court. Make sure in this case that you talk to the person who customarily makes referrals. You could also try law professors whose specialty is in the same area as your problem — not only are they familiar with those in the city who might be interested in taking on your case, but it could possibly be of interest to them — or they may have ex-students who specialize in your problem area.

Local counties and states also have lawyer referral services.

D.C. Bar Lawyer Referral and Information Service
1426 H Street NW, Suite 840
Washington, DC
638-1509
Monday-Friday: 9 am to 5 pm

Lawyer Referral Service of the Bar Association of DC
Washington, DC
223-1484
Monday-Friday: 9 am to 5 pm, excluding holidays

Maryland State Bar Association
(800) 492-1993
A statewide referral service available to Maryland residents who live in communities not served by local bar referral services.
Monday-Friday, 9 am to 5 pm

Lawyer Referral Service of Montgomery County Bar Association
762-4940
Monday-Friday: 9 am to noon and 1 to 3 pm

Prince George's County Lawyer Referral Service
277-1180
Monday-Friday: 8:30 am to 4:30 pm

Virginia State Bar Association
(800) 552-7977
Monday-Friday: 9:30 am to 4:30 pm

Arlington County Bar Association Lawyer Referral Service
558-2243
Monday-Friday: 8 am to 4:30 pm

Lawyer Referral Service of the Fairfax Bar Association
273-6860
Monday-Friday: 8 am to 4:30 pm

Alexandria Bar Association
City Hall
Alexandria, Virginia
548-1105
Monday-Friday: 9 am to 1 pm

In order to best utilize a referral service, you should specify the nature of your problem, as well as the amount of money you are willing or able to spend on it. If you are really in bad shape, then you should also let the service know, for they can refer you to a service which offers reduced rates, or even to an attorney who does *pro bono* work — who may take on your case at no charge.

Among the Referral Services in this area, the one which offers the most services, and goes beyond the referral function, is the Lawyer Referral and Information Service of the DC Bar (LRIS). This relatively young organization adds a long list of information functions to its traditional service of referral. This information includes facts about the law, legal procedures — what they are like, what you can expect, time limits, like statutes of limitations on certain types of cases, residency requirements, etc. This is basically "pre-attorney" work. The service starts out by letting you do a lot of talking — and they do a lot of listening, with the purpose of trying to sort out what your problem really is, whether or not you really need a lawyer, and, if so, who could give you the best help. If you don't need a lawyer, but just need someone to speak for you, or clear up a minor problem, they will function much like an Action Line, and make the necessary call or write the letter in simple cases.

The LRIS also gives information about fee structures, and how lawyers charge for their work. When they feel that they have adequately assessed your problem, and determined that you do need an attorney, they will give you the names of three qualified individuals from their directory who have time to take your case on, and who have experience in your type of case. They will give you information about what languages the attorney speaks, his fees, and his education. You choose one, and they will make an appointment for you. The maximum fee for the first half-hour consultation is $15.00.

The LRIS does not lose interest once you receive your referral — they also have a feedback function built into the program. When the client is referred to the attorney, the attorney receives a form, which he or she is to return, stating whether or not the client kept the appointment, what the fee basis is, and, when the case is terminated, what the outcome was. Feedback from clients is also encouraged.

Because of this feedback system, the LRIS keeps a rein on the competency and quality of the attorneys who belong to the service. They check beforehand with the certification board to see if the attorney has had any problems with clients in the past. They request that the attorney be able to demonstrate at least one year in practice. All participating attorneys must have malpractice insurance. And before an attorney can sign up for an experience panel, he or she must have handled a minimum of four cases in the chosen specialty area.

Anybody who has problems in the District of Columbia can use the service. There are 200 attorneys who participate in the service, 10% of them being located in Maryland and Virgina. However, you need not be a resident of the District, Maryland, or Virginia in order to use the services of the LRIS. And there are no minimum or maximum income restrictions on using the service. Of the many who call the LRIS, only about 20% are referred to lawyers: some individuals receive immediate help or information (for example, calls are made or letters written on their behalf, clearing up their problem); others are routed to other organizations that can help them. The LRIS attempts to arrange graduated or reduced fees when necessary.

Other referral services are not as elaborate in their functions. For example, the Fairfax County Referral Service lists those attorneys who are members of the Fairfax County Bar, with their specialties and education — and sometimes their fee schedules. They also publish a directory of these attorneys, which is publicly available.

For the Low-Income

In the poor to moderate income category, there are a large number of organizations which offer free or reduced-fee legal services. So, if you are hard-core poor, or just find yourself in temporarily impoverished circumstances, there are a multitude of places to turn to for help. Among these is the Legal Services Corporation. The Legal Aid Societies can be of assistance. They function in small money matters, like claims for wages; disputes between clients and landlords, lenders, or installment sellers; and domestic issues. The Public Defender's Office represents the poor in criminal cases. And a number of law schools provide legal clinics to those at the lowest end of the income scale. But only in the District of Columbia are law students allowed to represent their clients in the courts.

For the Not-So-Poor, Not-So-Rich

If you don't qualify for any of the free or reduced fee services, there are a number of options open to you: legal clinics, group plans, or prepaid legal plans.

In one article written for an ABA publication, legal clinics were called the "illegitimate child of permissive advertising rules" — since, without advertising, most could not generate the high volume of business necessary for them to stay in business.

A legal clinic is usually a storefront operation which offers flat rates for a limited number of types of routine cases, and many offer initial consultations at no fee. Many of these clinics are highly automated and computerized, which is one of the ways they keep overhead low. They also depend heavily on paralegals for client screening, filling out forms, general processing, and research. The presumed advantage of these clinics is the ability to provide legal services efficiently and economically. Most of these places are simply furnished, which indicates to their clients an attitude of no-waste. Those that are storefront operations advertise less heavily than those located on second floors of office buildings, or in shopping centers.

The modus operandi varies greatly. Some of these clinics are really oriented toward helping low-income individuals with routine problems; others are in business merely to generate volume (and income); and there are those which combine both of these goals. Many feel that by specializing they can give the best service to the client, can cut down excessive costs, and can more easily charge a flat rate. It is generally not to the advantage of legal clinics to deal with issues that go into appeals or lengthy litigation, or to deal in such matters as criminal or juvenile issues.

However, some do deal with cases like personal injury and criminal cases, and criticism has been raised as to how effective they can be in these cases. Advocates of legal clinics who practice in such cases suggest that the actual legal work is much the same as in more routine cases — only the use of an outside investigator is the difference.

Some legal clinics tell you about their fee schedules in advance, or in a pamphlet which they will give you. Some have no charge — or only a minimal charge — for the first visit. Some have a flat amount for every procedure, or a low per-hour cost, with a maximum limit on the total bill guaranteed. Some take contingency cases — and some ask for payment in advance.

Regardless of the mode of operation of these legal clinics -- and they do vary widely — they can be very effective in routine cases. A survey conducted recently by the University of Miami School of Law indicated that people who went to legal clinics were more satisfied with treatment of their cases than were clients of more traditional services. The results showed that, on the average, husbands wound up paying less for child support and wives got more for alimony when they were represented by clinics.

A growing type of prepaid legal plan is called *Group Legal Services.* These plans are most frequently seen now offered as employee or group benefits. They function very simply. Basically, the management of a group makes an arrangement with a law firm whereby members of the group can choose to use the services of that firm at reduced rates, and usually with no fee for the initial consultation. In return, the group endorses this firm to its members. The firm is usually geared solely to this type of work. The advantages are many: For the law firm, an aggregate client group is practically delivered into their waiting hands. For the client, if he saves nothing else, he gets a free initial consultation, and many such programs offer free immediate action letters — like notes to landlords for action, to stores with which the consumer has had a problem, etc. The consumer also gets a reduction in rates, which can — if truly reduced from the rates of comparably equipped firms — be of great value.

One drawback to this type of plan is that it uses a *closed panel* arrangement: the group member is limited to this one firm, unless the group has an arrangement with more than one such firm, or unless the member elects to pay the going rate elsewhere. But if he is unhappy with the lawyers available to him, he loses nothing by going to another attorney. Mackey and Klein provide this service in the Washington area to

140 credit unions — and yours may be among them, so check to make sure you haven't missed this potentially free benefit.

More and more often, *prepaid legal service plans* are being offered as additional employee benefits.

Prepaid legal services work very much like health insurance plans or health maintenance organizations: for a flat yearly or monthly premium, you are entitled to a limited amount of legal services without charge. Usually, there are a considerable number of exclusions to this plan — these generally include contingency fee cases, suits against the employer or union which forms the group, business matters, or preparations of tax returns. Many do not cover the individual in criminal cases.

For all practical purposes, there are two basic types of prepaid plans: *open* and *closed panel*. An open panel arrangement can be likened to having health insurance: You can go to any lawyer you want, and, in covered cases, the plan reimburses the lawyer (after a deductible, and usually up to a certain maximum). In a closed panel arrangement, which is like a health maintenance organization, you are limited as to which lawyers you can go to — either geographically or to certain ones who have signed up to serve the group.

The advantage of the open panel form is that the client has free choice. The lawyer has no obligation to accept a case — for example, if his workload were too full, or if he did not feel he had sufficient expertise in the subject. However, administrative costs with the open panel are higher, because increased recordkeeping is necessary, and because of the extra effort necessary to ensure that the lawyers file the claim forms promptly. Further, the employer has no control over the charges that will be incurred, since the choice of attorney is open — from the cheapest to the most expensive. This also, with the open panel form, is the reason for putting a limit on liability — otherwise the premium would have to be excessive.

The closed panel system lowers costs by reducing the administrative costs, as claim forms are routinely filed. Further, the easy availability of paralegals and secretaries takes some of the burden off of the attorneys, and frees them up for cases in which their skills can be maximized. There are several disadvantages to the closed panel. For one thing, the lawyer who participates has difficulty in rejecting a case, yet he could be overloaded or not really specializing in the necessary area of expertise. Further, the client does not necessarily get the option of choosing his or her own lawyer.

No plan covers all of the legal problems a person could encounter, nor does any plan provide unlimited service. The best that the plans do is to cover the individual over the mid-range. They claim to help with preventive legal maintenance, because you can have someone look over any contracts you might sign; write immediate action letters to landlords, etc., with whom you have small claims-type problems; draw up your will, etc.

In this area, Fortemont charges $8 per person per month and offers what they term a "modified closed", or, alternatively, "modified open" plan — meaning that you have the choice of several firms in the general area in which you live. Joining this group gives you direct access to a "law firm on retainer," so that you can get accurate answers to your questions over the telephone or in person, depending on what you prefer. Other benefits include having a lawyer to write your will, and to handle primary residence real estate transactions, customer-merchant relations, credit actions, and adoption proceedings. You can get: help collecting claims (up to a limit); assistance with your divorce, separation, or annulment proceedings; representation in juvenile court; defense in cases of motor vehicle violations; defense in civil actions and federal and state criminal actions; non-business tax advice; assistance in the preparation of simple family federal and state income tax returns; and legal assistance for your dependents. Of course, there are limitations on a number of these items. But coverage begins from the time you receive your membership card. Certain costs and expenses outside of legal fees are not covered, and pre-existing conditions are excluded (legal actions which occurred before the effective date of coverage) as are requested actions arising out of something that occurred before coverage.

Guardian Legal Services also offers a closed panel preventive legal service — review of contracts, advice on consumer problems before suit, and guidance on problems before litigation begins. Fees include a $20 one-time enrollment charge, and $30 per quarter, or $57 per 6 months, or $110 annually, depending on how you elect to pay for it. Individuals can sign up for this plan. Guardian's services cover some part of real estate transactions; consumer law; claims against insurance companies or uninsured motorists (with a contingency fee after the first $1000 of each such claim); divorce, separation, or annulment; wills (short ones); birth certificates; unlimited consultations as needed; bankruptcy; traffic violations (excludes parking); change of name; family coverage; adoptions; probate; preparation of non-complex legal documents; landlord-tenant actions; criminal violations; civil actions; administrative and other judicial recoveries; and judicial proceedings. Benefits are said to be provided after payment of the one-time enrollment fee, but actually there is a thirty-day waiting period for preventive law and consultations, and a ninety-day waiting period for all other services (except divorce, for which there is a six-month waiting period). This is not unreasonable: they are trying to protect themselves from those who might join just to take advantage of these reduced rates for a pre-existing problem.

A third area group which offers a prepaid plan is Family Legal Services, which is located in Reston. This closed panel plan is offered primarily through groups such as credit unions (which offer it to their shareholders). Individuals pay a $10 one-time enrollment fee and $88.50 annually to join. They exclude criminal actions, business law, taxes, and parking tickets; and they include most of the same items as the other plans. They also have a pre-existing conditions clause. To group members, they are offering an enhancement to their plan, which is considered to be the first such in the nation: For an additional payment, you can get a rider to your policy providing *victim assistance* — 24 hour attorney service to victims of violent crime, such as rape, assault, etc. They act immediately to inform the victims how to decide whether they want to prosecute, and what their legal rights are. The attorneys for this plan are generalists, but each does have an area of specialty.

The Greenbelt Cooperative also operates a prepaid legal services plan called Consumer Services Cooperative, Inc. Anyone can join. If you are already a member of the Greenbelt Cooperative or the Greenbelt Federal Credit Union, you pay a one-time registration fee of $10, and $40 annual dues. If you are a member of neither of these groups, you must first join the Greenbelt Cooperative by paying $10 in dues for a lifetime voting membership. This services offers a legal checkup for each member family, one hour free consultation annually, reduced rates for legal fees, and seminars on legal problems. The system uses a closed panel format.

For a group or individual considering joining a prepaid legal services plan, the National Resource Center for Consumers of Legal Services offers a comprehensive list of considerations. Concerning the history and operations of the legal services plan, they suggest asking questions about the length of time for which the program has been operating; how many groups have joined; references from groups similar to yours; what proportion of total group membership has enrolled in the program; (for individuals) how many individuals have enrolled; how many attorneys are eligible to provide services; how members and lawyers get in contact with each other; who the plan's attorneys are and where they are located; whether they can be introduced to the group's management before signing up for the program; what their experience in the legal matters which the plan covers is; how conflicts between group members and lawyers are resolved; whether there is a grievance or complaint system; what proportion of premium payments goes to management; and how much in actual benefits is paid to lawyers.

Questions to ask about coverage: Are you really getting the legal services which you want and need? What are the limits to coverage? And are these limits clearly noted in promotion materials? You should also ask about risks: What if the company goes out of business? Will the client's premiums be refunded if the company folds; Do the attorneys have to follow through on cases in progress if the company folds and they do not continue to receive payments? And, under what circumstances can an attorney drop out of the program? This last could be disastrous to you if your attorney decided to drop out in the middle of your case.

USING A LAWYER

The First Meeting

If you did not speak directly to the lawyer on the telephone, confirm the cost of this first consultation before proceeding. At this meeting, you should be well-prepared, in order to avoid wasting time. You should bring with you a summary of your problem in outline form, or notes detailing the problem. You should include the names, addresses, and other relevant information about all involved parties, witnesses, and any insurance companies, as well as all relevant documents — letters, bills, notices, etc.

Don't hesitate to ask about the lawyer's experience with your type of problem. If he is really not familiar with your type of case, he should feel obliged to tell you so — and to recommend someone who is. When you find the right specialist, don't necessarily be put off by high rates — remember that the lawyer's experience could save you money in the long run. But if you find two of equal reputation and experience in your field, there is no reason not to take the one whose fees are lower.

Ask who is really going to be working on your case. Your fees should be adjusted to reflect a lower rate if the senior attorney is handing the bulk of the work on your case over to a young attorney or to paralegals.

In working with your attorney, realize that, the more active the client, the greater the probability of satisfactory results. If you want to take an active part in your case, make this known to your attorney. Ask that he keep you informed — by sending you copies of all documents relating to your case and informing you of any new developments as they occur — and ask him to consult you *before* he makes any major moves.

Regardless of your role, it is important to ask about the timetable for your case. Make sure you ask about the statute of limitations, which defines how long you have a right to act for justice in a given case. By waiting too long — or by letting your lawyer wait too long to take action — you can lose all of your related rights in the case.

The DC Bar suggests that you ask questions like the following: "Can you give me a list of events that are likely to occur in my case and a timetable for them?" "Will you give me your best estimate of how long this case will take to complete?" "What will you do next?" "When will we talk again?" "Is there a statute of limitations on the case? When does it expire?"

The Decision to Hire

Based on your first interview with the lawyer, your decision to hire or not to hire should hinge on a number of elements. The personality of the lawyer is important — you must be able to feel comfortable with him, and be able to put your trust in him. You should also feel secure that the attorney has had ample or sufficient experience in your type of case. And communications should not be difficult or strained — if they are, you should look elsewhere. Fees should be reasonable in comparison with other firms. And, finally, the attorney should have given you a clear explanation of the manner in which he or she plans to represent you. If the attorney does not rate satisfactorily by these criteria, you ought to keep looking until you find someone who does.

Fees

You should not feel embarrassed asking how much something is going to cost you. In 1975, the Supreme Court prohibited minimum fee schedules. Rates can vary from $20 to $100 or even more an hour, and you can probably find someone who can competently handle your case at almost every price range — assuming they answer the questions and issues which have been discussed to your satisfaction. And some large, ordinarily high-priced firms may offer reduced rates — ask on the telephone in advance of your appointment.

Fees and payment arrangements should be fully understood before you complete the first consultation. It is in your best interest to ask to be billed at regular intervals, in order to see how your time charges and expenses are mounting up. You can also ask that fees not exceed a certain limit of time or money without having the attorney get your permission first.

In order to avoid any future problems, it is important to have a written agreement setting forth not only the lawyer's charges, but also the services which are to be performed in exchange for the fee. At present, most such forms benefit only the lawyer.

Attorneys' fees are based on the following considerations: the time and labor required to complete the case, which involve the novelty and difficulty of the questions raised and the skills needed to perform the service. Also, another factor is the likelihood that accepting your case precludes other employment for the attorney — the opportunity costs of your job. Customary fees, the amount of damages sought and results received, time limits imposed by clients or circumstances, nature and length of professional relationship, experience, reputation and ability of the lawyer, and even overhead — all contribute significantly to the fee schedule of the attorney.

There are basically four alternative fee arrangements:

- *Standard fees* (sometimes called "specific job fees"): This is where a given fee is charged for a given service, such as drafting a will, probating an estate, handling an uncontested divorce, or handling an uncomplicated real estate settlement. If you have such a case, you should ask for an immediate estimate of the total bill: fees plus estimated other expenses, which can include lawyer's travel, meals, phone calls, postage, and copying. You should always ask precisely what is included in a flat fee payment.

- *Hourly charges:* For cases which are more complicated, attornies often charge by the hour; the per-hour charge ranges from $20 to $100 (or sometimes more). Some may offer reduced rates — ask during the first consultation, or even earlier, on the telephone. With hourly charges, you should also ask for an approximate cost estimate in advance. In most cases, lawyers bill for all the time they spend on the case — including telephone time, precourt waiting time at the court, etc. If you use this basis, stipulate how much time you want the attorney to spend before he asks your permission to go any further.

- *Retainer agreements:* A retainer is a fee paid in advance, which can cover a specific case, or any work which comes up. Always be sure to get a receipt if you pay in advance. This fee usually represents a number of hours of time. If you do not use as much time as you pay for have an agreement which will refund you the amount due. You should also have an agreement as to how you will be billed for additional hours over the amount the retainer covers. Occasionally, a retainer is a flat fee to cover the costs of service, regardless of the amount of time — this should be written into the agreement. Always determine if the initial consultation is included in the retainer.

- *Contingency fees:* These are usually agreed upon in cases of accident or personal injury, and this means that the attorney is paid a percentage of what you win. If there is no recovery, you would be responsible only for expenses incurred, such as court fees. In a contingency case, the client usually pays expenses out of his share. A few attorneys take their share after expenses are paid. This should be understood in advance. While the usual fee is ¼ to 1/3 of the award, you could suggest an alternate arrangement to your lawyer if you had high expenses. You could ask to have those expenses covered first from your award, and then give the lawyer a larger percentage of what remains.

Payment

To prepare yourself for the final bill, you should ask the lawyer in advance for a number of financial items: an advance estimate of the total cost; a written fee agreement listing both costs to you and obligations of the attorney; how often you are billed and told how much you are owing; estimated total costs, aside from fees — and how and when you will be billed for these; and what payment schedule you are expected to follow. Many attorneys accept credit cards, and a few will charge interest on overdue bills. Some may ask for a promissory note or cognovit note in advance as security for payment — but don't sign one of these unless you have read it fully and understand what it means.

Problems

If you have been working with an attorney and are not satisfied with the progress of your case, it is in your best interest to talk over the problems first with your present lawyer and try to solve them together. If you cannot resolve the problems and cannot part on good terms (with all of your materials returned to you so that you can give them to another attorney to use), or if you have any kind of problem and need help dealing with the attorney — you have recourse. In Maryland, the Attorney Grievance Commission of the Maryland Court of Appeals in Annapolis handles complaints against lawyers. Each county bar in Virginia has a grievance committee, but final decisions are made by the 10th District Committee of the Virginia State Bar on the regional level. The DC Bar's Board of Professional Responsibility handles problems with lawyers in the District. Each panel functions differently, and only the DC Bar includes non-lawyers on the panel.

Do It Yourself

There's nothing new or illegal about doing some things yourself in a legal sense. In small claims and traffic court, it has been going on for a long time. Now there are divorce kits, offered by some firms for a relatively small fee, or books on the subject to help you take care of an uncontested divorce yourself (although many practicing attorneys believe that, even in an uncontested action, the client could do better with alimony and the like by contesting the case and utilizing an attorney). Further, in the case of a relatively simple will, you could write it yourself. And many have felt that probate — the execution of a dead person's will — is relatively simple and the use of a lawyer is unnecessary.

Law Schools

Most law schools in the area offer free legal help through clinics (to low income persons, and only in some types of cases). By law, they are prohibited from handling felony cases, contingency cases, or suits seeking monetary relief of more than $750.

American University:
Public Interest Law Clinic (686—2741), also called National Veterans' Law Center, handles claims of veterans before VA.
Maryland Criminal Justice Clinic (686-3872), representing people charged with criminal offenses and jailable traffic offenses in Montgomery County or Prince Georges County District Court.
Lawcor Program (686-2629), represents residents of the Lorton DC Corrections Facility before prison disciplinary and parole boards.

Antioch Law School, Urban Law Institute (265-9500)
Private Law
Public Law
Criminal Law
Open 9 am to 5:30 p.m. Monday through Friday

Catholic University Law School (526-5800):
Clinic covers cases except worker's compensation, immigration, and criminal charges. Open 9 am to 5 pm, Monday through Friday.

Georgetown University Law Center: 624-8262
Information and Referrals
Criminal Justice Clinic
Property Rights Clinic
Open 9 am to 5 pm, Monday through Friday.

George Washington University Legal Aid:
Community Legal Clinics: 676-7463
Protection for Elderly Persons: 265-4900
Martin Luther King Clinic: 678-8089
Open 9 am to 5 pm, Monday through Friday.

Howard University Law School: 686-6440
Open 8:30 am to 5 pm, Monday through Friday.

LEGAL CLINICS

District of Columbia
CAWLEY & SCHMIDT, 1552 Connecticut Ave., NW, 387-5900. Covers a range of services including criminal and personal injury cases. First consultation free.

COMMUNITY LAW OFFICE, 2226 18th St., NW, 265-2336. A nonprofit organization handling family law, personal injury, and consumer problems. First consultation is $15.

RAPPAPORT LEGAL ASSOCIATES, 1212 Wisconsin Ave., NW, 337-5775. Handles all types of cases. First consultation free.

RENT CONTROL SERVICES, 1025 Connecticut Ave., NW; 659-4345. Handles landlord-tenant problems and real estate settlements. Consultation $15.

Maryland
BETTIS, FOSTER, HUNTSMAN & GOLDBERG, 1903 Seminary Rd., Silver Spring, 585-9555, 589-6910. General practice, free first consultation.

CAWLEY & SCHMIDT, 5402 Kenilworth Ave., Riverdale, 779-0004. Wide range of services. First consultation free.

RAPPAPORT LEGAL ASSOCIATES, 108 Park Ave., Rockville, 424-7797. All types of cases. First consultation free.

Virginia
BETTIS, FOSTER, HUNTSMAN & GOLDBERG, 6708 Arlington Blvd., Falls Church, 534-4710. General practice. First consultation free.

RAPPAPORT LEGAL ASSOCIATES, 1515 N. Courthouse Rd., Arlington; 243-6700. All types of cases. First consultation free.

S&M LEGAL CLINICS, 1730 N. Lynn St., Arlington, 522-7900; 8150 Leesburg Pike, Tysons Corner, 821-3990; Marumsco Shopping Center Woodbridge, 494-5188. Handles routine services

ASK THE LAWYERS
Each Tuesday, from 11 am to 1 pm, WTOP-AM offers *Ask the Lawyers* as part of its regular *Call for Action* program. Lawyers answer questions about specific problems, but the program is not broadcast. Phone number is 686-8225.

Free or Low-Cost Aid in Civil Matters

Neighborhood Legal Services
666 11th Street, NW, 628-9161

Ayuda — for the Spanish-speaking   387-4848

Columbus Community Legal Services
1709 North Capitol Street, 526-5800

Legal Counsel for the Elderly
234-0970

Legal Aid Society of D.C.
613 G Street, N.W. — NA 8-1161

Women's Legal Defense Fund
683-1123

Judicare, Montgomery County Dept. of Social Services
5630 Fishers Lane, Rockville, MD, 468-4363

P.G. County Legal Aid Bureau
3705 Rhode Island Avenue, Mt. Rainier, MD, 277-7830

Fairfax Legal Aid Society
4029 Chain Bridge Road, Fairfax, VA, 691-0600

Arlington Co. Legal Aid Society, Inc.
2009 North 14th St., Suite 705, Arlington, VA 22201
841-0304

Alexandria Legal Aid Society
815 King Street, Suite 611, Alexandria, VA 22314
750-6420 or 750-6438

For those who are interested in having more knowledge of and control over their legal environment, arrangements can be made for church or civic groups to hold Street Law Courses. This is available through the Community Legal Education Program of the Harrison Institute Street Law Program. The Harrison Institute also runs programs for community groups, which deal with community (rather than individual) legal problems. In the District of Columbia, contact Pat McGuire for information at 624-8235. In Maryland, contact the Law-related Eudcation Project in Burtonsville. Similar programs are available in Virginia. For general information, call the National Street Law Institute, which can provide information, books and materials, at 624-8235, 605 G Street NW, Washington, DC.

Other Legal Resources

American Civil Liberties Union
638-6263

Children's Defense Fund
1520 New Hampshire Ave. NW, Washington, DC 20036

Disabilities Rights Center
1346 Connecticut Ave. NW, Suite 1124, Washington, DC

Employment Discrimination Complaint Service (referral and advice)
683-1509

Equal Employment Litigation Clinic — Howard University
686-6416

Food Research and Action Center
2011 Eye Street, NW, Washington, DC 20006

Lawyers' Committee for Civil Rights under Law
733 15th Street, NW, Washington, DC

Legal Research and Services for the Elderly
1511 K Street, NW, Washington, DC 20006

Mental Health Law Project
1220 19th Street NW, Washington, DC 20036

National Center for Law and The Deaf Legal Defense Fund
9th and Florida Avenue, NE, Washington, DC 20002

National Committee against Discrimination in Housing
1425 H St. NW, 783-8150 (referrals)

National Veterans' Law Center
686-2741

Public Defender Service — Mental Health Division
562-2200

Washington Lawyers' Committee for Civil Rights
347-3801

Women's Legal Defense Fund
1010 Vermont Avenue NW, 683-1123 (referrals)

MEDICAL SERVICES

You've got a high fever, bad cold, and backache, and you've been out of work for a week; your 10-year-old daughter fell and apparently broke her arm; your spouse has had a heart attack at work and you're frantic. Who do you call and what do you do in each of these cases?

That heart attack turns out to be severe, and your spouse is spending many expensive days in the hospital, requiring specialized care and procedures which will run your bill easily into thousands, if not tens of thousands of dollars. Or your elderly parent is suffering from cancer and requires an intensive and comprehensive course of treatment, including chemotherapy, radiation treatment, and periodic stays in the hospital to accomplish it. How can you possibly pay for it?

These are questions which we always assume will have to be answered by *other* people — but the odds are that someday they will be your questions too. And too many people turn to the local hospital's Emergency Room for help with problems that are not really emergencies, or that require more specialized care. And many people (fortunately fewer than in the past) face financial ruin in the case of catastrophic illness.

Because people in the Washington area are often newcomers, here for a short stay, finding a fulltime family doctor seems to many to be an exercise with limited long-term value. The exception to this is people with children, who are more concerned with consistent and regular treatment for the children than for themselves. Thus, for too many, only when a crisis occurs does the search for a family doctor begin. But you can save yourself time, aggravation, and even money if you find yourself a primary care physician before you are in a tight situation. In the following pages, recommendations are given about finding and evaluating a primary care physician.

This chapter also discusses how to find and evaluate a health care plan which helps to minimize your contribution to your health care expenses. A wide range of possibilities is available to Washington metro area residents, yet few really look into these options. This section covers the advantages and weaknesses of health insurance carriers, Blue Cross/Blue Shield, health maintenance organizations, and Medicare, and also mentions other available health care resources.

FINDING AND SELECTING A PHYSICIAN

In one of its brochures on this subject, the American Medical Association (AMA) stresses that, although a doctor's duty as dictated by tradition and ethics is to provide medical care to anyone in need, his first loyalty is to his own patients. Thus, it is unwise to assume that, in times of crisis, a doctor with whom you have had no previous dealings would be willing to jump to help you. It should be obvious, then, that you should find a doctor who will be willing to take care of you in times of crises, and will also provide everyday preventive care, like checkups.

Physicians are usually M.D.s (medical doctors) or D.O.s (doctors of osteopathy). Because the phone company does not screen those who are listed in the Yellow Pages, it is estimated that about 5% of those listed are not M.D.s or D.O.s. Of that 5%, a small number are homeopathic practitioners.

Most people should start looking for a *primary care physician* as their first link into the medical system. Primary care physicians fit into four main categories:

- The Family Practitioner: a multispecialist who provides continuing and comprehensive care to the whole family, can treat most health problems, and practices preventive maintenance;
- Pediatrician: From birth through adolescence, the pediatrician watches over the care of children, practicing preventive medicine through regular examinations and immunications — the inoculations for measles, mumps, diphtheria, etc. that most children dread.
- Internal Medicine: Technically, the internist diagnoses and treats diseases of the organ system of adults. In this area, the internist is quite frequently the point of entry into the medical system, particularly for the single professional. The nine subspecialties of internal medicine are cardiovascular disease, endocrinology, gastroenterology, hematology, infectious diseases, medical oncology, nephrology, pulmonary diseases, and rheumatology.
- Obstetrics and Gynecology: The gynecologist/obstetrician is basically concerned with the reproductive tract in women. The obstetrician assumes responsibility for the woman during pregnancy, and the gynecologist other times. Many women use a gynecologist as their primary care physician.

In general, the family practitioner has replaced the old-fashioned general practitioner, as there are fewer and fewer physicians who bill themselves as GPs in this era.

The primary care physician will arrange necessary referrals to consultants in any of the specialties as they see fit. It is considered preferable not to self-diagnose, but to go to a primary care physician, who can lead you to the right specialist.

Qualifications

Most people find it easier to learn about a house they are going to buy than about a doctor who may hold their lives in his hands. It isn't for want of trying — but finding out about the quality of care takes a lot of investigation, and a lot of material which isn't readily available.

Part of the lack of availability of materials stems from the closed nature of the medical profession: It is considered bad manners — almost bad sportsmanship — to denigrate a fellow member of the medical profession. But you should nevertheless thoroughly examine the credentials of potential family doctors to ensure yourself the best chance of medical care available — at a price you are willing to pay. A representative of the AMA candidly stated that half of the doctors in this country graduated in the bottom half of their medical school class — not a very original statement, but still a meaningful one.

There are general qualifications which a physician — a medical doctor — must meet in order to be licensed and to practice in this area. After college, the aspiring MD attends medical school, completes an internship at a hospital, then specializes if he or she so desires. Completion of a specified number of years of specialized training (depending on the specialty) qualifies him to take a specialty examination. Upon passing the examination, he is certified by the body which governs the specialty. This is called "board certification". In some specialties, the physician must have continuing study to keep up with current developments and periodically be recertified. Within some specialties, the MD can become a subspecialist, which requires both further training and certification.

But before you can go ahead getting quality information about a doctor, you must find some candidates to take care of your families health.

The Medical Society of the District of Columbia runs a Physician's Referral Service at 223-6333, which makes available lists of physicians who are accepting new patients. Other local medical societies also have such referral services (see list at end of this section).

You can also turn to the American Medical Directory of the AMA, a who's who of doctors in this country, giving education, training, and other relevant information about them.

Local medical schools have lists of those physicians who are on their staffs. These include Howard, Georgetown, and George Washington University Medical Schools and hospitals. Health personnel at your place of business may be useful in suggesting a primary care physician. Hospitals in the area also have lists of physicians and specialists to whom they can recommend you. Pharmacists, too, who deal with the medical profession daily and hear a lot of talk about the various doctors, may be able to recommend someone to you.

One excellent source of suggestions can be your relatives, friends, or business associates, assuming that they are satisfied with the quality of care which they are receiving.

By now, you should have a list of physicians whom you are interested in using. Choose two or three names and get some more information about them, such as is suggested in the following paragraphs.

Questions about Quality and Suitability

You ought to match the physician you choose to the needs of your family. First, make sure he or she is willing to take new patients. Then get answers to these questions:

Does he have a location convenient to your home and place of business? Are his office hours flexible, or do they suit you by including evening or weekend hours? Will the doctor see you only by appointment, or does he take walk-in patients in an emergency or at other times? If you prefer someone older or younger, make sure you follow that preference, whatever your reasoning in this choice. Does he or she make house calls? House calls are of particular importance to senior citizens or those with mobility impairments. (Note, however, that they are relatively rare these days, for doctors claim that the expense in terms of their travelling time is not worth the quality of care they can give in the home. They indicate that, if there is really a situation in which the individual cannot get to the doctor's office, and in which immediate care is necessary, it would be better to meet you at the hospital, which has good diagnostic tools and superior care. Taking an ambulance to get there — in spite of the obvious cost to you or your insurance company — would actually be more beneficial to you than having the doctor deal with your emergency out of his "little black bag".) Do any members of your family have handicaps or continuing conditions which require special care? If so, is this doctor sensitive to and capable of dealing with this need? Does he have staff privileges at a hospital near your home? (Physicians must apply to each hospital where they want to join the staff and have admitting privileges.) If English is not your primary language, is he fluent in your primary language, or at least proficient enough to communicate well with you or with members of your family who need help?

Doctors can practice solo or in a group practice. In a solo practice, they arrange for someone else to handle patients when they are unavailable. Make sure you know how to get medical help 24 hours a day — regardless of whether your doctor practices solo or in a group. Group practices can be for multispecialties or one specialty, and the advantage is often that the second opinion is only a few steps away. One criticism that has been made of doctors who practice alone is that they may fail to keep up with recent medical developments — but this is not necessarily so, and the same thing could occur in group practices. An advantage to the group practice is that, when your primary care physician is away, the doctor who takes over from him may be more familiar with your case history, if only because he has the records in the office. Also, sometimes (but not necessarily always) the larger staff needed by a group practice can give you better service and more prompt attention than the smaller staff (sometimes only one person) handling everything from billing to appointments or ordering supplies for a doctor in practice by himself.

You may prefer to have a doctor who can take and analyze diagnostic test samples in his office. This is more likely to occur in a group practice, as the economies of scale in getting equipment and people to handle the equipment are maximized. But this is merely a matter of convenience.

While time allotted is not a measure of quality of care, it is worthwhile to you to know what the average time allotted is — and what the fee for that time is.

You should also look into the doctor's policies about medicine, immunization, and frequency of routine check-ups. For example, a doctor may be morally opposed to prescribing birth control pills — and you should find this out before you go. Routine immunizations are desirable, particularly for children, who need full shot series and boosters. (Adults should have tetanus and diphtheria shots every ten years.)

Although *where* and *how long* a doctor went to school may be of some interest to you, it does not necessarily indicate much about the quality of care you can expect to receive. The date when he graduated from medical school does tell you how long he's been practicing. Better signs include residency training — which indicates the breadth and depth of background and experience. Residency comes after the doctor has completed medical school and his internship and is a specialized training period which enhances his previous training. Board certification — that is, certification that the doctor has passed the examination in his specialty — is desirable; board eligibility means only that he has completed the other requirements but has not yet taken the test.

Staff appointments may indicate the esteem in which this doctor is held by others. University appointments are good, but still not an absolute seal of quality.

Complaints

Should a complaint arise, you should know how to handle it. You should know in advance whether the doctor will discuss complaints about fees or treatment with you directly, or if he will refer to you his secretary or nurse. Some doctors deal with this in a two-step process, allowing you to talk first with the nurse or secretary, and if you don't receive satisfaction, then discussing it with them personally. Many people are afraid that making complaints will lead them to be regarded negatively by the doctor; so they avoid raising even legitimate questions with the doctor. Either they meekly accept what the doctor does or without explanation switch to another physician. If you are otherwise happy with a doctor but have one minor complaint, it makes more sense to work it out. After all, you are paying for service, and if you feel you haven't received full value for your money, as with any other goods or services, you should complain.

Despite the fact that there are many things to look out for when choosing a doctor, there is absolutely no way for you to find a source which will do anything like rate the available area doctors. The Health Research Group (a Nader group) published a directory of doctors in Prince Georges' County several years ago. This listed much of the information mentioned above but did not rate the doctors.

After you have done all your research, go to the doctor who best fits your needs for a routine checkup. At that time, see whether his or her manner and style impress you. If so, continue to see that physician. Should you, after a few visits, become dissatisfied, express that dissatisfaction to the doctor, and ask him whether he will recommend another physician, and whether he will cooperate by sending your records on to that person. Or you can go to another of the doctors on your initial list. But beware of "doctor shopping" just to get the reassurance or answer you want. You can't make an inconvenient illness or an unwanted disease go away just by changing doctors.

On the other hand, if your doctor suggests something major — especially a serious operation or an extreme course of treatment — it is always in your best interest to get a second opinion. Most insurance policies will pay for this, and it has been found to cut down on a substantial amount of unnecessary surgery-benefits the plan would otherwise have to pay: it is often cheaper for them to pay for a second or even third opinion.

It is worth mentioning that the Health Research Group, under the direction of Dr. Sidney Wolfe, has been pursuing the issue of quality and hopes to be able to make more information available to people in this area in the near future.

Fee Information

Doctors' fees are often an expensive mystery. Fees can vary tremendously for the same procedure from doctor to doctor. And if you are going to pay even a part of those fees, fee shopping should be at least a small part in your search for a primary care physician. You should not be ashamed to be frank and forthright about your desire to know how much medical services are going to cost, any more than you would be to ask a salesperson how much a suit or pair of shoes costs.

While the fee clearly depends on the complexity of the problem, you should ask in advance the cost of a routine office visit — and what that cost covers in terms of time and activity. For specific procedures or problems, the doctor should at least be able to give you an estimate, if not an exact amount, of expense. You should also ask about the format of billing and payments, as some doctors require payment before you leave the office. Also inquire as to whether they routinely accept Medicare assignment and Medicaid patients, if this affects you or your family.

Other Issues

While **advertising** is not strictly proscribed by the AMA, soliciting of clients is. Because everyone is afraid of breaching these rules, the most common practice is to be conservative; and the extent to which most physicians go is listing themselves in the Yellow Pages of the telephone book, and sending out cards when they change addresses or acquire a new staff member.

The official stance of the AMA is to encourage **continuing medical education.** This is strongly in your benefit, because this indicates that a physician is keeping up with new advances in his or her field. This should also be a determinant in choosing competent medical care.

Minimizing the Need for Health Care Services

If at all possible, it is in your best interest to minimize the need for health care services: You can save yourself money and time, as well as pain and suffering.

The best, easiest, and most often made recommendation made is merely to stay healthy! You may think you're really good at doing this . . . but if you consider how often you stay up late, go out when you're a little under the weather, have too much to drink, or just wear yourself out . . . besides eating candy bars for lunch, skipping breakfast altogether, and getting no exercise . . . you may have a hard time convincing yourself of what a good job you are doing.

There are many free guides to taking care of yourself available — medical societies, local government resources, and local clinics all provide a significant number of free pamphlets and literature. You can go to the library for added information, or buy one of the plethora of books available at the bookstore. Regular medical care, such as an annual or semi-annual checkup, is a good preventive measure. This is true for dental needs as well, since good dental hygiene (such as brushing and flossing) can cut down on your need for extensive dental care and painful problems as you get older.

Despite the fact that there are many things to look out for when choosing a doctor, there is absolutely no way for you to find a source which will do anything like rate the available area doctors. The Health Research Group (a Nader group) published a directory of doctors in Prince Georges' County several years ago. This listed much of the information mentioned above but did not rate the doctors.

The general recommendations are not hard to follow, but you have to have an interest in staying well in order to motivate yourself to be consistent in preventive medicine.

A good diet and exercise are among the first steps to continuing good health. You should also try to avoid small accidents by eliminating hazards in your home — and train your children to avoid accidents, too: they should learn obvious thing like staying out of the street, not touching a hot iron, etc. You should use seat belts in your car — no matter how hokey that sounds. Because stomach upsets and other infections can be a result of careless home practices, you should work to reduce causes of infection, like dirty pet areas, food not put back into the refrigerator promptly, etc. And you should keep yourself on a schedule of vaccines — particularly tetanus. If you step on a rusty nail, you don't want to have to worry about whether your tetanus shot is current, or whether you should run to the emergency room to get one.

The AMA puts out a leaflet called "When to Call or See Your Physician", and, in this booklet, they offer general rules about when to go. When the patient's complaints are too severe to be endured, when what appear to be minor symptoms persist for more than a few days, when symptoms return repeatedly, and when in doubt. These are good general rules. In this leaflet, they list 18 possible causes for a visit to the doctor, and at what point or according to what symptoms a visit is necessary. This can be very useful.

Even more useful, however, are some of the new books which are just a step away from telling you how to be your own doctor. It is probably good to have this type of publication around the house, as most of them give good explanations of illnesses and symptoms, easy first aid remedies, and advice as to when you need to see a doctor. This is not to suggest that you never need see a doctor, but rather that you should do it selectively. Beware a book which purports to answer all your health care needs — the better books tell you when to see a physician.

Saving money on health also means spending less on drugs. This is discussed in detail elsewhere in this book. You can seek drug stores which offer discounts, expecially if you are a senior citizen. You should not buy useless pills — for example, a bottle of a sleeping remedy which you want for only one sleepless night — nor should you buy too many. Buy only as many pills as you are going to take; if you are buying a drug that you expect to take over a long period of time, check with your doctor to see if buying it in quantity makes sense, or if the shelf life of the drug is too limited.

When it comes to surgery, make sure you and your doctor communicate well about it, and that you understand what the procedure is. Ask if there are other courses of action. If your doctor insists on surgery — which is not only expensive, but may be unnecessary — then make sure you get a second opinion. A Health Research Group study between 1965 and 1973 indicated that common unnecessary operations included disc operations, hysterectomies, and prostate surgery.

You should take advantage of free medical services that are available. Most jurisdictions in this area offer mental health services to their residents — regardless of income, and with payment on a sliding scale. Clinics run by Boards of Health and Health Departments usually have a maximum income limit, but in certain cases provide services such as blood pressure readings, TB tests, VD tests, etc., free of charge to all who come in. Your employer may have a health center or may have an arrangement with specific health organizations, e.g., The Cancer Society, to do testing or offer you help for free.

Medical or dental schools in this area may use you for a guinea pig for their more advanced students — and charge you a fee well below what you would pay a full-fledged professional. This really isn't as much of a gamble as it sounds — they are well supervised, and if you go to them for a relatively routine procedure, you are not putting yourself to any great risk.

Learn hospital and emergency room fees in advance, and learn about the various kinds of health insurance available to you. If you should choose to buy commercial health insurance, whether individually or through a group, study the tradeoffs between costs and benefits, and see what makes the most sense for you. For certain simple procedures, it's not always necessary to spend a night in the hospital. Much of the diagnostic work can be accomplished before you go into the hospital. Some hospitals are trying new programs in which you go home from surgery a few days earlier than usual; your case is then handled by a visiting nurse. You should check to see whether this is available at the hospital to which you are going, and whether your health care payment plan covers the nursing. And don't bother entering the hospital for a weekend stay — little ever gets done over the weekend. Usually treatment won't begin until Monday, and you are just paying for extra days.

For your health, you should avoid overexposure to X-rays. Thus, whenever one is recommended, ask for an explanation of how it will help your diagnosis, and how necessary it is. Let your doctor know about similar X-rays you have had — it is wise to keep a list in your purse or wallet. Dental X-rays should not be automatic — a complete screening of the teeth first is suggested. And don't you insist on getting an X-ray when your doctor doesn't think it is necessary.

PAYING FOR HEALTH CARE

In the Washington metro area, the odds are that you work for the federal government — and if you don't, you probably work for a consulting firm or a company doing some other government-related work. In that case, you're lucky. All of these employers offer you health insurance plans of which they pay the bulk — all you need to pay is an additional sum for family coverage, or for any additional services or illnesses you want covered. And if your organization consists of 25 or more employees, your employers are required by law to offer you a choice of commercial insurance or a Health Maintenance Organization — a prepaid medical services plan.

If you are unemployed, you may be lucky: your group coverage may still be temporarily in force. Or perhaps you were able to get *conversion* privileges — by paying a larger premium, you get the right to convert your participation in a group policy to an individual policy.

If you are self-employed, you may be seeking the right health care plan that will minimize the costs of health care for you and your family — and avoid the catastrophic effects of a major illness.

If you're 65 or over, you are covered by Medicare, a government creation meant to help the elderly out with the burden of medical payments -- but which fails to do its job as well as it could. You may not know how to maximize your use of this program.

The maze of health care payment programs available may seem confusing — or you may not even be aware of the choices open to you. Like many people, you may just enroll in the program closest at hand and hope it works, or just do what your neighbor or best friend does. But if you really want to save money and provide yourself with the most suitable health care plan, you ought to read the following section.

Health Care Alternatives

There are five major ways to cover yourself for health care expenses: commercial health care insurance; Blue Cross/Blue Shield plans; Health Maintenance Organizations — which can be either open or closed panel; and Medicare. Or you can just leave it to fate and not use any of these alternatives.

Most people in this area have a choice of plans. If you work for the federal government, you may or may not know about a series of informational brochures which describe in detail all of the many plans offered to government employees. These brochures include information on benefits, location of services, how to make claims, and everything else you might want to know, all in a format clear enough to make it easy to compare the different plans. These pamphlets are available from the Office of Personnel Management (formerly the United States Civil Service Commission). Except for Medicare, all of the plans available to government employees are described in detail.

Health Insurance

Most states require that insurance companies that wish to offer lucrative forms of insurance, such as life insurance, are required to make health insurance available also to the same audience. Many of these commercial carriers use health insurance as a type of loss leader, offering it at a reasonable price, in the hope that the client who buys health insurance from them can be induced to buy life insurance from them as well. However, the ever-rising costs of inflation and hospital beds, as well as medical fees, has caused their premium rates to increase to be competitive with alternative health care payment strategies.

If you are getting some kind of group policy at your place of work, the best possible situation is one in which your employer is paying all expenses for a very comprehensive policy for you and your family. Your employer may pay only for a basic policy for you and your family, or just for you; in this case you will be able to buy additional coverage for your family and for specific or supplemental coverage. But the group policy — even if you do not receive it as a fringe benefit — is the cheapest way to buy health insurance from a commercial company.

The next most inexpensive way is to buy what's called "baby group" coverage — usually for a group of two to ten individuals. This way you get the benefit of group premiums, though they won't be as low as a larger group's.

Various experts divide the types of coverage up into different categories. We have decided to use the framework laid out by the US Department of HEW to explain what is available.

- BASIC: This includes two types of basic coverage: basic hospital and basic medical/surgical. Sometimes these are spoken of together as BASIC. Basic coverage is usually more expensive than major medical, as it covers a wide range of items. Basic hospital generally includes treatment and care in a ward or in a semiprivate room; it should contain routine nursing services, hospital supplies, and drugs, and it has a relatively limited annual benefit. Basic medical and surgical can be bought separately or in combination with a hospital policy. It covers doctor bills while you are hospitalized, surgery being the biggest benefit of this type of policy. Most policies lay out the total amount which you will be paid in benefits for each procedure. Some pay a certain percentage of your fees. Some of these plans cover doctor visits in the office, and a few cover in-home visits.
- MAJOR MEDICAL: If you can afford only one type of coverage, then this is what you should get. Generally, after a deductible of from $500 to $1000 annually (the higher the deductible, the lower the premium), this policy will take over where basic coverage ends. Usually your basic policies cover the deductible amount. Major Medical usually has a high annual limit and includes expenses both in and out of the hospital. Once you have satisfied the deductible, the policy then usually pays only a certain percentage of the bills, generally about 80%.
- EXCESS MAJOR MEDICAL: This supplements your major medical and enhances it. It should be considered if you have a low lifetime limit on your major medical benefits. But this plan is rarely used, and only about four companies in the US write policies for it.
- COMPREHENSIVE MAJOR MEDICAL: This usually costs less than separate policies with separate benefits, because it requires a deductible and that you pay a small percentage of your bills. It combines hospital, surgical, and major medical in one policy.
- DISABILITY INCOME: Sometimes called "loss of income" insurance or "income protection", this type of policy pays you a set sum for every day which you are in the hospital. A form of supplemental insurance, it usually involves a waiting period of from a few days to

several months. Most pay after the first week you are in the hospital, but as studies have shown the average length of stay to be eight days, it isn't used very often. The more you pay, the better your benefits.

There are a number of variations which you can get, and combinations, as well as additional riders. For example, to cover yourself more fully, you can get policies which have overlapping benefits. But, if you do, make sure that both companies allow you to accept full payment from the other. In general, it is best to keep duplicate coverage to a minimum, as you are paying twice for the same thing.

Many policies don't cover pregnancy, and those that do pay a pregnancy benefit may pay only a relatively small amount. The reasoning behind this is that the purpose of insurance policies is to protect you against unforseen hazards — which pregnancy isn't (or shouldn't be). Also, offering pregnancy benefits would lead to what consumer writer Jane Bryant Quinn calls "gamesmanship": you could sign up for the coverage, deliver the baby, and then quit that insurance company, placing the burden of your costs on others — unless, of course, the company has a preexisting benefits clause. Some companies that don't include pregnancy in their basic policies do have coverage available at additional cost.

Dread Disease coverage is available to allay your fears of expenses incurred due to major illnesses like cancer or a heart attack. While the premium is relatively small, so are the odds that you would run up great bills for these diseases. It makes more sense to build up your major medical coverage with the would-be premium for this type of coverage.

There are a few companies which offer short-term medical coverage of from 60 to 180 days for those laid off or between jobs. Some are non-renewable, others will renew only once, and most cover hospitalization only.

If you are not offered a policy through your place of employment, sometimes being a member of a group like a credit union can help you to get insurance at a group rate.

Regardless of what you do, you should get estimates on health insurance coverage from a number of companies, and, when speaking to them, you should make it clear that you are looking for the best value for your dollar.

You want to watch out for a number of items when getting information on the various policies.

1) How much of your bills are covered? Is it 100% after a deductible, or 80% after a deductible, or only 80% of what is considered a "reasonable" bill? You should know what the maximum payments by the insurance companies for each procedure would be in these cases. Some policies pay a flat rate per day, or per operation. This is not desirable in inflationary times: although it keeps the price of the policy stable, the payments do not go up to meet inflation — or, if they do go up, they don't keep pace with inflation. In general, the more coverage that you want, the more you pay for.

2) Ask about the lifetime maximum — most policies limit you to a total number of benefits. Sometimes the limit is placed on a certain kind of illness or condition, other times it is for all illnesses. Most hospital policies also set a minimum number of consecutive days you must be in the hospital before you can collect benefits.

3) Are there deductibles, and, if so, how much are they? The larger the deductible, the cheaper the premium. Also, find out if the deductible is for each separate occurrence, or for all illnesses put together. There may be a deductible for each member of your family, or a total for the family put together. In larger families, the second method is often an advantage: for example, if the individual deductible would be $100 per person, or $300 for a family, any family with over three individuals would benefit. Whatever policy you are buying, try to estimate what your maximum expenses would be if you got stuck with deductibles and percentage payments.

4) What conditions are covered? Each policy has a slightly different list. You should attempt to find a policy which includes any medical conditions or illnesses which have occurred often in your family history. Basic hospital coverage should include payments to hospital staff doctors, routine nursing care, minor medical supplies, hospital room and board, laboratory tests, X-rays, use of the operating room, anesthetics, drugs and medication given in the hospital, surgical dressings, ambulance service, illness, and accidents. Basic medical/surgical should cover a long list of surgical procedures performed either in the hospital or in the doctor's office. It is preferable to find a hospital policy which covers convalescent nursing home stays, or at-home care, but not all do.

5) Check for *exclusions*. An exclusion, quite simply, means a condition which is not covered by the policy. Preexisting conditions — conditions you were aware of when or before you got the policy — are usually excluded for a certain period of time called a *waiting period*, either for a time period after the policy goes into force, or until after the disease is cured. Preexisting conditions are defined differently by each company. Some policies put riders on, claiming that they will not cover payments for certain chronic conditions. If you have a chronic condition which makes it worthless to get — or impossible to get — commercial health insurance, Blue Cross/Blue Shield plans and Health Maintenance Organizations have open enrollment periods, during which anyone can join — more about this in a following section.

Individual policies may cover from a maximum of 30 days to 1 year in the hospital, yet research shows that for individuals under 65 years the average hospital stay is only eight days. Bear this in mind when choosing coverage, as you pay more for the one with the longest maximum — and it is unlikely that you will ever take advantage of it. If you have two hospital stays that run consecutively, they would be considered to be one stay by some companies. Look also for a *waiver of premium*, which allows you to avoid making premium payments while you are sick or in the hospital.

And remember, the cost of most policies rises as you get older. Some will cover you for a lifetime, but most turn to "medigap" insurance when you are 65 (see Medicare section which follows).

Also look for non-cancellable and guaranteed renewable clauses. With non-cancellable, as long as you pay the premiums, you can get coverage. Otherwise, the company could decide to cancel your policy whenever it felt you had too many claims — just when you need it most. With guaranteed renewable, they can increase the premium at renewal time, but only if they do so for all persons owning your particular type of policy.

One way to judge the effectiveness of the company is the loss ratio. This reflects the way the funds are used — how much of the funds actually go into paying claims, and how much to administrative. The more that goes for claims, the better. It has been found that the Blues are the most effective, since they are non-profit.

Coverage for your children is essential from the time of their birth. Childhood illness can be expensive. It is your responsibility to notify the company and pay the premium within 30 days of the child's birth. This is also applicable to adopted and step-children, if you are responsible for their support, and for dependent, single, full-time students from the ages of 19 to 23.

Spouses covered under group policies, particularly wives, should know that if they are covered under the group plan, and the wageearner dies, the policy will expire — usually within 30 days. Make sure, then, that the spouse will be covered in case of the wageearner's demise. Also, know that the premium should be reduced when the wageearner dies, particularly if it is the husband. Spouses are also out of the group plan when they are legally separated or divorced.

Plans commonly used in the government include the American Postal Workers Union Plan, the Indemnity Benefit Plan (administered by the Aetna Life Insurance Co), and the AFGE Health Benefit Plan (underwritten by The Mutual of Omaha Insurance Co.) For information on other plans: If you work for the government, ask the office of Federal Employee Health Benefits for relevant brochures. If you are an individual or small business, contact the insurance companies directly.

MEDICARE

Medicare is a federal health insurance program designed to help the elderly cover their medical costs. It was never designed to meet all of these costs – in 1977, in fact, only about 38% of costs were met by Medicare. Despite its drawbacks, it has been effective for many. This section tells you more about Medicare perhaps than you have ever wanted to know. But, assuming things continue for the next 40 years in much the same way (although there's little security in this premise), you will want to know a lot about Medicare. And even if things don't stay the same, if you have a parent or older friend or relative who will soon turn 54, you will benefit by knowing about Medicare.

Medicare is available to all US citizens who are 65 or older. You do not have to retire to qualify, but you do have to register for the program some time shortly before your 65th birthday. Medicare consists of two parts — Part A: hospital care, which includes some post-hospitalization care in a skilled nursing facility or in the patient's home; and Part B, which covers doctors' bills and other costs.

The hospital care section is free to anyone 65 or over if he/she is entitled to retirement or survivors' benefits under the Social Security or Railroad Retirement System; to people under 65 with certain disabilities or who are entitled to Social Security benefits or Railroad Retirement benefits for at least two consecutive years; to a disabled widow 50 or older who is receiving mothers' benefits to take care of children, but otherwise would have been eligible under the two-year requirement; and to people under 65 who, due to kidney failure, need dialysis or a kidney transplant. Those who are 65 or over and are not eligible because of not having worked enough, as of this writing, pay $69 per month; and they must buy Part B coverage (doctors' bills coverage) in order to be able to buy this first type of coverage.

At the time of this writing, Part B (coverage of doctors' fees) costs everyone $8.70 per month, which is automatically deducted from your social security check, unless you decide not to enroll — or you can pay directly every three months. It is suggested that you enroll when you turn 65, because you receive good benefits for a relatively small payment. And, for every year after 65 which you delay, the premium is hiked 10%.

The Part A Hospital Insurance pays for all covered services in the hospital for up to the first 60 days, after a $160 deductible charge. Covered expenses include a semiprivate room, regular nursing service, all meals, drugs provided by the hospital, rehabilitation services, and the cost of operations and the recovery room. After 60 days, the *coinsurance* clause goes into effect, whereby you pay $40 a day until the 90th day, and the government pays the rest. After the 90th day, you can begin to draw on 60 "lifetime" reserve days, which can be used any time, but only once. During those days, you pay $80 per day.

This is what happens during every benefit period. A benefit period is defined as starting 60 consecutive days after leaving the hospital or other "qualified" institution (not one that provides only custodial care). This insurance also shares with you the cost of a qualified phychiatric facility for up to 190 lifetime days.

For most people, this far exceeds the number of days which they will spend in the hospital, and the problem is the $160 deductible. Only about 3% of the individuals with this policy have wound up paying coinsurance costs after the first 60 days in the hospital.

This Medicare policy also covers care in a skilled nursing facility. The facility must meet strict requirements, and must offer not just custodial, but also medical care. In order for this to be covered, you must be admitted (generally) within 14 days of discharge from the hospital.

Medicare will share the cost of up to 100 days in this facility with you. The first 20 days, you pay nothing; then for the succeeding 80 days, you pay $20 per day. This is true as long as these requirements are met: you have been in the hospital at least three days, not including the day of discharge, before you are transferred to this facility; you are in the facility because of the same condition for which you were put in the hospital; a doctor certifies the need on a daily basis for skilled nursing care; and your stay is not disapproved by the facility's Utilization Review Committee or by the area's Professional Standards Review Organization.

This policy also covers home health care of up to 100 visits after a minimum hospital stay of three days, for the further treatment of the same condition, when the patient is confined to the home. This must occur within 12 months of discharge from the hospital. It must be necessary for the doctor to develop and supervise this home care program, and the help must come from a home health agency which participates in the Medicare program.

Part B of the Medicare policy covers doctors' fees, outpatient hospitalization, and other charges. It offers an additional 100 home health care visits if: you need parttime skilled care or physical or speech therapy; the doctor determines that you need these services; you are confined to the home; and the home health agency participates in Medicare. It covers doctor bills, certain ambulance services, diagnostic tests, physical therapy, prosthetics, outpatient physical therapy, and speech pathology. Of this you pay a deductible of the first $60 per year. Then the government pays 80% of all *reasonable* charges.

And this is the catch in Medicare, where many feel, justifiably, that the elderly are being ripped off. "Reasonable" payments can often be two years or more out of date, because, for each procedure, the reasonableness of a payment is based on a plethora of data about previous customary and prevailing charges and a certain Economic Index for the geographical area.

When a surgeon tells a patient how much he or she charges for a particular procedure — or when the patient receives the bill — he has no way of knowing how that surgeon's fee compares with those of other surgeons. The way to combat this is to inquire of a number of surgeons what the fee is — and to inquire of the Medicare carrier what the maximum payment is for an operation – so that the amount you will be stuck paying will be no more than the 20% minimum you'd have to pay in any event.

The amount that Medicare will pay is based on the use of customary, prevailing, and reasonable charges for a procedure. The customary charge is the median charge for any specific procedures charged by your doctor. The prevailing charge is set at the 75th percentile of all doctors' customary charges. The reasonable charge is determined among these, as the lowest of the actual charge, the physician's customary charge, and the prevailing charge.

For example, if a physician's customery charge is $800, but the prevailing charge is $700 for the area, and the physician charges the patient $850, Medicare would determine the reasonable charge to be the lowest -- which is $700 — and would elect to pay only 80% of this, or $560.

What you, the patient, would then have to pay would be determined by how the physician elected to be reimbursed. He can choose to be paid in either of two ways.

He can agree to accept the Medicare reasonable charge of $700, which is called "accepting assignment", and directly bill the Medicare carrier (which will pay him the $560) and bill you for the remaining $140. In this case, he cannot collect the $150 dollar difference from either you, the patient, or from the Medicare carrier; and the $140 is all you will have to pay.

But the physician can *refuse* assignment and bill you for the entire $850, which you'll have to pay. You will be able to get only $560 reimbursement from the carrier, leaving you with a burden of $290 — a whopping 34% of the $850 bill.

From this discussion, it should be abundantly clear to you the importance of inquiring whether the physician *routinely* accepts assignment.

This Medicare insurance does not pay for: private nurses, prescription drugs given outside of the hospital, custodial care in a nursing home, eyeglasses, hearing aids, dentures, or regular checkups — this last is particularly counterproductive, since some of the more expensive and debilitating diseases may be avoided or caught early by using regular checkups.

The Medigap

It should be obvious that certain gaps occur between Medicare coverage and actual needs — both from those things that are not covered and from the deductibles and coinsurance requirements. You can buy insurance to cover this gap, but it is always advisable *not* to buy duplicate coverage — for most commercial carriers state that they will not pay benefits that are covered elsewhere, particularly by Medicare.

Alternative ways to cover the Medigap are to extend existing group insurance if you can convert it when you retire, or extend an individual major medical policy — some can be extended for life. Blue Cross/Blue Shield policies can also help cover the gap, with their open enrollment periods for individuals. Certain policies which claim to fill these needs are available by mail — these should be examined closely. Retirement organizations offer policies to cover these needs, which range in price from $55 to $220 per year, and more for the very elderly. Some of these policies focus on special needs, e.g., outpatient or nursing care (it is very hard to get one which will cover custodial care). The more comprehensive the policy, the more expensive it will be. Some will pay both deductibles and coinsurance; some will provide extra cash for days you are in the hospital.

The two basic types of Medigap insurance are indemnity benefits, which (like hospital income policies) give you a fixed dollar amount per day, or a fixed rate per procedure. The advantage of this type of policy is that the premiums remain relatively stable over the years, not keeping pace with inflation — but that means that payments to you do not keep up with inflation either. But, if Medicare covers all expenses incurred, you can use this cash to pay other bills.

Then there is the service benefit policy, which pays all or a share of actual costs. The premium and the payments go up with inflation. These may even increase to cover adjustments to the amount of coinsurance which you must pay, and for surgical procedures.

Protective Steps

In order to avoid the squeeze of Medigap, you can follow a number of steps now:

1) Try to extend the existing group or major medical coverage which you now have into the retirement years if it seems like a good deal;

2) Make sure that you understand Medicare coverage, and then decide what gaps you want to fill;

3) Concentrate on the long-range, more catastrophic illnesses if you will have no problem paying the short-range costs — first dollar deductible;

4) Examine both the indemnity and service benefit policies available, or combinations of the two;

5) Buy the second part of the plan — it's worth it;

6) Check on pre-existing conditions and waiting periods when buying gap insurance — look for the shortest waiting periods;

7) Study renewal clauses before you have this problem — and be sure to buy a policy with "guaranteed renewal";

8) Make sure before you go into the hospital or facility that it is Medicare approved;

9) Look for a doctor who routinely accepts Medicare assignment;

10) Try to get cost estimates from your doctor in advance, so you can see how much will be covered under the Medicare reasonable clause;

11) Try to find out what the current maximum payments from the Medicare carrier are;

12) After 60 days in the hospital, it makes sense to go to a skilled nursing facility; then your coinsurance requirement is only $20, not $40;

13) Beyond 90 hospitalized days, try not to use the reserve Medicare days. Use insurance instead. If you do this, you must notify the hospital in writing.

14) If you disagree with a payment made by the Medicare carrier, ask for a review;

15) Try not to get sick!

BLUE CROSS/BLUE SHIELD

One effective way to pay your medical bills, whether you work for the government or purchase your own coverage, is to participate in the Blue Cross/Blue Shield programs. These provide broad coverage at a reasonable price, providing an excellent benefit/premium ratio, in part because they are non-profit and have tax-preferred status. Also, it is possible to convert from a group to an individual policy without raising your expenses.

These are actually two separate plans. Blue Cross covers just hospitalization bills; and Blue Shield covers doctors' bills, laboratory and diagnostic procedures. In some geographic areas, these two organizations have merged and function together.

Blue Cross was the first, founded in 1929 as a prepayment plan to provide health care coverage. It was subsequently endorsed by the American Medical Association, and grew in popularity. Blue Shield was created in the late 1930's and the early 1940's.

Locally, the Washington area Blue Cross plan, called Group Hospitalization (each plan has its own name) was started in 1934. There is also a Maryland plan. The Blue Shield plan of this area, which started in 1948, has the corporate name of Medical Services of the District of Columbia. Both plans are non-profit corporations, and are completely separate entities. But Blue Cross performs administrative functions for Blue Shield, they are marketed together, and the patient makes one premium payment, while getting one bill with a dual statement. The rates for each vary independently, depending on the performance of each program and its costs. The two programs also share information departments.

Blue Cross is similar to a hospitalization insurance policy, and it pays for all services rendered by the hospital. One of the advantages of both programs is that the physician or hospital files the claim for the patient, and the patient does not have to worry about getting the bills paid.

Blue Shield pays for the physicians and lab fees, anesthetics, procedures performed by a physician, diagnostic tests and X-rays, as well as a whole range of physician services and in-office diagnostic procedures.

Under the next level of coverage, you would get a joint contract from Blue Cross and Blue Shield, which would provide you with Major Medical coverage. The only things not covered under this program are prescription drugs and office visits.

An individual subscriber can purchase coverage for his family without being a group member. At the time of this writing, the fee was $111.68 per month for a family. However, the individual subscriber cannot get the best benefit package which is available to group members. Additionally, if there are any questions about an individual's medical fitness, Blue Cross/Blue Shield can place a rider on the policy, or ask for a medical checkup. However, during "open season", which is in July, they have to accept everyone who applies — up to a certain number of subscribers. And, for Medicare complementary coverage, anyone can get coverage within 3 months of his or her birthday.

One of the major advantages of this type of ocverage is that it is uniform for all. Blue Cross/Blue Shield has a network of participating hospitals and doctors throughout the country. Outside of this country you pay, and can be reimbursed for, 100% of covered claims.

HEALTH MAINTENANCE ORGANIZATIONS (HMOs)

An HMO is a prepaid medical care plan, in which you pay a fixed fee (usually on a monthly or quarterly basis) for your medical and hospital treatment. One of the earliest HMOs was begun in 1938 by industrialist Henry J. Kaiser, who, dissatisfied with fee-for-service medicine offered to his workers on the Grand Coulee Dam in the state of Washington, sought an alternative means of assuring their well-being. He gathered together a group of physicians who, on a prepaid basis, provided all necessary care to his workers. That original venture has grown into what is now the Kaiser Permanent Plan, which provides medical services to over three million people in six states.

Despite the early forms of HMOs, their growth really began when Congress passed the Health Maintenance Organization Act of 1973, which attempted to provide financial aid for the development of HMOs, but which set broad requirements for federal qualifications, and vague guidelines for meeting them. In 1976, amendments to the HMO Act simplified and clarified the previous work, which in turn stimulated renewed development and growth of HMOs.

The principal of an HMO is that of prepayment for all your medical needs, rather than reimbursement. Nationally, the cost of service runs from about $80-$130 per family per month, and from $30 to $40 per individual per month.

One of the touted advantages of this type of plan is *preventive care.* Most HMOs try to educate their members to act before crisis state — and the members can afford to do so, because they pay little or nothing for each medical visit. Also, preventive maintenance helps keep people out of the hospital for unnecessary procedures.

The value of the HMO in encouraging preventive medicine is debated by some. According to Dr. Melvin Small, Chairman of the Northern Virginia Consortium for Continuing Medical Education, who is charged with directing feasibility studies for an IPA-HMO in Northern Virginia, the preventive aspects of HMOs have been overestimated. He claims that, except for good diet and adequate exercise, there are few effective means of preventing diseases. Rather, he says, early detection is impsortant, citing certain diseases and conditions for which free or nominal-cost screening is available (often through an organization dealing specifically with that condition, or through local health departments).

There are three basic types of HMOs — group practice, staff model, and individual practice association. Group practice and staff model are basically similar. In the group practice, the HMO provides care by contracting with a physicians' group and with area hospitals. Physicians for the group work for a salary. The difference between this and a staff model is that, instead of contracting with the physicians, the staff model HMO directly hires the physicians on staff. These are both called "closed panel" models, as the patient is limited to certain doctors.

The Individual Practice Association is different. While your care is still prepaid, you can usually continue to see your own physician, although individual physicians have to decide whether or not they want to participate in the program.

Some of the advantages of the group practice/staff model over the IPA include one-stop health care in most cases; better coordination of care; and better follow-up and preventive care. According to Dr. Himman, Executive Director of the Group Health Association, a staff model organization, this model leads to greater continuity in the quality of care, better record handling, collegial atmosphere, implicit peer review, and single and consistent laboratory and X-ray facilities.

Unfortunately, in some cases there is a long waiting period for an appointment. Some health plans have found this to be an unexpected benefit — by the time the patient gets seen, the symptoms or disease may have cleared up spontaneously. This may be a tribute to nature's curative powers — but it says little good about the HMOs.

IPA-HMOs offer more convenient location of health services and a wider choice of physicians. Proponents of IPA-HMOs also contend that in the staff model, the patient does not always get to see his or her chosen physician.

Another advantage of the IPA-HMO is that it gives the doctor an incentive for doing better — to sell his product. He must provide good performance. In a staff model, desultory practice can be accepted because the physicians are accountable, not to the patient directly, but to the HMO.

The potential disadvantages of this form are that, although there is utilization and peer review, the doctor is still functioning as a private entrepreneur, which may not affect his hospital utilization as much as could be hoped. Another potential disadvantage is to the doctor. Payments for a certain procedure could get frozen at a certain level, but actual costs could get greater. The nature of the open panel model could actually lead to a slightly higher annual payment by the consumer.

Both forms subject themselves to peer review and utilization review, so that the patient has a better chance of avoiding both inadequate treatment and over-treatment.

One advantage of all HMOs is that they are part of a national network, so you are assured necessary and inexpensive health care while away from home. Also, because there is no benefit for the doctor in prescribing hospitalization, a lower rate of hospitalization occurs. FTC data released in July of 1977 indicated that the presence of HMOs tends to lower hospital costs, not just for the members, but for everyone in the community, and also tends to increase the benefits of Blue Cross programs by forcing them to become more competitive.

Federal Regulations for HMOs

In order for an HMO to become federally-qualified, it must provide certain basic services to its members without limit as to time, cost, or health status: physician services, outpatient services, and inpatient hospital services; medically necessary emergency health services; short-term mental health services; medical treatment and referral services for abuse of or addiction to alcohol and drugs; diagnostic laboratory and diagnostic and therapeutic radiologic services; home health services; and preventive health services. They may offer supplemental benefits such as intermediate and long-term care; and vision, dental, and mental health services beyond those required as basic services.

Other requirements which they must meet include fiscal soundness; acceptance of full financial risk with limited reinsurance allowable; enrollment of persons broadly representative of the service area; provisions for open enrollment period (when anyone will be accepted, regardless of physical condition); provisions insuring that reenrollment or expulsion from membership is not dependent on health status or requirements for health services; provision for a policy-making body composed of at least one-third members of HMOs; provisions for grievance procedures to protect consumers' legitimate interests; provision of medical, social services, and health education for enrollees; provision of continuing education for HMO health professionals; ability to report accurate data on cost and utilization of services to enrollees, the public, and the Secretary of the Department of Health, Education, and Welfare; and provision of a specific set of health services, as mentioned above.

What is the point of being federally qualified? There are two major benefits to the organization: one is directly financial — it qualifies the organization for grants, loans, and loan guarantees from the government.

Further, and more important to the consumer, is that it makes the organization eligible under the ruling that any organization which employs 25 or more workers must provide the option of a health insurance policy or a federally qualified HMO to its employees, enforceable under the Fair Labor Standards Act. This option is referred to as "Dual Choice" and is monitored by the Department of Labor (Section 1310, HMO act). Either the individual has the choice, or, where there is a union, it bargains collectively for the health coverage. Obviously, the HMO benefits in being qualified by gaining more members. One interesting note though — an HMO can be qualified for everyone but the federal government. Because the federal government automatically excludes itself from any legislation passed by Congress, it has a separate system for deciding which programs can be offered to its employees. It is therefore possible for an HMO to be federally qualified, but not qualified for offering to government workers, and vice versa.

How to decide whether an HMO is for you and your family
- How do costs compare for an HMO versus a health insurance policy?
- Consider whether the physicians are board certified or board eligible.

- Make sure the location is convenient for you. Some programs have only one center, others have several.
- Find out if the HMO is federally qualified, because, if it is, it usually offers more services.
- Are you willing to sever ties with your private physician (assuming a staff model)?
- Are you prepared to accept limited choice as to physicians (again, assuming staff model)?
- Do the hospitals affiliated with the HMO have good reputations?

There are five HMOs in this area: The Columbia Medical Plan, Georgetown Medical Plan, Group Health Association, George Washington University Medical Plan, and Health Plus.

The Columbia Health Plan is small and limited to serving the geographic area around Columbia, Maryland. Though it is not federally qualified, it does meet the requirements of the Office of Comprehensive Health Plans in the Office of Personnel Management; and thus it is offered to federal employees. It has only one medical center and is a staff model plan.

All of the other plans are federally-qualified and are also qualified for offering to federal employees under Office of Comprehensive Health Plan regulations.

The Georgetown Medical Plan, also a staff model, is considered by many to be the most successful plan in the entire SMSA, considering its high enrollment after only six years of existence. It offers its members a large number of centers throughout the metropolitan area.

Group Health Association is the oldest plan in the area and is also a staff model. It has several centers throughout the metro area.

The George Washington University Plan again is a staff model and operated solely out of a downtown Washington location, tied to the GWU hospital center.

Health Plus, which operates in Prince George's county, is a new open panel (IPA-HMO), in which about one-half of the physicians in the county participate. Its rates at the time of this writing are $125.91 monthly for a family, and $48.43 for a single membership, with a 3% increase anticipated in 1980.

Bob Helfrich, director of this plan, indicates that, while at this point rates are higher than or just about the level of comparable insurance policies, he feels that in the long range HMOs will be better at holding costs down due to lower hospital utilization and preventive care, and that insurance companies will start putting more restraints and exclusions on their policies, in order to keep their premiums competitive with HMOs. They will also more willingly stress second opinions on elective surgery.

Federal law requires that within five years, or when enrollment of 50,000 or more is reached after federal qualification, the plans must offer open enrollment, meaning that at that time, there has to be a period during which everyone is accepted, regardless of medical condition.

UNIVERSITY MEDICAL AND DENTAL CLINICS

One alternative to high-priced health care is the use of available medical and dental school clinics. This makes a lot of sense for dental care, in particular, which is usually covered by only the best group insurance policies and HMO plans. This coverage is usually very expensive, and individuals are unlikely to purchase it unless they have a reason to need extensive dental work.

Two area schools offer dental clinics where supervised senior students work on you. Georgetown University offers a full range of diagnostic services, X-rays, and whatever else you need, from cavity work to bridge work to periodontal work. The clinic is open to everyone, and the prices are lower than a regular dentist's charges. The building is located on Reservoir Road, adjacent to the Medical School. Call 432-1234 the first Monday of the month for an appointment.

Howard University offers a similar clinic, where students do the work — just about all dental services you would need. You basically pay the cost of the materials. They always have a tremendous backlog. Appointments are taken only once a month. The clinic is located at 600 W Street, NW, Washington, DC.

COMMUNITY HEALTH SERVICES

In this chapter, we planned to include all of the medical services offered free or on a sliding scale by local departments of health. However, lack of centralized information by most of these departments made the information-gathering too time-consuming a task. All offer free VD testing; and other services, like TB tests, chest X-Rays, glaucoma and cataract screening, are available free or at a minimal charge. Also, groups like the American Cancer Society and the Lung Association frequently have sponsored screening for the diseases they deal with. Community health fairs are another place where you can get free screening for a variety of conditions and diseases.

FREE INFORMATION

One great and convenient resource is the telephone-accessed medical information system called Tel-Med. In this area, it is offered by two local hospitals.

The Greater Southeast Community Hospital's Tel-Med number is 561-9500, and operates from 9 am to 9 pm on Monday through Sunday. They have 100 tapes, each of which discusses an ailment or disease and lasts for about three minutes. They do not tell how to treat the disease or condition, but tell about the disease, its symptoms and course. Among other things, these tapes discuss childhood diseases, high blood pressure, hypoglycemia, and sexual problems. For a free brochure that has a list of tapes and tape numbers, call 574-6646

The Prince George's Hospital, co-sponsor with the P.G. County Health Department and the County Library, operates a Tel-Med number at 345-4080. Ask for tape No. 429, which tells about the Tel-Med program, and call 773-1400, extension 344, for a free brochure listing tapes and their numbers. Brochures are also available at P.G. County libraries, chain stores, and health centers. This system is open from 10 am to 9 pm on Monday through Wednesday, Thursday from 10 am to 6 pm, Friday from 1 pm to 6 pm, and Saturday from 9 am to 5 pm. These Tel-Med tapes last from 3 to 5 minutes and are prerecorded messages dealing with subjects from pregnancy to home health care and preventive maintenance. 240 tapes are available. All tapes have been reviewed by the Prince George's County Medical Society and the Dental Society of Southern Maryland.

In Prince William County, call 368-9171 for similar information.

Note: All systems stress that they are no replacement for a doctor's or dentist's care, do not diagnose illness, and do not serve as emergency treatment.

HEALTH SCREENING COUNCIL

Staffed by nurses, health educators, and other health professionals, the Health Screening Council assists community groups in putting together health fairs. Preparation for these fairs includes setting up screening tests, such as for glaucoma and blood pressure; and providing information to be directed at the general public. The groups with which the Council works — community groups, older Americans, and high school students — are provided with written materials and free phone consultation about organizing health fairs. All of those who wish the aid of the Health Screening Council must follow the five part model which they use. It consists of screening, health education, counseling, referral, and follow-up. In the Washington Metro area, this group is a co-sponsor of the Health Fair Week. For further information contact anyone at the Council at 657-8480 or at 5161 River Road, Building 20, Washington, DC 20016.

LOCAL PHYSICIAN REFERRAL SERVICES

Location	Telephone	Hours
District of Columbia	223-6333	Monday through Friday 8:15 am to 4:30 pm
Maryland		
Howard County	(301) 730-7986	Monday-Thursday, 10 am to 1 pm
Montgomery County	949-9497	Monday-Friday 9 am to 5 pm
Prince George's County	779-0179	24 hours a day
Virginia		
Alexandria	751-4611	Monday-Friday 9:30 am - noon, 1:30 pm to 4 pm
Arlington County	528-0888	Monday-Friday 9 am - 1 pm & 2:15-4:30 pm
Fairfax County	532-0500	Monday-Friday 9 am - 4:30 pm
Prince William County	(703) 378-6505	Monday-Friday 9 am to 3:30 pm

SECOND PRINTING: ADDITIONS

Since the publication of the first printing of this book, many stores have opened or closed branches, new businesses have developed, and some firms have gone out of business. In this section, we have included new businesses and those missed in the first printing. We know we have not mentioned all openings and closings. But next year's edition *will* be totally updated; so we would appreciate your contacting us with any relevant information for inclusion in future editions.

Bag Boutique
7613 Wisconsin Avenue
Bethesda, MD
652-5317

If you want a gorgeous handbag, belt, umbrella, or other small leather goods, but don't feel like paying designer or boutique prices, then you have just got to visit the Bag Boutique. This long narrow store is well-laid-out, offering the customer an interesting and attractive display of American designer and other well-known brands found in major department stores and boutiques. Prices are from 15% to 20% below retail. Everything is first quality and in season. Anything can be ordered from designer sketchbooks. A deposit of 50% is requested on special orders, and these usually come in within 2 weeks of ordering. Seasonal clearance sales are held, and there is a mailing list.

Store hours are Monday through Saturday from 9:30 am to 5 pm and Tursday until 8:30 pm. Personal checks up to $150.00 are accepted, as are Master Charge and VISA. The layaway policy requires a deposit of at least 50% and 30 days to pick up. Store credit or exchanges are made for returned merchandise.

Basics Food Warehouse
3931 St. Barnabas Rd.
Marlow Heights, MD
899-2776

Basics is essentially a very large supermarket, which has a more limited selection of goods and lower prices than the customery retail supermarket. It achieves its lower prices with a no-frills policy, wherein customers choose their purchases from aisles which are neatly stacked with cartoned, rather than with shelved merchandise. All major brands are carried in selected varieties. The management here estimates that the average shopper can save 30% off the average food bill. Both produce and meat can be purchased here. Everything is first quality. You ought to bring your own bags, or else you pay for theirs. People are also welcome to use the cartons to box their groceries.

Other location:
Sugarland Plaza, Route 7, Herndon/Sterling Park

The stores are open 24 hours. Parking is ample. Cash or foods stamps are accepted.

Cape Craft Pine
10334 Main Street
Fairfax, VA
273-6556

Part of an East Coast Chain, this store specializes in Ponderosa pine items, prints, ceramic figurines, colonial decorative goods, candles, and brass goods, all of medium quality. The pine and brass are produced by the parent company. They also carry Fieldcrest and Martex linen and bathroom items, kitchen items, Carolina brass, and Cape Craft wood and candles, with prices ranging from 20% to 60% below retail. The reason prices are so low is because stock consists of overstock and seconds. The store is quite large and neatly laid out

Other locations:
Rte. 3 and St. Stevens Church Rd., Gambrils/Crofton, MD, 721-7009
9117 Fort Meade Rd., Laurel, MD, 953-1417

Store hours are from 9 am to 9 pm Monday through Saturday, and Sunday from noon to 5 pm. Personal checks, Master Charge, and VISA are accepted. Holds are possible. Returns can be made for credit within 30 days of purchase. Parking is ample.

Citizens Furniture
8715 Colesville Road
Silver Spring, MD
588-3000

Furniture of moderate quality for the whole house can be bought here at discounts averaging 20% to 30%, and up to 50% on closeouts. Brand names include Clyde Pearson, Lane, De Soto, Schweiger, Flexsteel, and Serta. All merchandise is first quality. A 50% deposit is required on special orders. Delivery is available free with a purchase over $500 and within a 5-mile radius. Most items come with full guarantees, and repairs are done here. Seasonal and clearance sales are held. The store is large and well lit and has a pleasant appearance.

Store hours are Monday through Friday from 10 am to 9 pm; Saturday from 10 am to 6 pm; and Sunday from noon to 5 pm. Personal checks, Master Charge, VISA, Central Charge, and NAC are accepted. 10% minimum deposit is required on layaways. They will hold items for up to 24 hours. Ample parking in rear.

Crest Books
115 Harry Flood Byrd Highway
Sterling, VA 22170
(703) 450-4200

In this large neat store can be found books and games, posters, prints, sculptures, Alva museum replicas (at what they say are the cheapest prices around), New York Graphic Society prints and more. Discounts range from 15% to 35% on selected paperbacks and hardbacks — many are remainders and out-of-print items. Some things sell for as little as $.99. The owners specialize in personalized service, taking special orders, and even giving discounts on them where feasible. They hold special sales twice a year, at which an additional 10% discount is granted customers. Maps and guidebooks are also discounted, with the popular Rand-McNally maps selling at prices 15% to 20% below the publisher's list price.

Store hours are from 10 am to 9 pm Monday through Thursday and Saturday, Friday until 10 pm, and Sunday from noon to 5 pm. Checks with proper identification are accepted, as are Master Card and VISA. Returns are accepted within 30 days of purchase, with receipt.

Drapery Land Discount Center
640-B Pickett Street
Alexandria, VA
370-6980

This store is much smaller than many others offering similar merchandise in this metro area, but it just might answer your needs for reasonably priced draperies, sheers, spreads, throw pillows, and Kirsch drapery rods. Labels are cut out of the merchandise, but they say you can expect to save 25% to 50% below retail prices, and 25% on special orders. About half of the merchandise is first quality, and the rest irregulars. They ask a 10% deposit on special order. You are encouraged to open everything and check for imperfections. Also sold here are comforters, bath carpets, and an even more limited selection of towels and Beacon blankets.

Store hours are Tuesday through Saturday from 10 am to 4 pm, Sunday from 2 to 5 pm. Master Charge and VISA are accepted. They will hold goods from 2 to 3 days without a deposit. All sales are final. Ample parking available.

Entenman's Bakery
1327-A Rockville Pike
Rockville, MD
762-1215

Entenman's is a fresh little bakery factory outlet, with price reduction policies clearly marked on neat signs around the store. Merchandise varies with bakery overruns, but generally consists of cakes, cookies, doughnuts, and the like. Merchandise includes products which were unsold at the retail stores (thus, day-old), and imperfections ("cripples"). Items marked with a black line are returns, which are priced at 40% below normal retail; items marked in yellow are promotionals, and have neat prices like 3/$2.00; items marked in red are fresh, but cripples, on which you save 25% of the usual retail price. Wednesday and Sunday are bargain days: black-line items are two for the price of one.

Hours are Monday through Saturday from 9 am to 6 pm and Sunday from 8 am to 4:30 pm.

Fan Fare
4624 Wisconsin Avenue NW
Washington, DC
244-7615

The management here claims to have the best prices in the area on Hunter, Casablanca, and Emerson ceiling fans and related accessories, such as lights, blades, etc. All merchandise is first quality, and 95% of orders are in stock. Samples are carefully displayed on shelves around the small salesroom. A minimum of 50% deposit is requested on special orders, which take from 7 to 10 days to fill. Delivery is available when convenient to the store. All fans come with a manufacturer's 5-year warranty, and satisfaction is guaranteed by the store.

Hours are Monday through Friday from noon to 6 pm; Monday and Thursday until 9 pm; and from 10 am to 5 pm on Saturday. Personal checks are accepted, as are Master Charge, VISA, and Bank of Virginia. Return policy is liberal. Metered on-street parking.

Hess Shoe Bargain Box
White Oak Shopping Center
593-2422

Hess Shoe Bargain Boxes operate stores in the Washington area, in addition to those in the Baltimore area, which were mentioned in the "Clothing and Shoes" chapter of the first printing. Here they sell men's and women's shoes of medium quality and up, with such name brands as Bally, Pierre Cardin, French Shriner, Selby, Joyce, and Anne Klein, as well as other designer and name brands. Savings range from 15% for the more expensive shoes up to 50% and more, depending on the item. Among ladies' shoes, about 50% are in season and about 50% are last season's merchandise. They get many overstocks from their regular stores.

Other location:
White Flint Plaza at Nicholson Lane, 468-1862

Open at White Oak from 10 am to 9 pm Monday through Saturday; at White Flint, only until 6 pm on Saturday. Personal checks, American Express, Master Charge, VISA, Central Charge, and NAC are all accepted. They will hold items for 24 hours without a deposit. All sales are final. Ample parking.

Home Lawn Discounters
4582 Eisenhower Avenue
Alexandria, VA
751-5051

A small, dark warehouse shop this is, where you can find large lawn and garden tools and equipment at prices 10% below list price, and up to 40% on featured items. The brands they carry are True Temper, Lawn Boy, Ortho spreaders, Boss gloves, Swan hose, and McGuire bamboo rakes. Everything is first quality, and it usually takes only 3 days for delivery on special orders. They are an authorized service dealer for Lawn Boy and offer full warranties.

Store hours are Monday through Friday from 9 am to 7 pm and Saturday from 9 am to 5 pm. Personal checks are accepted, and Master Charge and VISA may soon be. Parking is ample.

Kramer Equipment, Tools, & Supplies
7835 Richmond Highway
Alexandria, VA
360-4777

If the ebullience of the younger Kramer doesn't overwhelm you when you enter this store, then the sheer mass of products in their topsy-turvy environment is sure to. For if it's tools and equipment that turn you on, then Kramer's could be the greatest find of the season. Not only do the Kramers sell equipment and tools, electrical supplies, and anything in the hardware line, but *everything* is discounted — at a 20% average discount. You can expect far better buys on used and surplus stock. For example, we recently noted all different kinds of special light bulbs priced from 10c to 25c each — well below their normal list price. Looking into every nook and cranny in this vast warehouse, and in the two acres of surrounding land, we spied empty steel drums, scrap steel, bolts, iron tools, odd cans of paint, a vast array of rope and chain (their specialty), levels, trowels, gloves, paintbrushes, saws, rakes, blades, brooms, shovels, ladders, and much, much more.

Open Monday through Friday from 8 am to 4:45 pm. Personal checks are accepted, as are Master Charge and VISA. Return policy is liberal. Parking is more than ample.

Nat Lewis Feminine Apparel
1731 Eye St. NW
Washington, DC
396-1880

Nat Lewis shops are a satisfying find in the world of discount shopping. Until just recently, they were operated as normal retail stores, but the management decided that the trend to discounting could benefit both them and the consumer — so they now offer moderately priced brands of contemporary misses and juniors' clothing at prices 20% below retail across the board on all first quality in-season merchandise. There is always at least one promotional item offered at a discount of 50%, and prices are further reduced at the end of the wearing season. Separate dressing rooms are available at all locations. Alterations are available at a nominal fee, and they stand behind all of their merchandise. The stores are pleasant and well-designed — the only thing discount about Nat Lewis is the prices. Service and style have not suffered in the least.

Other locations:
Marlow Heights Shopping Center, 4237 Branch Avenue, Marlow Heights, MD, 423-3151.
Iverson Mall Shopping Center, Hillcrest Heights, MD, 423-1230

Store hours are from 9:30 am to 6 pm Monday through Friday downtown; at Marlow Heights from 10 am to 9 pm Monday through Saturday, Sunday from noon to 5 pm; and at Iverson from 10 am to 9:30 pm Monday through Saturday and from noon to 5 pm on Sunday. Personal checks are accepted, as are American Express, Master Charge, VISA, Central Charge, and NAC. A deposit of 1/3 is required on layaways, with 30 days to pick up. They will hold items for up to 24 hours without a deposit. Exchanges with receipt can be made within 5 days of purchase.

New Yorker Bakery
7041 Blair Road
Washington, D.C. 20012
726-1626

This bakery outlet store impressed me for one very simple reason — their bagels were the first bagles I've had in years that were true to my Chicago childhood notion of what a bagel should taste and feel like. Besides the bagels, you can buy either fresh (at the going price) or day-or-more-old (at half price and less) French breads, regular white breads, rolls, and a variety of sweet rools. The store is small and very clean, and everything is plainly marked. All items are checked for edibility. We recently paid 25c for a bag of six onion rolls that were over a day old — they tasted wonderful despite their age.

Hours here are from 8 am to 7 pm Monday through Friday, and Saturday from 9 am to 3 pm. Personal checks are accepted. Parking is limited, in a small lot in front of the store.

Pfaltzgraff Factory Outlet
10334 Main Street
Fairfax, VA
591-6141

We think this store is a truly good find for moderate to high priced dining and kitchen ware. They carry firsts and seconds on Pfaltzgraff pottery, firsts from other companies, special purchase items, and closeouts. On the latter, you can save from 20% to 50%, and seconds are approximately 50% less than retail Beware: some complementary items are priced at the going retail price. Organizations can get additional discounts on large quanitity purchases.

Other location:
1821 East-West Highway, Hyattsville, MD, 422-7977

Hours are the same at both stores: from 9 am to 9 pm Monday through Saturday, and Sunday from noon to 5 pm. Personal checks are accepted, as are Master Charge and VISA. Items can be held for up to 5 days without a deposit. Return policy is liberal. Cash refunds are made with receipt. Parking is ample.

Record and Tape Exchange
8606 Baltimore Boulevard
College Park, MD
345-9338

The Record and Tape Exchange sells used records and tapes, as well as cutouts — records which have been discontinued by the manufacturer. They also *buy* used records and tapes. The average price for an album runs from 99c to $5.99, and all are fully guaranteed. There are also some collectibles.

Other location:
M Street, Washington, DC, three doors down from Crazy Horse, 337-7970

The store is open from 11 am to 8 pm Monday through Saturday, and from 1 to 6 pm on Sunday. Personal checks are accepted, as are major credit cards. For return policy, you should check with the manager before you buy.

Record Collections
8231 Woodmont Avenue
Bethesda, MD
652-5500

In this extremely well-organized shop, the record lover can find collectible records, used 45s and LP records and tapes, and even some factory-sealed records at extraordinarily good prices. The shop gets its stock from people who may be liquidating collections or whose tastes are changing, or from those who buy albums merely to tape. They do not carry 8-track tapes. Non-collectible used albums cost 50% or less of the original retail price. Much current stuff goes for from $3 to $4 each album. Collectible prices are based on the quality of the disc and how much in demand the artist is. All items are checked by the management to be in as near-perfect condition as possible.

Hours here are from 11 am to 7 pm Monday through Friday; Thursday until 8 pm; Saturday from 11 am to 5 pm; and Sunday from 1 pm to 5 pm. Personal checks are accepted, as are Master Charge and VISA. A deposit of one-third is required on layaways. And they will hold items from 2 to 3 days without a deposit. Returns can be made within 3 days with receipt. Parking in the area is metered, and there is a pay garage across the street.

Robert Slate Ltd.
3644 King Street
Alexandria, VA
379-6200

Until quite recently, Robert Slate Ltd. was a fine quality menswear shop with *normal retail* prices. Seeing the trend to discounting, the owners decided to offer discounts of 20% to 50% on the men's clothing, sportswear and furnishings they carry — without changing the impeccable look of the store or the personalized and caring service for which they are noted. The result is that you can comfortably buy well-known brands like Cricketeer, Haspel, Pendleton, Hathaway, Izon La-Coste, and Jockey Underwear for substantial savings in season, all first quality.

There are four separate men's dressing rooms. Alterations are available at a nominal charge. Seasonal sales are held and promotional items are sometimes featured.

Monday and Thursday, open from 10 am to 8 pm, and Tuesday, Wednesday, Friday, and Saturday until 6 pm. Personal checks are accepted, as are Master Charge and VISA. On layaways, a deposit of 1/3 is requested, with 30 days for pickup. Items are allowed out on 24-hour approval with a deposit. Exchanges or returns for credit are accepted within 10 days on all merchandise. Parking is ample.

Sasan Shoe Salon
7301 Wisconsin Avenue
Bethesda, MD
652-4107

What makes Sasan's salon special is that every item here is first quality and in season. They specialize in women's shoes and bags in Bethesda and also sell children's shoes in the Potomac store. Well-known brands include Bandolinos, Capezio, Amalfi, Bass, Garolini, Nickels, Nike, Tretorn, Jumping Jack, and Capezios for children. The discounts average from 10% to 25%. The store itself is very pleasant and well-designed. A display of Stone Mountain and Borelli Collection handbags graces the walls.

Other location:
9812 Falls Road, Potomac, MD, 299-6525

Store hours in Bethesda are from 10 am to 6:30 pm Monday through Saturday, and Thursday until 8 pm. In Potomac, hours are 10 am to 6 pm Monday through Saturday. Checks, American Express, Master Charge, and VISA are accepted. Layaways are allowed. Items can be held for a few days without a deposit.

Sassafras
Pan Am Center (3069 Nutley Rd.)
Fairfax, VA
560-1800

This is a large, well-laid-out store specializing in discounted misses and juniors clothing, including sportswear, dresses, petite sizes, separates, coordinates, and some lingerie. Name brands range from moderately priced on up, with such names as Breckenridge, Junior House, Bobby Brooks, Cucumber, Fancy Props, Rumble Seat jeans, Underalls, and many designer names found in the better department stores. Discounts start at 20%. All merchandise is first quality, and most is in season. The selections are good. Alterations are available. Separate dressing rooms with curtains are used. Clearance sales are held seasonally, and there is a mailing list.

Other location:
Behind Lake Forest Mall, Gaithersburg, MD, 840-0390

Store hours are Monday through Saturday from 10 am to 9 pm, and Sunday from noon to 5 pm. Different hours at Gaithersburg. This is part of a regional chain. Personal checks are accepted, as are Master Charge, VISA, and Central Charge. Layaway terms are 1/3 down with 60 days to pick up. They will hold items for up to 5 days. Returns must be made within 5 days of purchase for merchandise credit only. Parking is ample.

Shoe Factory
5512 Leesburg Pike
Baileys Crossroads, VA
578-1327

This store is an outlet for Mushrooms, Bernardo, and Quaddy brands of men's and women's shoes, and also for children's slippers. They also carry socks and stockings. Mushrooms and Quaddy are priced at 25% to 30% below retail, Bernardo's at 20% to 25% below retail, and hose at about 50% off. Half of the merchandise is first quality, the rest seconds. There are factory closeouts, and much of the first quality merchandise is from the previous wearing season.

Other location:
Next to Jay's, in back of Old Keene Mill Center at the intersection of Rolling and Old Keene Mill Roads, Springfield, VA, 569-6308

Store hours are Monday through Friday, from 10 am to 9 pm; Saturday from 10 am to 7 pm; and Sunday from noon to 5 pm. Springfield store hours differ on Saturday: they are open only until 6 pm. Personal Checks are accepted, as are Master Charge and VISA. They will hold items for up to 3 days without a deposit. Return policy is liberal. Large parking lots.

Shopper Stopper
14753 Main St.
Upper Marlboro, MD
627-8288

This is a no-frills type of operation, selling canned and dry goods. The Indian Head store also carries frozen foods, such as meats, ice cream, and packaged lunch meats. The Upper Marlboro store may soon carry these frozen foods and a line of dairy/deli products. 50% of the brands carried are national; the other 50% of merchandise is the house brand — Food Club. Prices here average 20% to 40% off the cost at a conventional supermarket. All merchandise is first quality, and satisfaction is 100% guaranteed. You bag or box your own goods: boxes are free; you can bring your own bags or pay 3c each for theirs.

Other locations:
805 N. Strauss Avenue, Indian Head, MD, 743-5218
Also two locations in Glen Burnie, MD.

Cash, food stamps, and manufacturers' coupons only are accepted. Ample parking is available.

Shoe World
6120 Greenbelt Road
Beltsville, MD
345-3588

Featured here are ladies' shoes to size 11, including a house brand, and such well-known medium brands as Joyce, Hushpuppy, Miss Capezio, and Naturalizer. Most items are in season and come here as factory overruns or late shipments. All shoes are priced at $9.88; pocketbooks at $7.88; leather boots at $29.88 per pair; and vinyl boots at $19.98. At the end of the season, boots are marked down. There are no special orders, but they will transfer a pair from one store to another if they have it. There is a mailing list.

Other locations:
933 Fairlawn Avenue, Laurel Shopping Center, Laurel, MD, 766-4880.
5129 Indian Head Highway, Oxon Hill, MD, 839-4629
Waldorf Shopper's World, Waldorf, MD, 843-0322
2818 Alabama Avenue SE, Washington, DC, 582-9886
6200 Annapolis Road, Hyattsville, MD, 322-9600
140 Halpine Road, Rockville, MD, 881-3289
Beltway Plaza, 6120 Greenbelt Road, Greenbelt, MD, 345-3588
1315 Jefferson Plaza, Woodbridge, 491-6265

Stores are open from 10 am to 9 pm on Monday to Saturday at most locations. A few are open Sunday from noon to five pm in winter, and most open Sundays the rest of the year. They accept Master Charge, VISA, NAC, and Central Charge. Items will be held without a deposit. Return policy is liberal. Ample parking at shopping center locations.

Sportique of Washington
1120 W. Broad
Falls Church, VA
532-1500

Sportique is a typical large store which specializes in discounted misses and juniors clothing of medium quality. Name brands include Villager, Bobby Brooks, Calvin Klein jeans, Vanderbilt jeans, Time and Place, and Eccobay, at prices roughly 30% below normal retail. All merchandise is first quality, and most in season. They feature a lot of sportswear, and they also show a more limited selection of suits and dresses. Clearance sales are held once a month, and there is a mailing list.

Store hours are Monday through Saturday from 10 am to 9 pm and Sunday from 12:30 to 5 pm. Personal checks are accepted, as are Master Charge and VISA. Layaways on coats only. Items can be held for 3 days without a deposit. Returns must be made within 7 days of purchase. No cash refunds.

The Store has had a name change: to Clothes Corner; and branches are located in the Pan Am Center in Fairfax, VA; the White Oak Shopping Center, and the Aspen Hill Shopping Center. It is part of an East Coast chain of women's clothing discounters.

Three Wishes
1633 Wisconsin Avenue
Washington, DC

Finding Three Wishes was a surprise for us — we must have passed it by at least a hundred times. But crammed into this little hole in the wall is an amazing variety of sportswear and sports gear for the whole family — all at discount prices, and some amazingly super bargains. In addition to all of the sports paraphernalia, this store also carries a variety of ladies' dresses, including Kay Winter — all with labels cut out. The secret of this store is that it serves as an outlet for a chain of well-known high quality New York stores, and everything in it is first quality, including many one-of-a-kind items and overbuys. All dresses are current, but other items, such as men's shirts, may be last year's or last season's merchandise. You can find the basics for many sports, lots of backpacks, totes, tennis balls, books on sports, and more. And they even take special orders. There is one unisex dressing room available.

Hours are Tuesday through Saturday from 11 am to 6 pm, closed Sunday, Monday, and holidays. Personal checks are accepted, as are American Express, Master Charge, and VISA. Layaways are permitted, with weekly payments required. They will hold items for up to 24 hours without a deposit. No cash refunds.

Tiffany House
1800-E Rockville Pike
Rockville, MD

When you can't afford a real antique Tiffany shade, then you may find yourself at Tiffany House buying a copy. Tiffany House is part of a regional chain of factory outlets which specialize in selling Tiffany-style shades in a variety of colors, styles, and sizes, and coordinated brasslike fixtures. The average savings is 60% off retail, and they guarantee the lowest price in the area. Everything is first quality. All lights come with a standard set-up, which includes 3 feet of chain, 4 feet of wiring, and a ceiling plate.

Open Monday, Thursday, and Friday from 10 am to 9 pm; Tuesday, Wednesday, and Saturday until 5 pm; and Sunday from noon to 5 pm. Personal checks are accepted, as are Master Charge, VISA, and NAC. Layaway and hold terms are negotiable. On returns, you can get merchandise credit or exchange for an item of equal or greater value than the one you returned. Parking is ample.

Tuesday Morning
4950 Wyaconda
Rockville, MD
770-5623

Tuesday Morning, part of a regional Dallas-based chain, is one of those treasure troves which, once discovered, will seem an indispensable source of dinner and kitchenware, gifts, and accessories. It is not open full-time, but four major sales are held per year — in March, June, September, and December; and merchandise is geared to the season of the sale. On a recent visit, we saw china, stoneware, stainless flatware, Scandinavian kitchen accessories, baskets, paper goods, toys, lucite bathroom accessories, napkins, trays, picture frames, crystal, glass decanters, bar glasses, linens and bedding, luggage, tote bags, cookware, brass and copper items, ceramics, ice buckets, and many more items. All were nationally known fine quality brands, at prices 50% to 75% below retail. Most are first quality.

Other location:
Soon to open in Virginia. Call number above or (214) 387-3562

Opening day of a sale, the hours are 8 am to 8 pm. After that, Monday through Saturday from 9 am to 6 pm, and Sunday from 11 am to 6 pm. Personal checks are accepted, as are Master Charge and VISA. There are no layaways. Return policy is extremely liberal Parking is ample.

U.S. Merchandise Mart
5055 Nicholson Lane
Rockville, MD
881-3050

This store is everything the name "Merchandise Mart" implies — it is a true market for everything for the home and for home decorating, including furniture, appliances, wallpaper, drapery, shades, bedding, and carpeting — all of medium to high quality — with top-of-the-line brands like Baker, Kittinger, and General Electric. You can expect to save an average of 20% to 40% off list price. All merchandise is first quality, and there are many factory closeouts. You can order from the many catalogues available, or you can choose bedding or large appliances which are in stock. Bedding brands include Englander and Serta. The Mart offers a price-beating policy on appliances. The finest carpet lines are represented here, and you can buy televisions, and even diamonds (by appointment) at this multifaceted store. Upstairs on the second floor are many greatly reduced floor models. Delivery is available. And there is a full guarantee on everything. Sales are frequent: for inventory clearance, on floor samples, or on factory closeouts. There is no mailing list. The Mart has a Consumer Bulletin Board with government, manufacturer, and designer information, ratings, and ideas about the many products they sell.

Monday, Tuesday, Thursday, and Friday from 10 am to 8 pm; Wednesday and Saturday until 5 pm; Friday from noon to 8 pm. Personal checks are accepted. Merchandise can be returned if defective.

Villa Roel
102 N. Lee Street
Alexandria, VA
683-4260

The Villa Roel is a charming and attractive store which specializes in kitchen and dining room accoutrements and accessories, from the finest quality china, earthenware, crystal, and kitchen gadgets to more moderately priced lines. While Villa Roel does not bill itself as a discount store, it sells all of these items at surprisingly reasonble prices, usualy within 10% to 15% less than suggested retail prices. Most merchandise is in stock, but they will take special orders, for which they request a 50% down payment.

Other location:
Opening July 1, 1980: 922 19th Street, NW, Washington, DC

Hours are Monday through Saturday, from 10 am to 9 pm, and Sunday from 12 to 6 pm, in Alexandria. Washington store hours will differ. They accept personal checks, Master Charge, VISA, and Central Charge. Items can be taken out of the store on approval. Store credit or exchanges are made on returns. In Alexandria, they are members of the Park and Shop lot, directly across Lee Street from the store.

Wallpaper Boutique
6035 Chatsworth Lane
Bethesda, MD
530-1310

In two lovely homes in Maryland, there is a store well worth discovering — not only for wallpaper, as the name implies, but for anything at all concerned with home decorating. Not only can you find a range in quality from the finest designer wallpaper, carpets, blinds, shades, vertical blinds, shutters, drapery and upholstery fabrics, and custom spreads, to the least expensive lines; you can also expect to save anywhere from 25% up off the suggested list prices. Nothing is in stock, but the number of sample books they have is overwhelming. Discounts start at 25% and run up to 33%, depending on the quantity purchased and the price. You get best prices on the house selections. And by buying from the Wallpaper Boutique, you are guaranteed the lowest prices: even when a manufacturer's sale is run at other shops, the Boutique's owners can still save you 10% to 15% of the sale cost.

Other location:
9925 Bedfordshire Court, Potomac, MD, 350-2245

Hours are by appointment and Monday through Saturday from 10 am to 1 pm — always call first. Personal checks are now accepted, and credit cards will be soon. Mail orders are available. On custom made items, there are no returns.

386   *Inflation Fighter's Guide*

To locate a store with a street address in: See this map:

Alexandria	Alexandria
Annandale	Annandale/Landmark
Arlington	Arlington, some in Alexandria
Baltimore	Baltimore City or Baltimore Area
Baileys Crossroads	Falls Church
Beltsville	Silver Spring
Bethesda	Bethesda/Wheaton/Kensington
Bladensburg	Central Prince George's
Burke	Springfield
Cheverly	Central Prince George's
Cockeysville	Baltimore Area
College Park	Central Prince George's
Cottage City	Central Prince George's
Elkridge	Baltimore Area
Fairfax	Fairfax
Falls Church	Falls Church
Forestville	Southern Prince George's
Fredericksburg	Metro Area
Gaithersburg	Rockville/Gaithersburg
Germantown	Metro Area
Glen Burnie	Baltimore Area
Hyattsville	Central Prince George's
Kensington	Bethesda/Wheaton/Kensington
Landmark	Annandale/Landmark
Landover	Central Prince George's
Langley Park	Silver Spring
Lanham	Central Prince George's
Laurel	Metro Area
Linthicum Heights	Baltimore Area
Manassas	Manassas
Marlow Heights	Southern Prince George's
McLean	Tysons
Merrifield	Fairfax
New Carrollton	Central Prince George's
Oxon Hill	Southern Prince George's
Reisterstown	Baltimore Area
Rockville	Rockville/Gaithersburg
Seabrook	Central Prince George's
Seat Pleasant	Central Prince George's
Seven Corners	Falls Church
Shirlington	Alexandria/Shirlington
Silver Hill	Southern Prince George's
Silver Spring	Silver Spring
Springfield	Springfield
Suitland	Southern Prince George's
Takoma Park	Silver Spring
Timonium	Baltimore Area
Tysons Corner	Tysons
Vienna	Tysons
Warrenton	Metro Area
Washington	Washington, DC or Downtown Washington
Wheaton	Bethesda/Wheaton/Kensington
Woodbridge	Metro Area

Maps

The maps in this section were prepared to help you find all of the stores which are discussed throughout the book. The Washington metro area was split up into a number of separate regions according to the rough concentration of stores. The scale on each map is different because of this. The stores which are located on each map are listed alphabetically in the accompanying legend. Should you require more information about the store, refer to the index at the back of the book, which lists the number of the page upon which the store description can be found. For areas which are crowded with stores, one number is often used to represent a general area. Once you have reached this general area, you should have no trouble finding the store. This method has been used in cases such as the Rockville Pike and Randolph Road area of Rockville, which is congested with stores offering discounts.

Providing the finest in professional real estate services.
MANARIN ODLE AND RECTOR
REALTORS
277 SOUTH WASHINGTON STREET   ALEXANDRIA, VIRGINIA 22314
(703) 549-8200

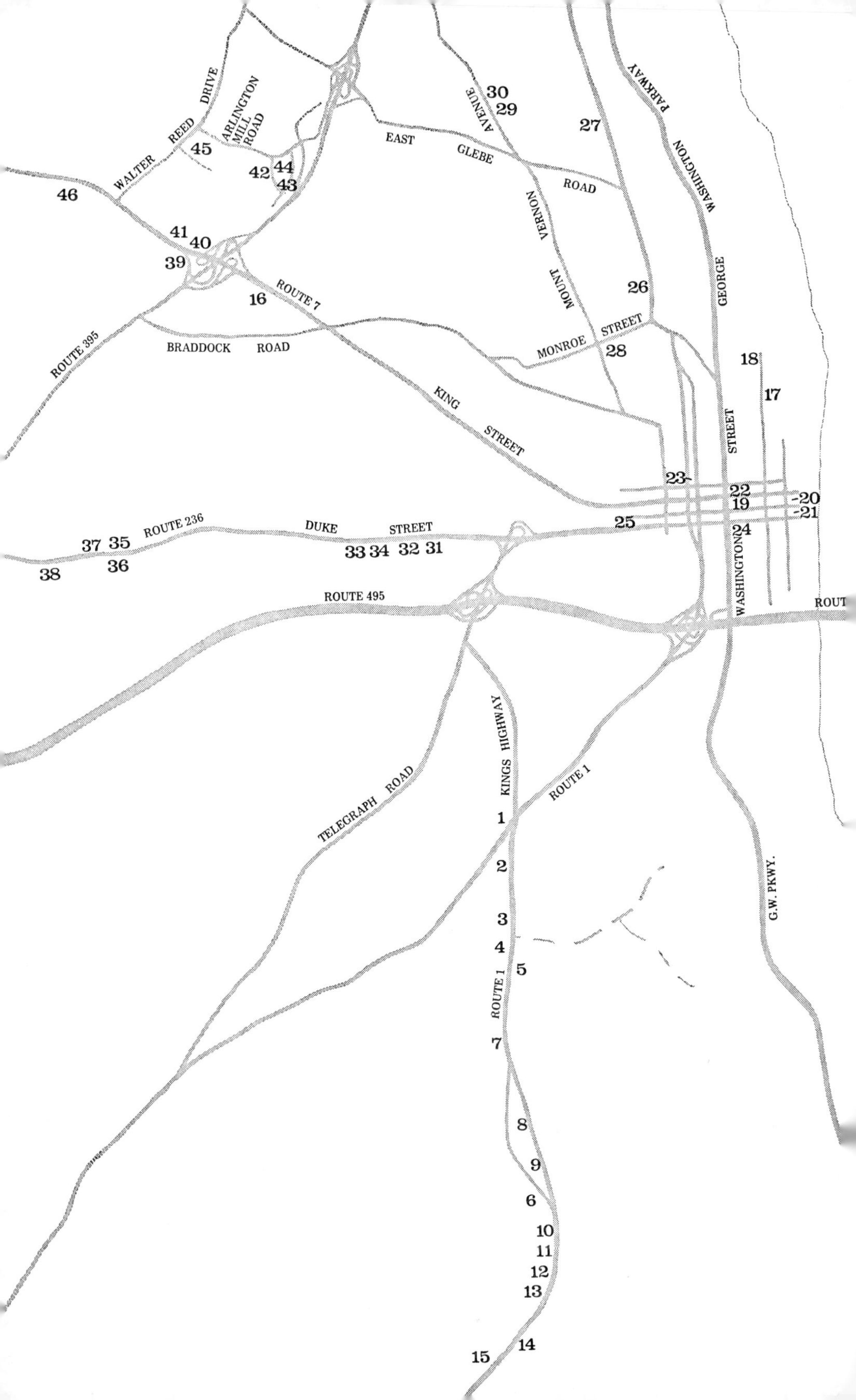

WALTER REED DRIVE
ARLINGTON MILL ROAD
EAST GLEBE ROAD
MOUNT VERNON AVENUE
GEORGE WASHINGTON PARKWAY
ROUTE 7
BRADDOCK ROAD
MONROE STREET
ROUTE 395
KING STREET
ROUTE 236
DUKE STREET
ROUTE 495
WASHINGTON STREET
ROUT
KINGS HIGHWAY
ROUTE 1
TELEGRAPH ROAD
G.W. PKWY.
1
2
3
4
5
6
7
8
9
10
11
12
13
14
15
16
17
18
19
20
21
22
23
24
25
26
27
28
29
30
31
32
33
34
35
36
37
38
39
40
41
42
43
44
45
46

ALEXANDRIA

45 Abbington Design Associates, 2709 S. Wakefield
15 Amp Auto Parts, 8655 Richmond Highway
23 Allstate Carpets, Cameron and Henry Streets
29 Arlandria Carpet, 3825 Mt. Vernon Avenue
44 The Back Door of David's Village Store, 4047 28th Street South
42 Best Products, 2800 S. Randolph Street
41 Belmont TV, King Street
5 Bedding and Furniture Discount Center, 6801 Richmond Highway
11 Bill's Carpet, 7812 Richmond Highway
33 Carpetland, 3240 Duke Street
8 Color Tile, 7500 Richmond Highway
2 Decor Furniture
34 Decorative Rugs and Carpets
43 Desks & Furnishings Clearance Center, 2810 S. Quincy Street
32 DeVaris Fabrics, 3104 Duke Street
42 Discount Typewriters, 2758 South Randolph Street
16 Fashion Action, 3672 King Street
46 Fabric Guying Service
20 Frocks at the Docks
43 General Store, 2800 South Quincy Street
6 George's, Hybla Valley
35 Hi Gear, Shirley Duke Shopping Center
4 Hit or Miss, 6770 Richmond Highway
30 Home Tile, 3903 Mt. Vernon Avenue
9 Home Tile, 7684A Richmond Highway
12 House of Shoes, 7822 Richmond Highway
18 Interstate Office Supply

3 Juvenile Sales, 6612 Richmond Highway
1 King's Smarten Up, Penn Daw Plaza
42 Lamps Unlimited Clearance Outlet, Shirlington Shopping Center
36 Luskin's, 5150 Duke Street
22 Marboro Books, King Street
27 Market Tire, 3300 Jeff. Davis Highway
31 Mattress Discounters, 3000 Duke Street
19 Medco Drugs, 605 King Street
37 Merchants Tire and Auto, 5220 Duke Street
4 Minnesota Fabrics, 6702 Richmond Highway
25 Morris Katz and Sons, Prince St.
10 Nationwide Tire, 7800 Richmond Highway
21 Old Towne Gemstones, Prince Street
7 Penguin Feathers, 7116 Richmond Highway
28 Penn Jersey, 1501 Mt. Vernon Avenue
15 Penn Jersey, 8853 Richmond Highway
6 Pop Shoppe, 7802 Richmond Highway
24 Professional Bookcenter, 226 S. Washington Street
39 Schwartz Tailors, 4618 King Street
17 Second Story Books, 816 N. Fairfax Street
44 Sloane's Clearance Center
44 Ted Louis Clearance Center, Shirlington Shopping Center
13 Tunz A Fun, 7844 Richmond Highway
38 Universal Beauty Supply, 5235 Duke Street,
26 Walmer's Doll House Factory, Jeff. Davis Highway

ROUTE 495
ANNANDALE ROAD
COLUMBIA PIKE
9
10
13
11
14
12
LITTLE RIVER TURNPIKE
6
7
BACKLICK ROAD
DUKE STREET
VAN DORN
STREET
4
1
8
5
3
2
BRADDOCK ROAD
ROUTE 395
ROUTE 495
ROUTE 495

ANNANDALE/LANDMARK

13 Baths Etc. Value Center, Little River Center
4 Carpet Bargains, 304 S. Pickett
13 Carpeteria, 7422 Little River Turnpike
1 Dinette World, 4558 Eisenhower
6 Evans Catalouge Showroom, 6200 Little River Turnpike
12 Juvenile Sales, 4415 John Marr
13 Lamp and Shade Center, Little River Center
1 Lee Furniture Warehouse, 4596 Eisenhower
6 Marshall's, Route 236 at I-395
12 Merchants Tire and Auto, 4206 John Marr
9 Minnesota Fabrics, 7343 Columbia Pike
2 The Parts Place, 5408 Eisenhower
14 Penguin Feathers, 7345 Little River Turnpike
3 Performance Discount Tire, 5426 Eisenhower
5 Rug Man, 648 S. Pickett
7 Sam's Tailoring, 6245 Little River Turnpike
10 Springfield Surplus, 4220 Annandale Road
8 3 Rs Book Store, 5111 Backlick Road
11 Vacuums Unlimited, 4229 Annandale Road
4 Warehouse Sleep Centers, 366 S. Pickett

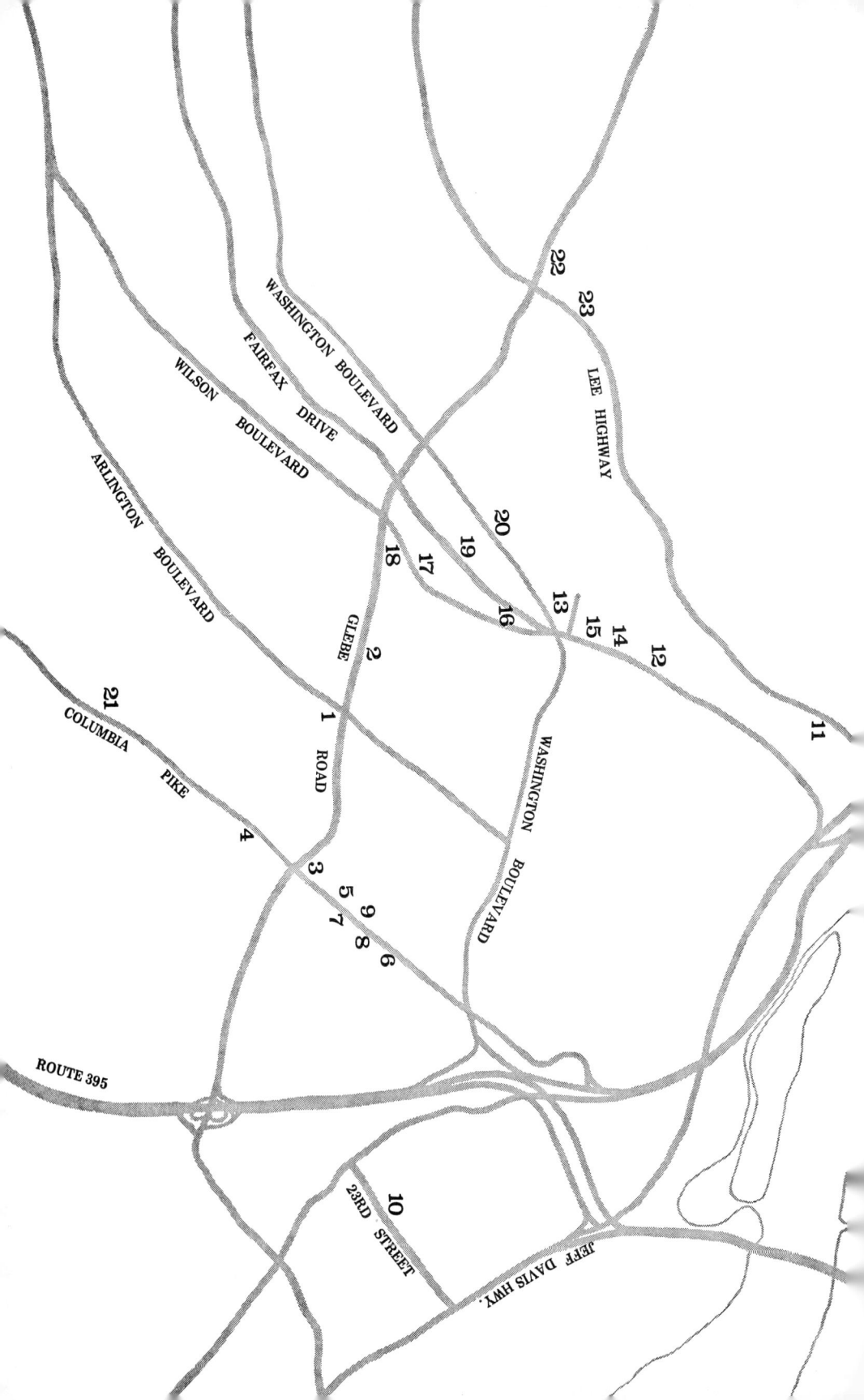

WASHINGTON BOULEVARD
FAIRFAX DRIVE
WILSON BOULEVARD
ARLINGTON BOULEVARD
LEE HIGHWAY
COLUMBIA PIKE
GLEBE ROAD
WASHINGTON BOULEVARD
23RD STREET
JEFF DAVIS HWY.
ROUTE 395

ARLINGTON

15 ABC Liquidators, 3185 Wilson Blvd.
13 Antiquities Brass Beds and Bedding, 1114 N. Irving St.
8 Associated Carpets and Interiors, 2630 Columbia Pike
12 Baby Products, 2731 Wilson Blvd.
22 Discount Fabrics, 2219 N. Glebe Road
4 Erol's, 3610 Columbia Pike
21 Fabrics Unlimited, 5015 Columbia Pike
3 Georgetown Carpet, Columbia Pike & Glebe Rd.
7 Giant Music Centers, 2615 Columbia Pike
18 Hecht's Parkington Warehouse Store, Wilson Blvd. and Glebe Rd.
16 Home Tile, 3409 Wilson Blvd.
14 Luskin's, 2901 Wilson Blvd.
17 Market Tire, 4125 Wilson Blvd.
19 Mattress Center, 3451 N. Fairfax Drive
23 Merchants Tire and Auto, 4801 Lee Highway
11 Merchants Tire and Auto, 1503 Lee Highway
6 Military Personnel Buying Service, 2516 Columbia Pike
9 Shoe Box, 2809 Columbia Pike
20 Surplus Center, 3451 N. Washington Blvd.
2 Vacuums Unlimited, 311 N. Glebe Rd.
5 , Wall Street Clothing, 932 S. Walter Reed Dr. at Columbia Pike
10 Zavarella's Music, 507 23rd St. S.

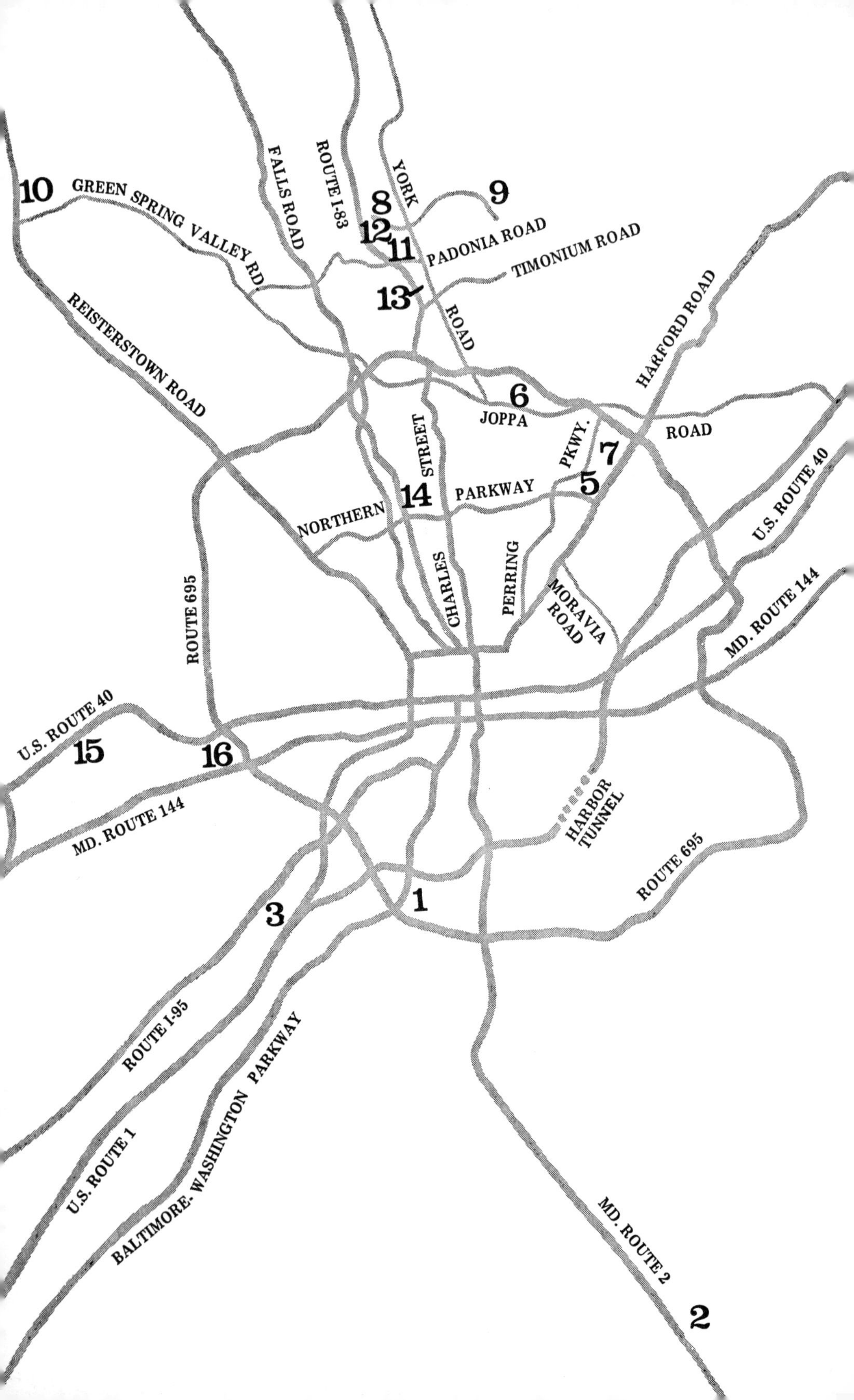
10
GREEN SPRING VALLEY RD.
FALLS ROAD
ROUTE I-83
YORK ROAD
8
9
12
11
PADONIA ROAD
TIMONIUM ROAD
13
REISTERSTOWN ROAD
HARFORD ROAD
6
JOPPA ROAD
PKWY.
7
STREET
5
14
NORTHERN PARKWAY
U.S. ROUTE 40
PERRING
CHARLES
MORAVIA ROAD
ROUTE 695
MD. ROUTE 144
U.S. ROUTE 40
15
16
MD. ROUTE 144
HARBOR TUNNEL
ROUTE 695
1
3
ROUTE I-95
U.S. ROUTE 1
BALTIMORE-WASHINGTON PARKWAY
MD. ROUTE 2
2

BALTIMORE AREA

13 Anders of Timonium, Green Spring Drive
1 Anders of Baltimore, 821 Oregon Avenue, Linthicum Heights
12 Ambach Mill Outlet, York Road, Cockeysville
4 Bata Shoe Warehouse, 6677 Moravia Park Drive
2 Bata Shoe Warehouse, 125 Penrod Court, Glen Burnie
15 The Clothes Connection, 16 Normandy Shopping Center, Ellicott City
8 The Clothes Outlet, 22A Church Lane, Cockeysville
2 Color Tile, 315 Ritchie Highway, Glen Burnie
6 Gordon Miller Music, 8802 Orchard Tree Lane
7 Harford Men's Shop, 6818 Harford Road
16 Hudson Wallpaper, Catonsville
14 The In Outlet Shop, 5730 Falls Road
10 Modern Photographic Supply, 140 Chartley Road, Reisterstown
11 Place Setting Outlet, York & Padonia Roads, Cockeysville
3 Stereo Discounters Warehouse, 6730 Santa Barbara Court, Elkridge
9 Tee to Green Golf Shop, 582 Cranbrook, Cockeysville
5 Triple S Discount Center, Perring Parkway Shopping Center
2 Triple S Discount Fabric Center, 8090 Ritchie Highway, Glen Burnie

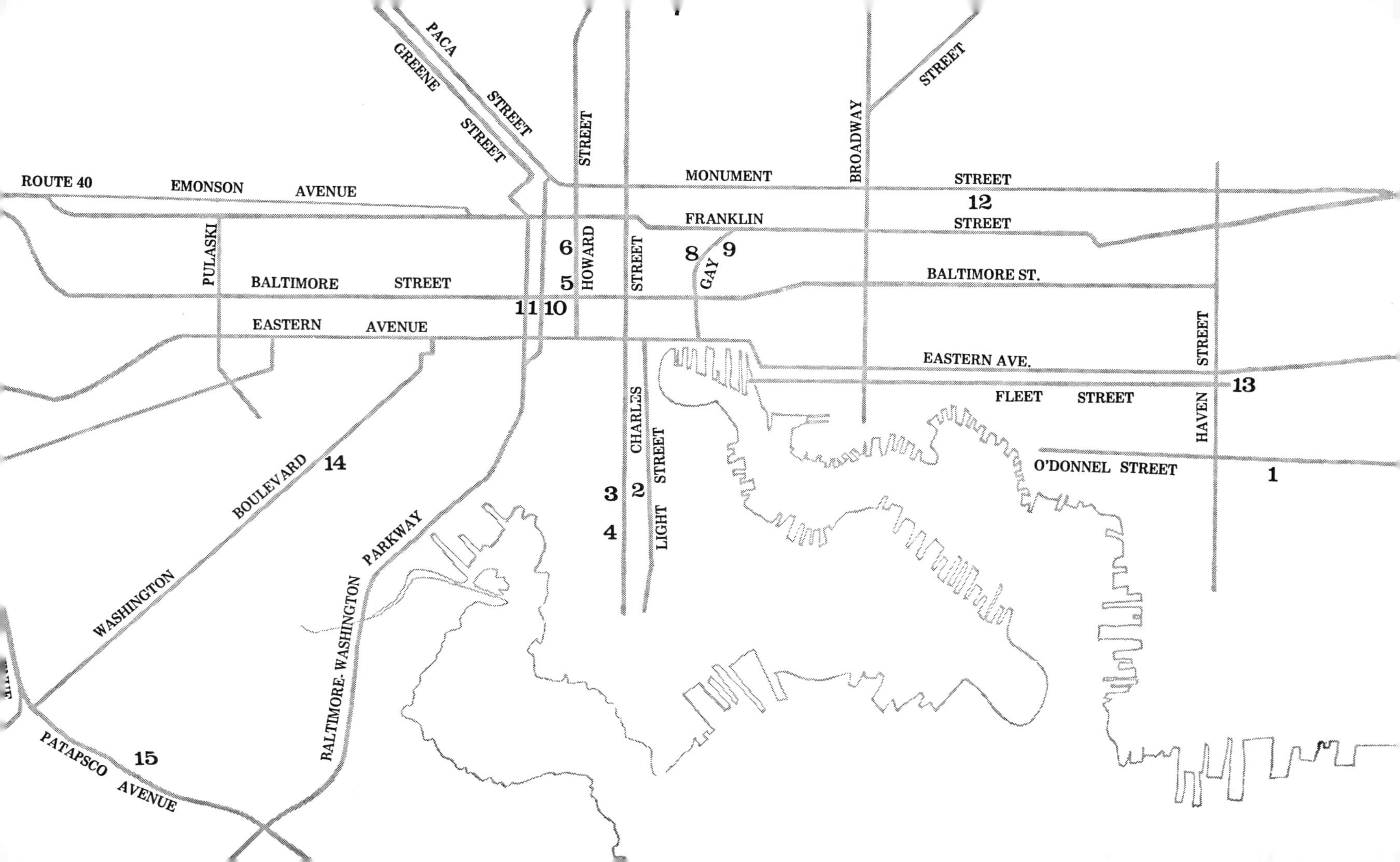
ROUTE 40
EMONSON AVENUE
PACA STREET
GREENE STREET
STREET
MONUMENT STREET
BROADWAY
STREET
12
FRANKLIN STREET
PULASKI
BALTIMORE STREET
6
5
HOWARD STREET
STREET
8
9
GAY
BALTIMORE ST.
11
10
EASTERN AVENUE
EASTERN AVE.
FLEET STREET
HAVEN STREET
13
O'DONNEL STREET
1
CHARLES
3
2
4
LIGHT STREET
14
BOULEVARD
WASHINGTON
PARKWAY
BALTIMORE-WASHINGTON
PATAPSCO AVENUE
15

BALTIMORE CITY

2 Dan Brothers Discount Men's Shoes, 1016 Light Street
2 Dan Brothers Discount Men's Shoes, 1032 S. Charles Street
14 Debois Textile Mill Outlet, 1835 Washington Blvd.
10 Glenbrook Coat Company, 333 W. Baltimore Street, 4th Floor
12 Greenbaum's, 2200 E. Monument Street
5 Greenbaum's, 104 N. Howard
6 Hess Shoe Bargain Box, 318 N. Howard Street
7 Max Rubin Factory Outlet, 113 W. North Avenue
13 Montgomery Ward Catalogue Surplus Store, Fleet & S. Haven Sts.
9 Sam Glass and Sons, 301 N. Gay Street
11 Sam Oidick, 413 W. Baltimore Street
8 Simon Harris Sporting Goods and Hardware, 200 N. Gay Street
15 Stofberg Bros. Inc., 2626 W. Patapsco
16 T.I. Swartz, 600 S. Pulaski Street
1 Triple S Discount Fabric Center, 4701 O'Donnell St.

LAMBERTON
DRIVE
11
ARCOLA AVENUE
BOULEVARD
VEIRS
10
MILL
ROAD
8
GEORGIA
AVENUE
UNIVERSITY
RANDOLPH ROAD
MILL
ROAD
9
PLYERS
HOWARD
KNOWLES
DETRICK
CONNECTICUT
AVENUE
ROUTE I-270
7
HIGHWAY
DEMOCRACY
BOULEVARD
OLD
GEORGETOWN
ROAD
CORDELL
FAIRMONT
EAST-WEST
ROUTE 495
4
6
5
BETHESDA
AVENUE
BRADLEY
BOULEVARD
1
2

Maps 399

BETHESDA/WHEATON/KENSINGTON

8 Attic Books, 2442 Ennals
5 Bethesda Ave. Coop, 4949 Bethesda Avenue
8 Catalogs Unlimited, 11151 Georgia Avenue
2 China Closet, 6807 Wisconsin Avenue
7 Christina's, Wildwood Shopping Center, 10251 Old Georgetown
9 Circuit City, 10530 Detrick Avenue
1 Circuit City, 6932 Wisconsin Avenue
8 Crazy Sally's, 2309 University Blvd. West
6 Crown Books, East-West Highway at Wisconsin Avenue
8 Crown Books, 11181 Veirs Mill Road at Wheaton Plaza
12 Discount Records and Books, 5454 Wisconsin Avenue
7 Fashion Tree, 10231 Old Georgetown Road, Wildwood Shopping Center
8 G. W. Imirie, Inc., 1322 Fern Street
4 G. W. Imirie, Inc., 4949 Fairmont
4 Jay's Designer Discounts, 7750 Woodmont
8 Juvenile Sales, 2321 University Blvd. West
8 Lee's Dinettes, 11201 Grandview Avenue
11 Kemp Mill Records, 1351 Lamberton
1 Lu Ann Warehouse, 6930 Wisconsin Avenue
8 Luskin's, 11305 Georgia Avenue
13 Marty's Auto Radio, 2412-14 University Blvd. W.
9 The Math Box II, 2627 University Blvd. West
4 Merchants Tire and Auto, 7851 Old Georgetown Road
8 Nationwide Tire, 11149 Veirs Mill Road
4 Nationwide Tires, Old Georgetown Road at Cordell Street
8 Penn Jersey, 2655 University Blvd. West
3 P. J. Nee, 7126 Wisconsin Avenue
10 Rodman's Discount Drugs, Randolph and Veirs Mill Roads
4 The Shoe Horn, 7770 Woodmont Avenue
7 Shoe Stop, Wildwood Shopping Center
14 The Store, Aspen Hill Shopping Center
4 Super Surplus Centers, 8008 Wisconsin Avenue
9 United Floor and Wallcoverings Inc., 3923 Plyers Mill Road

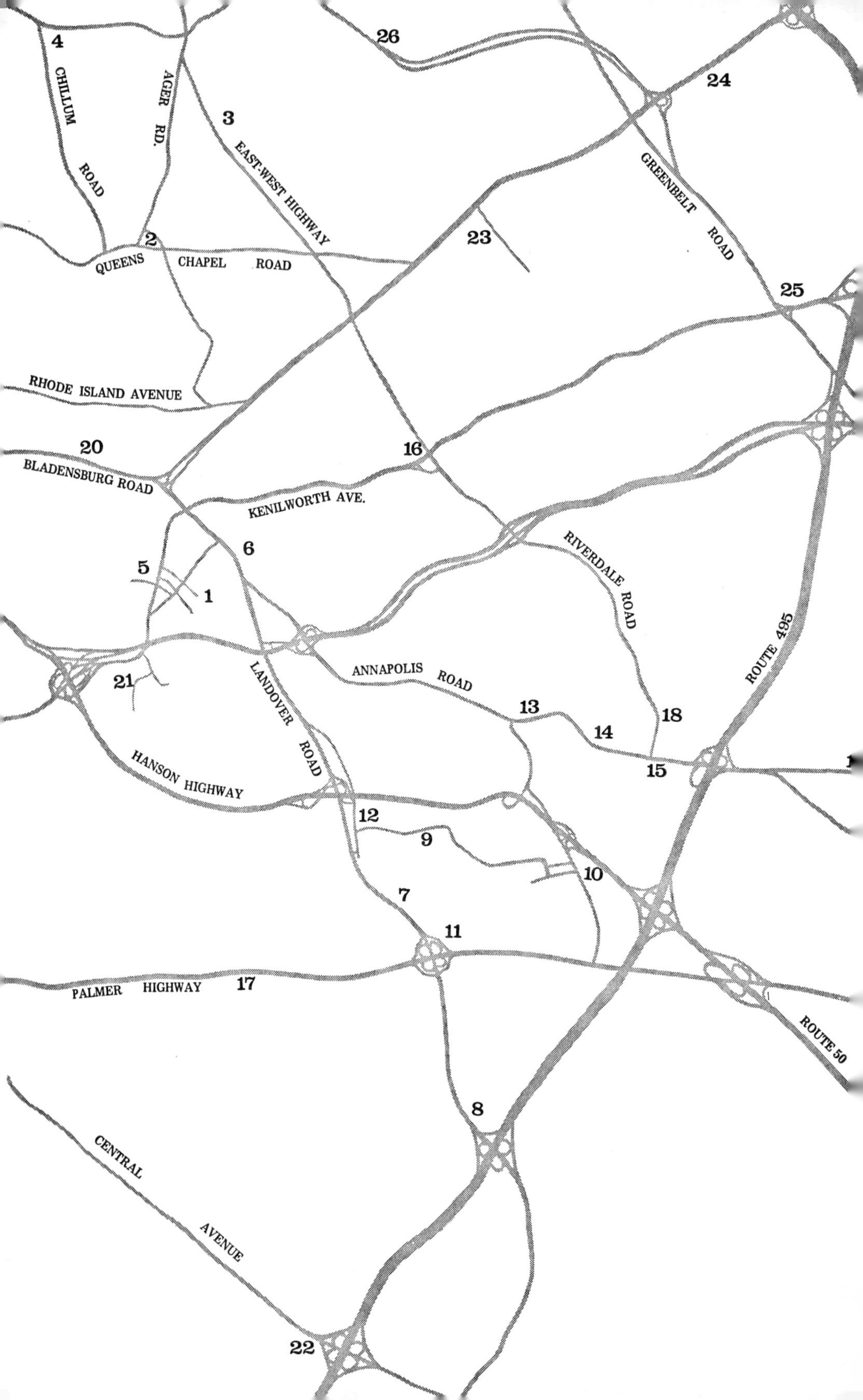
4
CHILLUM ROAD
AGER RD.
3
EAST-WEST HIGHWAY
26
24
GREENBELT ROAD
23
2
QUEENS CHAPEL ROAD
25
RHODE ISLAND AVENUE
20
BLADENSBURG ROAD
16
KENILWORTH AVE.
6
RIVERDALE ROAD
5
1
ROUTE 495
21
ANNAPOLIS ROAD
LANDOVER ROAD
13
18
14
15
HANSON HIGHWAY
12
9
10
7
11
PALMER HIGHWAY
17
ROUTE 50
8
CENTRAL AVENUE
22

CENTRAL PRINCE GEORGE'S

25 ABC Liquidators, 6419 Marlboro Pike
10 Ardmore Discount Auto Parts, 8520 Ardwick Admore Road
17 Ardmore Discount Auto Parts, 6737 Palmer Highway
18 Best Products, 7710 Riverdale Road
15 Beltway Kawasaki, 8807 Annapolis Road
13 Carpet Barn, 7423 Annapolis Road,
5 CED Prince George's Electric, 4822 Lawrence Street
26 Color Tile, 2012 University Boulevard
23 Contemporary Sounds, 7418 Baltimore Boulevard
9 Cort Furniture Rental Clearance Center, 3137 Pennsy Drive
27 Crouch Music Store, 5817 Baltimore Avenue
6 Custom Bedding, 4826 Annapolis Road
24 Dinette Gallery, 9213 Baltimore Blvd.
2 Discount Auto Parts, 2490 Chillum Road
2 Discount Beauty Supply, 3116 Hamilton, Hyattsville
26 Discount Rugs and Carpets, 6222 Baltimore Blvd.
13 Fabric Man, 7401 Annapolis Road
16 Fashion Action, 5831 Riverdale Road
25 Fashion Factory, Beltway Plaza Mall
7 Furniture World Factory Outlet, 7329 Landover Road
8 General Store, Landover/K-Mart Plaza
25 George's, 6192 Greenbelt Road
3 Hi Gear, Chillum Terrace Shopping Center
13 Hi Gear, 7454 Annapolis Road
11 Hi Gear, Dodge Park Shopping Center
19 Home Tile, 9350 Lanham Severn Road
13 House of Shoes, 7432 Annapolis Road
23 Kemp Mill Records, 7417 Baltimore Boulevard

15 Lamps Unlimited, Carrollton Mall
2 Luskin's, Landover Mall
15 Market Tire, 8801 Annapolis Road
22 Market Tire, Hampton Mall
23 Maryland Book Exchange, 4500 College Avenue
23 The Math Box I, 4431 Lehigh Road
13 Mattress Discounters, 7430 Annapolis Road
4 Merchants Tire and Auto, 909 Chillum at Riggs Road
14 Merchants Tire and Auto, 7911 Annapolis Road
8 Minnesota Fabrics, Landover Plaza, 8575 Landover Road
12 Montgomery Ward Bargain Room Sales, 7100 Old Landover Road
15 Nationwide Tire, 8511 Annapolis Road
20 Nationwide Tire, 3550 Bladensburg Road
1 Paper Mart, 5214 Monroe, Hyattsville
16 Penn Jersey, 5614 Kenilworth Avenue, Riverdale
2 Penn Jersey, 5407 Ager Road, Hyattsville
7 Penn Jersey, 7511 Landover Road
23 Performance Discount Tire, 5103 College Ave.
26 Rodman's Discount Drugs, 2510 University Blvd. E.
16 Russell Stover Factory Outlet, Riverdale Plaza
16 Slumberland, 5620 Kenilworth Avenue
15 Star Vacuum Cleaners, 8815 Annapolis Road
24 Surplus Electronics, 9600 Baltimore Avenue
2 Tire Man, 2901 Hamilton, Hyattsville
15 Toys R Us, 8201 Annapolis Road
21 University Tire, 2509 Schuster Drive
25 Veneman Music, 6000 Greenbelt Road
14 W. Bell and Co., 7933 Annapolis Road
12 Wholesale Carpets, 6605 Old Landover Road

Map

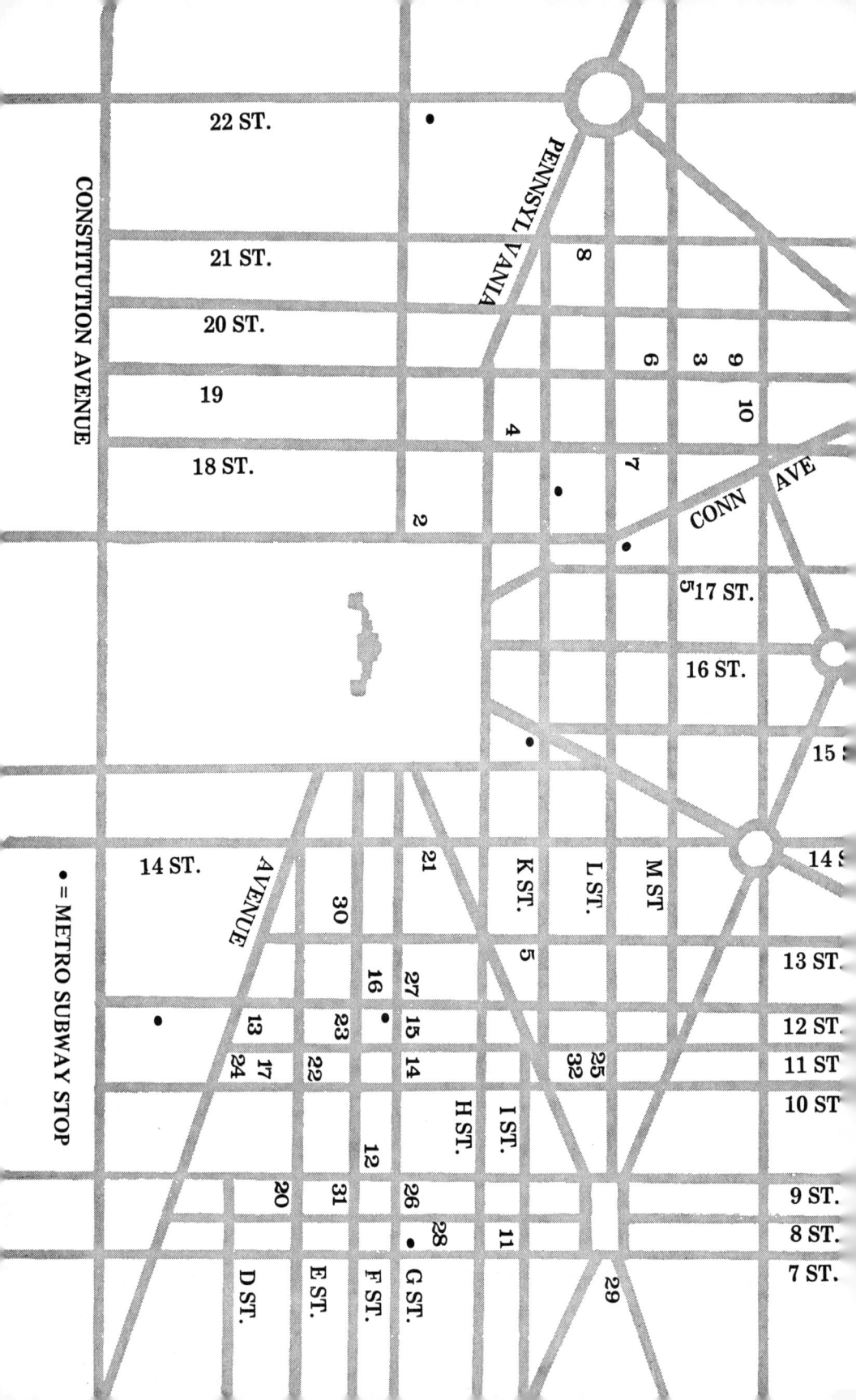

CONSTITUTION AVENUE

22 ST.
21 ST.
20 ST.
19
18 ST.
17 ST.
16 ST.
15
14

PENNSYLVANIA
CONN AVE

14 ST.
13 ST.
12 ST.
11 ST
10 ST
9 ST.
8 ST.
7 ST.

K ST.
L ST.
M ST.
H ST.
I ST.

D ST.
E ST.
F ST.
G ST.

AVENUE

● = METRO SUBWAY STOP

Numbered points on map: 2, 3, 4, 5, 6, 7, 8, 9, 10, 11, 12, 13, 14, 15, 16, 17, 20, 21, 22, 23, 24, 25, 26, 27, 28, 29, 30, 31, 32

DOWNTOWN WASHINGTON

16 Attic, Phillipsborn Retail Outlet, 1201 F St. NW
8 Crown Books, 21st and K Sts. NW
2 Crown Books, 17th and G Sts. NW
30 Dash's Designer, 1308 F St. NW
10 For Eyes, 1829 M St. NW
26 G Street Remnant Shop, G Street between 8th and 9th Sts. NW
31 George's, 816 F St. NW
11 General Store, 810 7th Street NW
7 Jos. A. Bank Clothier, 1015 18th St. NW
22 Linn Maternity, 513 11th St. NW
27 Luggage Center/Surplus Sales, 714 12th St. NW
4 Medco, 812 18th St. NW
12 Medco, 914 F St. NW
13 Medco, 1107 Pennsylvania Ave. NW
14 Medco, 717 11th St. NW
15 Medco, 1113 G St. NW
25 Office Furniture, 1206 K St. NW
5 Office Furniture Mart, 1680 L St. NW
28 Office Furniture Mart, 728 7th St. NW
17 Penn Camera, 414 10th St. NW
6 Record and Tape Ltd./Book Annex, 19th and L Sts. NW
32 Reliable Home Appliance, 919 11th St. NW
21 Seventh Heaven, F St. between 11th and 12th Sts. NW
20 Sunny's Surplus, 14th and H Sts. NW
24 Tanen's, 409 11th St. NW
3 T.H. Mandy, 1118 19th St. NW
9 W. Bell and Co., 19th and L Sts. NW

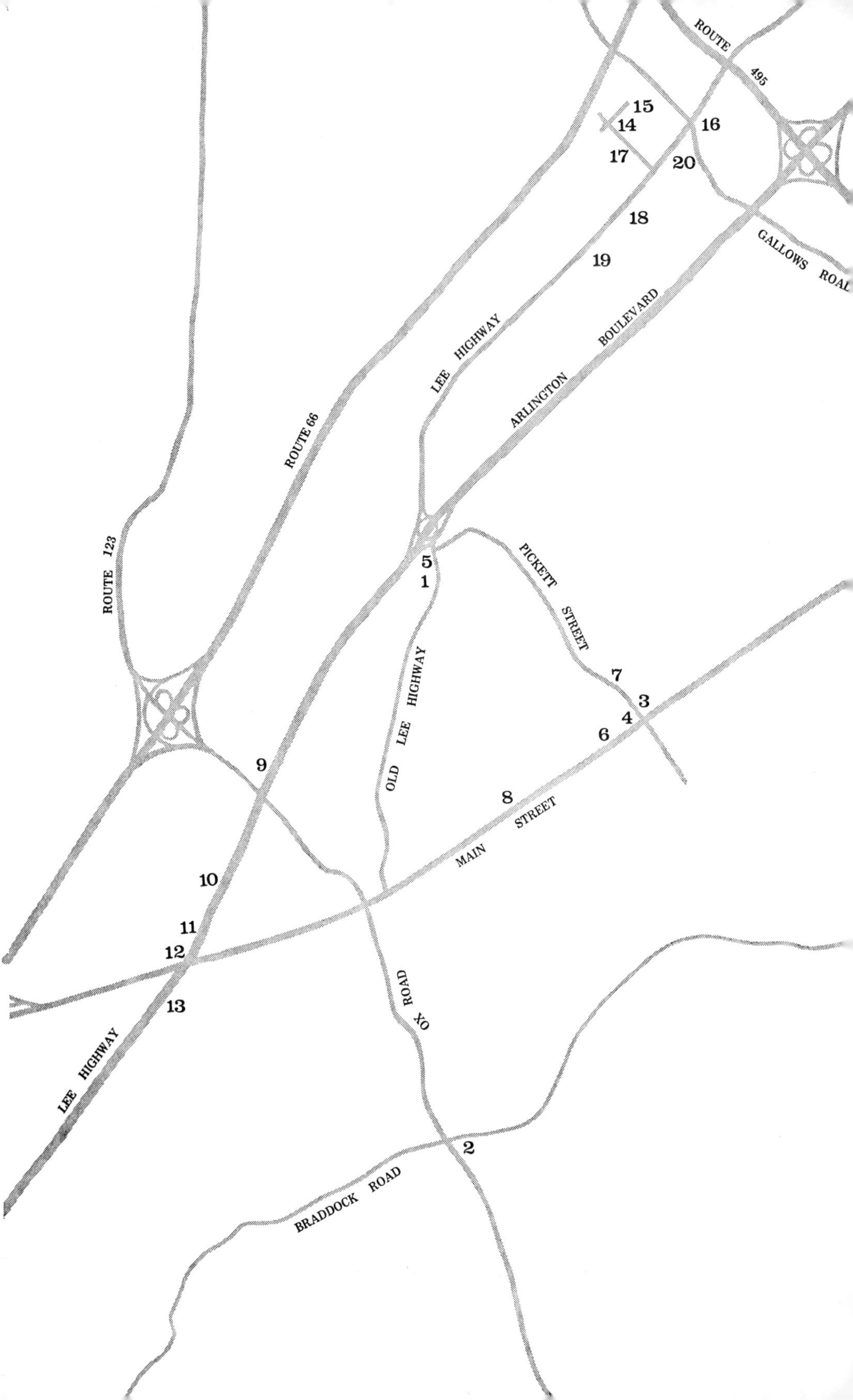

ROUTE 495
GALLOWS ROAD
15
14
16
17
20
18
19
LEE HIGHWAY
ARLINGTON BOULEVARD
ROUTE 66
ROUTE 123
5
1
PICKETT STREET
OLD LEE HIGHWAY
7
3
4
6
9
8
MAIN STREET
10
11
12
13
OX ROAD
LEE HIGHWAY
2
BRADDOCK ROAD

FAIRFAX

- 20 Bargain Tire, 8217 Lee Highway
- 2 Bazaar Knitting, 9543 Braddock Road
- 15 Beck Arnley Auto Parts, 2740A Gallows Road
- 21 Bill's Carpet, 10980 Lee Highway
- 9 Cardinal Lighting, 10358 Lee Highway
- 3 Custom Carpets, Turnpike Pickett Shopping Center
- 7 Economy Auto Parts, 3855 Pickett Street
- 11 Fairfax Auto Parts, 10912 Lee Highway
- 19 Fairfax Auto Parts, 8701 Lee Highway
- 3 Giant Music, 9416 Main Street
- 18 Interstate Electric, 8435 Lee Highway
- 4 Kidswear Outlet, 9540B Main Street
- 5 Lamp and Shade Center, 9691 Lee Highway
- 6 Math Box III, Fair City Mall
- 11 Market Tire, 10784 Lee Highway
- 16 Mattress Discounters, 2831 Gallows Road
- 6 Minnesota Fabrics, Fair City Mall
- 1 Record Lords, Old Lee Highway
- 9 Rodman's Discount Drugs, 10362 Lee Highway
- 17 Stanis Furniture, 2800 Dorr Ave.
- 13 Toys R Us, 11151 Lee Highway
- 8 Turnpike House Furniture, 9960 Main Street
- 17 Universal Beauty Supply Co., 2800 A Dorr Avenue
- 14 Universal Tire, 8304 Merrifield Avenue
- 5 Warehouse Sleep Centers, 9629 Lee Highway

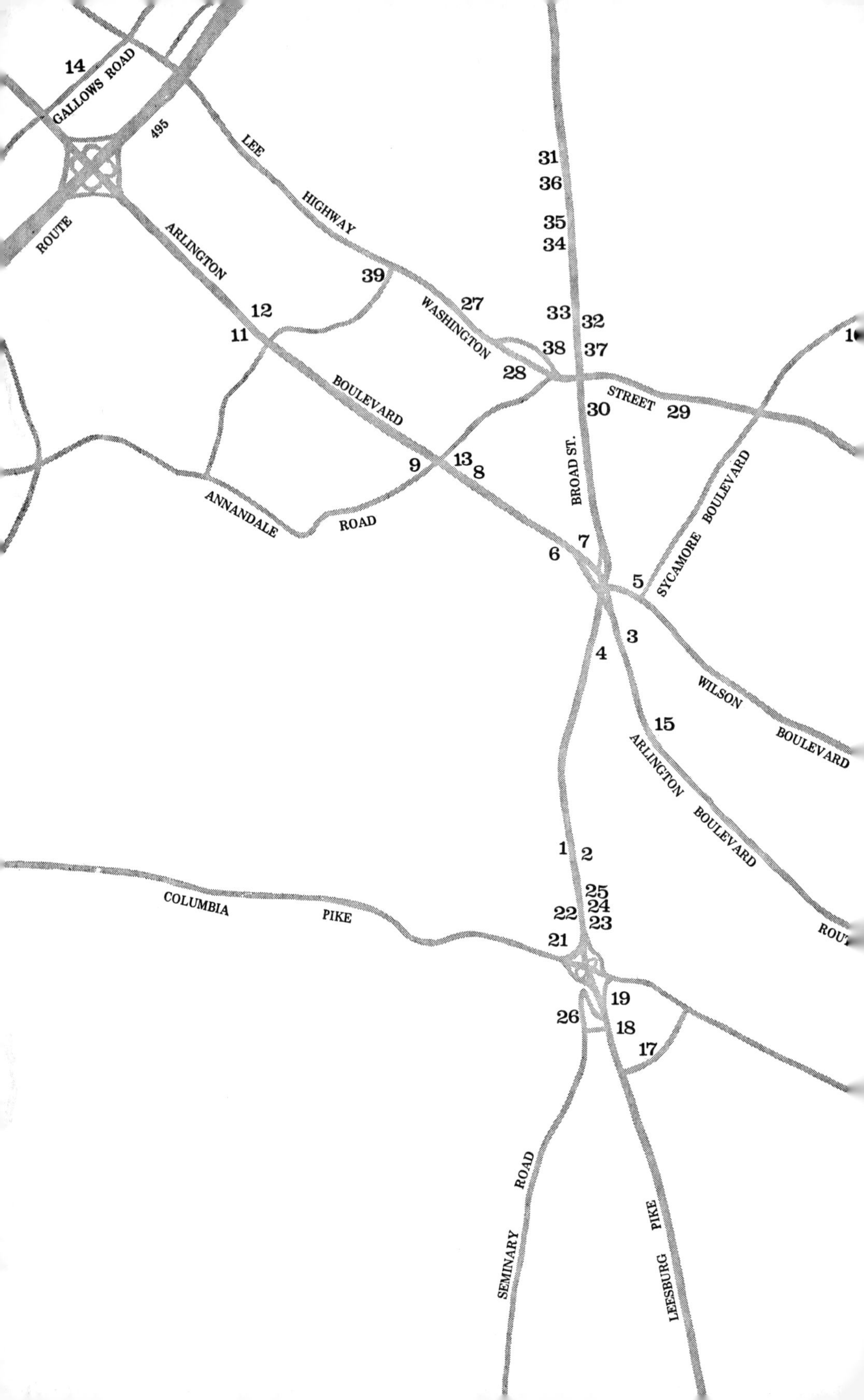
14
GALLOWS ROAD
495
LEE
HIGHWAY
ROUTE
ARLINGTON
BOULEVARD
12
11
39
WASHINGTON
27
31
36
35
34
33
32
38
37
28
STREET
30
29
BROAD ST.
SYCAMORE
BOULEVARD
ANNANDALE
ROAD
9
13
8
7
6
5
3
4
WILSON
BOULEVARD
15
ARLINGTON
BOULEVARD
1
2
25
24
23
22
21
COLUMBIA
PIKE
19
26
18
17
SEMINARY
ROAD
LEESBURG
PIKE

FALLS CHURCH

14 Alexander Wallpaper, 2964 Gallows Road
38 Amp Auto Parts, 431 S. Maple
27 Angel's Car Radio, 800 S. Washington St.
14 Best Products, 2982 Gallows Road
3 Bicycle Discount Center, 6148A Arlington Blvd.
32 Bill's Carpet, 134 W. Broad St.
10 Calico Corners, 6400 Williamsburg Blvd.
17 Carpet Barn, Korvette's Shopping Center
19 Carpets USA, 2810 Graham Rd.
11 China Closet, Loehmann's Plaza
19 Circuit City, 5520A Leesburg Pike
8 Color Tile, 6600 Arlington Blvd.
5 Dennis Tile, 6775 Wilson Blvd.
14 Danneman's, 2970 Gallows Road
19 Fabric Man, 5524 Leesburg Pike
34 For Eyes, 809 W. Broad St.
9 George's, 3036 Annandale Road
30 Giant Music Center, 109 E. Broad Street
29 Greg's Auto Radio, 554 N. Washington Street
15 Heel and Toe, 6178 Arlington Blvd.
21 Hi Gear, Baileys Crossroads Shopping Center
25 Honeycutt's, 5866 Leesburg Pike
6 Jay's Designer Discounts, 6535 Arlington Blvd.
11 Jos. A. Bank Clothiers, 7237 Arlington Blvd.
35 Jos. M. Catalano Co., 929 W. Broad St.
11 Kemp Mill Records, Loehmann's Plaza
30 King's Smarten Up, 2908 Graham Rd.
4 Kitchen Bazaar, Seven Corners Shopping Center
33 Koko's Color TV, 305 W. Broad St.
4 Lamps Unlimited, Seven Corners Shopping Center
11 Loehmann's, 7241 Arlington Blvd.
17 Market Tire, 3526 S. Jefferson St.
13 Merchants Tire and Auto, 6680 Arlington Blvd.
37 Mr. Sunshine, 1119 W. Broad
37 Nationwide Tire, 1121 W. Broad
22 Nationwide Tire, 5709 Leesburg Pike
5 Office Furniture Mart, 6769 Wilson Blvd.
24 Penguin Feathers, 5850 Leesburg Pike
31 Penn Jersey, 114 W. Broad Street
11 Pottery Fair, 7273 Arlington Blvd.
14 Reliable Home Appliances, 2986 Gallows Road
36 Rolls Music Center, 1065 W. Broad St.
11 Shoe Town, Loehmann's Plaza
11 Show Off, Loehmann's Plaza
2 Show-off, Spring Garden Shopping Center
12 Sleep King, 7240 Arlington Blvd.
19 Southern Furniture Surplus, 5522 Leesburg Pike
6 Sunlighting, 6533 Arlington Blvd.
7 Sym's, 1000 E. Broad Street
18 T. H. Mandy, 5510 Leesburg Pike
14 T. H. Mandy, Levitz Plaza
23 Tire Man, 5854 Leesburg Pike
20 Toys R Us, 5521 Leesburg Pike
36 Universal Beauty, 1055 W. Broad St.
5 Universal Beauty Supply, 6773 Wilson Blvd.
1 Vacuums Unlimited, 6041 Leesburg Pike
28 W. Bell and Co., 435 S. Washington St.
26 Wonder Bread Bakery Thrift Shop, 5820 Seminary Road

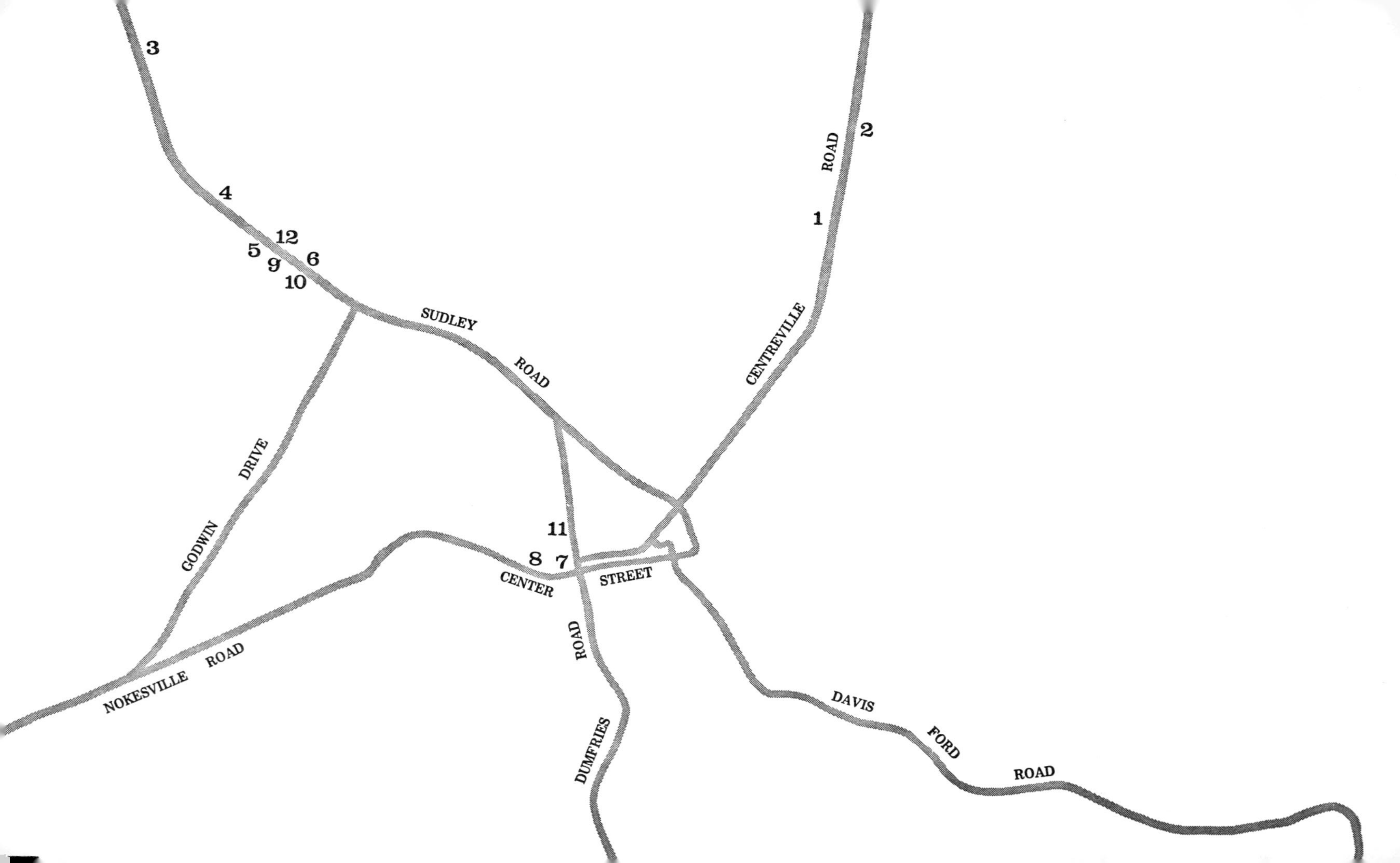
3
4
12
5
9
6
10
SUDLEY
ROAD
ROAD
2
1
CENTREVILLE
DRIVE
GODWIN
11
8
7
CENTER
STREET
ROAD
NOKESVILLE
ROAD
DUMFRIES
DAVIS
FORD
ROAD

MANASSAS

- 1 C. L. Barnes Clearance Center, 8219 Centreville Road
- 11 Consumer Discount Tire, 9412 Grand Avenue
- 5 Crown Books, 8339 Sudley Road
- 7 Discount Consumer Tire, 9248 Center Street
- 2 Fairfax Auto Parts, 7809 Centreville
- 10 Hi Gear, Manassas Mall
- 4 Home Tile, 8104 Sudley Road
- 12 Market Tire, Manaport Plaza
- 3 Merchants Tire and Auto, 7860 Sudley
- 9 Sugar's, Manassas Mall

BALTIMORE
ROUTE 695
GERMANTOWN
LAUREL
ROUTE I-95
ROUTE 1
BALTIMORE- WASHINGTON PKWY.
ROUTE I-270
WISCONSIN AVENUE
ROUTE 495
WASHINGTON
ROUT
ROUTE 29-211
ROUTE 295
ROUTE 50
ROUTE 495
WARRENTON
MANASSAS
ROUTE I-95
ROUTE 1
JEFFERSON DAVIS HIGHWAY
WOODBRIDGE
FREDERICKSBURG

METRO AREA

Arnold W. Hurt Discount Fabrics, 1505 Forest Heights Drive, Annapolis
Baby Products, 389 Main Street, Laurel
Bill's Carpet Route 1 in Laurel, opposite Laurel Shopping Center
Budget Food Outlet, Laureldale Road at 198, Laurel
Carolina Furniture, 4507 Jeff. Davis Blvd., Fredericksburg
Carpet Barn, Jefferson Davis Highway, Woodbridge
Carpet House, Route 1 at 198, Laurel
Crown Books, 6828 Race Track Road, Bowie
Fashion Action, Gordon Plaza (U.S. Route 1 at 123)
Fashion Action, Free State Mall, Bowie
Gallahan's Furniture, 105 Old Greenwich Drive, Fredericksburg
Heel and Toe, 9636 Ft. Meade Road, Laurel
Hi Gear, Woodlawn Shopping Center
Hi Hear, Laurel Shopping Center
Hi Gear, Belair Shopping Center, Bowie
Hi Gear, Featherstone Mall
Kemp Mill Records, 9709 Ft. Meade Road, Laurel
Luskin's, 14647 Jeff. Davis Highway, Woodbridge
Market Tire, Route 1 and Bowie Road, Laurel
Merchants Tire and Auto, 13980 Jeff Davis Highway, Woodbridge
Merchants Tire and Auto, Laurel Shopping Center
Reliable Home Appliances, Route 450 at Race Track Road, Bowie
Sears Surplus Store, Maryland City Plaza, Laurel
Slumberland, Laurel Plaza at 9608 Ft. Meade Road, Laurel
The Store, Hub Plaza, 197 and 198, Laurel

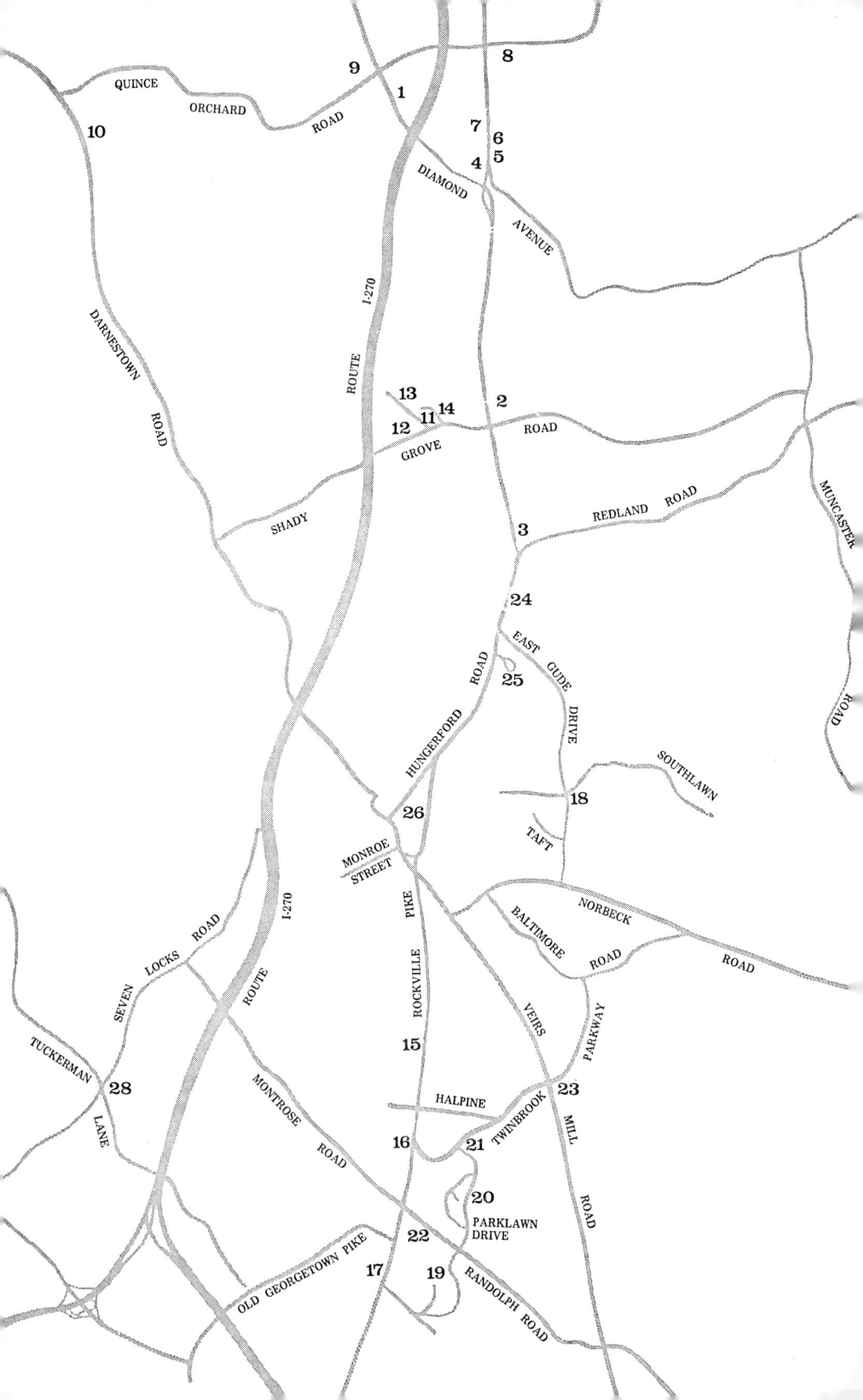

QUINCE ORCHARD ROAD
DIAMOND AVENUE
DARNESTOWN ROAD
ROUTE I-270
SHADY GROVE ROAD
REDLAND ROAD
MUNCASTER ROAD
HUNGERFORD ROAD
EAST GUDE DRIVE
SOUTHLAWN
TAFT
MONROE STREET
ROCKVILLE PIKE
NORBECK ROAD
BALTIMORE ROAD
VEIRS MILL ROAD
PARKWAY
SEVEN LOCKS ROAD
TUCKERMAN LANE
MONTROSE ROAD
HALPINE
TWINBROOK
PARKLAWN DRIVE
OLD GEORGETOWN PIKE
RANDOLPH ROAD
1
2
3
4
5
6
7
8
9
10
11
12
13
14
15
16
17
18
19
20
21
22
23
24
25
26
28

ROCKVILLE/GAITHERSBURG

19 Alexander Wallpaper, 12221 Nebel
18 American Physical Fitness Co., 14650 Southlawn Lane
18 Audio Expo, 701 E. Gude
18 Beck Arnley Auto Parts, 1321 E. Gude
4   Bedding and Furniture Discount Center, 101 N. Frederick
18 Bedding World, 1304 E. Gude
20 Best Products 12345 Parklawn
17 Bill's Carpet, Rockville Pike at Randolph Road
19 Carpet House, 5544 Nicholson
19 Ceramic Tile, 12081 Nebel
15 Chafitz, 856 Rockville Pike
22 Children's Wear Market, 5556 Randolph Rd.
25 Consumer Discount Tire, 273 Derwood Circle
16 Crown Books, 12111 Rockville Pike
9   Crown Books, 602 Quince Orchard Rd.
15 Danker Furniture, 1616 Rockville Pike
18 Dennis Tile, 1057 Gude
13 Design Store Warehouse Clearance Center, 9201 Gaither
19 Dinette World, 12053 Nebel
18 Discount Food Outlet, 1011 E. Gude
22 Discount Sound, 5618 Randolph Road
17 D&F Clearance Center, 11850 Rockville Pike
18 D&R Tire Wholesalers, 1301 E. Gude
19 Evans Catalogue Showroom, 5060 Nicholson
19 Everfast Fabric Mills (Danneman's), 5041 Nicholson
19 Fabric Man, 11760 Parklawn
15 Fashion Action, 1659 E. Montgomery, Congressional Plaza
15 Fashion Factory, 785 Rockville Pike
6   Fashion Tree, Gaitherstown Plaza, 230 N. Frederick
22 Foam Fabricators, 5560 Randolph Rd.

18 Fred O. Harris and Sons, 1315 E. Gude
15 Furniture and Carpetland, 1582 Rockville Pike
16 George's, 12125 Rockville Pike
12 Georgia Discount Carpets, 15916 Shady Grove Rd.
20 German HiFi Discount, 12350 Parklawn
15 Giovanni's Bed Bath and Table, 80 Halpine Court
23 Hi Gear Discount, Twinbrook Shopping Center
26 Home Tile, 779 Hungerford
22 Interior Wall, 5542 Randolph Rd.
15 Jay's Designer, Congressional Plaza
22 Jos. A. Bank Clothier, 5222 Randolph Rd.
24 Karpet King, 15551 Frederick Rd.
22 Karpet King, 5600 Randolph Rd.
28 Kidswear Outlet
1   Kidswear Outlet, Diamond Square Center
2   Knockdown Outlet, Walnut Hill Shopping Center
11 Kole's Lighting Showroom, Shady Gove Rd.
15 Lamps Unlimited, 1509 Rockville Pike
17 Lamps Unlimited, 11610 Rockville Pike
20 Lighting Gallery, 12340 Parklawn
17 Linen Loft, 11134 Rockville Pike
19 Loehmann's, Randolph Rd. at Nicholson Lane
17 Luskin's, 11132 Rockville Pike
17 Mandy's, White Flint Plaza
17 Market Tire, 11800 Rockville Pike
7   Market Tire, 457 N. Frederick
18 Mastercraft Interiors, 14650 Southlawn Lane
26 Merchants Tire and Auto, 379 Hungerford
19 Minnesota Fabrics, White Flint Plaza, 5100 Nicholson Lane
19 Modern Age of Maryland, 5544 Nicholson Lane

continued on page 424

CHERRY
HILL
ROAD
ROUTE 95
RANDOLPH ROAD
4
POWDER MILL ROAD
5
NEW HAMPSHIRE
COLESVILLE ROAD
ADELPHI ROAD
ROUTE 495
AVENUE
RIGGS
UNIVERSITY
BOULEVARD
FRANKLIN
6
FLOWER
2
GEORGIA AVENUE
ELLSWORTH
AVENUE
1
SPRING
NOYES
EAST-WEST HIGHWAY
SEMINARY ROAD
BROOKVILLE ROAD
FENTON
3

SILVER SPRING

18 Beltsville Menswear, Powder Mill Road at New Hampshire Ave.
1 Blouse House, 8623 Colesville Road
2 Box and Bag, Piney Branch Road
6 Carpet Carnival, 1506 University Blvd.
16 Circuit City, 10140 Bacon Drive
4 Colesville Hardware, 13423 New Hampshire Avenue
6 Dennis Sleep Shop, 7681 New Hampshire Avenue
1 Discount Musical Instruments, 1015 Noyes Street
7 Discount Rugs, 6600 New Hampshire Avenue
16 D&R Tire Wholesalers, Inc., 10112 Bacon Dr.
1 Estes Office Machine, 8309 Fenton
1 For Eyes, 8407 Georgia Avenue
6 The General Store, 7645 New Hampshire Ave.
1 George's, 8239 Georgia Avenue
1 Heel and Toe, Colesville Road
6 Heel and Toe
6 Hi-Fi Buys, 1362 Holton Lane
6 Hi Gear, 7665 New Hampshire Ave.
16 Hollywood Carpets, 10212 Southard Drive
6 Home Tile, 7641 New Hampshire Ave.
6 Juvenile Sales, New Hampshire Avenue

8 Market Tire, 2214 University Blvd. E.
1 Market Tire, 8010 Fenton
6 Minnesota Fabrics, 1173 University Blvd.
6 The Music Box, 8006 New Hampshire Ave.
8 Nationwide Tire, 2074 University Blvd.
1 Office Boy, Inc., 8605 Cameron Street
2 Penn Jersey, 8637 Flower Avenue
16 Shamrock Supply Company, 10226 Southard Dr.
6 Shoe Giant, 7601 New Hampshire Ave.
1 Standard Discount, 1500 University Blvd. E.
1 Stephen's Men's Clothing, 717 Ellsworth Drive
5 The Store, White Oak Shopping Center
2 Surplus Sales/Luggage Center, 8710 Flower Avenue
16 Susan Kay Cosmetics, 10551 Ewing
16 Tires by NTW, 10745 Tucker
8 Toys R Us, 2277 University Blvd.
16 Universal Tire, 10714 Hanna Street
3 Universal Tire, 8825 Brookville Road
16 Warehouse T-Shirt, 10768 Tucker

RITCHIE MARLBORO ROAD
CENTRAL AVENUE
ROUTE 495
FORESTVILLE RITCHIE ROAD
MARLBORO PIKE
PENNSYLVANIA AVENUE
ROAD
SUITLAND ROAD
SILVER HILL
SUITLAND PARKWAY
BEECH DRIVE
BRANCH AVENUE
ST. BARNABAS ROAD
ROUTE 495
OXON HILL ROAD
ALLENTOWN ROAD
LIVINGSTON ROAD
INDIAN HEAD HIGHWAY
1
2
3
4
5
6
7
8
9
10
11
12
13
14
15
16
17
18
19
20
21
22
23
24
25

SOUTHERN PRINCE GEORGE'S

25 ABC Liquidators, 6419 Marlboro Pike, Great Eastern Shopping Center
18 Beck/Arnley Auto Parts, 4469 Beech Drive
17 Bill's Carpet, 3914 Bexley Place
21 Carpet Barn, Marlboro Pike at Forestville Road
3 Carpet Carnival, 6304 Allentown Road
16 Circuit City, 4501 St. Barnabas Road
4 Consumer Discount Tire, 309 Ritchie Road
21 Discount Sports, 7824 Parston Drive
8 Fabric Man, 3120 Branch Avenue
10 Fabric Man, 5000 Indian Head Highway
14 Famous Furniture and Bedding Barn, 4724 Suitland Road
3 Fashion Action, 6292 Branch Avenue, Allentown Mall
20 Fashion Action, 3924 Donnell Drive
7 Foam Fabricators, 3211 Brinkley
11 Furniture Surplus, 7313 Livingston Road
9 George's, 3801 Branch Avenue in Iverson Mall
3 George's, 6200 Branch Avenue in Allentown Mall
20 Hi Gear, Penn-Mar Shopping Center
1 Hi Gear, Waldorf Shopper's World
5 Hi Gear, 4731 Marlboro Pike
10 Hi Gear, Eastover Shopping Center
6 Home Tile, 6433 Marlboro Pike
10 J.C. Penney Clearance Center, Eastover Shopping Center
21 Kemp Mill Records, 7728 Old Marlboro Pike
12 Kidswear Outlet, 9558 Livingston Road
16 Luskin's, St. Barnabas Road near Branch Avenue

15 Market Tire, 4410 Suitland Road
13 Market Tire, 6105 Livingston Road
9 Marvin's Sport City, Iverson Mall
16 Mattress Discounters, St. Barnabas and Branch Avenue
2 Merchants Tire and Auto, 3306 Indian Head Highway, Forest Heights
8 Merchants Tire and Auto, 3130 Branch Avenue
12 Merchants Tire and Auto, 9210 Livingston Road
20 Minnesota Fabrics, Penn-Mar Shopping Center, Penn. Ave. at Donnell Drive
13 Nationwide Tires, 6101 Livingston Road
15 Nationwide Tires, 4412 Suitland Road
14 Penn Jersey, 4823 Silver Hill Road
16 Reliable Home Appliance, 4516 St. Barnabas Road
3 Rodman's Discount Drugs, 6305 Allentown Road
23 Schmidt's Sunbeam Bakers Inc., 8008 Cryden Way
1 Sears Surplus Store, Waldorf Shopping Mall
14 Star Vacuum, 4733 Suitland Road
14 Suitland Electronics, 4712 Suitland Road
16 Sunlighting, Marlow Heights Shopping Center
5 Tire Man, 4863 Marlboro Pike
22 Tires by NTW, 7701 Penn Belt Drive
24 The Tire Shop, 1292 Ritchie Road
16 Toys R Us, 4444 St. Barnabas Road
19 Universal Tire, 5008 Beech Place
1 Wholesale Clothing Distributors, Village Square, Waldorf
23 Wholesale Merchandise Inc., 8056 Cryden Way

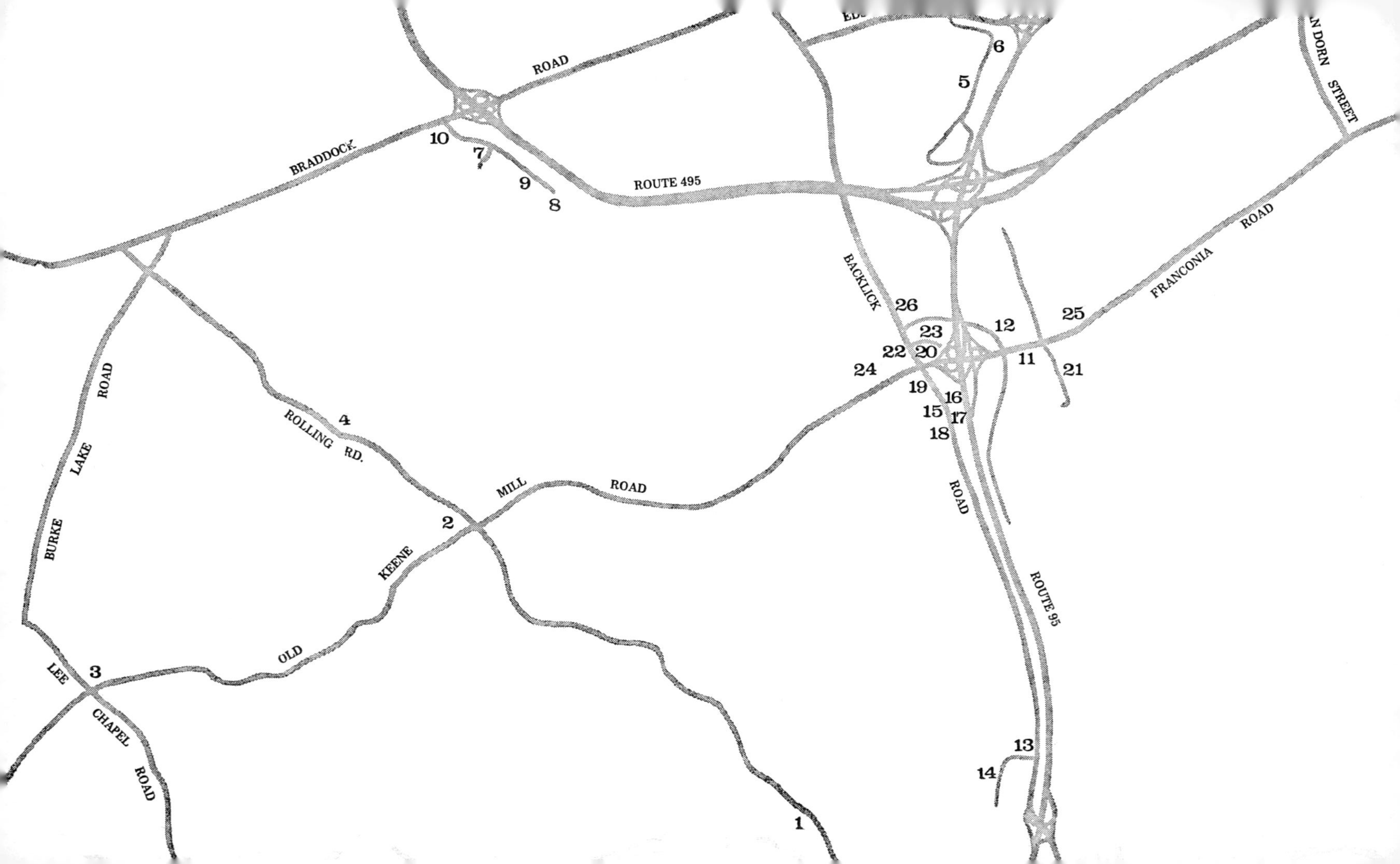

ROAD
BRADDOCK
10
7
9
8
ROUTE 495
6
5
N DORN
STREET
BACKLICK
26
23
22
20
24
19
16
15
17
18
12
11
25
21
FRANCONIA
ROAD
ROAD
BURKE
LAKE
ROAD
ROLLING
RD.
4
MILL
ROAD
2
KEENE
OLD
LEE
3
CHAPEL
ROAD
ROAD
ROUTE 95
13
14
1

SPRINGFIELD

18 Arnold Bakery Thrift Shop, Brookfield Plaza
7   Catalogue Furniture Sales, 7970 Forbes Place
21 Circuit City Warehouse, 6512 Frontier Road
5   Consumer Discount Tire, 6704 Industrial Road
24 Crown Books, Springfield Plaza
4   Designer Sales Showroom, 5803 Rolling Road
25 Danneman's, 6150 Franconia Road
20 Fashion Action, 6840 Franconia Rd.
3   Fashion Factory, Old Keene Mill at Lee Chapel Road
12 George's, 6400 Commerce Street
22 John Greenan and Sons, 6320 Backlick Road
26 Heel and Toe, Springfield Shopping Center
10 Heel and Toe, Ravensworth Shopping Center
18 Hi Gear, Brookfield Plaza
20 Circuit City, 6840 Franconia Road
11 Lamps Unlimited Springfield Mall
17 Lighting Gallery, 6715 Backlick Road
23 Marketplace Foods, 6801 Bland Street
15 Merchants Tire and Auto, 6620 Backlick Road
1   Minnesota Fabrics, 8042 Rolling Road
20 Pepperidge Farm Thrift Store, 6554 Backlick Road
20 Pop Shoppe, Brandon Avenue
18 Reliable Home Appliance, Brookfield Plaza
2   Showroom, Old Keene Mill Center
19 Springfield Surplus, 6530 Backlick Road
8   Star Radio, 5560 Port Royal Road
24 T. I. Swartz, Backlick and Keene Mill Roads
9   Tires by NTW, 5258 Port Royal Road
13 Tires by NTW, 7890 Backlick Road
14 Universal Tire, 7234 Fullerton Road
24 Universal Beauty t/a Perfumers International, 6809 Springfield Plaza
22 Veneman Music, 6319 Amherst Avenue
11 VIP Creative Yarns and Crafts, Springfield Mall
11 W. Bell and Co., Springfield Mall
6   Woodward & Lothrop Warehouse Store
2   Zippers, 8430 Old Keene Mill Rd,

TYSONS

3 American Physical Fitness Co. 8524 Tyco Road
7 Carpet Barn, 1448 Chain Bridge Road
9 Carpet Barn, 303 Mill St., Vienna
3 Consumer Discount Tire, 8524 Tyco Road
9 Crown Books, 1449 Chain Bridge Road
6 Custom Carpets, 111 Maple Ave.
13 Dash's Designer, 8133 Watson Street
6 Discount Sound, 127 Maple Avenue W.
17 George's, 8387 Leesburg Pike
1 Greg's Auto Radio, 8455 Tyco Road
8 Hi Gear, 128 Branch Road
14 Knockdown Outlet, Old Courthouse Road and Route 123
1 Koko's Warehouse, 8455-C Tyco Road
11 Lamps Unlimited, Tysons Corner Shopping Center
17 Market Tire, 8397 Leesburg Pike
16 Merchants Tire and Auto, 8350 Leesburg Pike
10 Merchants Tire and Auto, 1431 Chain Bridge Road
1, Modern Mart Furniture, 8455-G Tyco Road
17 Off the Rax, 8355 Leesburg Pike
5 Penguin Feathers, 521 Maple Ave. E.
4 Records Works, 2916 Chain Bridge Rd.
9 Record Works, 1392 Chain Bridge Road, MCLean
2 Tyson's Clothes-Out, 1524 Springhill Road
12 W. Bell and Co., 1991 Chain Bridge Road
15 Zippers, 7515 Leesburg Pike

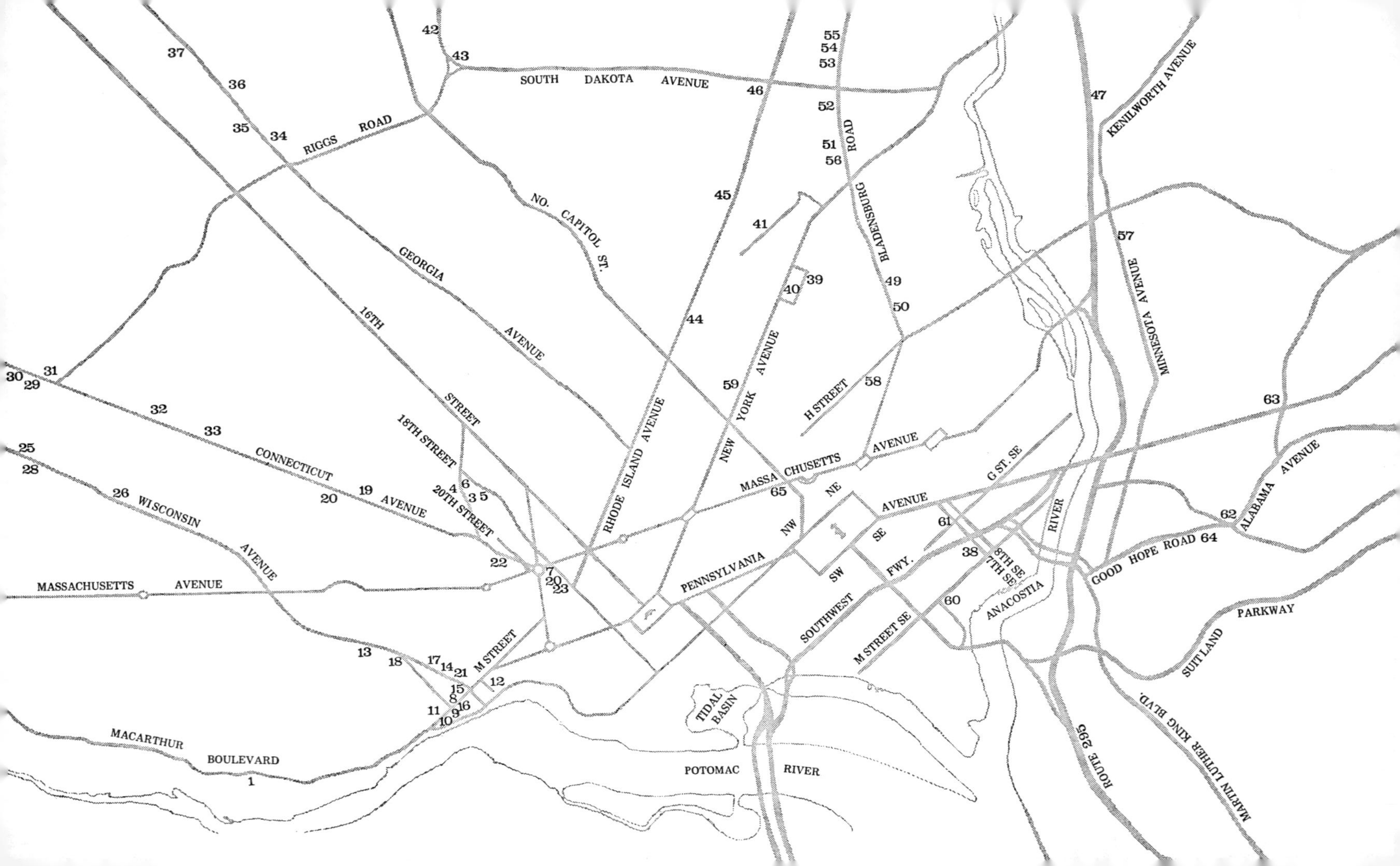
SOUTH DAKOTA AVENUE
RIGGS ROAD
NO. CAPITOL ST.
GEORGIA AVENUE
16TH STREET
18TH STREET
20TH STREET
CONNECTICUT AVENUE
WISCONSIN AVENUE
MASSACHUSETTS AVENUE
M STREET
MACARTHUR BOULEVARD
RHODE ISLAND AVENUE
NEW YORK AVENUE
BLADENSBURG ROAD
H STREET
MASSA CHUSETTS AVENUE
PENNSYLVANIA AVENUE
NW
NE
SW
SE
SOUTHWEST FWY.
M STREET SE
G ST. SE
8TH SE
7TH SE
ANACOSTIA RIVER
TIDAL BASIN
POTOMAC RIVER
KENILWORTH AVENUE
MINNESOTA AVENUE
GOOD HOPE ROAD
ALABAMA AVENUE
SUITLAND PARKWAY
ROUTE 295
MARTIN LUTHER KING BLVD.
1
2
3
4
5
6
7
8
9
10
11
12
13
14
15
16
17
18
19
20
21
22
23
25
26
28
29
30
31
32
33
34
35
36
37
38
39
40
41
42
43
44
45
46
47
49
50
51
52
53
54
55
56
57
58
59
60
61
62
63
64
65

WASHINGTON, DC

35 A&A Appliance, 7614 Georgia Ave. NW
41 Ace Restaurant Equipment, 1917 New York Ave. NE
27 Arnold Hurt Fabrics, 3420 Wisconsin Ave. NW
64 Arrow Discount Auto Parts, 2501 Good Hope Rd. SE
16 Bicycle Discount Center, 3405 M St. NW
11 Bon Marché Furniture, 1213 Banks St. NW
21 Book Annex, 1239 Wisconsin Ave. NW
42 B&S Auto Supply, 302 Riggs Road
5   Capital Cycle Corp., 2328 Champlain St. NW
34 Carolina Auto Parts and Supplies, 6213 Georgia Ave. NW
10 Carpetland, 3272 M St. NW
15 Dash Designer, 3229 M St. NW
47 Dennis Tile, 1215 Kenilworth Ave. NE
43 Design East, 151 Riggs Rd. NE
44 D&F Clearance Center, 513 Rhode Island Ave. NE
48 Discount Medical Supplies, 615 Division Ave. NE
20 Discount Records and Books, 1340 Connecticut Ave. NW
46 District Sound, Inc., 2316 Rhode Island Ave. NE
18 For Eyes, 1666 33rd St. NW
62 General Store, 2834 Alabama Ave. SE
3   General Store, 2424 18th St. NW (at Columbia Road)
56 George's, 2135 Queens Chapel Rd. NE
33 George's, 3509 Connecticut Ave. NW
19 Heel and Toe, 1327 Connecticut Ave NW
32 Kitchen Bazaar, 4455 Connecticut Ave, NW
17 Knockdown Outlet, Wisconsin Ave. at P St. NW
7   Kramerbooks, Connecticut Ave. NW
30 Lamp and Shade Center, Chevy Chase Circle
65 Lerner Law Books, 53 E St. NW
25 Luskin's, 5023 Wisconsin Ave. NW
60 Market Tire, 114 M St. SE
53 Market Tire, 3156 Bladensburg Rd. NE
39 Marlin Sales, 1415 Okie St. NE
22 Melody Record Shop, Connecticut Ave. NW
49 Merchant's Tire and Auto, 1141 Bladensburg Rd. NE
13 Murrell's Discount Sales, 2140 Wisconsin Ave. NW
54 New Town Auto Parts, 3170 Bladensburg Rd. NE
51 Office Furniture Mart Clearance Center, 2122 24th Pl. NE
1   Once Is Not Enough, 4830 MacArthur Blvd.
8   Orpheus Discount Records, 3224 M St. NW
29 Pottery Fair, 5534 Connecticut Ave. NW
14 Reed Electric, Wisconsin Avenue NW
36 Rodman's Discount Drugs, 7723 Georgia Ave. NW
28 Rodman's Discount Drugs, 5100 Wisconsin Ave. NW
63 Rodman's Discount Drugs, 3839 Alabama Ave. SE
37 Royce's TV and Audio, 7808 Georgia Ave. NW
6   Saxitone Tape Sales, 1776 Columbia Rd. NW
50 Sears Furniture and Appliance, 911 Bladensburg Rd. NE,
31 Second Story Books, 5017 Connecticut Ave NW
26 Slattery's, 4309 Wisconsin Ave. NW
61 S&S Office Supply Inc., 711 G St. SE
57 Standard Drug, 3929 Minnesota Ave. NE
4   Standard Drug, 1805 Columbia Rd. NW
    Standard Drug, 1125 H St. NE

continued on page 424

Rockville/Gaithersburg (continued from page 413)

- 16 Nationwide, 12103 Rockville Pike
- 17 Office Furniture Mart, 11534 Rockville Pike
- 17 Outergear, 11135 Rockville Pike
- 22 Paper Mart, 5540A Randolph Rd.
- 2 Penn Jersey, Walnut Hill Shopping Center
- 15 Penn Jersey, 1614 Rockville Pike
- 19 Performance Discount Tire, 11910 Parklawn
- 2 Performance Discount Tire, 8509 Grovemont Circle
- 13 P.J. Nee Clearance Center, 9128 Gaither Rd.
- 19 Price Right, 11910 Parklawn Drive
- 24 Pro Golf Discount, 15811 Frederick
- 20 Read Plastics Inc., 12331 Wilkins Ave.
- 22 Reliable Home Appliance, 5546 Randolph Rd.
- 5 Rodman's Discount Drugs, 218 N. Frederick
- 17 Rug Man, 11501 Rockville Pike
- 20 Scherr Furniture, 12340 Parklawn
- 19 Showroom, White Flint Plaza
- 26 Sloane's Clearance Center, 517 Monroe St.
- 15 Spreads and Things, 1327 Rockville Pike
- 15 Sugar's, Congressional Plaza
- 18 Suitland TV and Electronics, 1209 Taft
- 15 Sunlighting, Congressional Plaza
- 8 Sunlighting, 568 N. Frederick
- 22 Surplus Center, 2094 Veirs Mill Rd.
- 18 Tennis Warehouse, 1131 Taft St.
- 9 T.H. Mandy, Quince Orchard Plaza
- 19 T.I. Swartz, 11714 Parklawn
- 15 T.I. Swartz, Congressional Plaza
- 19 Tires by NTW, 12174 Nebel
- 14 Tires by NTW, 9025 Comprint Court
- 17 Toys by Garrison, 11130 Rockville Pike
- 17 Toys R Us, 11800 Rockville Pike
- 22 Universal Beauty Supply, 2120 Veirs Mill Rd.
- 18 Universal Tire Surplus Centers, 14628 Southlawn Lane
- 15 Universal Tire, 866 Rockville Pike
- 6 Universal Tire, 15615 Frederick Rd.
- 18 Urdong's Outlet, 1305 E. Gude
- 15 Veneman Music, 1150 Rockville Pike
- 12 Village Sleep Shop, 15900 Shady Grove Rd.
- 19 VIP Yarn and Creative Crafts, Loehmann's Plaza
- 22 Walls by Daizee, 5414 Randolph Road
- 22 Wall St. Clothing, 5560 Randolph Rd.
- 15 Zippers, Congressional Plaza
- 10 Rodman's Discount Drugs, Randolph and Veirs Mill Roads

Washington, D.C. (continued from page 423)

- 23 Star Radio, 1220 Connecticut Ave. NW
- 9 Sunny's Surplus, 3342 M St. NW
- 12 Telephone Warehouse, 1055 Thos. Jefferson St. NW
- 1 3M VQC Washington Photocopy, 4830 MacArthur Blvd.
- 43 Thrift Business, 151 Riggs Rd. NE
- 38 Tires by NTW, 67 K St. SW
- 59 Washington Beef Co., 1240 Fourth St. NE

GLOSSARY OF TERMS

Bakery thrift stores get their supply of goods from the plant or distribution center. These should be surplus goods. Some of these thrift stores sell other items for purposes of convenience. Stick with the day-old or surplus for best buy. Arrive early in the day, when the goods are the freshest and the selection is best.

Cancellations, closeouts, discontinued items, cutouts: Cancellations are items for which a customer's order has been cancelled, leaving the retailer with the merchandise. Discontinued items are those whose style, color, finish, etc. is no longer being manufactured or is being discontinued by the store or by the manufacturer. Closeouts are items or lines of items that the retailer (or sometimes the manufacturer) wants to clear out of stock — because their selling season has ended, because only odd items are left from a full line of merchandise, or for a variety of other reasons. Cutouts are discontinued records.

Clearance centers are usually operated by large retailers such as department stores, who get rid of their floor samples, discontinued styles, leftover pieces, damaged items, and some fresh merchandise through these centers. Some have turned to bringing in slightly lower-priced lines or special purchase items regularly.

Discount is a meaningless word unless you know what percent off of a true "list" or "manufacturer's suggested" price is being offered. Retailers really work on a "markup" basis. For example, an item that costs the retailer $50 would carry a 100% markup if it sold for $100. If this discount were sold to a consumer for $75 at a discount store, this would be a 25% discount.

Distributors or wholesale outlets usually represent several manufacturers. When such businesses sell directly to the public, they can get a bigger markup than they do when they sell to their retail store clients — but the consumer still pays less. In this case, the consumer is buying from the middleman, much as the retail store would. Some retailers insert the word "wholesale" into their names, but sell only to consumers.

Factory outlets are a special type of manufacturer's outlet, generally located in the factory. They usually feature overruns, seconds, irregulars, samples, and returned merchandise. Only a few of the stores in this book are true factory outlets, although many more claim to be.

First quality, seconds, irregulars, flawed, and intermediate merchandise: First quality merchandise is sold as unflawed merchandise (whatever the line's quality in relation to the rest of the market); it is sometimes called "perfect". The rest of these terms indicate merchandise that in some way do not fit the first quality standards. Irregular merchandise is usually better than seconds. Most such items are unaffected in appearance and utility. But whenever an item is sold as other than "first quality" or "perfect", you should examine it closely to make sure you know what the problem is and that it won't affect your use of the merchandise. Sometimes you will find that "seconds" or "irregulars" of a top-of-the-line item are actually higher in quality than "firsts" of a less-well-made brand. You should also be aware that some companies deliberately manufacture "seconds" with uniform flaws for use by discount operations and other retailers. The idea behind this is that the consumer will automatically assume that the unimportant flaw accounts for the low price — when, in fact, the merchandise may not be of a high quality otherwise. So if you see a pile of 100 sheets (for example), all uniformly imperfect, at a low price, be sure to check other criteria, such as thread count.

Importers' outlets are shops where importers sell the excess or late shipments of ordered merchandise.

In-season and LY refer to clothing that is either current (in-season) or of seasons past (LY meaning "last year"). This is commonly found in items that get dated by fashion, such as clothing.

Jobbers and job lots. Jobbers are middlemen who buy in bulk, then sell to retail outlets. They buy large quantities, which are called "job lots". When these items are offered to the public, the offering outlet is called a "jobber's outlet".

Manufacturers' outlets are where a manufacturer sells goods him/herself rather than through a jobber or retail store. These are variations on the factory outlet, but are not necessarily located inside the factory.

Manufacturer's suggested retail, sticker, or list price is the price which is most often quoted in manufacturers' advertisements for their goods. In most cases, this is the highest price which should ever be paid for this merchandise.

Mill ends and remnants are small quantities of yard goods like fabrics, carpets, and sheet vinyl, which are left over at the plant, or from a large job the retailer performed.

Overcuts, overstocks, and overruns are that supply of merchandise which was produced in excess of the needs of retailers. These are usually what is found in factory and manufacturers' outlets.

Retail is any store which sells directly to the public.

Samples are usually examples of merchandise shown to buyers in retail stores by the manufacturers' or distributors' salespeople. At the end of the retailers' buying season (which is of course before the end of the selling season), the manufacturers dispose of these samples by selling them to retailers at a reduced price or by selling them in factory or manufacturers' outlets. Choice may be limited in these sample lines: most companies make samples of clothing in only one size; and samples of furniture are often made in only certain upholstery and wood finishes. A retailer's floor samples or display samples are also offered in sales from time to time.

Index to Stores

A&A Appliance, 136
Abbington Design, 166
ABC Liquidators, 166
Ace Restaurant Equip, 110
Alexander Wallpaper, 215
Alexander Lighting, 189
Allstate Carpet, 216
Ambach Mill Outlet, 110
American Phys. Fitness, 284
Amp Auto Parts, 238
Anders of Timonium 75
Angel's Car Radio, 239
Antiquities Brass Beds, 167
Arlandria Carpet, 216
Arnold Bakery Thrift, 44
Arnold Hurt Fabrics, 118
Assoc. Carpet, 216
Atlantis Sound, 136
The Attic, 107
Attic Books, 284

Baby Products, 75, 167
Back Door, 76
Bargain Tire, 239
Bata Shoe Warehouse, 76
Baths Etc. Value Center, 111
Bazaar Knitting, 118
Beck Arnley, 239
Bedding & Furn, 167
Bedding World, 168
Belmont TV, 136
Beltsville Menswear, 177
Beltway Kawasaki, 240
Best Products, 251
Bethesda Ave. Coop., 444
Better Homes Furn., 168
Bicycle Village, 284
Bill's Carpet, 217
Blouse House, 77
Bon Marche Furn., 168
Box & Bag, 44
B&S Auto, 240
Budget Foods, 55

Calico Corner, 119
Cardinal Lighting, 189
Carolina Auto, 240
Carolina Furniture, 169
Carpeteria, 217
Carpet Barn, 218
Carpet Carnival, 218

Carpet House of MD, 218
Carpet House, 219
Carpets USA, 220
Capital Cycle Corp., 240
Catalogues, Unltd., 220
C. D. Majors Carpet, 220
CED Electric, 189
Central Office Supply, 194
Ceramic Tile, 221
Children's Wear Market, 78
China Closet, 111
Christina's 78
Circuit City, 137
C. L. Barnes, 169
Clothes Connection, 79
Clothes Outlet, 79
Colesville Hdwre, 221
Color Tile, 221
Consumer Disc. = Tire, 241
Contemporary Sound, 138
Cort Furniture, 170
Crazy Sally's, 80
Crown Books, 285
Custom Bedding, 170
Custom Carpets, 222

Dan Bros. Disc. Shoes, 80
Danielle Sportswear, 81
Danker Furn., 170
Danneman's Fabrics, 120
Dash's Designer, 81
Debois Textile, 112
Decor Furniture, 171
Decorative Rugs, 222
Denis Sleep Shop, 171
Dennis Tile, 222
Design East, 172
Design Resource, 172
Designer Sales Showroom, 17
Design Store Whse, 173
Desk & Furnishings, 196
Devaris Fabrics, 119
Dinette Distributors, 174
Dinette Gallery, 174
Dinette World, 174
Discount Beauty Supply, 52
Discount Fabrics, 119
Discount Food Outlet, 45
Discount Mart, 112
Discount Musical, 285
Discount Record & Bks., 286

Discount Rugs, 223
Discount Rugs & Carpets, 223
Discount Sound, 138
Discount Typewriter, 196
District Sound, 138
Division Med. Supply, 46
Dominion Electric, 190
Douglas Speed Sport, 241
D&R Tire, 241

Eagle Electric, 190
End of Roll Carpets, 224
Erol's, 139
Estes Office, 197
Evans Distributors, 251
Everfast Fabric Mill, 120

Fabric Man, 121
Fabric Man, 121
Fabrics Unlimited, 120
Factory Car Service, 242
Famous Funiture & Bedding, 175
Fashion Action, 81
Fashion Factory, 82
Fashion Tree, 82
Fashion Tree, 82
Fashion Fabricators, 113
For Eyes, 46
Frocks at the Docks, 83
Furn. & Carpetland, 175
Furn. Surplus, 175
Furn. World Outlet, 176

Gaithersburg Whse, 176
Gallahan's, 177
Georgetown Carpet, 224
General Store, 84
George's, 140
German Hi Fi, 139
Giant Music, 286
Giovanni's Bed, Bath, 113
Glenbrook Coat, 84
Gordon Miller Music, 287
Graham, Van Leer, & Elmore, 114
Greenan, 252
Greenbaum's, 85
Greg's Auto Radio, 243
G St. Remnant, 122
G. W. Imirie, 242

Harford Men's Shop, 85
Harris Carpet, 224

Hecht Clearance Ctr., 177
Heel and Toe, 85
Hess Shoe Bargain, 86
HiFi Buys, 141
Hi Gear, 243
Hit or Miss, 86
Hollywood Carpets, 225
Honeycutt's Fabrics, 122
Home Tile, 225
House of Shoes, 87
In Outlet Shop, 87
Interior Wall, 225
Interstate Electric, 190
Interstate Office, 197

Jay's Designer, 88
J. C. Penney, 252
Jos. A. Banks, Clothiers, 89
Jos. A. Catalano, 190
Juvenile Sales, 288

Karpet King, 226
Kemp Mill Records, 287
Kidswear Outlet, 89
Kings Smarten Up, 226
Kitchen Bazaar, 114
Knock-down Outlet, 178
Koko's, 141
Kole's Lighting, 190
Kramerbooks, 288

Lamp & Shade Center, 191
Lamps Unlimited, 191
Lee Furn. Whse, 178
Lee's Dinettes, 178
Lighting Gallery, 191
Linen Loft, 114
Linens & Spreads, 115
Linn's Maternity/Uniform, 90
Loehmann's, 90
Lowenthal & Hess, 90
Lu Anne Whse, 179
Luskin's, 142

Macon Tile, 226
Marketplace Foods, 46
Market Tire, 244
Marboro Books, 288
Marlin Sales, 47
Marshall's, 252
Marty's Electronics, 142
Marvin Sports, 289
Mastercraft Interiors, 179
Mattress Center, 180
Mattress Discounters, 180
Math Box, 142
Max Rubin Factory Outlet, 91
Medco/Standard Drugs, 47
Melody Records, 289
Merchants Tire, 244
Metro Discount, 253
Metro Office, 198
Military Buying Svce, 180
Minnesota Fabrics, 123
Modern Age of MD, 181
Modern Mart, 181
Modern Photo, 289
Mont'y Ward Bargains, 181
Mont's Ward Catalogue, 253
Morris Katz Car Radio, 245

Mr. Sunshine Carpet, 227
Muehly's Bakery, 48
Murrell's TV, 143
Music Box, 290
Myer-Emco, 143

Nationwide Tire, 245
New Town Auto, 249

Old Town Gemstones, 92
Office Furn., Inc. 198
Office Furn. Mart, 199
Off the Rax, 91
Once is Not Enough, 92
Orpheus Discount, 290
Outergear, 94

Paper Mart, 115
Parts Place, 246
Penguin Feathers, 290
Penn Camera, 291
Penn Jersey Auto, 246
Pepperidge Farm Thrift, 48
Performance Tire, 247
P. J. Nee, 182
Place Setting Outlet, 116
Plymouth Wallpaper, 227
Pop Shoppe, 52
Pottery Fair, 116
Price Right, 228
Prof. Book Ctr., 291
Pro Golf Discount, 292

Read Plastics, 116
Record & Tape Ltd., 292
Record Works, 292
Reed Electric, 192
Reliable Home Appliances, 144
Rodman's Discount Drugs, 49
Rolls Music, 293
Royce's 144
Rug Man, 228
Russell Stover Outlet, 49

St. Clair Kitchen, 145
Sam Glass, 94
Sam Oidick, 95
Sam's Tailoring Co., 95
Saxitone Tape Sales, 145
Scan Furn., 183
Scherr Furn., 183
Schmidt's Sunbeam Bakery, 50
Schwartz Tailoring, 95
Sears Furn., 184
Sears Surplus, 253
Second Story Bks., 293
Seventh Heaven, 96
Shamrock Supply, 228
Shane's Shoes, 97
Shoe Box, 98
Shoe Giant, 98
Shoe Horn, 98
Shoe Stop, 99
Shoe Town, 100
Show Off, 99
Showroom, 100
Simon Harris Sportg., 293
Slattery's, 145
Sleep King, 184

Slumberland, 184
Southern Furn., 185
Spreads & Things, 117
Springfield Furn., 185
Springfield Surplus, 254
S&S Office, 200
Stanis Furn., 185
Status II, 101
Star Appliances, 146
Stephen's Men's Clothing, 100
Stereo Discounters, 146
Stofberg Bros. Furn., 186
The Store, 101
Sugar's, 102
Suitland Electronics, 147
Sunlighting, 192
Sunny's Surplus, 254
Super Surplus, 254
Surplus Centers, 256
Surplus Centers/Luggage, 256
Surplus Electronics, 147
Susan Kay Cosmetics, 51
Sym's, 102

Tanen's, 147
Ted Louis Clothes, 104
Tee to Green, 294
Telephone Warehouse, 148
Tennis Warehouse, 294
T. H. Mandy, 103
Three Rs Books, 294
Thrifty Business, 200
Tire Man, 247
Tires by NTW, 247
T. I. Swartz, 104
Total Auto, 248
Toys by Garrison, 295
Toys R Us, 295
Triple S Discount Fabrics, 123
Tunz A Fun, 295
Turnpike House Furn., 186
Tyson's Clothes-Out, 104

United Floor & Wall, 229
Universal Beauty Supply, 50
Universal Tire, 248
Urdongs, Outlet, 105

Vacuums Unlimited, 148
Veneman Music, 296
Village Sleep Shop, 186
VIP Yarns, 124

Walls by Daizee, 229
Wall St. Clothing, 105
Walmer's Doll House, 296
Waxie Maxie, 296
W. Bell & Co., 256
Whse Sleep Centers, 188
Washington Beef Co., 50
Washington Photocopy, 200
Wearhouse Inc., 105
Wholesale Clothing, 106
W. J. Sloane Clrnce Ctr., 187
Wonder Bread Thrift, 51
Woodmont Carpet, 230
Woodward & Lothrop, 189

Zavarella's Music, 297
Zippers, 106